## Praise for *Return to Point Zero*

"In this highly original and sensitively written analysis, Murat Somer elucidates how the Kurdish Question became the Kurdish Conflict, and in doing so provides a cogent and clear-headed explanation for why the Kurdish-Turkish conflict has continued to persist and what needs to be done if it is to be transcended."

— Mark R. Beissinger, Princeton University

"Somer's deeply informed monograph puts emphasis on multiple and contradictory processes that determined and still determine the evolution of the Kurdish conflict in Turkey and opens new theoretical avenues to understand dynamics of ethnic conflicts throughout the twentieth and twenty-first centuries."

— Hamit Bozarslan, École des Hautes Études en Sciences Sociales (EHESS)

"This is a major contribution to the understanding of nationalist politics. Eschewing reductionist or mechanistic explanations, Somer provides a theoretically sophisticated and empirically rich account of the emergence of Turkish and Kurdish nationalisms and shows how the conflict is not historically inevitable or predetermined."

— Michael Keating, University of Aberdeen

# Return to Point Zero

# Return to Point Zero

*The Turkish-Kurdish Question and How Politics
and Ideas (Re-)Make Empires, Nations, and States*

MURAT SOMER

Cover image courtesy of Mr. Serdar Çömez.

Published by State University of New York Press, Albany

For information, contact State University of New York Press, Albany, NY
www.sunypress.edu

**Library of Congress Cataloging-in-Publication Data**

Name: Somer, Murat, author.
Title: Return to point zero : the Turkish-Kurdish question and how politics
    and ideas (re-)make empires, nations, and states / Murat Somer.
Description: Albany : State University of New York Press, [2022] | Includes
    bibliographical references and index.
Identifiers: ISBN 9781438486710 (hardcover : alk. paper) | ISBN 9781438486734
    (ebook) | ISBN 9781438486727 (pbk. : alk. paper)
Further information is available at the Library of Congress.

10 9 8 7 6 5 4 3 2 1

# Contents

# Illustrations

## Figures

## Tables

## Maps

# Preface

How did the Kurdish-Turkish Conflict arise? Why have Turks and Kurds failed for so long to solve it? How can they solve it today? How can social scientists better analyze this and other protracted conflicts and propose better conflict resolution methods for sustainable peace?

This book develops a novel framework for co-analyzing the historical-structural and contemporary-intentional causes of ethnic-national conflicts that highlights an understudied dimension: politics. It argues that longue durée structures present dilemmas that cannot be ignored by contemporary social and political actors. However, while these dilemmas must be addressed, political dynamics determine whether actors are in fact able to find successful solutions. Further, studying intramajority group politics can help better understand conflicts involving ethnic/national minorities than can be achieved by studying majority-minority differences alone.

Hence, I argue that the divisions among Turks are the key to understanding the Turkish-Kurdish Conflict. Though it was nationalism that produced the Kurdish *Question* during late-Ottoman imperial modernization, it was the political elite decisions that created the Kurdish *Conflict* during the postimperial (Turkish) nation-state building. During this process, the Muslim Ottoman imperial state identity was metamorphosed into modern Turkishness. Today, ideational rigidities, which are products of more recent periods, reinforce the conflict. In this book, I will analyze the evolution of the conflict from "premodern" times to today. While doing so, I will emphasize two periods and puzzles: how political elites inadequately addressed three fundamental dilemmas about security, identity, and cooperation during the formative era of 1918–1926, and why peace attempts have failed since the 1990s and since a re-formative period began in 2011. I will also develop new conceptual and theoretical tools to analyze ethnic/national conflicts and present concrete policy proposals for sustainable peace.

My discussion brings together my research and thoughts on the Turkish-Kurdish Conflict with my work and reflections on several other, broader topics. The latter include Turkey's modern history with respect to religion, secularism, social and political transformations, polarizing politics, democratization, and, more recently, democratic breakdown. They also involve my interdisciplinary and comparative inquiries on topics such as identities and names, ethnic conflicts and conflict resolution, religious and secular politics, polarization, and processes of democratization and autocratization in the world at large.

The writing and publication of this book have followed an unusual path. The current book is an expanded, updated and substantially revised and developed version of my book *Milada Dönüş*, which came out in Turkish in 2015 and had a second printing in 2016. I started writing it in 2010–11, during my sabbatical year as a Democracy and Development Fellow at the Institute for International and Regional Studies at Princeton University and later a visiting scholar at the Center for Middle Eastern Studies at Harvard University. One month into the writing, I decided to switch to my native language, Turkish. At that time Turkey's government, led by Prime Minister Recep Tayyip Erdoğan and his Justice and Development Party (AKP), was involved in what seemed to be an unprecedented peace initiative with the PKK (*Partiya Karkeren Kurdistan*—Kurdistan Workers Party). The latter had fought the Turkish government and other Kurdish groups since the 1970s in a struggle to obtain Kurdish rights and self-rule. This was a conflict that had begun in the early twentieth century and had since cost millions of people their lives, homes, cultures, or welfare. The timing and the subject matter of the book deepened the unease I felt about the more usual publishing path for Turkish academics with international experience, such as myself, whereby a work is first published in English or another Western language before being translated into Turkish, leading to a time lag of several years or more. By the time the book would have been published in Turkish, the peace process would likely have been long over, concluding either in success, or, as I predicted based on my research, in failure.

But what primarily motivated my decision were my reflections on academia, social sciences, universities, and publishing. If, as I believe is needed, the social sciences are ever to become truly more universal, pluri-versal, or "decolonized"[1] than they are today, there should be more theoretical-conceptual contributions to social sciences that are originally conceived in languages other than the dominant languages. This implies that they should first appear in print in the languages in which they were created and then be translated into such languages as English—the language in which I, too, write, disseminate, and often also think most of my academic work. Even more important than these considerations, of course, research in any language should first and foremost have sufficient scholarly and intellectual merit that is demonstrated based on time-tested academic standards and practices such as rigorous peer review and multi-methodological scrutiny. However, provided that a work meets these standards, readers should not, as they often do, automatically perceive it as "empirical" without general theoretical value, or as a case-specific study applying general theories to a particular context, only because it was first published in a location physically outside the Western world or in a nondominant language of social sciences. People should not expect it merely to *inform*, rather than develop, general theories. Such contributions, an example of which I aim to provide with this book, should be read—if it aims to make such a contribution and achieves its goal—as a theoretical-conceptual contribution to general knowledge.[2]

In its previous form and content in Turkish, the book won the prestigious Sedat Simavi Social Sciences Award in 2015, the selection committee commenting that the work constituted a major contribution by showing how a social scientist can properly research and theorize about a contemporary social and political problem and a difficult and complex subject "that can easily trigger emotions."

The peace initiative of 2009–11 and a subsequent one in 2013–15 both collapsed. Defying many overly optimistic expectations, Erdoğan, the AKP, and their allies in government shifted in a fiercely Turkish nationalist, militaristic, and authoritarian direction, while the PKK resumed its violent struggle, all of which my theory in the book had predicted and my policy proposals had been intended to help prevent. Despite the impossibility of completely assessing the Turkish book's real-world impact, I am certain that it made a long-term contribution to the social sciences and to the academic and public/political discourses in Turkey. It introduced new perspectives based on which Turks and Kurds can rethink this conflict and find the peace they deserve, while building a more inclusive secular democracy and by embarking on a more sustainable path of socioeconomic development at the same time.

My efforts to translate and publish the book in English for more international audiences began in 2016. It was no easy task finding a translator willing and able to translate a noncommercial academic book in Turkish, which, among other things, introduced new concepts and concocted new terminology.

The current book is a substantially and formally revised, updated, expanded, and developed version of the first book, which was initially translated into English by Hande Eagle. After Hande completed her translation in early 2018, and by taking her translation as the starting point, I worked on the manuscript for two more years. In the summer of 2020, I made further extensive revisions based on the useful suggestions of the two anonymous reviewers who evaluated the manuscript for SUNY Press. In its final form, the book significantly developed the original manuscript, especially in terms of its theoretical claims and presentation. I also made every effort in the current book to reflect the political developments since 2015 and acknowledge the more recent writing on the issue.

# Acknowledgments

Many people and institutions helped me in this nearly decade-long project.

I am grateful for the institutional support I received throughout the project from Koç University in Istanbul, my home institution, and its College of Administrative Sciences and Economics. A six-month-long visiting scholarship at the Stockholm University Institute for Turkish Studies in 2013–14 gave me the time to complete the first manuscript, while another visiting scholarship on the Abbasi Program in Islamic Studies at Stanford University in 2019 greatly helped me to improve and complete the current manuscript. The course on the history of modern Turkey, which I co-taught with Ali Yaycıoğlu during the spring of 2019 to a wonderful group of students at Stanford, provided great inspiration for developing the arguments in the book.

I am thankful to Michael A. Rinella, my acquisitions editor at SUNY Press for his patience and support, and the two anonymous reviewers at SUNY Press for their reading and helpful suggestions and criticisms.

Mark Beissinger, Hamit Bozarslan, Reşat Kasaba, and Michael Keating kindly read the book and wrote generous blurbs for its back cover, for which I am grateful.

Over the years, the comments and questions I received in talks, presentations, and lectures at many institutions, conferences, workshops, and webinars contributed to developing my argument and the book. Among others: Middle East Institute, Washington, DC, 2009; Conference on Secularism, Arbil, Iraq, 2009; Stanford Humanities Center, Stanford University, Palo Alto, CA, 2010; Middle East Studies Association annual meeting, San Diego, CA, 2010; Florida State University, Tallahassee, FL, 2011; Bilkent University Political Science Department, Ankara, 2013; Stockholm University, 2014; Association for the Study of Nationalities annual conference, Columbia University, New York, NY, 2015; Yıldız Technical

University, Istanbul, 2015; Weatherhead Center for International Affairs, Harvard University, Cambridge, MA, 2016; Bilgi University, Istanbul, 2017; Boğazici University and the Turkish Industry and Business Association (Tusiad) Foreign Policy Forum meeting, Istanbul, 2017; Workshop on Ethnic Conflict and Post-Conflict Strategies to Institutionalize or Avoid Reference to Ethnicities, New York University Florence, 2018; Heinrich Böll Stiftung, Brussels, 2019; Webinar on Race, Ethnicity and Democratic Erosion in Comparative Perspective, Brown University, Providence, RI, 2020; Barış Vakfı (Peace Foundation), Istanbul, 2021.

I would like to thank many individuals who contributed to my thinking about the arguments in this book through their invitations, questions, and comments or by providing information, material, and feedback (in alphabetical order): Bekir Ağırdır, Murat Aksoy, M. Ali Birand, Lisa Blaydes, Melani Cammett, Hasan Cemal, Bernard Crick, Cengiz Çağla, Cengiz Çandar, Larry Diamond, Tarhan Erdem, Aslam Kakar, Atilla Kart, Michael Keating, Elisabeth King, Paul Levin, Lenore G. Martin, David McCrone; William L. Miller, Kerem Öktem, Behlül Özkan, Ahmet Abdullah Saçmalı, Zeki Sarıgil, Cyrus Samii, Yüksel Taşkın, Baki Tezcan, Güneş Murat Tezcür, Gönül Tol, Ali Yaycıoğlu and Anna Zadrozna.

I am grateful to Emre Kongar for writing a long series of columns in the *Cumhuriyet* newspaper discussing the first book, Mehveş Evin for her interview at *Milliyet* newspaper, and to Bekir Ağırdır, Merve Calimli-Akgun, Fuat Dündar, Deniz Sert, and Kumru Toktamış for writing book reviews. Ali Değermenci at Tvnet, Dilaver Demirağ at Kültür (KRT), and Başak Şengül at CNN Türk television stations interviewed me on the book. David Dumke and Katie Coronado at WCUF in Central Florida interviewed me on the Kurdish and Turkish question. These all encouraged me to write and refine the arguments in the current book.

This book would not have been possible without the support and patience of my family. I am grateful to Ayda and Fethi Somer, my parents, who raised me and Selçuk free from any ethnic, religious, or national prejudices; Anna, my unapologetic love, friend, and critic; and the greatest gift and inspiration I received at the end, my son Nazım Erenay Somer.

The book is dedicated to Şefik Kocaeli, my grandfather whom I know from his stories as a humanist and first Turk Ottoman and later Turkish cavalry officer.

Cambridge-Istanbul-Graz-Stanford-Istanbul,
November 1, 2020

CHAPTER 1

# Introduction

*Structures, Choices, and Politics in*
*Creating and Solving Conflicts*

Turkey's Kurdish *Conflict* has been among the most violent and durable ethnic/regional conflicts in the world, since 1984 costing at least 55,000 lives—counting only those that could directly be linked with the conflict and discounting those that could not be documented.[1] It has continued in evolving forms and intensities and periodically seeming to subside and then resurge with a vengeance since the conflict's *formative* period between 1918 and 1926. Furthermore, the roots of this conflict stretch as far back as the nineteenth century, beginning with what I will call and describe as a Kurdish *Question*. This informs the conflict to this day.

How did the Kurdish Question arise? Why did Turks and Kurds fail to find a solution for such a long time? What would it take to resolve it, or at least begin to properly address it, today? What does this complex conflict teach us about how we can explain and resolve other conflicts in the world? Despite the presence of substantial corpora of scholarly as well as popular and journalistic writings[2] on the subject, we do not yet have satisfactory explanations of the Kurdish Conflict's origins, contemporary causes and dynamics, and its persistent resistance to conflict resolution. Nor do we have workable, theoretically and empirically informed guidelines based upon which future attempts at peace can succeed.

Available studies have produced rich and critical knowledge on historical and contemporary facts. However, as I will elaborate later in this chapter, rather than producing causal explanations, they have mainly generated noncausal or descriptive narratives that shed light on what has happened and the consequences. Further, they usually focused on one

1

specific period. Thus, they fell short of explaining the enduring causes of recurring violence as well as political deadlocks across different periods. Without a broader understanding, the existing literature could not offer policies that might effectively address the violence and redress political obduracy. Instead, this collection of writing has merely criticized the Turkish state and Kurdish insurgents for their actions, invited actors to adopt less violent, nationalistic, and authoritarian ways and embrace democracy, and condemned general and longue durée phenomena such as "nationalism." More specifically, descriptive studies cluster around two themes, which I will exemplify later in this chapter: "actors with predetermined intentions" or "the inevitable consequence of nationalism and the nation-state." Thus, the existing literature has failed to produce sound theory and policy implications beyond general theoretical and normative prescriptions.

However, producing causal explanations of the Kurdish Conflict is a challenging task. Such an explanation should tie the origins and formative periods of this conflict to the more recent and current, while carefully laying out what changed and what remained unchanged—or unresolved—across different periods and explain why. In other words. it takes a comphensive analysis that spans multiple historical periods based on a common causal story and theoretical framework. Hence, the challenges are both theoretical and empiricial.

The reasons why current research has not yet met these challenges are not only related to the weaknesses of studies on the Kurdish Conflict per se. They also result from some shortcomings of general theories of ethnic/regional conflict. These weaknesses undermine the usefulness of general theories when applied to particular conflicts such as the Kurdish one. Suffice it to say here that—pending a more elaborate review and discussion of current research at the end of this chapter and then throughout the book—general, metatheoretical, and mid-range[3] explanations of ethnic regional and national conflicts can be grouped into two types. These highlight two quite different kinds of explanatory factors, from the perspective of policy makers and, in general, of people affected by these conflicts.

On one hand, "structuralist,"[4] and, partially, some identity-based explanations highlight factors that are exogenous to the conflict itself and evolve by themselves. Insofar as these factors can be modified through human interventions, this tends to happen only gradually, at "critical junctures"[5] of history and outside any single individual or collective actor's control. People affected by a conflict must take these causes as more or less given at any point in time. These entail longue durée factors such as geopolitics and socioeconomic conditions. They also include history, nationalism and the nation-state, and cultural identities. History, more accurately whichever records and collective memories of it are available, can be rewritten and reinterpreted over time but cannot be erased or ignored in the short run. The nation-state has developed and spread across the globe. It may be surmountable in the future but now is the dominant mode of governance, just as empires or feudal states were beforehand. Some aspects of our cultural identities were historically shaped, especially during crisis periods and at critical junctures. They can be transformed only across generations or at new critical junctures.

On the other hand, "instrumentalist," "constructivist," and "ideological" explanations[6] emphasize factors that are largely endogenous to the conflict and more subject to human will, creativity and choice. In other words, these are more amenable to the interpretations and interventions of individual and collective social and political actors. State institutions, including electoral rules, constitutions, and state borders, for instance, can be made and remade. Hence, this second type of factors includes for example political and economic institutions, material incentives, and those aspects of our cultural identities that are given shape by contemporary social and political processes.

The Kurdish Conflict showcases how most conflicts cannot be attributed to any single major cause, be it geopolitical, economic, or institutional. Usually, multiple and interactive factors are at work. More importantly for my purposes, the Kurdish case also shows how it is often very hard to simultaneously account for the two types of causal factors that I outlined above when applied to a particular ethnic/regional conflict. The second type of factors—where the wills of actors play causal roles through their direct or indirect consequences—coexist and interact with the first type of factors. But it is very hard to conceptualize and explain how the two work together and influence each other. This is especially true if one wants to keep the explanation and theoretical framework as simple and accessible as possible and be able to derive realistic policy implications at the same time.

To cope with this difficulty, in this book I cast the longue durée causes of the Kurdish Conflict as "dilemmas," rather than treating them as deterministic or fixed constraints. I argue that social/political actors must address these dilemmas in some form or fashion. Although political actors cannot eliminate the dilemmas entirely, they can "resolve" the dilemmas, that is, mitigate the pernicious and conflict-reproducing effects of the dilemmas on actors' behavior. Such solutions may, for example, include constructing new institutions and discourses. Hence, the dilemmas do not directly generate the conflict, I argue, but rather the inadequate responses to these dilemmas by social/political actors cause the conflict. Unfortunately, most of the responses and counter-responses by various Turkish and Kurdish actors during the Kurdish Conflict have reproduced distrust between the actors and the conflict. Nevertheless, in this book I will discuss how it was and still is possible to resolve these dilemmas and ultimately better manage the Turkish-Kurdish Conflict.

In short, the root cause of the conflict in my explanation is the historical emergence and then irresolution of three dilemmas. These "three fundamental or structural dilemmas" relate to *external* (territorial) *security*, *common identity*, and *elite cooperation*, which I will define shortly. The outcome—or the dependent variable—is conflict versus sustainable peace, i.e., conflict-resolution.

However, if it is possible to resolve these dilemmas, this brings up the question of why Turks and Kurds have failed to successfully resolve them and move forward toward conflict-resolution since the formative period. In other words, what determines the outcome in my explanation, that is, whether or not actors will be able to successfully address the dilemmas? I build my answer to this question by employing a combination of methods. I will utilize process tracing[7] and historical event analysis to analyze the different periods of this conflict from its emergence to the present, by analyzing in depth and unpacking the formative period and recent conflict resolution attempts. By referencing crucial official documents and public political discussions and drawing comparisons with other conflicts in the world, I will construct "analytical narratives" and new theoretical constructs. I will also present findings from my content analysis research to shed light on elite beliefs and values in the 1990s and 2000s, and I will reference public opinion polls to illustrate my various arguments and theoretical propositions.

Thus, I argue that, while the root causes of this conflict are the three dilemmas, two explanatory factors primarily explain why Kurds and Turks—particularly the political elites—time and again failed to acknowledge and resolve the fundamental dilemmas. The first of these two factors that obstructed conflict resolution is the "politics" of intra-Turkish elite conflicts. Political considerations prevented Turkish political elites from properly addressing the dilemmas rather than factors such as ideology, nation-state, and actor intentions, which most current explanations emphasize. Politics[8] here refers to processes such as building and consolidating political movements, parties, leadership, and institutions including state organizations, which include such mechanisms as bargaining, pact making, deliberation, representation, and coercion. More generally, it captures all the dynamics, potentials, and pitfalls of collective and authoritative decision making and employing "legitimate violence" and state organizations to distribute power and resources.

The second explanatory variable is "ideational factors,"[9] which became more influential after the formative period and over time. These break down into *ideational bottlnecks* and *ideational gaps*. The former denotes rigid and limiting ways of defining, expressing, and understanding key concepts such as nation, equality, and sovereignty, which came to prevail in mainstream Turkish public/political discourse after alternative interpretations were marginalized due to the political developments in the formative period. I will exemplify these bottlenecks throughout the book and then elaborate and conceptualize them into several categories in chapter 7. Ideational gaps refer to wide differences between how Turkish and Kurdish actors conceive and express key concepts such as nation and democratization as well as the causes and possible solutions of the Kurdish Conflict. As I will elaborate and theorize in chapters 6, 7, and Conclusions, for decades the Turkish mainstream public/political discourse silenced real discussion and knowledge on Kurds and the Kurdish Conflict. Thus, unlike Kurds, who have some concrete—whether feasible or not—demands and solution proposals, Turks lack sufficient knowledge and tangible solution proposals.

Together with politics, ideational bottlenecks and gaps undermine actors' ability to imagine new political/institutional solutions, make different decisions and overcome (or reconstruct) the dilemmas.[10] Thus, they also help explain the failures of conflict reolution attempts in recent decades.

Hence, and as will become more clear after my literature review at the end of the chapter, my explanation involves a dialogue between structuralist, constructivist/ideational, institutionalist, and agentic and voluntarist approaches to theorizing ethnic, national, and, in general, political conflict and change.[11]

## The Goals of this Book

In a nutshell, this book has four main goals. The first is to transcend extant, "standard" explanations that implicitly or explicitly suggest, or assume, that the paths on which this conflict was born and evolved were more or less the only possible paths. Instead, I will develop a "nonstandard"[12] causal explanation of why and how this conflict came about in its formative period, and why and how it has become a protracted conflict since then. In other words, I will explain both the actual path on which this conflict emerged and progressed, and the alternative paths it could have followed. I will analyze which logical and theoretical possibilities existed at various time periods then and show that these different paths were in fact imagined, considered, and discussed by contemporary political and intellectual actors. I will investigate the particular ways in which political elites tried to resolve these dilemmas in the formative period, why they did so, and what the consequences were.

Second, while my primary motivation is to develop a causal explanation of the Kurdish Conflict per se, I also aim to contribute to the development of general theories of conflict and conflict reolution, and, indirectly, those of democratization and social/political change, by treating this conflict as a "crucial case."[13]

Third, following a brief exposé of the "premodern period," I will walk through the evolution of this conflict from its formative period to the present, emphasizing recent events and peace attempts. In doing so, my objective will be to construct not so much a historical as an analytical narrative.[14] That is, rather than presenting a fully fledged account of how the historical events unfolded, I will focus on narrating what did and what did not change during these periods in terms of the three fundamental dilemmas, and explaining which factors led to the enduring irresolution of these dilemmas. Through historical event analysis and process tracing, examination of political and intellectual debates, and a systematic content analysis of pro-Islamic and pro-secular press, I will analyze the factors that undermined attempts at finding a political resolution and peaceful settlement.

Fourth, I will focus on the recent and present periods and try to imagine possible resolutions to this conflict. Acting not only as a scholar *of* the present but also as a scholar *in* the present, I will try to develop practical proposals for how scholars, domestic and international policy-makers and observers, as well as ordinary Turks and Kurds can rethink this conflict and develop mutually acceptable solutions.

## A Roadmap for the Rest of the Book

In the rest of this chapter, I will first offer a very brief synopsis of the Kurdish Conflict for readers less familiar with it. Then, I will explain the difference between the Kurdish Question and Kurdish Conflict—two distinct analytical constructs for my explanation, and how one cannot explain the creation of the Kurdish Conflict without properly undertanding the "Turkish Question." Next, I will define the three dilemmas, which are the cornerstone of my explanation.

The remaining second half of the chapter will consist of a review and critical discussion of current research on Turkey's Kurdish Conflict and then general theories of ethnic/regional conflict, ethnicity and nationalism, and how my explanation contributes to them. In this part, I will exemplify the two standard stories on the emergence of the Kurdish Conflict present in extant research and explain how they fail to offer satisfactory causal explanations. I will also explain crucial concepts in the historical analytical narratives and causal explanations I will develop in the chapters ahead, such as nation, nation-state, state-nation, ethnicity, ethnic categories, and ethnic groups, by critically reviewing relevant literatures.

Having summarized my main arguments in relation to extant research and having defined most of the key concepts for my casual story in the Introduction, I will be ready to start developing my nonstandard explanation. The goal of the second and third chapters is to show how the three dilemmas limit but still allow for different policies toward the Kurdish *Question*, that is, how different possible responses have been available to governing elites. The second chapter will elaborate the demographic, geographical, and institutional parameters of the Kurdish Question and draw comparisons with a "most different case," the Scottish case, as well as with the Kurdish questions in neighboring countries, to illustrate the diversity and limitations of possible policies. The third chapter will narrate the historical evolution of the Kurdish Question since the premodern times and show that, at the dawn of the formative period, there were in fact different, "imaginable and imagined" ways to address the Kurdish Question.

The fourth chapter will focus on the formative period (1918–1926) and explain how the Kurdish Conflict was *created* when political elites addressed the three dilemmas challenging them in particular ways. By building an analytical narrative, this chapter will show how political developments and processes primarily explain the governing elite decisions in this period. It will also summarize the main political and socioeconomic developments between the formative period and the 1990s.

The fifth chapter will narrate the political and discursive but not necessarily ideational changes during the 1990s and 2000s, which laid the groundwork for the "re-formative period" in the 2010s, which I will define shortly. In particular, it will explain how Kurds were transformed from an "unseen" minority to a "seen but unrecognized" minority.

The sixth chapter will focus on the re-formative period and explain why and how peace attempts—to properly address the three dilemmas this time—have so far failed. It will illustrate the reincarnation of the risks and opportunities that prevailed in the formative period to resolve the dilemmas. It will show how, in addition to the political dynamics, ideational bottlenecks—particular beliefs regarding Kurds and general categories such as nation that have become internalized by Turks since the formative period—and ideational gaps between "moderate" actors have been major barriers before resolution.

The goal of the seventh chapter is to elaborate the ideational bottlenecks, whose evolution was exemplified in the previous chapters, especially the sixth chapter, and conceptualize them into various cateagories.

The concluding eighth chapter will recapture my empirical and theoretical arguments and employ them to make concrete policy recommendations. In other words, after summarizing my analysis and conclusions as a scholar *of* the conflict, based on these, it will offer my prescriptions toward conflict resolution as a scholar and intellectual *in* the conflict.

## A Short Synopsis of the Kurdish Conflict

As I will discuss in detail in the next chapter, Kurds constitute a trans-state ethnic/national group that constitutes sizeable—and geographically adjacent—demographic minorities in Turkey, Iraq, Iran, Syria, and smaller minorities in other countries. They are estimated to form close to 20 percent of Turkey's population. Following the World War I, an independence movement founded the Republic of Turkey in 1923, encompassing the Ottoman territories that it could liberate from the control of the allied powers through war (1919–1922) as well as diplomacy and treaties. During this process, Ottoman Kurds were divided between the new Turkey and the British and French mandates of Iraq and Syria. After this and through the policies of the new, pro-secular governing elites led by Mustafa Kemal (Atatürk, Ataturk), a wave of ambitious modernization and nation-state formation, nation building, and state centralization swept across Turkey, including in Kurdish lands. This was followed by a series of Kurdish insurgencies during the 1920s and '30s. The state's main response was repression and assimilationism, which has continued unabated despite a transition to multiparty electoral democracy in 1950, socioeconomic modernization, governments of numerous ideological and political persuasions, and "promissory"[15] military coups in 1960–61, 1971, and 1980–83. Until the 1990s, the official state discourse denied even the existence of a Kurdish minority.

In 1984, the PKK (Partiya Karkeren Kurdistan—Kurdistan Workers Party), started an ongoing and violent war against the state for Kurdish rights and self-rule from within both Turkey and neighboring countries, in particular Iraq and Syria. A short-lived era of relative peace and reforms started in 1999 when the state captured and imprisoned the PKK leader Öcalan and Turkey became a candidate for EU membership. The PKK resumed its armed struggle in 2004. There were peace talks between the PKK and governments led by the Justice and Development Party (AKP) and its leader Recep Tayyip Erdoğan and relative nonviolence in 2009–10 and then again in 2013–15. Since the collapse of these last negotiations, violence has resumed.

As I will elaborate in chapter 6, the current, post-2011 era is very similar to the formative 1918–1926 period in terms of the opportunities and risks faced by the political elites to resolve the dilemmas. In fact, I will call the current era the *re-formative* period of this conflict because it presents a *reincarnation* of the fundamental domestic and external conditions that prevailed during the formative period. Hence this book's title, *Return to Point Zero*.

Just as in the founding, in pursuit of regime legitimacy and social/political unity on the basis of an overarching common identity, Turkey's Constitution categorizes all citizens simply as Turks,[16] regardless of ethnicity, race, and religion. But actual laws and policies favor Sunni Islam and "Turkish"[17] ethnicity, culture, history, and identity. For instance, even though the—until recently illegal—"teaching of" minority tongues has been legalized in schools in elective courses, "teaching in" any language, that is to say, as the language of education, other than Turkish is banned. The state grants "minority status" to some non-Muslim minorities only, who comprise less than 1 percent of the population.[18] But the state as well as mainstream social norms do not consider as minorities numerous other indigenous ethnic/linguistic and sectarian groups who are nominally Muslim, such as the Alevis, Arabs, Bosnians, Circassians, Laz, and Kurds. Hence, they have no separate minority rights, constitutional recognition, or autonomy. Many such groups became politically mobilized to demand mainly cultural recognition and rights, especially since the 1990s. But by far the most extensive and forceful mobilization with far-reaching rights-claims has been that of Kurds.

## Kurdish Question versus Kurdish Conflict

Developing a nonstandard causal explanation requires us to distinguish between the Kurdish Question and the Kurdish Conflict. The Kurdish Question is a product of history: more specifically, the historical ascent of nationalism and ideas of nation-state in the eighteenth and nineteenth centuries and their spread to the Ottoman world in a period when the Ottoman state was engaged in major modernization efforts.[19] Thus, the Kurdish Question would have existed regardless of the will and particular decisions of political actors. It emerged out of the modern development of nationalist visions and projects in areas where Kurdish people lived (e.g., Ottoman Muslim, Kurd, Turk, Turkish,[20] Armenian, Iranian, Persian, and Arab nationalisms, and Ottoman nationalism among the Ottoman ruling classes, i.e., the Ottoman "political society").[21] All of these nationalisms presumed a type of self-governance and sovereign state formation on more or less the same, or at least partially overlapping, territories. This gave rise to a series of questions. Which ones of these nationalist projects would succeed and which ones would not? Which ones of these nation-state or autonomy projects were more viable than the others? What would be the initial status of the Kurds in the Ottoman and Persian empires, and, later on, in successor states with majority populations and state identities such as Turkish, Arab, Persian, and Azeri-Turk? By aiming to remake the world order based on U.S. interests as well as Wilsonian ideals—which were not envisaged as racially and culturally impartial ideals—at the end of World War I, President Woodrow Wilson rendered these questions significantly more legitimate, urgent, and complex than they already were. He declared his famous fourteen principles—one of which was specifically on "Turkish and non-Turkish portions" of the Ottoman Empire—and promised to defend "the right of all peoples to self-determination."[22] This spelled the end of the era of empires. How could Kurdish nationalists'yearnings for self-governance become realized in the presence of rival nationalist projects? To what extent was a Kurdish independent nation-state or autonomy possible? Through which institutional configurations, identity formations, and ideological justifications could the Kurds' ethno-cultural differences be recognized in practice? These are and were the Kurdish Question(s).

The Kurdish Conflict emerged because the major political actors, primarily the governing political elites, failed to address the Kurdish Question in a manner that could produce sustainable, peaceful, and agreeable solutions for both Kurds and Turks. Hence, while the Kurdish Question was a product of global historical developments, the Conflict was a product of political decisions and choices, which need to be analyzed and explained.

The claim in this book is that the Kurdish Conflict was not the only "logically or objectively possible"—à la Max Weber—consequence of the Kurdish Question. By drawing on conparisons with other cases, public/political discussions in the formative period, and general theoretical insights, I argue that more accommodative and conciliatory paths were within the realm of logical and objective possibility, which could have prevented the Kurdish Question's transformation into the Kurdish Conflict.

The rise of nationalism presented difficult challenges to all of the world's multiethnic and multiconfessional political entities, particularly to empires such as the Ottoman, Qajar, Habsburg, and British. Yet, while the realm of possible responses to these challenges by the ruling elites and the populations they mobilized must have been limited, these challenges were not always met in the same fashion by the governing elites of these polities at different times. What's more, I will show that the contemporary Ottoman imperial political elites were aware of the different possible and imaginable strategies, as indeed were the nationalists themselves.

In a nutshell, giving a causal explanation of the Kurdish Conflict is almost the same as explaining how the Kurdish Question was transformed into the Kurdish Conflict.

## The "Turkish Question" and the Kurdish Conflict

Unpacking the processes that produced the Kurdish Conflict and have been preventing a peaceful resolution of the Kurdish Conflict indicates that they pertain to unresolved divisions of identity, security, and ideology that could be found both among Kurds and Turks, but especially among Turks. In other words, I argue that, to a large extent, the Kurdish Conflict emerged as a byproduct of intra-*Turkish* divisions, conflicts, contradictory ambitions, and feelings of insecurity. Similarly, finding a peaceful resolution has depended on the Turks' ability to successfully address these issues. Hence, my main, political and ideational explanatory variables that account for the failures to resolve the dilemmas pertain to intra-Turkish political and ideational rifts.

Thus, the Kurdish Question and Conflict and their protracted nature cannot be explained without simultaneously analyzing a Turkish Question: the Turks' own political struggles in attempting to form a viable and secure national identity and state. The latter involved efforts to resuscitate the Ottoman/Muslim state project and nationalism based on a reinvented and reconstructed Turkish identity and on particular narratives regarding why and how the Ottoman state disintegrated. These narratives feed Turks' fears of territorial loss and ethnocultural diversity and their ongoing quarrels about how "Turkic," how "Muslim and Islamic," how "Anatolian," how "Western," and how "secular" the Turkish identity and nation-state should be.

Complicating these disputes are two additional and broader challenges. The first one is how to overcome the never-ending search for singular-hegemonic names and meanings of shared identities, places, and social and political categories. The second is how to express in language, live with, and indeed embrace as richness, the social and historical fact of plural, polysemic, polyonymous, and polynomial identities and categories present in Turkey. Indeed, the ethnic/cultural diversity of people who identify themselves as Turks in one way or another is a well-known social and historical fact among (often fiercely Turkish nationalist) Turks as well as non-Turks. However, it has been a challenge for Turks to embrace this based on more pluralistic political values and institutions. Simultaneously, they struggled to find ways to embrace and express it in language, for example in terms of hyphenated identities, such as Bosnian-Turk or Christian-Turk, or, better yet, in some fashion that does not privilege one identity over the other.

Hence, it would not be wrong to say that this book is more about the Turks and the Turkish Question than it is about the Kurds and the Kurdish Question.

## The Three Dilemmas and the Explanation in This Book:

Figure 1.1 illustrates my nonstandard causal explanation.

### External Security Dilemma

This dilemma regards—from the point of view of the ruling political elites—the question of how the Kurdish Question can be resolved while at the same time ruling out the possibility of Kurdish secessionism. This dilemma grew out of the partitioning of the former "Ottoman Kurdish" population between three post-Ottoman nation-states: Turkey, Iraq, and Syria. At the beginning of the War of Independence, the independence

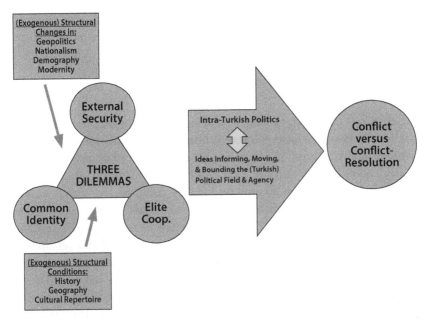

Figure 1.1. Summary illustration of the causal argument.

movement envisaged that most Ottoman Kurds and the territories in which they formed majorities would be included within the nation-state they aimed to establish. Hence, this state would comprise two major ethnic groups not so unequal in size, Turks and Kurds. However, following the war and a period of multilateral negotiations between 1923 and 1926, "Southern Kurds" were left outside of Turkey and remained within the British and French–mandated Iraq and Syria respectively, as decided by the League of Nations. As I will discuss further in chapter 3, there is weak evidence to support Kurdish nationalist claims that Turkish nationalists, or for that matter, secular nationalists led by Mustafa Kemal, *intended* to leave Mosul outside of Turkey. The exclusion of Mosul rendered pan-Kurdish secessionism a potential threat while turning the Kurdish population in Turkey into a smaller and thus more negligible minority for the ruling elites to control. This dilemma continues to exist because the potential of pan-Kurdish separatism[23] has not credibly been eliminated through measures such as a domestic or international political settlement.

I will maintain that one way in which Turks and Kurds might resolve this dilemma is through the "flexible socioeconomic integration" of Turkey with Kurds in Iraq and Syria. The realization of such a policy would require ideational innovation as well as the formation of particular political elite coalitions I will discuss.

## COMMON IDENTITY DILEMMA

This dilemma concerns the challenge of constructing a common identity[24] that would simultaneously address Kurdish and Turkish identity-related demands and concerns. The form, if not the essence, of this dilemma has changed since the formative period. In the formative period, the dilemma regarded whether or not a common identity could be found that would simultaneously meet Kurdish nationalists' demands for the recognition of the Kurdish identity and culture in the new Turkey, and the Turkish nationalists' concerns to form a cohesive nation out of the remaining non-Kurdish population that also comprised an ethnically and linguistically diverse lot. In the current period, when there is a well-established national identity and nation-state of Turkey, this dilemma concerns the question of how to reformulate the national identity or reconstruct existing common identities so that the Kurds feel that their identity enjoys equal respect and recognition while the remaining majority of the population, who now zealously identify themselves as Turkish (even though the origins, content, and boundaries of Turkishness remain contested among the Turks themselves), do not feel anxious and defensive about the future and integrity of their own identity.

This dilemma involves an asymmetry between how (a sizeable number of) Kurds and Turks view the Turkish identity. While for many Kurds, Turkishness unquestionably is an ethnic identity, Turks tend to have a more variegated, mixed, and contested image. The reasons for this asymmetry lie in a metamorphosis of Turkishness before and during the formative period. At some point during this process, some elites, whose primary goal was to rescue the Ottoman state and the majority of whom were ethnic Turks, decided to defend their campaign as a "Turkish" rather than a Muslim Ottoman project and as "Turkish" rather than Muslim Ottoman nationalists. In other words, they tasked Turkish nationalism and identity with taking over the roles and "missions" of Ottoman state nationalism and state-national identity. Yet, during this process they did not merely replace a well-established Muslim Ottoman identity with a predetermined Turk identity;[25] they also reinvented and transformed the meaning and boundaries of the Turk identity that they wanted to uphold. This new

Turkishness became a broader project in view of its geography and target audience. From then on, and in the eyes of its upholders, the historically preexisting ethnic Turk *category*—which I will define shortly—was transformed into a national *identity* and expected to encompass a multiethnic and, to some extent, multiconfessional population. Such a transformation did not take place with Kurdish nationalists and with Kurdish nationalism and national identity, which remained projects mainly of and for ethnic Kurds and Kurdish speakers.

I will argue that, in order to resolve this dilemma, it may be necessary to formulate and foster a common identity that allows people to embrace it with different names and contents, as in Turkish (*Türk*), which most Turks prefer as the name of the common identity or "of-Turkey"[26] (*Türkiyeli*), which many Kurds prefer as the name of the common identity in the country. Clearly, ideational innovation and flexibility—about identities in general and about Turk and Kurd identities in particular—politics and political agency would play key roles in realizing the legal and discursive changes to implement such a policy.

## ELITE COOPERATION DILEMMA

This dilemma regards the question of which political actors can work together to address the Kurdish Question, by establishing inter-elite trust and managing inter-elite power struggles over differences not necessarily related to the Kurds. These differences involve ideological disagreements—mainly, but not exclusively, over secularism—and discords over power sharing, which have been more pressing for Turkish elites than the Kurdish Question and Conflict.[27]

The resolution of the Kurdish Question requires significant elite unity,[28] that is, the presence of a group of elites who can agree on certain strategies and reforms and cooperate with each other to implement them, and who are not divided by goals and interests that are more important to these elites than the Kurdish Question. This last condition means that these elites should prioritize the Kurdish Question, that is to say, they should not see their policies vis-à-vis Kurds as an instrument to settle other elite power struggles.

Such elite unity is needed for intra-Turkish, Turkish-Kurdish, as well as intra-Kurdish elite cooperation. My focus will be on the first two elite divisions. The intra-Kurdish elite dilemma is more straightforward. During the formative period, Kurdish elites were suppressed as they were fragmented, weak, and distant from the masses. Over the course of the republican history, Kurdish elites achieved more unity and support of the masses.[29] We will see that this is especially true for secular/leftist Kurds. They have thereby organized greater challenges to the nation-state of Turkey, notably under the violent leadership of the PKK and its political formations during the last three decades or so. Further, and understandably, the Kurdish Question and Conflict were a priority for most Kurdish elites. That is, even though they are by no means immune to power struggles and ideological and other rifts, the Kurdish Question is not instrumental to other objectives for them.

Intra-Turkish elite divisions are more complex. Time and again different elite groupings have instrumentalized the Kurdish Question to achieve domination over other, Turkish elites. Hence, in both the formative and current re-formative periods, the ruling "Turkish"[30] elites formed their policies vis-à-vis Kurds primarily with a view to prevailing in intra-Turkish elite struggles, and to achieving elite goals unrelated to the Kurds. For these elites, the Kurdish Question was secondary to other questions, such as the secular-versus-religious nature of the state.

In the formative period, the intra-Turkish dilemma mainly pertained to divisions, first between Islamist/Muslim conservative and secularist elites, and then, following the partial purge of the former from power, between radical revolutionary and moderate evolutionary secularist Turkish elites. I will argue that as the radical revolutionary secularist elites monopolized power and the regime coalesced around their ideas and base in the formative period, the kind of inter-elite cooperation that would be required to address the Kurdish Question also became less and less possible.

Since the formative period, the elite cooperation dilemma has become more multilayered. It still involves a major inter-elite rift between Islamist and secularist elites, and, to some extent, between Muslim conservative[31] and secularist Turkish elites. In addition, it now involves problems of collective action and consensus building to address the Kurdish Question between "moderate" Turkish and Kurdish actors within each of these political-ideological groupings. As we will see, since the 1960s, and especially since the late 1980s, Kurdish politics has produced many explicitly Kurdish parties and movements while many Kurds have also participated in majority Turkish political parties and movements. In addition, while Kurdish nationalist party politics consolidated behind political parties close to the PKK, Kurdish movements have significantly diversified with new generations of women, youth, ideological orientations, and visions of peace.[32] Hence, in the current period, as I will elaborate in chapter 6, the elite cooperation dilemma also pertains to problems of cooperation between Turkish and Kurdish actors within and across these groupings: for example, between Turkish and Kurdish left-wing actors or between left-wing Turkish and religious conservative Kurdish actors.

Solving this dilemma hinges on legal/political institution building and transformations and the emergence of a more balanced and accountable political system. These, in turn, require political learning, agency, and ideational factors. Ideational gaps between Turkish and Kurdish actors—and the ideational bottlenecks affecting especially Turkish actors—undermine cooperation between nonviolent actors who are otherwise willing to work together. In general, this dilemma underscores how the resolution of the Kurdish Conflict is closely interlinked with the overall question of democratization.

## This Book and Current Research on the Kurdish Conflict

### OVERCOMING STANDARD EXPLANATIONS

Whether academic or not, every explanation of historical events and developments actually forms a story (a narrative). And, as in every story, these stories also have actors, protagonists, and, often, antagonists. These actors are described as playing specific roles in a chain of events.

"Standard stories"[33] take place between self-propelled actors. They explain the reasons behind the actors' behavior through the actors themselves, that is, through the actors' distinctive characteristics and own volition, which are considered evident. Most importantly, standard stories are conveyed in such a way that it seems impossible for events to unfold in any other way.

In contrast, causal, nonstandard stories emphasize—implicitly or explicitly—not only what happened, but also what could have happened. That is, à la Max Weber, they shed light on "counterfactual outcomes": "outcomes which have not been realized but do not conflict with logical or objective possibilities."[34] This of course does not imply that "anything can happen"; counterfactuals are bound by what we know about how the social world operates, based on history, other empirical evidence, and available theories.

Counterfactuals are the essence of every causal explanation. Being able to state: "A happened because of B" requires being able to state: "If B is causally relevant and hadn't happened, A wouldn't have transpired (and something else would have happened)," or "A would have happened differently."[35] In the background, there is an alternative story in which there is no B, and, hence, A cannot come into being or cannot happen in the same way. Nonstandard stories explain why alternative causal paths—chains of events—did not unfold and why the factual path unfolded the way it did.

The ubiquity of standard stories in academic and popular writings on the Kıurdish Conflict is a major factor in itself, which undermines a resolution because they prompt people to search for spurious, unhelpful, or counterproductive remedies. Standard stories mislead people to think of actions, beliefs, and discourses that are actually products of conflict as the causes of the conflict. Hence, they lead people to see actors themselves and their purportedly pre-fixed intentions, identities, and ideologies as the causes of the problem, instead of focusing on institutional reforms, conceptual innovations, and wiser political decisions.

Two standard stories have dominated analyses of the Turkish-Kurdish case.

## Standard Story 1: Actors with Predetermined Intentions

The research that produces this story aims to explore the goals and intentions of the actors during the formative phase by examining historical records and documents. For example, it attempts to understand how Mustafa Kemal (Atatürk, Ataturk), the Young Turks, or Kurdish nationalists *wanted* (or intended) to solve the Kurdish Question.[36]

In line with this approach, Kurdish nationalists and many other analysts have argued that Turkish or "of-Turkey" nationalists promised a kind of autonomy and equality to the Kurds who joined them during the War of Independence.[37] However, they have argued that Turkish nationalists never intended to fulfill this promise.[38] As this narrative goes, any promises made were tactical.[39] In the words of Mehmet Bayrak,[40] a Kurdish and "of-Turkey" researcher and intellectual who has published many books on Kurds, Turks, and Alevism:[41]

> During the Treaty of Lausanne in 1923, Kurdistan was actively and officially split into four as a country and a nation. The Kemalist regime had forgotten its previous promises to Kurdistan relating to Kurdistan's autonomy from and equality with Turks in political, social and cultural life and blatantly mani-

fested its *secret aim* to create a uniform society by suppressing the 1925 Kurdish National Resistance Movement: The Kurdish identity was to be eradicated with oppression and by brutal force and a Turkish nation would be created by the hand of the state [emphasis mine].[42]

According to this narrative, from the very beginning there was a plan to found a Turkish nation-state that was imagined as a homogeneous, mono-ethnic nation-state, namely, a nation-state that disregarded and denied any recognition to ethnic components. There was consensus in this matter among the leaders of the independence movement (including those who were later politically sidelined), and thus, there were no other possibilities. When Turkish nationalists no longer needed the support of the Kurds, they put their plan into practice.[43]

Other (mainly Turk) authors who critically examine the development of the Kurdish Question from this perspective give less place to the importance and validity of any promises of Kurdish autonomy made by Turkish nationalists. However, they too refer to the statements of the leaders of the time, primarily those of Mustafa Kemal, and attempt to infer the leaders' intentions. This methodology has produced two conclusions: (1) There was no incoherence or fundamental change between the narratives and policies during the war and those after the founding of the Republic;[44] and (2) both prewar and postwar policies and discourses were natural extensions of Turkish nationalism and of the aim of founding a nation-state.[45]

In the words of one author, "The pluralism of the National Campaign [*Milli Mücadele*] was a consequence of the political requirements of the period. These requirements pushed the nationalist cadres that founded the republic to form alliances they would not sustain after establishing the political order for which they *aimed*. These alliances were made with Muslim-conservative and Islamist groups and non-Turkish Muslim ethnic groups" [emphasis mine].[46] However, the emphasis in these studies is as much on the intentions of the actors as it is on "the assumed agentic role" of "nationalism," which I will discuss next.[47] Meanwhile, other writers emphasize as causal factors the intentions of external powers such as Great Britain and the United States, and Kurdish secular-nationalist and Islamist actors.[48]

These studies help us grasp the perceptions of the major social, political, and military actors of the time. However, even the best examples of such research can only make a limited contribution to building a causal, nonstandard narrative.

A significant number of events as well as the thoughts and intentions of key actors from this turbulent period were not recorded. Further, most of what has reached us today consists of the thoughts and intentions of those actors who came to attain dominant political positions later on. Furthermore, during the National Campaign years, very few participants would have foreseen the founding of the republic or the events that took place afterward. At that time, there were different imaginations and expectations of the future, and, thus, preferences and perceived interests were formed accordingly.

Had events unfolded differently, other actors and their thoughts might have become more influential, potentially creating room for other unthinkable or "unthought" scenarios and dominant narratives. If we fail to include the views of subsequently marginalized actors as part of our explanation, or the views that were not entertained but were possibilities, our explanations will ignore alternative scenarios that were objectively and logically possible.[49] The process ultimately becomes based on the ostensibly unchanging and determinist intentions of the "winning" and prominent actors. It might be the case that the principal causal factors were those that allowed the winning actors to win, rather than the winning actors' intentions themselves. These factors could be political, military, or socioeconomic. One should also keep in mind that the National Campaign might have failed, and the Republic of Turkey might not have been founded, without the participation of those who were later politically marginalized. Hence, it would be inadequate to determine the possible "intentions" and goals of Turkish nationalists vis-à-vis Kurds and other ethnic components based on the postwar actions of a smaller set of political elites, which, as I will argue, rose to power as the victors in intra-Turkish political conflicts. Last, but not least, the intentions and visions of the winning actors in this process most likely did not remain stable either. I will make the case in the third and fourth chapters that leading actors' intentions and plans changed and adjusted to unforeseen and changing circumstances.

Thus, my nonstandard explanation helps overcome a major weakness of extant research on the Kurdish Conflict and the formation of modern Turkey in general: the limited conceptualization of Turkey's nation-building elites as, more or less, consisting of the revolutionary secularists and notably the persona of Mustafa Kemal (Atatürk) alone. More specifically, my explanation contributes to transcending personalist explanations and, in particular, "methodological Kemalism . . . the practice of referring to Mustafa Kemal—or to his name—as a means for spontaneously periodizing and conceptualizing Turkish history."[50] This does not mean to downplay the immensely critical, agentic, and charismatic role that Mustafa Kemal personally played in shaping the formative period of Turkey and the Kurdish Conflict. However, my nonstandard narrative contextualizes and clarifies why he and other founding elites made the choices they did.

## STANDARD STORY 2: THE INEVITABLE CONSEQUENCE OF NATIONALISM AND THE "NATION-STATE"

According to this story, the Kurdish Conflict was caused by nationalism and the pursuit of forming a nation-state, and its solution is to "overcome" "nationalism" and the nation-state. Hence, one should conclude, it was inevitable that the Kurdish Question—which did indeed emerge with the rise of nationalism in the world—would transform into the Kurdish Conflict.

In no way unique to Turkey, this narrative claims that national identities are more artificial and inherently flawed than other identities, and that nationalism itself—not nationalists—is responsible for many of the world's problems. Hence, argued a video published by *New York Times*, "nationality . . . the idea that you identify with millions of strangers based on borders . . . is weird . . . that's because nationality is made up."[51] The video did not question that based on the same reasoning most of the social identities that give meaning to people's lives, such as religion, socialism, or environmentalism, would also be "weird," because they too were constructed by people at some point in history and they too enable people to identify with millions of strangers. Nevertheless, as I will elaborate in chapters 6 and 7, examples of this standard story among critical Turkish academic and intellectual circles translate Benedict Anderson's concept of imagined community (which he utilizes to refer to nation) into Turkish as *hayali cemaat* (literally, "*imaginary* community").[52] This translation undermines critical discussions in pursuit of peace by trivializing nationalism as if it were something that could be eliminated if only people "woke up." It also bypasses the actual question about nationalism: given the reality of explicit and implicit national sentiments, nationalist ideas, and nation-states in the world, how can we explain the role of nationalism in the creation of conflicts and how can we convince people from different nations and "nationalist" mindsets to embrace conflict resolution?

During the last few decades, studies of Turkish and Kurdish nation-alisms have created an important body of knowledge regarding the his-torical course of these two ideologies and how they were constructed.[53] However, particularly popular texts have produced a problematic tendency. Rather than considering nationalism an ideology, sentiment, movement, or doctrine, they personify it as if it were an *agent* with its own will, desires, and ability to learn, enabling it to make independent decisions and "speak to" or enter into conflict with other nationalisms.[54] Examples of commonly used pseudo-causal statements include: "Turkish nationalism [not nationalists] *wanted* to create a homogenous nation," or, "Turkish and Kurdish nationalisms excluded each other."

This "nationalism treated as an agent" is charged as the cause of a series of phenomena, from the Kurdish Conflict to Turkey's democratic deficits, rather than the decisions taken by nationalist actors or their actions. As a result, these studies propose solutions such as overcoming nationalism and introducing new identities that are allegedly not nation-alist or are less artificial. In the words of one author and book, Turkey should evolve "towards post-nationalism" and promote "post-nationalist identities."[55]

This perspective overlooks the fact that any sustainable conflict res-olution and peace would need to involve "nationalists," whether hardline, moderate, or "banal,"[56] and must take into account their fears, grievances, and demands. We will see in chapter 5 how political actors such as Recep Tayyip Erdoğan, who denounced nationalism in the name of postnation-alist peace, Islamic solidarity, and ostensibly democratic values in 2011, actually harbored nationalist preferences in more indirect ways that were not free of the notion of "national" interest.[57] Indeed, Erdoğan ended up coalescing with Turkish hardline nationalists and adopted a fiery nation-alist orientation after the collapse of peace talks with the PKK in 2015.

Meanwhile, critical analyses often conflate criticisms of nationalism with those of nation-state, without properly defining "nation-state" and by simply equating it with the notion of "homogeneous nation-state." They seek solutions to the conflict by abandoning the nation-state, as well as nationalism. Consider the following passages from two Turkish intellec-tuals, one secular/liberal and the other Islamist:

[N]ation-state and Turkish nationalism put this country in a straitjacket from head to toe since the founding of the Republic in relation to the Kurds, Alevis, Muslims and non-Muslims.

Now this tight outfit is weakening at the seams. This is an unstoppable state of affairs that will take time. . . . There is still much to be done. Remember, the nation-state still continues to exist with its numerous flaws.[58]

The Kurdish conflict is, to a great extent, rooted in the nature of the nation-state. This is a new model of governance that emerged with the Enlightenment and the French Revolution. The nation-state is territorial, it selects an identity and makes it into the official identity. Everyone becomes homogenized in the same identity within national boundaries. This is what lies at the heart of the problem.[59]

In these quotations, the nation-state itself is given a causal role, rather than particular models, institutions, or interpretations of the nation-state, specific policies of the nation-state or the political dynamics that lead state founders to adopt a monocultural—rather than pluralist or diversity-friendly—version of nation-state. The nation-state is criticized *in toto*; the implication being that it needs to be replaced with something else rather than reformed.

In Turkey's political discourse and practice, people tend to think of mainly two models when they hear or talk about "overcoming (transcending) the nation-state." Some Kurds interpret this to imply either Kurdish secession or the transition to a federal or confederal system, while others interpret it to imply the transition to a state based on a religious common identity or religious principles, meaning, an Islamic or Islamist state. Hence, in the later parts of the second quote above, the Islamist intellectual pondered:

[If] the Republic of Turkey used the Turkish identity in its religious meaning there would not have been a problem. Then the Kurds would not have had to deny their own identity and could speak their mother tongue as they wished.[60]

To be clear, my point here is not to defend or denounce nationalism—or, for that matter, particular nationalist ideologies. Nationalism is too broad and vague a category to explain political outcomes—such as the Kurdish Conflict and others—on its own. Surely, nationalism should be part of causal explanations as an ideology, movement, doctrine, or emotion that has varying tones and forms. However, it is ultimately the *acts* of nationalists that shape political and social outcomes, not the ideology itself. Moreover, if nationalism is part of people's social and ideological environment,[61] this may be a byproduct rather than cause of various unresolved political or social conflicts, which problem-solving efforts should target rather than nationalism. Finally, one wonders whether it is an effective approach to hinge the solution of social/political problems on the transcendence of nationalism. Nationalisms are part of social reality and will probably remain so for the foreseeable future.

For sure, national identities are neither fixed nor sacred; people can become—and should in my opinion—"disenchanted" with nationalism in the same way that they can become disenchanted with religion either when they stop in believing in religions or when they consider "unbelief" possible[62] even when they continue to believe themselves. In fact, ethnic and nationalist politics can be understood as fields of social/political struggles to contest, preserve, or redefine/rebuild identity definitions and intergroup boundaries.[63] This is yet another sense in which "politics," as I discuss in this book, can help resolve the three dilemmas of the Kurdish Conflict and others.

Thus, without denying the role of nationalism in ethnic/regional conflicts, my explanation unpacks and explains the decisions and particular choices of nationalists, and explicates why particular forms of national identity and nationalism rose to dominance in the public political sphere in Turkey, based on political and ideational dynamics.

## This Book and Current Research on Ethnic/National Conflicts

My analysis and explanation informs and contributes to theories of group conflict and conflict resolution at large, in at least three major ways.

First, it shows how ethnonational conflict, and majority group nationalism, can arise as a byproduct of intra-elite rifts within the majority group. Accordingly, I argue that solutions to ethnonational conflicts should primarily be sought in the political and ideational dynamics of the majority group. This challenges the conventional wisdom that relatively more homogenous majority, dominant, or "core" groups,[64] and those having more united and self-confident elites, would be more willing and able to suppress minority groups, ultimately generating more "conflict."[65]

Concomitantly, groups would be less willing and able to repress minorities if they were less homogeneous and had less coherent elites. This would happen, for example, if they were fragmented by internal disagreements and cross-cutting divisions[66] they share with the minority, such as class, religion, and ideology. By contrast, I argue that conflict may be more likely when the majority group, especially its elites, is fragmented by internal disagreements.[67] As my causal analysis of the formative and re-formative periods of the Kurdish Conflict will suggest, at least four causal mechanisms can influence and operate through the actions of the majority group, promoting ignorance of and disregard for minority demands that directly extend the conflict.

In the Turkish-Kurdish case, these causal mechanisms include: (1) a preoccupation with settling internal disagreements and ignorance of the minority concerns, which are less important than the cleavages within the majority group; (2) a failure to develop, agree on, and organize political action to implement concrete policies of conflict resolution and accommodative reforms; (3) the exploitation of the conflict with the minority by some majority elites as an instrument to sideline rival elites and to prevail in internal power struggles; (4) the spontaneous rise and willful use of majority group nationalism by social/political elites to unify the majority group and the nation-state, and the inability to accommodate the minority demands as an unintended consequence.

Second, I show and maintain that ethnopolitical conflicts such as the Kurdish Conflict are not automatic products of nation-states and nationalism. As I will elaborate in my review of theories of nationalism and nation-state shortly, nation-states differ widely in their ability to accommodate differences among their citizens and thus manage conflict. My explanation draws attention to politics and ideational dynamics—especially those of the majority group—as possibly the most important yet least investigated factors that determine to what extent a nation-state is able to do so.

Third, and relatedly, I argue that political and ideational factors enable researchers to apply general explanations of ethnic/national conflicts to particular cases such as the Kurdish Conflict, and explain the historical evolution of these cases with higher degrees of "internal validity."[68] By their very nature, these general explanations are probabilistic, not deterministic. Structural determinants of conflicts such as geopolitics can be very powerful but are ultimately amenable to reinterpretation through ideational development and surmountable via political action. Similarly, politics and ideas directly shape a particular conflict while general explanatory factors highlighted by extant research only condition and constrain the field of possibilities. In other words, political action informed by ideational innovation can either aggravate and perpetuate or cancel and modify the conflict-producing effects of general explanatory factors. As I already discussed, I show a way to conceptualize the relationship between longue duree–structural and actor-based, purposeful causal factors by formulating the former as "dilemmas" that political actors need to address.

Similarly, I argue that metatheoretical perspectives such as constructivism and primordialism and different midrange theories on nationalism, state formation, and democratic transition—cannot by themselves account for the emergence and durability of this conflict. Again, I show a way to combine the causal factors highlighted by these general explanations to explain a particular case. I argue that these factors become influential through the intermediation of political and ideational variables. That is, on a different path of politics combined with different dominant ideational features, these factors might have been present but not as influential.

For example, on one hand, theories of ethnic/national conflict based on "material," "intersocietal," and "ontological" security dilemmas[69] explain a great deal of Turkey's Kurdish Conflict, as I argue through the conceptualization of the external security and common identity dilemmas. Similarly, arguments based on geopolitical rivalry[70] are relevant and embedded in my concept of external security dilemma. On the other hand, by analyzing the formative and re-formative periods through process tracing, I show that these security dilemmas and geopolitical conflicts became causally important only after power relations in domestic and external politics evolved on a particular path, and simultaneously particular ideas and beliefs became dominant. Hence, on different paths of politics and dominant ideas, security dilemmas and geopolitics might not have become as important.

Instrumentalist explanations[71] that highlight the role of political elites in mobilizing ethnic/national groups, making decisions that lead to group conflicts, and defining group interests according to their own interests are also relevant. These insights are captured in my argument by the elite cooperation dilemma. However, elite decisions and interests became so important precisely because of the failures of political processes that could have produced more cooperative paths of resolving elite power struggles, where ideational rifts and conceptual bottlenecks played crucial roles. Similarly, institutionalist theories[72] that emphasize how territorial and functional centralization of state institutions inevitably produces intergroup inequalities and induces conflict—and, conversely, how decentralization reduces conflict—help explain the Kurdish Conflict because Turkey's elites could not find political and ideational solutions to the three dilemmas.

Indeed, I will argue that decentralization—as in devolution or federalism—would be feasible in Turkey only after the three dilemmas are adequately addressed. I also maintain that because this did not happen, past periods of reforms featuring administrative decentralization have been followed by periods of re-centralization. Similarly, democratization's eventual[73] dampening effects on conflict shown by large-N empirical studies would only materialize in Turkey after the three dilemmas are resolved. Because this did not happen, as we will see, the direct and indirect effects of the Kurdish Conflict have instead undermined Turkey's democratization. Once again, the key link between general theories and particular cases is the unique politics and ideas surrounding the three dilemmas and informing Turkish democratization.[74]

"Microlevel" and "resource-based" explanations[75] of conflicts can help explain the territorial distribution of violence in the Kurdish Conflict. I refer to explanations focusing on economic grievances, inequality, and deprivation[76] when I discuss whether economic development can cure the conflict; however; I argue that economic grievances are not a main cause of this conflict, compared to other factors such as identity, security, and political power.

Finally, geographical "diffusion theories"[77] and the legacy of past violent conflicts[78] also help explain the endurance and evolution of Turkey's Kurdish Conflict. I capture the role of the former partially in the external security dilemma. In addition, I refer to their roles in my historical narratives of how Kurdish movements in Iraq affected the Kurds of Turkey, how external developments triggered transformations in the Turkish mainstream discourse on Kurds, and how the ascendance of the PKK and its violent war with the state affected the trajectory of the conflict. Ultimately, however, the roles of these factors are also not deterministic; they are endogenous to the failures of politics and ideas in resolving the three dilemmas, which constitutes the thrust of my argument.

## This Book and Theories and Categories of Nation, Nation-State, and Ethnicity

Lastly, I need to discuss the relevant theories of nationalism, nation-state, and the formation of modern states in relation to my argument and clarify how I employ critical terms such as *nation, ethnic group* and *ethnic category, nation-state, homogenous nation-state,* and *state-nation,* which undergird my explanation. In chapter 4 I will explain rival and compatible images of identities: two other crucial concepts for my explanation.

The concepts of nation, nation-state, and ethnicity are among the constitutive ideational innovations that gave rise to the modern world. Yet, their meanings are constantly contested and differ considerably across countries as well as when used in laws, politics, media, academia, and everyday life, not to mention fiercely debated scholarly disagreements.

## What Is a Nation? Visionary and Realistic Projects

Do the Kurds constitute a nation, as Kurdish nationalists and many Kurds believe, or an ethnic group,[79] as the Turkish government and many Turks think and argue? Throughout this book, I draw on a definition of "nation" that I borrow from Lowell W. Barrington (all emphases are mine).

> What makes nations different from other groups is that they are collectives united by shared [or believed to be shared] cultural features (such as language, myths and values) and *the belief in the right to territorial self-determination* [in other words, the belief that the people who constitute this collective have the right to decide how and by whom a particular territory should be governed]. Put another way, they are groups of people linked by unifying cultural characteristics and the *desire* to control a territory that is *thought of as the group's rightful* homeland. "Culture" here includes a range of traits and beliefs, and the particular ones stressed by one nation may differ from those stressed by another. Likewise, while the belief in the right to territorial control is common to all nations, the particular type of territory and even the degree of control will vary from case to case.[80]

According to this definition, what makes a group of people a nation is not the specific content or nature of those people's common characteristics and identity. Rather, it is the presence of the claim to political rights derived from this content. The common identities of nations may have various specific contents and also be based on different types of bond. Different nations can establish their common identities on different prevalent foundations, such as ethnicity, geography, and religious as well as secular values, which I will elaborate in future sections. In other words, they can believe that their common identities stem from different shared features.

In some cases (actual or nominal), religious belonging might come into prominence (e.g., the people who were divided into the nations of India and Pakistan) as a result of social and political conflicts and mobilizations, and in others, a common history, law, ethnicity, or language might be more central (e.g., the people who were split into the nations of Pakistan and Bangladesh).[81] In any case, we cannot expect each and every member of a nation to come to an agreement on the same content. As in the case of other identities, the specific foundations of national identities are contested by those who embrace those identities as well as by those who don't, giving rise to different perceptions of what makes a specific group of people a nation. These typically are ongoing and sometimes constitutive disputes within nations. For example, in America, discussions about who is a "true" American and who is merely an "American citizen,"[82] or what makes an American or America "great," operate in the same way as arguments over the modern Turkish nation's links to Islam, Ottoman heritage, the specific territory and "cultures" of Anatolia, and Turkic or "Turkish-speaking peoples" elsewhere in the world. Regardless of how fiercely people debate these "formative rifts"[83] regarding the bases and contents of their nationhood, however, the actual condition that qualifies them for nationhood is the belief (or the claim) that they have "the right to territorial self-determination," in other words, the assertion and/or recognition of sovereignty.[84]

In the social sciences, there are two different perspectives on what constitutes a nation.[85] According to the primordialist view, present-day nations are founded upon their ethnic and cultural roots in ancient history, that is to say, the "ancient nations."[86] Nations and national identities demonstrate continuity and permanence in view of their existence and fundamental features.

In turn, the constructivist perspective emphasizes that the nations we presently observe are modern identities and categories constructed particularly by elites who govern the state.[87] According to Hans Kohn:

> Nationalism as we understand it is not older than the second half of the eighteenth century. Its first great manifestation was the French Revolution which gave the new moment an increased dynamic force . . . .For its composite texture, nationalism used in its growth some of the oldest and most primitive feelings of man, found throughout history . . . .They correspond to certain facts—territory, language, common descent—which are entirely

transformed in nationalism, charged with new and different emotions and embedded in a broader context.[88]

The constructivist perspective points to the key roles played by the elites who reenvisage common identities in these processes and build narratives that explain foundational questions concerning national belonging, boundaries, and the future of the nation. These include the physical boundaries of their nation's homeland, who are or should become members of the nation and why, as well as which state policies (educational, military, linguistic, and media) should help build the nation. While acknowledging that modern nations are often built on past historical categories, constructivism asserts that during nation building, the elites rewrite and reinterpret history either deliberately or unwittingly in a selective and creative manner in view of their own imaginings, political preferences, and interests.

According to constructivism, modern states emerged before the seventeenth and eighteenth centuries, thus, before modern nations.[89] That is to say, the claim that modern states have created modern nations is more realistic than the thesis that nations created nation-states. Andreas Wimmer maintains that, while building national identities during the process of modernization, the main concern of the state and the nation-founding elites was to create a new social contract between the rulers (the state) and the ruled (the people) and to establish a new connection (common identity) that would serve as the source of legitimacy for this contract.[90] Through this new bond and in order to increase their means of warfare so they could better compete with other states, the elites tried to persuade the people to do more for the state, for instance, to pay higher taxes and volunteer for military activities.

If so, which factors might have determined the emphasis placed on the historical ethnic origins of the people—in other words, on ethnic nationalism? According to Wimmer, while building common identities, the central governments' or rulers' resources and means to provide services are what determined how much emphasis they placed on ethnicity—a concept I will discuss in more detail shortly. The more powerful and resourceful central governments and power holders were vis-à-vis local power holders, the more successful they were in including the local elites of the different ethnic groups in the process. Thus, the common national identity they constructed became more inclusive of different ethnic groups, emphasizing political belonging, rather than religious or ethnic origins. The more limited the central rulers' resources, the more national identities were constructed based on ethnic origins and (assumed or often reconstructed) ethnic homogeneity.[91] From this perspective, the fact that ex-Ottoman nation-states including Turkey, Greece, and Bulgaria all pursued policies highlighting ethnicity and religion—in discourse if not in practice—to varying degrees in their nation-building processes[92] should be explained with references to state resources and war making, in addition to ideology and historical identity categories.

Ultimately, constructivists argue that political dynamics shaped how people, particularly the ruling classes, constructed ethnic and national identities. These dynamics may include both the "will" of some elites to build a particular form of a sovereign state and its people (i.e., the people to form a nation), as in the example of early-twentieth-century Iranian nationalism, as well as the political and emotional reactions of others who feel alienated by these projects, as in the example of the Kurds of Iran. Hence, argues one author, while Iran's Kurds previously lacked a collective consciousness, during the first half of the twentieth century such consciousness became "constituted by its [Kurdish identity] otherness, and hence its differences with the sovereign [Iranian state national] identity."[93]

Just like other social identities, each project of nationalism is in essence a project of "creative" identity building. It not only generates a new identity with a particular name but also reenvisions the past and the future in a selective manner. But only some of these projects become successful. Khazanov states, "It is not enough to construct identities. To be successful, these identities have to be accepted."[94] Anthony Marx noted that choices about who were excluded and who were included in European nation-building practies were "shaped by a combination of 'rational' and historically determined calculations."[95] That is why it is more meaningful to question and discuss which visions, imaginations, or "projections" of particular nations and which nationalist narratives associated with them are more realistic (plausible) rather than visionary (implausible) instead of focusing on whether or not nations are real (or whether they are constructed or historical). Accordingly, Hamit Bozarslan refers to periods in which Kurdish historiography was more realistic and more "visionary" but states that the periods reflecting the latter played a role of conservation.[96]

In the case of Turkey's nation-building process, certain already existing terms, as well as new and reinvented constructions such as Ottoman, Turkey, Of-Turkey (*Türkiyeli*), Muslim components or ethnicities (*Anasır-ı Islamiye*), Anatolia, Turkish-Kurdish and "nation of Turk" (*Türk milleti*), and other associated imaginings of nationhood were all brought to currency as potential names and descriptions of the nation in the making. Which one or which ones of these could become successful?

Nationalists endeavoring to construct a national identity always have to develop two types of narratives. One of these relates to land and has to explain why the boundaries of a nation-state must encompass a certain territory. The other regards identity and relates to what the nation (i.e., the name and content of the national identity) is, whom it involves (or should involve), and whom it excludes. The narratives of every national identity project constantly compete with the narratives of other identity projects, which may or may not be national. For example, during the final periods of the Ottomans, in addition to Ottomanism, Islamism, and Turkism projects, ideologies, and teachings such as socialism, liberalism, and Sufism presented people with other narratives about who they were, what they should consider their sovereign homeland to be, and on what basis. Meanwhile, Turkism itself proposed different narratives that emphasized ethnic origins, on one hand, or territory (Anatolia, Rumelia,[97] or both) and culture on the other.

The most successful national narrative projects have quite a few attributes in common, which account for their relative success. Firstly, they must establish a reasonable degree of linkage or congruence with social and political realities such as economic integration or military defensibility. These narratives must mobilize the public toward new goals, be it independence or equality and "development" or even "attaining the highest level of contemporary civilization," as was the case in Kemalist Turkish nationalism. They must also enumerate values such as homeland, sovereignty, and common language, history, and brotherhood, as well as enemies or rivals. Finally, successful national projects include symbols such as a flag, national heroes, and patriotic songs, which need to be produced in aesthetically inspiring ways.

However, as we will see, projects that included each of these previous attributes still risked failure. What ultimately emerges as the dominant narrative was the result of a complex web of sociopolitical domestic and international processes and critical events. Even though a homegrown independence movement managed to play a predominant (but not exclusive) role in the foundation of Turkey as a nation-state, in most cases elsewhere in the Middle East—with exceptions such as Iran—external powers were predominant players during the building of nation-states.[98]

Historical and cultural repertoires also play key roles, because building a new nation that never previously existed, using a brand-new name and content is a very difficult and risky project. The state- and nation-founding elites would prefer to take the existing names and historical categories (regardless of how changed their meaning and contents are) as their basis in order to persuade the public to adhere to a new social contract and common belonging. Therefore, the success of the elites' newly created narratives depends on the extent to which these narratives agree with historical and cultural legacies and can inspire and mobilize the target population as well as on contemporary conditions. In turn, the ruling elites can be as creative and innovative as their material possibilities allow.

In keeping with this perspective, Ronald Suny's "radical middle position" offers a useful perspective on how nations emerge:[99]

> For me the nation is (1) modern and constructed but built on prior associations, communities and identities, which in turn were constructed, though at a different time and in a different way. Ethnicity itself, for all the primordialism that accompanies its spokespersons, is like every other human category or group, a social construction—though one with deep roots and considerable longevity—and it evolves and changes over time, is contested by its members and outsiders, and requires effort by actors to maintain some coherence or make changes.
>
> The nation is (2) certainly influenced, shaped, often driven, even created by elites, but on the basis of themes, traditions, and symbols that resonate in the population. "Experience" as understood and explained, is the context for the creation of the nation. "History" is doubly implicated: what is remembered as having happened, and what historians, journalists, and politicians select and promote as collective or official memory.
>
> The nation is (3) more often both civic and ethnic than either one exclusively. As Barrington mentions,[100] these forms of nationalism are useful, perhaps, as ideal types but seldom exist in isolation from one another. They overlap and blend into each other. For one thing, civic requires a stable community, which in some sense is a culture, though the markers of it may be different from those more easily recognized as ethnic.
>
> The nation is (4) both situational and constantly shifting. At the same time, it is much more persistent and indelible than many constructivists would have it. If nations are successful and maintain themselves, imagined communities are soon institutionalized communities.

In summary, even though there is an "umbilical cord"—à la Anthony Smith—between nations and their preexisting names, frames, or foundations, the nation represents something different. Regardless of how commonplace national identities drawing on a particular ethnicity are, a nation is "something more" than an ethnic group.[101] The vital requirement for nationhood is the (socially and politically constructed) *belief* in the existence of commonalities rather than their actual existence.[102]

## NATION-STATE AND CULTURAL HOMOGENEITY

The simplest way of defining "nation-state" is as a type of state that is based on a "nation," believed to belong to a nation, and is identified with it. It is a state that represents, or claims to represent, a specific nation and is legitimated by the "existence" and support of that specific nation.

All (emerging and evolving) nation-states have attempted to ensure that the boundaries of the state and the nation coincide for legitimacy and representation purposes.[103] There are two different ways of accomplishing this. From the primordialist viewpoint, the boundaries of states would have to comply with those of existing historical nations, which—given that the number of viable states in the world far exceeds the number of historical nations—means that some nations would remain nation-stateless, or "destroyed."[104] Indeed, many emerging nation-states forcefully altered demographics by seceding from an existing state, by excluding, suppressing, or exiling certain groups from the state territory, and population exchanges[105] or, alternatively, by annexing other lands. Hence, before the formation of nation-states, secessionist and civil wars escalate, while, during and after the formation of nation-states, both civil and interstate wars increase.[106] The gravest and cruelest examples of these processes are genocide and ethnic cleansing.[107] All of these different painful, tragic, and destructive processes were experienced during the formation of post-Ottoman states including Turkey.[108]

Since nation-states are not necessarily built upon preexisting historical nations with fixed and self-evident boundaries, however, the second way of coinciding the boundaries of nation and state is by political and cultural elites adapting the boundaries and contents (the building blocks) of existing, evolving, and new nations to the boundaries of the state. Hence, all nation-states implemented some nation-building policies, which often involved cultural homogenization, among their people who lacked an awareness of shared sovereignty. People were first and foremost told that they were members of the same nation. For example, the states recognized a single language, usually that of the majority or "core" group—or the standardized version of different dialects—as the standard and taught it to everyone, while they neglected, left out, discriminated against, and sometimes outright disregarded or banned other languages and cultures. When existing nation-states—typically, influential large countries—recognize and support the existence of a new nation-state with a particular name and dominant group representing it, they too contribute to this process. This was the case with the United States in 1783, Greece in 1829, "Yugoslavia" (originally named the Kingdom of Serbs, Croats, and Slovenes)[109] in 1922, Eritrea in 1993, and South Sudan in 2011.

It is important to highlight, however, that while cultural homogeneity is important for the nation-state, it is neither necessary nor sufficient for its viability. It is easier—but not necessary—for people who share a common language and cultural characteristics to develop a common national identity and a sense of "us," and perceive their states as legitimate and sovereign.[110] Thus, cultural homogenization policies are not "ends" in themselves but rather "means" for nation-states.[111] As the next section will illustrate, nation-states differ widely in terms of how much they recognize and often promote cultural diversity within their territories.

STATE-NATION

What happens if a state, or would-be nation-state, at the moment of state foundation, already comprises more than one group of people who view themselves as a separate nation? Who has political sovereignty if more than one group of people is present on more or less the same land and possesses national awareness? What happens if a group of people from within a nation-state over time gains such national awareness? In such situations, how can nation-states consistently guarantee equal democratic civil and political rights as well as universal human rights for all, while simultaneously addressing the question of sovereignty and the expedience of ensuring political/territorial integrity and discouraging conflict-prone centrifugal political dynamics?

Under such circumstances, assert Stepan, Linz, and Yadav, these polities should adopt a "state-nation model" based on "four empirically documentable characteristics":

(1) a high degree of positive identification with the state;
(2) multiple but *complementary* [emphasis mine] political
[including national] identities; (3) a high level of trust in the
state's institutions; (4) a high degree of positive support for
democracy among all the extremely diverse groups of citizens
in the country.[112]

Crucially, "state-nations" do not expect their citizens to embrace a
single national identity and they abstain from cultural homogenization
policies. This is not to say that they do not rely on the common sense
of political belonging and sovereignty held by their members. But rather
than basing their political/territorial legitimacy to rule on the existence
or creation of a *single* nation, state-nations

include mechanisms to accommodate competing or conflicting
(national) claims . . . without imposing or privileging, in a
discriminatory way, any one claim. . . . [They craft] a sense
of belonging (or "we-feeling") with respect to the state-wide
political community, while simultaneously creating institutional
safeguards for respecting and protecting politically salient
sociocultural diversities. The "we-feeling" may take the form of
defining a tradition, history, and shared culture in an inclusive
manner, with attachment to common symbols of the state, or
of inculcating some form of "constitutional patriotism."[113]

Thus, state-nations are able to recognize multiple nations. Stepan,
Linz, and Yadav do not distinguish between political and cultural notions
of nationhood, a distinction I will offer in chapter 7 and will argue is
necessary for the viability of state-nations.

Conversely, these states must also avoid "pure multination[alist]"
policies. Even though they might recognize multiple nations on their
territory, they must also incentivize citizens to embrace some common
national identities. More specifically, it is necessary that citizens in
state-nations view their plural attachments of political/national belonging
as "complementary." For example, in a state-nation arrangement, both
French speakers and English speakers in Canada, or Gujarati and Tamil
in India, can define themselves as nations, but these national identities
should be understood as complementary to the national identities of
Canada and India respectively.

Stepan, Linz, and Yadav propose the state-nation model as an abstract "ideal type,"[114] which in the real world is approximated by "Switzerland, Canada, Belgium, Spain, and India," and present it as an alternative to the "ideal type" of nation-state. Examples close to the nation-state pole are given as "Germany, Austria, the United States, Argentina, and Brazil," as well as Japan and Sweden.[115]

In fact, "state-nations" might be conceptualized as a subcategory of nation-states, since they share the fundamental characteristic of state legitimacy being rooted in the claim of representing a nation or, in the case of state-nation, a set of complementary nations that share a common sense of belonging. Indeed, state-nations and nation-states are not so categorically different as to prevent the adoption of each other's basic institutional practices. The authors argue, for example, that unitary nation-states can adopt policies associated with state-nations in order "to respond to the demands of a potentially secessionist, territorially concentrated minority by creating constitutionally embedded federal guarantees":

> We explore . . . how to utilize many state-nation policies within a unitary state, and whether a mixture of state-nation and nation-state policies can enhance inclusionary democracy and ethnic peace. We propose a strongly revised theory of "federacy" to address this situation . . . federacies have actually been used to democratically manage "robust multinational" problems by the otherwise unitary nation-states of Finland (with the Åland Islands) and Denmark (with both Greenland and the Faroe Islands). We also show that the "scope value" of federacy arrangements can extend to the postwar reconstruction of Italy (with its once-separatist 86% German speaking population of South Tyrol) and to Portugal's 1975 response toward the emerging secessionist movement in the Azores. . . . In a federacy, the unitary nation-state follows nation-state policies everywhere in the state except for the federacy itself, where it employs state-nation policies.[116]

For groups with national awareness, state-nation policies include the provision of maximum autonomy to regional governments where necessary and whereby political sovereignty would be retained by the central state. Most of these policies are described as asymmetric autonomy and foresee the devolution of power to regional governments. Unlike decentralization, where central governments transfer powers of making administrative decisions to local units, in devolution, central governments also delegate legislative and policymaking powers to regional governments. In asymmetric autonomy, devolution is not implemented in the same way and proportion in all regions but only in regions where there is a need and a demand. Such policies of devolution are implemented in different forms and to differing degrees in dozens of places, such as Scotland and Wales within the UK, as well as in Hong Kong, the South Tyrol in Italy, the Åland Islands in Finland, the Tuareg region in Mali, Gagauzia in Moldova, and Tatarstan in the Russian Federation.[117] The concept of state-nation can be compared with Arend Lijphart's model of consociationalism and Will Kymlicka's notion of multicultural citizenship.[118] While these focus solely on "setting up institutional safeguards for ethnoreligious diversity" and "recognition of certain forms of diversity" in respective order, the state-nation model also pays heed to the "task of nurturing countrywide loyalties" and "a coexistence of centrifugal and centripetal institutions."[119]

## Ethnic Group versus Ethnic Category

According to Max Weber's classic definition, ethnicity relates to the belief in and myth of common descent,

> a subjective belief in [a group of people's] common descent because of similarities of physical type or of customs or both, or because of memories of colonization and migration . . . it does not matter whether or not an objective blood relationship exists. [It] differs from the kinship group precisely by being a presumed identity, not a group with concrete social action, like the latter.[120]

Regardless of how real this connection to the same ancestors is, it doesn't change the fact that these conceptions too emerged from social/political configurations in ancient history. To quote Weber again:

> [I]t is primarily the political community, no matter how artificially organized, that inspires the belief in common ethnicity. This belief tends to persist even after the disintegration of the political community, unless drastic differences in the custom, physical type, or, above all, language exist among its members.[121]

Hence, myths of common descent can be developed by people who share collective experiences such as political association, migration, and colonization. Ethnic identities are constructed[122] like other identities. Still, ties arising from real or imagined common ancestry resemble family ties and are therefore thought to invoke greater warmth and sense of authenticity than other ties.[123] Furthermore, even though ethnic identities are by no means entirely given and unchangeable for individuals, they have certain relative qualities, such as "constrained change" and "visibility," which may make them more "real" in the minds of people.[124] As was the case in our earlier discussion of the role of elites in the construction and reconstruction of national identities, the preferences of the elites have played a great role in ethnic identities becoming more important in modern times.[125]

Just as it is for all group identities, it is possible to define ethnic group identity both internally (emic) and externally (etic); hence, Anthony Smith's distinction between ethnic category and ethnic group.[126] *Ethnic category* defines a people referred to with the same name and thought by outsiders to share the same ancestry and origins due to their common geographical, linguistic, and other cultural characteristics. *Ethnic group*, on the other hand, indicates a people, or community, who might carry the characteristics of ethnic category *and* subjectively view themselves as such, that is, they possess a group awareness and, possibly, a certain spirit of solidarity.[127]

Thus, a people possessing the status of ethnic category might not constitute an ethnic group. That is to say, this name and group identity might not be very important to the people who form this category.[128] The group characteristics and boundaries "seen" by outsiders might be very different from what is seen and felt by the insiders. The "insiders" might see the divisions within the group much more clearly and/or identify with wider identities than that of the group. While the elites of an ethnic category might possess such a consciousness, ordinary people from the same category might not have ethnic group consciousness, or vice versa. Of course, in reality, many groups can stand somewhere between the two analytical reference points (or "ideal types" à la Weber) of ethnic category and ethnic group.

## CHAPTER 2

# The Three Dilemmas Explained

## The Lens of a "Most Different Case"

The goal of this chapter is to elaborate the demograhic, geographical, and institutional shapers of the three dilemmas of the Kurdish Conflict, which I introduced in the previous chapter and which form the basis of my explanation. While describing the dilemmas, and for heuristic purposes, I will utilize a "most different case,"[1] by referring to the absence of these dilemmas in the British-Scottish case.[2] I will also make some comparisons with the Kurdish Questions in Turkey's neighboring states. My goal in doing so is not to engage in any systematic contrast and comparison with the Scottish case and others. Instead, my objective is to use it to better illustrate the dilemmas of the Kurdish Conflict.[3]

As of 2018, Scotland comprised roughly 8.2 percent of Great Britain's population and one-third of its territory.[4] Compared to the Turks and the Kurds, the Scots and the English (or at least their respective ruling elites) had a longer history of warfare. However, since the 1707 Acts of Union that united Scotland and England into "a single sovereign people," there have been no episodes of organized deadly violence between Scots and Brits.[5] In modern times, Scottish nationalism stands out as a generally peaceful movement that rejects violent modes of expression.[6]

Over time, however, the Scots were able to win much more self-rule, prosperity, and security than Turkey's Kurds could. In sharp contrast to Kurds, who have no separate rights or authorities whatsoever "as Kurds" apart from their rights as Turkish citizens, Scots achieved devolution and autonomy. In 1999, Britain granted the Scots a parliament and government with wide-ranging authority over taxation and administration of issues ranging from energy policy to education.[7]

Thus, the Scottish case looks remarkably different from the Kurdish case and lacks the "justifications" that Turks and Kurds tend to use to blame each other and defend their own actions. Compared to the path of repression and denial, which Kurds rightly accuse Turks of having meted out to them, the English mainly used negotiation, politics, economic and other incentives to address the Scottish question and gradually recognized past injustices and Scottish rights. In turn, in addition to utilizing mainly peaceful political means to assert their interests, the Scots accepted gradual, evolutionary refoms.

In 1949, two million Scots signed a petition demanding the devolution of political sovereignty and continued to push the British government for self-rule, which was realized only in 1999. The efforts of the autonomous Scottish branch of the Labour Party (the Scottish Labour Party) have been especially important in forwarding and securing Scotland's political demands.

Scotland held a referendum in 2014 on full independence. Despite studies that showed widespread support among Scots for further political autonomy, fewer than half (44.7 percent) of voters voted in favor of full independence.[8] Support for independence might have risen since the 2016 "Brexit" referendum, when a slight majority in the United Kingdom voted to leave the European Union, but only 38 percent of Scots did so.[9]

The English had shown in Ireland that they were more than willing to resort to violence and other repressive means to stamp out expressions of nationalism—in Scotland, they have instead navigated the problem through peaceful negotiation. If the 1949 petition demanding political autonomy for Scotland had been presented to the government of Turkey instead, it would have been labeled "divisive and subversive," and those responsible for it would have been severely punished. The UK government, however, permitted its circulation even if the government felt no obligation to respond to the demands. Going farther back, in 1870, the British government passed a bill aimed at standardizing education across the country. The Scots responded negatively, fearing the bill was an effort at forced assimilation. In 1924, the Kurds responded in a similar fashion to a law unifying the education system, which, as we will see, was among the reasons for a Kurdish/Islamic rebellion in 1925 that the government brutally crushed. By contrast, the British government created a "Scottish Ministry" that was intended to meet some of the Scots' demands, despite being limited in scope. In time, by increasing the powers of both the ministry and the Scottish officials in it, the Scots were able to address their own problems as Scots.[10]

If they had a magic bullet that could put an end to the violence and erase the legacy of the violence between Turks and Kurds in Turkey, would the two parties then act more like the English and the Scots? Or would violence and the culture of violence return after a brief honeymoon? What factors beyond tradition and culture might help us understand the differences between these two cases?[11]

## External Security Dilemma

If Great Britain were not an island and the Scots lived in high concentrations in adjoining countries, one could imagine a similar dilemma to prevail in the Scottish case. Kurds comprise a significant minority population of several neighboring states; yet they do not possess a nation-state of their own. This situation has created a sense of anxiety among the governments and dominant populations (whether Turk, Arab, or Persian) in these countries about the possibility of Kurdish secessionism.

Many Kurds of Turkey feel that as a result of its concerns, the state has worked to weaken Kurdish collaboration and organizations both in Turkey and in neighboring countries. Turkish state policies have been shaped by this mistrust and have further alienated the Kurds. This alienation may stoke separatist political preferences, but it might also kindle demands for self-government through devolution and autonomy similar to those the Scots enjoy, which could provide insurances of cultural and material security for Kurds without independence. In line with this idea, a recent study reveals that in 2011 and 2013, 23.3 and 32.1 percent respectively of the Kurdish respondents in a nationally representative survey declared that they would support an independent state, while 54.6 and 66.1 percent stated a preference for autonomy.[12]

As I have already argued, this dilemma has its origins in the division of former Ottoman Kurds between the Turkish Republic, Iraq, and Syria. The domestic and external political decisions that led to this outcome comprise the Sykes-Picot Agreement (1916), the Armistice of Mudros (1918), the Treaty of Sevres (1920), the Lausanne Treaty (1923), the League of Nations decision to award the Province of Mosul to British Iraq (1925), and the 1926 Ankara treaty between Iraq and Turkey. These developments divided former "Ottoman" Kurds among three independent nation-states.

How and to what extent does this dilemma continue today? Iran, of course, also has a major Kurdish minority, and Russia, Azerbaijan, various Central Asian states, the EU, and the United States all possess significant

Kurdish populations.[13] I will, however, limit my discussion to the four states (Turkey, Iraq, Syria, and Iran) that rule over the territories identified by Kurdish nationalists as their historical homeland and potential basis of a Kurdish nation-state.

## THE KURDISH POPULATION IN TURKEY AND FORMER OTTOMAN LANDS

According to current population statistics, Kurds comprise a substantial minority in Turkey, Iraq, Syria, and Iran, but form a majority of the population over a singular, more or less continuous and broad expanse of territory divided by these four states' borders, which run through it.

Ethnic and national population estimates typically vary depending on how they define ethnicity and nationality and their methodology, whether they define ethnic identity based on ascriptive and innate factors, such as descent and "mother tongue" (*anadil*)[14]—the term used in Turkish to denote one's native language—or based on acquired characteristics and a person's subjective self-identification.

For example, in the censuses conducted in the former Soviet Union, native language and "nationality" were separate questions on the census forms, and millions of people gave different responses to both questions.[15] Similarly in Turkey, a 2010 study titled "Who Are We?" found that responses to the questions "What is your native language?" and "What do you identify as your ethnic identity or ethnic background?" frequently differed from one another. While 12.7 percent of respondents over the age of eighteen indicated that Kurdish was their native language, 13.49 percent reported Kurdish as their ethnic identity.[16] While this discrepancy might appear negligible, out of an estimated population of seventy-three million, this corresponds to more than five hundred thousand people identifying as being ethnically Kurdish but not declaring Kurdish as their native language. Another concern is the assumption that a person should possess only one native language. Another poll conducted in 2014 revealed that around half (7.9%) of the 15 percent of respondents who reported being Kurdish speakers identified Kurdish as one of their two native languages along with Turkish.[17]

The data reveal even more important insights into Turkish identity. While 84.03 percent of respondents reported Turkish as their native language, only 76.74 percent reported Turkish as their *ethnic* identity. This evidence adds further weight to my arguments regarding the common identity dilemma and the nature of Turkishness I will elaborate next; millions of

Turkish citizens (according to the 2010 census, perhaps more than five million) do not see themselves as ethnic Turks but nonetheless speak Turkish as their native language and, as other research has revealed, embrace the label *Turkish* to describe their national identity. Hence, nearly one in ten people in Turkey who are native Turkish speakers identify with an ethnicity other than Turkish. It can be assumed that millions more Turkish citizens with non-Turk ethnic roots over time embraced both Turkish as their native language and their ethnic identity; thus, these figures taken in 2010 greatly underestimate the number of people who have non-Turk ethnic origins but identify themselves as Turkish in one way or another. One reason for this is that since the founding of the republic, education in languages other than Turkish has been banned, resulting in subsequent generations forgetting the native languages of their forebears. Societal and cultural intermixing is another factor. For example, an individual with a Kurdish father and a Turkish mother may identify as Kurdish, but, if Turkish is the primary language spoken at home, might report Turkish as his or her native language.[18]

With all this being said, and keeping in mind that this is a rough estimation, as of the 2000s—and before the Arab Uprisings and the Syrian Civil War—Kurds comprised approximately 18–19 percent of the population of Turkey[19]—including all age cohorts—20–25 percent of Iraq's population[20], and 10 percent of Syria's population. Meanwhile, Iran's Kurds comprise about 7–13 percent of that country's population.[21] Table 2.1 reflects these population estimations and percentages. Accordingly,

Table 2.1. Kurdish Population in Turkey, Iraq, Iran, and Syria.

|  | Turkey | Iraq | Syria | Iran |
|---|---|---|---|---|
| Estimated Kurdish Population (in millions). | 14–15 | 7–9 | 2–2.5 | 6–10 |
| Estimated percentage of total population. | 18–19 | 20–25 | 9–10 | 8–13 |
| Percentage of region's total Kurdish population resident in each country. | 41–48 | 24–25 | 7 | 21–27 |
| Percentage of Kurds living in Ottoman successor states. | 57–61 | 30–34 | 9 | — |

nearly 41 percent of the combined Kurdish population living in these four countries resided within the borders of the Turkish Republic. If we further restrict ourselves to the three Ottoman successor states, Iraq, Syria, and Turkey, the number swells to 57–61 percent.[22] This is to say that a majority of the descendants of the Ottoman Kurdish population—let us call them "Ottoman Kurds"—live within Turkey's borders.

## THE SEMI-MIXED NATURE OF TURKEY'S KURDS

What would be the consequences of any hypothetical Kurdish secession from Turkey, similar to a future Scottish secession from the UK, for example, as one of Brexit's long-term consequences? These consequences could not be understood without taking into account how mixed Kurds are with the rest of Turkey, both socially and geographically. Table 2.2 and Maps 1 and 2 show the available data based on "mother tongue" and regional distribution.

Table 2.2 shows my estimates, based on the 2011 Konda survey, for the percentage of Kurds in the total population of various regions in Turkey, as well as the percentage of the country's total Kurdish population that resides in each region. Accordingly, including ethnic Zaza speakers,[23] who often identify as Kurdish, Kurds in Turkey geographically form a

Table 2.2. Percentage of population in various regions in Turkey who report their ethnicity as Kurdish*

|  | Percentage of total Kurdish population | Percentage of total regional population |
|---|---|---|
| Istanbul | 18 | 14.8 |
| Western Marmara | 0.5 | 0.9 |
| Aegean Coast | 5 | 6.1 |
| Eastern Marmara | 3 | 4.9 |
| Western Anatolia | 4 | 7.7 |
| Mediterranean Coast | 3 | 4.9 |
| Central Anatolia | 0.5 | 1.3 |
| Eastern Black Sea Coast | 0 | 0.1 |
| Western Black Sea Coast | 0.3 | 0.3 |
| Northeastern Anatolia | 10 | 32 |
| Central-Eastern Anatolia | 29 | 79.1 |
| Southeastern Anatolia | 27 | 64.1 |

*Konda, *Kürt Meselesi'nde Algı ve Beklentiler*, 91–92.

"semi-mixed" minority. Forty-four percent of Turkey's Kurds resided in 2010 in regions of the country in which Kurds represent a minority; this number falls to 34 percent if we do not include Northeast Anatolia. One in five Kurds in Turkey live in Istanbul, Turkey's largest city, where they comprise 15 percent of the total population.

A majority (56 percent) of Kurds live in central-eastern (26 percent) and southeastern (27 percent) Anatolia. But, as Map 2.1 illustrates, Kurds

Map 2.1. Percentage of Kurdish Population in Each Statistical (NUTS-1) Region of Turkey.*

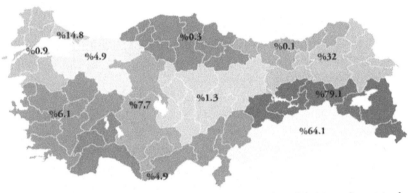

*Nomenclature of Territorial Units for Statistics (NUTS) classifies subdivisions of countries for statistical purposes, based on standards developed and regulated by the European Union.

Map 2.2. Kurdish Population in Each Statistical (NUTS-1) Region as Percentage of Turkey's Total Kurdish Population.

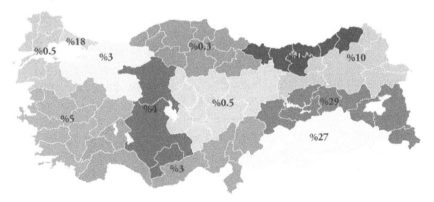

form significant majorities of the population in these two regions (79.1 and 64.1 percent respectively), which share a border with the Kurdish-majority regions of northern Iraq, and Kurdish-majority regions, or pockets, of northern Syria. Together, these areas comprise the geographically—if not always politically—recognized region of Kurdistan, the borders of which have nonetheless never fully been defined.

Other findings reflect relatively low barriers to social integration between Kurds and others, with significant rates of intermarriage; but the Kurds are still not—as I will argue in detail in chapters 7 and 8—a well-known group for the Turkish majority based on personal relations. According to the Konda survey, Turks who reported having a Kurdish parent or spouse totaled 4.4 percent of the country's total population, while given the Kurds' smaller numbers, 12.6 percent of Kurds had a Turk family member. Another study reported that at the end of the 1990s, 8.4 percent of married Kurds had a Turkish spouse.[25] Social barriers might have risen in the 2010s due to the conflict with the PKK and the failed peace initiatives, as I will elaborate later.

These geographic and demographic conditions render pan-Kurdish nationalism and secession possible, as well as being highly destabilizing for Turkey. In this respect, for example, Turkey bears little resemblance to the much less "mixed" population of the former Czechoslovakia. Czechs and Slovaks for the most part lived in separate regions of the country, and when the country officially split into the Czech and Slovak republics in January 1993, it happened relatively smoothly and nonviolently. In 1991, just before the split, ethnic Czechs comprised only 1 percent of the population of Slovakia, while ethnic Slovaks represented 3.1 percent of the population in the region that would become the Czech Republic.[26] Hence, in terms of interethnic mixture, Turkey is closer to Bosnia in ex-Yugoslavia, particularly Sarajevo, where Bosnians of different religions were geographically and socially intermingled. Marriages and friendships between people of different groups were common and people shared a sense of belonging to common identities alongside being Muslim, Serbian, or Croatian.[27] Hence, the attempted ethnic-religious unmixing of Bosnia caused a very painful and bloody civil war and genocide in the 1990s.

In addition to history, nationalism, and demography, great power interests, in particular British, German, and French ambitions, and rivalries played a pivotal role in creating this external security dilemma.[28] Following World War I, Western states led by Britain supported the creation of an independent Kurdish state as a way to frustrate both Soviet interests and the growing power of pan-Turkist and pan-Islamist political movements. This independent Kurdish state was to serve as a buffer separating Turkey under great power mandate from Azerbaijan and Central Asia—where pan-Turkist and pan-Islamist ambitions could find cultural roots and ostensibly sympathetic populations—and weaken the Soviet-backed Armenian state. With the emergence of the Republic of Turkey (1923) and Kingdom of Iraq (1922), Western powers instead saw a "moderate Kurdish nationalism" as more amenable to their interests. This Kurdish nationalism would not pose a serious threat to the territorial stability of regional states but would nonetheless counterbalance Arab nationalism and the regional power of Turkey, Iran, and Iraq.[29]

Come the twenty-first century, the United States as well as a wide range of outside powers including Russia and China are major economic and/or military players in Iraq and Syria. A complex combination of military, economic, and geopolitical interests shape each country's position vis-à-vis the others. However, even today in the midst of the Syrian civil war, many in Turkey, including Kurds, are convinced that Western powers are intent on building a Kurdish state.

Middle Eastern states have their own realpolitik rationales for opposing or supporting Kurdish secessionism, fueling problems concerning democracy and human rights. Throughout the twentieth century, the governments of Iran, Iraq, Syria, and Turkey have at varying times supported Kurdish separatist movements outside of their borders in efforts to weaken rival neighbors. At the same time, they have worked together to weaken and quash Kurdish nationalist and pan-Kurdish political movements.[30] A main goal of the 1937 Saadabad Pact, signed between the governments of Turkey, Iraq, Iran, and Afghanistan, was cooperation to contain Kurdish nationalism. However, for the Kurds, perhaps the most bitter example of states collaborating against their interests took place when the Shah of Iran supported the Kurdish nationalists during the second Iraqi-Kurdish war, only to abandon them after he secured key gains from the Iraqi government over the Shatt-al Arab border dispute in the 1975 Algiers Agreement.

While perhaps providing the state elites with a false sense of territorial stability, such efforts suppressed but did not resolve the external security dilemma. Rather than de-securitizing the Kurdish Question by finding sustainable political/institutional solutions for the external security dilemma, these maneuvers reinforced the politicization and securitization of Kurdish demands, and, indirectly, other societal demands for equality and justice, such as those of women, religious minorities, and working classes in the region. These suppressive and military-security oriented policies have taken a heavy toll on these countries by undermining their democratization and fostering authoritarianism.[31]

Following the 2011 Arab Uprisings, the entire geopolitical order in the region came into question. The Syrian and Iraqi civil wars transformed the Kurds in both countries—including the PKK affiliate Democratic Union Party PYD, which Turkish governments saw as the PKK's extension—into important players on the international stage, reinforcing the external security dilemma as perceived by Turkish governments.

## Common Identity Dilemma

In the Scottish case, there has been only one, limited identity question focusing on policies and the extent of Scottish representation in government and the larger public/political sphere with their separate identity. The British government and the English have not challenged the right of the Scots to express their own identity or the authority of autonomous and "Scottish" institutions such as the Church of Scotland. Scots have also been able to retain their identity within British political parties: major British political parties had their Scottish members form their own "Scottish councils or conferences" centered on issues and concerns particular to Scots.[32] Hence, the conflict revolves around questions of sovereignty, political and adminis-trative authority, the division of economic resources, and relations with the EU, rather than questions of identity and belonging. The issue of critical importance, and upon which the central government was unwilling to concede, is that *political* sovereignty jointly belonged to all citizens of the UK—for example, one single referendum was held on Brexit to determine the fate of the UK as a whole.[33] In sharp contrast, Turks and Turkish governments have contested the separate identity of Kurds in almost all spheres albeit in changing degrees over time, as we will see in detail in later chapters. The presence of a "Kurdistan" even as a historical-geographical category devoid of any political administrative connotation continues to be contested and considered anathema—and even offensive or criminal—in official and mainstream nationalist discourses to this day.[34]

Perhaps more importantly for my argument here, when any Scottish identity concerns are discussed by the Scots and other Brits, there is no simultaneous debate of the anxieties related to the English identity. By contrast, in Turkey, the Kurds' identity-related demands immediately give rise to emotionally charged debates about the *Turkish* identity. Thus, in Turkey, there are two interrelated identity questions, and one (the Turkish) has eclipsed and led to the neglect of the other (the Kurdish):

> *The Kurdish Identity Question*: How (i.e., through which legal/institutional, social, and political arrangements and reforms) to meet the Kurds' need to feel that their identity can be freely expressed, secure, and viewed as an equal to the identity of Turks?

> *The Turkish Identity Question*: When the Kurdish identity is recognized in one way or another, how to address the fears of many people who identify as Turkish that this process would weaken their own identity, which they define as a common national identity and a glue for the nation?

Given Turkey's denial of Kurds' distinct identity, the Kurds understandably felt a sense of unease about the future of their identity and their own futures, and indeed felt victimized by this denial. But the reasons for the concerns that Turks feel about their own identity are less patent. Why do Turks feel anxious about their own identity when Kurds want to publicly and freely act as Kurds? Why should recognizing the Kurdish identity weaken Turkish identity?

The common-identity dilemma grew out of metamorphosis of the Turk identity as a substitute for the Muslim Ottoman identity through processes driven by political elites. The political and intellectual decisions in the formative period, transformed the process of creating a Muslim Ottoman national identity for an ethnically diverse population into one of developing a Turkish national identity.

This process made their identity "vulnerable," if not fragile for many Turks, even though the Turk identity has a long historical legacy as an ethnic/linguistic and political category. Heir of the multiethnic Ottoman Empire and having received major waves of Muslim migrations during the nineteenth and early twentieth centuries, the population inhabiting the territory where Turkish nationalists aimed to form a nation-state was a multiethnic, multilingual, and multiconfessional lot. The Kurdish identity question itself was one major challenge that came out of this process. However, it was not the only one. The other was the question of how to ensure that the common national identity would hold among the remaining (non-Kurdish) population of the nascent imagined nation.

While the great majority of the non-Kurdish population were native speakers of Turkish, a large proportion comprised Muslims who had fled massacres, expulsions, assimilationist policies, and changing conditions (or were descendants of those who had fled) in the Balkans, Russia, and the Caucasus as the empire's borders retreated and people were "unmixed" in the late nineteenth and early twentieth centuries.[35] Many of these refugees and their descendants did not speak Turkish or identify as ethnically Turkish. They were an ethnically diverse lot, including Bosnians, Albanians, Laz, and Arabs. Perhaps more importantly, regardless of their native language or ethnicity, a vast majority had no sense of national identity or common belonging. This situation was made only more acute following the end of the War of Independence and the subsequent mass expulsions and population transfers, most notably the "population exchange" between Turkey and Greece in the mid-1920s.[36] How could a sense of common identity and national consciousness be instilled among such a heterogeneous population? What should be the name of the nation and the basis of the common national identity? These were more salient challenges for the ruling elites than the Kurdish Question.

The names and common identities that were considered and circulated during the War of Independence possessed some potential to resolve the common identity dilemma. These included "the People of Turkey" (*Türkiye Halkı*), "Of-Turkey" (*Türkiyeli*), "the Turkish-Kurdish Nation" (*Türk-Kürt Milleti*), and "Islamic Components" (*Anasır-ı Islam*). By and large, these names all referred to the same "people" as the new nation. On one hand, as newly constructed composite categories, they had more potential than the "Turk" identity to substitute for the multiethnic Ottoman state identity. On the other hand, they lacked historical depth and mass awareness. Compared to the proposed new identity constructions, the Turk identity was a known and historically well-established category, but it was also a narrower ethnic/linguistic category that had long been subordinated to the cosmopolitan Muslim Ottoman category.[37]

However, predominantly political goals and developments, rather than ideological and cultural considerations explain the ruling elites' choice of Turkishness as *the* hegemonic common identity of the new nation-state of Turkey. Rapid nation building, secular political regime consolidation, and, hence, denunciation of the Ottoman ancient regime were urgent prerogatives for the political elites. These priorities were reinforced when the external security and elite cooperation dilemmas could not be resolved. Hence, these elites abandoned the search for options that would resonate with the Ottoman and Muslim legacy and novel categories that would take time to take root. They bestowed the role of carrying on the Muslim Ottoman state identity upon (a reinvented and reformulated version of) the Turkish identity.

Since this national identity formulation—in its eventual form, as I will elaborate in chapter 4—recognizing the Kurds as members of the ambiguously nonethnic "Turkish" nation,[38] Kurds' demands for recognition create a sense of anxiety among Turks about the nature of their own identities, not just Turks' political and economic interests. The conflict often revolves around names, symbols, and concepts such as nationhood. Turks and Turkish governments did not negotiate with Kurds "as Kurds," that is, by recognizing them with their own identity.

This distinguishes Turkey's Kurdish Conflict from those in neighboring countries. For example, the Kurdish question in Iraq primarily revolves around questions of land, natural resources, and political power. The Iraqi central government, which derived its political legitimacy from Arab nationalism, did not deny the existence of the Kurds even during its most violent efforts to quash Kurdish nationalism. Even though it failed to follow through with its legal and institutional promises, the Iraqi government endeavored to negotiate with the country's Kurds. The 1958 Iraqi Constitution, which grew out of a military coup that overthrew the monarchy, declared that "Arabs and Kurds are considered partners in this county where the constitution will state their national rights under the Arab unity."[39] By contrast, Turkey's laws and official institutions nowhere mention Kurds by name, whether as a people, partner, component, or minority. The Iraqi-Kurdish Sovereignty Agreement of 1970 provided Iraqi Kurds with regional sovereignty and cultural rights, allowing for Kurdish-language education and expanding the Iraqi cabinet to include five "Kurdish ministers," and providing for the creation of a Kurdish Academy of Sciences. These articles recognized the Kurdish identity in Iraq and were largely honored by the Iraqi government. Articles that were not honored dealt mainly with the definition of political autonomy, especially in regard to "sensitive issues," such as control of natural resources in contested regions such as Kirkuk and Khanaqin.[40]

Similarly, since the creation of the de facto quasi-independent Kurdish Regional Government in Iraq in 1992, which was recognized and guaranteed by the 2005 Iraqi Constitution, the primary source of conflict between Arabs and Kurds in Iraq has centered on control of land and economic resources.[41] In addition to recognizing the Kurdish Regional Government, the Iraqi Constitution recognizes Kurdish as the country's second official language. Since the transition to multiparty rule in 1950, Turkey has generally been a more democratic country, formally speaking, than Iraq. Ironically, however, it has been much more reluctant to recognize the historical, sociological, and cultural fact of Kurdish identity. This suggests that procedural democratization by itself does not solve the three dilemmas.

In 1978–79, the minister of public works, Şerafettin Elçi, stirred great public controversy when he openly declared: "There are Kurds in Turkey, and I am one of them." This was a shocking statement at the time. Hence, Iraqi Kurdish leader Jalal Talabani (1933–2017) was extremely excited and pleased when Turkish President Özal was willing to host him as a *Kurdish* leader in 1991. He is reported to have said: "This is like nothing else. No one who is not a Kurd can quite understand what it means for me as a Kurd to be accepted and recognized as such by the President of the Turkish Republic."[42]

The denial of the Kurdish identity created an asymmetrical perception of what it means to be Turkish among many Turks and Kurds. For many Kurds, Turkishness is only an ethnic or mono-ethnic national identity, while many Turks also view it as either a nonethnic national identity or one with multiple meanings.

Many people self-identifying as Turks indeed link it to their ancestry, which lends credibility to Kurds' claims about the ethnic nature of Turkishness. However, research shows that these people form a minority among Turks.According to one survey, only 21 percent of those polled felt that ethnic Turkish descent was one of the two most important defining characteristics of the Turkish nation. In contrast, 46.5 percent cited speaking Turkish as a mother tongue—which, in practice in contemporary Turkey, corresponds to the language spoken at home, not to the language of one's forebears; 40.7 percent cited sharing a common Turkish culture—which is a diffuse category, often linked with Muslim or Anatolian culture; and 33 percent cited being a citizen of the Republic of Turkey among the two most important characteristics of being Turkish.[43]

As I will discuss later in more depth, when peace settlement efforts were made in Turkey during the 1990s and 2000s, this did not only invoke public debates about the Kurdish identity but even more bitter debates about the Turkish identity. For example, in 1999, Abdülmelik Fırat (1934–2009), an MP for the center-right True Path Party DYP and grandson of Sheikh Said, leader of the 1925 Islamic-Kurdish rebellion, remarked:

> If you are an Arab, Kurd, Albanian, Bosniak, or Circassian, as long as you say "I am a Turk," as long as you do not acknowledge your Kurdishness, you may find bestowed upon you the loftiest positions in the land. You will be much like the Ottoman janissaries of old. Not long ago our nation was in search of a prime minister. Among those names at the top of the list were three Kurds: Bülent Ecevit, İsmet Sezgin, and Yalım Erez. Inscribed on the grave of Ecevit's grandfather in the city of Kastamonu are the words "Kürtoğlu [son of a Kurd] Mustafa Bey." If you are Bosniak or Circassian, how can you say you are Turkish? [The famous actor and writer] Cem Özer once said, "I am Turkish and Chechen." How is that possible? This is nothing less than fraudulent.[44]

Meanwhile, Hasan Cemal, a prominent journalist, intellectual, and defender of Kurdish rights, and grandson of Cemal Pasha, who, along with Talat and Enver Pashas, ruled the Ottoman Empire during World War I, pondered:

> There is nothing fraudulent about this. One can be Turkish and Kurdish at the same time. It is possible to be, like Yaşar Kemal [1923–2015], "a Turk of Kurdish background." [45] Even if one's native language is Kurdish, one can still write great novels in the Turkish language. Some are Turkish while also being Kurdish. One can be Turkish yet still feel that they are Kurds.[46]

Hasan Cemal, like many of the millions of people in Turkey who come from ethnically diverse backgrounds, embraced a sense of Turkishness as a common identity open to all citizens. Such individuals feel they can embrace this common Turkish identity while simultaneously acknowledging their non-Turkish ethnic backgrounds and belongings. In the following chapters, I will call upon and conceptualize this state of self-perception as the "compatible image" of Turkishness vis-à-vis these other ethnic identities.

However, many people justify this compatibility by creating a hierarchy of importance between these identities in their minds, for example, when some people identify and some people label others as having a

"Kurdish background" (*Kürt kökenli*). According to this hierarchy, Kurds can simultaneously be Turkish and Kurdish only if they embrace the former as their primary and national identity and the latter as their secondary and ethnic identity.

I argue in this book that this is not necessarily a built-in, inherent quality of these identities and of identities in general. Two identities can exist on an equal footing, and often do, especially in "state-nations," as I discussed in the Introduction. A Kurd can identify as Kurdish with his Kurdish friends and as Turkish with his Turkish friends. There are thousands of Kurds in Turkey who project this image of compatibility with their dual Kurdish and Turkish identities.

All of these perceptions and self-definitions are social facts. A tension clearly exists between those who view Turkish and Kurdish identities as mutually compatible and those who view them as being mutually exclusive. From this perspective, a conflict exists, not between the Turkish and Kurdish identities per se, but between the upholders of different images of these identities, as I will conceptualize in the next chapter.

Take the famous Kurdish intellectual Musa Anter (1920–1992), who, throughout his life, sought to peacefully defend Kurdish rights before being the victim of an unresolved murder in the 1990s. Anter, who viewed Kurds who embraced a Turkish identity as "traitors to their own kind," also said the following about "non-Turks" who claimed a Turkish identity:

> Now let us turn our attention to prominent Turks. I can find no prominent Ottoman statesmen of the Turkish race [*sic*]. Those Ottoman elites, janissaries[47] and graduates of the Enderun School,[48] were all kidnapped from Europe as part of the devşirme[49] child levy. Damat Ibrahim Pasha was of Greek descent, Ahmet Melek Pasha was Italian, and the famous Sokollu Mehmet Pasha was of Serbian background. So let's turn to the Republican period. Ismet [İnönü] was Kurdish . . . Rauf Orbay was Circassian[50] . . . meanwhile prominent Kurds openly state "We are not Kurds," but [those] prominent "Turks" [whether of Kurdish, Arab, or Circassian ethnic background] nonetheless declare, "We are Turks."[51]

While Anter's views might be understandable in light of state polices that refused to acknowledge Kurdish identity, his assertion that people should only embrace an identity that aligns with their ethnic ancestry and background found its counterparts among its seeming ideological opposites, Turkish *ethnic* and *racial* nationalists:

> Atatürk's statement, "The people of Turkey who have created the Turkish Republic shall all be called Turks," was, from our perspective, said in light of the political conditions of the time and thus was a diplomatic statement. Because as far as we are concerned, *one does not become a Turk, one is born a Turk.* If we accept this to be true, then it follows that one does not become a Kurd, one is born a Kurd. Are we supposed to recognize Jews who only speak Turkish as Turks, or Armenians who do not speak Armenian, Circassians who do not speak Circassian, Georgians who do not speak Georgian?[52]

Tension and distrust born out of different understandings of what Turkishness is or is not undermine the basis for dialogue and compromise between different political and social actors. I witnessed this firsthand during an interview with Kurdish politician and statesmen Şerafettin Elçi (1938–2012).[53] Although Elçi, a senior figure associated with the Kurdish movement in Turkey, happily agreed to meeting with me and the interview began very amicably, I soon began to feel that I was facing a stone wall and that he was holding back.

The turning point was a question I asked him about Turkishness. I had been trying to understand how the Turkish identity was perceived by politicians such as Elçi. My question was asked in the context of then-ongoing public debates over legal/constitutional reforms and discursive changes in state policies that would replace Turkishness (*Türklük*) with *Türkiyelilik* (Being "Of-Turkey") as the umbrella identity that would unite the nation. The protagonists of these changes thought that the latter identity was a more civic, ethnically neutral, and inclusive national identity and provided a better constitutional basis of citizenship in Turkey compared to Turkishness. Because of certain methodological principles that I now understand to have been too rigid, I restricted myself to merely asking questions that were brief, standardized—across other interviews I was conducting—and open-ended along the lines of whether Elçi thought Turkishness was primarily an ethnic identity, or whether he believed it could be acquired through voluntary association[54] and citizenship. I did so in the hope that I could hear his own personal narrative, even though I could, to some extent, anticipate his responses.

From his perspective, however, it was offensive of me to pose this question about an issue that should instead be accepted as self-evident truth. My question represented discourses that served to reinforce and legitimate the very policies of assimilation that denied the Kurdish identity. The fact that I am an ethnic Turk could have only reinforced this sense of discomfort. For him, this was a sensitive subject for which there was little room for dispassionate intellectual and theoretical debate; there was simply no question in his mind that Turkish identity was ethnic. The very act of questioning it shut down dialogue.

This scene was repeated in my discussions with other Kurds from various social classes and political perspectives. At the same time, I encountered many people who identified as Kurdish (or as being of Kurdish descent) while at the same time self-identifying as Turkish, even though they did not have ethnically mixed parents. This, of course, implied that they perceived Turkishness as a nonethnic category, one that ethnic Kurds could acquire through voluntary association, citizenship, territorial belonging, or patriotism without its necessarily conflicting with their ethnic identity.

My conversations with many liberal (Kurdish and Turkish) intellectuals and academics echoed these tensions. Asking such questions always ran the risk of being perceived as an assimilationist Turkish nationalist. One explanation for this may be that liberal Turkish intellectuals imported the perception of Turkishness held by many Kurdish nationalists, or that these intellectuals subscribed to a rather rigid form of liberal multiculturalism.[55] Alternatively, the reason may be the absence in Turkey and in the Turkish language of terminology that can express hyphenated identities and those with plural and equal meanings and names—that is, polysemic, polyonymous, and polynomial identities.

How could individuals who equally embrace Kurdish and Turkish identities (i.e., without seeing one identity necessarily as more important than the other) express their identity? How would such individuals, who in a variety of contexts may identify equally as Kurdish or Turkish, be described by society? Hyphenated categories that may make sense in English, such as "Turkish-Kurdish" (*Türk-Kürt?*), "Turkish Kurd" (*Türk Kürdü?*) or "Kurdish Turk" (*Kürt Türkü?*) sound strange, artificial, and confusing in the Turkish language. The distinction between Turk and Turkish in the English language, where the former reflects a more ethnic and the latter a more national or citizenship-based meaning (as in "a Turkish national"), does not exist in the Turkish language. *Türk* can mean an ethnic category, nation, or citizenship depending on context, and it can be used as a noun as well as adjective.[56] The phrases "Turkish of Kurdish descent" (*Kürt kökenli Türk*) or "citizen of Kurdish descent" (*Kürt kökenli vatandaş*) are frequently used in Turkish, but impose a hierarchy on the individual's two identities, which is unacceptable to many Kurds in Turkey.

## The Elite Cooperation Dilemma

The elite cooperation dilemma would equally complicate the Scottish Question if, for example, the disagreements and the distrust between the conservative, liberal, and left-wing political elites over questions unrelated to the Scottish Question were so great that they could never cooperate in matters regarding the Scottish question, and instead instrumentalized and weaponized policies such as Scottish rights and devolution—or opposition to such policies—to sideline and outbid each other. Scottish and English actors with respect to the definitions of key concepts such as Scottishness and Scotland or the meanings of nationhood and sovereignty in general were so great that they could not develop policies agreed upon by both groups to address Scottish affairs. Similarly, if pro-peace Scottish and English actors could not develop mutually agreeable policies regarding the definition of Scottishness, Englishness, or nationhood, an elite cooperation dilemma would prevent them from generating mutually agreeable policies to address Scottish grievances.

In the formative period, this dilemma pertained to inter-elite rifts, first among Islamist/Muslim-conservative and secularist elites, and later, following the partial exclusion of the former, between radical revolutionary and moderate-evolutionary secularist elites. The nation-building elites were divided over the meaning and means of modernization and nation building: between those skeptical of modernization and concerned with preserving the Islamic tradition, those who imagined an Islamic model of modernization—similar to their contemporaries[57] in India, Iran, or Egypt, and those envisioning revolutionary versus evolutionary Westernist/secularist modernization. These divisions as well as questions were by no means unique to Turkey, even though it was an early, ambitious, and trailblazing case among such efforts of nation-state formation and modernization.[58]

The disagreements between secularists and Islamists were deep enough to derail new regime formation. However, the rifts among the secularists who saw eye to eye on many fundamental goals of modernizations were not resolved based on power sharing, either. Instead, power was concentrated in the hands of revolutionary secularists who stipulated reforms "for the people, in the name of the people, and despite the people."[59]

> [I]t is hard to imagine that practices such as alphabet and language reforms, which were implemented in haste and in a way that caused a permanent interruption in social memory, as well as the introduction of a Turkish History Thesis, the university reform of 1933, and the recital of the *azan* in Turkish could be implemented in an environment that allowed for criticism. In return, there seems no reason to think that reforms in line with the long-standing fundamental projects of the Turkish progressive-nationalist movement, such as unifying the (modern and traditional) education system, the dissolution of the Sharia courts, civil law reforms, the granting of women's rights, the alphabet reform, calendar and measurement reforms, would be attacked by the opposition [mainly evolutionary secularist Progressive Republican Party].[60]

From the point of view of these elite divisions, the Kurdish Question was of secondary importance. In the contemporary period, the dilemma is more multifaceted, as I will elaborate in chapters 5 and 6, and as vivid as ever.

## CHAPTER 3

# From Empire to Imaginable and Imagined Nations

## *How Did the Kurdish Question Arise?*

Erstwhile world empires and imperial identities such as Spanish, Habsburg (later Austrian-Hungarian), British, and Ottoman faced particular challenges when subjected to the forces of modernization and nationalism. In response, they—especially the state elites and the intelligentsia—tried to reinvent and remold their ways of governing and the identities with which they were familiar. These elites found themselves restrained and influenced by a myriad of factors including the new methods, technologies, identities, and values spreading through the world at that time, as well as geopolitical developments and the resources at their disposal, as we discussed in the Introduction with reference to Wimmer's work. Different national imaginations were fired in this kiln.

My goal in this chapter is to discuss how the Kurdish Question arose from the Ottoman Empire's encounters with the forces of modernization and the rise of nation-states in the world. Thus, I also aim to demonstrate how malleable identities, and, in particular, imperial identities can be, as well as how and by whom they can be reinvented in response to changing conditions. I will also attempt to underline both the necessity and the difficulty of constructing hybrid and representative identities in this process.

## "Turk" as a Historical Ethnic Category

A paradigm of continuity, innovation, and synthesis seems especially thought-provoking where the history of the Turks is concerned. Their history begins so far away in space from what is today Turkey and includes so many transformations that it is a challenge to say what the Turkic peoples have all shared across time and space.[1]

Historically, "Turk" did not have the same meaning for insiders and outsiders, common people and the elites. For all these groups, however, it seems to have been an ethnic category rather than group, albeit for different, instrumental reasons.

For outsiders, Westerners in particular, the term carried a broad meaning. Westerners generally referred to the Anatolian Seljuq and Ottoman territories as Turkey, after Muslim Turks—more specifically various Turkic groups—became the dominant ruling group, but not necessarily the majority, through conquest and migrations from the eleventh century on.[2] The Muslim people from this territory, including those whose mother tongue wasn't Turkish, were categorized by employing the exonym *Turks*.

Take *The Prince*, Machiavelli's (1469–1527) famous book, which frequently employs the terms *Turk, Turks, Turkey,* and *Turkish* in relation to the Ottoman Sultan, the Ottoman ruling class, the Ottoman people, and their lands. Rather than serving to describe a people they denote, these terms seem to serve as images of conrast with other categories, which Machiavelli constructs for his readers—whether you call them modern, Western, Christian, or European.[3] Hence, he uses the Turk category as a (positively or negatively charged depending on the context) reference point, by using which he describes new "Us" categories and "our ways"—new and more effective principles of ruling for emerging centralized states in "Europe." Take the following quotes:

> The Emperor of Constantinople (Byzantium), to resist his neighbors, sent ten thousand Turks into Greece. When the war was over, they did not want to leave; this was the beginning of Greek servitude under the infidel.[4]

> It is more necessary now for every prince to satisfy the people rather than the soldiers, because the people are stronger—with one exception: the sultans of Turkey and Egypt.[5]

> The entire Turkish empire is governed by one ruler—the rest are his servants.[6]

> (It) would be difficult to acquire the Turkish state, but, once conquered, it would be very easy to hold on to.[7]

The reason for the obstacle in taking possession of the Turks's [sic] is that there is no possibility of being called in by the local rulers of that kingdom, and there is no hope of facilitating your attempt by means of a revolt of those men the local ruler has around him—this fact follows from the reasons given above.[8]

Thus, when speaking of the "Turks," Machiavelli refers interchangeably to Turkic- or Turkmen-Ottoman tribes and warriors, as in the first quote, the name of a land and state, as in the second and third quotes, and, presumably, the Ottoman ruling class of any ethnic/linguistic origin, as in the fourth quote. Outsiders can often cross over the internal differences that exist within a group they want to distinguish from their own. Hence, non-Muslims who lived in Ottoman Rumelia lumped together all Muslims as part of a single group and tended to call them Turks, even though Muslims among themselves could opt for different identifications based on their mother tongue and origins.[9] However, the political instrumentality of the Turk category for Machiavelli also seems clear, as he uses a constructed and often imagined—"Turkish"—example as a useful contrast with the political principles he aims to promote. Hence, at least in modern times, Kurdish writers who imagined a Kurdish nation by contrasting it with other categories such as Ottoman and Turkish, too, often employed a presumably multiethnic and political definition of "Turk." They referred to Ottomans, Ottoman administration, and Ottoman armies, which included Kurds, and Ottoman sultans as "Turks," "Turkish administration," "Turkish armies," and "Turkish Sultans," in respective order.[10]

As for the insiders of the Turk category, they had a more variegated perception of their identity, but their perceptions could be politically instrumental in other ways ways, depending on the social and regional context.

For the territory outsiders called Turkey, the "Turks" themselves gave names such as *Diyar-ı Rum* (Rumelian Realm, i.e., the land of the Romans) and did not find this offensive. If the Turks (or Turkic people) were an ethnic *group*—as opposed to category—during that period, it surely would have made them uncomfortable to use a name for their homeland that referred to an ethnically and religiously different group (Roman, or *Rum* in Turkish). Further, people who changed their religion and name and came under the service of the Ottoman state and learned Turkish, whether they were of Serbian, Armenian, Polish, or Circassian origin, could be called "Turkish" without their origins necessarily being forgotten by themselves or by others. Had the Turks constituted and seen themselves as an ethnic group, they would have objected to this practice of including people with known non-Turkish ancestry as Turks, for the ancestral and historical/linguistic connotations and linkages of the Turk category were well known.

> Ottoman elites and Rumi urbanites called their language "Turkish" and knew well that it was related to other kinds of Turkish spoken and written by "Turks" elsewhere. Müter-cim Asım's [Ottoman Turkish lexicographer and historian 1755–1819][11] eighteenth-century translation and elaboration of a Persian dictionary occasionally points to usages in *bizim Türkî* (our Turkish) as opposed to the Turkish spoken in Iran or in Turkistan, highlighting a sense of "we" as defined by language. Genealogies of the House of Osman (Ottoman) proudly linked them to the tribal tradition of the Oghuz Turks; in their own conception of their history and identity, Ottoman writers inserted the formation of the polity into a narrative of Seljuk and post-Seljuk Turkish (*etrāk*) *political* [emphasis mine] communities. Moreover, the Ottoman literati (and presumably their audiences) were aware that, no matter what they preferred to call themselves, others called them Turks. It is striking that Ottoman sources often use the word "Turk(s)" to refer to themselves when they are quoting or paraphrasing Byzantine and European characters.[12]

"Turks," however, did not share a common—ancestral or present—homeland as we would expect in an ethnic group. Presumably, during this period, people who were part of the ethnic Turkish category included those who considered as their homeland Anatolia as well as the Balkans, the Caucasus, Transoxania, Iran, the "Middle East," and Central Asia. Further, they did not necessarily call each other as Turks.

As Ottoman historian Cemal Kafadar put it, by using the example of how the chronicler of one Turkic ruler wrote about another Turkic ruler and his army he had defeated in the fifteenth century:

> When writing of the Ottoman forces vanquished near Ankara in 1402 by his patron, Timur, the chronicler Nizamüddin Şami mentions the *Efrenc* (Frankish, Eurochristian?), presumably implying the forces under the command of the Serbian king, an Ottoman vassal, but reserves most of his disparaging remarks

for the Rūmīyān, that is, Turkish-Muslim soldiers serving Sultan Bayezid. To add insult to injury, he cannot resist the temptation to cite the second verse of the sura al-Rūm (Qur'an 30), "The Romans [i.e., the Byzantines] have been conquered." This is harsh but not particularly creative. Many learned and presumably some not-so-learned Muslims of Asia Minor knew the verse well, as did others in the rest of the Muslim world, but saw nothing wrong with identifying themselves as Rumis, or people of the lands of Rum.[13]

Who, then, did the insiders of the Turk category call Turks among themselves?[14] This seems to have depended on political class and social/ geographical context. In Anatolia, "Turk" appears to have been reserved for Turkish speakers who were not part of the ruling class and did not transcend the "tribal ways and cultural codes"[15] in favor of urban ways and Ottoman cosmopolitan cultural codes. Research suggests that the Ottoman governing elites had many different ethnic and religious origins, and hence ancestries, and regardless of their identification with various ethnic categories (Turk, Kurd, Arab, Albanian, Serb, Ukrainian, or Circassian) or the solidarity they felt with any such groups, we can presume that most of them primarily thought of themselves as Ottoman.[16] These elites considered identities such as Turkmen (Turcoman, *Türkmen* in Turkish) and Kurdish as exclusive to common people and separated themselves from the masses, emphasizing their (social and political) class belonging.

However, in regions of the Ottoman Empire outside Anatolia, the "Turk" could be used to describe the ruling and dominant social and cultural classes as opposed to the ruled. For example, in the Balkans, "Turk" was a category that was particularly identified with those in power. It was an identity that was given to and adopted by those from the ruling class and the dominant "religious nation" (the Muslim *millet*). While many people who adopted this identity surely developed their own ethnic mythology regarding their Turkic or Turkmen roots, the role of imagination and truth in these narratives is not always clear. Indeed, in Ottoman Rumelia, Turkish-speaking people who arrived from outside of Rumelia following conquest and the previous inhabitants of the lands, many of whom were Turkified Slavs, constituted an important portion of the ruling class. Therefore, adopting the Turk identity might have made it easier to distinguish oneself from the ruled and join the ruling class. According to Kemal Karpat, "The noun Turkish is one that is given to the elites that have control over the state and the language they speak rather than the villagers and tribes that live in many places in Anatolia and Rumelia. Ziya Gökalp was to later appropriate the noun Turkish to the nation."[17]

Arguably, then, the Turks were not a people who shared an ethnic group awareness through a common feeling for a homeland with (more or less) certain boundaries and group solidarity. Turks across vast territories formed an identifiable category with common linguistic and cultural characteristics sufficient to distinguish them from others in the eyes of outsiders. For Turks themselves, however, rather than serving as a source of common "Us" sentiment, it was a category associated with language and culture, and determining social class, depending on the regional social/political context.

## Kurdishness as a Historical Ethnic Category

Until the forces of modernization and nationalism began to affect the Ottoman lands in the modern period, Kurdishness, too, was an ethnic category. David McDowall put it succinctly:

> With the exception of the seventeenth-century poet, Ahmad-i Khani, there is virtually no evidence that any Kurds thought in terms of a whole Kurdish people until the later years of the nineteenth century. There is no doubt that a Kurdish people had existed as an identifiable group for possibly more than two thousand years, but it was only in the early years of the twentieth century that they acquired a sense of community as Kurds. [This occurred] at more or less the same time that Turks and Arabs also began to embrace an ethnic sense of identity in place of the two previous basic forms of solidarity—the idea of Ottoman citizenship[18] and membership of a religious community, or *millet*.[19]

The region inhabited predominantly by Kurds was referred to as Kurdistan across various periods by many groups, including the Ottomans. The first Turkic ruler who named the region Kurdistan is thought to be Ahmad Sanjar, the Seljuq ruler of Khorasan, in the twelfth century. However, this geographical term, which at times also carried administrative meanings, did not have its current political meaning, so fervently upheld by Kurdish nationalists seeking recognition as a nation and so fiercely rejected by Turkish nationalists and governments.[20]

To illustrate the futility of discussing ethnicities through today's identity categories, Sultan Saladin was ethnically Kurdish but is believed to have had a "Turk" or Turkmen mother; however, he fought neither for the Kurds nor the "Turks." Renowned for his triumphs against the Crusades, he fought for the Muslims, for justice as he saw it, and for his own estate or "property." As McDowall writes, "Had his Kurdish identity been relevant to him it is unlikely that he would have given the fertile Shahrizur Plain in the heart of Kurdistan as a fiefdom to one of his Turkish mamluks."[21]

In the Ottoman context, being Kurdish meant speaking some version of Kurdish and being a Muslim who lived in the hard-to-reach eastern border regions governed by the tribal political organizations exclusive to the Kurds. In regions such as present-day Eastern Anatolia, where Turkish- and Kurdish-speaking people mixed, it was the norm to be multilingual. In any case, even if ethnicity involved a sense of belonging to a specific homeland, it had nothing to do with political "sovereignty" over that territory because states and other ruling structures were not based on popular sovereignty.

## Turkish Identity Taking on Multiple Meanings

In the nineteenth century, as a result of various bottom-up social, political, and intellectual processes, and state-driven policies, Turkishness began to acquire the characteristics of an ethnic group, parallel to other group identities in the empire.[22] Some Ottomans who were part of the Turk ethnic category and others began to develop a consciousness of a common culture, history, solidarity, and homeland.

According to Kemal Karpat:

Even though [S]ultan Abdülhamid did everything he could (parallel to his Islamist policies) to get closer with the Arabs in order to win them over between 1880 and 1900, from 1900 onwards he placed importance on Turkishness and asserted that he himself, his dynasty and even the founders of the state were Turkish. The primary force that determined his contradictory attitude was that Rumelian and Anatolian *citizens* who constituted the foundations of the state embraced a unique and *new* identity and that they identified it as 'Turkish.' The 'Turkish' identity derived from Ottoman history, Ottoman political culture and social experience, not from race [emphases mine].[23]

However, when these processes were just beginning from the mid-1870s to the 1920s, multiple wars and large migrations critically shifted the feasible boundaries of "homeland" and the demographics of the erstwhile empire. These developments also affected the political priorities as well as the identity perceptions and imaginations of the elites themselves. For these elites, it became an increasingly urgent goal that the Ottoman state be rescued by being reinvented as a nation-state or state-nation based on a common national identity, homeland, and nationalism.

Land loss and migrations led to a rapid shift and narrowing of the imagination of a homeland. As first "Rumelia" and then the Ottoman "Middle East" remained outside of the state's borders, the projection of the homeland and the associated narratives had to be Anatolia-oriented due to the developments taking place outside the control of the elites. Thus, while earlier imaginations encompassed a much broader territory, a devotion to Anatolia quickly developed, its having now become "the only homeland."

Against this background, just as "Turkish" was undergoing the transition from being an ethnic category to being an ethnic group and the concept of homeland was changing, Turkish was made the name and the foundation of a *national* identity project that encompassed a larger target audience than just those belonging to the Turk ethnic category, due, among other things, to migratory and political developments. In the second half of the nineteenth century and until the Balkan Wars, great surges of immigration took place, particularly from the Caucasus to Rumelia and Anatolia, and then from Rumelia to Anatolia.

Considering these rapid shifts of material conditions, it may not be surprising that the homeland, Anatolia, took on an abstract, symbolic, and objectified, so to say, quality for many of the elite. What was fundamentally attributed to and exalted in Anatolia was an idea, an envisagement of an abstract land that took a back seat in comparison to the state. "State patriotism" and state nationalism developed partly independently of the actual land itself;[24] a patriotism that was primarily committed to the state. This patriotism focused on the symbols and the cult of the state and on the idealized image of Anatolia, more than on the latter's actual nature, geographical characteristics, and history.[25]

Throughout these processes, Turkishness gained new plural meanings. In addition to denoting an ethnic category and ethnic group, it became the name and basis of a national project tailored to encompass also other ethnic groups and categories. In Kemal Karpat's words, "We have to distinguish between ethnic and linguistic Turkishness and political Turkishness. Political Turkishness [referring to its use as a basis of political solidarity and sovereignty] appeared for the first time in the twentieth century . . . this reality was very well expressed by Atatürk."[26]

Hence, as we will see in the next chapter, in the speeches of state-founding elites, particularly Atatürk, "a nation of Muslims composed of Turks, Kurds and other ethnic components" was first transformed into *the* "People of Turkey" (*Türkiye halkı*) and later to *the* "Turkish people" (*Türk halkı*). Among other factors that appear to have motivated these changes was the political experience of the decline of the Ottoman Empire and the lesson some elites drew from this experience that "religious belonging was not sufficient to found a state, or at least one that is national."[27]

## The "Premodernization" Period

Keeping in mind that they then were ethnic or cultural/linguistic *categories*, the first time some "Turks" and some "Kurds"—presumably, the ancestors of today's Anatolian Turks and Kurds—united within the same major political organization that could be considered a "state" can be traced back to the eleventh century, under the Great Seljuk Empire.[28] To offer some comparative perspective, this means that the political union of Turks and the Kurds in "Turkey" has relatively deep historical roots. For example, even though it took place under quite different conditions, the political union of the Scots and the English (after the Anglo-Scot Wars) dates back to 1707.[29] Another example is the unification of Catalonia (the Kingdom of Aragon) with the Kingdom of Castile, later to become the center of Spain, which dates back to 1469.[30]

The army of the (Turkic) Seljuk Emperor Sultan Alp Arslan included a considerable number of soldiers from Kurdish *beyliks* (principalities). Together they defeated Byzantine Emperor Romanos IV Diogenes in the Battle of Manzikert in 1071 and ushered in the beginning of the Turks' permanent settlement and domination of Anatolia. The Seljuks established many Turkmen *beyliks* in Anatolia, together with the Kurdish *beyliks* that came under their domination.

Turkmen and Kurd tribes and principalities found ways of living together while competing for domination and it was common for Turkmen and Kurdish *beys* (princes or chiefs) to give one another their daughters' hands in marriage, or for a Kurdish clan to enter under the rule of a Turkish *bey*, and vice-versa.[31] At the same time, these *beyliks* took advantage of the rivalries and shifted their loyalities between the Seljuk and Ayyubid dynasties. In the fourteenth century, the Mongols invaded Anatolia. In the post-Mongolian period, the Kurd and Turkmen areas of the region witnessed a race for dominance, initially between the Turkmen states of the Aq Qoyunlu and Qara Qoyunlu, later between the Ottomans and the Aq Qoyunlu (literally, those with the white sheep), and finally, between the Ottomans and the Safavids who ruled Iran.[32] In order to rule the Kurdish *beyliks*, the Aq Qoyunlu and the Safavids sought to weaken the power of the Kurdish clans' chiefs by appointing Turkmen and Persian governors in their place.[33]

Then came a second and more consequential "Turk-Kurd" political union in the sixteenth century. Ethnic Kurd scholar and statesman Idris Bitlisi, the intellectual architect of this unification, was first a consultant for the Aq Qoyunlu Turkmen State (brought down by Shia Muslim Safavids, another Turkmen dynasty) and later at the palace of the Ottoman Sultan Selim I. After the conquest of Istanbul in 1453 and the Balkans, the Ottomans were poised to continue their expansion into Europe. However, the fact that their borders to the east were not safe from the Safavids in Iran and the Mamluks in Egypt posed a significant barrier for them. Long-term campaigns to the west weren't feasible while their eastern territories were vulnerable to attacks. Meanwhile, the rule of the Kurdish *beys* was threatened by conflicts among themselves and by the Aq Qoyunlu and Safavids who wanted to rule them with their own appointed governors.

In the period following the Battle of Chaldiran in 1514, "Kurdish provinces"—in reference to the Ottoman term *Bilad-ı Ekrad,* denoting a vaguely defined geocultural zone and governing category—became part of the Ottoman State. After this, the Ottomans safeguarded their eastern border with conquests in the Middle East and the creation of a buffer region on the Iranian border composed of Kurdish towns loyal to the Ottomans. According to the *Sharafnama,* penned by Sharaf al-Din Bitlisi in the sixteenth century, twenty-five Kurdish *beys* announced their loyalty to the Ottomans before the war and supported them. Rather than ethnic loyalties, the intelligent diplomacy adopted by the Ottomans played a role in this outcome. The Ottomans strayed from the policies of the Aq Qoyunlu and the Safavids, and allowed the powers of the Kurdish *mirs* (a princely aristocratic title in Muslim tradition) whom they appointed to be passed down from father to son.[34] In addition to the relative political autonomy of the Kurdish ruling classes, sectarian ties and considerations of religious freedom might have contributed to Sunni Kurds' siding with the Ottomans as opposed to Shia Safavids.[35]

From this time until the nineteenth century, the Kurdish provinces were partially self-governed by governors directly appointed by the Ottomans and by Kurdish *beys* whose powers were handed down from father to son in bordering regions. *Bilad-ı Ekrad* was not a state with definitive borders and a single ruler; instead, it was an administrative zone and loose confederation of *beyliks*. At the same time, this relationship between Istanbul and Kurdish provinces imparted significant levels of power to local Kurd power holders.

In this indirect state/society relationship, Kurdish *beys* were fighting for power among themselves and the victor was recognized by the central Ottoman State. According to Şerif Mardin's conceptualization, this reflected a "tacit contract" between the local rulers or power holders and the Ottoman dynasty. When the Kurdish *beys* were in disagreement among themselves or when they had demands from the state, they would initially convey their demands through a petition, and later through rebellion, and the central state would "meet" their demands in a manner that would ensure that its own power was not weakened.[36] The state increased its power by manipulating the power struggles among the *beys*, and did so at every opportunity.

What did the "Turks" and the "Kurds"—more appropriately, Kurd and Turk power holders—at that time gain, so to speak, out of this historical union? The weakness of Kurdish *beys* caused by the endless power struggles among themselves, and their security problems with the more powerful political configurations surrounding them, were "resolved" through the agency of the Ottoman Palace. Kurdish elites became part of a world state through their affiliation with the Ottomans. They had become Kurdish *beys* in their own domains, and Ottoman ruling elites—a much more prestigious status in the world at large—when they related with the external world as Ottoman soldiers and officers, or, in other words, as members of the state elite. According to Martin van Bruinessen:

> Many tribal chieftains, and sometimes entire tribes, prided themselves on real or fictitious Arab descent. Kurds who entered the civil service and other town-dwellers often preferred to call themselves *Osmanlı* (Ottoman).[37]

The Ottoman "Turks," that is, the multiethnic Ottoman state elites, gained control over the Middle East with the aid of this union and attained the status of a global empire. The absolute "losers" could be identified as the tens of thousands of Alevi, Shia, and Qizilbash—whether Kurd or Turkmen—who were massacred or exiled from Anatolia due to their association with the "enemy rulers of Iran" in the eyes of the Ottoman state.[38] In any case, it is difficult to evaluate what changed for the common people.

## "Modern" Turkish and Kurdish Identities Becoming Imaginable

### TRANSITION FROM INDIRECT TO DIRECT ADMINISTRATION AND NATION BUILDING: A STYLIZED DEPICTION

The question of when, how, in what sense, and to what extent the Ottoman state began to modernize is a matter of ongoing inquiry and heated debate among historians. Earlier scholarship focused on the late eighteenth and nineteenth centuries as the main periods of "modernization."[39] More recent scholarship maintains that the encounter of the Ottoman state and ruling elites with the forces of modernity might have begun earlier: "Its vast reaches needed consolidation and from the reign of Süleyman I (1520–1566), [the empire] turned its synergies inward and slowly, if painfully, joined the ranks of early modern states."[40] During the seventeenth century, the state administration and governing elites were transformed, enlarged, diversified, and professionalized to such an extent that a recent contribution called it a "second empire."[41] Still, Ottoman modernization remains elusive. " 'Modern' " means many things to a great many people."[42] Ottoman modernization was a gradual, uneven, and contested process, which is as yet only poorly understood. It is hard to pinpoint the decision-makers and major turning points and explain the causes and consequences.

Hence, in the following discussion, I will offer a highly stylized narrative with a focus on highlighting the transformative forces of "modernity" that made it possible to imagine nations rather than present a "historical" account per se. Modern nation-states and state-nations historically emerged more or less parallel to the rise of direct governance, another contested concept. As I discussed in the Introduction in reference to constructivism and Wimmer's work, and to make a gross simplification and empirical generalization for analytical purposes, "premodern" states had governed their subjects *indirectly;* or, more precisely, they hadn't *governed,* they had *ruled.* Indirect governance or rule, however, has four different aspects, which do not always develop in the same direction in the same state and time period.

The first aspect is perhaps the simplest and refers to the territorial distribution of resources and authorities between the central and local rulers and administrations.[43] Lacking the information, organization, and technology to make most local decisions, especially in peripheral areas far from the center, central states ruled indirectly through local rulers and powerholders loyal to them. The tributary states are a good example of this. They required little more than submission and periodic payment of dues from local rulers. Second, as premodern states lacked the financial resources and well-developed bureaucracies to rule over or govern people by interacting with them directly, they instead ruled indirectly through partnerships with intermediaries including local powerholders and traditional institutions, such as tribal organizations and religious foundations.[44] Hence, they established relationships, which could be called "ruling partnerships" with local elites and organizations, in often vaguely defined territories, and ruled over people through these partnerships.

Third, premodern states had neither the sufficient capabilities nor reasons to involve themselves in the private, social, and economic lives of people in the same way that modern states do when they, for example, provide education and welfare and monitor and regulate civil affairs, from traffic to economic transactions, hygiene, and sexual relations. Functions of social regulation were viewed as the realm of "society" itself, and, more specifically, the domain of families and traditional organizations, such as clans, religious communities, and charities.[45] Finally, with the exception of small city-states, premodern states were not built upon the direct participation of the people, that is, the "masses," although many premodern and early modern states had institutionalized the legislative, advisory, or electoral participation of provincial elites and aristocracy through institutions such as assemblies or—in Islamic tradition—councils called *shura.*[46]

Since premodern states were not present in common people's daily lives in the ways modern states are, it was neither necessary nor possible to imagine and construct state-level identities (such as political, national, ethnic, and linguistic) shared by the masses and the ruling classes alike. In fact, both central and local rulers would probably have fiercely opposed such imaginations, considering them absurd and dangerous, as they might place limitations on whom and which territories they could legitimately rule. Moreover, such imaginations and common identities might encourage the masses to demand a say in political and state affairs. The rulers' legitimacy did not depend on a state-level identity shared with the masses. As for the masses, it was probably too far-fetched an idea that they should necessarily share a common identity with the state rulers—or with the inhabitants of faraway lands simply because they were ruled by the same states. Both were too unknown and too distant from their daily lives.

The development of modern, central states directly ruling over their well-defined territories and populations changed all of this. From the fifteenth century onward, feudal structures, an example of indirect governance in Europe, began to regress and central states started to gain power—a result of processes thought to have been driven by changes in military technology and warfare, commercial developments, and ideological/philosophical transformations.[47]

During these processes, central states demarcated their territories, authorities, and institutions by drawing ever thicker and more salient boundaries and by establishing rules and symbols, thereby strengthening their strong image, privileged status, and legitimacy vis-à-vis people and highlighting their distinctness vis-à-vis society, competing states and non-state organizations. On the other hand, state and society were becoming ever more engaged with one another. The state's ability to penetrate society (i.e., to influence society from within, through creating rules, discourses, symbols, and practices) dramatically increased, as more people joined the state apparatus.[48] As the resources of central states increased, direct governance became a growing possibility. The developing modern state began to interfere with and regulate more and more spheres of social life, eventually to shape people's mental worlds and private lives, and to turn its hand to areas such as education, the environment, morality, welfare, and economic development, which were previously of no interest to states.[49] While in some ways this meant that "society was losing or regressing for the good of the state," social actors were also participating in this process as they couldn't inhibit it, and, to a certain extent, they were actually shaping it.[50] Hence, for the "state," mobilizing the public on issues such as military service and paying taxes became easier to the extent that this relationship became voluntary and based on shared identities with the rulers.[51] States that established such relationships with their people began to become more successful and powerful.

Meanwhile, Western Europe and the Americas had already entered a long period of ethnic and religious homogenization with the purging of Muslims and Jews from Spain from the twelfth to the fifteenth century, and, later, with the religious wars among Christians and racially and religiously exclusionary immigration policies.[52] The Peace of Westphalia (1648) was one major turning point among many that reflected the modern state's emergence as the ideologically dominant actor during this stage of history. European central rulers increasingly accepted each other's sovereign right to determine the religious and ethnic identity of the territories they were ruling.

In addition to all this, first mercantilism and then the development of capitalism and the attendant developments in transportation and communication technologies, such as the postal services and the printing press, increased the ability of the literate classes scattered across large territories to be connected with each other through the dissemination of information, knowledge, and news. Inventions such as newspapers, and faster means of distribution, created populations that received the same news and were concerned with the same questions at similar times, thus able to conceive of themselves as a people attached to a specific land and affected by the same chains of events.[53]

All of this made it possible to imagine, construct, and promote "national" identities that would simultaneously identify the people, the ruling classes, and the states united by shared features of belonging such as language, nationalism, religion, ethnicity, laws, and culture. As direct governance began to emerge through the establishment of modern bureaucracies, the question arose of which language and culture to use to establish relationships between these bureaucracies and the public. Also arising was the *possibility* and *opportunity, imaginability* and—according to the assertions of nationalist thought which had begun to develop—*necessity* to standardize the language in which information was conveyed. Similarly, according to the nationalists, there was now the need to develop a *national* "high culture" supported by the state—not merely one reflecting the "high culture" of the ruling state elites as in the Ottoman or Mandarin but that of the "nation." Nationalist thinkers thought that such a culture facilitated the socioeconomic relationships between citizens from different cultural roots and regions by producing a common language and shared aesthetic values, social norms, and economic standards.[54]

Modern states identified—in a manner of speaking—the easiest and most effective way of governing and ruling for themselves. People sharing a common identity through a common economy, legal order, language, and/or culture—as well as preexisting notions of common ancestry and homeland patriotism that were now reinterpreted and justified—and who internalized the concept of nation, voluntarily paid taxes, enlisted for war, and worked for their countries.[55] All of this also had a consequence that had not necessarily been desired or intended by the powerful but that came to be accepted by them and internalized in time. This consequence was that the concept of popular sovereignty also became increasingly imaginable and, over time, feasible, even though the ideas of "republicanism," "populism," and "free people," that is, free from arbitrary power and domination, had long premodern pedigrees.[56] Further, the idea that the ultimate governing authority may be vested in a body including the "people" or *demos* began to be associated with the nation.

Imperial states with vast territories and vastly diverse populations, such as the British, Spanish, Habsburg (later Austria-Hungarian), Ottoman, and Romanov (Russian) empires, tried to cope with these trends by reinventing and popularizing their imperial identities and developing their own state nationalisms, with varying degrees of success. In general, however, they were eventually much less successful in doing this than were demographically, territorially, and in terms of identity more consolidated nation-states.[57] Arguably, empires' capability to transform themselves was constrained also by the very logic of (traditional or not) imperial governance itself: "a sovereignty that lacks a community," which tends to transform "distinct societies with autonomous institutions and regional elites into politically subordinate civil societies," based on "limited political participation of segments of the population" and "the non-involvement of the majority."[58]

Parallel to the development of the nation-state model, the West, or more precisely Western Europe and North America, progressed militarily, socially, and economically and came to occupy the "center" of the world. Along with the rest of the world, both Eastern Europe and the Ottoman Empire gravitated toward this model perforce. As the modern states developed, they formed a "community" or "club," so to say, even when they were fighting and competing with each other, which other states either wished to or were coerced to join. In order to be recognized in the international system and to establish relationships with other states, they were forced to adopt their practices.[59]

The implementation of this model was painful and problematic in all of the places in which it was tried. Coherent with the reasoning of the modern state which gained international currency, state apparatuses managed people's lives in the name of ideals such as progress and modernization, regardless of the people's will or consent. The state apparatus perceived society and the environment as objects and considered it as their right to implement transformative policies that were more often than not exploitative.[60] The preferences and characteristics of majority, politically dominant, or "core" groups were always represented more.[61] Those who formed minorities in terms of numbers, politics, or economics were forced to comply. "People of the periphery" who inhabited the bordering regions between existing states were underrepresented. Groups located closer to the center had more influence on the centralized state's choices on matters such as language, culture, and economic development.

Among the peripheral people, those with the most ambiguous status were people living in remote places (i.e., distant from the capital), with distinct languages, cultures, and lifestyles and traditionally autonomous governing structures yet with insufficient social and political unity, institutions, fortune, and external support to form their own state. The inclusion of these people (e.g., Kurds in Turkey and Berbers or Amazighs in Morocco) in the state often involved tough and painful measures in the processes.[62]

Even though the nation-state was de facto spread to Muslim countries mostly through colonialism, these ideas had begun influencing Muslim ruling classes and intelligentsia long before. Independent or semi-independent states and societies that had a predominantly Muslim identity began to adopt and utilize the concept of the nation-state of their own accord. The intellectual developments and endeavors of modernization in Iran and the Ottoman Empire are among the best examples of this.[63]

As the Ottomans were influenced by and became part of these processes, imagining, constructing, and promoting *national* identities such as Ottoman, Turkish, and Kurdish became possible, albeit with some important differences from their Western counterparts and among themselves.

According to Stefanos Yerasimos, the formation process of the nation-state in Turkey "in essence was not different from the formation of the nation-state in Western Europe or the Balkans. However, what was lacking was its period of maturation." In other words, the nation-state in Turkey had to be developed through an accelerated process because its maturation process had been truncated by "the Ottomans' imperial ambition," which was threatened somewhat by nation-state formation, and because of the Ottoman elites'—initially including also those elites who became the republic-establishing Kemalist elites—hopes of saving the empire until its very end.[64]

For the same reasons, the search for "state-nation" models, rather than "nation-state" per se, was always present in the endeavors of Turkish Ottoman elites and nationalists. This distinguished Turkish nationalism from other otherwise similar nationalisms in southeastern Europe, and, as I highlight in this book, from Kurdish nationalism, too.

Hence, on one hand, Southeastern European nationalisms, such as Greek nationalism, were fundamentally subject to similar dynamics, and influenced one another.[65] They implemented homogenizing policies by producing common identities through promotion of religious and ethnic symbols and attachments, as well as through educational policies, and by unmixing communities, who had mixed and merged on their lands over time, through the employment of organized state violence, which produced forced migrations, pogroms, and population exchanges. However, the development of modern Greek nationalism, which dates back to the 1830s, was spread across a relatively longer period of time compared to the Turkish form of nationalism. In modern Greece, nation formation preceded state formation. That is to say, the imagined borders and context of the modern "Greek" nationhood were formed—even though these of course were always contested by some, for example in "Macedonia" and Anatolia, and never entirely clear—before those of the independent Greek state; the state then *tried* to make its borders overlap with those of the nation. By comparison, Turkish nationalism mostly evolved from a state to a nation, that is to say, state formation and state nationalism preceded or coincided with nation formation. First, the borders of the state were shaped, and, then, the nationalists tried to adapt the definition and context of the nation to those of the state. In the process, the borders of both the state and the nation underwent major changes from what their defenders and protagonists had initially imagined.

In a nutshell, questions of ethnic "minority" and nationality were inherent products of the emergence of modern nation-states throughout the world; but in different cases, these questions found answers that were more or less socially/politically disruptive, sustainable, and violent. To draw an analogy, similar puzzles arose vis-à-vis working and capitalist classes with the rise of modern capitalist economies. This is because one of them owes its wealth to the maximization of profit and to keeping the cost of labor as low as possible, while the other naturally strives to maximize the value of its labor. This tension originates from the structure of the capitalist economy and cannot be completely eradicated. Unless managed well, it can lead to class conflict and violence, which are suppressed by oppressive regimes in the name of either capital or labor. If managed well, violence and conflict can be minimized and relatively fair and stable democratic systems can be established that offer reasonable protection for both the working classes and the capitalists' interests and enable economic development.

## OTTOMAN MODERNIZATION AND THE RISE OF THE KURDISH QUESTION

While trying to adapt to the features of nation-states in line with global developments, the Ottoman elites tried two things in their attempts to produce projects in the name of the state, during these processes protecting, privileging, or persecuting specific ethnic and religious groups, or specific social and professional classes. The latter included the members of the ruling and state-managing bureaucratic classes, the military classes who also formed powerful occupational and economic interest groups (e.g., the janissaries), official Islamic clergy, or society-based Sufi Islamic leaders. The first was to shift from "indirect to direct governance" by restructuring the traditional Ottoman state apparatus, namely, by building a new type of state and a societal consensus on which it would be built.[66] They thought that this approach would financially and militarily empower the state, get separatist movements under control, and help compete with Western countries. While some attempted to achieve this goal—a New Order—by strengthening and modernizing the central state, others pursued the same goal through decentralization, albeit one that would be built upon a more modern, formal, and stable partnership and cooperation between the central state and provincial elites.[67] Second, they generated different imaginations and ideologies of modernization and shared national identity.

## THE SHIFT TO DIRECT GOVERNANCE

Many legal, economic, political, and administrative changes were attempted in this vein. Examples of these include: the first authorized use of Muslim printing press (for nonreligious books) in Ottoman Turkish (1727); efforts to increase tax revenues from agriculture by replacing the ancient *timar* system (state distribution of land tenure and revenues in return for military service) with various forms of tax farming (throughout the eighteenth and early nineteenth centuries); the Deed of Alliance—reflecting a short-lived effort by some reformist central state and provincial elites to

establish a more equal and enhanced "partnership" (1808);[68] beginning the
building of a modern postal system (1825); attempts at first disciplining
and modernizing and then the abolition of the rebellious *janissary* corps
(1826); the establishment of an Imperial Ministry of Pious Foundations
(*Vaqfs*), with a view to centralizing their administration and increasing
state revenues (1826); the publication of an official gazette to enable the
state to communicate with its own bureaucracy (1831); the first general
census (1831–32); the abolition of the Mamluk rule in Baghdad (1831);
the establishment of a centralized and unified army by abolishing local
units (1838); issuing passports to the subjects of the state; the Edict of
Gülhane, proclaiming legal rights and equality for citizens (1839); the
passing of a new criminal code, based on the French criminal code, parallel to Sharia-based law and courts (1858); the recognition of private land
property through a new land law (1858); the First Constitution (1876);
the passing of a new civil code called *Mecelle,* which modernized Islamic
Sharia law based on the Hanafi *fiqh* school (1878). Moreover, new schools
were founded that provided Western education and efforts were made to
develop a local manufacturing industry.[69] Nomadic groups were encouraged
to settle down in order to be registered and taxed by the state.[70]

What the Ottoman elites really hoped to do with all of these reforms
was to increase state revenues and strength by exerting more effective control and by "rationalizing," disciplining and mobilizing not only the state
apparatus but also society, thereby enhancing the state's ability to compete
with Western states. Wars, military expenditure, and losses of territory,
which directly reduced the state's tax base, were major compelling factors
driving these changes. A war indemnity payment to Russia in 1775, for
example, amounted to "almost half of all state revenues for that year."[71]

As part of these reforms, the Ottomans tried to standardize and
control the governance of border regions and to weaken the resistance of
"peripheral groups," such as the Albanians, Bedouins, Druzes, and Kurds,
who had their own distinctive tribal structures and were hard to control
through stern military measures. As Hamit Bozarslan quotes:

> The Ottoman authorities achieved their greatest successes
> within the borders of the settled world. They first succeeded
> in stopping the pressure from the Bedouins and later in reg-
> ulating it, and from the 1850s onwards they took long-term
> precautions such as continuously using the armed forces, but
> more importantly, building a series of small forts to monitor

the water sources in the moors in general and encouraging the settlement of small tribes.[72]

In order to include the Kurds in this project, inspired by the Cossack regiments in Russia, the Hamidiye Corps were founded, comprised of Kurdish tribes and boarding schools (Hamidiye and Imperial Tribal schools) for the children of Kurdish elites. The Hamidiye Corps was part of the Ottoman State's efforts to modernize, settle tribes permanently, and to shift from indirect to direct governance. During this period, the Ottomans also undertook efforts to permanently settle the nomadic Turkmen, Albanian, Arabic, and Circassian populations, so Kurds were not the only targets of these policies.[73] Some of the principal ambitions of the state were to safeguard the Kurds' loyalty to the state and to transform this group into a more trusted and reliable military resource.[74] In turn, it was hoped this would create a power that would balance the rising Armenian nationalism in the region and "civilize" (Kurdish) tribes. However, this project should not merely be seen as a process solely determined unilaterally by the state; its essence and outcomes were also shaped by parties, mainly local elites, which benefited from this process.[75] At a time when private ownership of land was just beginning to develop, the ownership and power relationships in the region changed fundamentally. The Hamidiye Corps also became a hard component for the state to control, and one that could tyrannize both Muslims and non-Muslims, particularly the Kurdish villagers and the Armenians, thereby straining ethnic relationships and deepening regional class inequalities.[76]

With a *firman* (Sultanic decree) issued in 1846, the *Eyalet* (Administrative Region) of Kurdistan—later renamed the Eyalet of Diyarbekir—was founded to initiate the shift to direct governance, and continued to function from 1847 to 1867.[77] Unrests such as the Badr Khan (1843–48) and Sheikh Ubeydullah rebellions (1880) mainly reflected the Kurdish ruling classes' efforts to preserve their own status in response to centralization policies by the Ottomans and the Qajar Dynasty in Iran.[78] Rather than being "national" uprisings, these instances were individual rebellions ignited by Kurdish *beys* wanting to share their autonomy neither with the central state nor with anybody else. Another key reason for the Ubeydullah rebellion was the freedoms given to Armenians through the reforms undertaken by the central state as a result of pressures from Europe, which triggered fears among the Kurdish elites that this would threaten their privileges and economic interests.[79]

However, since the state did not have the power or the resources to truly put in place direct governance, the actual effect of these developments was to change the local balances of power in the region. The power gap that arose as a result of oppressing tribal leaders who had previously enjoyed the status of *emirs* was filled by *aghas* and *shaikhs* with religious authority. For instance, the state did not have the capacity to build direct governance by establishing and administering courts in rural areas. Thus, new local power holders filled the gap generated by the state oppression of communal leaders who had previously performed such tasks as conflict mediation.

Another factor underlying the rise of the *aghas* and *shaikhs* was the land act of 1858. Enacted during the rule of Sultan Abdülmecid, the aim of this act was primarily to increase tax revenues, as well as to dismantle the tribal structures and to encourage the permanent settlement of nomadic tribes. The act dissolved the right of communal use and stipulated that the tenure of all landed property had to be registered with a title deed in the name of private persons. In this process, *shaikhs, aghas,* and urban merchants used their powers and took advantage of the weaknesses of civil servants to sign the landed property in their own names. Consequently, the *aghas* and *shaikhs* strengthened their powers by attaining the status of feudal landlords, while other tribal members became tenants.[80]

While such developments were underway in Kurdish provinces, great transformations were also taking place across the Ottoman Empire and in the central state as a result of administrative and military measures and reforms. "A new political imagination" emerged in which the concept of nation and the trailblazing role and top-down force of the army came into prominence:

> Although the Ottoman State did not back down from its greatest promise, delivering justice to its subjects (which sadly became also its most questionable claim in implementation), it was attempting to safeguard its permanence by building a "nation" that it could use as groundwork for mobilization and legitimacy. Military units that were formed with the aid of European officers were perceived as prototypes of what the new society would be like. The army that could neither solely be identified with imperial guardianship nor with a professional body commissioned with the duty of territorial defense became an organic component of the new administration. As

the army became more prominent for its domestic use of force rather than its effectiveness in (defending) borders, it gradually identified with the "nation" and towered as hope for its construction and welfare.[81]

In fact, this process of nation building was not only a top-down process, involving the initiative and force of the state. Meanwhile, Ottoman society was experiencing an intellectual revolution as a result of the modernization efforts and the processes of integrating with the global economy.[82] In the nineteenth century, the number of printing presses, newspapers, and magazines increased greatly, as did schooling rates. In parallel, a bourgeoisie and a middle class were also developing, which many theories associate with the development of nationalism as well as democratic aspirations.[83] These socioeconomic transformations were even reflected in the construction materials used by the new middle classes and their aesthetic tastes, still visible today in the buildings of the period.[84]

All of these developments affected the elites as well as the masses. Had the intellectual developments and new imaginations of state and society, imposed top-down by the state and the military, not had a socioeconomic and class basis, their influences would have been short-lived. According to one viewpoint still influential in Turkey's public/political discourse, collective memory, and mainstream as well as critical, leftist, and Islamist historiographies—partially informed by Marxist theories of development and dependency theories[85]—particularly after the Tanzimât Reforms, the Ottoman economy entered a process of distorted and foreign-dependent economic development, during which the state lost control and semi-colonization began.[86] This theoretical narrative reflects one aspect of what transpired, and from the point of view of state elites. Among the most significant dynamics that shaped this period were the efforts of various state elites to gain a grip on developments involving domestic and external actors.

However, to view this as merely a period of collapse would produce an incomplete and state-centered interpretation of the factors that led to the Ottoman decline. In fact, there was economic and social development throughout this period. New middle classes were emerging. As an indicator of this, in the late nineteenth century, the dime levy (aşar vergisi), which the state collected from agricultural land, had tripled from the levels of the 1840s and 1850s.[87] While Greeks and Armenians undertook highly profitable commercial occupations in towns and cities—thereby dominating the commercial and industrial bourgeoisie—the majority of the ownership of agricultural land gradually fell into the possession of Muslims, thus possibly generating a sharper religious belonging-based occupational division in society than before and sharpening perceived ethnic and religious differences and tensions. However, as a result of this, both the Muslim and the non-Muslim middle classes were developing. According to Kemal Karpat:

> It's possible to state that after the 1860s capital directly related to agricultural production was in the stronghold of the Muslim middle class. . . . This way a new social group composed of Muslims—which we call the new middle class or small agrarian bourgeoisie—emerged in the Ottoman State. A considerable number of these were immigrants.[88]

These new classes were also the breeding grounds of Muslim Ottoman as well as Turkish (and Kurdish, Arab, etc.) ideas and sentiments of nationhood. All this could not but affect people's sense of their relationship with the state, too. They supported the state for as long as it protected their own interests and property, and did not refrain from resisting when the state acted against their interests.[89] As Karpat emphasizes, in order to be able to satisfactorily explain the political history of both the Ottoman State and the Turkish Republic, the roles of these new classes have to be examined, as indeed do the roles of the official and civilian *ulema* (Muslim religious scholars and clergy, who often also acted in other capacities such as judges) classes, intellectuals, and military/civilian bureaucrats. The same is valid for comprehending transformations relating to identity (the bottom-up development as well as elite-construction of the Muslim Ottoman and Turkish national identities).

## New Imaginations of Nation Generated by Ottoman Modernization

During this period, the Ottoman State elites tried to create a common identity for the developing classes as other modern states did. At first, they attempted to create a multiethnic and multiconfessional Ottoman identity and consciousness among the state's diverse subjects.[90] With the Imperial Reform Edict of 1856, Muslims and non-Muslims were declared to be equals, as "Ottomans" (*Osmanlı*). Although the state had tradition-ally classified them as Muslims and non-Muslims, from 1869 onward, it identified all of its subjects as Ottomans and distinguished them from "foreigners." All of this was a reflection of the efforts to shift from being a traditional state to becoming a state with a well-defined territory and citizenry—i.e., developing narratives and rules that specified the locations of the state's lands and who its "people" were. This involved borrowing from modern Western states as well as the logical implications of state modernization such as a certain degree of standardization, and the desire to be included in the family of European states was a major motivation.

However, the 1856 edict provoked indignation among many Mus-lims, who considered themselves the dominant *millet,* and it also failed to create a sense of joy for many non-Muslims, who feared they would be burdened with additional duties such as military service. When this new identity fell off the radar, particularly because it was thought that it would not be embraced by non-Muslims, Sultan Abdulhamid tried to create a common identity and a union of ideals among the Muslims with his pan-Islamist policies.

During this period, a new Ottoman elite class formed that had been educated in the schools established as a result of the modernizing efforts. These elites organized under names such as the Young Ottomans and, later, the Young Turks. The formation of this new "state society" was not limited to the capital and urban centers, that is, the elites of the "center." A provincial "state society" also developed from among the ethnically as well as confessionally diverse, traditional provincial elites. The following description and keen observations describe well the plural ethnic nature of this emerging provincial state elite, among whom imaginations of nation presumably developed, and which was later also carried over partially to the republican cadres in the same provinces.

> [In] the old Ottoman province of Trabzon (Old name Trebi-zond, in Black Sea region), participants in the imperial system included large numbers of Turks, Lazis, Greeks, Armenians, and Kurds, as well as some number of Circassians, Georgians, Bosnians, and Albanians. Representatives of these same peoples would have also been participants in the imperial system in other Ottoman provinces, along with still other peoples, most notably Arabs, Persians, and Jews, not to mention some scat-tering of Hungarians, Poles, Russians, Italians, Frenchmen, and

Germans. The imperial project was joined by peoples of diverse backgrounds, and in so joining it, they acquired behaviors that featured its peculiar "Turkish" and "Islamic" qualities.[91]

For my purposes here, I should also highlight that these "peoples of diverse backgrounds" could not possibly and logically be merely acquiring preexisting and fixed "Turkish" and "Islamic" characteristics. Undoubtedly, they were also reshaping what they were acquiring. They thus contributed to the making and cultural nature of what started as a Muslim Ottoman state society and then became a Turkish state-society and state-nation, and, eventually, nation-state.

At first, the common aim of these elites (ethnic Turk, Kurd, Albanian, Arab, and, until the final periods of the Empire, also non-Muslim) was to save the Ottoman State from demise and the unity of the Ottoman territories, regardless of their ethnic origins.[92] However, they had many different projects and imaginations for the future. Due to the changing external conditions and possible borders of the country, imaginations of homeland, people, and nation were continuously shifting as well. Hence, the late Ottoman period was an era in which numerous different narratives relating to identity and land emerged among Ottoman intelligentsia and state elites, which could justify different political projects vis-à-vis the survival of the Ottoman order; that is to say, different nation-building projects, and different imaginations of the past and the future were being produced, which would involve more or less the same people and the same lands.

The most renowned classification of these imaginations was made by Yusuf Akçura in his 1904 essay "*Üç Tarz-ı Siyaset* [Three Directions of Policy]," published in the Cairo-based journal *Turk* (*Türk*). In his essay, Akçura advocated "Turkism" together with Ottomanism, and Islamism. Coming from a Tatar family—from Russia where Turkic Tatars constitute a major ethnonational minority based on their ethnic/linguistic differences from majority Russians to this day—his vision of Turkism was based on ethnicity. Akçura's categorization particularly reflected the views of those who had a Muslim and Turk *ethnic group* consciousness. Tatar Turks acquired an ethnic group awareness long before those in Anatolia. While Turkish-speaking Muslims were the demographic majority and politically dominant group in Anatolia, Tatar Turks were a minority subject to domination because of their ethnicity, thus having good reasons to develop a self-awareness of their ethnic/cultural differences, whether these differences were linguistic or based on religion and culture.

In addition to Akçura's, there were other ethnic/nationalist imaginations and projects with relatively narrower territorial and demographic boundaries, such as Kurdish and Albanian. While some of these imaginations produced independent nation-state projects, others envisaged cultural or regional autonomy within broader and multiethnic state projects.[93] The first type of nationalist imaginations, which demanded independent nation-states, were hard to reconcile with the macronationalist imaginations that sought to save the Ottoman State—at the very least, they were hard to reconcile in terms of how the territory would be divided. However, this was not the case for the second type of imaginations, which had autonomy in their sights. Imaginations that aimed at cultural or political autonomy might theoretically be compatible with projects such as *Ottomanism* and *Turkey-ism* (based on Of-Turkey identity).

The fact that the macronationalist projects were rather flexible and adopted different and changing names reflected both this possibility of coexisting macro (based on state-nation) and micro (autonomy-seeking) nationalist imaginations and the political and intellectual efforts to translate them into reality. These projects that were aimed at saving the Ottoman State with a different identity and territorial borders were put forward with different names, such as *Turkism, Ottomanism, Islamism, Türkiyacılık* (a contemporary term for Turkey-ism), *Türkiyelilik* (*Of-Turkey-ness*), and *Anadolululuk* (*Anatolian-ness*). For example, *Anatolian-ness* and the ideological project promoting it, Anatolianism, remained on the agenda as both a concept and a project for a long period of time and were defended by prominent Turkish nationalists, such as Halide Edip Adıvar.[94]

Simultaneously, the imagination of Turkism was diverse within itself. It was not against "logical or 'objective' possibility," à la Weber, as we discussed in the Introduction chapter, that some of these imaginations could cohabit with various imaginations of Kurdism; they didn't have to be rivals. The Committee of Union and Progress, which would govern the country from 1908 until the end of World War I and seal its fate, was established in 1889 under the name Committee of *Ottoman* (emphasis mine) Union as a pluri-ethnic and pluri-faith organization.[95] However, over time, particularly in the aftermath of the Balkan Wars, it became homogenized and more Turkist, both because of the changing ethnic and religious composition of its members and more importantly due to the changing perception of identities and ideologies.[96]

Whilst the macronationalist aim of saving the Ottoman State was of interest, among the elites an awareness of the distinct cultural identities of Turk and Kurd was also growing stronger. The fact that the fall of the Ottoman Empire gradually seemed to grow ever more unavoidable also initiated and cultivated micronationalist ideas based on these identities. In this context, ideas of Turkish and Kurdish nationalism (in other words, imaginations/ideals of Turkish and Kurdish nation-states) began to develop.

While reinventing, reimagining and building on Turkic history, Ziya Gökalp constructed an imagination of Turkishness that could be acquired through education and socialization and a Turkism based on cultural and linguistic unity and a reconstruction of the Turkish ethnic category and ethnogenesis. He became the best-known theoretician of the transformations and semantic changes that influenced the nation-formation processes that I try to capture and narrate here.[97] Gökalp's goal was not merely to revive and reconstruct a preexisting Turkish identity. His identity-related efforts were part of his broader ideals vis-à-vis the secularization and modernization of the people who would make up the Turkish nation and tackled issues of cultural authenticity and hybridity that were raised by his ideals.[98] This echoes the idea we discussed earlier, that nation-building efforts and the associated identity-construction projects are often complementary, if not instrumental, to broader projects, such as those related to modernization, power, and development. Alongside the cultural meaning that Gökalp's formulation exemplified, the ethnic meaning of Turkishness as asserted by Akçura also preserved its existence. It evolved and later developed racist versions, which would be expressed by ethnic nationalists such as Nihâl Atsız.[99]

For a long time, being a "nation" in the sense of forming a people that could determine its own fate was only an idea, which was expressed based on various projects of nation making. The language used reflected the various assertions, longings, and imaginations vis-à-vis *becoming* a nation. People were referred to as Turks or Kurds in the context of their ethnic/linguistic categories, but they were referred to as people who could *become* Turks and Kurds in the context of nations and nation-states.

Hence, a statement such as "resistance against a Kurdish attack" (*bir Kürt taarruzuna karşı mukavemet*)[100] could be referring to the ethnic/ linguistic identity of the attackers as Kurds or to the political aims of the attackers as Kurdish nationalists. Other statements, which may at first sound tautological, such as "those who feed Kurds with the goal of Kurdishness" (*Ekradı Kürtlük amali ile besleyenler*)[101] employed two meanings of "Kurd," first as a preexisting ethnic category, and second as a prospective, national category. Similarly, leaders of the National Campaign made references to "Kurdishness" (*Kürtlük*), "Circassianness" (*Çerkezlik*)—as if they were talking about ideas and projects—and "being open to or enthusiastic about Turkishness" (*Türklüğe hevesli olmak*).[102] Had Turkishness been considered only an innate and historical characteristic linked to blood and descent, what could "being enthusiastic toward Turkishness" mean? A national identity based on blood and lineage cannot be attained through "enthusiasm," that is, volition; it can only be a characteristic that an individual possesses, or doesn't possess, by birth.

## The Metamorphosis of Ottoman State Nationalism into "a" Turkish Nationalism

The Ottoman, Turkish, and Kurdish nationalist organizations that developed during the late Ottoman periods shared many similarities because they were the products of similar historical conditions and similar ideational and ideological sources. They also influenced one another. Within each of them, there were secular or Islamic modernist streaks, different imaginations based on ethnicity and language, culture, or territory, and they were all concerned with modernization, development, and achieving parity with the Western world.

However, a major group of Turkish nationalists also turned to the fundamental aim of saving the Ottoman State by taking over the mission of Ottoman nationalism and fulfilling the role that the Ottoman national identity project was expected to play but had failed to do. That is to say, for many Turkish nationalists, the ideal of a Muslim Ottoman nation turned into Turkish nationalism, albeit in a smaller territory. Because of this metamorphosis, the "homeland" that Turkish nationalists imagined became more ambiguous, more flexible, and broader, and the "people" whom they aimed to mobilize became ethnically and culturally more heterogeneous. Hence, while the ethnic/linguistic version of Turkish nationalism can be likened to Kurdish nationalism in terms of its content, Turkish nationalists also developed other versions, with the dominant ones acquiring a composite, state-nation-like quality.

According to Frank Tachau,[103] the loss of territories after World War I triggered a crisis in the Ottoman intellectual realms, severely shrinking their erstwhile imagined homeland. There was a need for new political projects that were suited to the new conditions, as well as for a new ideology to support these projects, to replace the overthrown old social and political order.

Thus, notwithstanding the certainty and force with which the dominant Turkish nationalism and state ideology were upheld and reified later, the exact forms and contents of the nation-state project were not clear and predetermined in the minds of the political actors of the time. A new Turkish identity was in the making, that is, undergoing a process of development and construction.

During and shortly after the Turkish War of Independence, Mustafa Kemal began to prefer terms such as *Turk* and *Turkey* rather than *Ottoman* and *Anasır-ı Islamiye* (components of the Islamic nation), but he never clarified the exact meanings and contents of these. According to Tachau, the reasons behind this were political and not ideological.

> There were two potentially troublesome points at issue here, one involving the relations with Turkic peoples outside the boundaries of the Republic, the other embodying the problem of the minorities remaining within the confines of the new state. What was needed was a criterion for national identification that would appeal to the emotions of the Turkish majority while neither over-emphasizing the cultural kinship with the Turks of Central Asia and elsewhere nor alienating the non-Turkish groups within the new body politic.[104]

According to Kemal Karpat:

> Indeed, a new and modern Turkish nation was emerging. But even though this nation was preserving its pre-Islamic language, some of its traditions and its name, it was a new entity due to both its internal and external structure and in its foundation there was the Rumelian and Anatolian Ottoman-Muslim community. In fact, the elites were striving to define their own sociocultural identities rather than that of society . . . .This new identity began to be introduced as "Turk" from as early as the 1890s onwards. . . . [This name Turk] is not only used for people who are of Turkish ethnic origin, people who live in villages and tribes but to the new society that emerged as a result of the demographic mixing that came about as a consequence of

migrations that gained momentum in the nineteenth century. Regardless of their ethnic origins (and even though they might have continued to speak their mother tongues at home usually for one or two generations) the elites considered themselves as having a Turkish identity in the sense of this new meaning and gave precedence to it.[105]

In this process, the Ottoman religio-political category of *millet* assumed a dual meaning and usage both as its former religio-political category as well as "nation" in the European sense.[106] Those, such as Yusuf Akçura, who supported ethnicity-based nation building justified this idea by pointing to the fact that ethnic Turks formed the majority. Others envisioned a process of nation building based on qualities that can be acquired, such as language (Turkish) and culture—in which Ottoman Muslims of various ethnicities could participate.

The latter types of projects and imaginations did not consider Turkishness to be an adjective that excluded Muslims of different origins. The emphasis was on the Turkish ethnic *category*, rather than on the ethnic group. In other words, it did not emphasize the members of an existing group, but rather the symbols and names (associated with the ethnic category) that people were invited to adopt. Hence, for many Turkish nationalists, Anatolia was, first, an *acquired*—rather than ancestral—and second, an *imagined* homeland. Similar things could be said about *"the Red Apple"* as literalized by Ziya Gökalp to refer to the Turks' mythological homeland (in Central Asia, i.e., "Turkistan"). As a result of this, in Ziya Gökalp's imagination (partially ethnic Kurd), ethnic Kurds could be natural members of a nation building despite their different ethnicity and mother tongue.

Carter Findley holds that Turkish nationalists' loyalties shifted from the land to the state during this period because there wasn't a fixed and safe homeland on which Turkish nationalists could rely—or, more precisely, because the borders and the demographics of the homeland were continuously changing.[107] Even as late as the Balkan Wars (1912–13), for many a Turkish nationalist leader, the actual (or primary) homeland was the Balkans.[108] Within less than a decade, however, even Thessaloniki (Atatürk's place of birth, now in Greece) was left outside what eventually became the territorial scope of the nationalist project, namely, the borders of the National Pact (*Misak-ı Millî*).[109]

There is a search that exists in varying degrees in all nationalist movements: to find and preserve values that are thought to be unchangeable and reliable and that can act as a kind of emotional safe harbor in response to the security concerns created in people by the uncontrollable external world and the resulting changes in social and cultural life. This shelter is found in land (or in the notion of a homeland), in national history, in common culture and (*our*) law, in the context of ethnicity (lineage), and in the concept of state—insofar as the latter is considered to be a representative and guardian of all of these notions. It seems unsurprising, then, that the state would become prominent when the reliability and contents of other resources are constantly changing—which was the case in the evolution of Turkish nationalism. The relative importance and contents of concepts used to define (national) identity, such as descent and territory, would then be adapted to the evolution of the struggle to save the state.

Hence, even ethnic Turkish nationalists, in their own ways, endeavored to include the Kurds in their projects of state-centered nation building. They did so by trying to "demonstrate," so to speak, that Turks and Kurds have common ethnic/racial roots or that most Kurds are rural Turks who have undergone cultural alienation, and that they have the same origins. As mentioned in the Introduction, different ethnic groups can adopt different strategies to protect or rebuild the boundaries of the group. They produce various forms of ethnic politics that are compatible with these strategies.[110] In this sense, ethnic Turkish nationalism can be seen as an example of the strategy to "include, incorporate."[111]

Kurdish nationalism followed a different course than Turkish nationalism in these respects. While Turkish nationalists were attempting to build the "people" for an existing state to safeguard or resurrect its political unity, Kurdish nationalists were endeavoring to unite a people which they considered to be politically fragmented and deprived of a state of their own. Political disunity was a dominant theme in the historical sources to which Kurdish nationalists referred. This was not a common theme in Turkish nationalism despite the presence of Turkic people across Eurasia under different states. Take the example of *Mem û Zin*, which is believed to have been written in the seventeenth century by Ehmede Xani and was originally read as a poem of mystical love before it was elevated to the status of Kurdish "national epic" with the development of Kurdish nationalism in the late nineteenth century. The poem, which depicts the story of "two tragic lovers . . . who—despite being buried together—remain separated by a thornbush, even in death, is usually seen as an allegory of the division of Kurdish society by outside forces and of the Kurds' inability to unite among themselves."[112] In it, Xani wrote:

If we had had a sultan . . .
These Rûms would not have outwitted us . . .
Undefeated and unresigned we would be to the Turks and
    Tajiks.[113]

Hence, Kurdish nationalism was not shaped by concerns such as saving or inheriting the Ottoman state nor a desire to meet the goals of Ottoman nationalism. Compared to Turkish nationalists, Kurdish nationalists identified with a relatively more limited and defined territory (Mesopotamia or Kurdistan) and directed their attention at mobilizing a people with—for all their linguistic and political differences—a comparatively higher degree of cultural homogeneity. By adopting Anthony D. Smith's theory, Martin van Bruinessen maintains that a "lateral-aristocratic ethnic" consciousness formed between "Kurdish emirs and tribal elites" as early as the seventeenth century, but that this consciousness never resulted in political integration.[114]

Kurdish nationalists envisaged a nation formed of ethnic Kurds, but they were split into autonomist (autonomy within a common state established together with the Turks) and pro-independence groups. Despite this main difference, however, they both strived to mobilize a people formed of ethnic Kurds (real or assumed) by imagining and defining a nation.

As a result, the imagined Kurdish nation highlighted how Kurds were ethnically and culturally different from neighboring groups. This was quite different from Turkish nationalists, who emphasized how similar different groups were and tried to "prove" the Turkishness of various ethnic/cultural groupings.

Hence, in a letter said to have been written to Mustafa Kemal by Kurdish nationalist and intellectual Celadet Bedir Khan, the latter accused Turkish nationalists of trying to mix other ethnicities with Turkish ethnicity.[115] He refers to efforts to form a Turkish national consciousness as "a new nationality formed out of the blood of other nations." The reaction to such efforts in the formation of a Kurdish national consciousness is very clear. In the same letter, Bedir Khan writes of the Turkish Hearths (Turkish nationalist associations and houses of culture): "They educated as many Kurdists for us as they did Turkists for you."[116]

One of the striking characteristics of much Kurdish nationalist literature is the objection to "mixing," interpreted as assimilation by many Kurds. In order to oppose the mixing, they frequently referred to biological metaphors, such as the "wrongness" of breeding different animal species with one another or "thoroughbred" horses with others.[117]

It would certainly be misleading to conclude that Kurdish nationalists formed a homogenous group. Just like Turkish nationalists, they too were a diverse group and had developed ideas that emphasized ethnicity, religion, "race," and political belonging to varying degrees.[118] In other words, imaginations of Kurdishness based on voluntary association and geographical/cultural ties, rather than on "blood ties" and origin, existed as much in Kurdish nationalism as they did in Turkish nationalism. The difference is relative and stems particularly from Turkish nationalism taking over Ottoman heritage and nationalism.

For example, the name of the Kurdish Committee of Solidarity and Progress KCSP (*Kürt Teavün ve Terakki Cemiyeti*) is similar to the Committee of Union and Progress CUP (*İttihat ve Terakki Cemiyeti*), which initially defended the ideal of Ottoman nation building, and later, Turkish nation formation. They both idealize progress. The difference between them is that the word "*teavün*" emphasizes the idea of solidarity, while "*ittihat*" connotes unity. The CUP had a heterogeneous membership in terms of ethnicity and mother tongue—hence no ethnonym in front of the name—and sought to ascertain the *union* of a population with heterogeneous lineage, inviting them to come together and form a new nation under a given state. Instead, the aim of the Kurdish Solidarity and Progress Committee was to ensure the *solidarity* of the Kurds, a relatively more homogeneous group of people, inviting them to realize their given "nationhood" and support each other.

However, the emergence of these nationalistic ideas and different imaginations didn't automatically give rise to the Kurdish Conflict. There were sufficient commonalities and similarities between Kurdish and Turkish nationalists for them to cooperate on common goals. They were not doomed to conflict. In addition to a shared religion (apart from some sectarian differences) and a partially overlapping history, they shared the same ambition for modernization.[119] They both had secularist and Islamist versions. Therefore, they could, for example, have formed a singular nationalist ideology that took as its basis either a geographical identity (Turkey or Anatolia) or a religious identity (Islam). Alternatively, they could have coexisted in a single nation-state or state-nation, pursuant to cultural or territorial rights. Under these scenarios, Kurdish nationalists' aspirations would be met by symmetrical or asymmetrical autonomy and individual cultural autonomy and rights.

There are examples where such arrangements were realized. Pakistan, also meaning the "Pure Land" or the "the Land of the Pure," was given a name concocted in the twentieth century based on an acronym formed from the ethnonyms and toponyms of Punjab, Afghan, Kashmir, Sind, and Baluchistan. It was also established as an Islamic republic, the nation-state of Pakistani Muslims (in the Muslim-majority eastern and northwestern regions of British India), and as a federal republic, in which regions and the inhabitant ethnic groups and tribes are relatively autonomous from the central state.

The subject at hand is not how "successful" and sustainable these arrangements are. Pakistan, for example, has long suffered from ethnic/regional conflicts. Rather, these examples show that it is possible for different logical and political routes to be taken by nationalist movements.

Multi-ethnic and multi-confessional Ottoman Parliament in session in Istanbul, 1908. Symbol of eventually failed efforts to revive the empire through representative institutions and multicultural nation-formation. Photo: Unknown photographer. Shutterstock Item ID: 785841214.

Ottoman Hamidiye corps soldiers, a product of Ottoman era efforts to make Kurds part of state modernization and, arguably, a "state-nation". Photo: Unknown photographer, in H.F.B. Lynch, *Armenia: Travels and Studies* (London: Longmans, Green, and Co. 1901).

U.S. President Wilson and French President Poincare, 1919, during Wilson's European tour to attend the Versailles Peace Conference. Wilson's 14 principles, which he announced at the end of World War One to promote peace and democracy in the world and which promised the right of self-determination for national minorities, significantly altered the normative international environment of the nationality questions in Ottoman territories, such as the Kurdish Question, and in other imperial and colonial contexts. Photo: Unknown photographer. Shutterstock Item ID: 239398993.

CHAPTER 4

# How Was the Kurdish *Conflict* Created?

## *A Non-Standard Explanation*

America, Europe and the whole world of civilization should know that the people of Turkey (*Türkiya halkı*) have absolutely decided to live freely and independently without any conditions and limitations like every civilized and capable nation.[1]

—Mustafa Kemal (Atatürk)

There aren't any material interests to present to the French and English nations for the destruction of the Turkish nation. [Their] project is one of leaders who take pleasure in greedy invasion and tyranny.[2]

—Minister of the Chief of General Staff İsmet İnönü

Turks and Kurds should always share the status of two brothers whose interests are known (or recognized) to be common (or shared) and who have a direct dialogue between themselves.[3]

—Ahmed Emin Yalman,
"Kürtler ve Kürdistan [Kurds and Kurdistan]"

### The Formative Period of the Kurdish Conflict: 1918–1926

It is crucial to explain this period, because by the end of it, the new republican regime considered the Kurds and Kurdish cultural/linguistic differences as vital threats and had adopted a long-lasting policy of oppression and assimilation.[4] State-nation discourses and definitions of identity, which governing elites used during the National Campaign, vanished, giving way to those reflecting the notion of nation-state, and, additionally an ethnically/culturally homogenous nation-state. The regime had single-handedly removed the option of reconciliatory responses, such as cultural or regional autonomy, dialogue and persuasion, or a more pluralist legal/political discourse. Since this time, some Kurds have struggled against the state of Turkey in the cause of changing this nonpluralist conception of nationhood, seeking to either gain autonomy and rights within Turkey or achieve independence.

As I already discussed in the Introduction in reference to the short-comings of standard stories, this outcome should not be taken as preordained, unavoidable, or foreseeable, in accordance with standard stories based on "preexisting actor intentions" and "inevitable consequences of nationalism." Rather, these outcomes need to be explained by developing a nonstandard causal story of what happened and why. This is my main goal in this chapter. Before doing so, however, I need to introduce the concept of rival and compatible images of identities that I will use in my explanation.

## Compatible and Rival Identity Images

*Turk I am with the Turks,*
*and Kurd I am with the Kurds*[5]

Which properties of ethnic, religious, national, or other group identities would prevent these identities from posing a threat to one another within the same territory and polity? Peaceful coexistence, of course, depends on many factors, which may be historical, economic, and institutional in nature, as I discussed in previous chapters. Setting all these factors aside for a moment and focusing on how the people in a society construct and make sense of their identities, however, which qualities of these identities would facilitate harmony and peace? Here, I am not only referring to those identities that people readily embrace as their own. Identities are relational. They gain their full meaning in terms of their own content as well as how they are understood in relation to other identity categories, as in how an identity is considered to be different from and similar to another; whether these identities are viewed as oppositional and antagonistic to each other, or as harmonious, even supplementary. The positive content of an identity is just as important as how that identity relates to and interacts with others. For example, it not only matters whether someone is a Serb, a Muslim, an environmentalist, or a political conservative, but also whether the Serb can be Muslim or the environmentalist can be a political conservative. Do these different identities logically or empirically contradict one another, or can they coexist harmoniously?

When I discussed state-nations in the Introduction, for instance, I argued that for a state-nation to be sustainable, the plural national belongings in that polity should be seen as complementary to each other—allowing for the possibilities of plural belonging, hybridity, and mixing. Which properties would make such complementarity possible?

The relation between even the seemingly most mutually exclusive identities at a particular point in history, say, being Jewish and Christian, or Hindu and Muslim, can change over time as a result of material, social, and ideational transformations. Suditap Kaviraj, for example, narrates a historical period in India during the times of Akbar when different people from different religions borrowed beliefs and practices from each other and developed multiple and syncretic belongings.[6] Rajeev Bhargawa relatedly discusses the theological, cultural, social, and political conditions of people moving easily back and forth between different religious soteriologies.[7] Similarly, Maria Rosa Menocal describes Medieval Spain where Muslims, Jews, and Christians crossed theological barriers and "positively thrived on holding at least two, and often many more (what many would consider today) contrary ideas at the same time."[8]

The inclination to create an "other" can be inherent in nationalism just as it is in other ideologies (for example, socialist and Islamist ideologies also create their own "others"). As we discussed above, narratives that express who is part of a group also express almost axiomatically who is not; and by doing so, they draw a line. However, they do not always describe these "others" negatively or portray them as a threat, and the line they draw between the two may not always be thick, impenetrable, and unchangeable. In fact, negative and relatively fixed images about the "others" usually grow as a result of competition for material and symbolic resources and conflicts, not necessarily vice-versa. They are not inherent properties of identities that include ethnic and national identities.

In order to differentiate between the different ways in which identities can define an "other" in relation to themselves, I employ an analytical distinction between the "rival and compatible images of identities."[9] Whenever two or more identities are present, I argue, there will be rival and compatible images of these identities in circulation, which are all constructed by social and political actors at some point, each reflecting a different impression of how these particular identities relate to each other. These images can portray the relation between widely different identity pairs, for example, being American yet born outside of the United States, being Polish and Protestant, American and Muslim, Muslim and secular, and Turkish and Kurdish. These images answer four crucial and interrelated questions about the relationship between these identities:

- To what extent do they compete with and exclude each other as identity categories (e.g., being vegetarian and meatatarian—eating meat)?

- To what extent do the groups associated with these identities have zero-sum versus positive-sum interests (e.g., the zero-sum and positive-sum interpretations of American and Chinese trade and security interests, the economic interests of capitalists versus workers, or, for that matter, the interests of younger and older generations vis-à-vis global warming)?

- Are these identities thought to have a hierarchical relation, meaning, one being more important or essential than the other (e.g., whether one's nationality comes before regional, ideological, and partisan identity)?

- Can the same individual logically and practically be both of these things at the same time, that is, hold these identities simultaneously?

Note that these questions can be posed vis-à-vis the relation between identities of the same type, such as Mexican versus Argentinian, both referring to a national identity, as well as across different identity types, say, national versus religious identity (for example, whether one's nationality is more important than one's religion, whether non-Jews can be Israeli nationals). Further, individual constructions and perceptions may differ from the dominant social and political understandings in one's environment. For example, a communist who lives in a capitalist society may think that capitalists and workers have antagonistic (zero-sum) interests, but dominant understanding in the person's social and political environment may be that these interests can be reconciled and be mutually beneficial (i.e., positive-sum).

*Rival images* describe two or more identity categories as opposites of each other and assert that the same individual cannot simultaneously hold them because of the very nature of these identities and/or the associated group interests. They reflect beliefs and impressions that portray two identities as competing with and threatening each other. The *compatible image*, in turn, portrays two or more identity categories as harmonious and potential complements, with positive-sum interests, which implies that the same individual can simultaneously embrace them both.

While my focus in this book is on ethnic and national identities, an advantage of the "rival and compatible images" distinction is that it is more general than other analytical distinctions, such as the "ethnic and civic" national identities distinction.[10] Unlike the latter, it can be applied to any kind of identity.

Table 4.1 summarizes the key features of the rival and compatible images of identities.

I provided an example of the rival image relating to Turkish and Kurdish identities in the introduction chapter by the quote showing how Kurdish politician Abdülmelik Fırat perceived the relationship between these two identities. He stated that identities such as Turk, Kurd, and Chechen are categories that cannot be simultaneously held by the same

Table 4.1. The Rival and Compatible Images of Identities

| Type of Definition | Interest Relationship | Identity Relationship |
|---|---|---|
| **Rival Image** | Zero-sum relationship. Oppositional. | • Substitutes.<br>• Binary choice between identities.<br>• Usually hierarchical relationship.<br>• Low attachment to comprehensive categories that are jointly belonged to and to jointly valued sources of belonging. |
| **Compatible Image** | Positive-sum relationship. Complementary. | • Complements.<br>• Simultaneous holding of identities.<br>• No hierarchical relationship.<br>• High attachment to comprehensive categories that are jointly belonged to and to jointly valued sources of belonging. |

person, and gave a typical example of the rival image: "[Being both Turkish and Chechen] how can it be? This is an example of fraudulency." Hence, the rival image forces individuals to make "either-or" choices between two or more identity categories. Another example of the rival image was put forward by Kurdish intellectual Musa Anter, who said, "Because in the laws of nature a Kurd is a Kurd, a Turk a Turk and Arabs and others are themselves."[11]

However, many other social and political actors perceive—or would like themselves and others to view—the relationship between Turkish and Kurdish identities differently. The compatible image allows individuals to develop a sense of belonging to plural identities. If we return to the example above, individuals who embrace the compatible definition believe that they—or others in their social environment—can simultaneously identify themselves as both Chechen and Turkish, Muslim and secular, or Turkish and Kurdish. They don't consider it a contradiction for others to possess such a self-image and identity awareness. The words of Hasan Cemal in the Introduction present an example of the compatible definition.

Martin van Bruinessen—an anthropologist and expert on Kurds— witnessed the compatible image when he was talking to a villager in northwestern Iran in the 1970s. The man he conversed with surprised him by telling him that he was Azeri, Kurdish, and Persian, just like his father.[12] Bruinessen highlights that there are people living in Eastern Turkey who consider themselves Turkish but who speak both Turkish and Kurdish. Bruinessen, whose own theoretical expectations seem to have led him to think that these testimonies are self-contradictory, explained his observations by concluding that assimilationist policies must have forced people who were "objectively" Kurdish to forget their ethnic identities. While this might well have been the case, there could also be an alternative explanation. Such testimonies might also be explained by the villagers having a compatible image of these identities. As Bruinessen notes, the villagers attributed a linguistic, rather than ethnic, meaning to these identities. And since they didn't consider these identities in relation to their ancestry (or because the presence of ethnic mixing and multiethnic identification were considered natural), it seemed normal to them that different identities could be simultaneously adopted by the same individuals.

Social and political actors who believed that many ethnic/national categories (such as the Albanians, the Kurds, and the Circassians) in Anatolia and Rumelia were compatible with Turkishness played a vital role in the construction of Turkish nationalism and the "Turk" (Turkish) as a national identity. This image of Turkishness vis-à-vis these other categories is as vivid in social/political discourse as the rival images of these identity categories. Hence, to cite a prominent Turkish journalist's biography of Sami Frashëri (his name in Turkish, Şemsettin Sami):

> Son of Halit Bey of the Albanian Frashëri family who were descendants of *timar*[13] holders, Sami Frashëri was born in 1850 in the Vilayet of Janina. He started his education in the Greek language Zosimea Gymnasium. He was well-versed in Greek, Italian, French, Arabic, Persian, and also Turkish and Albanian. He wrote the first two-volume modern Turkish dictionary titled, *Kamus-ı Türki. Kamus-ul Âlem*, the first Turkish encyclopedia comprising six-volumes, and *our* [emphasis mine][14] first novel, *The Love Between Talat and Fitnat* (1873) are his works. He was a defender of women's rights. He contributed greatly to the development of the idea of Turkishness by studying *Orkhon inscriptions*[15] and *Kutadgu Bilig*. He rejected the terms "Ottoman Turkish" [*Osmanlıca*] and "Chagatai" [*Çağatayca*] and argued that these language families should be referred to as "Turkish" [*Türkçe*]. Ali Sami Yen, one of the greatest names in our history of sports, is the second son of Sami Frashëri.[16]

The quote by Şükrî Bitlis-i: "Turk I am with the Turks, and Kurd I am with the Kurds," offers a perfect example of the compatible image.[17] That it became difficult for many Kurds to adopt such a compatible image can be attributed to conflict and state policies that denied the existence of Kurds in Turkey in the name of Turkishness or Turkish nationalism. However, a version of the compatible image with which many Kurds still feel comfortable is: "*Türkiyeli* (Of-Turkey) I am with the Turks, and Kurd I am with the Kurds." I will discuss the Of-Turkey identity extensively in chapters 5 through 7 as part of my analysis of why peace initiatives in recent decades failed and my ideas about how the common identity dilemma can be resolved.

Discursive practices may be necessary, but by themselves would not suffice to alter the dominant images of identities in society. Arguably, compatible and rival definitions of the same identities are typically present simultaneously in the same society, but it is usually the case that one of these becomes dominant in the official, social, or political narrative. What is dominant may change, however. For example, in a society where the compatible image is dominant, certain political actors—rival identity entrepreneurs—can begin to use or express the rival image to suit their own ideological or political interests, and over time, the rival image can become the dominant image. In fact, this is exactly how we can define polarization: the process by which the rival definition becomes widespread and attains a dominant status, thereby dividing society into "Us versus Them" camps.[18] The more widespread the rival image in a society, the stronger the polarization. The reverse can also happen, and a dominant rival image in a polarized society can be replaced by a compatible image, thereby reducing polarization. Hence, we should take a closer look at how rival and compatible images are generated and popularized. My analysis of how the Kurdish Conflict was created in the formative period will focus on why and how political elites and state policies came to promote the rival image of Turkish and Kurdish identities. However, these images became internalized by people and dominant in social/political discourse later though the mechanisms I explain here. These mechanisms also provide insights into how the dominant image of the Kurdish and Turkish identities in society and politics can change again in the future.

On one side, there is the discourse of the states, governing elites, and of social and political actors. These discourses reflect the elites' existing beliefs and perceptions, as well as their agentic attempts to construct and reconstruct the social and political reality through their own narratives regarding the true, imagined, or "desired" nature of the identities in question. On the other side, there are government institutions, policies, and structures, such as economic relations and geography, which determine whether social and political interests related to group identities are compatible or rival.

Figure 4.1 explains this relationship. Sometimes, certain actors use the rival image for political ends, for example, to gain votes, to outbid competing actors, or to further their financial interests or stop members of other groups from applying for the same jobs. At other times, the complete opposite is pertinent. Even if it might suit their political interests, some people refuse to use the rival image because they don't believe in it or think that it will have negative social and economic consequences.

Hence, there might be a circular relationship between the identity and the interest components of these images (see Figure 4.1).[19] Collective actions constitute the cause-and-effect mechanism that connects identities to perceived interests.[20] If the dominant discourses around people reflect the rival image, in other words, if the discourses portray groups of people

| Scenario 1: | Rival image discourse →* Opportunities for joint collective actions decrease and become difficult → Perception of being different and adversarial is developed → The plausibility/credibility of rival image increases →* Even less joint collective activity → Rival definition becomes stronger → "One or the other" type of shifts between identities increase and are encouraged. |
|---|---|
| Scenario 2: | Compatible definition discourse →* Opportunities for joint collective actions increase and become easier → Perception of being complementary is developed → The plausibility/credibility of compatible definition increases →* Further joint collective activity → Compatible image becomes stronger → Plural, hybrid and composite identities develop and are encouraged. |

*Intervening variable: Existing mono-ethnic and common collective action opportunities.

Figure 4.1. The formation of compatible and rival identity images.

as being exclusive "others," individuals cannot participate in joint collective actions. During the 2013 Gezi protests, for example, many Turkish and Kurdish activists did not attend the protests together, even though they both opposed the government, the main target of the protests.[21] They avoided joint participation, at least openly and with their own political insignia, because they saw an oppositional relationship between the two identities, at least in the political sphere, and doubted that they could have shared goals. This was an example of the rival image affecting collective actions. But I am not referring here only to taking part in political activities, such as attending a joint rally or becoming a member of the same political party, but also to engaging in civic activities or those related to civil society, such as working at the same foundation or nongovernmental organization, commercial partnerships, marriage, and social relationships.

The fewer shared collective activities groups of people undertake, the greater their perception of being different grows, and, as such, the perception that their mutual interests are zero-sum is strengthened to that degree. In the above example, had the opposite happened, that is, if more Turkish and Kurdish protesters had held the compatible image and joined the protests together, then their perception of having positive-sum interests would have been reinforced as a result of this political experience.

One discursive practice that would have facilitated this for the Kurds would be for the Turkish protesters not to draw a hierarchical relationship between Turkishness and Kurdishness (based on the belief that the former is *the* national identity and the latter an ethnic identity), which many Kurds see as unequal treatment of their identity and a reminder of assimilationist policies.

On the other hand, causality can also work in reverse, leading from interests to identity images. As people keep thinking that their interests are positive-sum, they undertake common collective activities and, thus, gradually develop compatible definitions in relation to their identities.

In social psychology, "Robbers Cave" experiments provide a classic example. In these experiments at a youth camp, Muzafer Sherif and his team randomly split teenagers who had never previously met into two separate groups and engaged them in competitive games. Thus, the teenagers, in striving to defeat the other team in various team games, were given a common group interest that was by definition in a zero-sum relation with the interests of the other team. During the experiment, it was observed that the teenagers of both teams, who previously shared no other common characteristics with their fellow team members, quickly began to form a group identity and to define the members of the opposite team as "the others," attributing to them negative characteristics.[22] To recapitulate, if we explain this in relation to our hypothesis, being split into two teams and starting to play games in which there is a winner and a loser defines both teams' interests as contrasting and zero-sum. As a result, this creates a pressure to change the identity definitions according to the rival image. Feelings of conflicting interests lead to the development of the perception of the rival image. However, the opposite might also take place. In other words, people who have no conflict of interest can become estranged from the other group because of the development of the rival images in social/political circulation and begin to think that there is a conflict of interest between them.[23]

One way state policies can impact the evolution of rival and compatible images is by affecting the opportunity structures for various collective actions. For example, as we will see later, state policies in Turkey long suppressed "moderate" Kurdish political actors who advocated the compatible image and worked together with Turkish actors for cultural rights, alongside hardliner Kurdish activists employing violent methods. Thus, these policies hindered the development of political movements with mixed (Turkish-Kurdish) membership that promoted the compatible image. Since its establishment, the PKK has undertaken actions to the same effect by targeting and oppressing nonviolent Kurdish activists.[24]

So, how do people form their perceptions of which image the state favors?

Figure 4.2 summarizes my hypothesis. Defending a compatible image successfully depends on the state adopting narratives and policies that are consistent with the compatible definition. The box in the bottom-right corner depicts this, while the box in the bottom-left corner explains that compatible policies will be unsuccessful for as long as they do not coexist with a suitable parallel narrative. The reason for this is that the narrative is not credible in the absence of consistent policies. Actors who support the rival image will damage the credibility of the policies in question by asserting that the compatible image does not reflect the long-term strategies of the state. For instance, a narrative of "intergroup brotherhood" that is not supported by laws and socioeconomic policies aimed at creating equal rights and opportunities will be unsuccessful in building the compatible image. Policies that support the compatible image might include: creating opportunities for realizing collective actions that express the compatible image; development policies that will help create positive-sum results for the economic integration of group members; creating conditions that don't exclude certain groups from public service; ensuring that identities are respected and creating a sense of equality; implementing policies that will enable group members to perceive the steps that the state has taken in this direction.

Sometimes, actors within a group defend the rival image in order to hinder the assimilation of group members. However, while this strategy might dissuade some members of the group from assimilating, it still represents

| | | DE FACTO POLICIES OF THE STATE | |
| --- | --- | --- | --- |
| | | Consistent with the rival image | Consistent with the compatible image |
| **THE NARRATIVE OF THE STATE** | Consistent with the rival image | Outcome: Perception of the Rival Image | Outcome: Perception of the Rival Image |
| | Consistent with the compatible image | Outcome: Perception of the Rival Image | Outcome: Perception of the Compatible Image |

Figure 4.2. The formation of the perception of the identity image favored by the state.

| | Defended by Group A | |
|---|---|---|
| | The Rival Image | The Compatible Image |
| **Defended by Group B** | | |
| The Rival Image | **Outcome:** Perception of the rival image | **Outcome:** Perception of the rival image |
| The Compatible Image | **Outcome:** Perception of the rival image | **Outcome:** Perception of the compatible image |

Figure 4.3. The formation of the dominant identity image between two groups.

a double-edged sword, which can give rise to unintended results. In fact, this strategy can actually accelerate the assimilation of some group members. When compelled to choose between two groups, with no chance of having relations with both, some group members whose desire to integrate with and gain acceptance by other groups is stronger than their loyalty to the group—but who would have preferred to preserve their original group identity had the compatible relations prevailed—may choose assimilation into the other group, suppressing their attachment to their initial group identity.

The most important effect of the rival definition is that it greatly facilitates the emergence of the "clashing image," in which the "other" who is excluded and considered to be a rival also becomes the "hostile other."[25] For some actors, this is an unintended effect, while for others it is an outcome that is undoubtedly intended. However, the consolidation of the rival definition increases polarization in society and the possibility of intergroup conflict.


## The Outcome to Be Explained:
## The Change in the (National) Identity Model during the Formative Period

### When Did the Shift from the Compatible to the Rival Model Take Place?

During the War of Independence, the leading participants of the national campaign outlined several models that more or less fit the state-nation model, which by themselves appeared more inclusive and realistic—given the nature of the people the nationalists wanted to mobilize—than the nation-state model that ensued later. These models accepted the Kurds as a component of *the* nation with their own distinct identity and lawful rights. In other words, the Kurdish identity was portrayed as an identity that was compatible with the national identity and expressed as such. This model was later forsaken and a stricter model began to be upheld, whereby the Kurdish identity started to be seen (by the ruling elites, the state, and the Turkish majority) first as a rival identity and later sometimes even as a clashing identity.

Since research on the Kurdish Conflict does not distinguish between compatible, rival and clashing images of identity as I do here, there is no consensus on when and how this change came about. Even though the change from a "Muslim Ottoman" to a "Turkish" nation-state model occurred almost immediately after the foundation of the republic, this did not necessarily reflect a rival image of Turkish and Kurdish categories. The latter change from the compatible image occurred later, and took some time and major domestic and international developments.

The records of the proceedings of the first assembly during the war years are extremely interesting, exemplifying how the speakers saw and sought to frame a national identity in the making, how they experimented with notions of nation-state and state-nation while doing so, and how their efforts were bounded as explained by the "radical middle position" perspective I discussed in the introduction.[26] Members of the parliament mentioned a singular Ottoman Muslim *people* or *nation*, but also freely referred to the Kurds and "Kurdish people" as part of this.[27] Neither was the term *Kurdistan* taboo; Atatürk saw no harm in speaking of leading his heroic troops in "Anafarta, [in Galipoli] *Kurdistan* [the emphasis is mine], Syria."[28]

British documents assert that a draft law relating to the autonomy of the Kurds was being discussed. The existence of such a vote is questionable as it could be a figment of the imagination that the administration of the Grand National Assembly leaked in order to mislead the British.[29] However, even if this were so, the fact that such a leak took place makes one think that the subject of Kurdish autonomy was thinkable and a credible possibility in the conditions of the day. Thus, during the war years, the recognition of Kurds as a people having distinct legal rights was a subject that could be discussed and imagined within the bounds of the imagination of a single nation.[30] Perhaps as significant is the fact that—whether or not it was truly discussed—this autonomy draft remained in the collective memory of Kurdish nationalists. Its content is still seen as a framework by some Kurdish actors for conflict resolution.

In a message to Nihad Pasha, commander of the Elcezire Army—established with various aims, such as ensuring Kurds' loyalty and the support of the National Campaign, and preventing the loss of the Mosul province to the British[31]—Mustafa Kemal stated that "a local government (*mahalli idare*) would gradually be founded in regions inhabited by Kurds (in consideration of) both foreign and domestic policy." This pointed to a general and symmetrical plan in relation to the founding of local governments across the land in circumstances when the people demanded such local administration.[32] In 1923, before the proclamation of the Republic, he mentioned just such a form of autonomy (and rights for other ethnic/religious groups) to journalists as part of general decentralization.

In his writings and memoirs, Mustafa Kemal conveyed information about his correspondence with prominent Kurdish figures and how many of them actively supported the National Campaign through such contacts.[33] As Kurdish sources confirm, "The majority of the Kurds were arguing against leaving Turkey and becoming part of today's Syria and Iraq."[34] In a letter to Kazım Karabekir (1882–1948)—Ottoman Turkish general, leader of the National Campaign and commander of the eastern armies that fought against Russian and Armenian forces during the War of Independence—Kemal wrote that the "prominent Kurdish beys" supported the National Campaign and that they were ready to do all it would take "so that *the* homeland and *the* (emphases mine) nation could be completely independent and free." He also claimed that those who wanted an independent Kurdistan formed a small minority.[35]

During and in the aftermath of the Lausanne Treaty Conference (1922–23), İsmet (İnönü)—commander of the Western Front that fought against mainly Greek forces during the War of Independence and later president of the republic—stated the following:

> The government of the Grand National Assembly of Turkey is as much the government of the Kurds as it is of the Turks. The true and legitimate representatives of the Kurds have been elected as members of parliament and participate in the government and governance of the *country to the same degree as the representatives of the Turks* [the emphasis is mine]. . . . [Referring to the demands of the Kurds of *Kürddağı*—literally the Kurd Mountains—handed to the Assembly in Ankara in 1922] The Kurdish people to the south [those of the Mosul province]

have recently applied to the Grand National Assembly of Turkey and informed us of their firm decision to enable the return to Turkey of the countries that were invaded after the Armistice of 1918. . . . The Kurds have shown togetherness in earnest throughout the National Campaign; the Kurds were also side by side with the Turks as patriots during the Lausanne Treaty. In fact, during the Lausanne Conference we (us Turks and Kurds) defended our national cause *as one nation* [the emphasis is mine] and procured acceptance.[36]

These examples reflect a model that does not fuss over the existence, recognition, and rights of the Kurdish component in the National Campaign. That is to say, the Kurdish identity, which would be recognized with legal rights,[37] was considered as a compatible identity that could be adopted simultaneously with the national identity of the new Turkey, which was itself in the making, regardless of what its name would be. This model was abandoned and disappeared from circulation between 1923 and 1926. In the aftermath of the 1925 rebellion, İsmet Pasha depicted Kurds and other components as a source of threat, rather than as a partner for the Turkish majority, and as a people that needs to be assimilated by force. He thereby gave a stark example of the clashing identities image.

Nationality (nationhood) is our sole vehicle of unity. . . . Other components do not have the power to influence the Turkish majority. Our duty is to make those residing in Turkey Turkish no matter what. We will cut off the components that will oppose Turks and Turkism. The quality we look for in a man who will serve the homeland is that he is, first and foremost, Turkish and Turkist.[38]

When did this change occur? Mesut Yeğen, who analyzed the state narrative regarding the Kurdish Question, argues that change happened first before the Shaikh Said Rebellion, with the Constitution of 1924. According to him, the perception that "situated Kurds as an ethnic group (*kavim*)[39] with particular recognized rights into the political community" changed in 1924 and a perception that identified the Kurds as "prospective Turks" installed itself.

With the Constitution of 1924 the Republic did not object to the reality that there were other ethnic groups than Turks in the country but declared that this physical presence would not be allowed to translate into law. . . . The Kurds were no longer Kurds as judicial and political subjects. They had legally become Turkish like other citizens of the country. The Republic, which denied the judicial presence of Kurds with the Constitution of 1924, set to work on denying the physical presence of Kurds as of the 1930s.[40]

The Constitution of 1921 had not given a name to the nation or associated it with a specific ethnic category when it stated: "Sovereignty belongs without restriction to the *nation* [the emphasis is mine]."[41] By comparison, Articles 3 and 4 of the Constitution of 1924 named the nation and declared that sovereignty belongs to the Grand National Assembly of Turkey in the name of the "Turkish nation" (*Türk milleti*).[42]

Article 3—Sovereignty belongs without restriction to the nation.

Article 4—The Grand National Assembly of Turkey is the sole lawful representative of the Turkish nation, and exercises sovereignty in the name of the nation.

While the formulation in the 1924 Constitution no doubt marked a significant and exclusionary shift for Kurds, this being said, the provisions included in the Constitution did not completely stand in the way of obtaining Kurdish cultural rights in due course. Further, the main motivation of the state founders in instituting this change does not seem to have been the exclusion of Kurds, as I will discuss shortly.

The change in 1924 was a more moderate change in proportion to the aftermath of the 1925 rebellion. For example, the former did not contain any provisions ruling out potential policy changes in the future such as education in languages other than Turkish. The same applied to the Treaty of Lausanne.[43]

The first two articles of the Constitution determined the name of the state on a territorial basis rather than on an ethnic basis. The term used was *The State of Turkey* (*Türkiye Devleti*), and not *The Turkish State* (*Türk Devleti*).[44] It was possible for the notion of the State of Turkey to accommodate more inclusive policies toward the Kurds and other components in time. The parliament, which was established in 1920 with the name Grand National Assembly, took the name Grand National Assembly of Turkey in 1921 and the Constitution of 1924 registered this officially.

The Constitution defined the "official language" of the state as Turkish, thus being relatively open to polylingualism compared to, for example, the Constitution of 1982, which proclaimed the "language of the state" as Turkish. The notion of an official language is more open to the use of non-Turkish languages by, for example, regional authorities. Even when only one language is decided as the state's official language, the state can use other languages to better communicate with people at a local level.[45]

Article 1—The State of Turkey is a republic.

Article 2—The religion of the State of Turkey is the religion of Islam;[46] the official language is Turkish; the seat of government is Ankara.

The Constitution of 1924 was based on the definition of the Turkish nation, but it did not define the Turkish nation or base the criteria for being Turkish on ethnic origin or culture. Being included in the Turkish nation was described as a legal and attainable attribute, rather than one based on lineage:[47]

Article 88—Everybody in Turkey is called a Turk from the point of view of citizenship, without distinction of race and religion. Every child born in Turkey, or in a foreign land of a Turkish father; any person whose father is a foreigner established in Turkey, who resides in Turkey, and who chooses upon attaining the age of majority to become a Turkish subject, and any individual who acquires Turkish nationality by naturalization in conformity with the law, is a Turk.

Several inferences can be made from these expressions. First, the constitution implicitly accepted that being Turkish was polysemic, that is, having ethnic, political, civic (citizenship), and legal meanings, by stipulating "Turk from the point of view of citizenship." Second, every citizen was declared a Turk in terms of this latter meaning. Third, while imposing *a* Turkish identity on every citizen from above, it also imposed a legal/political version of Turkishness on the state, at least in regard to matters of citizenship.

Reflecting institutional and discursive "path dependence" and continuity during regime change,[48] in terms of its rationale and language, Article 88 is quite similar to the article on citizenship in the Ottoman Constitution of 1876. Written by "Young Ottomans,"[49] the 1876 Constitution was aimed at forming an Ottoman national consciousness. Its Article 8 stated: "All subjects of the empire are called Ottomans without exception, and without distinction whatever religion or sect they profess; the status of an Ottoman is acquired and lost according to conditions specified by law."[50]

The fact that the Constitution of 1924 applies the same criteria to being Turkish corresponds with my thesis here that the Turk category was given the role of the Ottoman identity. But the Constitution of 1924 differs from that of 1876 in three aspects. The first is the addition of "without distinction of race" to "without distinction of religion and sect"[51] (in contemporary usage, the term race was often used to refer to ethnicity and language).[52] The reason for this must be the material conditions, which had changed since 1876 from the viewpoint of nation building. In 1876, the key issue—from the perspective of the Ottoman elites—was to build a nation from peoples of different faith, specifically from religiously defined millets. Hence, the use of the term: "without distinction of religion and sect." By comparison, in 1924, the people who were meant to develop a national conscience had become much more homogeneous in terms of religion (as a result of changing borders, genocides, migrations, and deportations across the Ottoman lands from the Balkans to Anatolia). Instead, linguistic and ethnic differences had become prominent among Muslims, who had now become the overwhelming majority in a newly defined homeland. Thus, the governing elites saw it crucial that a people who were religiously homogenous but linguistically and ethnically heterogeneous could gain national consciousness. In particular, it had become a critical question as to how indigenous Kurds and Muslims who came from the Caucasus and the Balkans (who had different ethnicities) would adopt the national identity.

However, the fact that the Constitution of 1924 only states: "without distinction of religion" and does not refer to "sect" (differently to the Constitution of 1876) can be viewed as a step backward for the recognition and equality of diverse beliefs. The Muslims were not homogeneous in terms of sects. The Alevis constituted an important minority. The way Article 88 was penned points to the rise of Sunni Islam and the oppression of sectarian differences. Indeed, "In the creation of the nation the most important criterion, in fact at times the only criterion, for belonging to Turkishness was to belong (emphasis mine) to Islam [i.e., religious identity by birth rather than actual belief]. This can be seen in the involuntary population exchange of 1923 . . . .A Turk is Muslim, a Turcophone who is not Muslim is far from us, a Muslim who is not a Turcophone can be Turkified."[53] In keeping with this viewpoint, when Article 88 was put to a vote, the parliamentary discussions were not generally about ethnic differences or about the Kurds in particular. Instead, they were about religious belonging and non-Muslim citizens. Since it was thought that cultural Turkishness required one to be Muslim and a citizenship-based definition of Turkishness could also include non-Muslims, questions were raised regarding how non-Muslims can be considered Turks.[54] That is, the grand question regarded nation building among Muslims of different ethnicities and how to achieve "national cohesion and collective morality" through a "sacred synthesis," by cooperating with religion and religious elites whenever nation builders deemed it necessary and possible.[55]

Thus, while important, the Kurdish Question was not a prioritized and urgent issue for the state builders. While rival and clashing images of Turkishness and non-Muslimness were already established as a product of wars and intercommunal clashes during the disintegration of the empire and the War of Independence, such images were not yet there vis-à-vis Turkishness and Kurdishness. According to Bozarslan:

> [W]hy did a strong Kurdish resistance emerge immediately after 1923? . . . It is difficult to explain this change solely as a reaction against the heavy hand of the Kemalist government. It is difficult to state that there was a systematic oppression of the Kurds [from 1922 to 1924]. Moreover, despite the fact that the Kemalist government didn't keep its promises of Kurdish-Turkish brotherhood, it didn't ignore the possibility of local autonomy for Kurdish provinces, at the very least not in 1922 and 1923. In August 1924—just six months before the Shaikh Said Rebellion—a Kurdish delegation met with representatives of the state in Diyarbakır and they proposed specific middle-of-the-road nationalist demands related to local autonomy; this step did not lead to retaliation, violence and oppression by the state.[56]

Among the most crucial issues for the state builders were: the development of a common identity among the Muslim population in general, particularly those who migrated to Anatolia; non-Muslims who were seen as untrustworthy; the issue of Mosul and not playing into the hands of the British; elite disagreements on the model of modernization (Islamic or secular) and related questions of political regime and leadership; and, perhaps most importantly, distrust of adversaries more sympathetic to the Ottoman heritage. These issues pushed the Kurdish Question into the background and affected attitudes toward the Kurds.

From the vantage point of the Kurdish Question, the greatest weakness of the 1924 Constitution was not the name of the nation; it was its lack of any principle or legal status on which any educational and cultural rights of Kurdish "Turks" could be based. The Constitution did not include any principle that would safeguard diversity. Meanwhile, for the Kurdish elites, there was no assurance that decentralization would be implemented and secular reforms posed a threat to their local statuses and powers.

Yet, many Kurdish sources date the change much earlier—in terms of the Kurds' own perceptions. Seasoned politician and writer Tarık Ziya Ekinci wrote:

> From 1923 onwards the process of forming a mono-cultured, homogeneous nation was initiated. Gazi Mustafa Kemal Pasha used the term "Turkish nation" for the first time in March 1923. After his speech on 29 October 1923, he never used the term "the nation of Turkey" and instead replaced it with the "Turkish nation."[57]

It is understandable how important this discursive change was for the Kurds. While the notion of "the nation of Turkey" was an acceptable one for the Kurds, the notion of the "Turkish nation" was exclusionary, and thus unacceptable. However, in terms of a causal narrative, the shift from "the nation of Turkey" to the "Turkish nation" in Mustafa Kemal's speeches can be interpreted in two ways. As Ekinci speculates, Atatürk might have forsaken the term "the nation of Turkey" and started using the preexisting definition of an ethnic Turkish nation when the conditions became suitable. Or, he might have substituted the term *Turkish nation* for the term *the nation of Turkey*, but to denote more or less the same meaning and people, thus redefining the Turkish category. That is to say, he might have started using it as a notion based on land, culture, and political belonging instead of ethnicity. Perhaps a combination of both interpretations may be valid at a time of nation making and identities in flux. According to Sadi Borak, Atatürk wrote as follows in his notes dated 1926:

> [A] nation is a community who inhabit the same piece of land, who are subject to the same laws, and who are united by morality and language. One can refer to the French nation, the German nation, the Spanish nation. Most of the time, the words "nation" and "people" are confused in use. However, the difference between them is that the word "nation" denotes a political establishment, whereas the word "people" recalls, first and foremost, origin and race.[58]

In the 1930s, *the clashing image* became hegemonic, and even the physical presence of the Kurds began to be denied. In 1926 and 1934, two important settlement laws were passed that reflected the changing perception of the state. With the law passed in 1926, which had limited scope, Kurdish elites who were deemed to have participated in Kurdish rebellions or to have the potential to do so were subjected to mandatory settlement in western provinces. The law passed in 1934 divided Turkey into three regions in terms of settlement policies: (1) "Areas populated by groups who share Turkish culture," (2) "Areas where groups who can assimilate into Turkish culture will be settled and resettled," and (3) "Areas that are barred from settlement due to sanitary, economic, cultural, political, military and security reasons."

Bosnians and Pomaks were included in the first group alongside Crimean Tatars. The Kurds were considered as a group that did not share Turkish culture but could potentially do so. In light of this, the aim was to settle Kurdish nomads in the first area where Turks were the majority; to settle (with an additional bylaw passed in 1939) the "Turkish" migrants who arrived from abroad in the second area where Kurds also lived, and, where necessary, to deport nomadic Kurds.[59]

The 1930s also witnessed regime-led and intellectual attempts to reinvent the Turkish nationhood based on race, which would eliminate questions over the Turkishness of all Anatolian groups once and for all.[60] This was attempted through developing pseudo-scientific theories such as the "Sun Language Theory," which was also expected to prove "Turks" belonging to the European race, against the background of growing racism and fascism in Europe.[61] Still, however, the aim of these "theories" was to include the Kurds as Turks, rather than to exclude them as a foreign element.

## Why Did the Transition Occur from the Compatible to the Rival Image?

### IDENTITIES IN FLUX IN RESPONSE TO CHANGING MATERIAL CONDITIONS

Challenging standard stories based on the assumption of fixed actor intentions and ideological determinism, major shifts in the environmental conditions changed the nature of the three fundametal dilemmas during the formative period. Following Thomas Schelling's method of "vicarious problem-solving," these changes could not but reshape the priorities and policies of the postimperial nation-building elites. While highlighting the continuities between the Second Constitutional Era policies in the Ottoman era (1908–1918) and the early policies of the republic, Erik Jan Zürcher observes that major demographic and geographical shifts disrupted this continuity:

> The Turkey which was born out of post-war chaos in 1923 was—from a geographical and demographic perspective— greatly different from the late Ottoman Empire which had shrunk considerably. Most of the Arab territories that were under Ottoman rule in the pre-war era had been lost. Syria and Lebanon (under French mandate), Iraq, Jordan and Palestine (under British mandate) had emerged. New Turkey was primarily composed of Anatolia with the addition of some land from the Southeast Balkans. Famine, mass exiles, civil war, migration and finally, the population exchange realized at the helm of the League of Nations caused the annihilation of the Greek and Armenian communities in Anatolia. As a result, Anatolia became an ethnically and religiously monolithic country composed of a Turkish majority that was primarily Sunni Muslim and a Kurdish minority. Alongside this homogeneity, the population had declined further due to the severe losses caused by the wars in the last decade. It can be stated that in percentage, this population decline is unmatched—possibly except Cambodia—in the history of the modern world.[62]

By 1919, Turkey had become a much more homogeneous country in terms of religious belonging and was territorially much more limited compared to the prewar period. It had become a people that could possibly be envisioned as either Muslim "Turkish-Kurdish" or "Turkish" nation.[63] These names and definitions would have been unthinkable in Anatolia before World War I, when Armenians and Greeks were major minorities and Muslim immigrants—or more precisely, refugees—were fewer in numbers. We do not have accurate data about 1919, but we know that in 1912 about 20 percent of the population of Anatolian Turkey was non-Muslim and that this decreased to 2–3 percent in 1927. Meanwhile, the Muslim population rose through forced and voluntary emigrations.

Among the Muslims, the second biggest ethnic/linguistic group after the Turks was the Kurds. As of 1927, about 9 percent of the population was Kurdish.[64] However, this percentage had been even higher in 1919 because Mosul (more or less today's Northern Iraq and Syria)—which was later lost—was still a part of the imagined nation-state. Thus, the Erzurum Congress of 1919 proclaimed that it represented a "Muslim nation composed of Turks and Kurds." "All Muslim citizens" were considered "natural members" of the assembly.[65]

As the "target audience" of the envisioned nation changed, so did the way nation builders envisioned it. A pragmatic quest regarding the name and content of the aspired nation-state can be found in the discourses of Mustafa Kemal (Ataturk) as well as those of other nationalists. Ahmed Emin Yalman's—prominent Turkish nationalist journalist, author, and academic with evolutionary secularist views—statement below implies how concepts such as Ottoman-ness, Turkishness, and "Muslim from Turkey" were used by the intellectuals of the period in interchangeable and intertwined ways shaped by perceived political realities and exigencies.

> The notion of an Ottoman manifests itself among people who include such a group that openly expresses its lack of loyalty to the country . . . .The insincerity that consequently pervades the term "Ottoman" leaves no other choice but the use of terms such as "Turk" and "Turk and Muslim.[66]

Yalman wrote as an intellectual who defined himself as "Turkish and Muslim" but who at the same time distinguished between "a positive Turkism" (*müsbet Türkçülük*) that aimed for the cultural development of the Turks and "an official Turkism" (*resmi Türkçülük*) that wanted to hinder the development of other components people such as "Albanians, Arabs and Kurds," supporting the former and condemning the latter.[67]

In their search for a postimperial national model, Ottoman Turkish elites were not unique in the world. Echoing the Habsburgs who restructured themselves as the Austro-Hungarian Empire, Ottoman elites experimented with visions such as reinventing themselves as a Turkish-Arabic confederation, or as a "Muslim nation of Turks and Kurds."[68]

Hence, Zürcher observes that the national resistance movement "had three factors that determined its aims and the social strata on which it would be built." These were political, territorial, and religious factors; in other words, "state, homeland, and *millet*."[69] He highlights that the most distinctive of these was the political factor: "The borders of the piece of land on which the movement demanded independence were determined by the realities of the post-war conditions."[70]

For instance, despite the factor of "Muslim solidarity" and the fact that the leaders of the movement at first considered themselves as Ottoman Muslims, many areas where Muslims and Arabs formed the majority were not included within the borders of the National Pact.[71] The province of Batum, where the National Pact stipulated a referendum would be held and where Muslim Georgians (Meskhetian Turks) constituted the majority, was handed over to the Russians with the Treaty of Alexandrapol in 1920 "on the basis of realism and conciliation."[72] For political and strategic (and not identity or ideology-related) reasons, Atatürk placed special importance on relations with the Soviet Union and considered the nationalist movements in Islamic countries to be fellows but having secondary importance.[73]

> Matters of ethnicity and mother-tongue played only a small role in the mind of [national resistance] leaders. The term "race" was used a few times. However, it can be stated that this was used with a highly ambiguous content to emphasise "origin," "foundation" or "component" rather than "race" in a biological sense.[74]

Even those who considered it ill-advised to use the notion of Turkishness did not necessarily claim that the category of Turkishness in question referred to an existing ethnic *group*—in the sense I discussed in the Introduction—or culture. What they opposed was *not* the assimilation of different cultures into the already existing culture of a specific ethnic (Turkish) group; on the contrary, they were concerned that such a model would fail because there was no developed ethnic group culture that could serve this purpose. This supports my thesis that, during this period, Turkishness was not an ethnic group, but an ethnic category. For example, Ziyaeddin Fahri—a prominent philosophy and sociology professor—who was critical of Ziya Gökalp's project of Turkishness based on culture and who, instead, supported the category of "Anatolianism," pondered:

> There is nothing established, concrete [*uzuvlaşmış*], sovereign to speak of . . . .[Had there been] a national culture that could inject the national conscience and national life, i.e.—to put it across in a single word—Anatolianism to them [to different cultural components] then—as mentioned by Ernest Renan and [the way it was] conveyed by Ziya [Gökalp] Bey—in order to be Turkish it would have been sufficient to think and feel like a Turk.[75]

In other words, Ziyaeddin is stating that there was no ethnic or national group with an identifiable and distinct culture called "Turkish." Turkishness was an ethnic category. Therefore, what the proponents of Turkism in lieu of Muslim Ottomanism argued was to *build* a Turkish national culture and belonging through educational, cultural, economic, and other public policies. In fact, before the leaders of the National Campaign used it, the term *Turkish nation* was used in the constitution of another Muslim nationalist republican project in the aftermath of the Ottoman defeat in World War I. This was the short-lived Provisional National Government of the Southwestern Caucasia (1918–19), employing the "Turk" category in a particularly multiethnic region that borders Eastern Anatolia and Southern Caucasus.[76] Hence, political and strategic considerations gave rise to a national project from which many ethnic Turks were excluded like many ethnic non-Turks.

Mustafa Kemal's criticisms about Western Thrace becoming part of the National Pact laid bare his way of thinking:

> It has been said that if we appeal to a plebiscite, Western Thrace's accession to us will be guaranteed. Will the addition of Western Thrace make us stronger or weaker [vulnerable]? In my opinion, it will make us vulnerable. There is Bulgaria to the north, sea to the south, and Greece to the west of Western Thrace. This terrain extends towards two hostile terrains.

The power that will be consumed to keep this terrain under control will not add up to the advantages that can be gained from this terrain. Giving up Western Thrace is necessary for the welfare of the homeland.[77]

As the way the nationalists named the national identity changed alongside the changing political conditions, their own identities might have changed in this process. According to Zürcher:

> Mustafa Kemal . . . often refers to the terms, *us* and *them*. *Us*, in this instance, refers to the *Ottoman Muslims* . . . .Overwhelming documentary evidence shows that the leaders of the movement considered themselves as *Ottoman Muslims* and that this identity emerged through a contradictory [conflicting] relationship with Ottoman Christian communities, particularly the Armenians and the Greeks. [However, above and beyond this], the terminology used by the pioneers of the resistance movement wasn't entirely consistent. Mustafa Kemal himself mentioned the *Ottoman nation* at least once. During this period, Mustafa Kemal did not use the concept of an ethnic nationality. The word, *Turk*, is not encountered in his speech texts . . . .[However], it is misleading to think of this as evidence of Mustafa Kemal envisioning [but concealing] the founding of a new Turkish State to replace the Ottoman State as early as this. There is no evidence [to prove he had a hidden agenda or a "national secret"].[78]

In other words, this appears to have been a period of "identities in flux," and of identity seeking, shifting, and remaking;[79] it was not one of predetermined goals and hidden intentions. Certainly, these possibilities are not mutually exclusive. Some actors might have changed their discourses in the process as a result of prior intentions, others might have done so due to political realism, pragmatism or opportunism, while yet others might have been transformed through genuine identity re-formation and remaking under changing conditions.

While some identity reinvention and remaking is common among all nation-building experiences, the period during which the Ottoman Empire collapsed and modern Turkey was established in its place as a nation-state seems to have been a period during which identities, names, and perceptions went through a particularly slippery process of evolution. This is because of rapidly changing territorial and demographical conditions.[80] In the end, Anatolia became a country composed of a Turkish majority and a Kurdish minority—both of which were predominantly Sunni Muslim—and the imagination of a "Turkish-Kurdish" nation or "the nation of Turkey" came to prominence.

The borders outlined by the National Pact reflected the "national borders" of the homeland that the nationalists had set their sights on. These were also accepted as the official aims of the National Campaign, which hinged upon two criteria: the borders controlled by the Ottomans on the day the Mudros Armistice was signed, and the lands where "Turkish and Kurdish" Muslim Ottoman people lived[81]—in short, territorial and linguistic-cultural criteria. Certain provinces where Kurds were concentrated, such as Mosul, had been invaded immediately after the armistice. Therefore, there are certain uncertainties about the text of the National Pact and where exactly its borders were. Some authors use the expression "within and outside the borders of the armistice."[82] There were also some uncertainties around how these criteria were implemented.

However, when the entirety of the National Pact and the military policies during the War of Independence are considered, the thesis that the National Campaign considered all Ottoman Kurds (including those in today's Iraq) as part of the imagined nation seems true. In places such as Western Thrace (where the population was Muslim and Turkish-speaking and both linguistic and religious criteria would demand inclusion) and "Arabia" (where the population was mainly Muslim Arab, for example, the province of Baghdad)—which could be part of the National Campaign but were excluded, the right to self-determination of the people was recognized and plebiscites were requested to determine their future. However, unlike these cases, the Ottoman Kurds were accepted *in toto*, automatically and unconditionally within the national borders, and self-determination was not stipulated. In the context of deliberations with the Russians, on July 3, 1920, Atatürk compared the National Campaign's view on Arabic, Armenian, and Kurdish people as follows:

> They consider the independence of Turkey to be natural; they also consider it appropriate for the Turkish land to remain with us. We have accepted Arabia and Syria [to become independent states outside our national borders] and this has already been proclaimed . . . . There is [only] one difference and that

is the issue of having recourse [to the vote of Muslims from different races within the national borders]. For all intents and purposes we have accepted [the independence of] people in both Syria and Iraq . . . .We have accepted [the independence of] Armenians who constitute and founded the Republic of Yerevan and their wishes in relation to this. However, not for Kurdistan, Lazistan, etc. [The various Muslim components that live within the circle we have drawn as national borders] are genuine [full] siblings.[83]

## THE DIVISION OF OTTOMAN KURDS

The Treaty of Lausanne in 1923 left the Mosul question, and, thus, the question of southern Ottoman Kurdistan unresolved. In the interviews he gave in İzmit in January 1923, Mustafa Kemal explained his thoughts on why the disintegration of the Kurds would be undesirable:

The province of Mosul is within our boundaries. Mosul is very valuable to us; first, because of the nearby oil reserves that constitute endless fortunes. Second, the issue of Kurdishness is as important as the previous reason . . . .The British want to form a Kurdish government there. If they achieve this, this idea can spread to the Kurds within our boundaries. In order to hinder this idea, our border needs to cross along the south.[84]

This speech can be interpreted in two ways. The first is that Atatürk was against any Kurdish autonomy (government). In this case, however, he might also have preferred the partitioning of the Kurds, who would then have become a smaller and more easily assimilable minority within Turkey, as many Kurdish writers have argued.[85] Another interpretation is that the real danger for him was that the Kurds might become a minority vulnerable to separatist influences. In another speech, Atatürk stated the following (the emphases are mine):

The Kurdish Question [Cause] can on no account be to *our, namely Turks,* benefit either. Because, as you know, the existing *Kurdish components* have settled within *our national borders* such that they form a majority only in limited areas. By losing population density and mixing with the *Turkish components,* a border has been derived. So much so that if we want to draw a line in the name of Kurdishness, it is necessary to exterminate Turkishness and Turkey . . . .Therefore, rather than *imagining* a Kurdishness in its own right, a kind of local autonomy will be formed by virtue of our Constitution. Under such circumstances, whichever province has Kurdish inhabitants will govern itself autonomously. Furthermore, when mentioning the people of Turkey, it is necessary to also include them. If they are not included, it will always be probable that they will develop some cause for themselves. Now, the Grand National Assembly of Turkey is formed of the authorized representatives of both Kurds and Turks, and these two components have combined their interests and fates. In other words, they both know that this is joint. It would not be right to attempt to draw a border separately.[86]

The language Mustafa Kemal used in this excerpt is in many respects consistent with other records from the time. Terms such as "our national borders" and "the people of Turkey" denote the "Turkish and Kurdish components" of a singular nation. Kurdishness is envisaged as an equal component (*unsur*) whose legal rights are recognized and whose interests overlap with the Turks in relation to this nation project.

On the other hand, at the beginning of the excerpt, Mustafa Kemal uses the words: "our, namely Turks." The reason for this can be understood from the context of his speech. He responds to a question by Ahmed Emin Bey, their previous discussion having been about the situation of Turks from Russia. Thus, in the context of this conversation, "Turkishness" appears to have been used in an ethnic and linguistic sense. It is also noteworthy that Mustafa Kemal refers to "Turkish components" just as he also refers to "Kurdish components" of the nation.

The province of Mosul (present-day northern Iraq) and the area between Alexandria and Aleppo (present-day northern Syria)—which, as already mentioned, were within the borders of the National Pact[87]— were shared between Britain and France as early as 1916 with the secret Sykes-Picot Agreement. When the Armistice of Mudros was signed on October 30, 1918, Mosul was still under the control of Ottoman troops. However, in the following two weeks, the British invaded Mosul, turning a deaf ear to Ottoman remonstrations.[88] In short, the disintegration of the Ottoman Kurds began with real military defeats.

Many Kurdish nationalists consider the Treaty of Sèvres, signed by the Ottomans in August 1920, as the moment in which they were closest to independence and view its fall into abeyance as a historical defeat. Article 24 of the Treaty of Sèvres really envisaged the founding of a Kurdish state in Kurdish regions including Mosul if the Kurds requested it. However, the British suppressed with all their power the Kurds' quest for independence under the leadership of Sheikh Mahmud Barzanji in Iraq, which would remain under British mandate after 1921. In view of this, it was not certain that the great powers would have allowed the Treaty of Sèvres to be implemented as requested by the Kurds.

According to Robert Olson, during World War I the British supported Kurdistan as a buffer state that would separate Turks from their ethnic and religious relatives in Azerbaijan and Central Asia, with a view to contain pan-Turkism and pan-Islamism. What's more, a Kurdish state might be beneficial in balancing Armenia under Soviet influence and to isolate it from the Middle East. However, the conditions changed once Iraq fell under British mandate. What was important from this point onward was to be able to govern Iraq and manage, that is, exploit its oil fields, and to do so, they had to take the Shi'a Arabs under their control. The British did not trust the Shiites after the uprisings in Basra. The Sunni Arabs, whom King Faisal (supported by the British in Iraq) depended on, were the minority, whereas with the Sunni Kurds, they formed a population that equaled the Shi'a. Therefore, opposing Kurdish independence and keeping Sunni Kurds as part of Iraq became a part of British policy, even though when required they did not refrain from supporting Kurdish nationalists in order to weaken Arab nationalism.[89]

In turn, according to McDowall, implementing the Treaty of Sèvres would most likely have sparked off new conflicts between the Kurds and the Armenians, the Nestorians and the Assyrians, and among Kurdish tribes. In this period, while some Kurdish notables defended cooperation with the Russians and the British, and advocated Kurdish independence, in general, Kurds supported the National Campaign. Various factors contributed to this outcome: the fear of an Armenian state that encompassed the Kurdish provinces; the massacres committed by Armenian gangs in areas taken over by Russians; the British supporting the Nestorians and waging war on Shaikh Mahmud Barzanji—whom they had previously encouraged; and, the effective exploitation of all of these by leaders of the National Campaign, first and foremost by Kazım Karabekir and Mustafa Kemal.[90]

Furthermore, there was a conflict between the national ambitions of Kurdish nationalist intellectuals and the interests of the landlords who were representatives of the traditional order and who wanted to preserve their influence, and this conflict led to the fragmentation of Kurdish nationalism.[91] Mustafa Kemal and Turkish nationalists took advantage of this and pulled Kurdish notables into the National Campaign. There was no semifeudal and powerful landlord class in Turkish-majority regions as there was in Kurdish-majority regions.

With the Treaty of Ankara, signed between France and the Grand National Assembly of Turkey on October 20, 1921, France recognized the new state of Turkey. Even though a decision on the final borders was postponed, Turkey's present-day border with Syria (which would later be recognized in Lausanne and which excluded Hatay) was de facto recognized. Present-day northern Syria—inhabited by a significant Kurdish population—was thus excluded. However, the Treaty of Ankara left places such as Antep and Maraş to Turkey, even though the Sykes-Picot Agreement had previously handed them over to France. Again, the main motivations of the Turkish side were military and political rather than ethnic or ideological. The question of the frontier with the French in the south was resolved and this made it easier for the National Campaign to concentrate its efforts in the west.

According to one viewpoint, "Even though Turkey's new Kemalist regime consciously and deliberately expressed otherwise, it was predisposed to abandoning Mosul." The fact that the regime "*wanted* [the emphasis is mine] defeat in the fight for Mosul" also played a role in this outcome.[92] Even if this claim were partially or completely true, it could be consistent with a different causal explanation. The reasons for this predisposition might have been military/strategic rather than directly related to the Kurdish Question. Thus, it may have been prompted by fears of the consequences of a new war, and a preference for peace with Britain, and the desire to start building a new regime as soon as possible.[93]

In the period from 1918 to 1923, it was possible to imagine a wide range of different borders and nation models. Cengiz Çandar asserts that in 1920 Atatürk considered the founding of a confederation among postwar Turkey, Iraq, and Syria within the realm of possibilities. Moreover, during the National Campaign, *Kuva-yi Milliye* (National Forces) officers "caused great distress to the British with their efforts to bring the province of Mosul under Turkish control."[94]

Kurdish members of parliament predictably resisted most strongly the possibility of excluding Mosul. However, records of the secret sessions reveal that neither did other MPs view the issue of Mosul as being any different from Karaağaç, Western Thrace, and the Aegean islands, where ethnic Turks resided. These reactions were consistent with the imaginations of homeland that motivated the National Campaign. A letter the nationalists distributed to the Istanbul press in 1919, for example, stressed the great danger that arose with "the occupation of our most important provinces such as Istanbul, *Mosul* [emphasis mine], Adana and İzmir, each of which has [equal] importance as they are all essential to our existence."[95] Thus, the members of the parliament saw these western and southeastern provinces including Mosul as equally falling within the borders of the National Pact and reacted vehemently to the possibility of their separation. The same records reflect that members of parliament from Kurdish as well as non-Kurdish regions were deeply concerned about the signing of the Lausanne Treaty without a decision on Mosul. They were anxious about the emergence of a Turkish-Kurdish Question should Mosul be lost, but they also assessed the financial and military considerations.[96]

During the Lausanne talks, the Turkish side insisted vehemently for the province of Mosul to be included within Turkey, arguing that "it had been under Turkish sovereignty for a thousand years," ethnic Kurds and Turks formed the vast majority in the region, and Anatolian and Iraqi Turks (Turkmens) shared the same dialect. Turkish and British representatives did not agree on the percentages of the ethnic Kurdish and Turkish populations in Mosul but agreed that the sum of these two Muslim populations constituted the great majority compared to other groups.[97]

In comparison to objectives such as the abolition of capitulations—legal and economic privileges the Ottoman state granted to select European powers and foreign citizens[98]—unity of law—supremacy of Turkish law in Turkish territory—and peace with Britain, the Mosul question might not have been a top priority for the Turkish side in Lausanne; nevertheless, they insisted until the end. The chief negotiator of the Turkish side, İnönü was deeply concerned about "the division of Kurdistan."[99] When the deliberations in Lausanne came to a deadlock because of the Mosul question, as a diplomatic tactic, Lord Curzon offered the Turkish camp the mountainous regions without oil fields. İnönü was later blamed for following an all-or-nothing strategy, his allegedly poor diplomacy, not having made a counterproposal, and for not having attempted to harm the British-French alliance by bringing up the issue of the Syrian border. Regardless of how valid these criticisms are, and how clever the Turkish delegation's tactics were, the records show that the Turkish camp put up a real fight for the whole of Mosul with the claim that "Turks and Kurds are one." But when they were unsuccessful, they did not take the risk of starting another war and, to a great extent, gave up on Mosul despite the opposing voices of the MPs in the assembly.[100]

In his memoirs, İsmet Pasha discusses the "loss" of Mosul despite a "great struggle" by the Turkish side during the Lausanne talks and afterward, and attributes this outcome to the realities on the ground, the risks of forsaking peace, the government's preoccupation with domestic political struggles, and the pro-British biases of the League of Nations.[101] In his own memoirs, Kâzım Karabekir, arguably an "evolutionary-secularist" critic of İsmet and Mustafa Kemal, also writes that he was fiercely critical of İsmet for leaving the Mosul question undecided in Lausanne and that Mosul should have remained part of Turkey, but he was equally opposed to and actively campaigned against any military campaign to regain it.[102] While it is clear that the Kurdish Question was one of the most important factors that determined the Turkish camp's strategies on Mosul and other matters in Lausanne, the military and economic "balance of power" carried more weight.[103]

Following the failure to resolve the Mosul question in Lausanne, İnönü delivered a speech at the Istanbul Conference on May 19, 1924, as the representative of the Turkish committee:

> In the face of the sacrifices endured by the Turkish and Kurdish brothers of the Turkish nation in their fight for independence, [the allies] have recognized the Turkish nation's [right to live] within its own ethnographic borders. The Mosul question is vital to Turkey. The people of this province populated by a great Turkish and Kurdish majority do not under any circumstances regard themselves under the governance of Baghdad. As long as Mosul is under foreign governance, the Turkish people will always feel threatened by the south of its territory and in order to counter both this threat and other political provocations that may extend from Mosul, Sulaymaniyah and Kirkuk to the north, the Republic of Turkey will assign a part of the resources needed for the development of the homeland to defense cautions.[104]

However, Lord Curzon, who was representing the British camp, succeeded in putting across his own theses during the Lausanne Peace Conference. No agreement could be reached on the Mosul question and the task of making a decision was handed over to the League of Nations. Established in 1924, a commission formed by the League of Nations proposed that Mosul be controlled by Iraq, a British mandate. Turkey accepted this with the signing of an agreement in 1926. It was during the period from January to July 1925 that the commission undertook work on Mosul. Shortly before that, in the fall of 1924, the power struggle between moderate (evolutionary) and hardline (revolutionary) secularists had escalated and the government was faced with a rebellion by Nestorians in the Southeast and British pressures to give up Mosul.[105] Then, the Shaikh Said Rebellion erupted in February.

These facts do not support the standard story that the Kemalist regime sacrificed Mosul in order—that is, with the intention—to divide the Kurds. A more plausible explanation is based on economic and military/strategic considerations, namely, the military difficulties of invading and defending Mosul by taking the risk of war with Britain—even today, the Kurdish government in Iraq which controls the area in question is facing major military challenges in defending its southern border—and the inter-elite political struggle for supremacy within the new republican regime, which took precedence over the question of Mosul and the Kurds in the eyes of the ruling elites.

After 1926, the Kurds who remained in Turkey could overcome the external security dilemma by credibly rejecting pan-Kurdish nationalism. However, it would have been difficult to achieve this even if the Kurdish actors had wanted to, given the problems of credible commitment and time-consistency.[106] Who among the Kurdish elites could speak and make promises for the rest of Kurdish elites? Could they make any commitment on behalf of future generations? Although Kurdish nationalism did not enjoy much support among the masses, it mobilized many Kurdish elites. In 1924, around two years after the Koçgiri rebellion during the War of Independence, former Ottoman Kurdish military officers started a small-scale local rebellion in Beytüşşebap. Moreover, Kurdish nationalists had good reasons to believe that the only way to come to an agreement with the state was a violent rebellion like the one they started in 1925; this was the traditional path Kurdish elites had taken to compromise with the Ottoman State.[107] Alternatively, they might have hoped to force the state to give autonomy to the Kurds by threatening to separate.

One may also link the Kurds' problem of credible commitment (to nonseparatism) with a problem of representation. As we will see below, from the 2nd Parliament established in 1923 onward—for reasons indirectly related to the Kurdish Question—the institutions of the Republic (notably the Grand National Assembly) became less representative, participatory, and democratic.[108] Therefore, through which representatives, on which platforms, and through which opposition mechanisms could the Kurds credibly commit to nonseparatism?

## DIVIDED NATION-BUILDING ELITES

In Meeker's words, the challenge for Turkish nationalists was "the difficult task of transforming a citizenry (and I would add subjects, i.e., not necessarily having a consciousness of being citizens) of Ottoman Muslims into a citizenry of Republican Turks."[109] Pursuing this goal based on a state-nation model whereby the Kurdish component would be recognized as a social group with legal rights would have required inventiveness as well as a broad-based consensus, trust, and agreement among the diverse group of elites who established the republic.

Let me define, as I discussed in the Introduction chapter, the "nation-building"—or founding—elites in the context of Turkey as being all elites who led or actively supported the National Campaign in Anatolia, including those in occupied Istanbul and even abroad. This is an "unconventional" definition. Conventional writing on modern Turkey's establishment identifies the founding elites as being the "secular," "Kemalist" elites, and among those, especially Mustafa Kemal and the small circle of military, bureaucratic, and literary elites who were his close companions. This definition more or less limits the founding elites to the revolutionary secularist elites as I define in this book. An unconventional definition, however, is crucial for developing a nonstandard explanation, as I already discussed. The question of who would compose the ruling elites and how broad-based the ruling regime would be was not a predetermined and inevitable one at the beginning of the formative period. The reasons that explain why some elites who had contributed to the National Campaign but had become disempowered and thus "invisible"—at least within the power bloc of the regime and mainstream historiography—by the end of the regime consolidation process should be part of explaining the nature of the nation-state that came to existence, and the consequences for the Turkish-Kurdish question.

Within this broad group of nation-building elites, a wide diversity prevailed in terms of ethnicity, sect, and professional groups (e.g., soldiers, bureaucrats, *ulema*, small merchants and shopkeepers, and intellectuals such as writers, journalists, and academics), and a broad range of differing views, such as secular nationalism and modernism—within it, members and former members of the Union and Progress Party and socialists included—religious conservatism and modernist Islamism, which partially overlapped. The military/bureaucratic senior officials who led the war and the members of the First Parliament (1920–23) were more or less representative of this diverse group.

Thus, the elites who were marginalized between the First and the Second Parliaments of Turkey, and later during the period from 1925 to 1927, were sidelined and excluded from ruling elites as a result of the political developments that are part of my causal explanation of the outcomes at the end of the formative period. Without their exclusion, outcomes might have been different. If anything, without them the National Campaign could probably not have been won and the Republic could not have been founded.

Four subgroups can be identified within the nation-building elites. One of them is comprised of the Muslim conservatives who joined the Turkish War of Independence in order to save the Ottoman Sultan and Shaykh al-Islam. They most likely would have supported neither the subsequent abolition of the Sultanate nor the Caliphate (nor most of the secular reformations). A second group, to whom we could refer as Islamist—or Islamic—modernists, consisted of elites who were not necessarily against the republic (i.e., the abolition of the Sultanate) but would have supported a republic with a stronger Islamic foundation or constitutional monarchy that preserved the Caliphate, and modernizing reforms inspired by Islamist rather than secularist blueprints.

A recent contribution even asserts that one could refer to a Turkish Ottoman "republicanism" and that it had an Islamic variety, in addition to its "radical and liberal" versions, which were more secular and inspired by Western examples and tradition:

> [It] took its inspiration from the Islamic state in the period of the four caliphates and medieval Islamic thought [and] the Ottoman political thought of the Classical Age . . . .In the republican debates of the 1920s, a group of *ulema* and political conservatives believed that the most suitable type of regime for

the new Turkey was an Islamic Republic, because the indigenous Islamic state exhibited elements of direct democracy and
republic, and monarchy was a deviation from it.[110]

One might question whether these were well-established schools of
thought, notwithstanding their richness and complexity. I think it would
be more appropriate to describe them as "perspectives"[111] that also justified—and were justified by—key practical issue positions vis-à-vis the
major sociopolitical questions of the age, such as the status of the Sultanate,
Parliament, and Caliphate, and, almost always, gender relations and social
rules and hierarchies.[112]

Hence, Islamic modernists might have endorsed a republican form of
government, even the eradication of Sultanate. Like conservatives, however,
they too would have opposed most of the postwar secularist reformations,
especially in the areas of education, culture, the official narrative about the
Ottoman ancient regime, and, probably, the repression of the Sufi orders.
Instead, they would have upheld a modernization founded upon Islamic
principles, historical memory, and narratives.

In turn, those elites who wanted to modernize the country based
on ideas of secularism and nationalism, "secular nationalists" for lack of
a better term (often referred to as Kemalists, a term initially concocted
by sympathetic Western observers)[113] were divided among themselves
between evolutionists and revolutionists. They had different views on the
means and form of secular modernization: *evolutionary secularists* did
not oppose the essence of the republic, that is, a political order founded
upon the ideal of a sovereign body of citizens rather than some form
of monarchy, but disagreed with the revolutionists with respect to how
this would be formed and administered. Hence, they could for example
have preferred the preservation of the Caliphate as a symbolic authority
once it was separated from the Ottoman dynasty and stripped of any real
political power, and a more inclusive and influential legislature. Similarly,
they disagreed with the pace and the authoritarian implementation of the
subsequent cultural and political reforms, albeit not necessarily with their
essence.[114] Gradualist and society-centered critics of revolutionary reforms
have long argued, for example, that while top-down reforms secured
unprecedented civic and political rights and freedoms for women, they also
rendered women reliant on the state and had a dampening impact on the
bottom-up dynamism of women's movements that had been developing
in the early twentieth century.[115] By comparison, *revolutionary secularists*

proposed a faster-paced, authoritarian/revolutionary process of secular modernization and the foundation of a republic.

These groups were not homogeneous within themselves, and individuals could move across different groups within their lifetime. My goal here is to establish an analytical distinction. Naturally, there was mistrust between the holders of these views; but this grew over time, and from the point of view of the subsequent political developments, the crucial questions regarded which view would dominate the nation building, and the very *political* question of to what extent the distrust and conflicting visions could be reconciled based on consensus, power sharing, and cooperation, as opposed to conflict, power concentration, and coercion. In other words, it is possible to envision more or less exclusive and hegemonic and more or less inclusive and participatory paths than the ones that ended up being followed

These elite divisions were not necessarily unique to Turkey and affected Muslim and non-Muslim societies alike, albeit at a different pace and under different, imperial, colonial, and semicolonial power configurations.[116] Certainly, those in Turkey can be considered particular manifestations of the divisions present in the Muslim world.[117] The particular revolutionary secular-nationalist manifestation that emerged and later became hegemonic in the context of Turkey had its counterparts throughout the post-Ottoman world of nation-states, and for many nation-states, it became a model and inspiration.[118] Hence, such elite divisions emerged almost everywhere in the world, but were more divisive, intractable, and conflict-prone in some places, or, to put it obversely, were managed relatively more cooperatively, based on more compromise and reconciliation, in other places. Hence, the reasons why one of the more deep-cutting and distrustful divisions in the world emerged in Turkey can be neither found in the inherent and general properties of these cleavages nor in the logical impossibility of coexistence of the defenders of these views. Instead, the reasons should be sought in the political developments that established particular power hierarchies, as I will explore ahead.

These four elite groupings did not disagree on all fronts. For example, Islamist modernizers could be nationalist like their pro-secular counterparts and they could also, for instance, be inspired by the Muslims in India seeking a nation-state and independence. However, their comprehension of the nation and the state would involve a far greater emphasis on Islamic symbols and concepts.[119] The quest for an umbilical cord holding the nation, the past, and the future together in the face of the constant changes brought about by modernization prevailed among Islamist as well as pro-secular modernizers. While the latter tended to look for the umbilical cord in ethnic, cultural, and geographical identities and belongings, Islamists sought it in Islamic identities, texts, and reinvented and reinterpreted notions of an Islamic golden age. In turn, many secularist modernizers did not disregard religion altogether, but asserted that they upheld a "pure," anti-clerical, and authentic Islam, one that prevailed in a golden age and had not yet been spoilt by corrupt rulers, and one that they would imagine and interpret much more rationalistically and instrumentally in the service of fast-track modernization.[120]

Religious homogenization was a pursuit for both pro-secular and Islamist modernizers, a feature they shared with other nationalists that tended to emerge in post-Ottoman nation-states.[121] Hence, for pro-secular modernizers too, " 'Turk' came to mean 'Muslim' as well (and) secularization—as an expansion of state control over religion, rather than the simple removal of religion from public life—had an official project starting with the Ottoman Tanzimat reforms of 1839 . . . subsequent Turkish secularization can best be seen as an ongoing struggle over the nature and development of an 'official Islam,' characterized by the public use of religion to promote national cohesion and capitalist development."[122] The differences between these elites could also be mapped onto different strategies of institutional change, rather than being rooted in rifts over resisting versus supporting institutional change and innovation.[123] Late Ottoman reforms, of which many Islamist modernizers were supporters as well as "agents," were based on "institutional layering." For example, new and secularized institutions, such as secular schools or "Nizamiye courts" enforcing laws modeled on European codes, were built parallel to "old ones," such as Koran schools and Sharia courts.[124] By comparison, Kemalist republican secularization, which was a product of revolutionary secularism, built on Ottoman reforms, too, but was mainly based on "institutional replacement and innovation."[125]

Positivist and materialist ideas were only partially influential on secular modernist elites.[126] There were many scholars, journalists, and intellectuals among them, but the vast majority of the elites in question were pragmatic political/military elites rather than intellectuals or ideologues. Atatürk, for example was a rationalist man of action and a brilliant strategist first and foremost, regardless of his intellectual interests and his ideological and intellectual resources.[127] Despite their philosophical distinctions, the elites of this period attempted to develop new political and social strategies with the intent of saving the state and elements of Islam under rapidly changing conditions. For example, recent studies show that the Ottoman *ulema* were not homogeneous and, rather than being completely against change, many of them considered themselves both as the "actors and the agents of change as well as the guardians of traditions," and strived to synthesize these two roles.[128] However, there wasn't sufficient time and groundwork to develop consistent doctrines. For many elites who lacked the opportunity and intellectual capital to develop coherent doctrines, ideological and philosophical distinctions had instrumental characteristics. Furthermore, differences regarding means might have been more decisive than those concerning goals and ideals.

The title of Ziya Gökalp's classic text openly summarizes the aspirations of the elites of the time and the alternatives about which they partially differed: Turkism, Islamism, and Modernism. Various elites were divided according to how compatible they thought these three were and on which one they placed more emphasis. Secularist modernizers gravitated more toward Turkism and modernism and Islamist modernists toward Islamism and modernism. However, the majority of them did not wholly disregard any one of these three values. As in the case of Ziya Gökalp, most of them endeavored to pursue all three.[129]

Hence, Carter Findley uses the adjective *comparative* when defining the significant fractures modernization brought about among Turkey's elites. He states that two alternative approaches emerged among the elites as they aspired to synthesize these three values (religion, ethnicity/language, and modernism): "A comparatively radical, secularizing current, and a more conservative, Islamically committed current."[130] Both currents constituted a wide range within themselves. For example, Ahmet Mithat, Fatma Aliye, Hâlid el-Bağdâdî, and Said Nursî, individuals with widely different backgrounds and ambitions, were all involved in the Islamist modernist movement.

Evolutionary secularists blamed the revolutionary secularist elites for the collapse of consensus. Historian Mete Tunçay states that Adnan Adıvar—Turkish politician, writer, and historian who supported the Ankara government and Mustafa Kemal during the National Campaign but then turned critical—attributed the lack of philosophical interaction between secularists and Islamists solely to Kemalists' obdurate stance and that Adıvar thought Islamists were inclined to reach a consensus. Tunçay himself states that he is doubtful of this judgment and concludes that neither party was particularly intent on a philosophical conciliation.[131]

This question is important because even though political cooperation does not necessarily require philosophical reconciliation, widely different and incompatible worldviews can undermine trust, moderation, and cooperation—a problem that has endured in Turkey to this day.[132]

Mustafa Kemal's testimony below reflects the revolutionary secularist viewpoint:

> In the First Parliament, we made countless sacrifices regarding our views and perhaps it was necessary. As a result of this, wholly unnecessary mentalities influenced articles of the Turkish Constitution of 1921. And perhaps because of this we are having difficulty abolishing the judicial capitulations[133] (in the Lausanne Treaty). The chaps [the Allied powers in the negotiations, *herifler*] say that the laws we will pass will be based on Islamic jurisprudence, etc.[134] If Turkey has any credit in the Lausanne Peace Conference and in the world today it is because of the abolition, annihilation of the old way. Had our reformation been like the reforms of the Constitutional Monarchy Eras and those before them, no one would attribute any importance to it. It is possible to say, "Let us satisfy the Muslim scholars, the Islamic world and everyone else"; they will all be satisfied but we will become distanced from our purpose. Those who work with half-way measures basis cannot make a revolution (or reformation).[135]

Hence, Atatürk thought that the late Ottoman modernization tried to build the new side-by-side with the old and that this was deficient and ineffective. He was of the opinion that this was not convincing to Western powers, and, presumably, Western public opinion, from whom they sought recognition as an equal and "modern" state. For example, he felt that attempting to modernize Sharia law was a futile endeavor. A modernization that might ensure equality with the West could only materialize with radical and transformative reforms that replaced old concepts and institutions with new ones, such as a new and secular civil code. Hence, revolutionary secularists were skeptical about conciliation and collaboration with the Islamic elites because the latter supported reforms that preserved existing institutions such as the Caliphate and *Mecelle*, the Sharia-based Ottoman code of civil law,[136] which itself was a major product of Ottoman modernization efforts.

Again, none of this amounted to disclaiming or disdaining Islam:

Republican secularism has never officially and publicly opposed the essence of religion but rather confined itself to attacking superstition that is allegedly against Islam and misuse of religion. For example, in the Republic of Turkey freedom to propagandize against religion was not permitted as it was in socialist countries.[137]

Power struggles and disputes over the means and pace of reforms also shaped national identity models to be upheld. For example, the following excerpt itemizes a scholar's historical analysis of the reasons why Anatolianism (an example of the evolutionary secularist view) did not become popular, even though "in essence it overlapped with Mustafa Kemal's goals." The reasons do not regard the inherent weakness—whether for historical or sociological reasons—of Anatolianism as an identity or nation-building model but political events, personalities, material conditions, and power relations such as organizational dynamics, that is to say, politics:

[Even though Anatolianism was previously defended within Turkish Hearths, it later lost the support of] *the influential individuals* [emphasis mine] of the period and consequently failed to shape public opinion . . . [and events] such as the Shaikh Said Rebellion [which led to a crackdown on the opposition as a whole][138] . . . .Anatolianists aspired for a gradual transformation [which clashed with] the "radical" nature of Mustafa Kemal's reforms . . . .The greater potential [power] of Turkish Hearths which were organized into 43 branches across Anatolia in May 1923 [in an attempt] to sway public opinion . . . .Anatolianists distanced themselves from Mustafa Kemal and his circles [because of their opposition to a "one man" mentality].[139]

Hence, the most significant intra-elite disagreements were over leadership and the distribution of power.[140] Accordingly, Özoğlu argues that the fundamental dynamic determining the major decisions that shaped the face of "New Turkey" "was not a result of a predetermined vision but a pragmatic synthesis of political realities and opportunities to silence the opposition."[141]

## POLITICAL DYNAMICS AND THE AUTOCRATIZATION OF THE REGIME

Before the proclamation of the Republic, a new parliament (Second Parliament) was elected under the "guidance" and shadow of Atatürk's charismatic authority. There were no MPs elected into the new parliament from the Second Group, the opposition in the First Parliament. While the Second Parliament still had a diverse composition in terms of ethnicity and region, during the transition from the First National Parliament, which led the War of Independence, to the Second Parliament, the vast majority of the Islamist elites (a main ideational current within the nation in the making) were excluded from the main lawmaking body.

Hence, the main opposition and the source of pluralism that remained with respect to the fundamental characteristics of the nation-state in formation were the aforementioned divisions among the secularist modernizing elites. In 1924, some elites within the People's Party (later to be renamed the Republican People's Party) who were evolutionists, as well as evolutionists from outside the party, founded a new party, the Progressive Republican Party. The latter included National Campaign leaders such as Kazım Karabekir, Rauf Orbay, and Ali Fuat Cebesoy and proposed pro-secular modernizing reforms that were "for the people and with their consent"—as opposed to the revolutionist motto "for the people despite the people."[142] This gradualist and consensus-seeking attitude rendered them more tolerant of autonomous religion and ethnic expressions, even though they shared the revolutionary secularists' zeal for modernization and nationhood. Hence, they were equally opposed to "religious reactionaries and retrogression" as they were to Kurdish separatism. But they supported a softer transition and cooperation with local elites.

When the Shaikh Said Rebellion broke out, Prime Minister Fethi Okyar's government maintained that rather than overstating the rebellion, it should be quelled with moderate measures. However, Mustafa Kemal and İsmet İnönü did not share this view, contending that the rebellion should be seen as a great threat that could imperil the new regime. This sharp division was concluded with Okyar's resignation, the accession of an İnönü-led government, the bloody suppression of the rebellion, and the marginalization of the evolutionists by the Independence Tribunals established with the consequent Law on the Maintenance of Order.

While the Shaikh Said Rebellion did indeed seriously threaten the new republic, it is highly debatable whether it aspired for a separate Kurdish state and had the power to endanger the survival of the new regime. The rebellion had both Islamist and pro-Kurdish dimensions, thus targeting both the secularist and nationalist ambitions of the new regime.[143] Hence, it was destined to trigger a serious reaction from the regime, which would also be divisive by invoking opposition criticism; nevertheless, there were different potential means and scales of reactions with which the government could respond to the insurgency.

The violent suppression of the rebellion had a great psychological and political impact on the Kurds. Up until the late 1930s, there were nineteen more Kurdish rebellions, and they too were suppressed very harshly.[144] The fact that there was never more than one rebellion in a particular place and by the same tribe (*aşiret*) suggests how heavy-handed the military operations to suppress the insurgencies were and how much "fear and exhaustion" they caused among the specific Kurds targeted.[145] Moreover, this heavy-handed approach produced and strengthened the rival image of Turkish and Kurdish identities. It can be expected that as a result, while some Kurds became more open to assimilation, (Kurdish) nationalism and rejection of the Turkish identity were reinforced among others.

Two implications are important here in terms of our analytical narrative. First, during this period, a problematic relationship of distrust was established between a vast majority of the Kurds and the state; these images "developed" and were "made" by political, social, and military developments rather than being inevitable products of history and culture. Second, not singular but various modes of identity, nationalism, and state-society relationship emerged among the Kurds. Therefore, the Kurdish modes of politics that developed decades later (including the PKK) should also be interpreted as a reflection of the struggles between Kurdish movements that can be partly traced back to different responses among Kurds to state repression.[146]

Still, the most important consequences of the Shaik Said rebellion were on the intra-elite struggles among the (Turkish) ruling elites and on the emerging regime of the new Turkey. The rebellion started on February 13, 1925, a few months before it was planned to start. "Gazi Pasha (Mustafa Kemal) decided that they could only suppress this rebellion with the collaboration of İsmet Pasha." In a meeting lasting twelve hours on March 2 at the headquarters of the Republican People's Party with the attendance of the Gazi, the motion "for the government to portray a determined and astute stance" was passed by ninety-two votes to sixty. This can be interpreted as a sign that evolutionist elites were present in the Republican People's Party. Despite proclaiming martial law in the eastern provinces on February 25, Fethi Okyar's government was forced to resign, as it was accused of "not being energetic enough."[147] Soon after, İsmet İnönü's government was established, and two days later, Fethi Bey was appointed as Turkish ambassador in Paris.

It was not only Okyar's government that was sidelined after the rebellion. In the period after the rebellion, Independence Tribunals were established with the Law on the Maintenance of Order, ostensibly to establish state authority and punish insurgents. With the expansion of the investigation into an assassination attempt against Mustafa Kemal in Izmir, however, all opposition was cracked down upon. The opposition Progressive Republican Party (PRP) was shut down, members of the party stood trial and the evolutionist elites who had previously supported the party were completely marginalized and intimidated. However, just like Fethi Okyar, who wanted to suppress the rebellion but to do so with a measured response, opposition leaders such as Kazım Karabekir, Rauf Orbay, and Ali Fuat Cebesoy, who had co-founded the PRP shortly before, had also not made light of the rebellion. They had only warned against extraordinary measures that would also hurt pluralism and freedom of expression.[148] Critical newspapers were shut down. According to Zürcher, the democracy that was "supported by the relatively free press of the period to a great extent" and which "had been in formation" (since 1923–24) "met an abrupt end in early 1925."[149]

With an amendment made to the Law of Treason right after the rebellion began, an article was added that deemed it treasonous to use religion for political ends. This article loaded the dice in the elections against the Progressive Republican Party—which argued for a reconciliatory relationship with religious elites, *ulema*, and those with religious sensibilities. As a result, of the twenty-nine MPs who joined the PRP, none were reelected into the assembly in the following term, and six of them were executed for the assassination attempt in Izmir.

Against this backdrop, the reasons for *the way* that the Shaikh Said Rebellion was suppressed seem to lie mostly in the power struggle among the ruling elites themselves. This does not mean that the revolutionists did not sincerely view the rebellion as a major threat (or, for that matter, a British provocation, as they argued). What is beyond doubt is that they used the rebellion to sideline the evolutionists. A byproduct of this was the disappearance of an opposition which would have supported relatively moderate and accommodative policies toward the Kurds. Thus, for political reasons, the odds against the implementation of such policies, which were objectively and logically possible, increased dramatically.

In a speech delivered at the Grand National Assembly in 1927 to declare the decommissioning of the Independence Tribunals, İsmet Pasha stated as follows:

> The most important of the developments we were faced with two years ago was not the uprising that became clear with the Shaikh Said Rebellion. The real danger was the ambiguity and confusion that accrued in the public life of the country. . . . The chaos in question was created by degenerate intellectuals who were accustomed to pursuing their small ambitions.[150]

This statement indicates three things. First, the emerging regime treated the Shaikh Said Rebellion as part of a wider problem not directly related to the Kurds. Second, the sole or most important reason behind the harsh state response to the rebellion was not that it was an insurrection that could lead to the division of the country or to the toppling of the new regime. The more important reason was that some ruling elites saw it as a sign of disunity and a lack of direction among the elites that might hinder the reforms they wanted to put in place. Third, the mistrust among the elites became manifest, and this mistrust is personalized. Rather than critiquing them for their views, İnönü accused the evolutionists of acting based on personal ambitions.

The Law on the Maintenance of Order had granted extraordinary authorities to the government for a period of two years "to fight against reactionism (*irtica*) and uprisings" and "to protect the social order, security and public peace." The government was able to ban "all institutions, provocations, acts and publications" without consulting the parliament and with the approval of the president. In response, the opposition put forward the following views:

> What could be more vaguely defined than "the social order of the country"? . . . All governments based on arbitrary regimes around the world have inserted all their wrongdoings through this gate . . . .We are all united in the hope that the uprising is suppressed quickly and mercilessly . . . .We are in support of

legal precautions . . . but we are not for acts that will undermine the natural rights of the nation. The brotherhood of Turks and Kurds is alive within the borders of the Republic of Turkey. In accordance with our Constitution, all who live within the borders of Turkey are Turkish . . . There is something happening in a part of Turkey that is Turkish. The Turkish nation cannot be doubted . . . .Sovereignty is its right . . . .The natural rights of the nation should not be violated while this fire is being put out.[151]

## Missed Opportunities between 1938 and 1984

The period between 1937–38—when the last major pre-PKK rebellion took place—and the 1960s was a misleadingly silent one for Kurdish nationalism. The British diplomat Anthony Parsons observed that during his three weeks traveling through the Kurdish provinces in 1956, he did not encounter the slightest trace of Kurdish nationalism in Turkey, in stark contrast with the situation in Iraq.[152] In Bozarslan's words:

During these decades, openly outspoken Kurdish nationalism became a rare phenomenon. Some leaders of the resistance of the 1920s and 1930s, such as Nurî Dersimî, Ihsan Nurî and the Cemilpaşazada brothers, who were dispersed in different Middle Eastern countries, became aware of the impossibility of realising their dreams during their own lifetimes. They had no other choice than to accept their own efforts as simply moments in a long struggle that would be continued after their deaths. They thus turned to writing, either memoirs or history and geography books, largely inspired by the Turkish nationalist models. The written legacy of this period of silence played a decisive role in the codification of Kurdish nationalism (with such accoutrements as a map; a unified historical narration; a flag; an idea of martyrdom and glorification of martyrs; the myth of Kawa, liberator of the Kurds; the notion of Mesopotamia as the cradle of the Kurdishness; and so forth). The period also contributed to the formation of a collective memory and to the integration of the years of revolts during the Kemalist regime into the history of the Kurdish nationalism.[153]

The lack of political activity and violence in this period also concealed social changes and dynamics with long-term political consequences. During these decades, a new Kurdish intelligentsia with rural roots gained upward social mobility through the education they received in cities such as Diyarbakır, Ankara, and Istanbul. This group replaced the traditional Kurdish elites, which had consisted mainly of large landowners and religious figures.[154] When this new class left their birthplaces, changed their socioeconomic environments, and became more aware of their ethnic/cultural differences, they gained and searched for a new consciousness of identity and origin. Like their Turkish counterparts (and often comrades), they too became acquainted with leftist and secularist ideas and movements, as well as with right-wing, political Islamist, and culturally conservative ones.

Another important dynamic with long-term implications was the Kurdish nationalism growing in Iraq.[155] The "new Kurds" of Turkey learned about the past Kurdish movements in Turkey as well as the current ones in Iran and Iraq. While Turkish governments were able to control domestic Kurdish politics, they could not restrain events outside of their borders. In 1946, the Kurds founded the Republic of Mahabad in Iran with the support of the Soviet Union. Even though this first experience of Kurdish statehood only lasted a year, it transformed Mustafa Barzani and his tribal units—who had formed the main military force of the Republic—into Kurdish national heroes and inflamed Kurdish national sentiments in Iran and Iraq. In 1958, when the Hashemite monarchy was overthrown, the Kurds became recognized partners of the Arabs in the new Iraqi constitution and acquired significant cultural rights. However, as I emphasize in this book, beyond cultural recognition, a yearning for self-determination and some form of self-rule constitutes the basis of Kurdish nationalism. When Barzani's demands for autonomy were denied, he launched another uprising in Iraq within three years. All of this had political and psychological repercussions in Turkey.

Had Turkey provided a liberal-democratic environment in which the new Kurds could freely express their Kurdish identity and conduct politics, perhaps the Kurdish Conflict—as defined earlier—might have been contained and over time resolved. Militant Kurdish politics would still have developed, but might have remained marginal. In other words, the violence and identity conflict of later years could have been minimized and politics could have concentrated on economic and administrative questions. These new Kurds also nurtured a strong *Türkiyelilik* (Of-Turkey) identity alongside their Kurdish identity. Many of them either spoke Turkish better than Kurdish or did not speak any Kurdish at all. As products of republican modernization, they fought for the Kurdish cause as "Kurds of Turkey."

Hence, 1950–1970 (from the transition to the multiparty period) represented a second missed opportunity to prevent the Kurdish Conflict. During the Democrat Party (DP) period, multiparty politics resulted merely in the traditional Kurdish elites being drawn into political patronage and in relative economic development and political liberalization.

However, little if anything was done to resolve the Kurdish Question or to enable the Kurds to engage in peaceful politics "as Kurds," that is, with their distinct identities. An environment of truly liberal and participatory democracy was not provided. Rather, mainly unintended transformations occurred through the indirect impacts of competitive and clientelistic party politics. To cite a striking account:

> [The success of the Democratic Party also affected the Republican People's Party.] In contrast to previous terms, MPs were now mostly [chosen from among] the local Kurdish power holders. From the perspective of the Kurdish power holders, the situation was as follows: People who were [persecuted] until five or ten years earlier for being [or being deemed as being] shaikhs, *pir, dede, sayyid* [local Alevi and Sunni Muslim religious leaders], feudal lords, *mütegallibe* [local power holders], tribal chieftains were now being honored for the same qualities, and becoming [and being made] more functional within the system. They specifically called Melik Fırat [Shaikh Said's grandson] and made him an MP. All of the prominent shaikh families from Said Nursî to the Naqshbandi shaikhs and *tariqat* [religious order] leaders were incorporated into the system. A similar process also took place for chieftains, prominent merchants and landlords.[156]

Yet, none of these people or any other Kurds were allowed to express their Kurdishness in public, for example, by publishing or broadcasting in Kurdish, or establishing associations or parties "for Kurds." The process of integrating Kurdish provincial elites into political party patronage networks reproduced and sometimes reinforced these elites' social and political influence. This was not unique to Kurdish areas. Hence, prominent families who had acted as intermediaries between the Ottoman state and local people in the provinces (and thus were members of the Ottoman state society) resurged in prominence through multiparty politics, after a setback during the single-party era, in non-Kurdish regions such as the Black Sea region also.[157] The complex relations of competition, difference, cooperation, and collusion between the central bureaucratic and provincial social/political elites have long underlain Turkey's political cleavages, especially the so-called center-periphery politics and culture wars.[158] For Kurds, however, the consequences have been much more deep-cutting because of the peculiarities of the Kurdish Question, the Kurdish areas' highly inegalitarian social structures, and the more enhanced cultural/ linguistic as well as political conflicts Kurds experienced when they were included in the political and economic system.

A military coup in 1960 culminated in the creation of a junta-commissioned, yet liberal, constitution, which, however, also provided a legal basis for military tutelage. The rights and freedoms laid out in the 1961 Constitution generated a pluralistic environment in which many social/ cultural minority groups, including Kurds, became publicly organized and expressive. In 1965, traditional right-wing Kurdish nationalists founded the underground Kurdistan Democratic Party of Turkey (TKDP), inspired by the Barzani movement in Iraq. Simultaneously, they tried to express themselves within the New Turkey Party (YTP), which proclaimed itself to be the successor of the DP. In 1962, the YTP joined a coalition government with the CHP (Republican People's Party). This demonstrated that they were "willing to cooperate in a project of national integration wherein being ethnically Kurdish was not seen as incompatible with being nationally 'Turkish.' "[159] In other words, this demonstrated an effort to generate a compatible image of sorts.

However, a dispute that took place in the coalition government exemplifies how mainstream Turkish actors wasted the opportunity to develop a compatible image and the reactions this dispute created among the Kurds. Many CHP members did not view being Kurdish and Turkish as contradictory as long as the Kurds subdued their Kurdishness in social and political life. The confrontation in question started when the minister of the interior from the CHP accused some members of the YTP of Kurdism. In response, some YTP members demanded that the Kurds be recognized as a nation in the Grand National Assembly. In a somewhat different reaction, the leader of the YTP said that "if there is someone whose Turkishness should be questioned it is [the interior minister]." The crisis ended with many Kurdish MPs resigning from the YTP and the minister being forced to resign from his post.[160]

Similar dynamics were also in play within the socialist movement that was growing at the time.[161] The Workers Party of Turkey (TİP) specifically tried to develop a compatible image from a socialist perspective. Left-wing Kurds initially entered politics through the TİP. Some of them continued to place the ideals of socialism before the ideals of Kurdism. However, another group of them who were discomfited by the postponement of issues relating to the Kurds split after a while and organized the "Eastern rallies" together with the conservative Kurds, and in 1969, established the Revolutionary Eastern Cultural Hearths (DDKO). However, in one way or another, all of these organizations were suppressed and closed down.[162] That is to say, the liberal freedoms brought about by the Constitution of 1961 did not encompass the right to peacefully defend communism, religious law (Sharia), or Kurdish nationalism. A setting in which a compatible relationship could be developed between Kurdishness and Turkishness (or *Türkiyelilik*) was not being created. The regional boarding schools that were opened in 1961 are an example of this. These schools, which might have otherwise promoted integration and Turk-Kurd solidarity, instead developed a Kurdish consciousness in many students who felt the pressure to become Turkicized.[163]

It was during this period that leftist thought became popularized and developed its own approaches to the Kurdish Question within the revolutionary secularist modernization perspective. For example, in line with its socialist ideology, the TİP defined the Eastern Question as an issue related to economic underdevelopment, not national identity. However, it also recognized the presence of a Kurdish "people" (*halk*) and thus of a related problem that could be resolved through autonomy and cultural rights. Simultaneously, the TİP recognized Turkey's integrity "with its country and people"—an expression used to denote a belief in one nation on the territory of Turkey. All of this was in line with the ideas of "National Democratic Revolutionist" intellectuals. Later, however, some leftists who considered this way of thinking inadequate founded organizations such as the Revolutionary Path (*Devrimci Yol*), which defined Turkey as multinational and argued that the Kurds had the right to self-determination. Once again, in the emergence of these divisions, too, personal distrust and power struggles played as great a role as ideological differences. Hence, one wonders whether some social/cultural factor might have been at play here, such as some weakness of social capital that undermined the sustenance of large-scale social/political collective action.

How did these attempts at developing compatible images among revolutionary-secularist modernizers impact the state-endorsed mainstream narratives? They seem to have made the state more defensive, simply because they united communism (or socialism) and Kurdism—two fundamental fears of the state. However, they also influenced the thinking of social democrats. Thus, during the 1980s and until the early 1990s, the Social Democratic People's Party (SHP) contributed to helping to prevent the Kurdish movements from radicalizing, by enabling the Kurds to conduct politics within the SHP with their own expressed identities as Kurds.

However, the Left did not have a comprehensive recipe to address the complex ingredients of the Kurdish Question beyond the question of socioeconomic development and social class, such as questions of nationhood, the sharing of sovereignty, external security, and cultural development. Having been the party that founded the republican state upon the legacy of the Ottoman state, the CHP's approach to the Kurdish Question has been heavily influenced (in addition to social democratic ideas since the 1960s) by the state's developmentalist orientation. Since the 1970s, for example, many state agents hoped that megaprojects such as the Southeastern Anatolia Project (*Güneydoğu Anadolu Project*, GAP)—a series of dams and hydroelectric power plants on the Euphrates and Tigris rivers and extensive irrigation networks, which affect as much as 10 percent of Turkey's land and population—would help depoliticize the Kurdish Question and "remove the ethno-political nature of the Kurdish question and redefine the conflict along the lines of socioeconomic development."[164]

However, the Kurdish Question could not be resolved solely through economic development and social justice.[165] Until the mid-1970s, the CHP had enjoyed a certain popularity among the Kurdish electorate. Bülent Ecevit's "simple and low-key" lifestyle and his slogans, such as "the land belongs to those who cultivate it and water to those who use it," "rights are taken, not given," and "no oppressed, no oppressor, humane and rightful order" struck a chord with the masses. In the 1973 parliamentary elections, "a significant proportion of the Kurds" voted for the CHP.[166] Yet, in 1975, Ecevit replied to those chanting, "Freedom to the peoples!" in Diyarbakır with: "There aren't peoples in Turkey, only one people!" According to Kurdish Islamist writer and politician Altan Tan, this response became the *beginning of the end* in the region for the CHP—which until that time had given many people hope.[167] Following Ecevit's vetoing of candidates who were "prominent for their Kurdish identities" in the 1977 elections, many former CHP candidates ran as independents.[168]

Global examples, from Quebec to Scotland, suggest that economic development does not solve ethnic/national questions, even though it might have a dampening effect on violent mobilization. On the contrary, prosperity can strengthen the demand for identity recognition and autonomy. Similarly, "while governmental development programs may reduce insurgent recruitment in rural and impoverished areas, they will be less effective in ending rebellions [such as the PKK insurgency] that develop significant social endowment through political mobilization."[169] The behavior of business associations in Diyarbakır, actors that one would expect to be the most pragmatic and most responsive to economic interests, is also revealing in this respect. When AKP governments pursued a strategy of weakening Kurdish nationalism by pitting economic interests against "unruly passions" through economic incentives, businesspeople tried to negotiate a middle ground between the "dual power" of the state and the Kurdish movement, but did not abandon the "passions" and demands such as education in their mother tongue.[170]

The belief that socioeconomic development can resolve the conflict seems to have been the pretext for ignoring Kurdish demands that cross-cut socioeconomic cleavages. This not only weakened conflict resolution efforts but also undermined developmental projects. Failure to address the ethnopolitical aspects of the Kurdish Conflict, for instance, led to the politicization of the perception and implementation of projects such as GAP, which could otherwise help peace and unify Turks and Kurds. The project instead invoked three clashing narratives: "GAP is a strategic 'anti-Kurdish' plot . . . GAP is a remedy for the conflict . . . GAP is a neutral and non-political project."[171]

Like their left-wing counterparts, center-right parties and the Islamist-nationalist National Salvation Party (MSP) adopted "a developmental discourse alongside a religious narrative." They did not envision taking "any political steps in relation to the Kurdish Question." Necmettin Erbakan and his team did not pave the way for candidates who "were interested in the Kurdish Question."[172] For, the MSP—just like the CHP—did not possess the conceptual and discursive resources to distinguish between political and cultural notions of nationhood and to enable them to imagine plurinational states or state-nations. Instead, they proposed to replace the secular Turkish national identity with an Islam-based one. They argued that an overarching Muslim identity would automatically reduce the tenacity of ethnic demands for recognition.[173]

In the 1990s, the Welfare Party, and in the 2000s the AKP, built up a significant support base among Kurds with their populist, anti-elitist, and anti–status quo politics and slogans such as "opposing all national-isms."[174] However, as I will elaborate in the coming chapters, they did not possess the intellectual repertoire or well-considered policy proposals and reform projects required to address the Kurdish Conflict. In 1992, Altan Tan observed:

> The administrators of the headquarters of the [Welfare Party] had never mentioned the word Kurd until after the general elections of 1991 . . . .They constantly referred to "southeastern brothers" solely to emphasize the backwardness of the region. The alliance between the Nationalist Work Party (MÇP) and the Reformist Democracy Party (IDP) led to heated disputes.[175]

Even though their ideas were deemed "radical" at the time, Kurdish organizations such as the DDKO were nonviolent organizations. The idea that "Kurds are a (distinct) people. They have a history, a language and a culture, and they should develop these," which was adopted by the Work-ers Party of Turkey in 1970 with the influence of the DDKO, was very "moderate" compared to the goals of independence and federation that were later demanded by the PKK through armed struggle. Yet, they were still sanctioned when, with a military intervention in 1971, organizations such as the DDKO were dismantled and many Kurds who had direct or indirect connections with them were either imprisoned or fled abroad.

The "ideal" conditions were being laid for Kurdish politics to become militant and go underground. First, socioeconomic and educational policies were creating opportunities for people to gain ethnic group conscious-ness, demand equality and rights, and form social/cultural and political organizations, and then, legal rules and government policies were refusing them the right to express their identity freely and to conduct legal politics with their own identities. It is not at all surprising that for many people, reductionist theories that explained ethnic conflicts through "internal colonialism" gained legitimacy.[176]

However, legal/political oppression did not eliminate these ideas; quite the opposite, they legitimized and politicized them. Sociologist İsmail Beşikçi, who wrote about the Kurdish Conflict from the 1970s onward and explained the conflict with his thesis focusing on (Turkish) colonialism, served seventeen years in prison because of his ideas. Of his thirty-six books, thirty-two were banned. However, rather than his ideas being quashed by such antidemocratic practices that restricted freedom of thought, Beşikçi was nominated for a Nobel Peace Prize in 1987.[177]

Similarly, the prohibitions did not wipe out Kurdish nationalism, they radicalized it. After an amnesty in 1974, those who previously founded organizations such as TKDP and DDKO reorganized under names such as Rızgari, Kawa, and Freedom Path. Compared to previous organizations, the violence and the tendency for armed struggle in these organizations escalated. This was also influenced by the right-left polarization and propensity for violence that captured Turkey in the 1970s. The PKK, which openly started out with the assertion that the Kurdish cause could not be resolved without arms, organized its first meeting in 1975 and was founded in 1978 under the leadership of Abdullah Öcalan. However, at the time, the PKK was a relatively marginal organization.[178]

The 1970s was also a decade in which the hopes dissolved for resolving the Kurdish Conflict in Iraq through relatively peaceful means and consensus. With the Algiers Agreement signed between the Shah of Iran and Saddam Hussein, the Shah withdrew his support of the Kurds in return for Shatt al-Arab. Thus, the autonomy agreement between the Iraqi Kurdish movement and the Ba'ath regime dissolved in 1975. Mustafa Barzani had to first flee to Iran and later to the United States.[179] While this experience deepened Kurdish nationalists' distrust of the countries of the region, it also created a shock effect among Turkey's Kurds. The lesson that Öcalan learned from this event was that Barzani was wrong to rely on traditional Kurdish notables, defend a "primitive" ideology that was not socialist enough, and fight for autonomy instead of independence.[180]

In summary, the new Kurds who were educated in large cities became politicized in the post-1960s pluralist setting and were initially organized in both leftist and rightist movements together with the Turks. However, as a result of the political system's intolerance of such activities in the name of Kurds and for Kurds and the tendency of their Turkish "comrades" to turn a blind eye to the Kurdish Question, the new Kurds gradually gained a stronger Kurdish consciousness and became political nationalists. What's more, they became conscious of the complicity of traditional conservative power-holding Kurdish elites in the political and economic order. Thus, a section of young Kurdish leftist-nationalists emerged and challenged the state in defense of the Kurdish cause, while at the same time disobeying the traditional Kurdish power holders who were associated with unfair proprietary relationships, tribal structures, tradition, and religious authority.

It is possible to consider the PKK as a product of these changes. Aliza Marcus notes that many members of the PKK are in fact educated Kurds who are fluent in Turkish.[181] If what was expected of them by the state had not been assimilation, but rather some sort of integration, keeping their "Of-Turkey" as well as Kurdish identities, and had they not been subject to state oppression and violence, they might not have joined the PKK.

Finally, there seems to have been another and paradoxical reason why more accommodating policies toward the Kurds could not be implemented even after the transition to a multiparty regime. So to speak, the "single and homogenous nation" discourse and policies, which, as I have argued, were advanced as a result of specific and revolutionary political circumstances during the formative period, "successfully" became normalized and gained hegemonic status among political elites as well as major segments of citizens. They continued to shape the thinking of Turkish political elites and average citizens even after the passing of the peculiar historical circumstance and political exigencies. This was nation building par excellence. Through education and other policies, they were internalized by the majority of the elites not only as the official ideology but as the one "truth." Within a matter of one or two generations, for many of them, the vocabulary and perception of Kurdish difference and nationhood became first "unthinkable" and then "unthought."[182]

## The 1980 Turkish Coup D'état

In 1980, the military overthrew the elected government and suspended democracy, citing government instability, economic crisis, left-right civil strife, and surging street violence.[183] In contrast with the short-lived 1971 intervention and the 1960 intervention that limited itself to political and constitutional restructuring, the hardliners within the military who came to control the junta embarked on an extensive project of political and social/ideological engineering, and heavily repressed civil/political rights and all social mobilization, especially of the Left.[184] Following the coup, in addition to the abolition of all political parties, "650,000 people were arrested, 1,683,000 prosecutions were prepared, and 517 people were sentenced to death; 49 of the death sentences were carried out. Furthermore, 30,000 people were fired from their jobs for holding political views incompatible with the state, 14,000 had their Turkish citizenship revoked, and 667 associations and foundations were banned."[185]

All this—which was not primarily motivated by the Kurdish Question—had critical consequences for the evolution of the Kurdish Conflict. The undiscriminating state repression and human rights violations in the Kurdish areas were very painful and consequential. The Diyarbakır prison became notorious for torture. Cemiloğlu, a fifty-four-year-old Kurdish politician who had previously run for mayor as a candidate for a center-right party, was taken into custody in 1982 and tortured. He said later: "If I had been young when I got out of prison, I would have taken to the mountains."[186]

Many younger Kurds did indeed take to the mountains, and violent Kurdish militancy—the PKK being the main beneficiary—was given a boost by the state's oppression. The PKK had been a marginal component of Kurdish politics before the military regime, but was now growing. The leadership and many members of the Kurdish nationalist organizations that had been powerful up to that point and were less violent than the PKK were put in prison and their organizations were dissolved. Öcalan had fled to Syria before the coup d'état. Hence, the PKK remained "unrivalled." Furthermore, while the PKK until then had mainly directed its violence at rival Kurdish groups and traditional Kurdish power holders, after its competitors were crushed under the military's fist it regrouped in a few years and began to target the state.

In addition to this "unintended" impact of state violence on intra-Kurdish politics, the identity-related unintended consequences were also vital. The fact that state oppression was undertaken by the military in the name of the Turkish identity and nationalism and the blatant contempt shown toward the Kurdish language and identity caused the victims and their relatives to gain a new ethno-nationalist consciousness. More importantly in terms of my theoretical framework, the victimization not only strengthened the Kurdish identity per se but also strengthened the rival and clashing images of the Turkish and Kurdish identities. Thousands of others fled to Europe, developing over time a new ethno-national consciousness semi-independently of the one they had held in Turkey.[187] While large segments of the Kurds thus developed stronger and more politicized attachments to their Kurdishness than before, the "either-or-else" choice the state and the conflict left for the people might have driven other Kurds to become more open to assimilation and to depoliticizing and privatizing their Kurdishness.

There were also other indirect consequences for the Kurdish Conflict. The 1980 coup d'état regime was not only Turkish nationalist and anti-Left. It "diagnosed" that the Left-Right polarization and political violence could be resolved through the empowerment of a more Islamized Turkish nationalism. Furthermore, many in the military saw communism as the number one threat and Islam as an antidote, which was in line with the U.S. "Green Belt" (green being the color of Islam) policies to contain the USSR—which had occupied Afghanistan to protect a pro-Soviet and leftist modernizing government in 1979—and the policies of other Muslim governments in the region at the time, such as those of Anwar Sadat in Egypt.[188] In Turkey, this policy found its expression in a "Turk(ish)-Islam synthesis." The emphasis on (Sunni) Muslimness was augmented in education, state institutions, the constitution, and laws. The ethnic Turkish element of the synthesis led to, among other policies, a constitutional amendment that allowed the banning of a language, as well as a new law that prohibited speaking Kurdish—echoing a similar ban against the Turkish language by the communist regime of neighboring Bulgaria at the time. The ban on Kurdish would only be lifted in 1991, long after the transition to democracy in 1983 and thanks to a Left-Right coalition government as I will discuss in the next chapter.

In general, by trying to institutionalize a guided illiberal democracy, the military hindered the development of what might have become the most important instrument for resolving the Kurdish Conflict. The leftist movement, which had demonstrated notable dynamism and potential for allowing actors to conduct legal politics with their Kurdish identity since the 1960s, received a severe blow during the coup d'état, from which it is yet to fully recover as of this writing. Kurdish and Turkish leftist politics still struggle to understand each other—especially with respect to how much Kurds have suffered state oppression because of their identity—and have difficulty cooperating toward common goals such as achieving peace. I will touch upon some significant advances in this regard in recent years at the end of the book. However, the following quote from an interview Uğur Mumcu—Turkish Kemalist/leftist journalist and intellectual who was slain in 1993 in an unresolved bomb attack—gave to aforementioned Kurdish politician Melik Fırat in 1990 speaks volumes:

[The] government which currently comprises ministers of Kurdish origin issued decrees of exile and censorship . . . which we [Kemalist Turkish Left] opposed first. [Put your hand on your heart and tell me.] The grandson of Seyid Abdülkadir, who was executed [after the Sheikh Said rebellion] with his son, was appointed the general manager of Sümerbank (State Enterprise founded by Atatürk). A few people from Shaikh Said's family were elected as MPs. The state harbored no ill will [was not vindictive], but if you are a Marxist or a revolutionary, the state will monitor you for life. You will not be able to work in public service or apply for a passport. Ruhi Su and Orhan Apaydın [two famous leftist intellectuals] were not issued passports even when they were on their deathbeds.[189]

## The PKK Insurgency and Movement

The latest and greatest Kurdish rebellion in Turkey began in 1984 with attacks against two military bases in the east of the country. This added a new dimension to the Kurdish Conflict, organized and sustained antistate violence, and a new dominant actor in Kurdish nationalism—the Kurdistan Workers Party PKK.[190] The PKK has become highly successful in mobilizing Kurdish nationalism, and has transformed into an international and mass political movement, compelling the state and Turkish-majority society to recognize the Kurds and the Kurdish Question more than any other previous actor.

Five characteristics separated the PKK from other Kurdish actors from the very beginning. First, the PKK prioritized armed over political struggle from the get-go. More adamantly than its rivals and predecessors, it set out with the assertion that the Kurdish Conflict could not be resolved without violence.[191] Strategic employment of violence has been instrumental to "the timing and ability" of the PKK's "rise as the hegemonic Kurdish nationalist organization in Turkey between the late 1970s and 1990."[192]

Öcalan explains retrospectively that "the PKK's declaration of a revolutionary people's war emerged as the only viable option [after the 1980 military coup]."[193] Yet, violence was central to the PKK's politics from the beginning, even before the coup. In the eyes of Öcalan, it served a greater purpose: "[The aim of violence strategy] is much closer to the objective of proving the existence of the Kurdish people and protecting their existence than of [becoming] a liberation movement. It should be pointed out that, in this regard, it has attained significant success."[194] Hence, violence has not only served the PKK as an instrument to challenge the Turkish state

and society but also as a cauldron of identity making. Political violence
(by the PKK as well as the state's counterinsurgency policies) led to identity consolidation and solidarity among many Kurds,[195] even though, as I
argued earlier and presumably, the rival and clashing images of Turkish
and Kurdish identities enhanced by the violence might also have induced
some Kurds to assimilate into Turkishness.

Violence was also key to eliminating the PKK's rivals. At the time
of the PKK's foundation, prominent actors, such as the Freedom Path led
by Kemal Burkay, while not ruling out violence, placed more importance
on political struggle for various reasons. For example, Burkay thought that
previous Kurdish rebellions had been unsuccessful because the people
were not ready and organized, and hence, the priority had to be given to
a political party.[196] By contrast, Öcalan decided from the start that there
was no choice but to take to arms. He initially used violence and a radical
discourse mainly against other Kurdish organizations, which he accused
of collaborating with the state and betraying the Kurdish cause. Later,
PKK violence focused on selectively targeting pro-government "village
guards" organized by the state, other "agents of the state" such as soldiers
and schoolteachers, and civilians.[197]

But it should be noted that violence has been a double-edged sword
from the point of view of the Kurdish cause. It deepened the association
of the Kurdish Question and the Kurdish cause with violence and terror
in the eyes of wide segments of the world and Turkish public opinion.
Thus, it also created a problematic legacy and deeply complicated the
efforts required to resolve the conflict.[198] Long-term evidence across the
world suggests that nonviolent campaigns have significant advantages over
violent insurgencies and might have a better record of achieving their
political objectives.[199]

Second, Öcalan gave up hope of legality and cooperation with Turkish
socialists and decided to directly appeal to the Kurdish people, bypassing
legal politics. He seems to have arrived at this conclusion in 1974 following seven months in prison (in 1972) and after his experiences in mixed
Turkish-Kurdish leftist associations such as Ankara Democratic Patriotic
Association of Higher Education (ADYÖD—later closed). At the same
time, he aimed to mobilize new Kurdish constituencies, gravitating toward
rural areas rather than urban activities. Other Kurdish organizations were
investing time in goals such as setting up offices in cities and publishing
magazines, all of which had little influence in the countryside. The PKK
opted not to waste energy on such activities and instead attempted to

reach Kurds in rural areas with one-to-one meetings to "change their ways of thinking."[200]

Third, within Kurdish nationalism and the leftist movement, Öcalan was a new actor. Therefore, while the other Kurdish organizations competed with each other and were intensely monitored by the state, the PKK drew less attention.

Fourth, the PKK came to represent a different class structure compared to many previous Kurdist organizations. It drew in youths and students with rural backgrounds and, later, urban middle-class youths. Besides Kurdish nationalism, it mobilized its supporters based on a discourse of rebellion against the unfair distribution of land in the east, the order of *aghas* and tribes, the feudal class system, and the patriarchal culture. Other leftist Kurdish organizations also criticized the traditional system but dared not risk armed attacks against the landlords. However, the PKK gained prestige among many people as an organization that could stand up to powerful landlords from 1978 onward, when they killed Mehmet Baysal—the leader of the Süleymanlar tribe. This was followed by the attack on Mehmet Celal Bucak's house in Siverek in 1979.[201]

Last but not least, the PKK skillfully sought and was able to obtain external state support for its operations more than any other Kurdish armed rebel group in Turkey. To different degrees and in different periods, for example, such disparate states as Syria, Iraq, Iran, Greece, Lebanon, Belgium, and the Netherlands either deliberately or "de facto" sponsored the PKK, by acting as a "safe haven" for its members or leaders, allowing it to open offices or training camps, or providing weapons and logistics aid.[202] Hence, the PKK could be seen as an early example of nonstate armed groups fighting their host states with some form of external state support.[203]

The PKK truly sought and received the support of external powers from the start. Leaving for Syria before the coup prevented Öcalan from being crushed like other Kurdish organizations by the military regime. After this, the PKK initially received external aid from the Palestine Liberation Organization. From 1980 to 1982, hundreds of PKK militants were trained in camps run by the Palestine Liberation Organization in the Beqaa Valley, Lebanon. Later, until 1998, they were protected by Syria, which had disputes with Turkey over water resources and the province of Hatay. Syrian governmental bodies actively helped the PKK find new members from among Syrian Kurds by allowing the latter to join the organization instead of doing military service.[204]

In the 1990s, after the First Gulf War, the no-fly zone created in the northern regions of Iraq provided a safe harbor for both the Kurdish administration there and the PKK, as I will discuss further later. Afterward, the PKK made great efforts toward political organization and internationalization. It established an extensive and professional organization with media and political connections, particularly in Europe.

From 1979, when he fled to Syria, to his capture in 1999, Öcalan remained outside of Turkey and the Kurdish regions of Turkey, and he has been in prison since then. Hence, he has not had a one-to-one relationship with ordinary Kurdish people during this time. These circumstances have exalted Öcalan to a superhuman cult status in the eyes of many Kurds.[205] They began to view the PKK and Öcalan as symbols or cult icons representing the Kurdish struggle even if they did not approve of the PKK's methods.

The PKK openly waged war not only on the security forces and civilian representatives of the state, such as teachers and imams, but also on all the Kurds who opposed them, who were labeled "supporters of the state." Therefore, since the 1980s, the war between the Turkish state and the nonstate pro-Kurdish actor, the PKK, has also been an intra-Kurdish war. Even if by force, it thus delivered relative "solidarity" among major segments of the Kurds. Even though it is very difficult to accurately measure the support for the PKK among Kurds, support for the pro-PKK political parties has hovered around one-half of the population whose mother tongue is Kurdish. Many who support or sympathize with the PKK's goals may not approve of its methods and ideology. However, in the eyes of the supportive and opposing Kurds alike, the PKK became the only actor that had the potential for violence and political power that could force the state to change. In this sense, at times, the PKK attained its respected status through fear and anger, and, at other times, through approval and admiration.

The diverse and, over time, changing membership and support base of the PKK is also significant to note. Despite the state's greatest efforts, the PKK continued to recruit across different periods, after the relative military defeat in the late 1990s and in relatively peaceful and violent periods.[206] Güneş Murat Tezcür found that tangible benefits such as pressing individual security concerns and, as the PKK increased its strength, expectations of social mobility and economic gain primarily motivated the PKK's early recruits. Over time, however, the share of well-educated and urbanized, idealist recruits rose. These "higher quality" members who were mobilized based on shared beliefs and ideals rendered the PKK more durable and mass-based, fitting "the pattern of a social endowment insurgency and [attracting] large number of committed and educated recruits despite the enormous risks and limited gains over many years."[207]

Finally, the end of the Cold War provided opportunities during the 1990s for nonstate actors such as the PKK. They could more freely frame their claims as ethno-nationalist demands, rather than as class-based demands, and many states found it more challenging to suppress them based on their external support from either socialist, capitalist, or independent camps.[208]

## Could the Kurdish Conflict
## Be Resolved if the PKK Did Not Exist?

If some Kurds had not formed a militarist movement such as the PKK and resorted to violence and terrorism in order to pursue their cause during the 1980s, would the Kurdish identity have continued to be the taboo subject that it was until the 1990s? Could a more peaceful Kurdish actor have emerged and more successfully promoted the Kurdish cause, given the long record of the Turkish state suppressing any demands the Kurds made "as Kurds" and in the name of Kurdishness? According to the PKK, the Republic of Turkey could only accept the Kurdish reality by force of arms.

The PKK and the war with the PKK during the 1990s itself were among the chief factors why Turkey's democratization process and the pro-democratic public's efforts to transcend the legacy of the 1980 military regime, came to a halt, or even regressed, in the 1990s—called the "Lost Decade." Arguably, the PKK never stood a realistic chance of military victory against the Turkish state. Nevertheless, the war took a very heavy toll on the Turkish state by boosting military expenditure, militarism, and corruption within the state.

The PKK conflict caused somewhere between 35,000 and 40,000 deaths between 1984 and 1999. By research standards, this qualifies as a "civil war," since the number of casualties surpassed one thousand per year between 1992 and 1999 (when the conflict was most violent).[209] No one knows to what extent these numbers include the thousands of unsolved murders or "extrajudicial executions" that took place in the 1990s and are widely attributed to pro-state paramilitary forces or clandestine forces supported by the state. According to the Human Rights Association and the Human Rights Foundation of Turkey, between 1990 and 2011, there were 2,872 unsolved murders, 1,945 extrajudicial executions, and 950 deaths or murders in prisons or under in police custody.[210] Other sources suggest that these deaths and murders number anywhere between five thousand and seventeen thousand.[211]

Yet, in the late 1980s, Turkey was just beginning to move beyond the 1980 regime and toward democratization. Following the transition to limited multiparty politics and civilian rule in 1983, in a 1987 referendum, the electorate openly voted for democratization by opening the doors to the politicians banned by the coup. It was in this spirit that Turgut Özal's government officially applied for EU membership. In 1991, the center-right and -left (SHP and DYP) established a reasonably successful coalition government—an unimaginable feat in the 1970s. Military tutelage was, of course, ongoing,[212] but civilian politics and civil society were rapidly strengthening.

The PKK war was a primary cause of the subsequent reversal of these trends. Instead of a democratic welfare state, the war-induced security state grew. The authority of the military and other intelligence and security units surged within the state. Tansu Çiller's—Turkey's first female prime minister—government decided with its chief of staff that the regular army could not succeed in its fight against the PKK. Similar to the Fujimori government's policies in Peru, the Turkish government resorted to handing over the "powers of the state" to the unlawful shadow state. Corruption rapidly spread in places where law was absent due to a state of emergency. The voices of civilian politics and civil society were muted. In the second half of the 1990s, these hawkish and authoritarian policies helped the military temporarily defeat the PKK. Even though these policies helped the state gain the upper hand in the conflict in a military sense, the conflict became even more intractable politically, and society in Turkey paid a very heavy price in terms of economic welfare and democracy.

The violence that had waned in the early 2000s began to escalate after 2004 and peaked particularly during electoral periods. By using force, the PKK attempted to preserve its position as the representative of the Kurds while also continuing a war of attrition against the state through violence. In fact, the PKK tried to render certain regions of the country impossible to govern, while also being careful not to escalate the violence to the point of losing the Kurdish people's support. The state, on one hand, tried to punish both the PKK and its supporters through violence, while, on the other, it attempted to politically weaken the PKK through limited compromises over Kurdish demands. Both sides refrained from increasing the violence to a point that would force them to change their basic strategies and would threaten their own survival.[213] The real victims were human rights, democracy, socioeconomic development, and Turkey's international reputation.

However, civilian Kurdish identity politics in the late 1980s developed independent of the PKK. It was not unthinkable that this politics might take root within leftist social democratic, center-right, and Islamist movements and parties, and later in pro-Kurdish parties, where Kurds would be given a platform for expression with their distinct identity. Under such scenarios, the possibility of conflict resolution through deliberation among nonviolent and with legal actors could emerge.

From feminists to political Islamists and from LGBT to Alevis and various ethnic identity groups, many constituencies have mobilized and developed enduring social movements that previously either did not exist or were marginal in Turkey during the 1980s. These have been quite successful in politicizing and rendering visible many identities and causes that used to be taboo, just like the Kurdish identities and Question. Without the war with the PKK, it is conceivable that the Kurds could enjoy similar, if limited, success, considering the impact of the external security dilemma, which affected the Kurdish Conflict but not these other identity-based conflicts in Turkey.

The Grand National Assembly ("of Turkey" after 1921) that led the War of Independence (1919–22). Simultaneously an effort to rescue the Ottoman state and parliament and a rebellion against them. Founded the nation-state and Republic of Turkey in 1923. Photo: Public Domain, http://www. eskiturkiye.net/1561/ankara-1-meclis.

Mustafa Kemal (Atatürk), on way to the Grand National Assembly with Diyap Ağa, Kurdish tribal leader and member of assembly from Dersim (later Tunceli). An effort to include the Kurds in "the nation". Photo: Maynard Owen Williams, March 22, 1921. https://commons.wikimedia. org/wiki/File:Mustafa_Kemal_Atat%C3%BCrk_and_Diyap_A%C4%9Fa. jpg

The last Ottoman Caliph (and briefly Caliph in the Turkish Republic), and former heir to the Ottoman throne Abdülmecid Efendi (Abdulmejid II), being informed of the parliament's decision in March 1924 to abolish the Office of the Caliphate. A major "secular" political reform that reflected and reinforced the "elite cooperation dilemma". Photo: Unknown photographer, Public Domain, https://upload.wikimedia.org/wikipedia/commons/8/84/Caliph_Abd%C3%BClmecid_dethronment.jpg

Store front soon after the "alphabet revolution" (1928), which abandoned the Arabic for Latin alphabet. Part of Turkey's pro-secular "remaking," which echoed and hardened the "elite cooperation dilemma". Photo: Maynard Owen Williams, with permission from National Geographic.

Sheikh Said, bottom-right, Kurdish religious leader who launched in 1925 a brutally suppressed armed rebellion against the state, opposing the new republic's "Turkish and secular" state-building and nation-formation policies. Photo: Unknown photographer, Public Domain, https://commons.wikimedia. org/wiki/File:Sheikh_Sherif,_Sheikh_Said,_Kasim,_Sheikh_Abdullah.jpg.

# The Changing Context of the 1990s

## *Seeing Kurds without Recognizing Them*

There is no harm in Turks and Kurds, two indispensable brothers to one another, freely debating issues relating to each other and the common homeland. By contrast, [if they deny the realities] and avoid debating, not only will [misunderstandings] manifest themselves but also those who are in pursuit of intrigue will have been handed a good opportunity.[1]

—Ahmed Emin Yalman, *Kürtler ve Kürdistan.*

On the surface, the 1990s was a dismal decade for Turkey when measured in terms of many criteria, such as peace between the Turkish state and the Kurds, and human rights, procedural democracy, and the economy. However, by no means does this mean that the period lacked some improvements in the supportive conditions of democracy, and changes in the social, political, and discursive environments of the Kurdish Conflict. Some of these transformations prepared the necessary ground for future democratization as well as conflict resolution efforts. During this decade, multiparty democracy was reestablished, albeit with growing political instability and corruption. Internationally, post–Cold War geopolitics raised hopes of "democratic hegemony"[2] in the world, while, domestically, Turkish society urbanized rapidly. A vibrant civil society and newly mobilized groups, such as feminists, Alevis, Sufi communities and movements, business associations, and political Islamists, transformed and diversified the social and political sphere. They politicized and raised new public questions on issues such as the environment, LGBTQ rights, "non-Turk" ethnic legacies, and tenets of a more pluralist and democratic secularism, often cross-cutting the Left-Right and Turk-Kurd divides.

Further, and most importantly for this book, a remarkable bottom-up transformation of the mainstream public/political discourse took place in the '90s, whereby the Kurdish identity became no longer a taboo. As a result, "silence" replaced "talking" about Kurds, and the "unseen, unarticulated and often unknown" social/political category of Kurds was transformed into a "seen, articulated, and known" category. However, this did not necessarily bring about greater recognition for Kurds. Here, I use the term *recognition* in reference to two interrelated but separate qualities: (1) having greater social knowledge about people who are thought to form a particular social group, thus, knowing more about their past, present and emic and etic identities, either as individuals, as a group, or both; and (2) having greater acceptance that these people form a group that may be entitled to distinct social/political rights, institutions, and, when necessary, mechanisms of representation and expression.[3]

Each of these qualities separately confers a sense of "dignity" upon those who are recognized. It is a fundamental, existential desire in most of us that we want to be "seen," that is, not ignored by others, *and* be treated with equal respect and rights. Ignoring Kurds' yearning for recognition in Turkey—or perceiving it as merely consisting of material demands such as territory and economic benefits and thus ignoring its multifaceted nature—would amount to a "failure to recognize how vulnerable humans are to being treated as if they didn't matter" and did not exist.[4] I think recognition extends to respecting that people involved in a conflict have lives and aspirations beyond the conflict in question. In this respect—and taking into account also the anxieties and aspirations of Turks in the process, as I do in this book—conflict resolution would involve an outcome where both sides "recognize and acknowledge each other's value"[5] and existence beyond their actions and roles in the Kurdish Conflict.

Thus, the task of this chapter is to explain why and how a remarkable discursive transformation occured in the 1990s regarding the Kurds, how and why this did not amount to recognition, and the resulting social/ political consequences for the Kurdish Conflict. I will do so by developing a nonstandard analytical narrative and generating new conceptual/theo- retical categories. My explanation will show that social/political learning, deliberation, and the resulting intra-elite divisions, coupled with bottom-up civil society efforts, the discursive implications of external geopolitical developments and cascade dynamics, were the major causal mechanisms that opened up the mainstream social/political discourse. These changes advanced a greater awareness of diversity, even in the context of a seemingly hegemonic social/political belief about homogenous nationhood and of a "strong state" [6] that fosters and guards these beliefs. Such a discursive change was necessary to permit any conflict resolution, since peace cannot be achieved with a people whose very existence as a group is considered taboo and closed for honest sociopolitical debate. Yet, I will also maintain that in the absence of a resolution of the structural conditions captured by the three dilemmas in this book, such discursive liberalization could not lead to conflict resolution. In fact, it did not necessarily bode well for social/political peace, recognition, or the democratic implementation of ethnonational pluralism and rights.

What happened discursively in Turkey during the 1990s can be seen as a "theory-infirming crucial case,"[7] that is, an example that challenges or disconfirms some theories and established opinions about ethnic and national conflicts and democracy. In an authoritarian or totalitarian regime, we expect that an ethnic identity may be erased from the popular discourse; however, extraordinarily, we witnessed this exact phenomenon in Turkey despite its electoral democracy and significant albeit limited civic and political rights. Yet, unexpectedly, this "closed discourse" was liberalized and opened new avenues for conflict resolution in the late 1990s. What's more, how and how fast this "closed discourse" became liberalized and its consequences for conflict resolution defied expectations.

## Seeing Without Recognizing

As we saw earlier, during the formative years, in the eyes of the Turkish state elites, the Kurdish identity became, first, a rival to the national identity and, later, gained a clashing image with the national identity. The state thus adopted a long-term policy whereby it began to restrict the expression of the Kurdish category, albeit with certain significant regional and temporal variations. With subsequent generations, this policy came to be considered normal, and talking about Kurds as "Kurds" became more or less unthinkable among mainstream Turkish actors. Therefore, for the average Turkish citizen, the Kurds became a category about which they had no knowledge and, whether positive or negative, judgment. This created a highly unfavorable setting for resolving the Kurdish Conflict based on democratic procedures. A democratic polity cannot address a social/political problem when the group categories—i.e., the linguistic and conceptual tools—necessary for discussing the problem are not there, and about which there is little public knowledge.

However, this situation also to some extent prevented the development of hostile attitudes toward the Kurds. Neither compatible nor rival and clashing images about the Kurds were freely expressed in the mainstream discourse. In short, the Kurds were rendered "invisible" and ignored as a people with a distinct identity. Of course, this is not to say that negative or positive views and expressions about the Kurds entirely vanished from social memory, private expression, and public political discourse.

The discursive changes in the 1990s allowed the public to learn more about the Kurds and discuss and deliberate the Kurdish Question. Hence, they enabled the development of a compatible image of the Kurdish and Turkish identities: the imagination of the Kurdish identity and the common national identity in ways that enable their simultaneous expression and development.

On the other hand, the new context also allowed the expression and development of rival and clashing images of the Kurdish and Turkish identities. Particularly with the influence of the PKK war, negative judgments about Kurds started to develop and find an expression in the public political discourse. A permissive setting was also created for the development of polarization through the rival image.

This led to a bifurcated development. A part of society began to accept the discussion of Kurdish rights as normal and desirable in a context of democratization. Yet, many others developed perceptions of the Kurds as being politically separatist and subversive, and socially and culturally degenerate.

## When and How Did the Discursive Change Happen?

Until the 1990s, the Kurds were rarely referred to publicly in Turkey. The Kurdish category was avoided in both official documents and in mainstream public political discourse. The word *Kurd* was more or less absent in mainstream media.

For example, between 1984 and 1985, *Hürriyet*, which could be considered the flagship mainstream newspaper of the period, published only twenty-five articles that were fully or partially related to Kurds in Turkey. Only three of these twenty-five articles (12%), included the word

*Kurd* one or more times. The media rarely covered issues concerning the Kurds, and when it did, it would not use the word *Kurd*, and employed terms such as "eastern citizens" instead, that is, it refrained from discussing and framing the issue as being about Kurds per se. By contrast, just in the first five months of 2003, *Hürriyet* published 114 articles related to Kurds in Turkey. Approximately 47 percent of these articles referred to Kurdishness as a group category at least once, using terms such as *Kurds, ethnic Kurds,* or *Turkish citizens of Kurdish origin.*[8] This transformation of the discursive environment took place between 1991 and 1992. In these two years, 658 articles were published in *Hürriyet* related to the Kurds in Turkey. In almost half of these (304 articles), the word *Kurd* was used at least once. This meant that twenty-six times more articles were published than in the 1984–85 period, and, in these articles, the word *Kurd* was used four times more frequently than in the earlier period.[9]

These figures come from a research project I conducted for which my graduate student assistants content-analyzed every issue of *Hürriyet* from 1984 to 1998.[10] After browsing the titles of all news articles and comments, and their contents when necessary, 4,277 articles were found to be directly or indirectly related to the Kurds, the Kurdish Question, or the Conflict. Then, we examined the contents of these articles in close detail.[11]

Each article was coded according to three qualitative and quantitative variables: (1) Does the article include the term *Kurd* or any of its variants, such as *Kurdish (Kürt), Kurd Of-Turkey (Türkiyeli Kürt), ethnic Kurd, citizen of Kurdish origin (Kürt kökenli vatandaş)* or *Kurdish insurgents,* to refer to a group or place? Or, were nonethnic terms such as *eastern citizens (doğulu vatandaşlar), bandits (eşkiya),* or *terrorists* utilized? (2) Does the article deal with domestic Kurds, in other words, Kurds living in Turkey? (The language used to refer to Kurds living in Turkey and abroad can be subject to different dynamics.) (3) What is the subject of the article, and, most importantly, does it address "security" (for example, the conflict between the PKK and the security forces) or other aspects, such as politics (for example, news articles about pro-Kurdish political parties), rights (for example, human rights abuses or linguistic rights) or sociocultural issues (for example, identity-related topics, education in mother tongue, and socioeconomic development)? Additionally, the reasons and triggers for the major shifts were investigated through historical event analysis and interviews with prominent journalists.

A total of 3,027 of these articles mainly related to domestic Kurds, with the remainder concerning "external Kurds"—Kurds based in countries other than Turkey—for lack of a better term. Tables 5.1 and 5.2 summarize the findings on domestic Kurds. The seven-year period from 1984 to 1990 contrasts with the period from 1993 to 1998 in terms of the visibility and recognition given to the Kurdish category.

From 1991 onward, not only did the total number of articles related to Kurds increase significantly, but a high percentage included the word *Kurd*. Within the space of two years, the terms *Kurd, citizen of Kurdish origin,* and *Kurd Of-Turkey* became widespread in mainstream media and in public discourse. Toward the end of 1991, Prime Minister Süleyman Demirel declared that he accepted the "Kurdish reality," the presence of a "Kurdish" population in Turkey.

More than one-quarter of articles used the term *Kurd* in the 1993–98 period. Part of the reason for this was a change in the issues covered. The subjects of the articles shifted from security to nonsecurity matters. Columns four and five of Table 5.2 show that the term *Kurd* was used far more frequently in articles about nonsecurity matters. Nevertheless, the use of the term *Kurd* increased in the "security" subject category, too, from 12 percent to 19 percent. Therefore, in addition to the increasing interest in talking about Kurds in nonsecurity contexts, the word *Kurd* became more frequently used when discussing security-related subjects as well.

Meanwhile, while the majority of the articles related to Kurds in both periods regarded security matters, in the period between 1991 and 1992 security- and non-security-related topics were afforded roughly even coverage. This is remarkable because these were the two years when the violence peaked; just as this was happening, articles on the social, economic, and identity aspects of the Kurdish Question also increased. In other words, civil society (in this instance, the journalists who could be considered part of the intelligentsia and the press) reacted constructively and self-reflexively, in search of democratization and conflict resolution. They attempted—successfully or not—to question and understand the social and political problems underlying the violence.

Another important finding is that not all of these changes came about in a continuous and gradual fashion. Sudden upswings and reversals also took place. Between 1987 and 1988, there was a short-lived surge in the number of articles containing the word *Kurd,* triggered by the statements of the ex-prime minister and leader of the left-wing nationalist Democratic Left Party (DSP), Bülent Ecevit. Ecevit's words were reported under the headlines: "Let Us Not Fear the Word 'Kurd' " and "Turks Who Don't Speak Turkish." However, this was followed in 1989 by a significant fall in the

Table 5.1. Yearly changes in use of the term "Kurd" in reference to a domestic group

| Year | Total Number of Articles on Domestic Kurds | Monthly Average of Articles | Number of Articles Using "Kurd" at Least Once | Percentage of Articles Using "Kurd" |
|------|-----|-----|-----|-----|
| 1984 | 18 | 1.5 | 2 | 11 |
| 1985 | 7 | 0.6 | 1 | 14 |
| 1986 | 40 | 3.3 | 8 | 20 |
| 1987 | 122 | 10.2 | 27 | 22 |
| 1988 | 65 | 5.4 | 19 | 29 |
| 1989 | 152 | 12.7 | 23 | 15 |
| 1990 | 129 | 10.8 | 18 | 14 |
| 1991 | 238 | 19.8 | 121 | 51 |
| 1992 | 423 | 35.3 | 186 | 44 |
| 1993 | 490 | 40.8 | 157 | 32 |
| 1994 | 300 | 25.0 | 90 | 30 |
| 1995 | 178 | 14.8 | 54 | 30 |
| 1996 | 253 | 21.1 | 64 | 25 |
| 1997 | 139 | 11.5 | 16 | 12 |
| 1998 | 473 | 39.3 | 95 | 20 |

Table 5.2. A comparison of the periods 1984–1990 and 1993–1998

| Period | Monthly Article Average | Percentage of Articles using "Kurd" | Percentage of Security-Related Articles Using "Kurd" | Percentage of Non-Security Articles Using "Kurd" | Percentage of Non-Security Articles |
|---|---|---|---|---|---|
| 1984–1990 | 6.34 | 18 | 12 | 49 | 19 |
| 1991–1992* | 27.54 | 47 | 25 | 71 | 48 |
| 1993–1998 | 25.46 | 26 | 19 | 44 | 29 |

*Transition Period

use of the word *Kurd,* despite the increased number of articles related to Kurds. As the third column of Table 5.2 depicts, the most significant and sustained transformation occurred in 1991–92. In these years, the number of articles related to Kurds, the use of the word *Kurd,* and the frequency of nonsecurity articles related to Kurds all peaked.

These changes surprised observers. For example, journalists such as Hasan Cemal, who followed the Kurdish Question closely, admit they were shocked when, in 1990, President Turgut Özal stated that the Kurds should cease to be a taboo subject and revealed that his own grandmother was Kurdish. The reaction was the same when, in 1991, Prime Minister Süleyman Demirel spoke of the "Kurdish reality."[12] Notably, the press used the word *Kurd* freely in the context of "external" Kurds, as in "Iraqi Kurds" or "Iraqi Kurdish leaders" but the term was avoided as a domestic category.

## Explaining the Discursive Change

How was it possible for this transformation to take place in such a short period of time? Addressing this question requires several analytical/conceptual steps and ruling out simplistic explanations.

### STATE VERSUS SOCIAL DISCOURSE

The discursive changes took place despite the active resistance of a good part of the state elites. Hence, we need to analytically separate the state's discourse from the mainstream social discourse; this distinction was often overlooked in contemporary studies on the Kurdish Question.[13] There is no doubt that the official state ideology and discourse about the Kurds were internalized by major segments of society through education and other means of nation building.[14] However, to assume that the state discourse was internalized without any modification by the *whole* society would be tantamount to asserting that Turkey had a totalitarian regime during the period. In fact, despite its authoritarian or illiberal predispositions, Turkey's state had neither the capability nor the will to penetrate society as such. Furthermore, its democratic qualities allowed for significant societal autonomy.[15] Turkey's powerful military/bureaucratic elites were equipped with both legal and extralegal powers that enabled them to restrict the autonomy of societal actors. However, these elites operated in a context of formal democracy and an economically and technologically developed, assertive, and pluralistic media. The elites' authority and power were not far-reaching enough to establish totalitarian control over the sociopolitical discourse.

## HARD-LINE AND MODERATE NATIONALIST ELITES DIVIDE

Intra-elite divisions played an important causal role in the discursive change. The state elites of the period—who could be defined as comprising the military, bureaucratic, and mainstream political elites—did not constitute a monolithic group. In broad terms, they had two sets of perspectives in relation to the ethno-linguistic diversity of the country. For lack of a better term and to comply with broader theories of democratic transitions, I will call them "hard-line" and "moderate" nationalist perspectives.[16]

This distinction partially overlaps with the radical/revolutionary and moderate/evolutionary secularist elite division we discussed previously, and crosscuts other divisions such as those between conservative and modernist Islamist perspectives, as well as Left-Right and center-periphery divisions. In other words, we can find hard-line and moderate nationalist perspectives among both the secular and the pious nationalists. At least partially, the ideational origins of these two perspectives lie in different—and perhaps equally flawed or incomplete—interpretations of the Ottoman decay.

According to the hard-line nationalist perspective, there is an insep-arable connection between the identity and security aspects of the Kurdish Question. In other words, there is a causal connection between the unity of language, culture, and religion and political and territorial integrity. What is understood by religion, language, and culture might vary; yet the assumption that they are requirements of political solidarity and territorial integrity does not change. Hard-line nationalists argue that politics that draws on sub-state identities has a built-in predisposition to evolve into separatism; they therefore oppose ethnic categories becoming prominent in the public/political discourse. They oppose political movements with prominent Kurdish identities and any cooperation with them, even if these movements shun violence and express themselves merely on cultural/lin-guistic matters; for the hard-line nationalists, the movements in question are simply stepping stones that lead to "political" goals such as founding a separate state. Well-entrenched interpretations of Turkey's pre-republican, imperial history that support such opinions attribute the dissolution of the Ottoman Empire to ethno-religious cultural and political movements that transformed into rival nationalisms. It was as a result of this, these narratives explain, that Turks and Muslims suffered losses and arrived at the very brink of annihilation. To prevent this from happening again, it is necessary to give priority to preemptive and coercive policies vis-à-vis any sign of Kurdish nationalism.

Moderate nationalist views separate the identity and security (i.e., state security and territorial interests) dimensions of the Kurdish Question—and, for that matter, other questions pertaining to ethnic/national diversity—when considering how these affect national solidarity and territorial integrity. As such, ethnic Kurds might have interests that can be upheld without harming Turkey's social cohesion or its political and territorial integrity. In fact, meeting the Kurds' demands regarding their language, culture, and identity might even curb their incentives for demanding political and territorial rights. Therefore, those holding moderate nationalist views argue for cooperating with moderate Kurdish actors in order to grant Kurdish cultural/linguistic rights and keep pro-Kurdish actors within the legitimate political system. According to them, the demise of the Ottoman Empire might not have resulted simply from rival nationalisms and external competition. The jittery center could not properly analyze the writing on the wall and manage the centrifugal forces—however difficult this might have been under the circumstances—offer fair treatment to and win over the moderates within different religious/ethnic groups, and establish effective legislative, judicial, and administrative institutions. Hence, while moderate nationalist views do not rule out the use of military measures against Kurdish rebels, relatively speaking, they mistrust exclusively security-centered and coercive policies and give more preponderance to broad-based consensus building, negotiation, and persuasion. The rift between the İnönü and Okyar governments over how to quell the Sheikh Said rebellion, as we saw in the last chapter, was a good example of the hard-line and moderate positions respectively.

There is a similar hard-line and moderate division among Kurdish actors. The main differences between the two groups lie in their views about the legitimacy of the Turkish political system and the acceptability and benefits of ideational and political cooperation and compromises with "Turkish" actors within the system. Abdullah Öcalan's opinions as expressed in 1991 are an example of hard-line views. In an interview, Öcalan described as "collaborators" any Kurdish actor who lived in Turkey, Iran, and Iraq and cooperated with the regimes of these countries at different levels, even if they defended Kurdish rights and autonomy. Hence, for example, Öcalan criticized the 1990 report by the Social Democratic People's Party (SHP), which demanded cultural/linguistic rights for Turkey's Kurds because the SHP referred to the Kurds as an ethnic group rather than as a separate nation.[17] By comparison, moderate nationalist Kurdish actors maintain that it is possible for Kurdish interests to be pursued within the system and by cooperating with mainstream actors. Despite the Turkish political system's suppression of openly Kurdish actors and interests, Kurdish actors with more moderate views have long been present in the Turkish political system. In fact, the system was "competent and elastic enough to integrate traditional Kurdish actors. In turn, those actors played a key role in the legitimization of the system."[18]

## INSTRUMENTAL VERSUS GOAL-ORIENTED BELIEFS

Most research on the Kurdish Conflict, and, for that matter, on ethnopolitical conflicts, focuses upon the *goals* of the actors in order to categorize them; but this may have limited predictive and explanatory power vis-à-vis political behavior.[19] As the hard-line and moderate nationalist distinction also implies, among both Turkish and Kurdish nationalists, what really distinguishes moderate from hard-line views is not necessarily what different actors want (e.g., territorial integrity, independence, or autonomy—their *goal-oriented beliefs*), but their *instrumental views* on how they aim to attain what they want. For example, when Erdal İnönü, the chair of the SHP and deputy prime minister, objected in 1994 to removing the parliamentary immunity of seven Kurdish parliamentarians charged with supporting separatism and the PKK, his *goals* were not very different from the goals of those who defended the removals. He argued that this decision would do more harm than good with regard to the goal—national and territorial integrity. That is to say, it was his instrumental beliefs that were not aligned with the views of those who argued for the removals.

Adam Przeworski argues that there are two types of instrumental belief: causal and equilibrium.[20] Causal (technical) beliefs are concerned with the cause-and-effect relationships between particular policies or actions and their outcomes. They reflect our expectations regarding which policies will lead to which outcomes. One such view regarding minimum wage policy would be the assertion that were we to raise the minimum wage, employers would hire fewer workers and unemployment would increase. Similarly, many actors including members of the military opposed coercive policies vis-à-vis the Kurds, arguing that oppressive policies backfire by steering people toward—rather than away from—the PKK. Hence, causal beliefs are strategic views that consider not only the direct outcomes of the individual's own actions but also the anticipated reactions of other actors to such actions.

In turn, equilibrium beliefs are beliefs about the popularity of different actions and outcomes; in other words, beliefs about what the majority of other people think and want. These might include beliefs about which party the majority of the people around us support, or whether the majority of Turkish people are in favor of or against education in Kurdish. The "majority" in question does not necessarily refer to a numerical size; it may instead denote sociopolitical power. The views of the groups that constitute our reference groups carry the most weight. These beliefs affect behavior since, all things being equal, there is always a potential social and political cost to pay when people deviate from the prevailing views of their environment. This does not mean that all people are conformists all of the time, but rather that it is easier to express and defend views approved by the people in one's social and political environment.

Goal-oriented beliefs can correspond to completely different choices and behaviors depending on the actor's accompanying causal and equilibrium beliefs. Take, for example, an imaginary Kurdish nationalist who has pro-independence goal-oriented beliefs. This person may still refuse to support separatism if he/she thinks that such a movement would fail given the lack of sufficiently widespread support among the Kurds for a separatist movement (unfavorable equilibrium beliefs) and the fact that separatism would face fierce opposition from regional states, and might even increase resistance against any Kurdish rights (unfavorable cause-effect beliefs).

This distinction between types of belief matters for conflict resolution. Altering goal-oriented views is more difficult because these opinions may be rooted in people's fundamental worldviews and emotional attachments, identities, and socioeconomic positions in society. For example, whether people place more value on economic security or on individual freedom, and, thus, whether they prioritize democracy or economic development, might only shift through long-term processes of socioeconomic change and education, and through the associated changes in one's relative social status and social class.[21] However, instrumental views may be more amenable to short-term changes through persuasion and deliberation. A person who cares about economic development but not so much about democracy may still support democratization if he/she is convinced that this would lead to more investment, employment, and, thus, economic development. Hence, one factor that facilitated the discursive transformation during the

1990s might have been the fact that it primarily encompassed instrumental views.

Indeed, during the 1990s, two opposing types of instrumental beliefs that prevailed among the Turkish elites competed in the public/political discourse to explain the causal relationship between the public/political expressions of Kurdishness and national integrity. These can be summed up by the following two examples:

> [If we lift the ban,] tomorrow there will be cafes where Kurdish folk songs are sung, theaters where Kurdish films are shown, and coffee houses where Kurdish is spoken. If this is not separatism [*bölücülük*], what is?[22]

> What would it mean if Kurdish songs and ballads were broadcast on TRT [Public Radio and Television], and at news hour, the newsperson delivered the news in Kurdish? The Kurdish citizens of this country would think, "My state recognizes and respects my presence and identity, and as such, TV and radio channels of the state broadcast in my mother tongue every day at a specific time . . . .The PKK won't disappear . . . [but] the heat of the conflict might subside . . . .But the political balances in this country, the military etc. would not allow it.[23]

The last sentence in the last quote, uttered by President Özal in 1991, also exemplifies an equilibrium belief, that those opposing ethnic/cultural rights are more powerful in the political system. Hence, some people who believed that ethnic/cultural rights can be instrumental to social cohesion and peace (favorable instrumental beliefs) might still have not supported reforms believing that they would not see the light of the day because the political majority would never allow it (unfavorable equilibrium beliefs).

## CASCADES AND CHANGING EQUILIBRIUM BELIEFS

The rapid and surprising nature of the discursive transformation was remarkable, which can be explained by cascade theories. Let us assume that some elites wish to initiate discursive liberalization so that one might openly refer to ideas and notions that were previously taboo. According to the cascade model, in order to succeed in this endeavor, the elites in question would have to change people's equilibrium beliefs of what the socially and politically dominant portion of society believe. Thus, if the individuals voicing a new discourse can cross a certain tipping point or reach a critical mass, they can then set into motion self-reinforcing changes called "cascade effects." In other words, they can initiate a discursive cascade. Earlier contributions to cascade theories asserted that it is almost impossible to know how likely and when a cascade may reach a tipping point.[24] Later studies focused on identifying the causal mechanisms producing the cascade effects and the facilitating conditions that increased the probability of a cascade; that is to say, even if we cannot know the exact point when a cascade may form, we can identify when and in which cases it may be most likely.[25] This increases the explanatory potential of cascade models.

I have identified two causal mechanisms that underlie discursive shifts, Interdependent Belief Changes, that is, remaking, and the Voicing of Held-Back Beliefs, that is, resurgence, as well as four facilitating conditions. These are listed in Table 5.3.

In order for my explanation to make sense, let me introduce the concept of civil beliefs and discourse, which I will distinguish both from private beliefs and discourse and, from a closely related but different concept, public beliefs and discourse. Private beliefs can be defined as those that people express among people whom they know and trust, and, thus, with minimum fear of social and political correctness. As cascade models emphasize, what people express openly can be misleading and very different from what people privately believe, because they may falsify their private beliefs outside of their private realm, especially, but not exclusively, in authoritarian regimes.[26] For instance, prior to a republican revolution, many may exaggerate their privately held loyalty to the monarchy; but in the postrevolution period, many may start overstating their private commitment to the republic.[27]

Hence, early research suggested that private beliefs are more real, stable, and consistent than what people express in *public*.[28] As I argued elsewhere, I believe this to be debatable.[29] Of course, there are many ways of defining "real beliefs," but let us assume that a belief is more real the more a person sustains this belief without regret and second thoughts. Based on this standard, in fact private beliefs may be less real because people often make statements in private that they come to regret or feel embarrassed about when they have to voice them in the company of strangers—and not merely due to the pressure of social/political norms. In this respect, private beliefs may also be less stable and coherent because they are less challenged. Among close friends, for example, a person may express many political beliefs that are not subject to scrutiny or careful consideration, especially if these friends have a limited interest in politics. Furthermore, different emotions and values such as fairness, care, and purity may be attached to the same belief when framed with different metaphors in different, more and less private social settings.[30] In this sense, besides holding onto deeply considered beliefs and opinions that they will defend even in the face of evidence proving the contrary, people might hold many "shallow" private beliefs and opinions that may change when challenged by counterarguments, contradicting evidence, and conflicting emotions. By contrast, in the presence of strangers, we might express beliefs that are more consistent with our emotions and principles.

Hence, I define "civil discourse" as what people write or say openly— that is to say, when their own identity is also known to others, which excludes many social media interactions where people feel "anonymous"— not just when communicating with "the people they know and trust. [Instead, it is] accessible to the entire public . . . .They have no control over who will be following what they have written or said."[31] Similarly, "civil beliefs and opinions" are those that people "express as part of their civil discourses."[32] The term *civil discourse* has an advantage over the term *public discourse,* which can be confused with political discourse and state or official discourse.

*Remaking* occurs when people change what they believe interde- pendently based on what others say and do. Since the dominant mechanism preventing change here is "horizontal restraints," meaning, restrictions

Table 5.3. Causal Mechanisms and Facilitating Conditions: Discursive Cascades

| **Causal Mechanism** | Interdependent Belief Changes: Remaking | Voicing of Held-Back Beliefs: Resurgence |
|---|---|---|
| **Dominant control mechanism** | Horizontal | Vertical |
| **Facilitating Conditions** | Low private belief resistance: shallow civil beliefs Powerful Network Effects | Low private belief resistance: thick suppressed beliefs |

people holding similar degrees of social and political status exercise upon each other (e.g., social norms and peer pressure), such changes would be the more likely the shallower the civil beliefs are and the more interconnected different peer groups are, that is, where there are powerful network effects. By contrast, the dominant control mechanism in *resurgence* is "vertical restraints," that is, restrictions imposed on individuals from above by people holding institutional and organizational power (e.g., an authoritarian state censoring speech). In this case, the facilitating condition is low private belief resistance. Here, strongly held but suppressed private beliefs may resurface with a vengeance when vertical pressures diminish or are overcome by powerful cascade effects.

Prior to the discursive transformation, some mainstream Turkish journalists had developed strong opinions on the Kurdish Question through the debates in which they had participated within the leftist movements of the 1960s. Some eschewed the use of the term *Kurd* in their civil discourse because of legal-political pressures, while others did so because they firmly believed in the hardline nationalist ideology. The former's civil discourse was subject to change through resurgence. But most people had little knowledge or had no strong opinions about the Kurds, as their only source of information about Turkey's ethnic diversity was the official education system, which avoided negative or positive references to the Kurds. Therefore, their civil beliefs were amenable to shifts through remaking.

## A Nonstandard Explanation of the Discursive Change

There were vertical restraints on the civil discourse before the transformation. The junta that had seized power on September 12, 1980, stepped aside in 1983. But the transition to civilian rule took place on the military's own terms and was guided. Semi-free multiparty elections in which only three parties vetted by the junta were allowed to participate were held, the military's favorite lost, and the victor, the newly founded Motherland Party ANAP of Turgut Özal, was permitted to assume power. Yet all this happened only following the approval of a new constitution in a referendum that institutionalized the military's praetorian powers and installed General Kenan Evren as president. Compared to Turkey's previous constitution— paradoxically, also proclaimed under military rule in 1961—the new one was highly restrictive in terms of civil and political freedoms in general and narrowed the legal space available for ethnic and religious politics.

In 1984, following the PKK's first attacks, full-scale military operations started in the predominantly Kurdish southeast. In reaction to how the news media were depicting the operations, the army organized a briefing and instructed members of the press on the appropriate language to use and on the news content. The army was particularly critical of the media's reference to the Kurdish category. According to the army, "Kurd" was "their expression," that is, the term preferred by the rebels. Therefore, the media's use of this term gave the impression that the security forces were battling Kurdish groups rather than "Marxist-Leninist rebels."

In 1987, a broader legal foundation was established for the direct or indirect censoring of the media when a state of emergency was declared in the southeastern provinces. In an unofficial meeting organized in 1990 with the participation of President Özal and high-level military officials, representatives of the media were warned about "irresponsible reporting and language."[33] The formal restrictions reached their peak with the passing of the Anti-Terror Law in 1991, which made it possible for all kinds of "separatist propaganda" to be punished by imprisonment.

Hence, the discursive shift that occurred in 1991–92 took place despite hard-liner attempts to control the discourse. In part, this shift might also have reflected a reaction against hard-line policies, or, perhaps, vice-versa. Even though restrictive laws were not always enforced, the threat of being labeled "pro-PKK" or "separatist" was generally sufficient for mainstream political actors, including journalists, to self-censor their own discourse. From this perspective, it is quite understandable why Ecevit defended his past attitude when asked why he had not made sufficient efforts to change the restrictive laws and practices. Ecevit stated that the Kurdist or separatist image could "glue itself to one's forehead and remain there."[34] This situation led to mainstream actors expressing their opinions indirectly and through coded words. In 1988, when defending the linguistic rights of the Kurds, Erdal İnönü did not once refer to the Kurdish category; without making a single reference to Kurdish, he stated that democracies should preserve "whatever are the mother tongues" of their people.[35] Even though most people could understand that he was talking about the Kurds, by distancing himself from certain terms and categories, he implied that he was operating within the mainstream (civil) framework and that his intention was to challenge the civil limitations from within, not from outside.

How then did the mainstream civil discourse shift in the face of such obstacles?

## INTER-ELITE DISPUTES, 1987–1990

In the formative period, splits within the ruling elites led to the emergence of a revolutionary, single-party authoritarian regime and a hegemonic discourse excluding Kurds. By contrast, in the semi-democratic multiparty context of the 1990s, inter-elite divisions led to discursive liberalization and bifurcation.

Ideational differentiations appeared among the elites in the period from 1987 to 1990, and moderate nationalists were able to influence civil discourse. Faced with the first PKK attacks, the initial reaction of the state was shock, followed by a purely military response. When it became clear that the PKK threat was only increasing, the moderate-hard-liner differences became increasingly visible.

At this time, one of the main fractures was between Prime Minister Özal, who later became president, and the hard-liners that dominated the military. From the start, Özal was against a hawkish military reaction that exaggerated the PKK threat. Özal also questioned paramilitary measures such as the deployment of rural guards. However, hard-liners in the military accused Özal of underestimating the PKK threat. They quoted Özal's 1984 speech in which he stated Turkey should not be afraid of a "handful of bandits." Moreover, they objected to issues of identity being discussed before the PKK rebellion had come to an end.

Özal was keen to enact reforms. He thought that regaining the Kurds (including those in Iraq) would be to Turkey's advantage and would increase its influence in the region. It would seem that he was already testing the water as early as in 1989, when he told the U.S. delegation that he was partially of Kurdish origin.[36] He encouraged President Bush to invade Iraq as he planned for the Turkish army to enter Mosul and Kirkuk—both inhabited by Kurds—so that it could help create a Kurdish domain in northern Iraq. Necip Torumtay, chief of the general staff, made his opposition to this idea known by handing in his resignation.

Within the scope of our theoretical argument, Özal was undoubtedly a nationalist, but a moderate one, because of his instrumental beliefs. To quote Cengiz Çandar, who at the time worked closely with Özal:

> Getting rid of Saddam . . . and Turkey having "political influence" over the new regime that will be established in Baghdad were very important for Turkey to appear as an influential player in the international arena and, most importantly, to guarantee its future.[37]

The difference lay in his instrumental beliefs, at least in Çandar's interpretation:

For this, it was imperative that there was a "Kurdish card." The "Turkmen card" was easy for Turkey to play, but it wasn't enough. The opening up to Iraqi Kurds would, perforce, also mean that Turkey had to face its own Kurdish Conflict and alter its customary official relations with its own Kurds . . . .Turkey could not become part of the Iraq equation through the Iraqi Turkmens, who were considered "ethnic brothers" according to the Turkish "nation-state" mentality. . . . [This is why Özal referred to "Iraqi peoples" and] stated that he would not distinguish between Iraqi Kurds and Turks of Cyprus, Western Thrace and Bulgaria.[38]

Çandar believes that Özal had a robust vision regarding the Kurdish Conflict.[39] At times, Özal approved the implementation of extremely harsh security measures against the separatists. However, in order to demystify and weaken the PKK, he defended having an open debate about the Kurdish Question.[40] Part of the strategy was to subtly encourage mainstream journalists to break taboos, such as conducting interviews with PKK leader Öcalan. One such interview conducted by Mehmet Ali Birand, a renowned journalist, hinted to other journalists that the norms of the civil discourse were being questioned from within. *Cumhuriyet*, a left-wing, Kemalist/ republican nationalist newspaper, broke another taboo and published news articles reporting on the abuses by the military during its struggle against the PKK. This was another example of intra-elite dispute, considering that Turkish journalists had long been activist members of the intelligentsia and acted as informers as well as opinion makers. There had been strong "party-press parallelisms" and the media functioned as platforms of elite recruitment, contestation, and deliberation.[41]

Özal was not the first actor to argue that the Kurdish identity should be respected. In 1987, Ecevit challenged public opinion by stating that the word *Kurd* should not be feared. As I mentioned earlier, SHP leader Erdal İnönü stood up for Kurdish rights without mentioning the Kurdish category. Moreover, İnönü, like many other politicians, realized that the PKK conflict could not be resolved through military measures. In 1991, the DYP-SHP coalition was presented with a golden opportunity to carry out reforms based on left-right (and thus partially secular/religious) elite cooperation. Prime Minister Süleyman Demirel declared that the state recognized the Kurdish identity (reality); but following the reaction of the military and of the public, he shelved the plan.[42] Demirel later expressed his bafflement with the public's reaction to his statement: "I didn't know that the Turks were so nationalist. There was a lot of violence, I couldn't do anything."[43] Nationalist beliefs, which can often be fueled by contexts of democratization[44] in unconsolidated democracies, was undermining discursive liberalization and encumbering conflict resolution. In 1991 and 1992, the PKK's "military" power climaxed. However, it then announced a unilateral truce, apparently because it failed in its goal of achieving the mass uprising (serhildan) it had been planning, in the face of the state's fierce military reaction. This created an opportunity for peace, and many people became hopeful of an end to the violence.

Without referring to the Kurdish category, Demirel also spoke of the need to make "them" "full citizens," and discussed eliminating the inequalities and harsh conditions prevalent in Kurdish areas and enabling the Kurds to feel equal as Kurds. Furthermore, he criticized the state oppression. Such attitudes were signs of an increasing inclination toward self-criticism among mainstream politicians and a quest for change. However, they failed to shift the civil discourse of a critical mass. When Mehmet Ali Eren—the SHP's MP for Tunceli—drew attention to the parallels between the Turks in Greece and Bulgaria and the Kurds in Turkey, other MPs accused him of violating the Constitution and being intoxicated.[45]

In comparison, Özal's 1990 statement to journalists about his Kurdish origins had a greater impact. First, Özal's statement was coming from the very top of the state. Second, Özal was effectively killing three birds with one stone by bringing his background into the limelight. He was making the Kurdish category undeniable, while also conveying a strong message to ethnic Kurds that he shared their identity. Moreover, he was underlining the legitimacy of the state, which had given him the opportunity to become president despite his ethnic origin. Therefore, he was appealing to different sensibilities simultaneously in a way that was hard to dismiss. Such mixed messages represented a significant step toward questioning the civil discourse from within without giving credit to hard-liner Kurds. Özal had also succeeded in creating a credible image in the eyes of the Kurds as being someone who had their best interests at heart.[46] Özal's attitudes created a powerful psychological effect.[47]

Still, the content analysis shows that the main discursive shift took place later, from 1991 to 1992. In fact, the immediate effect of Özal's statements led to a decrease in the use of the word *Kurd*, presumably because his rhetoric brought about a fear of legitimizing the PKK among other elites. Özal's influence had first to merge with two other factors before the discursive transformation would start.

## THE DISINTEGRATION OF THE COOPERATION BETWEEN KURDISH AND TURKISH LEFT-WING MODERATES

In 1989, seven SHP members were expelled from the party because of their participation in a Kurdish conference in Paris. This did not end the cooperation between Turkish and Kurdish left-wing moderates; it actually temporarily enhanced it. The expelled members founded the openly Kurdish political party, the HEP (People's Labor Party). On the eve of the general elections of November 1991, the SHP and the HEP established an electoral alliance, and HEP members ran for election on SHP lists. For the first time in Turkish democratic history, the cooperation among moderates was expanding to include an explicitly pro-Kurdish party, that is, a political actor that directly and openly voiced Kurdish demands. In the elections, the SHP achieved great success in the southeast, and twenty-two Kurdish MPs entered Turkey's Grand National Assembly under the SHP umbrella.

However, as a result of a series of actions by both sides, the cooperation collapsed and the dialogue ended. On November 6, 1991, before taking the oath, newly elected MP from HEP Hatip Dicle, speaking before Parliament, said: "I am being pressured to take this oath by the Constitution." This statement was met with loud protests. Session moderator Ali Rıza Septioğlu ordered that Dicle retract his previous statement and renew his oath for it to be deemed valid. Dicle was followed by Leyla Zana, who took her place at the lectern with a yellow, red, and green ribbon—the colors traditionally associated with the Kurds and the PKK flag. After taking the oath, she added in Kurdish: "I am taking this oath for the brotherhood of the Kurdish and Turkish peoples." Zana's words also met with loud protests in the hall, and she too had to return to the lectern, retract her previous statement, and renew her oath.[48] Whether the MPs in question were following the orders of the PKK (as prosecutors asserted in later years), or whether they had acted on their own initiative in the interests of brotherhood and against separatism, these events and their aftermath destroyed an important opportunity for cooperation.[49]

The HEP MPs were accused of separatism. Rather than discussing Leyla Zana's words about Turkish and Kurdish brotherhood, the debate focused on the colors of the ribbon on her head. It was not clear to what part of the oath Hatip Dicle was objecting. Was it the part that refers to "the indivisible integrity of the nation and the state" or the "indivisible integrity of the state"? Was he arguing for the recognition of different nations living within the same state or for the division of the state or its territory? It was impossible for such questions to be asked in an environment where even the term *Kurd* was a taboo in civil discourse and where there was very limited little public awareness of the Kurdish claims.

In such a climate, any SHP cooperation with the HEP was seen as nothing short of political suicide. Many HEP proposals, such as lifting the state of emergency in the southeast and debating cultural rights, were actually also embraced by the SHP.[50] However, it became impossible for such proposals to gain currency. In fact, the HEP was later banned by the Constitutional Court. Were these actions and their outcomes inevitable? Would it have made a difference had members of the HEP been more patient or had the public's reaction to the events been more cautious and matter-of-fact? I would answer yes in both cases. If the actors involved had made different decisions at the time, a different path might have been taken. Since these events might have transpired differently, the accompanying actions and decisions should be part of a causal explanation.

The breakup of the moderate-moderate cooperation had severe consequences. Trust between the moderates was undermined. In 1993, former members of the HEP founded the Democracy Party (DEP), which favored a hard-liner approach. The DEP, which defined the PKK as a political—i.e., legitimate—organization, was considered by both the state and the mainstream media to be an extension of the PKK.[51] Moderate Turkish nationalists who had held reservations about referring to the Kurdish category because they considered the Kurds to be part of the Turkish nation began to distance themselves from the Kurds. They began to see the Kurds as different, and were less reticent about using the word *Kurd* as a description of an ethnic other. In turn, hard-liner nationalists began referring more freely to the Kurdish category, as they now perceived their distrust of the Kurds as a distinct and unreliable group to have been vindicated.

Another chance for cooperation and peace initiatives arose in early 1993. The unilateral truce announced by the PKK in March sparked a mainstream debate and an elite rethinking of the Kurdish Question. However, in April 1993, Özal died of a sudden heart attack under suspicious circumstances. Then, in May, thirty-three unarmed soldiers were killed in a PKK attack. Öcalan first denied and then accepted PKK involvement. Many observers of the Kurdish Conflict see the hand of clandestine elements within the security state, or the so-called deep state, at work in these two events.[52] Afterward, violent conflict resurged with a vengeance. HEP MPs did not condemn the attack and interpreted it as part of a "war against Turkish colonialism."[53] Öcalan threatened to escalate the violence. The newly elected Prime Minister Tansu Çiller initially displayed a moderate stance. While campaigning in the eastern provinces, she voiced the possibility of providing education and radio and TV broadcasts in Kurdish to respond to the identity sensibilities of the Kurds. However, faced with escalating violence and stern opposition from the military, Çiller soon adopted a hard-liner approach. She handed carte blanche to the military to do as it pleased in its struggle against the PKK. Demirel declared that "cultural issues cannot be discussed as long as terror continues." The DYP's promises to its coalition partner the SHP of a democratization package were set aside.[54]

The final nail in the coffin of moderate-moderate cooperation came with Parliament's 1994 decision to remove the immunity of eight DEP parliamentarians who had entered Parliament on SHP lists. After the oath-taking crisis, relations had been further strained when the 1992 Nawruz celebrations were turned into an uprising by the PKK. The eight MPs did not distance themselves from the PKK and resigned from the SHP. After their immunity from prosecution was lifted, the parliamentarians were arrested, put on trial, and given long terms of imprisonment. The DEP was subsequently declared illegal and the party was shut down. Meanwhile, however, the People's Democracy Party (HADEP) had already been founded in its stead.

From 1994 to 1998, hard-line nationalist prerogatives reigned. During this period, security forces militarily isolated the PKK in the southeast. But this occurred at a very high cost economically, as well as in terms of human rights, and it led to the further politicization and radicalization of the Kurdish Question. The "total war" strategy of the Turkish hard-liners involved oppressing all Kurdish nationalists—regardless of whether they were moderate or not—as they were considered potential PKK members. The civil discourse regarding the Kurdish Question was suppressed by the state using legal, illegal, and extralegal instruments. Table 5.1 shows new lows in the number of articles about the Kurds. However, in contrast with the 1980s, the Kurdish category was now used in the debates. The vertical restraints no longer primarily targeted references to the Kurdish category; instead, they focused on talk that articulated Kurdish rights and demands.

THE EXTERNAL SECURITY ENVIRONMENT AND THE GULF WAR

Table 5.4 demonstrates that the years in which there was an increase in the recorded use of the word *Kurd* coincide with the years in which the number of articles published about external Kurds also increased. 1988 marked the beginning of the rise in the proportion of articles about domestic as well as external Kurds, and it was also the point when the use of the term *Kurd* increased in articles about domestic Kurds. However, both figures fell in the subsequent two years. In 1991 and 1992, there was a new upsurge in the number of articles published about the Kurds abroad.

External developments made it difficult for the Turkish elites to ignore the region's Kurdish reality (and therefore the Kurdish identity). In 1988, Saddam Hussein started the sinister Al-Anfal campaign against Iraqi Kurds, gassing thousands of them. Tens of thousands of Iraqi Kurds escaped to the Turkish border and their torment was covered in detail by the Turkish media. During this period, the Turkish media did not use the word *Kurd* and engaged in what may be described as discursive engineering, referring to the refugees instead as *Peshmerga,* a traditional term to refer to Kurdish tribal fighters.

Table 5.4. External Developments and Use of "Kurd" as a Domestic Category

| Year | Share of Articles on External Kurds in All Articles | Use of "Kurd" Within Articles on Domestic Kurds |
|------|------|------|
| 1984 | 0.14 | 0.11 |
| 1985 | 0.00 | 0.14 |
| 1986 | 0.17 | 0.20 |
| 1987 | 0.16 | 0.22 |
| 1988 | 0.55 | *0.29* |
| 1989 | 0.17 | 0.15 |
| 1990 | 0.10 | 0.14 |
| 1991 | 0.38 | *0.51* |
| 1992 | 0.25 | *0.44* |
| 1993 | 0.19 | 0.32 |
| 1994 | 0.24 | 0.29 |
| 1995 | 0.34 | 0.30 |
| 1996 | 0.38 | 0.25 |
| 1997 | 0.40 | 0.12 |
| 1998 | 0.35 | 0.20 |

Then, the First Gulf War, which started just before the 1991–92 transformation of the discourse, rendered it impossible to ignore the Kurdish category. In the aftermath of the war, the creation of a no-fly zone in Northern Iraq (not controlled by Baghdad) significantly changed once again the external conditions of the Kurdish Question. Iraqi Kurds, represented by the Kurdistan Democratic Party (KDP) and the Patriotic Union of Kurdistan (PUK), became the most important allies of the United States, as well as the region's most crucial actors. Mindful of the changing security environment in Northern Iraq and the ongoing PKK rebellion, President Özal took reconciliatory steps toward the Kurds as part of his plans to put into practice a more active Turkish foreign policy in Northern Iraq.[55] Meanwhile, surging Kurdish radicalization in Turkey's southeast was causing anxiety among the political and economic elites.

Envisaging the dissolution of Iraq, Özal was concerned that the Kurds would emerge from the crisis stronger. However, unlike the hard-line nationalists, he thought that Turkey's best response to the U.S.-backed Kurdish formations in Iraq would be to support them. This policy could also help address the economic hardships created in southeastern Turkey by the war in Iraq, which had previously been one of Turkey's foremost trading partners. Hence, by developing official relationships with Iraqi Kurdish leaders, Özal broke with a long-standing state policy. Ultimately, the change in Özal's and other elites' perceptions was also influenced by the end of the Cold War. They were considering how the country should acclimatize to a changing global environment that increased the salience of new ethnic and nonethnic actors on the international stage.

## Potential Effects of Discursive Changes on Intergroup Relations and Common Identities

### The Rival Image and the Consequences of the Kurdish Category Becoming Visible and Known

The theoretical framework of rival and compatible identity images I outlined in chapter 3 would predict that the replacement of "silence" with "visibility" with regard to the Kurds might produce two contrasting outcomes: recognition and acceptance, or, exclusion, boundary making and thickening (otherization), and stigmatization. Which outcome was more likely to materialize depended on whether the compatible or the

Table 5.5, Possible Consequences of Kurdish Category Entering Civil Discourse

| Dominant Image in Civil Discourse | Expected Impact on: | | | |
| --- | --- | --- | --- | --- |
| | Common Identities | Inter-Group Relations | Kurdish Identity | Kurdish Rights Freedoms |
| Rival Image | Weakened | Polarization | Strengthening for some Kurds and assimilation for others. | Lack of progress |
| Compatible Image | Strengthened | Integration | Strengthening | Progress |

rival image was dominant in the civil discourse. Table 5.5 summarizes these theoretically possible outcomes.

With the rival image dominant in civil discourse, the usage of the Kurdish category would weaken common identities and foster polarization. This is because many Kurds would have to make either/or choices between their Kurdish identity and their common identity, and the number of them embracing both identities would diminish. Meanwhile, non-Kurds would acquire a greater awareness of Kurds as an "other" that is different and competing with their own group identities, thus engaging in boundary thickening. Rival images would discourage intergroup mixing and investment in long-term relationships such as intermarriage and home ownership in mixed localities. By contrast, with the compatible image dominant, the opposite would take place. The increased visibility and awareness of the Kurdish category would not undermine plural identity attachments, intergroup mixing or investment in long-term relationships such as intermarriage because people (and their children) would not see the Kurdish identity as a rival or a threat to their other identities. Thus, by avoiding the need to make either/or choices between different identities, polarization would also be avoided.

It is hard to say whether either one of these images was strong in Turkey at the beginning of the 1990s. The suppression of both positive and negative judgments about the Kurds, which enabled "conditional upward mobility" (as long as they suppressed their ethnicity in their public involvements) for many Kurds, and, as I discussed in chapter 2, Kurds' being a "semi-mixed group" in Turkey, which limited the amount of knowledge Kurds and non-Kurds acquired about each other through social relations and day-to-day interactions, might have prevented the strengthening of any image. It appears, however, that the red flag was not the strength of rival images, but the weakness of compatible images and the weakness of norms of pluralism that would enable the creation of compatible images. Further, the problem was reformist actors' focus on issues other than addressing these weaknesses.

## Roadblocks on the Path of Recognition

### Weakly Pluralist Social and Political Norms and Discourse

It is not easy for new norms, beliefs, and causal narratives to be constructed out of thin air. Their historical, moral, philosophical, and intellectual foundations take time to establish and require civil debates that can address different groups' ontological insecurities.[56] When new norms are introduced, they can also be more effective and lasting if the civil debates producing them can build links with preexisting norms, values, and narratives that prevail in civil discourse and public memory, which people often take as reflecting moral and historical truths. The latter can be used as references to help justify, legitimize, and explain new norms to publics.

In Turkey during the 1990s, the discursive changes about Kurds did not extend to encompass a civil debate that properly addressed the ontological fears of both Turks and Kurds and generated new and pluralist norms by successfully making references to preexisting norms. It was either asserted that Turkishness was an ethnic (not national) identity (which was unacceptable to most Turks), and/or that the Kurdish identity would not be a threat to national cohesion simply because it would be subsumed under overarching national identities alternative to Turkishness such as Muslimness, Of-Turkey identity, or "citizenship of Turkey." In fact, without new norms, institutions, and policies that support the compatible image (and the notion of equal identities in a state-nation), these alternative identities might also come to represent the identity of the majority and confer secondary status to the Kurdish identity.

Two major references were used by the proponents of recognizing Kurdish difference to justify new norms about diversity: Europeanization and joining the European Union, and the so-called Ottoman heritage of multiculturalism.

As for the EU and Europeanization references, except for the period from 1999 to 2005, when Turkey's membership prospects looked relatively credible and which I will discuss later, the EU and Europeanization references did not have strong influence.[57] Either way, they could not be very effective against the "Sévres syndrome": a distrust of European intentions vis-à-vis Turkey, in reference to the Sévres treaty that led to the occupation and dismemberment of the Ottoman Empire at the end of World War I. Arguably, this distrust would only disappear completely were EU countries patently ready to embrace Turkey as a member, once Turkey fulfilled the membership criteria. However, Turkey's EU prospects were always weakened by weak policy commitments to full membership on both sides, among other reasons because they were not embedded in strong societal preferences favoring Turkey's accession.[58] Hence, statements by leading EU politicians such as Angela Merkel and Nicolas Sarkozy undermined Turkey's accession process from the very beginning, in addition to Turkey's democratic erosion and policies later.[59]

In turn, invoking the historical example, idiom, and metaphor of the Ottoman system, that is, the organization of Ottoman society, which featured a variety of different *millets*, had limited potential as a source of inspiration and justification. For, above all, Muslim and non-Muslim *millets* were not equal in the Ottoman Empire, both in a de jure and de facto sense, and nineteenth-century state attempts to establish de jure equality among all Ottoman "citizens" ended miserably. Intra-*millet* differences were not always respected; for example, Muslim minorities such as the Alevis were oppressed and not recognized within the Muslim *millet*. According to Karen Barkey, the notion of tolerance underlying the *millet* system did not translate into acceptance of differences among equals. It meant to keep those who are different separate and protected from tyranny.[60] In this sense, instituting rights inspired by the *millet* system carries traces of the Ottoman heritage where "that which is different was accepted but held separate, unequal and only tolerated."[61]

In fact, many scholars argued that the Ottoman legacy undermined the emergence of a nation-building model in Turkey that embraced ethnic/cultural and religious pluralism. For example, Ayhan Kaya states that, mirroring the dominance of the Muslim *millet* under the Ottomans, the Republic's ideal citizen reflected the "holy trinity of Sunni-Muslim-Turk." Thus, he argues, the discourse and belief prevailing among many Turks, that Turkey has a historically embedded culture of tolerance, is largely a myth.[62]

Similarly, talking about Kurdish "minority" rights made many Kurds uncomfortable for reasons related to Ottoman heritage. Aron Rodrigue argues that the modern Turkish understanding of "minority" (*azınlık*) lacks a "political language . . . [that is] needed to see and *accept* [emphasis mine] difference," that is to say, one that considers minorities as equal to and as valuable as the majority.[63] The dominant perception of minorities stems from the metamorphosis of the Ottoman *millet* category during the nation-state formation I discussed before. Partly as a result, it still implies a combination of difference, numerical and at times moral inferiority, and an ambiguous and precarious status of belonging to the nation.

What's more, there was no widespread civil debate about how to overcome the Sèvres syndrome. The Treaty of Sévres, a suburb of Paris, was signed by the last Ottoman Sultan's government in 1920. It had stipulated the total capitulation and dismemberment of Ottoman Turkey among new ethnonational states that would be founded, such as Armenian and, potentially, Kurdish states, territories under British, French, and Italian mandates, Greece, and a small Turkish rump state in Central Anatolia. The treaty was never formally approved by the (then closed) Ottoman parliament in Istanbul, was rejected by the "national" parliament in Ankara, and was later rendered defunct by the War of Independence.[64] Nevertheless, the public memory and particular interpretation of the treaty continue to foster diversity-phobic causal beliefs about ethnic pluralism and the intentions of Western powers vis-à-vis Turkey. According to these beliefs, unless ethnic expressions are carefully controlled by a strong, leviathan state, they might be manipulated by Western powers to dismember Turkey. There was no sufficient discussion during the 1990s to reinterpret history so as to discredit these causal beliefs.

Last but not least, there was no discussion of the plural meanings of *nation*. In other words, there was insufficient reckoning with the ideational bottlenecks that I started discussing in chapter 2 and which I will explore further in chapter 7. This does not mean, of course, that there were no historical and contemporary references that could form a basis for producing new diversity-friendly norms, from Muslim humanist Sufi poets and thinkers, such as Yunus Emre and Rumi, to Islam's "liberal" interpretations and interchanges with the pluralist Western traditions, and the "surpassing the level of contemporary civilization" standard that Atatürk had set for the nation, which could be understood as capturing the pluralist and minority-friendly standards of advanced liberal democracies in the context of the late twentieth century. However, these sources needed to be duly debated and reinterpreted so as to inform contemporary conditions in the civil sphere.

## Powerful Horizontal Restraints and Weak Self-Reflexive Civil Debates

Vertical restraints can be overcome to introduce new norms with the opposition of a relatively small elite group because it is easier to define targets, such as an authoritarian government or military rule. However, when horizontal restraints are in question, the path that leads to change goes through broad-based discussions and negotiations and the goals of the opposition become more complicated. In fact, most people are both the victims and the enforcers of these restraints. Hence, they must also question their own actions and norms. Turkey of the 1990s did not experience such broad-based and self-reflexive civil debates.

Horizontal restraints establish culturally specific signifiers and draw subtle borders between acceptable and unacceptable discourses and ideas. Usually, their trajectory can only be identified by observers and researchers with an astute and field-based familiarity with the social and political context. Word choices or specific pronunciations of words can signal membership in particular groups, for insiders, outsiders, or both. In Turkey, a person's use of words with an Ottoman Turkish origin for specific concepts—for instance, *millet* and *beynelmilel,* which mean nation and international—can signal one's political or social identity as being pious, conservative, or Islamic, while pro-secular, progressive, and left-wing persons would usually prefer to use the republican period Turkish synonyms of the same word—for instance, *ulus* and *uluslararası.* To give another example, PKK members and sympathizers, and people who view the PKK as a social/political movement, rather than merely a terrorist group, would pronounce the name "Pee-Kay-Kay," while most Turks, PKK-opponents and those who identify it as a terrorist group would pronounce it "Pa-Kuh-Kuh." Regardless of the content of one's speech, listeners could ascribe particular political identities and preferences to others based on these word and pronunciation choices, so many people would be careful in making these choices. When people are too afraid of being stigmatized based on their discourse through horizontal restrictions, a version of Gresham's law—the monetary principle that "bad money drives out good money"—can operate, too, in the civil sphere: demonstrably false beliefs and claims can remain unrivalled and enjoy civil acceptance if critics are too intimidated to confront these claims.

In such an environment, democratization cannot simply result from reforms that eliminate vertical restrictions, such as military tutelage. Such reforms would be ineffective against horizontal restrictions, and therefore could not eliminate the barriers to change that prevail in the civil discourse, and, thus, among civilian political actors.

## The Consequences of Seeing but not Recognizing Kurds

### SOCIAL NORMS, IMAGES, AND IDENTITIES

Vindicating the theoretical expectations above, when the Kurdish category became "visible" in the 1990s without the concurrent development of compatible images of Turkish and Kurdish identities, this fostered polarization (both between and among Turks and Kurds) and stalled progress of reforms.

For example, research conducted in the Aegean metropole of Izmir in 2006 and 2007 found that by that time, for many of the locals, Kurdish migrants had become a group subject to "exclusive recognition," that is, recognizing them with the consequence of excluding them, in daily life.[65] In in-depth interviews with locals, negative judgments about the Kurds were expressed by people from the middle classes, who were more likely to encounter Kurds in their daily lives. These negative judgments were not found among the upper classes, whose more privileged and sheltered housing complexes—a product of the neoliberal urban development of recent decades—rendered it less likely that they would encounter immigrant Kurds in their daily lives. One of the interviewees stated:

> [In the past] I didn't know much about the Kurds to tell you the truth. The only thing I knew was that . . . they live in the east, they have difficult lives, the problems they had with the state, etc. . . . [but] now you see them everywhere . . . .Frankly, I no longer think positively about them.[66]

Until the 1980s, the Kurds' migration to the western provinces was mostly economically motivated. The newly arrived migrants enjoyed greater opportunities for employment in these provinces thanks to the import-substitution industrialization policies of the time, which created less competition in the labor markets. Combined with the melting pot ideology that considered all Muslims as potential Turks, the Kurds came to constitute an invisible category. By contrast, the post-1980 migration was mostly motivated by necessity, hardship, and state coercion, byproducts of the war with the PKK and the state's hardline security policies. Combined with neoliberal economic policies, the slowing down of industrialization and the growth of the service sector, and the discursive changes, this wave of migration both gave rise to growing competition in labor markets and urban poverty and made Kurds a visible category. Absent strong pluralist norms, this cracked the door open for the development of anti-Kurdish perceptions along with a discourse that defined the Kurds as separatist, ignorant people who cut corners and made illicit profits.[67]

Still, the perception of the Kurdish Question as a predominantly political problem between the state and the Kurds, or between the state and the PKK, and not as a social problem or a clash of ethnic cultures, remained strong. Incidents that might potentially trigger widespread social clashes between Turks and Kurds remained isolated. Anti-Kurdish sentiments gained momentum among right-wing and left-wing ultra-nationalists with headlines such as "There isn't a Kurdish Conflict but a Kurdish Invasion," but could not become mainstream.[68] Sporadic but worrisome protests and lynching attempts occurred against Kurdish migrants in several western and central Anatolian towns. Racist and "racialized" discourses about the Kurds accompanied these events.[69]

In turn, one could imagine how the Kurds' own perceptions of their identity would be affected by being seen but not necessarily recognized as Kurds. My theoretical propositions expected that the propagation of the rival image would not significantly affect the identity perceptions and preferences of Kurds who identify themselves as exclusively Kurdish—that is, who have no attachment to common identities shared with Turks—are assimilated into Turkishness, or have social, political, and economic relationships bounded mainly by Kurds. However, the theoretical expectation was that many Kurds with multiple identity belongings and group relations would feel compelled to choose between their Kurdish and other identities and social relations—for example, by choosing between their Turkish and Kurdish friends—and at least some of them would begin to feel as exclusively Kurdish. Thus, the share of Kurds identifying exclusively as Kurdish would rise.

Indeed, survey and voting data indicate that the proportion of Kurds who exclusively self-identified as Kurds and voted for "Kurdish" parties increased throughout the 1990s. Table 5.6 presents the results of three national surveys conducted in 1996, 2002, and 2003–04.[70] In these years, respectively 9.24 percent, 11.35 percent, and 10.63 percent of all participants chose "Kurd" as one of their identities when picking from a list of ethnic, national, and religious categories, such as Turk, Kurd, Of-Turkey (*Türkiyeli*), and Muslim. These surveys almost certainly understated the real size of the total Kurdish population, on account of a variety of methodological shortcomings or respondent fears amid a violent political conflict. What concerns us here, however, is the ratio of those declaring multiple versus exclusive attachments to Kurdishness. The share of Kurds declaring exclusive Kurdishness rose from 2.71 percent to 5.76 percent and 5.20 percent in 1996, 2002, and 2003–04 respectively. In other words, it increased from less than one-third in 1996 to approximately one-half in 2002 and 2003–04.

Meanwhile, other Kurds could be expected to become more open to assimilation. We have indirect evidence that periods when the armed conflict escalated—and thus when the rival image can be expected to

Table 5.6. Kurdish Identity Perceptions and Votes for Pro-Kurdish
Political Parties

| Exclusive Kurdish / Plural Kurdish | | | Votes for HADEP-DEHAP | | |
|---|---|---|---|---|---|
| 1996 | 2002 | 2003–2004 | 1995 | 1999 | 2002 |
| 2.71 / 9.24 (Ratio = 0.29) | 5.76 / 11.35 (Ratio = 0.51) | 5.43 / 10.63 (Ratio = 0.51) | 4.17 | 4.74 | 6.23 |

gain ground—has had such an impact. In one study, two sets of in-depth
interviews were conducted with approximately three hundred inhabitants
of Izmir—half of whom were Turkish, with the other half being Kurdish.[71]
The first set of interviews was conducted in January 2011 (when the conflict was at a lower ebb), and the second in August 2011 (shortly after the
murder of thirteen soldiers by the PKK on July 14, 2011). Not surprisingly,
in the latter period, the social distance and negative judgments between
the Kurds and the Turks were greater, and social tolerance was lower. The
most informative finding for our purposes pertained to the statement,
"Some people should let go of highlighting ethnic identities and accept
that they are first and foremost citizens of the Republic of Turkey."[72] In
the conflict period, the support for this statement rose not only among
Turks but also among Kurds.[73]

Prime Minister Recep Tayyip Erdoğan greeting people in Diyarbakır, together with Masoud Barzani, President of the Kurdistan Regional Government of Northern Iraq, and renown Kurdish artist Şivan Perwer, November 16, 2013. Photo: Unknown photographer, various Turkish media outlets.

"Are Kurds a Nation?" An online newspaper headline from August 2013, representative of many others, during comprehensive constitutional reform talks in the parliament. The talks later failed among other reasons due to disagreements over the article defining citizenship (and Turkishness) and government proposals to switch to a presidential system. Photo: Unknown photographer.

Kurdish fighters in Baghouz, Northern Syria, the new focus of Turkey's "external security dilemma". March, 15, 2019. Photo: Shutterstock Item ID: 1454683397. https://www.shutterstock.com/image-photo/baghouz-north-east-syria-march-15-1454683397 .

One of President Erdoğan's highly symbolic projects, the new mosque in Istanbul's Taksim square, the focal point of pro-secular Gezi protests in 2013 (and for decades, of May 1, Labor Day rallies and others). Overshadowing the Republican Monument (featuring Atatürk) during construction in 2019. Surrounded by posters and an arc commemorating Atatürk's legacy following completion in 2021. November 10, Ataturk Memorial Day. Photos: Anna Zadrożna (first photo) and Kerem Öktem.

Kemal Kılıçdaroğlu, leader of the pro-secular, main opposition CHP (Republican People's Party) shaking hands with Selahattin Demirtaş, co-leader of the pro-Kurdish HDP (Peoples' Democratic Party), in prison awaiting trial since 2016 as of January 2022. October 16, 2015. Photo: Necati Savaş, Cumhuriyet, via Doruk Çakar and Murat Aksoy, Politikyol: www.politikyol.com.

(Clockwise) Selvi kılıçdaroğlu (wife of CHP leader Kemal Kılıçdaroğlu), Başak Demirtaş (wife of jailed Kurdish leader Selahattin Demirtaş), Dilek İmamoğlu (wife of Istanbul mayor Ekrem İmamoğlu) and Aygün Demirtaş (sister of Selahattin Demirtaş), August 16, 2019. New venues of dialogue, moderation and hope for future resolutions? Photo: Unknown photographer, via Doruk Çakar and Murat Aksoy, Politikyol: www.politikyol.com.

CHAPTER 6

# Return to Point Zero

## *Why Did the Peace Initiatives in the 2000s Fail?*

From 1999 onward came new opportunities to solve the three dilemmas, as well as new risks to add to those that had appeared in the 1990s. Indeed, many important legal reforms and discursive changes to address Kurdish demands took place during this period; yet, according to Kurdish nationalists' expectations, these were inadequate and insufficient. Even more importantly, in 2009 and 2013, the government initiated two major peace initiatives with the PKK to both solve the conflict and de-securitize the Kurdish Question. However, both Kurdish openings ultimately failed. Come the summer of 2015, violence between the PKK and state forces had resurged with a vengeance and government policies and the civil sphere had surrendered to hawkish and defensive-nationalist attitudes.[1]

Why did these attempts fail? Since 2015, a plethora of new "standard" stories have emerged to answer this question. In terms of their causal logic, these theories were very similar to those that claimed to explain the emergence of the conflict in the formative period. They either put the blame on "predetermined actor intentions"—this time involving new actors such as the AKP, President Erdoğan, Gülenist Islamists, the PKK, or the United States and other external actors—or they interpreted the conflict as being the "inevitable consequence of [Turkish and Kurdish] nationalism." However, this time it was not possible to put forward secularism, secular Turkish nationalism, or the military's nationalism as possible explanatory factors, as an increasingly religious/nationalist group of ruling elites, which were led by the AKP and its increasingly dominant and autocratic leader Recep Tayyip Erdoğan, was in power for most of the period and had over time subdued the military, too.

199

In this chapter, I will offer an alternative, nonstandard causal explanation and argue that the reasons for the failure were similar to those that explain the birth of the Kurdish Conflict in the formative period.

## RETURN TO POINT ZERO

The current transition and remaking of Turkey—and the domestic and external, structural, and ideational parameters of the conflict—bears a striking resemblance to its historical parallel—with all of the commensurate major accomplishments and flaws—almost a century ago, when the Ottoman Empire was dismantled, modern Turkey was founded, and the Middle East was remade. I labeled the first period, specifically the period of 1918–1926, the Kurdish Conflict's *formative* period. In turn, we can call the current period—which started in 2011[2] and is continuing—the *re-formative* period.

As we saw in previous chapters, in the formative period, a group of ambitious secular nationalist elites led by Mustafa Kemal (Ataturk) remade Turkey by building a secular republic. While the Kurdish Question was an important concern in the minds of these elites, it was overshadowed by other goals and concerns which they considered more important. These included building "secularism"[3] and a "Turkish" nation from an ethnically and culturally diverse target population, joining the emerging club of world nations as an equal member, preventing the return of the Ottoman *ancien régime,* and state security in the face of a Middle East in flux.

Almost a century later, during the last fifteen years or so, similar and arguably more opportune conditions have emerged for successfully addressing the structural dilemmas. Once again, however, the political elites have other priorities and dominant goals. This time, a new political class of "Muslim conservatives" and a new group of Islamists have taken center stage in Turkish politics, led by the AKP and Erdoğan. While the Kurdish resistance and conflict have been crucial concerns for them, they have been secondary to other political, ideological, and socioeconomic ambitions,[4] including the creation of a more Muslim, less secular, and less Western Turkish nation-state under—what evolved to be[5]—a would-be electoral authoritarian, competitive authoritarian, or neo-patrimonial regime.[6] And, once again, the external context is one of a Middle East in flux in the post–Arab Spring era, especially Syria with which Turkey shares its longest land border.

These external developments raised the possibility of a Kurdish nation-state or widespread autonomy, evoking the political/territorial uncertainties and changes of the formative period. The AKP enjoyed broad-based and cross-ideological support—including a honeymoon period with liberal and moderate secularist elites—and the backing of many Kurdish nationalists. This was similar to the popularity enjoyed by secularists during the War of Liberation—this time the common "enemy" being military tutelage plus rigid and "strong state"[7] structures. However, secularist/Islamist and intra-Islamist "formative rifts"[8] were alive and intensified afterward, particularly after 2013.

Further, the new elites' Islamist identity, their longing for the Ottoman past, and their ambition to refashion the national identity based on more religious (Sunni Islam) foundations all gave rise to new debates about Turkishness, which took priority over any debates revolving around Kurdishness. These triggered social and political attempts to promote alternative common identities, such as Islamic and Of-Turkey (*Türkiyeli*) identities in lieu of Turkishness. Hence, in this way too, this period resembled the formative era, when Turkishness was remade and became the official and dominant identity of the nation.

I will maintain that the main factor that undermined successful peacemaking was the failure to resolve, first, the common identity and elite cooperation dilemmas, and, after 2013, the external security dilemma, which was complicated again because of external developments, this time in Syria. Highlighting the structural difficulties of the dilemmas themselves, I will stress that the ideational bottlenecks that I introduced in the Introduction chapter and will elaborate in chapter 7, as well as Turkish Kurdish ideational gaps, help explain the political actors' failure to resolve the dilemmas.

## Opportunities for Resolving the Dilemmas

### Relative De-Securitization, Democratization, and EU Process

Toward the end of the millennium and into the 2000s, a combination of domestic and external developments contributed to the relative de-securitization of the Kurdish Conflict, political stability, and liberalization/

democratization. These created opportunities for the resolution of the elite cooperation by liberating civilian elites from military tutelage, thereby presenting a freer environment for negotiation and deliberation and offering EU recipes for consensus. The aforementioned developments also presented an opportunity to resolve the common identity dilemma by creating a more liberal public space for removing taboos, reconciling with history, and developing new and more inclusive identity constructions.

In 1998, when Turkey threatened to go to war with Syria, Öcalan was forced to leave Syria. He lived in exile first in Russia and later in Italy and, briefly, in Greece. Eventually, and with U.S. assistance, the Turkish National Intelligence Organization (MIT) captured him in Kenya, while he was making his way from the Greek embassy to the Nairobi airport. During his hearing, Öcalan was cooperative. He ordered the PKK forces to retreat from the country and announced that he was ready to cooperate with the state to resolve the conflict. His death sentence was commuted to life imprisonment upon the abolition of the death penalty in Turkey as part of the EU accession reforms.

This temporary cessation of the war with the PKK eliminated a major political obstacle that had undermined reforms throughout the 1990s: the fear of—and of being seen as—rewarding separatist violence. From 1998 to 2002, the percentage of Turkish citizens who considered "terror and security" to be the greatest threat dropped from 39.3 percent to 5.5 percent.[9] In the east, the state of emergency began to be lifted province by province.

At the end of 1999, the EU announced Turkey as a candidate for full membership. ANAP leader Mesut Yılmaz's statement that "the path to the European Union goes through Diyarbakır" signaled a new age. Moreover, Yılmaz criticized how broadly and without societal involvement the state interpreted the notion of national security. The EU process was a rare blessing because the Copenhagen criteria for membership—based on the rule of law and liberal democracy with minority rights—eliminated the need for politically divisive domestic debates about "which reforms will be made and to whose credit," by providing a ready road map that political parties could jointly support in the name of EU accession and democratization.[10]

Minister of Foreign Affairs Ismail Cem from DSP announced that TV and radio broadcasts in "mother tongues" other than Turkish should be legalized.[11] As part of the three extensive EU harmonization packages that the ANAP-DSP-MHP coalition enacted, constitutional barriers to broadcasts and education in Kurdish were removed. Military influence over the judiciary and the National Security Council was diminished. Shutting down "ethnic" parties—which Turkish Law deemed subversive—by the judiciary was made more difficult. Law No. 4771 was passed, which allowed broadcasts and education in private schools in "unofficial languages."

An economic shock and its political repercussions unrelated to the Kurdish Question interrupted this burgeoning reform process. In 2000 and 2001, Turkey suffered the deepest financial crisis of its history. With the support of the West and the IMF, the coalition government made wide-ranging reforms and strengthened financial institutions. While the economy shrank by 5.5 percent in real terms in 2001, it bounced back with 6.2 percent growth in 2002.[12] Yet, the coalition government committed political suicide by going for early elections before the fruits of the painful reforms had been felt by the electorate, who voted to leave all coalition parties and most other mainstream parties outside of parliament after the November 2002 elections. A 10 percent electoral threshold—a rule the 1980 military regime put in place to leave out Kurdish parties—was a key institutional factor that helped produce this outcome.

Only the CHP and the newly established AKP managed to enter parliament. The AKP gained 67 percent of the seats with 34.3 percent of the vote and formed a single-party government, thanks to the high threshold that had to be surpassed to win any seats. Thus, the pro-Kurdish DEHAP was not able to enter parliament with 6.21 percent of the votes, nor were sixteen other parties and independents that received a combined 46.2 percent of the votes—including a center-right party that received 9.54 percent of the votes. This weakened the representativeness and legitimacy of the political system and of the government, which would be needed to resolve such a long-festering problem as the Kurdish Conflict.

A new era had begun. In the 2002, 2007, and 2011 elections, the AKP became the first party in the history of the Republic to win three general elections with increasing votes (34.3, 46.5, and 49.8 percent respectively). Alongside these sweeping victories, it won three local elections, in 2004, 2009, and 2014, gaining 41.7, 38.4, and 45.4 percent respectively. In 2007 and 2010, the AKP won two historical constitutional amendment referendums, with the respective voting rates of 68.9 and 57.9 percent.

An average growth rate of 5 percent between 2003 and 2013 despite the 4.8 percent contraction in 2009 that resulted from the global financial crisis, and major improvements in public services such as health, were key to ensuring these electoral successes.[13] The AKP maintained the solid macroeconomic fundamentals put in place during the coalition period and had a zeal for neoliberal economic policies[14] and integration with world markets, which delivered significant domestic and international elite support for the government and foreign capital inflow into the economy.[15] Following legal/administrative reforms, EU accession talks officially began in 2005.[16] Despite many political crises and clashes with the opposition and judiciary, the government did not fall. The party obtained the backing of liberal democrats at home and the Western world outside, which was seeking positive examples of Islamist political actors who embrace democracy in the post–September 11 world.[17] Furthermore, AKP governments used their popular support to subdue the meddlesome military, albeit by using populist and polarizing politics and extralegal and illegal methods that subsequently sowed the seeds of democratic erosion.[18]

In a nutshell, elected AKP governments attained a level of decision-making power not previously achieved by other governments. Crucially, they managed to minimize the veto powers of the military, which was—together with Kurdish politicians' lack of autonomy from the PKK—a major barrier before the resolution of the elite cooperation dilemma. They obtained the autonomy to carry out policy as they willed even when the army disagreed.

## DEVELOPMENTS IN IRAQ

After initially exacerbating the PKK conflict, the developments in Iraq gave rise to an opportunity to resolve the external security dilemma by building trust-based and cooperative relations with external Kurds, whose appetite for a nation-state might be addressed with some sort of statehood short of full independence.

The U.S. invasion of Iraq in 2003 and the uncertainties that surfaced in the country thereafter rendered the KDP and the PUK critical actors in the region as well as major U.S. allies. Iraq's 2005 Constitution proclaimed Iraqi Kurdistan an autonomous state of Federal Iraq and Kurdish became the official language alongside Arabic. Under the Kurdistan Regional Government (KRG), Iraqi Kurdistan gradually started to become a de facto state. Meanwhile, the PKK found itself a safe harbor in Northern Iraq. However, Iraqi Kurds also vied with the PKK to lead Kurdish nationalism in the region. This contributed to the PKK's decision to end the ceasefire.[19]

However, all of these developments also generated an opportunity for Turkey to build a direct relationship with external Kurds. Establishing good relationships with Turkey would be wise for the Iraqi Kurds, both for their regional economic development and for the development of their autonomy from the central government in Baghdad. Iraqi Kurds were geographically and economically an extension of and dependent on Turkey.

Throughout the previous century, Turkey's policies that viewed Kurdish autonomy (let alone statehood) as a fundamental threat fed a perception that everything to the advantage of the Kurds was to the detriment of the Turks and alienated many Kurds from Turkey. The rival image was influential in a critical decision taken in March 2003, when Turkey's parliament rejected, by two votes, a government bill to allow U.S. troops through Turkey for the invasion of Iraq from the north. In addition to the strong antiwar sentiment among the Turkish public, many parliamentarians believed that allowing the United States to invade from the north would help Iraqi Kurds grow stronger and in turn foster separatism in Turkey.[20] As a result, Turkish-U.S. relations reached their lowest point since the Cyprus crisis (1955–1964).[21]

In fact, given that other countries of the region, such as Iran and Syria, were also against the founding of a Kurdish state, it was unlikely that autonomy would result in independence in the foreseeable future. Even if a Kurdish state were to spring to life, it would not immediately turn into a threat to Turkey's territorial integrity. Iraqi Kurds were going to want to maintain good relationships with their powerful neighbor to the north, who had been knocking on the EU's door, as Iraqi Kurds were economically dependent on Turkey. In other words, by developing economic ties with the Kurds and keeping its close relations with the EU, Turkey could minimize the chances of the autonomous Kurdish state becoming a threat to its territorial integrity. In any case, successful irredentist movements are quite rare across the globe.[22] Simultaneously, strong economic development in Northern Iraq would create a positive spillover effect in the southeast of Turkey. Hence, arguably, what really mattered was not whether a Kurdish state would be founded, but whether it would be hostile to Turkey.[23]

A PKK attack in 2007 provoked a nationwide reaction that caused the parliament to grant approval for a cross-border military operation in Iraq.[24] The U.S. government, which stepped into action to prevent Turkey, pressurized Iraqi Kurds to cooperate. In November, Prime Minister Erdoğan convened with U.S. President George W. Bush in Washington, and the United States actively started sharing intelligence about the PKK with Turkey. From 2008 onward, Turkey gradually developed a friendly relationship with the

KRG based on mutual dependence, in parallel with improved relations with the United States, and in 2010 Turkey opened a consulate in Erbil. Turkey had also tried to cooperate with Iraqi Kurds against the PKK in the 1990s, but this cooperation was limited to military assistance. By contrast, in 2011, "official" trade between Turkey and the KRG had surpassed 5.5 billion USD, and the turnover of Turkish companies in Northern Iraq totaled 3.5 billion USD. Thirty-five thousand workers from Turkey were working in Iraqi Kurdistan, including Dahuk and Sulaymaniyah.[25]

## PERIOD OF INACTION AND EXPERIMENTATION: 2002–08

In its first years in government, the AKP did not make much of an effort to address the Kurdish Question, except for lifting the state of emergency in those eastern provinces where it had not yet been lifted by the previous government and investing in social policies and infrastructure. The law granting freedom to air private broadcasts in Kurdish, which had been passed by the previous government, was put into effect in 2006. The reforms carried out between 2002 and 2005 were significant but below the expectations of the Kurds. Steps were not taken to address sensitive and complicated issues, such as amnesty for PKK members and the future of the PKK fighters, who were waiting in the mountains, gripping rifles.

Meanwhile, the PKK continued to recruit militants[26] but also faced inertia and uncertainty. In 2004, Osman Öcalan, Abdullah Öcalan's brother split from the PKK. DEHAP's loss of provinces such as Ağrı, Bingöl, and Siirt to the AKP during the 2004 local elections provoked concerns within the PKK that it was losing its base.[27] The PKK's conditions for negotiations were yet to be met. Simultaneously, the organization had to weigh up the opportunities and risks stemming from the developments in Iraq.

In mid-2004, the PKK cancelled its unilateral ceasefire, and clashes restarted. Only then did the AKP government begin to publicly address Kurdish grievances. In August 2005, Erdoğan delivered a historic speech of reconciliation in Diyarbakır. He acknowledged the past mistakes of the state and stressed the socioeconomic investments being made in the region. He also referred to the "Kurdish Problem" (Kürt Sorunu), that is, he acknowledged the Kurdishness of the problem, but later seemed to take back his statement.[28]

Contrary to his 2011 speech six years later, Erdoğan did not mention religion and Muslim brotherhood in this speech. Instead, he emphasized his wish to resolve the conflict based on democratization, the identity of

"Republic of Turkey Citizenship" (as stated by President Demirel in the 1990s), and socioeconomic development.

> [B]ecause the sun warms everyone, and the rain is a benediction to all. Because everyone belongs to the same land. This is what it means to be a nation. That is why I tell those who ask the question: "What about the Kurdish Problem?" As the Prime Minister of this country, this conflict is—above and beyond all, first and foremost—my problem. We are a great state and with the fundamental principles and tenets of the Republic bequeathed onto us by those who founded this country, we will resolve every issue within the scope of the constitutional system with more democracy, more citizenship rights and more welfare . . . .We have three red lines. And there is no space for ethnic nationalism, regional nationalism and religious nationalism. Everyone can be proud of their identity, but no one can state that they are superior. There is only one supra-identity and that is the [citizenship] bond with the Republic of Turkey.[29]

Hence, in 2005, Erdoğan specifically rejected "ethnic, regional and religious nationalism," whereas, as we will see, in his 2011 speech, he went on to condemn "all nationalisms." Notwithstanding the rhetoric, however, we will see that in both speeches, a kind of Sunni Muslim Turkey nationalism was apparent in the background. Hence, there was no indication that Erdoğan had any solution for Turkey's ideational bottlenecks related to key concepts such as nation and sovereignty, beyond giving them a more Islamized frame. Erdoğan's statements about the Kurdish Question followed a contradictory and confusing course; at times he even denied the existence of the question, as he would do again ten years later following the ending of the 2015 peace process.

Less than a year after his 2005 Diyarbakır visit, the city was shaken by the funerals of PKK members whom the PKK claimed had been murdered with chemical weapons. A call was sent out to "claim the bodies."[30] In the aftermath, PKK attacks and consequent losses began to surge.

These were the years when the AKP prioritized consolidating its own power. Electoral incentives would begin to change things when the AKP realized that Kurdish votes might be instrumental to their becoming the dominant party. As Table 6.1 shows, in the 2007 elections, the AKP came first in the eastern provinces with predominantly Kurdish constituencies;[31]

Table 6.1. AKP, DEHAP (2002) and DTP (2007) votes in the eastern Provinces with major Kurdish populations*

| | Total AKP | % AKP votes | Number of AKP MPs | Total Kurdish party votes | % Kurdish party votes | Number of Kurdish MPs |
|---|---|---|---|---|---|---|
| **2002** | 550,807 | 20.29 | 50 | 936,823 | 34.51 | 0 |
| **2007** | 1,470,502 | 49.25 | 52 | 898,783 | 30.10 | 20 |

*The provinces where the pro-Kurdish party received more than 10 percent of the votes in 2002 were Adıyaman, Ağrı, Ardahan, Batman, Bingöl, Bitlis, Diyarbakır, Hakkari, Iğdır, Kars, Mardin, Muş, Şanlıurfa, Siirt, Şırnak, Tunceli and Van. Calculated from the official election data.

between 2002 and 2007, the party almost tripled its votes in these provinces. The AKP benefited from introducing a new approach to the relationship between the state and society and the Kurdish Question—at least on a discursive level—and took advantage of the weak performance of its rivals, including the Democratic Society Party (DTP).

Attempts to transform the region into a food industry hub to maintain the Middle Eastern markets, primarily Iraq, met with mixed results, except for Gaziantep, which became an important center. As economic development in Diyarbakır steered toward the construction industry, the manufacturing industry experienced restricted growth; its exports to Iraq—which became a large market after the U.S. invasion—failed to grow sufficiently.[32] However, the government improved the conditions of the region's poor through better health services and developments in rural infrastructure. It was building an image of being a government whose policies focused less on security and more on the human needs of the local community.[33] At the same time, the AKP was gaining an image that it could challenge the status quo by openly challenging the army, and spreading the message that it could bring about a peaceful resolution through its Kurdish party members.

The party also benefited from the rise of Islamic conservatism in the region.[34] From the 1990s onward—the end of the Cold War—secular leftist Kurdish political actors from the PKK to the BDP also adapted to this situation and tried to win over Islamic voters. For example, the BDP attempted to do so with an emphasis on Islamic discourse and by organizing "civilian [i.e., not organized by the nationwide public agency Diyanet, which regulates Muslim religious affairs] Friday prayers."[35] The AKP government responded by recruiting traditional Kurdish imams, known as *mele,* to the Diyanet and directed harsh criticisms at the BDP.[36]

An important reform was made with the foundation of TRT 6, the first official TV channel in Kurdish, which went live in January 2009.[37] While this represented a historic progressive step in the eyes of the government and liberal-minded Turks, it was viewed as a rather humble step for many Kurds. Hence, by the March 2009 local elections, the AKP was facing diminishing support in the eastern provinces.

## First Resolution Attempt: The 2009 Opening

In May 2009, Öcalan made an announcement from the prison on İmralı Island that he would present a roadmap to resolve the Kurdish Question.

Shortly before this, the DTP had revealed its democratic autonomy projects.[38] The minister of the interior announced in July that the government had its own plans. Commentators generally coined this period the "Kurdish opening," while the government called it the "democratic initiative" or the "national unity project" in order to fend off the criticisms. The government later admitted that it had been negotiating with Öcalan and "indirectly" with the PKK.[39]

However, the government did not seem to have a very clear roadmap. It presented some important tangible proposals, such as a more generous pardon for PKK supporters, Kurdish education in state schools (at university level), changing back into Kurdish the Turkified place names in the east, and a new and democratic constitution. Optional Kurdish courses were opened in many universities, as was education of Kurdish in private schools. In December 2009, the Council of Higher Education (YÖK) decided to establish an institute at Mardin Artuklu University focusing on Kurdish, Assyrian, and Arab languages and literatures—tellingly naming it the "Living Languages Institute" (Yaşayan Diller Enstitüsü).[40] However, beyond these measures, it was not really possible to talk of a coherent set of reform plans, let alone one aimed at resolving the three dilemmas.

In October 2009, when the first group of PKK fighters entered the Habur Border Gate in order to surrender as a symbolic gesture, the massive crowds of PKK-cheering Kurds welcoming them generated a spectacle. When these images were broadcast, they were met with indignation among the Turkish public. Moreover, when the arrested PKK members were subsequently released by a makeshift court set up at the border, the resolution process arguably got off on the wrong foot from the get-go. The initiative set into motion far-reaching deliberations and public debates, which included the possibility of Kurdish independence.[41] However, serious doubts remained among the bases of both the AKP and the opposition.[42] The government's initiative did not introduce to the public any new values, symbols, or principles with which to make sense of the change. Mehmet Zekai Özcan, an MP from the AKP (who later resigned and joined MHP), stated that the initiative was void of tangible content, that the unitary state was being questioned, and that the DTP, which he called an extension of the PKK, had started talking about a second flag.[43]

The priority for the government and for the Turkish public was that the PKK lay down their arms, if not disarm completely. However, the PKK had very different expectations. For Öcalan's three-stage democratic resolution proposal, "retreating across the border" (not disarmament)

would take place after the founding of an investigation and justice commission within the parliament and the simultaneous release of "arrested
and imprisoned" PKK members; all of this would be audited by a commission formed of representatives from the United States, the EU, and
the KRG. The third stage would entail finding solutions to the Kurdish
Conflict through constitutional changes, whereupon armed struggle would
no longer be needed.[44]

Within a few months, the death of the initiative was announced.
While some had perceived the initiative as a "betrayal," others had seen
it as a new initiative to purge the Kurdish opposition. In December, the
Constitutional Court decided to shut down the DTP claiming that it posed
a threat to the integrity of the state in an environment where there was
danger of widespread street fighting. The activities of the KCK (Kurdistan
Communities Union)—a parallel administrative organization established
by the PKK to form the organizational basis of future autonomy—which
started in April 2009, even before the peace initiative had been placed
on the table, played an important role in this decision. With these operations, thousands were arrested, among whom were Kurdish activists and
politicians who were members of the BDP (Peace and Democracy Party,
which was founded after the DTP was closed down), as well as some
pro-Kurdish or pro-peace intellectuals.[45]

The KCK was founded by the PKK in 2005 and took its final form
in 2007. Hence, already in 2005:

> A number of "Free Citizen Councils" [sic] were organized . . . a
> Democratic Society Congress (Demokratik Toplum Kon-
> gresi, DTK) was founded in 2007, which acted as a kind of
> shadow parliament, although it only held its first congress in
> 2011 . . . various local councils were established to arbitrate
> in domestic cases, including blood feuds, divorces, domestic
> violence and honor killings.[46]

All this was to serve the purpose of forming autonomous administrative structures based on decentralization from Ankara across Kurdistan
without changing any official state boundaries.[47] On one hand, most of the
visible agents of the KCK were elected municipal officials; on the other
hand, they were assuming functions for which they were not necessarily
elected, that is to say, beyond the official and legitimate structures of the
state. In other words, the KCK was an attempt by the PKK, the pro-Kurdish

legal party, and the Kurds supporting them to build de facto autonomous governing structures—including illegal People's Defence Forces (HPG)—that were not based on any agreement with the existing Turkish state or with the Turkish majority. This process had an important place in Öcalan's three-stage democratic resolution plan[48] to establish "democratic confederalism," inspired by Murray Bookchin's idea of a "commune of communes."[49]

This is not to say that the 2009 opening bore no fruit. Both the initiative itself and some symbolic steps taken by the government were highly significant in terms of mending the relationship between the state and the Kurds.[50] For example, in 2011 the government changed the name of the military barracks in Özalp, Van,[50] from Mustafa Muğlalı—a general convicted of ordering the extrajudicial execution of thirty-three villagers in 1943. This sent out an important message to the Kurds. In the same year, Erdoğan apologizing on behalf of the state for the Dersim/Tunceli massacres of 1937–38—even though his primary motivation appeared to be to exploit the ongoing disagreements about history within the CHP—was highly significant for the people of the region. This gave Kurdish actors the courage and confidence to press charges over the unidentified (extrajudicial) murders of the 1990s. With the efforts of the Kurdish activists who wanted to enforce change, significant increases were seen in the number of children, streets, and roads being given Kurdish names (a considerable number of them were named after PKK members).[52] At the same time, one should note that, to this day, AKP governments have not apologized for or taken any effective steps to bring to account the perpetrators of state violence and human rights violations, such as the 2011 Uludere (Roboski) incident,[53] when Turkish jets bombed and killed thirty-four Kurdish villagers/smugglers of Turkish nationality along the Turkish-Iraqi border, which took place under the AKP government's authority, much to the chagrin of many Kurds.

## SECOND ATTEMPT: THE 2013 OPENING

This second and most extensive Kurdish peace initiative officially started in January 2013 when two pro-Kurdish party members held a meeting with Abdullah Öcalan in his prison cell, and then Erdoğan announced in the following month that Hakan Fidan, the head of the MIT national intelligence organization, had also met with Öcalan.[54] It was later revealed that indirect talks and negotiations with the PKK had been taking place in Oslo, Norway, since 2010, possibly even earlier.[55]

The 2013 opening went well beyond any previous attempt. Discursively, it represented radical change as the government openly negotiated with the pro-Kurdish party in a bid to work out a resolution, it acknowledged the indirect talks with the PKK and Öcalan (through the pro-Kurdish party and other channels), and partially involved the Kurdish members of the AKP in the process—the term *partially* is used here because the Kurdish AKP members were consulted as individuals, not as a caucus. The opening included attempts at preparing society and public opinion for peace by forming a "Wise People Committee," which consisted of journalists, artists, academics, and other opinion makers, although these were government-picked and excluded the opposition. This committee operated more as a government emissary and less as an intermediary between society and government or as a neutral arbiter. The opening produced some important reforms, such as the legalization of electoral campaigning, self-defense in courts, and education in private schools in Kurdish based on the legal category of "mother-tongues" that included Kurdish as well as other local languages.[56] The two sides tried to officialize the process first, by passing a law of immunity for state functionaries negotiating on behalf of the state, and then, by producing a memorandum of understanding specifying the scope, goals, and fundamental concepts of peace. The memorandum was signed by the government and the pro-Kurdish party (which indirectly represented the PKK) and announced on February 28, 2015, in the late-Ottoman Dolmabahçe Palace in Istanbul.

By that time, however, the process was already half-dead. Less than a month after the Dolmabahçe declaration, Erdoğan, now president of the republic, went back to the discourse of "there is no Kurdish Question in Turkey." Growing rifts had long been appearing between the Kurdish side and the government, as well as—in line with my argument in this book—within the "Turkish" side, including the government itself. After the June 2015 elections, when the AKP lost its majority, a spree of terror attacks against Kurds and pro-Kurd leftists, random civilians, and security forces took control of the country. The government capitalized on these attacks to crack down on all opposition and to wage a scorched-earth campaign against Kurdish militants in southeastern provinces. The "violence"—the sources and perpetrators of which are yet to be fully uncovered, with the main opposition blaming the government as well as the PKK and other nonstate organizations such as ISIS (Islamic State of Iraq and the Levant)—only began to subside after the AKP regained its majority in the repeat elections[57] of November of that year, upon which full-fledged clashes restarted between the state and the PKK. The AKP formed an informal coalition with the Turkish nationalist MHP (Nationalist Action Party), and adopted hawkish nationalist discourse and policies vis-à-vis the Kurdish Conflict and Question.

## Why Did the Resolution Attempts Fail? Unresolved, Deepening, and Diversifying Elite Cooperation Dilemma

### DEEPENING RELIGIOUS/SECULAR ELITE RIFT

The AKP's coming to power was a major opportunity to bridge Turkey's secularist/Islamist cleavage. The AKP was Turkey's first party with explicit roots in political Islamism to govern on its own, and even subdued the meddlesome military. Hence, had it governed in a more inclusive fashion, advanced pluralistic democracy and rule of law, and strengthened not only religious but also secular freedoms, this might have eradicated the religious/secular distrust.

On the contrary, however, the elite disunity, distrust, and polarization deepened under the AKP. The more the party consolidated its power, the more it felt emboldened and saw itself as a revolutionary party with a mandate to remake Turkey and the Turkish state based on a more Islamic model.[58] Hence, similar to the situation during the formative period a century ago, the government's Kurdish openings were secondary and instrumental to this overarching and self-anointed mission. Although there is no reason to think that AKP governments lacked a genuine interest in resolving the conflict as long as it was not politically too costly, they only took risks and serious steps toward this purpose when they saw an opportunity to electorally and institutionally dominate secularist elites by doing so. They had no clear recipes for addressing the three dilemmas and abandoned their peace efforts whenever they felt that Turkish-Kurdish peace efforts no longer looked like serving their goal of marginalizing the pro-secular opposition and achieving and consolidating elite dominance.

The coalition government that ruled between 1999 and 2002, formed by one pro-secular Center-Left, one Center-Right and one extreme-Right party (the last two representing major segments of religious/conservative constituencies) represented a significant case of elite cooperation across the secular/religious cleavage—even though the coalition excluded Islamist parties. The latter were dealt a heavy blow by the 1997 military intervention against the Islamist-led government and seen as the black sheep of mainstream politics. Secularist and Islamist elites for some time could cooperate more or less successfully after 2002, when the AKP came to power. The AKP was an offshoot of the banned Islamist party, but now called itself "conservative democrats" and avoided Islamist themes in civil discourse. Reform packages required to gain EU membership were generally passed through cross-party collaborations. Many liberal secular elites worked within the AKP or supported it from outside in the name of democratization and EU reforms. Still, many hardline secularist actors were suspicious that the government had a hidden Islamist agenda. However, they felt reassured by the existence of a secularist military and judiciary that drew a line on what the government could do vis-à-vis secularism. That was until 2007.

In the previous chapters, I have already discussed the origins of the secular/religious elite distrust in the formative period. It would be useful to summarize the developments since then in order to understand the division in 2007. In 1950, Turkey peacefully transitioned from an authoritarian single-party regime under the secularist CHP to multiparty democracy. External incentives were very important in motivating the transition: Western nation-states with which the CHP was seeking association in the context of an emerging Cold War had adopted democratic regimes in the aftermath of World War II. However, the transition was mainly a domestic affair presided over by Kemal Ataturk's comrade President İnönü. It reflected the founding elites' relatively democratic management of the deepening divisions occurring among themselves, which arose mainly with regard to economic policy, religion, and authoritarianism. To resolve these rifts, they reached an agreement on "going to the people," as the arbiters, based on free and fair elections. Hence, the transition resulted from successful elite cooperation between radical/revolutionary secularist elites dominating the CHP and the evolutionary/secularist and economically liberal and socially conservative elites, who split from the CHP and founded the Democrat Party (DP). This process was ideationally facilitated by the populist, republican, and modernist facets of the CHP's ideology, which allowed and justified electoral democracy (the other principles being nationalism, revolutionism, and laicism).[59] While Islamists were not part of this elite pact, at least not openly, later on both the DP and to a lesser degree the CHP courted the religious-conservative populace as well as Sufi orders and Islamists in a bid to win elections.

Hence, between 1950 and the 2000s, on the surface there was considerable de facto power sharing, cooperation, and compromise, as well as both Islamist and secularist moderation—Islamist elites adapted to the secular constitutional order and competitive politics, while secularists moderated their skepticism of public and political religion.[60] For example, the number of mosques, Quran courses, and religious high schools increased consistently with state support, and the call to prayer, which had been vernacularized briefly under the single-party rule, was changed back to Arabic. Officially banned Sufi orders—which in later years would be dominated by the Gülenist movement—became increasingly vital in social, economic, and political life through informal channels.[61]

When the CHP lost the 1950 elections, it peacefully handed over power to the DP, which represented religious interests.[62] Had power peacefully rotated back to the CHP through elections at the end of the decade, by which time the DP had become increasingly populist/authoritarian, liberal democracy might have been consolidated. Hence, it is conceivable that the religious-secular elites' distrust could also have been mended successfully then. However, what looked to some elites like an established (social/cultural) revolution that culminated in a successful transition to democracy was viewed by other elites as an "unfinished revolution."[63] A secularist military coup in 1960 prevented any possible reestablishment of elite unity based on democratic procedures by "going to the people." The coup initiated a pattern whereby the pro-secular military would supervise civilian politics from above and, on several occasions, temporarily overthrow elected governments and multiparty democracy—and thus the possibility of religious and secular elite reconciliation—in 1971, 1980, and 1997.[64] In addition, peaceful multiparty politics was increasingly troubled by growing Left/Right polarization and a spiral of violence on the streets in a context of rapid urbanization and industrialization.[65]

Against this backdrop, despite some efforts to do so, civilian elites did not, or could not, translate their de facto and practical power sharing and cooperation into de jure, programmatic, intellectual, and ideological reconciliation. They continued to interpret the past and the present through incompatible lenses and using clashing narratives—that is, in terms of the theoretical frame I introduced, through "rival and clashing images." They saw de facto compromises as concessions to be taken back in the future, rather than as the necessary compromises of democracy and coexistence.[66] Both sides remained conditional and instrumental democrats, believing that the future belonged to them.[67] Fragile cooperation, low trust, and weak consensus over "restrained partisanship" and power sharing, which prevailed among rival political elites, periodically polarized and destabilized Turkish democracy throughout this period.[68]

By the time the AKP came to power, the secular elites were also in a state of ideological inertia. The leftist movement, which since the 1960s had become the most dynamic segment of the secularist side without relying on the state (and in fact in opposition to the state) had been subjected to severe crackdowns by the 1980–83 military regime, which also promoted pro-state formations of Islamism.[69]

The coalition government, led by the Islamist Welfare Party and its leader Necmettin Erbakan, was forced to resign by a "postmodern coup" in 1997. Then, the younger and more pragmatic generation of Islamists, which were open to economic neoliberalism, linked with an emerging Islamic/conservative bourgeoisie and, led by Erdoğan, parted company with Erbakan, and founded the AKP in 2001.[70] In the same year, the Western world entered the post–September 11, 2001, context, when the AKP's "moderate Islamist" outlook would become increasingly more welcomed by a West that was eagerly seeking "moderate Islamists" at home, seeing democracy as an antidote to Islamic extremism.[71] The AKP elites also benefited from the fact that they were not considered politically responsible for the dirty PKK war or associated with the resulting political and economic corruption of the 1990s, which had dilapidated the mainstream secularist elites.

This does not mean there were no political or intellectual efforts to develop more liberal visions of secularism and citizenship, and to establish greater trust and cooperation with religious conservative and Islamist elites in order to resolve the Kurdish Conflict. In addition to efforts within the SHP and CHP,[72] the New Democracy Movement (YDH) of the mid-1990s was an important endeavor, which also prepared solution proposals that addressed the three dilemmas.[73] However, the YDH (and other efforts)[74] failed to construct a new and more liberal base for secularist elites, with the YDH garnering only 0.5 percent of the votes in 1995, amid the PKK war—a time when the public had little appetite for liberal solutions. In a nutshell, new and old political parties ultimately failed to successfully act as ideational "carriers"[75] between "politics"[76] and the civil society's demand for religious-secular reconciliation on the basis of an inclusive and stable democracy. Hence, by the early 2000s, secularist elites had become divided between moderate-liberal and hardline nationalist secularists, while the Islamist elites had achieved more internal unity based on the AKP. The latter attracted the sympathy and support of moderate-liberal secularists and the passive acceptance of radical secularists, in a context where the EU membership process and the veto powers of a secularist president, judiciary, and military still provided insurances against creeping Islamization.[77]

These conditions changed for political reasons, when the time arrived for the parliament's election of a new president in spring 2007. The AKP nominated as their candidate Abdullah Gül—the most important name in the party after Erdoğan. The hardline secularists were up in arms. The army published an ultimatum on its website and sent out stern warnings to the government. The secularists organized mass antigovernment rallies in protest and in defense of "secularism." The AKP did not cave in and won a landslide victory, receiving 47 percent of the votes in the July general elections. Soon afterward, Gül was elected president.

However, this did not stem the social and political polarization to come. The hitherto somewhat subdued "formative rift" in the religious/secular fault line was activated.[78] It would take a separate book to analyze all of the crises and swings of democracy that were to take place over the following decade. The result was a "downward spiral of polarizing politics coupled with democratic erosion." The AKP grew increasingly confident and populist; the secularist opposition reinforced the polarization with its own defensive mobilization, and the AKP was transformed from a potentially reformist to a revolutionary polarizing party.[79]

As a result, when the initiatives of 2009 and 2013 took place, secular and Islamist modernizing elites were not able to cooperate to attempt to resolve the Kurdish Question. On the contrary, they were engaged in a bitter battle for dominance, in the context of which the Kurdish Conflict had only secondary and instrumental significance.

Turkey became one of the most polarized countries in the world; first, based on a vague religious/secular dimension, and then, increasingly based on a partisan cleavage that pitted the supporters and opponents of Erdoğan (and his AKP) against each other.[80] A fiery and hostile rhetoric took hold of politics. The exchange between CHP leader Kemal Kılıçdaroğlu and President Erdoğan at the very beginning of the 2013 initiative should suffice to describe the lack of cooperation between the government rooted in political Islamism and the pro-secular main opposition. When the opening officially started, Kılıçdaroğlu declared his support, stating that "despite all its mistakes in the past, we offer [the AKP] new credit. Solve the problem." In a nonpolarized setting with more political elite unity, this gesture from the opposition would have been welcomed by the government, which after all had just embarked on a politically risky undertaking. However, the next day, Erdoğan's response was less than appreciative of the main opposition party's support: "Who do you think you are offering credit," he said. "You need credit yourself."[81] The consequences of such distrust or antagonism could be anticipated. The opposition, except for the far-right MHP, backed the process, but only with a sense of unease and making frequent criticisms of its lack of transparency, parliamentary oversight, and uncertain objectives. The initiative lacked the opposition parties' intellectual input, as well as the potential contribution they might have made by mobilizing their own constituencies in favor of the peace process.

More consequentially, the elite disunity severely weakened the government's own commitment to the peace process. Even though there is no reason to think that the government's interest in resolving the conflict was insincere, the peace initiatives were instrumental to the government's prioritized objective of amassing sufficient power to remake the country.

In particular, the government's interest in resolving the Kurdish Conflict appears to have been secondary to its interest in a super-presidential system and changing the constitution for ideological reasons as well as, arguably, a thirst for power and self-aggrandizement and a failure to find power-sharing compromises with the opposition. Many social and legal/political changes that the AKP wanted to secure in order to transform Turkey based on—call it *Islamic* or something else—prescriptions required constitutional changes. Similarly, they would benefit from an AKP-controlled and all-powerful president who could make crucial executive decisions without being subject to parliamentary or judiciary vetoing. Despite its electoral achievements, however, the AKP failed to obtain the parliamentary supermajority it needed to change the constitution on its own. Kurdish votes could deliver such a majority. In fact, the beginning of the peace process coincides with the failure and dissolution of an interparty parliamentary commission tasked with drawing up a new constitution. Between 2011 and 2013, the commission reached a consensus on rewriting more than one-third of the constitution, but failed to reach agreement in the last minute—according to opposition claims—on Erdoğan's desire to bring in a presidential system.[82]

The negative impact of these two priorities on the peace process was very clear. During the peace negotiations, one of the main complaints expressed by the pro-Kurdish HDP party—and by the rest of the opposition—was the weakly institutionalized structure of the talks, which depended on the personal final word of Erdoğan. After being elected to the presidency in 2014, Erdoğan immediately began to build a de facto presidential system that severely undermined institutional traditions and procedures. Hence, according to HDP leader Demirtaş, the talks were always on the edge (of collapsing) because the whole process might be ended at any moment based on Erdoğan's whim; moreover, the government representatives in the talks, who had no real authority themselves, were even fearful of communicating the full content of what was said to the president.[83]

Even more important than these problems of power concentration and communication, what brought the talks to an end was the HDP's unwillingness to support Erdoğan's planned presidentialism. There were certainly other factors that reinforced the mutual lack of trust between the sides, such as the changing conditions in Syria, which I will discuss shortly. However, because of the lack of trust, the PKK continued to recruit fighters, build up their armory, and install landmines, while the government went on building new heavy-security military bases in the southeast.[84] Nevertheless, both sides remained onboard. The point of no compromise was reached when Demirtaş declared that the HDP "will not give way" to Erdoğan's super-presidential ambitions, which sounded the death knell for the peace process.[85] Just days before this declaration, Erdoğan had urged voters, after complaining about the opposition and stressing the need for a presidential system in an election rally in the southeastern city of Gaziantep, to "give us 400 MPs [which would deprive the HDP of seats in Parliament and give the AKP a supermajority] and let this problem be resolved with peace of mind."[86] He was reiterating his statement made at another rally the previous month: "If you want a solution process you need to give us 400 MPs."[87]

These undermining dynamics would not have been in play had there been more religious/secular elite unity and consensus, which in turn would have curbed the AKP's hegemonic and revolutionary/transformative ambitions. Hence, the (political as well as ideational) inability of the AKP and the opposition to resolve the religious/secular elite cooperation dilemma during the 2000s is part of the causal explanation for the failure of the peace initiatives.

## Leftist/Secular Elite Cooperation Dilemma

Throughout the 1980s and 1990s, Turkish social democrats—mainly the SHP, which merged with the CHP in 1995, but also the left wing of the

CHP—were the leading defenders of a "democratic resolution" for the Kurdish Conflict. As I discussed earlier, the most important Turkish/Kurdish moderate elite cooperation occurred within left-wing parties, but this cooperation had broken down by the early 1990s. After the AKP came to power, the CHP, perceiving a fatal threat to secularism, put its weakened ties with social democracy on the back burner and concentrated on secular nationalism instead.

This change of focus diminished the ability of the CHP to engage once again in cooperation with Kurdish parties. Leaving aside the Kurdish Question, it was the pro-Kurdish parties, which were rooted in socialist ideology, that were closest to the CHP ideologically, especially but not exclusively to its social democratic wing. They advocated similar economic and social policies, and shared the ideal of secular modernization. Theoretically, by co-operating, these parties could not only work to resolve the Kurdish Conflict, they could also win the majority vote required to govern the country and implement pro–social democratic, progressive, and pro-secular policies, to the benefit of both parties and their constituencies.[88] Instead, it was the AKP that secured the cooperation of pro-Kurdish parties, but, as we have seen, this cooperation was based on weak and instrumental foundations.

Kurdish votes played an important role in the CHP losing the 2010 constitution referendum—a turning point of its *Kulturkampf* with the AKP.[89] Similarly, the 2013 Gezi protests represented a massive anti-AKP mobilization whose demands prioritized social equality and freedom of expression, secular freedoms, and opposition to neoliberal economic policies—causes shared by Turkish and Kurdish leftist parties.[90] One month before the Gezi uprising broke out, May Day celebrations were banned in Istanbul's Taksim Square—a highly symbolic space for the secular Left—and the AKP government literally shut down public transportation throughout the city. While the Gezi protests were motivated by such joint secular Turkish/Kurdish concerns, they were weakened by the precarious support they received from the Kurds. The latter were concerned about the Kurdish peace initiative being derailed and the mixed signals they received from Kurdish leaders.[91]

Despite the CHP's and SHP's major efforts during the 1990s to develop progressive solutions for the Kurdish Question, the reasons for the leftist/secular elite cooperation dilemma ran deeper and were organizationally and ideologically related to the CHP's past as a state-founding and national-developmentalist party.[92] Hence, overcoming this dilemma necessitated major programmatic efforts and discursive and ideological renewal on both sides[93]—but, as I argue in this book, more so among Turkish secular leftists.

## MODERATE ELITE NEED FOR AUTONOMY

A major theoretical explanation of democratization offered by democratic transition theories argues that "moderates" need to have sufficient vigor and autonomy (from veto players) so that they can reach and honor agreements among each other and build democracy-constructing pacts against hardliners who resist democratization.[94] What does this insight imply, therefore, with respect to resolving the Kurdish Conflict?[95] The weaknesses of Turkish and Kurdish moderate actors and their lack of autonomy from veto players—mainly the Turkish military and the PKK respectively—hampered their efforts to cooperate and address Turkey's greatest democratic deficit: the inability to resolve the Kurdish Question through democratic mechanisms.

Throughout the 1990s, the PKK's oppression of autonomous Kurdish actors and the state's policies that indiscriminately restricted Kurdish activism weakened, radicalized, or crowded out legal and nonviolent Kurdish actors—which, by definition, are less capable of resisting and surviving under repression. This situation actually provided an advantage to the PKK and other "radical" groups, such as Kurdish/Islamist Hizbollah.[96] In turn, military and judicial praetorianism damaged the capacity and autonomy of mainstream Turkish actors.[97] In the end, moderate-moderate compromises became unsustainable because neither side could find it credible that the other side would resist pressures from its hard-liners and deliver on its promises. Could Turkish actors believe, for example, that legal pro-Kurdish parties can categorically condemn and distance themselves from all kinds of PKK violence—not only against civilians but also against security personnel—and armed resistance, despite PKK pressures? Could the pro-Kurdish parties find it credible that Turkish actors would commit themselves to wide-ranging political and administrative reforms and, say, an amnesty for rank-and-file PKK members, despite resistance from the military and bureaucracy?

With the regression of the military's influence from 2008 onward, the autonomy of civilian governments increased substantially, despite allegations of ongoing interventions by the so-called Gladio or deep state—the opaque and unaccountable security establishment within the Turkish state apparatus[98]—and "parallel state"—a term denoting secret formations within the state linked to the Islamist/Turkish nationalist Gulen movement.[99] Similarly, the foundation of the Peoples' Democratic Party HDP in 2012 started a process whereby a civilian pro-Kurdish party could gain autonomy from the PKK. The HDP's establishment reflected a major change in the PKK's and Kurdish movement's strategy and an effort to form a more inclusive and broad-based party that might appeal to Turks as well as Kurds, and "a new attempt to build a stronger, pro-democracy, left-wing alternative to the existing mainstream parties in Turkey."[100] The HDP simultaneously represents a continuation of earlier pro-Kurdish and pro-PKK political parties and reflects the socioeconomic, political, and "spatial transformations"[101] that its constituencies experienced in recent decades. The imprisonment in 2016 of the party's charismatic leader Selahattin Demirtaş, who had garnered 9.76 percent of the national vote in the 2014 presidential elections, undermined the HDP and its potential autonomy from Qandil (the PKK's headquarters in Northern Iraq) and from Abdullah Öcalan, the PKK leader in prison since 1998.[102]

However, the factors undermining moderate-moderate cooperation are more complex and not limited to external restrictions and coercions. They are also intrinsic to the "moderates" themselves.

## WHO ARE THE MODERATES IN THE KURDISH CONFLICT?

Moderate-moderate cooperation in Turkey was complicated by the fact that moderate actors could not be identified on a violence/nonviolence basis. The actors who might be considered "moderate" based on their rejection of armed struggle (in favor of nonviolent politics) were more "radical" in terms of their political goals and closeness to compromise with Turkish political actors compared to pro-violence actors such as the PKK (and pro-PKK political parties), who seemed more flexible in their political goals and inclusiveness. Thus, determining who the moderate actors were depended on whether one based one's analysis on the actors' use of violence or on their political flexibility and on their conceptual distance from mainstream or "centrist" Turkish values.[103] Table 6.2 summarizes the programs of three Kurdish political parties (DTP, KADEP, and HAK-PAR) during the 2000s. These three parties by no means cover the whole spectrum of Kurdish political parties and movements; they are just used here by way of illustrating my point.

Based on the violence dimension, we would have to identify HAK-PAR and KADEP as moderate. KADEP's program, for example,

Table 6.2. The Programs and Policies of Kurdish Parties

| | KADEP | HAK-PAR | DTP |
|---|---|---|---|
| **The Structure of the State** | Democratic Federation.* | Federation. But its official 2002 program does not use this word and proposes "with authority on 'education, health, internal security and local taxes.'"** | "Democratic Republic" where the Kurdish identity is constitutionally recognized and respect for Turkey's "one state, one flag and territorial integrity."*** |
| **Identity** | Kurds are a people with right to self-determination (but they shouldn't use this right for independence). There is no reference to other group identities and rights. The Kurds are a nation: "The greatest nation without its own state." | No specific conceptualization in the program. No reference to other group identities or rights. No reference to the Kurds as a people in its 2002 program.† | Kurds are referenced as a "people," but no reference to their right to self-determination. Emphasis on other groups such as Chechens, Laz and Alevis, and non-ethnic identities such as class and gender, and multi-cultural solidarity with Turks, Kurds and other groups. |
| **Turkey's Problems in General** | The Kurdish Conflict is defined as the reason for the existence of the party and constitutes one fourth of the program. | The contention that the resolution of Turkey's general problems is dependent on the resolution of the Kurdish Conflict. Specific solutions for Turkey's general problems constitute nearly 40% of program. | Policies about the Kurdish Question constitute one tenth of the program, and these are addressed within the framework of non-ethnic rights such as Turkey's democratization, human rights and women's rights. The remaining 90% of the program address secularism, economic development and detailed policy proposals on areas such as foreign policy and the discussion of "how Turkey can become a model country |

| Cooperation with Moderate Turkish Actors | Not addressed | Not addressed | Special emphasis on cooperation "with Turkey's democratic forces" and "the rejection of nationalism and separatism." |
| --- | --- | --- | --- |

*"KADEP Party Program," last accessed April 4, 2007. http://www.kadep.org.tr/ (last accessed in English, January 30, 2015 http://www.kadep.org/sayfa.asp?sayfaid=1549)//, 189.

**HAK-PAR, *The Rights and Freedoms Party Program* (Ankara, 2002), 7 and 9. Also see, Özdemir and Yalçın, "Kürtler, CNN Türk'teki 5N 1K Programı" (Kurds, CNN Turk programme 5N 1K), March 22, 2007 for an interview with Reşit Deli (HAK-PAR'S deputy chairman). The federation proposal is cited in HAK-PAR's program as of 2014. "The Rights and Freedoms Party rejects unitary state and principally adopts the nations' right to self-determination in the Kurdish Conflict. For the resolution of the Conflict, it argues for the restructuring of Turkey in a democratic and federal style based on the equality of Kurdish and Turkish peoples." Last accessed, 17 June 2014, http://www.hakpar.org.tr/root/index.php?option=com_content&view=article&id=60&Itemid=86&lang=tr

***DTP, *The Democratic Society Party's Guidelines and Program*, 2005.

†Its 2014 program adopts the "nations' right to self-determination" as a principle. See footnote 52.

proclaimed that armed struggle could not resolve the Kurdish Conflict, that
the Kurdish Armed Movement (the PKK) would not be able to defeat the
Turkish security forces, and that it condemned all violence.[104] In return,
the DTP (the antecedent of BDP and HDP) had an organic tie with the
PKK. While we could therefore describe the DTP as radical, in terms of
its "conceptual-ideological distance from Turkish majority parties," the
DTP looked the more moderate one: it gave primary importance to the
*supra-identity of Türkiyelilik* (Of-Turkey identity), sensitivity and inclusivity
to all the problems of the country, and a "democratic Republic," which
was a more flexible and moderate objective than federation, given Turkey's
constitutional principle of unitary statehood.[105] The DTP also referred to
the Kurds as a people not a nation, without mention of self-determination,
and stressed working together "with Turkey's democratic forces."

No matter how flexible Kurdish actors were in the way they defined
their values and political goals, however, it would be difficult for them to
close the gap with the cognitive map of Turkish actors.

## The Cognitive Rifts between Turkish and Kurdish Elites

The cognitive rifts existing between Turkish and Kurdish actors are
highlighted by the fact that they both frequently made references to concepts such as "democratization," "Kurdish rights," "decentralization," and
"unity" (i.e., Turkish-Kurdish fraternity). However, they were assigning
quite different meanings to these terms.[106] This hindered the creation of
common strategies among actors and complicated cooperation. To make
a comparison, when Scottish and English moderates use terms such as
*devolution,* rights of *Scots,* and *Scottish* regions, there is little ambiguity
about the meaning of these terms. There are surely disagreements over
whether these things are desirable, or over how they can be achieved,
but much less over their meaning and content. By contrast, in Turkey, disagreements were frequently over concepts, categories, and their
meanings.

Hence, while Turkish actors believed that democratization did not
require changing constitutional principles regarding the fundamental nature
of the state, many Kurds felt that a more democratic constitution had to
recognize Kurds by name. Another sticking point was over the meaning
of "Turkishness." As I discuss extensively throughout this book, the Kurds
have tended to be very adamant about categorizing "Turkishness" as an
ethnic identity that by definition is incompatible with someone's being a

Table 6.3. Cognitive Rifts Between Turkish and Kurdish Actors

| | Democratization | Solidarity | Turkish Identity | Kurdish Identity |
|---|---|---|---|---|
| **Actors from the Turkish Majority** | More rights and respect for Kurdish identity and culture; policies of administrative decentralization; lower or no election threshold. | Unitary state, single nation. Socio-political integration and territorial integrity. The empowerment of local governments from a reformist perspective. | A mixture of political-territorial identity and ethnic identity. Definition based on citizenship, common religion or ties of affectionate fraternity and patriotism (*gönül bağı*) alongside ethnic definition. Kurds can simultaneously see themselves as Turkish or as Muslims Of-Turkey. Turkish or Muslim-Turkish identity can further recognize the differences of the Kurds. | Ethnic identity |
| **Kurdish Actors** | In addition to the views stated above, the recognition that Turkey is a state with two (or more) "nations"; local self-government (autonomy or devolution with partial lawmaking and taxing authorities, and possibly having its own security forces); amnesty and honorable re-integration of former PKK members into society; Öcalan's release and pardon. | A unitary or federal state in which Kurdish sovereignty and autonomy is recognized. There is territorial integrity but there doesn't have to be sociopolitical integration. Democratic autonomy: a flexible form of "bottom-up" devolution short of a federative state.* | Ethnic identity that excludes the Kurds. Kurds cannot see themselves as Turkish. Turkish identity cannot accommodate Kurdish differences. Even if Islam is unifying, it cannot prevent discrimination against the Kurds on its own. | Ethnic identity and ethno-nation. Sovereign nation or nationality. |

*Democratic Society Party, Demokratik Toplum Partisi'nin Kürt Sorununa İlişkin; Leezenberg, "The Ambiguities of Democratic Autonomy."

Kurd, while the Turks have tended to define "Turkishness" more broadly (and ambiguously).

According to a study conducted in February 2006, 70 percent of the participants thought what defined "Turkishness" best was "being a Turkish citizen." Only 11.7 percent felt that "having Turkish parents" was important.[107] In another survey, the participants identified patriotism ("loving Turkey") as the most important basis of Turkish citizenship. However, in a clear display of the flexibility, polysemy, contested nature, and perhaps also confusion that underlies the meaning of "Turkishness," nearly 46 percent thought that being ethnically Turkish was a prerequisite of being a Turkish citizen. This contradicted the answers to the previous question.[108] However, this apparent contradiction could also be interpreted as some respondents making no clear distinction between concepts such as "ethnicity" and "nationality."

In February 2007, together with one of my graduate students, I conducted a small survey with randomly selected members of DSİAD (Diyarbakır Industrialists' and Businessmen's Association)—which had eighty-nine members at the time.[109] The participants expressed their level of identification with a series of predetermined identity categories by giving them a score from 0 to 5, where 5 indicated full identification and 0 no identification, with no restriction on how many categories they could identify with. The primary identity of the overwhelming majority was Kurdish, with 75 percent (12 out of 16) choosing 4 or 5 for the Kurd-

Table 6.4. Identity conceptions of DSİAD members with primary identity of Kurdish

| Kurdish Respondents (I feel Kurdish ≥ 4/5) | |
| --- | --- |
| I feel: Turkish ≥ 2 (Türk) | 33% (4/12) |
| I feel: a Turkish citizen ≥ 2 (Türk vatandaşı) | 42% (5/12) |
| I feel: a citizen of Turkey (Türkiye vatandaşı) ≥ 2 | 92 % (11/12) |
| I feel: 'Of-Turkey' ≥ 2 | 58 % (7/12) |
| I feel: a Muslim ≥ 2 | 75 % (9/12) |

ish category. The same respondents that chose a score of 4 or above for "Kurdish" also identified as "citizen of Turkey," "Muslim," "Of-Turkey," and "Turkish," based on a score of 2 or higher. The most interesting finding was that 42 percent did not see a contradiction between their Kurdishness and also identifying as "Turkish citizen" (*Türk vatandaşı*), which suggests even more affinity with the Turk identity than with the "citizen of Turkey" category, which would appear more territorially based.

## RELAPSING EXTERNAL SECURITY DILEMMA

A major factor that reinforced the existing lack of trust between the government and the Kurdish sides, thereby undermining the resolution process, was the resurgence of the external security dilemma due to the developments in Syria, with which Turkey shares its longest (911 kilometers (567 miles)) border of continuous, flat land, similar to the U.S.-Mexico border. At the outbreak of Syria's civil war, Turkey together with U.S. and U.S.-led coalition forces actively supported the rebels against Bashar al-Assad's Baath regime in Damascus, in the expectation of a rapid collapse of the regime. The long heavily suppressed and disenfranchised Kurds of Syria first tried to stay outside of the conflict. Turkey held amicable talks with various Syrian Kurdish groups, including the increasingly dominant Democratic Union Party (PYD), an affiliate of the PKK. However, at some point, the PYD appears to have reached a deal with the Assad regime, which peacefully surrendered control of the Jazira region to the Kurds, who then declared democratic autonomy there in January 2014.

As the war was prolonged and radical Sunni Islamic groups such as the Islamic State of Iraq and Syria (ISIS) came to increasingly dominate the Syrian opposition, a rift emerged between Turkey, which saw both "an opportunity to enhance its regional influence" and "a threat to its centralized nation-state model" in Syria, and its Western allies.[110] The AKP government continued its enthusiastic support of the rebels; the government aligned its foreign policy ambitions with the emerging (later to collapse) governments ruled by Muslim Brothers (*Ikhvan*) in countries such as Egypt and Tunisia. Elements within the AKP government hoped that an Ikhvan-dominated regime would replace the Syrian Baath regime and become a major client state for Turkey.[111] Meanwhile, the United States began to see ISIS as a greater threat and target than the Assad regime, and gradually withdrew its support from the rebels, turning instead to backing and arming the Kurds, who proved themselves to be the most effective fighting force against ISIS.[112] The PYD established its hegemony over other Syrian Kurdish groups often by brute force, and began to establish autonomous rule in three growing pockets of land: Afrin, Ain al-ʿArab (Kobani), and Jazira, which the Kurds referred to as "Rojava."[113]

All of these developments led to the rise of the Syrian Kurds as a key player in the region, with Ankara beginning to see them as a double threat: the incubation of a Kurdish, PYD-PKK controlled (and potentially irredentist) independent state, and an enemy of the Ankara-backed rebels. Simultaneously, the PKK saw an opportunity for regional autonomy and leverage against Ankara in the peace negotiations and in other regional as well as global capitals such as Moscow and Washington.

A decisive turning point for the external security dilemma was reached in September 2014 when ISIS laid siege to the PYD-controlled town of Kobani, forcing sixty thousand civilians to flee to the Turkish town of Suruç just across the border. On both sides of the border, the Kurds expected the Turkish forces along the border to intervene and come to the help of Kobani, open a humanitarian corridor, and permit the passage of military reinforcements from other PYD-controlled areas in Syria and from the KRG in Iraq.[114] Arguably, doing so would have sealed Turkey's image as a protector and partner, as opposed to an oppressor, in the eyes of the Kurds. Hence, such a move, if it had proved successful, might also have gone a long way in resolving the external security dilemma, as it would have rendered external Kurds (in this case Syrian) and Ankara allies and jumpstarted a mutually trusting relationship between them. Ankara, however, hesitated. Erdoğan seemed to prioritize other goals such as the declaration of a no-fly zone (which would have hindered air attacks in support of Kurds) and a secure zone parallel to the region (splitting the Kurdish areas). He called for "the moderate opposition in Syria and Iraq to be trained and equipped," and for Kurds to join Ankara's proxy war against Damascus,[115] while, he argued, "Kobani is about to fall."[116] Pro-HDP Kurds' reaction consisted of the KCK's and HDP's call for "permanent action," which started mass protests and street clashes between HDP supporters and Kurdish-Islamist HÜDA-PAR supporters, leading to fifty deaths.[117]

The image of the PYD among Western democracies was boosted when the Kurds, on their own, successfully defended Kobani against ISIS and thereby shattered the invincible image that ISIS had held, in a war that was widely publicized in Western media and showed images of female PKK fighters battling bearded ISIS militants.[118] Had Turkey already established peace with Kurds domestically, the PYD and Syrian Kurds could have become Turkey's natural allies from the beginning of the Syrian quagmire. In turn, the emergence of a "rival," even "clashing image" with the Syrian Kurds caused a resurge in the external security dilemma, annulled the impact of the establishment of cooperative relations with Iraqi Kurds, and undermined the domestic peace process.

Before we move on to the common identity dilemma, one should note that weak EU support for Turkey's membership also represented an external factor that impaired possible moderate-moderate cooperation. EU membership—or even a strong prospect of membership—would have rendered any promises that moderate Turkish and Kurdish spokespersons would make to each other more credible through the Copenhagen criteria of liberal democracy, according to which both violent separatism and government oppression of minority rights are illegitimate.[119] Instead, Turkey's weak membership prospects had the opposite effect.[120]

In parallel with this, the AKP alternated between inclusionary discourses that emphasized "peace and prosperity for everyone" and exclusionary discourses that demonized a part of the Kurds and the opposition.[121] The party's narratives followed the short-term requirements of its prioritized political interests. The reasons for this might be interpreted either as a failure to resolve the contradictions between the inclusionary discourses the party used now and then and its long-term interests, or as an inability to build inclusionary narratives that were compatible with the party's interests.

## Failure to Resolve the Common Identity Dilemma and the Turkish Identity Question

### QUESTIONING MAINSTREAM NORMS AND BELIEFS IN THE 2000S

At the turn of the millennium, there were important discussions taking place regarding Turkey's ethno-cultural diversity, particularly its Kurdish component, and about the sociopolitical role of this diversity and how to organize it. These discussions criticized diversity-phobic views and values on factual and normative grounds. However, they could not overcome the standard stories (particularly the narrative of "the inevitable outcome of nationalism and the nation-state") I discussed earlier.

Why were these discussions not as successful as they were intended to be, in that they fell short of producing realistic narratives that could resolve the common identity dilemma?

## Overemphasis on Essentialized Identities Instead of Institutions and Politics that Produce Their Content

The discussions around Of-Turkey (*Türkiyelilik*) identity were an example of endeavors to construct an alternative national identity that was more inclusive of diversity but ultimately lacked sufficient social/political support.

First, the discussions on *Türkiyelilik* focused more on demonstrating why the Turkish identity was too narrow, rather than on demonstrating the inclusiveness of *Türkiyelilik*. They focused on a question that has multiple equally valid answers: whether or not the Turkish identity is ethnic, without distinguishing between ethnic category and ethnic group. Yet, as I discussed in the previous chapters, Turkishness, which historically had been an ethnic category, had—without losing its ethnic meaning—become the name and foundation of a national identity, which was expected to carry on the mission of the Ottoman state/national identity, and was adopted by a multiethnic population as their primary identity. Thus, Turkishness did not have a singular meaning.

Second, these discussions remained focused on identities per se rather than on institutions and politics that provide the contents of identities. They focused on the presumably unchanging traits of the Turkish identity and Turkish nationalism (which are in line with the standard narratives we examined in chapter 3) rather than on political dynamics (which are in line with the non-standard stories discussed in the Introduction chapter) as the reasons behind the failure to resolve the common identity dilemma and the exclusion of Kurds. The discussions appeared to be trying to demonstrate that the Turkish identity was "imagined or imaginary," artificial, or unsuccessful. By doing so, they essentialized Turkish and Kurdish identities as if they had singular, monolithic, and fixed meanings, and triggered a backlash among Turks.

Unintentionally or not, all of this gave rise to the following perception: "The problem is not the political attitudes and institutions (i.e., political, legal and social rules and norms) that exclude the Kurds (and other groups and pluralism) but the Turkish identity itself. Therefore, since (according to the above interpretation) the root of the problem is an identity, the solution must lie in rejecting that identity and supporting another identity." According to some, this new identity was *Türkiyelilik*, while for others, it was an Islamic identity.

Alternatively, public/political and intellectual debates might have focused on politics, political culture, the unequal relationship between state and society, institutions, and rights that provide identities with particular contents and meanings, rather than on identity per se.[122]

Third, these discussions focused on one component of the common identity dilemma: how to construct a common identity to satisfy the Kurds' longing for equal recognition, at the expense of the second component: how to make sure that this will not bring about anxiety among Turks about the erosion of the Turkish identity.

For example, a prominent left-wing Turkish scholar, public intellectual, and politician, Baskın Oran, put forward the following claims in an opinion piece. He argued that when nation building in France began to assimilate the country's linguistic and cultural minorities, in contrast with Turkey's case, the French nation (or a strong and ethnically neutral French identity) already existed.[123] This suggested that the French nation-building process was more realistic, peaceful, and inclusive compared to the Turkish process *because* (i.e., not for other reasons, such as socioeconomic and institutional development) the French identity was an already existing strong identity, while the Turkish identity was comparatively artificial and weak. Yet, as Eugen Weber showed, in the nineteenth century—the start of French nation building—the French language was a "foreign language" for at least half of the "French" population and the French nation-building process was only completed in the early twentieth century.[124]

Another implication of Oran's claims was that it was impossible to produce more democratic policies that would respect and recognize Kurdish and other minorities without rejecting the nation-state altogether. In fact, in a different op-ed, Oran asserted that "nation-states" could not become democratic:

> [T]aboo is the subject you cannot talk about because you fear it. . . . Just the way new enemies are immediately generated when one enemy (e.g., communism) disappears, new taboos are produced to replace them. Currently, the newest 'greatest' taboo is the notion of nation-state (N-S). *In other words, a form of state that denies the presence of subnational identities constituting the nation* [emphasis mine]. About this previously unheard-of N-S which is currently "in the making," they say, if it didn't exist, the Republic of Turkey would fall to pieces immediately. And to prove it, they give France as an example: See France? It denies it has minorities even though it's so powerful! A highly significant recent development: Article 75-1 which was added

to the French Constitution in August 2008 despite the great
opposition of the Academie Française states, "The regional
languages form part of the French heritage." Meanwhile, [N-S
defenders] are tearing out their hair thinking that France will
fall into pieces! Now, can you imagine a Turkey where Arabic
language and Syrian law is valid in Hatay, Russian language and
Muscovite law in Ardahan and Kurdish and Kurdish Federal
State law in Diyarbakır? Will you dare to give France as an
example of the nation-state in Turkey again? . . . *France is no
longer a nation-state* [emphasis mine], it is a democratic state.[125]

Oppressive public/political discourses also harden and radicalize
those discourses that are critical of them. According to the above quote
from Oran, in order to criticize assimilationist and oppressive state policies vis-à-vis diversity, one has to embrace a singular, monolithic, and
untenable definition of nation-states that does not distinguish between the
notions of nation-state and (ostensibly) homogenous nation-state. Oran
makes another somewhat untenable claim, when he contrasts democratic
states and nation-states. However, the constitutional reforms in the French
constitution that Oran himself presents suggest that nation-states can
democratize by embracing ethnic/national pluralism without necessarily
ceasing to be nation-states.

In fact, a revisionist narrative of republican history in a volume edited
by a prominent historian, which came out in Turkish in the same period
as Oran's piece above, implied that the evolution of Turkish nationalism
cannot be understood by merely looking into its ostensibly stationary and
monolithic characteristics of identities and the evolution of Turkish-Kurdish relationships.[126] Turkish nationalism has had other versions than the
ones that eventually became dominant. Four factors must be considered
in order to grasp the experience of Turkish nationalists and the development of the dominant version of Turkish nationalism: global political
and intellectual developments, demographic changes, rival nationalisms
that Turkish nationalists encountered, and relations with external powers
who negotiated the breakup of Ottoman lands into new nation-states.
Zürcher elaborates:

It is certainly not an exaggeration to state that the 100 years
spanning from 1850 to 1950 was a century of demographic
engineering in Europe. Large masses of people were either

expelled or deported from their ancestral lands or slaugh-
tered. What was experienced in the late Ottoman Empire and
Turkey fits in with this general scene. . . . The Russian state's
religiously biased ambition to ensure total control over the
newly-acquired territories caused Muslims to be expelled from
the Black Sea coast (post-1828), Crimea (1853–1854, during
and after the Crimean War), and the Caucasus (in the early
1860s) in masses and their emigration to (Ottoman territories)
under insufferable oppression . . . .After the Congress of Berlin
in 1878, the national states that emerged in the Balkans which
utilized the convenient conjuncture created by the politics
of the Great Powers were products of romantic nationalist
movements that tore off land (from the Ottomans). They fundamentally defined their national identities in opposition to
Ottoman rule. . . . They all had a strong religious component
in their definition of nation. This led to the massacre (as well
as to new migrations and population exchange agreements)
of Muslim populations . . . .The fate of Muslim refugees from
the Caucasus and the Balkans directly affected the situation in
Anatolia (inter-ethnic and inter-faith relations). [The analyses
in the book] help us understand how the Republic of Turkey
was a product of the ethnic policies and conflicts observed
from 1912 to 1922.[127]

An article by another historian in the same volume asserted that two
factors had a critical effect on the evolution of Turkish nationalism:[128] first,
the pressures from and conflicts with Armenian nationalists, and second,
the particular *political* decisions that international powers made in reaction
to the mass deportation and genocide of Armenians during World War
I. Şeker argues that Turkish nationalism might have evolved differently if
the allied powers had placed the blame for the plight of the Armenians on
individual perpetrators, as the Kemalists stated they should be, instead of
trying to divide the Ottoman Turkish country. A relatively more tolerant
attitude might have developed in relation to the country's minorities.[129]

Causal beliefs that political elites formed during a conflict with
one group at a particular time can also affect their beliefs vis-à-vis other
conflicts at different times. Hence, the experiences of Muslim and Turkish
refugees from the Balkans, Black Sea Basin, and the Caucasus also affected
Turkish nationalists' perceptions of the Kurdish Question. Many of them

had fresh memories of experiencing pressure from rival nationalisms and bloody religious and ethnic fissures. These memories also shaped their mental framing when they evaluated their new experiences. For example, judges raised the memory of Balkan nationalisms and conflicts (e.g., in Bosnia and Albania) during the trials of Kurdish rebels after the Sheikh Said rebellion.[130] In other words, the historical examples they used to interpret the causes and possible outcomes of the rebellion originated from Ottoman experiences in the Balkans. The political developments and conflicts across a wider territory influenced Turkish nationalists' attitudes toward minority issues in Anatolia.

With the forced migrations, Muslim communities, most of whom did not speak Turkish, emigrated en masse to Anatolia and were incorporated into the ethnic mosaic of Anatolia, which was already multiethnic.[131] As a consequence of these developments in the nineteenth and twentieth centuries, Turkish nationalists and the people they intended to mobilize formed an ethnically diverse population, the majority of whom did not constitute an ethnic group. Still, many people, such as Yaşar Kemal (one of the greatest novelists of Turkish literature), could adopt Turkishness as a national identity without hiding or abandoning their ethnic consciousness.[132] Hence, if they do not lie in the inherent nature of identities or of the Turkish identity, the sources of the Turkish state's conflictual relationship with particular groups such as Kurds may be found in the political failure of the state to form a state/society relationship with these groups based on mutual acceptance and ties of affection.

Regardless of how frequently the metaphor of "blood ties" is used in the definition of Turkish national identity, Turks acknowledge that their genealogical origins vary from Central Asia to the Middle East and the Balkans. In other words, the modern Turkish identity is based more on language and (a highly heterogeneous) cultural commonality than on descent. Hence, argues Jenny White, developments such as missionary activities, differentiation of religious practices, and globalization triggered concerns among Turks related to loss of identity because, "despite the powerful discourse about blood, [Turkishness] has weak ethnic roots."[133] Hence, one might argue that the discourse of lineage(blood)-based nationhood, which is incompatible with the historical and demographic reality, is itself a problem that undermines democratization.

However, as I will elaborate ahead in this chapter, the differences between secular (Kemalist) and Muslim Turkish nationalisms may be much less than White makes them seem in terms of how much they draw on assumed ethnic bonds. She asserts that only the former is based on descent (blood), while the latter is based on religious culture and Ottoman heritage (hence, why it is more flexible and less exclusionary).[134]

Religious nationalism can feed off a discourse of common ancestry and blood ties (as in "not having alcohol in one's blood" or being "grandchildren of Saladin") as much as secular nationalism can. Periods such as during the 1930s when Kemalist nationalists promoted pseudo-scientific and racist theories such as the "Sun Language Theory" and "Turkish History Thesis" underlie the image of secular Turkish nationalism as particularly and exclusively ethnic and "blood"-based.[135] The late Halil İnalcık, one of the doyens of Ottoman history, lived through and observed the formation process of the Turkish History Thesis both as a student and as a university assistant. His retrospective reflections—which may also be motivated by a desire to counter and qualify recent criticisms of the period—help one understand the motives and perceptions of the period, as well as many contemporary and new practices and discourses.

> Atatürk wanted to transform the Turkish nation from a state of religious community (a state of Ottoman society linked to the Middle Ages) into a modern nation. For this, . . . he wanted to give a sense of national conscience to the people, and to let it have pride in its history and Turkishness. . . . Atatürk was especially sensitive to how the image of Turk was etched with extremely dark lines in the Western world due to its six-century crusades struggle. In all Western literature, the Ottoman Empire was referred to as the "Turkish Empire" and the Ottomans as "Turkish" and Turkish history was seen from an adversarial angle. Distortions, wrong and malevolent interpretations superseded realities. He had adopted as his greatest ideal the goal of national Turkish state taking its place beside Western nations as an equal. Even then we thought (were aware) that romantic national historiography was getting stuck in hyperboles and being wrong like other nationalisms. I understood later that Atatürk spent his time to this end in order to realize a great political plan. Today, the "Turkish History Thesis" in its original form has been abandoned . . . .However, by founding the Faculty of Language and History-Geography—a center of social science working with scientific methods—the great leader prepared the groundwork for many important discoveries that

shed light on Turkish history and Middle Eastern civilizations. Anatolian archaeology thus made great progress.[136]

Hence, the "discourse of descent and blood" in (pro-secular as well as religious) nationalism can be understood as mostly instrumental to a political project of modernization. Rather than embracing and producing a new perspective that would reorganize and legitimize the plural meanings of the Turkish identity, however, the debates of the 2000s revolved around the question of whether Turkishness is ethnic-exclusive *or* national-inclusive. It was inevitable then that these discussions would foster identity concerns among one group or another. *Everyone* was experiencing an "identity crisis": those with non-Turk origins when they were told that Turkishness is (only) an ethnic identity based on descent; and those with non-Muslim, non-Sunni Muslim, or nonreligious beliefs, those with a secular worldview, and women and sexual minorities when they were told that *the* Turkishness went together with being Muslim, often understood as being Sunni Muslim.[137] Proclaiming that Turkishness *is* based on citizenship did not solve the problem either, as it led to a sense of unease among some Kurds (since this definition had been used to legitimize assimilationist policies in the past) as well as among some religious people and ethnic and cultural Turks (because a definition based on citizenship was considered superficial and devoid of any cultural depth).

Meanwhile, the recipe of associating the state and its nation with the Of-Turkey category (*Türkiyeli*) as opposed to Turkishness ignited fierce public/political debates.[138] Could it be successful?

As I discussed in the Introduction chapter, a degree of embeddedness in society, historical depth, and time-honored content are all major facilitating factors that permit an identity category to flourish as the basis of a unifying project. It was unclear whether *Türkiyelilik* had such rootedness, depth, and appeal. Further, *Türkiyelilik,* or, for that matter, any other identity category, could not be taken for granted as an automatically and permanently inclusive category. Depending on domestic and external political developments, *Türkiyelilik* could also become exclusivist. For example, some people might begin to assert that although the Kurds are *from* Turkey (i.e., living in Turkey and being citizens), they are not really *Of*-Turkey, that is, belonging to Turkey (as much as other groups) on cultural, historical, or political grounds. When group conflict evokes threat and "enemy" perceptions, some people can reinterpret any identity category.

While some welcomed the Of-Turkey identity because it made them feel more at home in their own country, other people felt that identities that played integrating roles in their lives were discredited. Hrant Dink, who was prosecuted for "denigrating Turkishness" in 2007 (the same year in which his political murder took place—which still remained unsolved when this book was being written), wrote:

I don't intend to insult Turks. My concern is to reflect my own state of mind. Do you think that the inclusive meaning of the "Turk" employed by Atatürk in his phrase: "How happy is the one who calls himself a Turk!" is the same as the meanings later subscribed to this phrase, the racist and ethnic meanings and the fascist discourses that dismantle the national-integrationist (unifying) content of the (original) phrase? . . . Atatürk's phrase can surely maintain its existence but why should those who say, "How happy am I to be Of-Turkey [*Türkiyeli*)]," be dishonorable?[139]

In turn, the following words of a prominent academic and public intellectual reflected the sentiment and perception that prevailed among many Turks in the 2000s:

It is possible to observe that the emphasis on "I am Turkish" is getting stronger even among fractions of society that previously did not feel the need to emphasize their Turkishness. Some of the underlying reasons that caused this were untimely and inconsiderate discussions conducted through certain symbols. It is inevitable for the fire to spread when the Turkish flag, emblem of the Republic of Turkey, and marginal discussions such as the definition of the Turkish nation according to the constitution are brought to the limelight as if they are the basis of the issue and everyone is of the same conviction. Such discussions that are savored by the media throw the whole of society into flames and no one realizes it. The comfort zone of those who have defined themselves as Turkish until today is gradually narrowing. In any case, they haven't felt the need to defend their own identities since the founding of the Republic because it's been defended by the state. However, at this stage the state is fading from the scene and a Kurdish identity is taking shape as the dialectic counterpart of the Turkish identity. This is an extremely perilous situation. For the first time in history, we may be embarking on a period which has the potential for internal (civil) conflict. To prevent this from happening there has to be coherence to show that the Turkish identity will not be lost while opening an area of freedom for the Kurdish identity.[140]

Hence, in another interview, the choices were described in the following zero-sum fashion, which unintentionally presented a stylized description of the common identity dilemma and were testimony to the fact that the ongoing debates were failing to resolve the dilemma:

—If citizens of the Republic of Turkey integrate under the supra-identity of Of-Turkey (*Türkiyelilik*), will the Turks consider it as defeat?

—(Yes.)[141]

—When all citizens of Turkey are called Turkish, will the Turks feel victorious and the Kurds defeated?

—Yes, that's how they will feel; and that's how they have felt all along.[142]

In a nutshell, the politics of the 2000s not only overemphasized identities at the expense of institutional and practical solutions. It also fell short of generating new narratives that would resolve the seemingly zero-sum conflicts between the identity-related ontological insecurities of Turks and Kurds. As I argued, new narratives were especially needed to address the ontological insecurities of Turks. This is because Kurds' insecurities are more straightforward and understood by both Kurds and outsiders, whereas Turks' concerns are more complex. They are the dominant group and less aware of both the sources of their own identity-related insecurities and any possible solutions that don't necessitate the negation of Kurdishness. In the words of a recent contribution:

Peace processes are easier to initiate because they offer the ontologically insecure minority groups a potential pathway to stability and legitimacy of being. Yet they are harder to conclude because on the one hand, ontological insecurity renders minority groups more vulnerable to spoilers, and on the other hand, ontological security renders majority groups more resistant to change . . . thus far, the peace process in Turkey has not included conscious measures to construct new narratives [aimed at addressing both insecurities]. Despite the asymmetric nature of the conflict, Kurdish ontological security cannot be reinstated at the expense of Turkish ontological security, or vice versa.[143]

## Emphasis on Ideology Rather than on Rights and Institutions as Recipes

To be clear, my point here is not that ideational factors, meaning, ideologies, ideas, and beliefs, do not matter as explanatory factors.[144] On the contrary, I maintain that an ideational factor, namely, the nature of the ideational debates in Turkey in the 2000s, which overemphasized identities and ideologies at the expense of rights and institutions, helps to explain why the common identity dilemma could not be resolved.

Since 2002, and in the two years between the end of the 2013 resolution process and the AKP's hard-line/nationalist turn, many writers explained the AKP policies at that time and its positive steps as being mainly based on the "Islamic," "new Ottoman," or "conservative democratic" ideologies that the AKP and its social base ostensibly held. Hence, many claimed, and even took for granted, that the Islamists and Islamic conservatives had an ideological advantage over secular nationalists when it came to addressing ethnic/national questions in general and the Kurdish Question in particular. This was used as a powerful discourse for justifying the continuation of AKP governments and Erdoğan's ascendance. The underlying logic was either that Islamists were less nationalistic because they took an "Islamic" identity (an identity that was understood as above and beyond ethnicity and nationality) as the basis of their political identity, or that they had a more flexible sense of nationalism, which was thought to be more open to diversity.[145] Overall, these ideas and claims were part of "post-Kemalist" criticisms of Turkish nation-building and republican ideology, and displayed the weaknesses and flaws of these criticisms.[146]

Hence, one contribution casually and retrospectively noted in passing that, when the AKP came to power, "For the first time, Turkish nationalism was also liberated from its policies of forced assimilation and the negligence of ethnic diversity in the country." The study also observes critically that the AKP strengthened "the Islamic Sunni elements of Turkish nationalism," but appears to assume that nationalism rooted in religion and religious culture (as opposed to, for example, language) is more liberated from assimilationist impulses and less threatened by ethnic diversity.[147] Is this assumption true?

## "Secularism is the Problem and Islam is the Solution"

These claims have a long history beyond Turkey.[148] Cases such as Sudan and Pakistan, both of which are Islamic republics with rather poor records of resolving ethnic/regional conflicts, and cross-country evidence showing that co-religiosity does not necessarily prevent or help end civil wars, imply that the evidence supporting such claims is weak at best.[149] So too is the evidence from the case of Turkey.[150]

Nevertheless, Turkey's pro-religious elites that formed the political and ideational backbone of the AKP, and especially its Islamists, argued throughout the 1990s and 2000s that a national identity that emphasizes Muslim values can accommodate the expression of Kurdish ethnicity much more successfully than a national identity that emphasizes secular Turkishness.[151] Their claims were not only prescriptive but also explanatory and historical. Hence, they also asserted that secularism and the secular national identity *caused* the Kurdish Conflict. One analyst summarized the Islamist position as follows:

> [They argued that] Turkish nationalism contributed to the birth of its twin sister, Kurdish nationalism, by supporting secularism and secular nationalism. When Islamic values were substituted with Western culture and thought, Islam—which nurtured peace and mutual compassion between Turks and Kurds who were brotherly Muslims—lost its influence. Feelings of brotherhood transformed into a desire to strangle one another.[152]

Hence, Necmettin Erbakan (1926–2011), the head of the Islamist RP, in a 1994 speech in the eastern province of Bingöl, said:

> [T]his country's children started school by reciting bismillah for centuries. You arrived and changed it to "I am a Turk, honest and hardworking." If you say, "I am a Turk, honest

and hardworking," my Kurdish brother will attain the right
to say, "Is that so? I am a Kurd, I am more honest and more
hardworking." This is how you made this nation's children
enemies to one another.[153]

Similarly, a Kurdish politician and head of a pro-religious human
rights association who became an MP for the AKP in the 2000s opined:

> [W]hether the US or the Republic of Turkey solves it, these
> resolutions will not benefit the Muslims or the people of the
> region. . . . We wanted to approach this issue "with the conscious-
> ness of Islamic ummah" and determine our attitude. . . . Will
> we be able to abandon perversions of concepts such as ummah,
> nation, state, millet, ethnicity, racism, separatism, national pact,
> flag and martyr caused by "knowledge [or consciousness] of
> citizenship" and return to their Quranic meanings?[154]

## ARE SECULARIST OR ISLAMIST ELITES IDEATIONALLY MORE OPEN TO DIVERSITY?

In order to compare and contrast pro-secular and pro-religious elite values
regarding nationalism, diversity, and the Kurdish Conflict, I conducted an
empirical research project that systematically analyzed the contents of three
"pro–religious conservative" and two "pro–secular"[155] newspapers published
between the years of 1996 and 2004. A team of twenty trained graduate
student coders examined the contents of 42,463 articles in a total of 4,850
newspaper issues, based on a common methodology and investigating a
common set of subjects and questions.[156] None of the coders analyzed
two consecutive issues of the same paper. The aim of the project was to
determine elite values. Journalists have long been an integral component
of Turkey's intelligentsia and political society and individual journalists
often had close links with political parties. Newspapers have been major
platforms where new and old political movements were introduced to the
public and deliberated among each other their ideas and projects. Hence,
all relevant articles in each newspaper issue were analyzed, including
opinion pieces, news articles, front-page articles, and guest columns, as
well as those in the other sections.

The terms *pro-religious* and *pro-secular* might not necessarily square
with the self-descriptions of all the journalists in these newspapers—or
with the perceptions of all of their readers—and were used for lack of

better terms. However, it should also be stated that they roughly corre-sponded to a common perception and widespread daily usage (*dindar/laik*) in Turkey at the time. Furthermore, the research did not presume a priori that the elites who wrote for these two categories of newspapers necessarily came from two separate worldviews (i.e., religious versus sec-ular) or necessarily formed two separate groups. But the findings showed that the two sets of papers on average constituted two different groups on issues related to religion (and secularism), even though the two groups did not necessarily differ significantly on other issues, such as electoral and liberal democracy and nationalism per se.[157] It should also be kept in mind that all of the differences identified only make sense in terms of group averages. There was significant diversity within each paper as well as among "pro-religious" and "pro-secular" sets of newspapers. Many pro-secular writers wrote in religious newspapers and vice versa. In the period researched (1996–2004), there was significant pluralism within the Turkish media, but this later dwindled due to social/political polarization and the government's "new authoritarian" policies.[158]

In any case, it should be noted that the adjectives *religious* and *secular* refer to institutions, ideas, and society, rather than to people. For example, "pro-religious" papers can generally be expected to use religious ideas more and support religion and religiosity in society and state, while "pro-secular" papers can be expected to use secular ideas more and support secularity in society and state.[159]

The year chosen as the starting point for the publications researched was 1996, the year when the Welfare Party RP came into power, and the chosen cutoff year was 2004, when the PKK restarted their armed struggle, and before the AKP government attempted its first and short-lived peace initiative. By picking this period as the time frame, I sought to capture the elite beliefs before the politicization of the AKP's initiatives and the recommencement of the PKK's attacks.[160] The content analysis reveals the ideas and judgments of the religious/conservative elites and the pro-secular elites concerning many subjects, such as democracy and modernization. However, in this book, I will limit myself to discussing only the findings relating to ethnic/cultural pluralism, nationalism, and the Kurdish Ques-tion. The same research was conducted later with a smaller sample of newspapers published in 2007 and 2010, and supplemented with some additional questions.[161]

The findings suggest that in the 1996–97 period, the pro-religious elites tended to be more skeptical about democracy than the pro-secular elites. However, in the early 2000s, the pro-religious elites' thinking about both notions tended to converge with that of the pro-secular elites.[162] But there were exceptions in both groups. For example, the pro-religious elites might turn a blind eye to the rights and freedoms of the Alevis, sexual minorities, and women, while the pro-secular elites could hold authoritarian views about the rights of covered women in the name of "preserving secularism."[163]

Some findings seemed to support the claim that pro-religious newspapers[164] were more open to reforms that accommodated ethnic/national diversity. For example, the elites writing in pro-religious papers were more willing to accept ethnic parties. As Figure 6.1 demonstrates, pro-secular papers discussed the question of ethnic parties more frequently. Comparing the findings for the two pro-secular and three pro-religious papers, the former mentioned ethnic parties about 50 percent more frequently than the pro-religious papers did, forty-four times per paper. However, pro-religious papers contained more positive ideas about ethnic parties (i.e., ideas that considered them as legitimate and constructive, for example, to express ethnic identities or as a requirement for democracy) and fewer negative ideas (opinions discussing them as a threat and negative influence, for example, by unleashing centrifugal dynamics and disintegration and weakening national identity).

As ethnic differences became more widely expressed in Turkey in the 1990s, the idea that Turkish society is a "mosaic of cultures" began to draw attention. Many similar metaphors were put forward and these tended to be embraced more positively by the elites writing for pro-religious papers. They supported Turkey's image as a multicultural mosaic

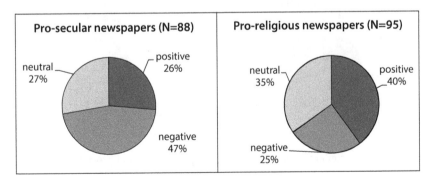

Figure 6.1. The right to establish ethnic parties.

(83 percent of 125 data codings), whereas the pro-secular papers held a neutral position (58 percent of 146 data codings), with blatantly negative views being very few in both groups.

There was more criticism of the nation-state principle in pro-religious press. In 2007 and 2010, when this question was covered, the subject was coded ten times in the two pro-religious papers, with six negative and three positive views. By comparison, the two pro-secular papers referred to the subject seven times, none of which were negative, with most of them being neutral.

As Figure 6.2 shows, the pro-religious and pro-secular elites imagined the national identity somewhat differently. They gave different weights to three potential sources of the national identity that were established prior to the content analysis: "Turkishness" (The Turk category, however it is defined), "Anatolianism" (or *Türkiyelilik*, territory), and Islam (Muslim religion). As was expected, the pro-religious elites thought Islam, whether as a religion, identity, or culture, was a critical marker of national identity and constituted a great deal of its content. On the surface, one could argue that this might create a potential for openness to ethnic pluralism, as ethnic identities may not threaten a religiously shaped identity. If this is indeed true, then we should also find that pro-religious elites are less nationalistic—since nationalist values would contradict the major tenets of a universal religion—and more supportive of legal/political reforms that accommodate ethnic/national differences.

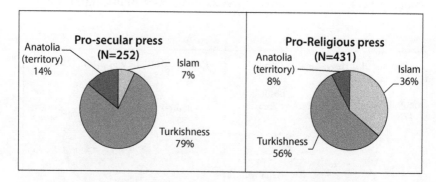

Figure 6.2. The content of national identity in pro-secular and pro-religious press, 1996–2004.

## Were Pro-Religious Elites Less Nationalist?

In his aforementioned 2011 speech, Prime Minister Erdoğan seemed unequivocal and confident in his vehement opposition to nationalism:

> For me there is neither Turkish nationalism nor Kurdish nationalism, or this or the other. They are all my brothers, my soul, my dear; I love them all the same, that is our difference [from the pro-secular opposition] . . . .The more we talked about national integrity and brotherhood, the more they defended nationalism and oppression . . . I say Diyarbakır should embrace freedom, democracy, *national* will [emphasis mine] and its own will . . . .My dear brothers, we are the grandchildren of Saladin, we are the grandchildren of the foot soldiers in Saladin's army that conquered Jerusalem. Turk, Kurd, Arab, Circassian, Zaza, Roman call it whatever you may, in the words of Yunus, we love the "created for the Creator's sake."[165]

Yet, as I maintained in previous chapters, this speech was not free of nationalist sentiments, values, and discourse, regardless of what Erdoğan's own perception and self-image might have been. The speech reflected at least two nationalist sentiments and assertions: nationalism based on descent (as Saladin's grandchildren); and national unity and will. As for the latter, it was clear from the speech that what Erdoğan meant by "national will" was the will of the whole nation of Turkey; it was unclear what would happen if Diyarbakır (the Kurds) exercised "its own will" to separate from the "national will."

Although not immune to nationalism, could it be true, nevertheless, that pro-religious elites were "less nationalist" than their pro-secular counterparts? In the content analysis, the subject of nationalism was defined for the coders as follows:

> Articles that contain views that particularly defend the identity and interests of Turks; national security; actions/policies against internal and external threats from non-Turkish sources; Turkish culture; the nation-state of the Turks; territorial integrity; unity against shared threats, or articles that argue for, criticize or emphasize struggling against the enemies of the Turks or

discuss the problematique/notion of nationalism or reflect
a nationalism other than Turkish nationalism (e.g., Kurdish
nationalism).

In the research, the coders first identified the articles that contained
this subject and then coded any views that affirmed (positive views),
criticized (negative), and discussed without judgment (neutral) any part
of the subject. Based on these codings, the pro-secular elites did indeed
appear to be more interested in the subject of nationalism (774 mentions
per pro-secular paper versus 392 per pro-religious paper), and they held
relatively more positive (i.e., nationalist) and less negative views.

Further investigation, however, reveals a more complex and variegated picture. As Figure 6.4 shows, both the "most nationalist" and the
"least nationalist" paper was a pro-secular one (indicated with "S" in the
figure), and the pro-religious papers (indicated with "R") lay in between.
Further, in the 2007 and 2010 findings, while the two pro-secular papers
contained slightly more nationalist views, they also reflected more critical
views of nationalism.

## Pro-religious and Pro-secular Elite Views on the Kurds

In pro-secular papers there were almost two and a half times more
references to Kurds (325 codings per paper) in the 1966–2004 period
compared to pro-religious papers (125 per paper). In other words, the
Kurdish Question and Conflict—one of the most important problems in
the country—was discussed less in the pro-religious press.

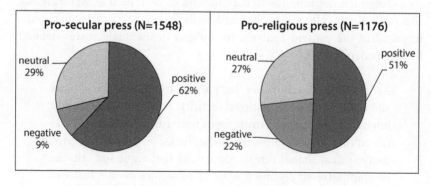

Figure 6.3. Normative views on nationalism, 1996–2004.

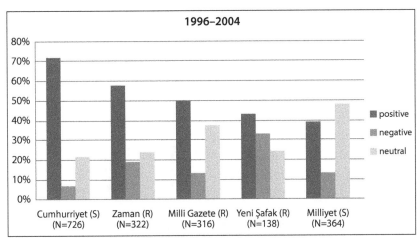

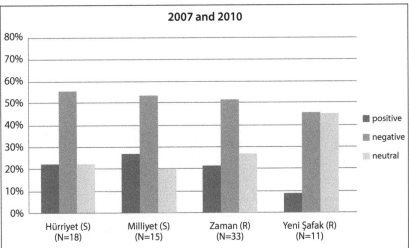

Figure 6.4. Normative evaluation of nationalism in individual newspapers.

There were internal divisions in terms of normative views. Reviewing the individual articles, one could see that the hard-line elites in both pro-religious and pro-secular papers were skeptical of Kurdish demands and reforms. The paper with the most positive references to the Kurds was a pro-religious one (*Yeni Şafak*); however, the fewest negative views were found in a pro-secular paper (*Milliyet*). The paper with the fewest positive views was also pro-religious (*Milli Gazete*). The findings from

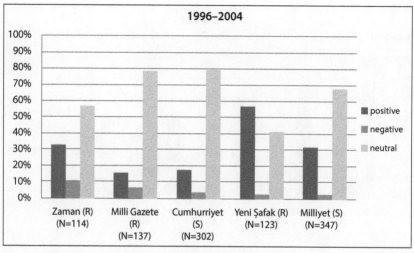

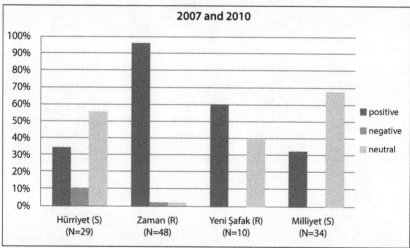

Figure 6.5. References to "Kurds" in individual newspapers.

the 2007 and 2010 research still showed more references to the Kurds in the pro-secular papers, but the difference between the two groups was less. Finally, there was no clear separation between pro-religious and pro-secular papers with respect to how frequently they employed the charged and negative term *separatist* in relation to the Kurds. The two papers that used the term most frequently were one pro-secular (*Cumhuriyet*) and one pro-religious (*Milli Gazete*).[166]

## IDEATIONAL PREPAREDNESS FOR REFORMS AND CONFLICT RESOLUTION

I used two criteria to assess the level of ideational preparedness—i.e., repertoire of knowledge and ideas—regarding whether and how to address any social/political problem—in this case the Kurdish Conflict: (1) the amount of prior discussion of the issue—more codings reflecting more preparedness;[167] and (2) the ratio of positive and negative views—more positive codings and fewer negative codings vis-à-vis target groups and specific reforms indicating preparedness. Hence, if the pro-religious elites were ideationally more prepared to resolve the Kurdish Conflict, then we would find them making more frequent and more positive references to the Kurds, to specific legal/political reforms and to conflict resolution proposals than the pro-secular elites.

Resolving a complex political conflict requires ideational preparedness about what to do and how, beyond general and abstract expressions of good will, such as, "We are all equal, we are all brothers," and, "This conflict should be resolved through democratic debate." Even though such expressions may in themselves be important and constructive, they are not sufficient. There is a need for reflection and discussion about questions such as: Which past and present policies and political and socioeconomic grievances underlie Kurdish demands? How (i.e., through which policies and social and institutional changes) can these grievances be addressed in politically and economically feasible ways, and in ways that can be accepted by the majority of society? In which language or languages, by whom, and for whom should education be provided? Can devolution happen in a unitary state? How can state authorities and responsibilities be shared between central and regional governments?

Based on the above two criteria, the pro-secular papers clearly had more ideational preparation for undertaking specific reforms. For example, Figure 6.6 shows that the two pro-secular papers (roughly 317 codings per paper) contained more than triple the amount of discussion that took place in pro-religious papers (roughly 95 codings per paper) about TV, education, and teaching[168] in Kurdish. Further, the pro-secular papers had more positive and three times fewer negative codings on the

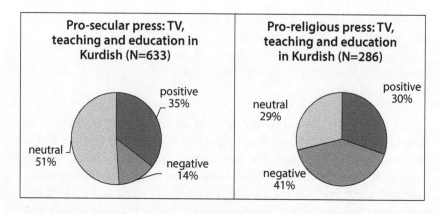

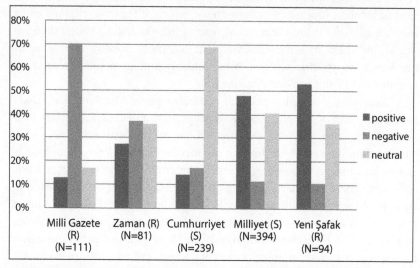

Figure 6.6. References to education on and TV in Kurdish in the pro-secular and pro-religious press, 1996–2004.

subject. With respect to normative views, however, there was a division within the pro-religious press. *Yeni Şafak* had the highest percentage of positive views among all the papers.

The data from 2007 and 2010 reinforced these findings. For these years, some additional subjects were covered, such as "the right to give Kurdish names to people and towns," "democratic autonomy," and "federation," which I aggregated with the others as "social, cultural and political rights." Again, the pro-secular newspapers (N = 50) contained more discussion than the pro-religious newspapers (N = 29), but the difference was now smaller (less than double the coverage).[169] Moreover, the fact that 44 percent of the views in the pro-secular papers were positive and 24 percent were negative suggests a discussion was taking place.

The rise in the amount of discussion in pro-religious papers could be considered an improvement in terms of ideational preparation, but the distribution was very skewed. *Yeni Şafak* had only three codings (all positive), which might have resulted from the uncritical acceptance of policies advocated by the pro-religious AKP government, especially in 2010. The *Zaman* writers discussed these subjects more often than their counterparts at *Yeni Şafak* (N = 26 versus N = 3), 44 percent positively and 20 percent negatively. This finding is interesting because *Zaman* belonged to the Gülen Islamist Movement at that time. The Gülenists were known to combine Islamism and Turkish nationalism and have been accused by the AKP government of opposing, indeed "sabotaging" the 2009 and 2013 initiatives.[170] For example, regarding an important institutional question, a 10 percent election threshold to enter parliament, which had long created a major disadvantage for pro-Kurdish parties, got only one coding in *Yeni Şafak* in 2007 and 2010, and this reference was critical of the threshold. By comparison, *Zaman* contained relatively more discussion (eight codings—one positive and seven negative). In the pro-secular *Hürriyet* and *Milliyet*, the same subject was coded nineteen times (sixteen negative and three neutral).

These findings suggest that the pro-religious elites' discursive support of ethnic diversity did not necessarily translate into actual support for the ethno-cultural and ethno-national rights and freedoms and legal/institutional reforms that would actually provide, protect, and regulate these freedoms and rights. At the very least, the pro-religious elites do not seem to have engaged in sufficient ideational discussion and preparation for well-considered reforms. Observations made in other studies support my theses here. For instance, in interviews conducted with pro-Islamic actors, questions such as "Do Kurds, Alevis, and Christians have equal rights and freedoms as other groups?" received only general answers, such as: "In principle, we believe in the equality of all." One AKP member, who described democracy as "people's ability to have the rights they want," responded: "That is a different matter," when he was reminded of the Kurdish demands for rights.[171]

One writer observed that there were three perspectives among Islamists on the Kurdish Question.[172] The Gülenists, whom the author referred to as "Statist Islamists," blend Turkish nationalist and Islamist ideologies. For the Gülenists, the problem is not Turkish nationalism itself but rather Turkish nationalism "which is deprived of an Islamic soul." Hence, they dismiss the existence of a Kurdish Question resulting from Kurdish differences among Muslims. A second perspective is held by "Turkish Islamists," who think that the problem is with Westernization and nationalism. In other words, they think that the Kurdish Conflict is an "invention" of Westerners. An Islamist writer expressed this as follows: "The Turks, Arabs and Persians did not occupy Kurdish geography. . . . The French Revolution occupied us with foreign and enemy ideals."[173] Therefore, Turkish Islamists expect Kurdish Islamists to forget about their separate problems and interests for the sake of the common problems of Muslims. Finally, there are the Kurdish Islamists, who do not want to reduce their problems to the "Kurds' Muslim egos" and wish to "maintain the struggle on the basis of cultural identity."[174]

All of this weakens the credibility of public/political claims that Turkish Islamists held an ideational advantage when it came to resolving the Kurdish Conflict and ideational explanations of the AKP's resolution attempts. As one critical observer put it:

By channeling the discussion of the emergence of Kurdish nationalism to its "root causes" identified as Ottoman-Turkish modernization, the Islamist writers shift the focus away from distribution and concentration of political power, the role of institutions and strategies of control which assume a heavy role for the evolution of Kurdish nationalism. In that sense, theirs is not a philosophical or structural critique of the history of modernization and its offspring concepts of nation, national identity, and citizenship. There is no historical and intellectual breadth in their analysis in terms of discovering the intervention of innate forces which gave rise to trajectories in the regime's drive to modernization without loss of its political control over the polity. Instead, spreading the contents and structures of European consciousness is assumed to give rise to what it does everywhere else, that is, the dissipation of religious values and beliefs as the most pervasive guide to moral conduct. The precondition for nationalism is then reduced to a decline in moral values caused by the onslaught of modernization.[175]

These observations are consistent with Sami Zubaida's more general analyses of political Islamism and ethnic/national diversity.[176]

> On the one hand, pan-Islamism has an anti-nationalist logic. On the other, this logic is not usually followed in practice. The Iranian Revolution, followed by the Gulf War, has, if anything, reinforced Iranian nationalism, to the detriment of the Kurds. In the short term, Islamic agitations are likely to lead to communalist strife between Sunni and Alevi Kurds . . . .But Islamists in power are no more attracted to democracy, pluralism and the rule of law than their pro-secular counterparts. They can be self-righteous in their rejection of democracy and pluralism as imperialist, Western divisive poisons. Note the antagonism of Algerian Islamists to Berber national expressions. Political Islam may be gratifying for some Kurds . . . .But it is not likely to lead to any novel solutions to the Kurdish question. It is more likely to attempt to eliminate the question in the name of Islamic unity, much as Atatürk denied Kurdish ethnic identity in favour of a national unity.[177]

In Turkey, the view that "Islam is the solution" for resolving ethno-political conflicts both Islamized ethnic politics and ethnicized Islamic politics.[178] Hence, Turkish and Kurdish religious elites embraced what one author called "religio-ethnic" categories, and, although they agreed that religion (Islam) can be a conflict-resolution tool, they "diverged in their interpretations of Islamic teachings and in their conceptualizations of religious and ethnic identities."[179] As a result, the Islamist ideology did not wipe out the ethnic/national differences that exist between Turkish and Kurdish Islamists: "Kurdish-Islamist writers tend to search for a 'space' for Kurdish ethnic distinctiveness within the framework of the suggested formula of ummah, the Islamic community of the faithful, while the position of the Turkish-Islamist writers leans heavily toward defending the integrity of the Turkish state rather than to acknowledging a Kurdish ethnic distinctiveness."[180]

A common religious cause does not eliminate the different priorities that are shaped by ethnic/national difference. The experiences of Turkish and Kurdish Islamists were not very different from those of Turkish and Kurdish socialists. As we saw in the previous chapters, when Kurdish socialists tried to create a space for Kurdish difference within the socialist project during the 1960s and '70s, Turkish socialists expected them to assimilate their Kurdish interests into the ideal of building socialism. This difference continues to reinforce the leftist moderate-moderate cooperation dilemma to this day. Between 2011 and 2013, for example, the "support" for the PKK as a "non-terrorist" organization and representative of the Kurds rose among both religious and nonreligious Kurds; this increase might have been caused, among various factors, by a cease fire at the end of the period. Another factor might have been the discrepancy that religious Kurds observed between the government's (and religious Turks') discourse of "Turkish-Kurdish religious brotherhood," on one hand, and its practice of securitizing and neglecting questions relating to Kurdish minority rights, on the other.[181]

The expectation that an Islamic national identity might solve the Kurdish Question much more easily than the Turkish identity drew on the assertion that the latter was an ethnic identity, the implications of which I discussed previously. At the end of the day, Islam also tolerates ethnic/national belongings as long as they do not take precedence over religious belonging.

It is debatable whether any identity or ideology can on its own be a guarantor of ethnic and cultural pluralism and human rights. Ideologies that seem relatively pluralist (including "moderate Islam" and "conservative democracy") can turn discursively authoritarian and be used to endorse authoritarian policies when political interests change and balances of power shift.[182] Focusing on ideology can lead to the holders of a single ideology becoming overconfident and shutting themselves off from criticism. At the very least, it may foster complacency and distract them from searching for complex legal, political, and institutional compromises. In a nutshell, pro-religious actors can lead the effort or contribute to resolving the Kurdish Conflict, but they must do so by contemplating legal/institutional reforms and by developing pluralist-democratic principles and values like other actors, rather than by singularly relying on their supposedly advantageous ideology or political identities.

In these respects, the political and intellectual explanations of the AKP's peace initiatives based on the party's built-in and ostensible, identity-based advantage (in circulation before and during the resolution attempts) became a causal factor themselves. They help to explain the failure of the initiatives and the AKP's authoritarian/nationalist turn. If the AKP—and the social and political elites it represented—had instead placed the emphasis on an ideational repertoire of specific policies, state/ society relations, institutions of checks and balances, and rule of law, this would have encouraged more self-restraint and sustainable policies. It would also have nurtured greater caution on the part of the supportive domestic and international actors.[183]

## CHAPTER 7

# Ideational Bottlenecks

My goal in this chapter is to unpack the ideational bottlenecks to which I referred in the previous chapters as causal factors that reinforce the structural dilemmas, among other things, by feeding the political beliefs, emotions, and attitudes that help reproduce the dilemmas and undermine efforts to resolve them. One can fully understand how structures and interests give rise to political conflicts only after accounting for the particular political beliefs and the discursive/interpretive lenses through which political actors interact with the structures and perceive their interests. It should be clear by now that what I mean here is not "ideologies" or "worldviews" as in Left/Right, conservative/liberal, religious/secular, or Kemalist/Islamist; rather, I am referring to particular beliefs and frames that often crosscut the major sociocultural and ideological divisions in Turkey, such as the interpretation of equal rights as same rights, the equation of cultural and political nationhood, and wariness of asymmetric governing systems and polynymous identities.

## Interpreting "Equal Rights" as "Same Rights"

Turkey's Constitutional Court emphasized the notion of equal rights when explaining its ruling to close the pro-Kurdish Democracy Party DEP in 1994:

> Since the French Revolution of 1789, "Equal Citizenship" has meant that all individuals who are part of the great majority are recognized as the ultimate and most valuable beings regardless of characteristics such as race, language, religion and denomination.[1]

How did the court envisage the provision of such equality? Any differential rights were anathema. The court's view was that if certain citizens had different rights due to their different characteristics, this would be contrary to the principle of equality. It reasoned that this could lead to a situation in which some citizens possessed either limited (i.e., more limited than others) or privileged rights. According to the court, the particular transformations that the Ottoman *millet* category had undergone during Ottoman and then Turkish nation building meant that such a question could only apply to "minorities"[2]—a term that came to take on a negative connotation in Turkey. By basing its judgment on this connotation, however, the court appeared to be legitimizing and reinforcing this connotation and perception:

> As previously stated, it is impossible to speak of any minority except "non-Muslim" citizens who are recognized as minorities [based on the 1923 Lausanne Treaty] within the integrity of the Turkish nation through certain international agreements. . . . Creating the feeling and idea among a group of non-preferential citizens that they are part of a minority and to request that they be subjected to a regime of *restricted rights* [emphasis mine] and that they become the minority while they are the nation itself cannot be interpreted in any other way than dismantling national integrity.[3]

This notion of strict equality might be understood within a framework of classical liberalism and republicanism. Empirically, and given the complexities of the Kurdish Question, granting differential rights based on multiculturalism may or may not successfully address the Kurds' demands for recognition.[4] Across the world, public/political debates on the pros and cons of multiculturalist polices are ongoing with respect to their consequences for intergroup equality, peace, and justice; nevertheless, a tradition of liberal communitarian—and feminist[5]—thought has long argued, and practice has shown, that at least some differential rights for disadvantaged groups such as women and ethnic/racial minorities might not conflict with liberal democratic norms of equality or with those of other traditions and schools of thought—and may strengthen rather than weaken equality in practice.[6] Hence, on normative grounds, having different rights does not mean having limited rights, or, according to the court's interpretation, fewer rights, than other citizens.[7] On the contrary, whether one works with a notion of equality of opportunity or outcomes, such equality may necessitate that different groups have additional rights arising from their different conditions and relative disadvantages.

Consider how an MP from the Central Anatolian province of Konya—who was representing the pro-secular and center-left CHP in an interparty parliamentary commission that was set up in the early 2010s to reform the constitution—explained the disadvantages he had suffered as a Kurdish boy at the very beginning of his education (where all classes were held in Turkish):

> In 1960 I went to primary school in the village. Later, we migrated to the center of Cihanbeyli in Konya as a family. I was in year two. I didn't speak a single word of Turkish. I was in utter shock. . . . Teacher Ismet assigned my classmate Bahar [a Turkish female name also common in Iran and other majority Muslim countries] a task. Who is Bahar? An unattainable person for me. A utopia. In a few years she helped me to adjust. I was lucky to have Bahar. Since not everyone could have a Bahar and a teacher like Ismet, the state should pave the way for everyone to learn their native language.[8]

As I discussed in previous chapters, a common language (Turkish) has been a key ingredient of both the Turkish identity and a common identity in Turkey in general; it is also a means of socioeconomic integration and achieving equal opportunities. Against this background, it might be in the best interest of both Turks and Kurds to offer bilingual or multilingual education, instead of education in Kurdish per se. A command of Turkish is crucial for Kurdish citizens to have equal opportunities in predominantly non-Kurdish areas; similarly, Turks wishing to work or do business in predominantly Kurdish areas would be disadvantaged if Kurds did not speak any Turkish. A simple application of the principle of Pareto-optimality could be useful here: any additional rights (such as bilingual education in predominantly Kurdish regions or even neighborhoods) that do not disadvantage any Turks but provide more equal opportunities for Kurds would strengthen rather than weaken equality. However, such notions of equality were not widely articulated and strengthened in Turkey during the 2000s. Options such as bilingual or multilingual education were discussed, but were primarily justified on the basis of the standard stories we have discussed in previous chapters.[9] Dominant notions of "equal rights understood as same rights" also continued to prevail.

## Not Distinguishing between Cultural and Political Nationhood: Cultural Nationhood with Positive-Sum Divisibility Versus Political Nationhood (Sovereignty) with Zero-Sum Divisibility

By not distinguishing between political and cultural meanings of nation-hood, both many Turks and many Kurds turn the Kurdish Question into a question with zero-sum answers. Many Turks perceive any minority demands for cultural rights as a net loss for themselves and as a threat that divides and diminishes something they possess. Likewise, they tend to perceive and dismiss as separatism (*bölücülük*, which literally means divisionism) all manifestations of Kurdish nationalism—even when it is peaceful and consists of exclusively cultural claims. In turn, many Kurds perceive the Turks' defining them as an ethnic group (rather than as a nation) to represent a net loss of what they have or should have. They interpret it as a loss of culture and identity, as well as a loss of political and economic assets. This contributes to a situation that hinders dialogue and negotiation.

As I have discussed in detail in previous chapters, Turkey was founded as a state based on the sovereignty of one single, political nation. This happened at the end of the War of Independence, in which ethnic Turks and Kurds generally fought together, and with the 1923 signing of the Treaty of Lausanne. Therefore, some Kurdish nationalist claims of separate nationhood—most clearly but not exclusively those claiming the right to external self-determination—pose a critical challenge as they aim to split an arguably indivisible asset: the national sovereignty that Turkish and Kurdish citizens jointly possess. It creates a potentially insurmount-able constitutional and political problem, unless changes are made to the fundamental structures of the nation-state of Turkey.

However, the nation has cultural meanings as well, which can more easily be absorbed and tolerated by a "nation-state"—the meaning of which is also controversial and contested, as previously discussed. The cultural meaning of nation is part of the Turkish lexicon and social discourse. A popular saying that is often used by even the most stringent advocates of single and ostensibly homogeneous nationhood in a political sense—seemingly without being bothered by the apparent contradiction with their political ideology—is, "[T]here are seventy-two nations in Turkey."[10] Cultural claims of the existence of multiple nationhoods in a "nation-state" can most easily be incorporated into "state-nation" models, which should be considered a subcategory of the nation-state model, as I examined in chapter 3, and into policies of asymmetric autonomy.

In fact, this may be the only possible and democratic way. As Stepan, Linz, and Yadav argue:

> [The idea that] every state must contain within itself one and not more than one culturally homogeneous nation, that every state should be a nation, and that every nation should be a state . . . .Given the reality of sociocultural diversity in many of the polities of the world, this widespread belief seems to us to be misguided, indeed dangerous.[11]

Political and cultural meanings of nation have different implications in terms of how nation-states can harbor differential rights for different "nations" among their citizens. External sovereignty—the basis of political nationhood—cannot easily be divided into its parts without diminishing the whole. A nation-state can decide to *share* its sovereignty with international and supranational entities, such as the European Union, or with ethnic or regional groups within itself; but it is hard to *divide* sovereignty without reducing it. In a sovereign decision, such as Brexit, a people can either have the right to decide jointly, or, if a part of them—say, the Scottish in the UK—possesses a separate decision-making authority, the remaining population cannot have the right to take decisions that are binding on them also. Similarly, constitutions can be amended by the approval of a whole sovereign nation or by the bodies representing the whole nation. If this authority were divided into several parts, this could produce multiple and conflicting constitutions. Hence, if a subgroup makes an amendment by itself, the rest would have to either accept this decision or else make its own constitution.

However, notions related to identity, culture, and territory can be divided without being diminished. The cultural "assets" that form cultural nationhood can be divided with a positive-sum outcome. The fact that some people know a city as Diyarbakır (the official name used by most Turks) and others know it as Amed (the name of the city preferred by many Kurds) does not reduce the value of the city; it may even increase it, as the city could more easily be seen as a site of multiple cultural/linguistic heritages. In the same way, the Kurds' claim to be a cultural nation does not diminish the Turks' own ability to be a cultural nation, or the ability of Turks and Kurds together to form another cultural "nation of Turkey," or, for that matter, one sovereign political nation. They can coexist.

Even though, as I will argue below, such a distinction is present in Turkey's historical political repertoire, it appears to have disappeared from common public/political usage. In Diyarbakır in 1975, when CHP leader and former prime minister Bülent Ecevit responded to those shouting out the slogan "freedom to the peoples" by saying, "There are not peoples (*halklar*) in Turkey but *the* people (*halk*),"[12] he had a monosemic understanding of people (nation) in mind. Clearly, Ecevit interpreted the slogan through the lens of political nationhood. He was concerned that recognizing multiple peoples (i.e., political nations) in Turkey would translate into divided sovereignty and secession. Had Ecevit perceived the slogan as an assertion of cultural nationhood, making a distinction between the concept of nation's cultural and political meanings, however, he might have felt less threatened.

Thus, the lack of such a distinction in Turkish public/political discourse is an ideational factor in itself that undermines the reform efforts to resolve the three dilemmas. Why this is so requires an explanation given that Turkey in fact has the historical precedence of making just such a distinction during its War of Liberation.

Turkey's nation builders did indeed distinguish between political and cultural nationhood (without naming them as such) during the War of Independence and, partially, during the initial founding years of the Republic. As discussed in chapters 3 and 4, this was apparent in the discourse of the leaders (of Turkish and Kurdish origin) of the national movement, most notably in the words of Mustafa Kemal (Atatürk). By mentioning both groups with their separate names and distinct identities, Kemal asserted that the "Turks" and "Kurds" shared *a common fate* as *a single body*. Simultaneously, there were frequent references by leaders of the movement to the separate (ethnic/cultural) "components" of this body. Hence, the nation that the National Struggle Campaign claimed to lead and represent was conceived of as a singular entity, and notions of "common destiny and will" denoted a shared sovereignty. This remained constant even when the nation itself was imagined using different names. For example, leaders of the campaign could use the term *nation of Turkey* but not *nations of Turkey*. The term *Turkish and Kurdish nation* could be employed but not *Turkish and Kurdish nations*.

While there thus was no indication that a state based on two different sovereignties or political nations was imagined, however, the same statements also referred to the Kurds as a group whose *separate identity and lawful rights and freedoms* (*Kürtlerin hukuku*) were recognized within the "nation." The idea of separate political nationhood was refused, but separate cultural nationhood was not denied. Critical steps and processes along the path to nation building, such as the Erzurum Congress, the Amasya Circular, the deliberations at the Grand National Assembly of Turkey, and the statements of Mustafa Kemal, demonstrate that the Kurds were considered as a people comprising a distinct cultural component within the imagination of a single nation sharing a common homeland and sovereignty.

In his letter to Cemilpaşazade Kasım Bey during the National Struggle, Mustafa Kemal wrote: "Turks and Kurds are full brothers who will not accept being separated from one another; our conscientious debt is to defend our independence as a single body and single heart as Kurds, Turks and all [the other] Islamic components, and to prevent the motherland from disintegration. We can be completely certain of the outcome thanks to the '*Turkish and Kurdish nation's*' [emphasis mine] ambition to attain this supreme purpose."[13]

Here, the expression "Turkish and Kurdish nation" echoes the name of Czecho-Slovakia (the hyphen is mine)—the state of the Czechs and Slovaks—which was founded after its separation from the Austro-Hungarian Empire in 1918, at the end of World War I. It was not uncommon in those postimperial times to imagine such nation names. The leaders of the National Struggle, who were closely following the international developments, must have been aware of these examples of building new states based on multiple political nationhoods, but did not follow them. In a telegraph to Kazım Karabekir—a major leader and commander of the eastern armies during the National Struggle—Mustafa Kemal wrote: "as a component [of the nation] . . . that has been the target of Armenian gangs' atrocities and attacks . . . I am determined to embrace the Kurds as full brothers and to unite the whole nation around one point."[14]

Mustafa Kemal's viewpoint and rhetorical acts of nation building are even more clearly in evidence in a famous address to the Grand National Assembly in 1920 (the emphases are mine):

The persons who are intended here and who make up your Supreme Assembly are not only Turkish, Circassian, Kurdish or Laz. They are Components of Islam[15] [*Anasır-ı İslamiye*], a genuine *collective (or collection) formed by all of them*. Therefore, the aims represented by this supreme council, the rights, lives, honor and glory of which we have resolved to save, are not particular to one component of Islam. They belong to *one mass* composed of Components of Islam. We all know this to be so. . . . It comprises my *national* boundaries . . . .Mosul, Sulaymaniyah and Kirkuk. We said that this is our *national* boundary! Even though north of Kirkuk there are Kurds as well as Turks. We did not distinguish between them. Therefore, *the nation* we are busy preserving and defending does not consist of a single component. It is formed of various Islamic components.[16]

During the War of Independence, names such as "Components of Islam" (or Islamic components), "the People of Turkey," and "Turkish and Kurdish nation" were used by nation builders interchangeably in reference to the same mass of people, that is, a still-polynymous nation in the making. After 1923, the term *Turkish nation* began to be used. However, even in 1924, Fethi Okyar referred to "the Turkish and Kurdish brothers of the Turkish nation."[17]

In chapters 3 and 4, I examined why and how this transition took place, offering a mainly political explanation. What needs to be highlighted here is that these statements distinguished between the political and cultural meanings of "nation." Terms such as *component, race,* and *folk (kavim)* were used interchangeably in reference to ethnic/cultural groupings that roughly correspond to cultural nations, thus, nations that can coexist within one sovereign nation but whose distinct lawful rights should be recognized. Meanwhile, the term *nation (millet)* was almost always used in the singular form and in reference to a political nation, meaning, a sovereign people.

The Turkish mission led by Ismet Pasha during the Lausanne Conference emphasized that the Turks and the Kurds were a single body and— to refer to my previous argument—that they had common sovereignty. They succeeded in having the notion recognized that among Muslims, no group was a minority (and by the same token, no group was a majority). In order to support the Turkish mission at Lausanne, MPs from various eastern provinces sent a message to the conference declaring that "the Turks and Kurds are a single mass. The Kurds can never separate from the community of Turkey."[18]

As a result, unlike other contemporary examples of post–World War I states such as Czechoslovakia and the "State of Slovenes, Croats, and Serbs" (Yugoslavia), the names of which reflected a multinational model, Turkey was not founded as a "State of Turks and Kurds" or as a "State of Islamic Components." The new government of Turkey managed to obtain international recognition of its claim that only religious minorities would have a minority status. This represented an exception to the common contemporary practice within the League of Nations whereby ethnic or linguistic minorities would legally be recognized as such upon the formation of new states.[19]

In a nutshell, Turkey became internationally recognized as a state with a single sovereign nation as a result of war making (World War I and then the War of Liberation), geopolitical developments, and the unwillingness of the Allied Powers to prolong the war, the decisions of Turkish nationalist leaders, and the bargaining power gained by the nationalist movement through their victory in the War of Liberation.

Nevertheless, Turkey could on its own recognize ethnic/cultural rights—as in the right to education, trial, and political activity in Kurdish—for the Muslim components of the new nation. Although it was not obligatory, the Lausanne Treaty did in fact allow such an interpretation.[20] Indeed, Muslim minority rights might have been established based upon the fact that the National Struggle distinguished between political and cultural nationhood and that Mustafa Kemal stated that "the people of Turkey who founded the Republic of Turkey are called the Turkish nation."[21] However, as I have argued previously, such a path was ruled out by the political decisions taken during the formative period, which addressed but were unable to sustainably resolve the three dilemmas simultaneously. Hence, the fact that the distinction made between cultural and political nationhood during the National Struggle appears to have disappeared from the public/political discourse after the formative period may also be interpreted as a product of these political developments, rather than a self-evident and inevitable outcome of culture, Turkish nationalism, or nationalism in general.

## The Rejection of Asymmetric Rights and Polysemic and Polynymous Identities

### SYMMETRY IN GOVERNANCE

The Ottoman order was based on asymmetric institutions and rights that applied to different territories, peoples, and social classes. For instance, there were differences in the models used to govern Albanian Muslims and Kurdish Muslims (both peripheral people inhabiting mountainous frontier regions). During the Ottoman modernization (and later nation-building) efforts in the eighteenth and nineteenth centuries, this asymmetry was initially—and briefly—formalized as a settlement between central and provincial state elites.[22] Subsequently, this settlement was increasingly replaced with a dominant trend toward establishing symmetrical rules, rights, and authorities that would prevail across different regions and social groups. Still, the Ottoman order, which prevailed across a vast, multinational, and multiconfessional terrain, remained a colossal assemblage of overlapping and asymmetrical institutions, principles, and practices.[23] This was perceived as a cacophony and a source of weakness by secularist modernizers, who might also have been overwhelmed by the difficulties of nation- and state building modeled on European examples, given their complex legacy. Hence, influenced by the example of France, Republican administrations vehemently rejected asymmetric practices and opted for symmetric governance practices and principles of rights.

During and after the War of Liberation, local autonomy was envisaged for the Kurds, but only in a symmetrical fashion that also applied to other regional groups. For example, in a speech dated 1922, Hüseyin Rauf Bey, MP from Sivas, stated: "The destiny of the Kurds is one with the people of Turkey, they share common goals and the same religion . . . .To speak of minority rights for the Kurds means to speak of it for the Turks."[24] In other words, it was thought that a status given to a Muslim component among the people of Turkey had to also be granted to other Muslim components.

Mustafa Kemal expressed his imagined symmetric autonomy or decentralization in a famous statement given to the press in January 1923:

> Kurdish components are settled within our borders [the borders of the National Pact, which encompasses Mosul] in such a way that they form the majority in very few places. Over time they have stopped being the majority and intermingled with the Turks to such an extent that if we wanted to draw a border for the sake of the Kurds, we would have to demolish Turkishness and Turkey . . . .Therefore, rather than imagining Kurdishness on its own, a kind of self-government will be formed [everywhere] in accordance with our Constitution. Under such circumstances, whichever *liva*[25] has Kurdish populations, they will govern themselves autonomously. Moreover,

whenever the people of Turkey are referenced, they should be expressed together with [the nation, people of Turkey] . . . .The Grand National Assembly of Turkey comprises the competent representatives of both Turks and Kurds and these two components have united all of their interests and destinies. That is to say, they know that this is something shared. It would be inappropriate to draw a separate border.[26]

Still today, it is common to find that Kurdish demands for such things as educational rights or autonomy are opposed on the basis of arguments such as: "Then groups such as the Circassians and the Laz should also be given these rights, but the state cannot absorb this." Legal and political elites strongly associate unitary state with centralized state administration, more so than other centralized unitary states, such as France, or decentralized unitary states, such as Italy.[27] Hence, all local and metropolitan governments and potential regional administrative structures are constitutionally subject to a strict interpretation of the principle of "administrative tutelage" (*idari vesayet*). Thus, theoretically, central governments can make any decision without consulting with local governments, and they can monitor and annul any local government decisions and cancel delegated local authorities based on the principle of deconcentration (*ademi temerküz*).[28] Based on this principle, for example, Turkey approved the European Charter of Local Self-Governments only in 1993 with reservations on several major articles, and, President Sezer vetoed a major reform law of decentralization in 2004.[29]

If there are no other groups expressing such demands, asymmetrical rights, or devolution, do not contradict the principle of the unitary state. On the contrary, asymmetrical decentralization poses a lesser challenge to a unitary state because it only requires a partial restructuring of state administration compared to symmetric decentralization, which necessitates a wholesale restructuring.

To differing degrees, unitary states as dissimilar as Britain, France, Finland, Morocco, the Phillipines, and Mali have delegated governance authorities and legislative prerogatives to local and regional administrations through asymmetric practices; they have done so to accommodate regional needs and to prevent and settle conflicts.[30] Reforming such domains as legislatures, education, economics, and teritorial self-governance, such rearrangements have led to peace in numerous post-conflict cases.[31] For example, in Finland—a country with a unitary state—the Åland Islands, inhabited by ethnic Swedes, have as much autonomy as the autonomy of regional governments in federal states, but such autonomy does not apply to the rest of Finland. Stepan, Linz, and Yadav term such practices "federacy" rather than "federation."[32] Federations can have drawbacks, the authors maintain, such as an inability to implement constructive social policies across a country due to the difficulty of reaching compromises between states. There are drawbacks to asymmetric practices, too, of course, and symmetric solutions may be ideal when there is no consensus among different regions over certain policies on matters such as the need for autonomous cultural and educational policies in a particular region but not in others.

In addition to their defensive positions aimed at protecting the unitary status quo, the actors who recognize the presence of a *Kurdish Conflict* have made two solution proposals with a view to reforming the unitary state structures in Turkey. The first may be called *symmetric multiculturalism*. According to this proposal, the problems of the Kurds should be addressed not only for the Kurds' sake but for all the different groups and regions in Turkey, and through recipes such as empowering local governments across the country and education in mother tongues or in multiple languages wherever needed. According to this perspective, if attempts are made to solve the distinctive sociocultural, political, and economic problems of the Kurds through social and political reforms that are only implemented for the Kurds, this can create greater problems for the Kurds and for Turkey in general. For example, local autonomy rights that are granted solely to the Kurds can give rise to negative reactions against the Kurds among other groups. It can decrease the feeling of equality and unity between the Kurds and other groups and lead to the pursuit of "identity justice" becoming more prominent, rather than the pursuit of social and economic justice. These are matters of global concern.[33]

The second perspective—mainly expressed by Kurds and pro-Kurdish parties—might be termed "*asymmetric multiculturalism*" or "*asymmetric autonomism*." According to this view, the historical, geographical, and demographic characteristics of the Kurds and the legacy of past Kurdish rebellions, oppressive state policies, and the war with the PKK all give rise to different needs and demands among the Kurds. Therefore, besides the democratization and multiculturalism that may apply to the whole country, this Conflict requires certain advanced reforms specifically designed and implemented for the Kurds, such as regional autonomy and the constitutional recognition of the Kurdish identity.

## Symmetry in Identity

A similar aversion to asymmetric solutions also exists vis-à-vis conflicting identity perceptions and identity-related demands. The most politically thorny and publicly controversial discussions about constitutional reforms often end up regarding the constitutional definitions and redefinitions of Turkish citizenship, national identity, and Turkishness, and proposals to make references to other identities such as Of-Turkey (*Türkiyeli*) and Kurdishness. A reason for this is that people symmetrically link discussions about recognizing the Kurdish identity with other identity questions as well, most consequentially with Turkishness, as I have discussed with examples in the previous chapter.

In fact, theoretically speaking, recognizing the Kurdish identity does not require a symmetric discussion of Turkishness and other identities. It is commonplace that identities have asymmetric and plural definitions and names. The same ethnonym or national identity name, such as "Turk" for example, can be polysemic. It can asymmetrically carry plural meanings held by different groups and be applied to different contexts. In different contexts and for some people, it can be associated with innate and ascriptive characteristics, such as ancestry, mother tongue, and ethnicity, while in other contexts and for other people, it can be associated with acquired and chosen characteristics, such as citizenship, homeland patriotism, and religious and cultural belonging. What's more, the same identity can be polynymous. It can asymmetrically be embraced with different names by different people.

As I have discussed extensively in this book, Turkishness has strongly polysemic characteristics. On one hand, it carries the meaning of an ethnic, historical, linguistic, and trans-national category and identity related to ethnicity, lineage, and mother tongue. It transcends Turkey's borders and creates a cultural bond and capital with other Turkic people across the world. This ethno-linguistic category has proved to be remarkably flexible, adaptive, and inclusive throughout history and across different geographies.[34]

At the same time, Turk has a meaning particular to Turkey, as a national or common identity that can be acquired or chosen through cultural assimilation, citizenship, and patriotism. This also creates a common bond and social capital among millions of Turkish citizens, regardless of their ethnic and linguistic origins. A great many people who adopt the Turkish identity in Turkey know that their ancestors (often as recent as parents and grandparents) originated from a very wide area extending from Bosnia to Greece, Syria, and the Caucasus. For most of them, their mother tongue is not Turkish, or was not Turkish until recently. In addition, there are millions of descendants of autochthonous Anatolian people, including Armenians, Laz, and Arabs, whose mother tongue is not or was not Turkish. Yet many of these autochthonous Anatolians still consider themselves to be Turkish. These include people who have been assimilated into Turkishness and have relinquished their other, ascriptive identity, as well as people who embrace Turkishness as a national identity in addition to embracing and expressing their own separate ethno-linguistic identity. The same person can simultaneously embrace these different meanings of Turkishness and use them in different contexts. When relating to an Azeri or Karachay Turk, a Turk of-Turkey may draw on a definition of Turkishness as an ethno-linguistic category and switch to a territorial and citizenship-based definition when relating to a Laz or Bosnian of-Turkey.

Then, there are members of the official non-Muslim minorities—the Greek (Rum), Jewish, and Armenian communities—who are typically either bilingual or monolingual Turkish speakers and embrace Turkishness as an emic, national, or territorial identity. There are also non-Muslim minorities that are officially nonrecognized—a historical product of politics rather than ideology and principle, as I emphasize throughout the book—such as Yezidis and Syriac Orthodox Christians, many of whom also display similar identity and language characteristics to those of recognized minorities. However, as already discussed, as an etic identity, many Muslim Turks have a hard time attributing Turkishness to these (recognized or nonrecognized non-Muslim) groups. In part, this is due to the historical legacy of the National Struggle's having been fought between Muslim and non-Muslim autochthonous people as well as external armies, but, ultimately, dominant perceptions were also determined through political processes such as the Lausanne Treaty negotiations and "intra-Turkish" elite power struggles. Finally, there are identities such as Anatolianness (*Anadoluluk*) and Of-Turkey (*Türkiyelilik*). Many Kurds embrace this identity since they perceive it as different from Turkishness. Many Turks, however, make little distinction between these identities and Turkishness; to them, somebody of-Turkey would also be a Turk, and vice versa. Hence, the ways in which Turkishness is perceived by Turks and Kurds is asymmetrical.

Therefore, this polysemic and polynymous nature of Turkishness *is* arguably the empirical and social reality in Turkey. However, this reality is not acknowledged by state institutions, laws, or civil discourse—or, for that matter, by academic research and discourse; as a result, there are no idioms offered to express it. The constitution and other laws do not make any reference to the multiple meanings of Turkishness or to hybrid and hyphenated identities. Nor did the civil discourse develop a language to express the prevailing multiple, hybrid, and asymmetric identity expressions as a richness; hence, as any casual conversation with ordinary people would reveal, many Turks also have a hard time formulating and expressing their Turkishness in a way that can simultaneously acknowledge their diverse backgrounds and identity consciousnesses. Indeed, the Turkish language does not even have the means to express hyphenated identities. Translating "Turkish-Kurd" or "Kurdish-Turk" (or other hyphenated identities) literally as "Türk-Kürt" or "Kürt-Türk" is not possible and sounds awkward. It would also be widely perceived as a negation of one identity or the other.

In this respect, this incongruity between the social reality, on one hand, and the laws, institutions, and language, on the other, is a causal factor that undermines efforts to address the common identity dilemma and helps to explain the endurance of the Kurdish Conflict. This incongruity is in turn rooted in the ideational bottleneck that presumes that identities should have single meanings and names that are symmetrically embraced by different groups. The debates on Turkey as a multicultural mosaic that I discussed in the last chapter fall short of producing a terminology capable of capturing polysemic and polynymous identities. When the public/political struggles pursue single meanings and names (even when they claim to reflect diversity), these automatically become struggles with zero-sum outcomes, where one group or the other is destined to feel defeated, neglected, or "less."

To what extent can the propagation of polysemic Turkishness help resolve the common identity dilemma and mitigate the identity conflict between Turks and Kurds? Given the history of the Kurdish Conflict, it is understandable that many Kurds (and some members of other ethnic groups) may feel that polysemic Turkishness is just another, indirect way of imposing assimilationist Turkishness on Kurds. Hence, the only solution may be an asymmetric one whereby Turks and Kurds accept each other's different understandings of Turkishness, one polysemic and one monosemic.

Contrary to a widely held view, the current constitution of Turkey allows for an interpretation that acknowledges the polysemic nature of the national identity. Article 66 states, "Everyone bound to the Turkish state through the bond of citizenship is a Turk." On one hand, this definition can be—and is widely—interpreted as defining who the citizens of

Turkey are, that is, defining them as Turks and negating identities such as Kurdish, which is the source of many grievances among non-Turkish ethnic/linguistic groups. On the other hand, what often misses the eye is that this article also defines who the Turks are (or should be in the eyes of the law and the state) and categorically rules out ascriptive definitions, such as those based on ethnicity and religion (since *everyone* who is a citizen is also a Turk).

Whether one accepts one interpretation or the other (or both), discussions on constitutional and citizenship reform also trigger discussions on the Turkish identity.[35] According to a popular liberal view, the constitution should not attempt to define identities. Article 66 can be transformed into an article that only regulates citizenship. However, while this may be a partial solution, there are many other references to national identity and Turkishness in the constitution. It is debatable whether constitutions that are free of any references to (common or particular) identity categories—for example, in line with the constitutional patriotism theorized and popularized by Jürgen Habermas—would be either possible or desirable, in terms of legitimacy, functionality, and holding a society together.[36] A main political obstacle to constructing such a model in Turkey is the fact that for many Turks, the references to Turkishness in state laws and symbols are not only a source of bonding with the state, they are also identity markers and a source of cohesion for their state-nation; therefore, to remove them would be perceived as a major loss and defeat. However, identity-based constitutional reform is one of the most important demands of the Kurds. How is it possible to resolve a conundrum wherein one part of society requests that the constitution express a common and specifically Turkish identity, while the other part considers this as a negation of its own identity?

I think that there may only be an *a*symmetrical solution to this question.[37] A constitution devoid of identity is also a symmetrical recipe (scrapping all identity references symmetrically from the constitution). The common national identity does not need to be adopted symmetrically by everyone with the same name and definition. It might be best if the constitution used a flexible notion of national identity, which recognized its polynymous nature and allowed different groups to embrace it with different names and contents. As I discussed in previous chapters, the 1924 Constitution was more advanced in this respect. It explicitly accepted that Turkishness had different meanings when it affirmed, "Everyone bound to the Turkish state through the bond of citizenship is a Turk *in terms of* *citizenship*"[emphasis mine]. Similarly, when National Struggle leader and later Prime Minister Okyar referred to "the Turkish and Kurdish brothers of the Turkish nation," he was also implicitly embracing a polysemic understanding of Turkishness, by using in the same sentence two different meanings of "Turk"—one as an ethnic/linguistic component and the other as the name of the nation.[38]

Hence, a viable reform might be to replace the current Article 66 with a statement such as: "In Turkey everyone is called a Turk or Of-Turkey (*Türkiyeli*) in terms of citizenship regardless of their religion, sect, ethnicity and race." Similar formulations might be used wherever identity is referenced elsewhere in the constitution. The preamble could also be amended to include quotes from the National Struggle (*Milli Mücadele*) that explicitly refer to different components such as "Turk" and "Kurd" and implicitly acknowledge the polysemic nature of Turkishness. While the references to "Turk" would prevent Turks from perceiving a sense of loss, the references to "Of-Turkey" and "Kurd" identities could address the Kurds' longing for identity acknowledgment and equality and fear of assimilation. In other words, such a formulation could help accommodate both groups' concerns about ontological and "societal security"[39] and "dignity"[40]

## Conflating the Notion of Imagined Nation with Imaginary Nation

As I have discussed in previous chapters, Turkish nationalism, whether in its "defensive" or "proto-liberal" versions, enjoys a privileged and hegemonic position in Turkey's civil discourse and ideological spectrum. It crosscuts Left/Right and religious/secular fault lines and is frequently used by the state and much of society to justify and normalize many past and present, authoritarian and diversity-phobic policies and practices.[41] In reaction to the democracy-undermining consequences of this form of normalization, and parallel to a massive scholarly and intellectual literature on the dangers of nationalism in the world, since the 1980s, there have been major intellectual and political attempts to dethrone nationalism.[42] Remembering the adverse consequences for the Kurdish Conflict of hardened nationalism, hawkish nationalist policies, and sacralized national identities and symbols, these dethroning attempts seem justified and might contribute toward conflict resolution and democratization. However, rather than critically deconstruct the actions of nationalist actors and desacralize national identities by showing that they are *imagined* social constructions like other social identities, these attempts have tried to demonstrate that nations (especially the Turkish nation) are *imaginary* or artificial. In my opinion, if not the project itself, then the way it was made might have hardened nationalism by triggering a defensive backlash rather than subduing it.

Hence, Benedict Anderson's seminal conceptualization of nations as *"imagined communities"* is routinely and wrongly translated into Turkish in critical writings as *"hayali cemaat,"* which actually means *"imaginary communities."*[43] In fact, a correct translation should be *"tahayyül edilmiş cemaat."* Anderson explains how modern nations have been socially and politically constructed by states and social/political elites, who drew on material conditions, such as the growth of print capitalism, that facilitated this process. Anderson is not implying that national categories are any more "unreal" than other social identities, which are also constructed.[44] On the contrary, what Anderson wishes to explain is the puzzle of how national identities (ones that are relatively successful) become so real that millions of people can at times voluntarily sacrifice their lives in solidarity with other group members, even though they have never had any physical contact with one another. By way of comparison, historically and for various reasons, socialist movements have been relatively less successful—despite their more "real" material bases according to Marxist theories—than nationalist movements in constructing class-based identities that transcend national borders and effectively mobilize the masses.

Certain national identities are relatively "artificial" categories, in the sense that they were constructed and imposed by external powers but remained as political projects that were never fully embraced and internalized by most of the peoples who comprised the nations in question. But none of this makes these nations more "unreal" than other, less widely held social/political identities.

All social categories and identities, including family, marriage, state, human rights and justice, sex and gender, religion and sects, have been imagined by people in certain periods of history and constructed through social and political processes, even though they are of course built upon the structures of human mind and material conditions.[45] Most of social reality has been imagined by someone at some point in history, including such key principles for modern democracies as the notion that people are born with inherent rights, which was envisioned in relatively modern times. For sure, these social constructions can be deconstructed and criticized, however, to characterize them as imaginary would conflict with analytical, practical, linguistic, and normative realities that give meaning to the lives of the millions of people who have internalized them. In the words of a historical and political sociologist and prominent scholar of the Kurds:

> [Nationalist historiography is] completely real from the moment it becomes part of a social and political activity. It is clear that historiography is a component of imagining a community and it is accepted to a great extent; but historiography becomes an area of interest to the social scientist not as an imaginary thing, on the contrary, as something that produces real effects. It is one of the ways of the social construction of reality.[46]

During the debates in Turkey, in addition to making implicit and explicit assertions that national identities are imaginary constructs, there have been implicit and explicit assertions made that the Turkish national identity is a particularly unsuccessful and artificial project. These claims are not borne out by the empirical and comparative data, which show that this identity is internalized by large portions of Turkey's population and constitutes an important part of their self-image, compared to, for example, other nationalist projects such as the construction of Iraqi, Syrian, Somalian, or Yugoslav national identities.

For example, in former Yugoslavia in 1981, only 5.4 percent of people adopted the Yugoslav identity (as opposed to identities such as Croatian, Serbian, or Bosnian) and by 1991, this level had fallen to 3 percent.[47] Instead, according to the World Values Survey conducted from 2005 to 2008, 81.3 percent of people living in Turkey were "very proud" of their country's national (Turkish) identity, while a further 15.1 percent were "rather proud." Only 2.9 percent and 0.6 percent respectively stated that they were "not very proud" or "not proud at all." Likewise, 61.7 percent and 31.9 percent of the people (93.6 percent of the total combined) respectively expressed that they "completely agree" or "agree" with the statement, "I consider myself to be a citizen of my country."[48] Just 6.4 percent "disagree" or "completely disagree" with the statement. It may be no coincidence that the percentage of people who disagreed with the statement more or less corresponded to the percentage of people who vote for pro-Kurdish political parties, i.e., somewhere between one-half and one-third of Turkey's Kurds. Hence, for a great majority of Turkey's population, with the exception of a minority (who may consist of people especially aggrieved by Turkish state policies in the Kurdish Conflict), the Turkish national identity seems to be a real, internalized, and valued category.

Other research supported these data. Konda found that 90.3 percent of people who self-defined as Turkish and 66.8 percent of those who self-defined as Kurdish expressed that it was "important" or "very important" for them "to be identified as Of-Turkey (*Türkiyeli*)." Similarly, for 95.1 percent of the Turks and 68.2 percent of the Kurds, it was either important or very important to be identified as "a citizen of the Republic of Turkey." Comparatively, it was important or very important respectively for 63.7 percent, 73.6 percent, and 81.8 percent of Turks and 67.2 percent, 75.2 percent, and 81 percent of Kurds to be identified in accordance with their birthplace, ethnic origin, and religion/sect. Only 4.4 percent of Turks and 13.8 percent of Kurds thought that being identified as being Of-Turkey was unimportant or very unimportant.[49]

## CHAPTER 8

# Return to Point Zero

## *New Political Choices Informed by New Ideas*

In this book, I have tried to show that ethnic/national and regional con-flicts can arise as derivatives of other, larger unresolved quarrels and, thus, their resolutions can also hinge on the resolution of these other cleavages.

### A Turkish Choice More than a Kurdish One

I have argued and explained that one of the world's most violent and protracted conflicts, Turkey's Kurdish Conflict, is predominantly—i.e., besides the dynamics that mainly concern Kurds—the byproduct of broader, more complicated disputes that are mainly intra-Turkish in nature and have little to do with the Kurds. I formulated these disputes in terms of three dilemmas: common identity dilemma, elite cooperation dilemma, and external security dilemma. These dilemmas are primarily about Turks: they prevail among Turks and require addressing by Turks.

For the resolution of the dilemmas, "Turks," and especially "Turkish" social and political elites, must successfully rise to the task of overcoming political and ideational challenges. In order to address the "elite coopera-tion dilemma," for example, Turkish elites need firstly to achieve sufficient unity among themselves. They can do so "politically" by agreeing on power sharing and by building inter-elite trust; and they can do so "ideationally" by reaching a degree of consensus over fundamental questions such as secularism, democracy, and Turkey's place in the world and ties to its Ottoman imperial past. Likewise, the "common identity dilemma" needs to be resolved, which predominantly depends on the ability of Turks to achieve sufficient self-understanding and confidence regarding the plural meanings and richness of their own identity, Turkishness. They can do so ideationally based on academic research and intellectual self-reflection and deliberation, and politically by embedding these plural meanings in laws and governing institutions backed by elite power settlements. The third puzzle, the external security dilemma, is the least dependent on Turks' agency, as regional developments outside Turkey's control, such as World War I and the Arab Uprisings of 2011 significantly change the parameters of this dilemma independently. However, here too, resolving the dilemma requires that Turks, and particularly the elites, make foresighted political decisions and develop new ideational perspectives. These perspectives concern, for example, the question of how Ankara can and should secure its southern borders and territorial integrity: whether it can and should do so through military hard power and by excluding Kurds, or through regional socioeconomic integration, soft power, and by cooperating with Kurds.

## Overcoming Structural Barriers through Politics and Ideas

I have also discussed and demonstrated in this book how the structural and ideational underpinnings of conflicts can be closely interlinked. Furthermore, I highlighted how "politics," "political action,"[1] and political actors as "carriers of ideas"[2] play critical roles in either reproducing or reshaping structures by mediating between structures and ideas. While the three dilemmas can be seen as "structural," I have offered a mainly political explanation of how they arose and can evolve, whereby ideational factors play crucial facilitating or reinforcing roles. Thus, recipes for conflict resolution should also be sought in ideational innovations as well as in politics. By negotiating, amassing, distributing, and exercising power, politics can reign over the conflict-reproducing structural dynamics, promote novel ideational frames, and establish a new status quo acceptable to both Turks and Kurds.

Hence, on one hand, the roots of the common identity dilemma lie in structural changes, such as the nation-state formation, geography, wars, and migrations that compelled Ottoman Muslims to make certain choices. On the other hand, however, this dilemma took its particular form when intellectual elites addressed the need for a common identity that arose as a result of these structural developments in particular ways, and political elites selected what was politically preferable for them from this repertoire. Hence, the outcome reflected political developments in a particular ideational context. Given the repertoire of identities available in society, what shaped the particular form and content of the common identity that was promoted by the state were the interests and agency of the elites that emerged as the winners of political power struggles. Hence, the resolution of this dilemma today also depends on ideational and political factors. The ability of social and political actors to adopt, remake, and synthesize existing identities and construct new ones is crucial. Ultimately, however, the success of any of these identities will draw upon the legitimacy of the political processes that promote them and the backing of political power. A winning majority or a plurality of political actors with sufficient legitimacy will need to act as two-way carriers of these new identities between the people and the state. They will then utilize political processes of representation, deliberation, and decision making in order to embed these identities in laws, institutions, and state discourse.

Similarly, the elite cooperation dilemma, arguably also a structural constraint that time and again undermines conflict resolution efforts, at least partly results from particular ideas and interpretations. It prevails because Turkish elites interpret Ottoman, and later Turkish, modernization in particular ways. These interpretations lead to incompatible narratives about how to reach key national objectives—on which these elites arguably agree—such as progress, socioeconomic development, and integration with the world. Hence, the resolution of this dilemma requires the development of inter-elite trust and cooperation partly by developing alternative and less conflicting interpretations of why the Ottomans fell behind the West, and what the flaws and the strengths were of first the Ottoman and then the Turkish modernization. At the same time, and after inter-elite trust has been established, Turkish elites need to find and agree upon concrete proposals to address the Kurdish Question. This, too, ultimately draws on collective and individual ideational processes, such as self-critical reflection, communication, and deliberation. But, ultimately, the implementation of any solution proposals will depend on a "winning" bloc of political actors to carry and represent these ideas and turn them into authoritative decisions—as politics does—such as in new laws, policies, and new institutions.

Similarly, the external security dilemma does not only result from structural factors, such as interstate borders, geography, demography, and military balances. It also stems from ideational/intellectual factors, such as military and political elites' understandings of the very concept of "security"—for example, state versus human security—and their beliefs about how security can be pursued, meaning, through which policies. Relatedly, with any given set of structural factors, such as geography and demography, the nature of the external security dilemma would also change, depending on how state elites conceive of and prioritize different foreign policy goals; for instance, whether they think an isolationist or activist foreign policy would best serve the interests of the state and their own.

## HUMAN AGENCY AND SCHOLARSHIP

In an alarmist recent book on the global democracy crisis, Larry Diamond observes:

> It is not abstract economic or social forces that bring about democracy or make it work. It is individuals—ordinary and extraordinary citizens—who stake claims, shape programs, form organizations, forge strategies, and move people.[3]

In other words, human agency, including leadership, is essential for democratization, even though structural improvements such as socioeconomic development can enable or facilitate it, as Diamond also discusses in his book. Similar things could be said about any conflict resolution. After all, one way to conceptualize democratization might be to picture it in the form of a series of conflict resolutions, which would minimize the potential for any major social and political actor to employ authoritarian means to prevail in these conflicts, whether through violent rebellion or state oppression.

Hence, I have also highlighted and tried to demonstrate in this book the role of human agency and leadership, both in the emergence of a conflict and in the creation of opportunities for conflict resolution. This can be true even against the odds, where there are seemingly insurmountable structural and ideational barriers. My explanation of how the Kurdish Question became the Kurdish Conflict during the formative period ultimately rests upon structural dilemmas and political decisions. However, I also emphasized that there were other counterfactual paths that were imagined by some people, and political agents could have pursued these. Some of these paths might have addressed the Kurdish Question without turning it into a conflict. In the contemporary period, too, human agency and creativity are crucial. This is because, as I will further highlight later on in this chapter, the resolution of the three dilemmas ultimately depends on the ability of social and political actors to generate and communicate to society new narratives, common beliefs, and policy proposals about identity, development, and security.

Political agency, however, can succeed only insofar as political actors adequately identify the structural and ideational bottlenecks and dynamics underlying a given conflict, and how they work. Here is where, I would argue, scholarship can actively contribute to conflict resolution and to achieving other goals, such as democratization, peace, and coexistence: by unpacking and bringing to light the structural and ideational under-pinnings of a conflict. Feasible, sustainable, and successful solutions can be built upon, and would have to be consistent with, this knowledge.

Remarkably, but also unfortunately for anyone who wants peace and democracy, most of the predictions made in this book have so far been borne out by the developments that have taken place since 2011, when I began to write this book. As I predicted (but hoped would turn out otherwise), there was the collapse of the 2013–15 peace process (as well as of Turkey's democracy), and violent conflict and militant nationalism resurged with a vengeance. That is, without adequate proposals and policies to resolve the three dilemmas, the conflict re-escalated, accompanied by concentration of power (most importantly the creation of an authoritarian, hyper-presidential system in 2017) and a general downslide of pluralism and power sharing in the political system. These developments happened through processes that I examine in this book: the failures were directly linked with the inability of the political actors—and of the Turkish actors more than the Kurdish—to offer solutions (in political as well as ideational terms) for addressing the three fundamental dilemmas.

One of the book's main observations—that Turkey is experiencing a reincarnation of the structural conditions and dilemmas that incubated the Kurdish Conflict in its formative period roughly a century ago—is as valid today as it was at the beginning of the 2010s. I argued that the formative period lasted eight years, between 1918 and 1926. Arguably, the reformative period of the Turkish and Kurdish Question began in 2011 and is still ongoing. Turks and Kurds face the same dilemmas that they tried to tackle a century ago, and their political representatives have an opportunity to restructure the nature of Turkish-Kurdish relations—and the related phenomena that I discuss in the book, such as the secularism question, state-society relations, and Ottoman heritage—based on a new and hopefully more egalitarian and democratic contract between the people and the state.

In the remainder of this concluding chapter, I will recapitulate and discuss the theory and policy implications of the book's arguments, and put forward projections and potential recipes for conflict resolution.

## Embracing the Protean and Polysemic Nature of the Turkish Identity and Understanding the Link between Turkish and Ottoman Nationalisms

Why do discussions about the Kurdish Question and identity turn into discussions about Turkish identity? Why do discussions about notions such as Turkishness and Of-Turkey (*Türkiyelilik*) turn into heated quarrels between rival meanings and identity claims?

One factor to consider when attempting to answer the above questions is that Turks have not yet come to terms with the historical relationship between Turkish nationalism and what we might call "Ottoman state nationalism." As I highlighted in previous chapters, the Kurdish Question emerged when some people living in predominantly Kurdish regions began to develop nationalist imaginations and projects (for example, Kurdish, Turkish, Armenian, and Arab nationalisms) because of the transformations taking place across the globe in the nineteenth century. Since all of these nationalisms envisaged some kind of self-rule or autonomy in overlapping territories, what would be the status of Kurds in the Ottoman and Iranian Empires, and, later, in the Turkish, Arabic, and Persian majority states that succeeded them? How might the Kurdish nationalists' yearning for self-rule become reality in the face of these other nationalist projects that rivaled one another? Ethnic and linguistic Turkish and Kurdish nationalisms, as well as Ottoman state nationalism, were three responses to this question, among many others. The first two were based on visions of nation-states, where the contours of land, citizenship, and common identity would be drawn by Turkish or Kurdish ethnicity and language. The latter, Ottoman state nationalism, however, envisaged an explicitly multilingual and multiethnic nation-state where the Ottoman state legacy and identity would constitute the basis of territory, citizenship, and common national identity.

One particular version of Turkish nationalism took over from Ottoman state nationalism. The latter disappeared in name, but continued to shape the claims, fears, aspirations, and practices of Turkish nationalists. In other words, a major strain of modern Turkish nationalism and national identity is the product of a metamorphosis of Ottoman state nationalism and identity.

The territory on which Turkish nationalists imagined building their nation was thus shaped pragmatically—i.e., based on a rationale of state revival and formation—rather than being historically and ideologically determined. Consequently, the people they aimed to mobilize and transform into a nation were a linguistically, ethnically, and culturally heterogeneous group. Meanwhile, the Turkish national identity, which had already begun to emerge rapidly on a cultural/linguistic basis, also was given the responsibility for securing the survival of the Ottoman state identity under a new name; hence, the polysemic nature of the Turkish identity.

During the period in which the Kurdish Question appeared on the Ottoman landscape, so too did a Turkish Question, an Arab Question, and an Armenian Question. However, unlike the others, the Turkish Question became integrated with the Ottoman state question, to wit, the issue of reinventing and saving the Ottoman State. This transformation took place over a few decades. On one hand, it was the result of historical and demographic/sociological factors: the majority status of Turks (or Muslims whose mother tongue was Turkish) in Anatolia; the renaissance that the Turkish language and its literature underwent in the nineteenth century; mass (Muslim and Turkish) migrations from the Balkans, Russia, the Middle East, and the Caucasus, which made Muslims and Turks a greater majority in Anatolia; and the loss of Rumelia (Ottoman Balkans), which used to be a central part of the homeland. "Turkish" nationalism was also rekindled through the personal life experiences of many Turkish nationalists, who were confronted with and persecuted by rival nationalists (e.g., Greek, Serbian, and Bulgarian) during the Balkan Wars because of their Muslimness and Turkishness, not only for being "Ottoman." All in all, however, Turkish nationalism and its dominant formulation were also products of political and strategic choices that nationalists made.

In intellectual and social-scientific terms, this historical trajectory and metamorphosis of identity is fascinating. In terms of practical and political potential, the polysemic, multifaceted, and protean natures of Turkish identity and nationalism can be seen as sources of cultural richness and political/economic advantage: they allow the inclusion of diverse groups in the nation and facilitate building social/cultural/historical and political/economic links with various people in a vast region that spans from Central Europe to East Asia based on different formulations of Turkishness.

In fact, however, its multiple meanings have been politicizing the Turkish identity. They give rise to tensions, misunderstandings, and a sense of insecurity among Turks. They foster intra-Turkish struggles between competing ways of perceiving, promoting, and belonging to Turkishness, such as between those that are more ethnic/linguistic (Turkic), religious (Sunni Muslim or Alevi), Ottoman/Muslim, territorial (Anatolian and those encompassing broader ex-Ottoman territories), cosmopolitan, and multicultural. To a significant extent, the recognition of a Kurdish identity has been hostage to this Turkish identity question.

## Solving the Common Identity Dilemma by Embracing Plural and Asymmetric Names and Definitions

As was also the case in the formative period, the common identity dilemma in the current reformative period consists of two parts. The first is the question of the Kurdish identity; that is, the Kurds' need to feel that their own identity is experienced freely in social and political life and protected and recognized as a valuable and equal identity alongside Turkishness. An important corollary to this is the recognition of the Kurds as a nation. The second part relates to the question of a common identity, and, relatedly, Turkishness; that is, how to ensure that common identities in Turkey are not weakened and that Turks are not concerned about their own identity—seen by many as *the* common identity—while Kurdish identity is also recognized.

Any solution for the common identity dilemma, I would argue, should avoid forming a relationship of hierarchy between these two needs and social/political demands. They need to be valued simultaneously and equally. In other words, social and political actors need to find a formulation that can turn a perceived win/lose question into a win/win question.

In Turkish vernacular, the defenders of Turkishness as an overarching national identity call it *üst kimlik* (literally meaning supra-identity, but could also be understood as superior identity), while categorizing group identities such as Kurdishness and Aleviness as *alt kimlikler* (literally meaning subidentities, but could also be understood as inferior identities). This may be a legacy of the metamorphosis of the Ottoman state identity into Turkishness. The "components" (*unsurlar*) of the Muslim Ottoman nation are considered subidentities, while the national identity, now called Turkishness, is considered the supra-identity. This, of course, literally creates a hierarchy of identities. Many Turks consider their own identity as a supra-ethnic (or supra-component) national identity that also constitutes the identity of their state. The Kurds, in turn, do not want to be a "sub-national" group because, to them, this means being unequal to Turks. Many Turks consider the references made to the Turk identity in the fundamental documents and symbols of the state, such as in the constitution, an acquired right and a guarantee of both their own national identity and the continuation of their nation-state.

Meanwhile, Turkishness is not a supra-ethnic identity for many Kurds, even though they may accept the Of-Turkey identity as a common national identity. For these Kurds, being recognized as a nation—as a social and cultural category, if not politically—is also a major demand, for this would establish equality with Turks, even for Kurds who want to remain part of Turkey. In the words of one author, "Turkey's Kurdish Question would no longer exist the day Kurds are acknowledged [in the constitution] as a state-forming [*kurucu*] partner."[4]

The only way to address both of these concerns simultaneously is to abandon the terminology and think of hierarchical identity categories. Instead, a nonhierarchical relationship can be constructed whereby different groups would be allowed to adopt common identities with different names.

For example, the article in the 1924 Constitution relating to citizenship might be rephrased by slightly altering the wording as follows: "In Turkey everyone is called Turkish *or* Of-Turkey (Türkiyeli) *in terms of citizenship* regardless of their religion, sect, ethnicity and race."[5] Thus, the common identity can be adopted by Turks with the name *Turkish*, while Kurds can embrace it with the name *Of-Turkey*. The qualification "in terms of citizenship" would implicitly acknowledge the polysemic nature of Turkishness by implying that it has meanings other than the one denoting citizenship. Simultaneously, the country's cultural and national diversity can be acknowledged in the preamble and in the later sections of the constitution. This might be done, for example, by using excerpts from Mustafa Kemal's speeches during the War of Independence in which he refers to Kurds, Turks, and other components by name.

## Recognizing the Cultural and Political Meanings of Nation

In chapters 2 and 7, I argued that "nation" has cultural and political meanings,[6] a difference that is often overlooked in social/political discourse, and one which has practically disappeared in current Turkish usage. I also discussed another frequently disregarded distinction between ethnic category and ethnic group. Acknowledging and utilizing these different meanings in conflict resolution and public policymaking are crucial. As we saw earlier, Turkishness was an ethnic category until its meaning began to change and diversify as a result of nineteenth-century Ottoman modernization, migrations, and political power struggles.

When identities gain new meanings, this does not imply, of course, that everyone agrees on their new meanings and that the old meanings disappear. The meanings of being Turkish as an ethnic category, ethnic group, and nation—and variations of the latter based on ethnicity, territory, religious belonging, and other criteria—have continued to co-exist and be upheld by different actors. Therefore, it is hardly meaningful to discuss which definition is correct, as these are all aspects of social reality. The presence of multiple meanings can either be interpreted as ambiguity, indeterminacy, and vulnerability or be embraced as richness, flexibility, and multilayered inclusiveness, because it can allow different people to connect with the same identity in different ways and at different levels. I would maintain that what politicizes identity and produces conflict is not so much the presence of these multiple meanings as the lack of recognition of plural meanings and the search for a singular, true meaning instead, and the weakness of discursive and conceptual tools that embrace plural meanings.

Let me give an example:

In 2011, a conference on "the Turkic Republics on the 20th Anniversary of their Independence" was held in Ankara, which brought together the representatives of six "Turkic republics"—Azerbaijan, Kazakhstan, Kyrgyzstan, Turkey, Turkmenistan, and Uzbekistan. The event was broadcast live on Turkish state-owned radio and television channels, TRT. The honorary speaker was Abdullah Gül, then president of the Republic of Turkey. In his speech, Gül proudly stated: "We are a single nation (*millet*) with six states."[7]

Keep in mind that the Turkish language makes little distinction between the categories of Turkic and Turk. The term *Türkî*, which corresponds to the term *Turkic* in English, was introduced to public discourse after the end of the Cold War for practical and political purposes. The motivation was to use a proper term to denote those post-Soviet states and nations, for example, Turkmenistan, that had majority populations speaking Turkic languages such as Turkmen, Uzbek, and Kazakh. In other words, the term was concocted to describe people and states that were culturally/ linguistically linked with the Turks in Turkey but were not "Turkish" or Of-Turkey politically, that is, in terms of citizenship and territorially.

In Turkish non-expert usage, however, the *Türk-Türkî* distinction hardly exists or makes any sense for ordinary people. In fact, while the adjective *Turkic* was used in the English translation of the conference name, in the original Turkish version, at which Gül spoke, the organizers did not in fact bother to make the distinction. The conference was simply presented as "Conference on the *Turkish* [emphasis mine] republics on the 20th Anniversary of their Independence" (*Bağımsızlıklarının 20. Yılında Türk Cumhuriyetleri Konferansı*).[8]

Gül's statement about being a single nation with six states could not possibly have had a political meaning, or, for that matter, have referred to the only meaning of Turkishness. Each one of these six nation-states and their people had nationalistic sentiments and official ideologies of their own. The six states had no intention of political/territorial integration and had vastly different political regimes and international orientations. Hence, any allusion to common political nationhood would have been fiercely contested and internationally controversial.

The statement could only make sense if a cultural and nonpolitical meaning were attributed to the term *nation*. This expression of nationhood could be considered natural and meaningful for the context and for the participants of the meeting in a cultural sense. It reflected a cultural/ linguistic sense of solidarity and connectedness, short of any claim to common sovereignty, rights, and statehood.

The same category of Turkishness (*Türk*), however, logically and practically must carry a different meeting, (a political/territorial meaning) when used in the symbols and fundamental documents of the Republic of Turkey. This is because millions of Turkish citizens (whom the constitution defines as Turkish regardless of ethnicity and race) have non-Turkic ethnic/ cultural and linguistic backgrounds. In these contexts, "Turk" refers to a legal/political rather than a cultural bond. These "Turks" have cultural and linguistic affinities, not necessarily with the titular people of Turkic republics, but with people of such places as Bosnia, Georgia, Syria, or, for that matter, the Kurdistan Regional Government of Iraq.

Yet, organizing a meeting in Turkey and stating that Kurds of, say Iraq, Syria, Iran, Turkey, and others form a "single nation" would have been politically explosive and possibly considered a crime of subversion by the legal authorities. How might this inequality and use of double standards for different citizens be eliminated? Is a political/constitutional order possible whereby Kurds could organize such meetings that celebrate their sense of trans-state nationhood without triggering Turkish fears of separatism, actual centrifugal dynamics, and oppression from the unitary state? By the same token, how might Kurds feel a sense of belonging to the same political nation as Turks while enjoying equal rights to celebrate their ethnic linguistic heritage and to bond with their ethnic/linguistic relatives in other countries just as Turks can?

In nation-states such as Turkey where at least one major minority group has already developed a distinct sense of nationhood, the only way to achieve the above aims—without dividing sovereignty and establishing a confederal state[9] and a "consociational democracy"[10] with more than one sovereign nation—may be by separating the nation's political and cultural meanings. In the Turkish context, this would allow Turks and Kurds, as well as other groups such as Arabs and Albanians, to be citizens of a single political nation, but simultaneously connect and harbor a sense of solidarity with Turks, Kurds, Arabs, and Albanians outside of Turkey as members of respective cultural nations.[11] This may also require discursive innovations or adaptations. For example, new terms might be introduced to distinguish between "nation" (*millet*) to denote nation in a political sense and "nationality or people" (*milliyet, halk,* or *unsur*) to denote nation in a cultural sense.[12]

Such an approach may also serve the political and economic interest of Turkey since it would make it easier for the country to deepen its cultural, economic, and political cooperation with neighboring countries by drawing on the common bonds that its citizens have with the multiple cultural nations of the region. The fact that Turkishness has plural meanings that express different ties in different contexts is not unique to this identity. Almost all identity categories—from ideological identities, such as socialist, liberal, and conservative, to regional identities, such as Mediterranean and European, to national identities, such as American, English, French, and Arabic—have plural meanings across people, time, space, and political/institutional context. There is "more than one way of being national, even in the same nation."[13] It is in the nature of all identities to possess plural meanings, though some may be more elastic and polysemic than others.

In this respect, all identities, but perhaps especially postimperial national identities such as Turkishness, can be likened to a tree with multiple roots and branches growing in different directions. The trunk of the tree would represent a common political nationhood, while the separate roots and branches would symbolize its connections to separate cultural nations.

## Cooperation of New Actors for Conflict Resolution

Ultimately, the elite cooperation dilemma, which I discussed extensively in previous chapters, can be resolved through two causal mechanisms. Either those elites who do not trust each other for ideological reasons might change their views that divide them, or new actors, such as parties and political leaders, might emerge who can trust and cooperate with each other. These two mechanisms are interrelated. Sometimes, instead of a new party, it can be an existing party that changes its positions on key issues when new leaders and cadres become more influential within the party, for example, through generational or ideational change. Hence, I use the term *new actors* broadly in reference to the ascendance of new social/political actors as well as political/ideational changes within the existing actors in politics.

New actors in these two senses can help resolve the Kurdish Conflict. In chapter 5, I analyzed why the peace initiatives in the 2000s failed to resolve the conflict. We saw that the main actors who gained sufficient political power and undertook initiatives to resolve the conflict were the right-wing, religious conservative elites led by the AKP and religious conservative Kurds within the AKP. These elites, however, were insufficiently prepared ideationally to produce sustainable legal/institutional solutions for the Kurdish Question, and ideologically too distant from the left-wing, pro-secular Kurdish nationalists with whom they attempted to negotiate the peace. In turn, pro-secular and left-wing Turkish elites, mainly represented by the CHP, were relatively more prepared to offer reform solutions. Nevertheless, as I argued, the lack of concrete proposals for resolving the Kurdish Conflict was an ideational weakness that crosscut the Left-Right divisions. The pro-secular actors were in the opposition and thus lacked sufficient political power; moreover, for a variety of reasons, they could not work together with pro-secular Kurdish actors such as the HDP.

In recent years, rising government authoritarianism has begun to bring together Turkish and Kurdish moderates, which might give rise to the emergence of new actors in the future. First, in the June 2015 national elections, many Turkish pro-secular voters voted for the HDP and its leader Selahattin Demirtaş, which enabled the party to cross the 10 percent electoral threshold and enter Parliament as a party (rather than as independents); a first for pro-Kurdish parties. Demirtaş was later jailed based on charges deemed by critics to be politically motivated. Then, in the March 2019 local elections, the HDP supported the electoral coalition that the CHP established with the newly formed right-wing Good Party (İYİ), which enabled the opposition to increase its votes and win the country's trend-setting metropoles, including Istanbul. These political developments and practical experiences raise the likelihood that pro-secular Turkish and Kurdish actors will further their collaboration and overcome the elite cooperation dilemma in the future, based on a democracy-autocracy cleavage.[14]

## Resolving the External Security Dilemma through Flexible Integration with Regional Kurds

Logically, the external security dilemma can be resolved in one of three ways.[15]

First, Turkish governments might try to oppress Kurdish nationalism and prevent at all costs the formation of a potential Kurdish state in the region. This is essentially what Turkey and other regional states did throughout the twentieth century. However, as Kurdish nationalism became more mass-based after the 1960s and 1970s, and with the emergence of a de facto Kurdish state in Iraq from the 1990s onward, this policy became more and more costly and unrealistic for Turkey. Following the civil war in Syria and the rise of Syrian Kurds—dominated by the Democratic Union Party (PYD), a PKK affiliate—as a major Western ally in the fight against ISIS, Kurdish nationalists emerged as key actors in the region's politics. The Kurds, of course, are not the same as the PKK, which is considered a terrorist group by Turkey, as well as by the United States, the EU, Iraq, and Iran. But the external insecurity dilemma does not only involve the possibility of a particular pro-Kurdish group forming a state, but any kind of Kurdish state formation, which, Turkish policy makers may argue, will develop pan-Kurdish ambitions sooner or later.

Second, instead of adopting a preventative strategy, Turkey might pursue a strategy of precluding the possibility of Kurdish separatism by merging and formally unifying with the Kurds. As I argued in chapters 4 and 5, this appears to have been the strategy that Turkey's nation builders pursued during the National Campaign but later abandoned during the formative period mainly for domestic and external political reasons. According to a frequently voiced theory in the region (and echoed by PKK representatives), Iraqi and Syrian Kurds would rather be part of Turkey than of an Arab state.[16] In addition to their shared Ottoman legacy and history of coexistence as Ottoman Muslims, Turkey's developing economy, integration with the Western world, relationships with the EU, and, despite all of its serious shortcomings, democratic experience render integration with Turkey an attractive option for Iraqi and Syrian Kurds.

The greatest weakness of this merger strategy is that it cannot be realized without risking war with regional states, and possibly also with external powers, which would react against a fundamental shift in the regional balances of power and territorial borders. Indeed, the external insecurity dilemma emerged in the formative period when Turkey could convince the Kurds but not the outside great powers—and, presumably, the Arabs—to include within the new Turkey all of the territories inhabited by former Ottoman Kurds, who were part of the National Pact, and thus also the energy-rich Mosul.

What's more, such a fundamental demographic and geographical change can probably not be accomplished without restructuring Turkey as a federal or confederal state. If Iraqi and Syrian Kurds joined Turkey, the Kurds would constitute almost one-third (approx. 32–34 percent) of Turkey's population.[17] Presumably, then, the Kurds who already have their own de facto state in Iraq would not agree to any model of merger other than as part of a federation in Turkey. Such a change to the political/ administrative system would not be easy, for reasons I discussed in the Introduction—for instance, the Kurds being a semi-mixed population in Turkey. Resistance to a transition to a federation would come from the Turkish state's unitary state reflexes—compounded by the ideational weaknesses I discussed in chapter 7—and from Turkish nationalists. Were Kurds to constitute such a large minority within Turkey, it might not be feasible for them to achieve devolution, which, as I have argued in this book, is a more realistic reform path for Turkey within a framework of state-nation.

A third and more realistic strategy for Turkey might be to pursue socioeconomic integration with regional Kurds—without any changes to state borders—based on the principles of mutual interest and interdependence in the economy, socioeconomic development, and security. This would render pan-Kurdist irredentism both unnecessary and unfeasible for the Kurds, who, by pursuing irredentism, would have to forsake the benefits of cooperation with Turkey. It would also render any Kurdish promises of rejecting irredentism more credible in the eyes of Turkish policymakers. By the same token and for similar reasons, Turkish pronouncements of fraternity with Kurds would gain more credibility in the eyes of the Kurds. In other words, political and economic relations based on mutual dependence would make policies that might destroy these relations adverse to the vital interests of both sides. Since the 1990s, and more so since a 2017 referendum in which most Iraqi Kurds voted for independence, Kurds have shown an ability to subdue and postpone—if not entirely abandon—their pro-independence ambitions in exchange for socioeconomic development and stability, security, and autonomy.[18]

## Transition from Nation-State to State-Nation

The model of nation building that emerged during Turkey's War of Independence and brought together Turks and Kurds based on the imagination of a state-nation seemed consistent with the historical, geographical, and demographic conditions of the time and might have prevented the emergence of the Kurdish Conflict. The existence and rights of ex-Ottoman Kurds were recognized within the vision of a single nation based on the joint sovereignty of Turks, Kurds, and other components. However, this model could not be implemented under the tumultuous conditions of the period. As I have argued in this book, in addition to the preferences and influential decisions of the great powers that divided the ex-Ottoman Kurds between three states, two mainly political factors informed by particular political beliefs precluded the implementation of this model. The first was the secular/modernist priorities of Turkey's dominant nation builders, who suppressed the demands of the Kurds while—and perhaps intentionally—establishing their political hegemony and consolidating the new regime. The second factor was the relative urgency of building a Turkish nation among the non-Kurdish portions of the new Turkey's population.

As seminal Ottoman historian Halil İnalcık stated, "[Anatolia] became an ethnic and cultural miniature of the empire . . . through successive migrations from 1783 onwards, every time the Russian army entered the northern Black Sea, the Balkans and the Caucasus. Other than the hundreds and thousands of migrants of solely *Türk* origin, hundreds and thousands of Albanians, *Boşnak* [Bosnian or Bosniak], *Pomak* [Slavic-speaking Muslims predominantly originating from modern-day Bulgaria],[19] Cretans, Circassians, Abkhazians, Chechens and Georgians whose mother tongue was not Turkish but who [in previous centuries] had adopted Ottoman Culture and converted to Islam came to settle in these lands."[20]

Hence, Turkey is a melting pot, but does not consider or pride itself as being such. In its formative period, its nation builders might have ended up putting forward homogenous images of the nation for the sake of facilitating nation formation, but these images have since been internalized by many as *the* images of the Turkish nation.

Homogenous nation-building policies that went beyond building a common national identity included, for example, sweeping name-changing policies that Turkified the official names of places. The Kurdish, Arabic, Persian, Armenian, Laz, Georgian, and Pontic Greek names of thousands of cities, towns, and villages were given newly concocted Turkish names. Between 1940 and 2000, the names of 12,211 villages (around 35 percent of all villages) were altered.[21] Many of these names came not from living ethnic languages, which could be associated with rival nationalisms, but from ancient languages, such as Sumerian and Akkadian. In this respect, far from being necessary for nation building, these excessive policies might have "undermined" nation building. Rather than strengthening the bonds of the people with their homeland—which nation-state builders want—for example, the name changes in Turkey might have served to cut people's ties with the history of the lands in which they lived because each and every name represents the identity of that particular place. In a country such as Turkey, which has been inhabited by numerous ancient cultures and civilizations, place names remind people of the land's ancient past and make them aware of the historical importance of where they live. Hence, the name changes might also have undermined popular participation in the preservation of cultural and natural heritage.

Roughly a century later, today's Turks of Turkey are no longer a nation in the making but a firmly established and fiercely nationalist nation. And, as I have maintained in this book, since 2011 the structural conditions of a "reformative" period have materialized in Turkey and its region. Time will tell whether a more multicultural imagination of Turkey as a state-nation can come back by the end of the reformative period.

In this context, it might be relevant to cite a metaphor used by Selahattin Demirtaş—the currently jailed Kurdish politician who was the co-leader of the HDP and whom the HDP had nominated for presidency in the 2014 presidential elections—to describe his vision of common

nationality and intergroup harmony in Turkey. Instead of the more frequently used metaphor of a mosaic that I discussed in previous chapters,
Demirtaş adopted the metaphor of a "pomegranate." This was a powerful
metaphor portraying a compatible image of the common identity that Turks
and Kurds share, which he likened to the skin of a pomegranate, and the
separate identities that Kurds, Turks, and other components have, which
he likened to the seeds of the pomegranate: "We will defend everyone's
right to raise their children in their own mother tongue. We will be like
a pomegranate. A single skin will unite us but when you break it open,
there will be thousands within. If we do not stand as a pomegranate, we
cannot taste freedom in this country."[22]

## A Glance at the Future: Obsolete Narratives that Sacrificed Diversity for Unity Versus New Narratives that Sacrifice Unity for Diversity

### A NORMATIVE EVALUATION OF THE POLITICAL CHOICES THAT CREATED THE KURDISH CONFLICT

Certain creations of the political elite decisions during the formative
period—which also generated the Kurdish Conflict—remained remarkably
stable and resistant to change throughout the last century. They survived
far-reaching transformations in many aspects of this conflict's domestic
and international environments since then, such as the interwar, Cold
War, post–Cold War, post–September 11, and post–Arab Spring global
and regional environments, and national governments with a wide spectrum of ideological and democratic credentials, just to name a few. These
"unyielding creations" include the territorial borders of the nation-state of
Turkey. Moreover, the country's secular/republican[23] and unitary constitutional order, and the contested, yet also hegemonic, natures of Turkish
nationalism and the Turkish national identity have displayed remarkable
constancy and stability. Many critical explanations of the Kurdish Conflict
pinpoint these creations as *the* causes of the conflict. While I concur with
these studies that these creations must be included as causal factors in
explaining the conflict, I have a different take on them. I have formulated
them differently and, rather than treating them as self-explanatory, I have
tried to explain what led to the political decisions that created them and
why they became rather inflexible and nonadaptive.

Notably, the legacy and durability of these decisions suggests that they were not "unrealistic" or "unimaginative" responses to historically produced challenges. As we have seen, they were political elite responses to the tumultuous, existential anxiety-generating and rapidly changing regional developments in the aftermath of World War I, which led to the end of the six-hundred-year-old Ottoman Empire. Having consistency with the exigencies of the historical contexts in which they were made, these political elite decisions offered certain solutions to the overwhelming real-world challenges facing the elites and the people they aimed to mobilize, represent, and serve.

Still, none of these "unyielding" constructs relating to national borders, identity, and constitutional regime are necessarily unchangeable. Indeed, against the backdrop of the longue durée history of "Turks," "Kurds," and other people in the region, these structures are relatively "recent" and "modern" creations. National identities, borders, and constitutional orders are socially and politically constructed and can be changed—although, this by no means implies that they are less "real" than other social constructs or necessarily transient.

The constructs that gave rise to the nation-state of Turkey with particular borders, identities, and constitutive institutions became, over time, institutionalized and normalized, being perceived as "structures" themselves.[24] They began to mold actors' imaginations and constrain their choices, shaping what people think they can change in the foreseeable future, what they consider fixed, and what they view as foundational or sometimes even sacred. Hence, these constructs became features that needed to be either defended or fought against, by using lethal force if necessary.[25]

Even though the political elite choices during the formative period were neither arbitrary nor necessarily self-serving, they were not the only logically and objectively possible reactions to the dilemmas. It is one thing to be *a* necessary response to historical developments, but it is quite another to be *the* necessary response. Hence, it was not necessarily the case that these decisions were morally defensible and practically optimal; nor were they the only responses that were imaginable or feasible at the time.

In 2013, when Turkey was going through a critical and intense period in the aftermath of the Gezi Park protests, I penned the following observations and sentiments in my personal notes:

A sense of alienation and balkanization prevails among the people I encounter in academic and political meetings and

day-to-day life. It is apparent that the *master narratives*[26]—call
them what you will, Kemalist, secular, republican or nationalist—that dominated mainstream society in the past have become
obsolete. These narratives of the past, present, the country and
the world unified society to some extent. However, they did so
by excluding and ignoring the identities, ideologies and social
segments that some state elites had decided were undesirable
or threatening for one reason or another. In other words, they
generated unjust and unequal conditions for various groups
in society. They sacrificed diversity and equality in the name
of preserving unity. While bestowing meaning on history and
the contemporary age, they excluded alternative narratives
and made absolute and self-righteous judgments—presented
through a sharp, "black and white" language—which did not
allow any grey areas and room for reflexive adaptation. Hence,
the users and supporters of these narratives could not adapt to
the changing world and the requirements of pluralist democracy
as rapidly and effectively as was needed.

Especially from the 1980s onward, these absolutist master narratives
were criticized and gradually worn out by academics, intellectuals, and
ethnic and religious politics. However, there was also a concern that these
narratives would be replaced by other absolutist narratives. The concern
was that the obsolete narratives might be substituted by alternatives based
on ethnicity and religion, which were equally if not even more lacking
in pluralism and were exclusive of one another.[27] In other words, could
rival micronationalisms end up replacing the assimilationist (Turkish)
macronationalism? Could hardliner Kemalist and republican narratives
that sacrificed diversity and pluralism in the name of unity be supplanted
by narratives that in turn sacrificed unity in the name of diversity?

The developments of recent decades suggest that these concerns
were well-founded. When the old master narratives, which continued to
be embraced by large segments of the society, lost their vigor, the AKP
came to power based on sharp criticisms of these narratives and with
promises to reform them and establish new and more pluralist, alternative
narratives. Yet, the AKP's seemingly and relatively democratic, inclusive,
and reformist discourse and orientation became increasingly authoritarian, exclusionary and majoritarian, and revolutionary.[28] Time will show

whether, in the future, Turkey's social and political actors will be able to develop new master narratives that can be both unifying and inclusive, while also agreeing on a new legal/constitutional framework of democracy.

## Polynymous and Polysemic Identities

The political claims and aspirations and the cultural realities of two nations constitute the basis of the Kurdish Question in Turkey. Until recent times, Kurdish nationhood had been fragmented, overlooked by the outside world, and oppressed by the states ruling over it. Turkish nationhood, on the other hand, became fully formed against great odds during the twentieth century and recognized by the world; it oscillated between exuding extreme self-confidence and extreme insecurity and a fear of "being abandoned." In the eyes of the Kurds, Turkishness is oppressive and dominant, but in the eyes of the Turks, who consider themselves to be either superior to or victimized by the world and who cannot agree among themselves on the content of their national identity, it is still quite fragile. Both Turkish and Kurdish nationalists view each other as rivals and as vital threats.

Can different nation-formation projects ever coexist peacefully in overlapping territories? Can ways be found so that they do not compete and clash with each other in a zero-sum competition, in which one must necessarily become dominant and oppress the other? One may answer "no" to both questions based on the "nature" of nationalism, nation-states, and national identities. In this book, I have taken a different view and argued that nation-state as a model and nationalism as a broad sentiment or ideology might be more resilient and less restrictive of possible outcomes at the state level than often thought. In other words, while the national identities and nationalist projects that come to exist on a territory might be bounded, there are multiple possible configurations of nation-state and different models of coexistence. Based on my analysis of the Turkish and Kurdish Question, I have argued in this book that the factors determining which possibilities become actual outcomes might be the structural dilemmas that nation builders have to resolve; moreover, these factors determine what critical political choices and decisions nation builders make in the process, and the ideational repertoire informing their decisions, in particular with regard to which nation and state models are possible and which are not. While most of my emphasis has been on domestic political actors and decisions, the roles and decisions of external and international actors are also critical, as implied by the external insecurity dilemma I have examined.

Nations and nation-states are not limitlessly flexible; they resist change. Nor are they carved in stone, however, and they can be reformed over time and at critical junctures. I have argued here that since 2011, Turkey has been in just such a potentially reformative period; one that is remarkably similar in its structural conditions to the formative period of 1918–1926. Time will show whether this time around, and with the benefit of hindsight, Turkish and Kurdish actors—and international actors, for example, with respect to the war in Syria—will make choices and arrive at decisions that can generate a more egalitarian, democratic, and nonviolent outcome to the Kurdish Question.

Unpacking and considering how political actors can resolve the three dilemmas has led me to think harder about the nature of identity categories as well as human cognition and agency regarding identity constructions, their names, and their contents. I have argued that one weakness of the public/political debates in Turkey during the 2000s has been their focus on replacing one set of mononymous and mono-semic common identity categories, which are rightly criticized for being insufficiently inclusive and democratic, with another set of mononymous and mono-semic categories, which are claimed to be more inclusive and democratic. However, these new categories might be as exclusive as the ones they were supposed to be replacing.

I have maintained that these debates might have been more effective had they instead focused on persuading people to accept polynymous and polysemic common identities. In other words, it may be a more promising path for conflict resolution, coexistence, and democracy if people embraced rather than tried to overcome polynymous and polysemic identities in general, and such common identities in Turkey in particular; these identities are by their very nature contested, multirooted, and context-dependent. It is often the case that different groups cannot agree upon the content and name of the very identities that they nevertheless share and that bring them together. Hence, in Turkey, when discussing the importance of an inclusive common identity (or identities), one does not need to impose the same name and content on Turks, Kurds, and others, whether the common identity in question is called Turkish, Of-Turkey (*Türkiyeli*), or something else.

## Rival Identities in a Divided Society and Autocracy Versus Compatible Identities in an Open Society and Democracy

While democracy, democratization, and policies and institutions based on peaceful coexistence can be seen as means to resolve ethnopolitical conflicts, successful conflict resolution is often a precondition for pluralistic democracy. In this book, I have discussed how the inability of mainly social and political elites to address the three fundamental dilemmas of the Kurdish Question has produced the Kurdish Conflict and has prevented Turkey's democratization, while fostering authoritarianism.

The most straightforward consequence of this has been that since the formative period, some Kurds have turned to armed struggle, violence, and secessionism to defend their cause, which has undermined peace and democratization. However, the Turkish political elite have lacked the ideational repertoire, the political agency, and the political mechanisms required to resolve their intra-Turkish struggles and the three dilemmas, even in times free of violence. Thus, they were also incapable of adequately taking advantage of relatively peaceful periods for conflict resolution and cooperation with nonviolent Kurdish actors.

Hence, in this book, I have discussed how, time and again, authoritarian Turkish political actors have capitalized on the Kurdish Conflict to sideline political rivals and limit opposition, and how concerns about the impact on the conflict derailed broad democratization attempts. Attempts at constitutional reform that would have expanded freedoms and rights for all have been derailed due to concerns about Turkish identity and Kurdish rights. Conflict resolution initiatives have lacked broad political support because political elites were fearful that peace might strengthen rival elites, and, consequently, also their rivals' policies in areas such as secularism and education. Military coups and authoritarian state-capturing by civilian forces have been legitimized based on the perceived and real threats of Kurdish separatism.

Since 2015, the developments in this respect have been predictable from the point of view of my argument, but still disappointing from the point of view of democratization and peace. Paralleling the collapse of the peace process and the re-eruption of violence in 2015, the erosion, or backsliding, of democracy that had been ongoing since at least the early 2010s culminated in a full democratic breakdown. A failed coup attempt in 2016 and the installation of a hyper-presidential authoritarian system in lieu of parliamentary democracy in 2017 can be interpreted as a continuation of this democratic breakdown.[29] These developments echo the autocratization of the political system following the 1925 Kurdish rebellion in the foundational period. The final regime outcome of the current period of autocratization, however, was still uncertain as of the writing of this book and, unlike what happened in the formative period, a return to democratization in the near future through a shift of power to the growing opposition seemed emerging, at least possible.

Democratization is not a linear process.[30] It has its ups and downs and may be strengthened by reversals and breakdowns. As I have highlighted, politics and political agency can remake structures, identities, and institutions, as long as political actors engage in learning and have an adequate understanding of the dilemmas they face. It is my sincere hope that this book can serve as a token contribution to enabling such an understanding of the dilemmas and to paving the way for peace in Turkey, as well as to identifying solutions in other cases in the world confronted by the threat of the ebbing away of democracy and of peaceful and respectful coexistence.

# Notes

## Preface

1. Branwen Gruffydd Jones, ed. *Decolonizing International Relations*. Lanham, MD: Rowman and Littlefield, 2006; Achille Joseph Mbembe, "Decolonizing the University: New Directions," *Arts and Humanities in Higher Education* 15, no. 1 (2016): 29–45; Eduardo Restrepo and Arturo Escobar, "Other Anthropologies and Anthropology Otherwise," *Critique of Anthropology* 25, no. 2 (2016): 99–129.

2. For a discussion of mine on how "Turkey Studies" can make more and better contributions to political science and international relations: Murat Somer, "Theory-Consuming or Theory-Producing?: Studying Turkey as a Theory-Developing Critical Case," *Turkish Studies* 15, no. 4 (2014): 571–88.

## Chapter 1

1. According to one international ranking that covers the post–World War II period of 1946–2018, in two episodes involving the Republic of Turkey and the PKK (Partiya Karkeren Kurdistan—Kurdistan Workers Party), 1984–2004 and 2004–2018, this conflict caused approximately 40,000 and 15,000 deaths in respective order. According to these two rough estimates, this conflict ranked thirty-fourth and fourteenth among the most violent conflicts in the world that occurred in this period, in the categories of "intrastate warfare involving the state agent and a distinct ethnic group" and "intrastate violence involving the state agent and a distinct ethnic group," respectively. "Death in Major Episodes of Political Violence 1946–2018" Dataset, Center for Systemic Peace. Available at: https://knoema.com/xzmbnbd/death-in-major-episodes-of-political-violence-1946-2018 (accessed October 15, 2019). As I will discuss throughout the book, the Kurdish Conflict has produced deadly violence not only in these two episodes but periodically since its formative period in early twentieth century. In addition, the

casualties that were direct or indirect consequences of the conflict since 1984 might be higher than the figures above and the violence and suffering involved many other forms such as forced migration, internal displacement, and social dislocation. Among others, Dilek Kurban, Ayşe Betül Çelik, and Deniz Yükseker, *Overcoming a Legacy of Mistrust: Towards Reconciliation between the State and the Displaced* (Istanbul: Turkish Economic and Social Studies Foundation TESEV, Norwegian Refugee Council and Internal Displacement Monitoring Centre, 2006); Djordje Stefanovic, Neophytos Loizides, and Samantha Parsons, "Home Is Where the Heart Is? Forced Migration and Voluntary Return in Turkey's Kurdish Regions," *Journal of Refugee Studies* 28, no. 2 (2014): 276–96; International Crisis Group, "Turkey's PKK Conflict: A Visual Explainer." https://www.crisisgroup.org/content/turkeys-pkk-conflict-visual-explainer (Accessed October 15, 2019). For a detailed discussion, see also Mehmet Gurses, *Anatomy of a Civil War: Sociopolitical Impacts of the Kurdish Conflict in Turkey* (Ann Arbor: University of Michigan Press, 2018), Ch. 1.

2. I will review and elaborate on these literatures later in this chapter and then throughout the book.

3. For metatheories and mid-range theories, see, among others, Atul Kohli, Peter Evans, Peter J. Katzenstein, Adam Przeworski, Susanne Hoeber Rudolph, James C. Scott, and Theda Skocpol, "The Role of Theory in Comparative Politics: A Symposium," *World Politics* 48, no. 1 (1995): 1–49; Mark I. Lichbach and Alan Zuckerman, *Comparative Politics: Rationality, Culture, and Structure* (Cambridge: Cambridge University Press, 1997); Gerardo L. Munck and Richard Snyder, *Passion, Craft, and Method in Comparative Politics* (Baltimore: The Johns Hopkins University Press, 2007).

4. For structures and structuralist and structural/institutional analyses see, among others, James Mahoney and Kathleen Thelen, eds., *Advances in Comparative-Historical Analysis* (Cambridge: Cambridge University Press, 2015); for a recent application and theorization see Jasen Brownlee, Tarek Masoud, and Andrew Reynolds, "Introduction," and "chapter 1," in *The Arab Spring: Pathways of Repression and Reform* (Oxford: Oxford University Press, 2015). For a seminal contribution, Theda Skocpol, *Social Revolutions in the Modern World* (Cambridge: Cambridge University Press, 1994). For two different analytical perspectives on the complex two-way relations between structures, identities, history, and political decisions at critical junctures see Mark R. Beissinger, *Nationalist Mobilization and the Collapse of the Soviet State* (Cambridge: Cambridge University Press, 2002); and David D. Laitin, *Identity in Formation: The Russian-Speaking Populations in the Near Abroad* (Ithaca: Cornell University Press, 1998).

5. Among others, Giovanni Capoccia and R. Daniel Kelemen, "The Study of Critical Junctures: Theory, Narrative, and Counterfactuals in Historical Institutionalism," *World Politics* 59 (2007): 341–69. See also Beissinger, *Nationalist Mobilization and the Collapse of the Soviet State*. See also endnotes 16, 17, and 20.

6. For these different approaches, see Mahoney and Thelen, eds., *Advances in Comparative-Historical Analysis*. See also Lichbach and Zuckerman, *Comparative Politics*; Mark I. Lichbach, *Is Rational Choice Theory All of Social Science?* (Ann Arbor: The University of Michigan Press, 2003); Munck and Snyder, *Passion, Craft, and Method*; Jeffrey T. Checkel and Peter J. Katzenstein, eds., *European Identity* (Cambridge: Cambridge University Press, 2009).

7. Andrew Bennett and Jeffrey T. Checkel, eds. *Process Tracing: From Metaphor to Analytic Tool* (Cambridge: Cambridge University Press, 2015).

8. For the sense in which I use "political" and "politics" here and throughout the book, see, primarily, Sheri Berman, *The Primacy of Politics: Social Democracy and the Making of Europe's Twentieth Century* (Cambridge: Cambridge University Press, 2006). For standard definitions, also see Daniele Caramani, ed. *Comparative Politics* (New York: Oxford University Press, 2008).

9. For a helpful conceptualization of the role of ideas in social science explanations, Sheri Berman, "Ideational Theorizing in the Social Sciences since 'Policy Paradigms, Social Learning, and the State,'" *Governance* 26, no. 2 (2013): 217–37, 232.

10. Hence, ideational factors "straddle the line between interest- and environmental-based explanations" and "matter by shaping actors' interests and preferences as well as the constraints and opportunities they face." Berman, "Ideational Theorizing in the Social Sciences."

11. Mahoney and Thelen, eds., *Advances in Comparative-Historical Analysis*. See also Lichbach and Zuckerman, *Comparative Politics*; Lichbach, *Is Rational Choice Theory All of Social Science?*; Munck and Snyder, *Passion, Craft, and Method*; Checkel and Katzenstein, eds., *European Identity*.

12. Max Weber, *The Methodology of the Social Sciences* (New York: Free Press, [1905] 1949); Philip E. Tetlock and Aaron Belkin, "Counterfactual Thought Experiments in World Politics: Logical, Methodological, and Psychological Perspectives," in *Counterfactual Thought Experiments in World Politics*, ed. Philip E. Tetlock and Aaron Belkin (Princeton: Princeton University Press, 1996), 3–38; Charles Tilly, "The Trouble with Stories," in *The Social Worlds of Higher Education*, ed. Bernice A. Pescosolido and Ronald Aminzade (Thousand Oaks, CA: Pine Forge, 1999).

13. Murat Somer, "Theory-Consuming or Theory-Producing?: Studying Turkey as a Theory-Developing Critical Case," *Turkish Studies* 15, no. 4 (2014): 571–88.

14. Robert H. Bates, Avner Greif, Margaret Levi, Jean-Laurent Rosenthal, and Barry R. Weingast, *Analytic Narratives* (Princeton: Princeton University Press, 1998).

15. Ozan O. Varol, "The Democratic Coup D'etat," *Harvard International Law Journal* 53, no. 2 (2012): 291–356.

16. As I will discuss throughout the book "Turk" and "Turkish" have multiple meanings, which has important implications for the conflict.

17. See previous endnote.

18. For a summary with a focus on non-Muslim religious freedoms, see United States Department of State, *Turkey 2020 International Religious Freedom Report* (Washington, DC: Office of International Religious Freedom, 2021). For the specific social and political meaning that the term *minority* has in Turkey, which can be traced back to its Ottoman past, see Aron Rodrigue, "Reflections on Millets and Minorities: Ottoman Legacies," in *Turkey between Nationalism and Globalization*, ed. Riva Kastoryano (London: Routledge, 2013), 36–46.

19. Among others, Şükrü M. Hanioğlu, "Modern Ottoman Period," in *The Routledge Handbook of Modern Turkey*, ed. Metin Heper and Sabri Sayarı (New York: Routledge, 2012), 15–25; Ali Yaycioglu, *Partners of the Empire: The Crisis of the Ottoman Order in the Age of Revolutions* (Stanford: Stanford University Press, 2016); Ethan L. Menchinger, *The First of the Modern Ottomans: The Intellectual History of Ahmed Vasif* (Cambridge: Cambridge University Press, 2017).

20. As I elaborate throughout the book, Turkish nationalism has at least two variants that produce different and contested imaginations of Turkishness. The distinction between the two may best be described in English as "Turk," i.e., based on the historical ethnic category of "Turk," versus "Turkish," i.e., based on the nation formation among the multiethnic category of Ottoman Muslims who began to see themselves and become categorized by outsiders as Turks in terms of national belonging. In the Turkish language, the same word, "Türk," has multiple meanings and usages that capture both variants depending on context.

21. Michael E. Meeker, *A Nation of Empire: The Ottoman Legacy of Turkish Modernity* (Berkeley: University of California Press, 2002).

22. Erez Manela, *The Wilsonian Moment: Self-Determination and the International Origins of Anticolonial Nationalism* (Oxford: Oxford University Press, 2007).

23. This means the possibility that the Kurds of Turkey might carve out a portion of Turkey's territory in order to found an independent state and/or unite with their ethnic brethren in Iraq and Syria.

24. As I will conceptualize and elaborate later, what I mean here is "identities that can be shared and held in common voluntarily and that are not necessarily viewed as superior to other major ethnic/national identities in society." Insofar as common identities are imposed from above rather than embraced voluntarily by individuals, and insofar as they are constructed in a hierarchical relationship with other ethnic/national identities in society, they would not be different from "overarching" national identities in terms of their social and political consequences.

25. In Turkish language, "Turk" (*Türk*) can have multiple meanings of ethnicity, nationality, or citizenship depending on context, as I will discuss in chapters 2 and 3 and throughout the book. Suffice it to say here that whenever I use the terms *Turk-ness* or *Turk identity* instead of Turkishness, I aim to highlight the meaning of Turkishness referring to an ethnic category or group rather than its meanings referring to national identity and citizenship.

26. Throughout the book, I will translate the *Türkiyeli* identity as "Of-Turkey." The latter can be contrasted with the expression "from Turkey," which indicates one's country origin but not necessarily belonging. As I will discuss further especially in chapter 5, *Türkiyeli* (literally meaning "being Of-Turkey) is an important umbrella identity that many have proposed the state should embrace as a less ethnicity-based and more inclusive alternative to Turkishness. Many Kurds in Turkey feel that Turkishness is an imposed identity on them but embrace Of-Turkey-ness (*Türkiyelilik*) as a common identity they share with Turks.

27. Hence, in terms of elite theories of regime formation, Turkey's nation-forming elites can be categorized as lacking unity in terms of "value consensus," which has been argued to be the "sine qua non of liberal democracy." John Higley and Michael Burton, eds., *Elite Foundations of Liberal Democracy* (London: Rowman and Littlefield, 2006), 28. Turkey's elites have also been disunited in terms of "ideology" and, possibly, "structural integration," though I will have less to say on the latter dimension in this book. Ibid., 8–13, 51.

29. Hamit Bozarslan, "Kurds and the Turkish State," in *The Cambridge History of Turkey, vol. 4: Turkey in the Modern World*, ed. Reşat Kasaba (Cambridge: Cambridge University Press, 2008), 333–56.

30. "Turkish" ruling elites often involve ethnic Turks as well as ethnic non-Turks including ethnic Kurds who subsume their Kurdish identity under other identities such as republican, conservative, or Islamist.

31. The meanings and contents of all of these categorizations can inevitably be contested, and I use them for lack of better terms. I use "Islamist" to refer to actors who are more ideologically inclined and informed by comprehensive projects inspired by Islam, while I employ "Muslim conservative" to denote actors for whom Islam is a more restricted and mainly social and cultural blueprint.

32. Cengiz Güneş and Welat Zeydanlıoğlu, eds. *The Kurdish Question in Turkey: New Perspectives on Violence, Representation, and Reconciliation* (London: Routledge, 2014).

33. Tilly, "The Trouble with Stories."

34. More specifically, "aspects of the empirical world that are contrary to fact but not to logical or 'objective' possibility." Margaret Levi, "A Model, A Method, and A Map: Rational Choice in Comparative and Historical Analysis," in *Comparative Politics Rationality, Culture, and Structure*, ed. Mark I. Lichbach and Alan Zuckerman (Cambridge: Cambridge University Press, 1997), 31–32; Max Weber, *The Methodology of the Social Sciences*.

35. B doesn't have to be a singular and simple cause or reason; it can be a combination of many causes or "B under certain conditions." The social sciences are open to contingent explanations with many causes. Similarly, they acknowledge the legitimacy of causal explanations with equifinality, i.e. A may result from different combinations of causal factors. Even so, this would mean that A

would happen differently without B. For related discussions, Henry E. Brady and David Collier, *Rethinking Social Inquiry: Diverse Tools, Shared Standards* (Oxford: Rowman and Littlefield, 2004).

36. Robert Olson, *The Emergence of Kurdish Nationalism and the Sheikh Said Rebellion, 1880–1925* (Austin: University of Texas Press, 1989); Baskın Oran, *Atatürk Milliyetçiliği* [Atatürk Nationalism] (Ankara: Bilgi Üniversitesi Yayınları, 1990); Martin van Bruinessen, *Ağa, Şeyh, Devlet* [Agha, Sheikh, State] (İstanbul: İletişim Yayınları, [1992] 2003), 50; Mehmet Bayrak, *Kürdoloji Belgeleri* [Kurdology Documents] (Ankara: Öz-Ge Yayınları, 2004).

37. Mahmut Akyürekli, *Türklerle Kürtler: Bin Yıllık Geçmişin Kısa Tarihi* [Turks and Kurds: A Brief History of a Thousand Years Long Past] (Istanbul: Tarih Kulübü Yayınları, 2016). Also see the statements of Şerafettin Elçi, " 'Hür Kürtler Grubu' Parti Kuruyor" ["Free Kurds Group" Forms a Political Party], *Milliyet*, July 8, 2006. https://www.internethaber.com/hur-kurtler-parti-kuruyor-31140h. htm (accessed October 11, 2019).

38. Mustafa Remzi Bucak, *Bir Kürt Aydınından İsmet İnönü'ye Mektup* [Letter from a Kurdish Luminary to İsmet İnönü] (Istanbul: Doz Yayınları, 1991); Tarık Ziya Ekinci, *Vatandaşlık Açısından Kürt Sorunu ve Bir Çözüm Önerisi* [The Kurdish Question in terms of Citizenship and a Solution Proposal] (Istanbul: Küreyel Yayınları, 1997), 136–66; Bayrak, *Kürdoloji Belgeleri*.

39. Sinan Hakan, *Türkiye Kurulurken Kürtler (1916–1920)* [Kurds When Turkey Was Being Founded (1916–1920)] (Istanbul: İletişim Yayınları, 2013), 362–63.

40. During the 1980s and 1990s, Bayrak faced persecution by legal-political authorities who considered his writings "separatist propaganda," but in a friendly settlement in the European Court of Human Rights (407/3.9.2002) the Turkish government conceded that its laws were in breach of the right to freedom of expression and information (Article 10 of the European Convention on Human Rights). Retrieved from: https://www.echr.coe.int/Pages/home.aspx?p=home. Also see Helsinki Watch, "Freedom of Expression in Turkey: Abuses Continue," *News from Helsinki Watch*, June 18, 1991. https://www.hrw.org/reports/pdfs/t/turkey/ turkey2916.pdf (accessed August 13, 2019).

41. Alevis constitute a major (Muslim) religious minority group in Turkey, even though they are not officially recognized as such. There are both Turkish and Kurdish Alevis. Among others, Markus Dressler, *Writing Religion: The Making of Turkish Alevi Islam* (Oxford: Oxford University Press, 2013); Kabir Tanbar, *The Reckoning of Pluralism: Political Belonging and the Demands of History in Turkey* (Stanford: Stanford University Press, 2014).

42. Bayrak, *Kürdoloji Belgeleri*, 23–24. The italic sections in the original text have been presented in nonitalic in order to highlight my personal emphasis.

43. Ekinci, *Vatandaşlık Açısından Kürt Sorunu*, 137–67; Bayrak, *Kürdoloji Belgeleri*. For Kurdish historiography in different periods, see Hamit Bozarslan, "Some Remarks on Kurdish Historiographical Discourse in Turkey," in *Essays on*

*the Origins of Kurdish Nationalism,* ed. Abbas Vali (Costa Mesa: Mazda, 2003), 14–39. See also Mohammed M. A. Ahmed and Michael M. Gunter, eds., *The Evolution of Kurdish Nationalism* (Costa Mesa: Mazda, 2007).

44. To explain the change after the war, these studies, too, implicitly or explicitly assume that the different policies and discourses during the National Campaign were mainly tactical, i.e., concealing the long-term intentions, even when this is argued in passing reference. See, among others, Oktay Uygun, "Federalizm ve Bölgesel Özerklik Tartışmaları [Discussions of Federalism and Regional Autonomy]," in *Demokratik Anayasa: Görüşler ve Öneriler* [Democratic Constitution: Views and Proposals], ed. Ece Göztepe and Aykut Çelebi, 91–139 (Istanbul: Metis Yayıncılık, 2012), 125.

45. Doğu Perinçek, *Kemalist Devrim—4: Kurtuluş Savaşı'nda Kürt Politikası* [The Kemalist Revolution—4, Kurdish Policies during the Turkish War of Independence] (Istanbul: Kaynak Yayınları, 1999).

46. Ahmet Yıldız, *"Ne Mutlu Türküm Diyebilene": Türk Ulusal Kimliğinin Etno-Seküler Sınırları 1919-1938* ["How Happy Is the One Who Can Say I Am a Turk": The Ethno-Secular Limits of Turkish National Identity 1919–1938] (Istanbul: İletişim Yayınları, 2001), 98.

47. For critical accounts from liberal, liberal/conservative, and Islamist perspectives in popular writing, see Hasan Cemal, *Kürtler* [The Kurds] (Istanbul: Doğan Kitap, 2003); and Mustafa Akyol, *Kürt Sorununu Yeniden Düşünmek* [Rethinking the Kurdish Problem] (Istanbul: Doğan Kitap, 2006); Altan Tan, *Kürt Sorunu: Ya Tam Kardeşlik Ya Hep Birlikte Kölelik* [The Kurdish Question: Proper Brotherhood or Slavery for All] (Istanbul: Timaş Yayınları, 2009). Also see Oran, *Atatürk Milliyetçiliği,* 122–32; Metin Heper, *The State and Kurds in Turkey* (New York: Palgrave Macmillan, 2007).

48. Uğur Mumcu, *Kürt-İslam Ayaklanması: 1919-1925* [The Kurdish-Islamist Rebellion: 1919–1925] (Ankara: Tekin Yayınevi, 1993); Heper, *The State and Kurds.*

49. One way of reckoning these counterfactual scenarios is the method of "vicarious problem-solving," as coined by Thomas Schelling. In this methodology, the researcher assumes that the principal aims of the primary actors remain the same but also constructs counterfactual scenarios that predict how the actors would behave toward each other under different conditions (Lichbach, *Is Rational Choice Theory All of Social Science?,* 12).

50. Nathalie Clayer, Fabio Giomi, and Emmanuel Szerek, eds., *Kemalism: Transnational Politics in the Post-Ottoman World* (London: I. B. Tauris, 2019), 4.

51. Max Fisher, Josh Keller, Mae Ryan, and Shane O'Neill, "National Identity Is Made Up," in *The Interpreter,* https://www.nytimes.com/video/world/100000005660651/national-identity.html. *New York Times* (accessed August 14, 2019).

52. For example, see Abbas Vali, ed., *Essays on the Origins of Kurdish Nationalism* (Costa Mesa: Mazda, 2003), 22–23. Bozarslan, whom Vali references in his

foreword, uses a different terminology. Özkırımlı acknowledges that Anderson's argument does not imply the "fakeness" of nations, but he nevertheless uses the term *hayali cemaat* (imaginary community). Umut Özkırımlı, *Milliyetçilik Kuramları: Eleştirel Bir Bakış* [Theories of Nationalism: A Critical Perspective] (Ankara: Doğu-Batı Yayınları, 2008).

53. Günay Göksu Özdoğan and Gül Tokay, eds. *Redefining the Nation, State, and Citizen* (Istanbul: Eren, 2000); Oran, *Atatürk Milliyetçiliği*; Tanıl Bora, ed., *Milliyetçilik* [Nationalism] (Istanbul: İletişim Yayınları, 2002); Bruinessen, *Ağa, Şeyh, Devlet*; Vali, ed., *Essays on the Origins of Kurdish Nationalism*; Erik Jan Zürcher, *Savaş, Devrim ve Uluslaşma, Türkiye Tarihi'nde Geçiş Dönemi: 1908–1928* [War, Revolution, and Nation-Formation, The Transition Period in the History of Turkey: 1908–1928] (İstanbul: İstanbul Bilgi Üniversitesi Yayınları, 2005); Mesut Yeğen, *Müstakbel Türk'ten Sözde Vatandaş'a: Cumhuriyet ve Kürtler* [From Prospective Turks to So-Called Citizens] (Istanbul: İletişim Yayınları, 2006); Ahmed and Gunter, *The Evolution of Kurdish Nationalism*.

54. I noticed, with surprise, that some of my own writings unwittingly reflect this tendency also.

55. Hans-Lukas Kieser, "Introduction," in *Turkey Beyond Nationalism: Towards Post-Nationalism Identities*, ed. Hans-Lukas Kieser (London: IB Tauris, 2006), vii–xvii, xii.

56. Michael Billig, *Banal Nationalism* (London: Sage, 1995).

57. Murat Somer and Evangelos G. Liaras, "Turkey's New Kurdish Opening: Religious versus Secular Values," *Middle East Policy* 17, no. 2 (2010): 152–65; Murat Somer, "Media Values and Democratization: What Unites and What Divides Religious-Conservative and Pro-Secular Elites?," *Turkish Studies* 11, no. 4 (December 2010): 555–77; and "Does It Take Democrats to Democratize?: Lessons from Islamic and Secular Elite Values in Turkey," *Comparative Political Studies* 44, no. 5 (2011): 511–45; Murat Somer and Gitta Glüpker-Kesebir, "Is Islam the Solution? Comparing Turkish Islamic and Secular Thinking toward Ethnic and Religious Minorities," *Journal of Church and State* 58, no. 3 (2015): 529–55.

58. Hasan Cemal, "Başörtüsü, eşit yurttaşlık derken, ulus-devlet . . ." [Talking about Headscarves and Equal Rights, but What of the Nation-State?], *T24*, October 5, 2013. http.//t24.com.tr/yazarlar/hasan-cemal/basortusu-esit-yurttaslik-derken-ulus-devlet,7570 (accessed August 14, 2019).

59. Banu İriç, "Bomba Kürt Devleti Kurulacak İddiası [Explosive Allegation: Kurdish State to be Founded]," exclusive interview with Ali Bulaç, *Internethaber*, May 4, 2013. http.//www.internethaber.com/bomba-kurt-devleti-kurulacak-iddiasi-529564h.htm (accessed August 14, 2019).

60. Ibid.

61. Berman, "Ideational Theorizing."

62. Charles Taylor, *A Secular Age* (Cambridge: Belknap Press of Harvard University Press, 2007).

63. Frederick Barth, ed., *Ethnic Groups and Boundaries: Social Organization of Cultural Difference* (Boston: Little, Brown, 1969); Andreas Wimmer, "Elementary Strategies of Ethnic Boundary Making," *Ethnic and Racial Studies* 31, no. 6 (2008): 631–65.

64. Harris Mylonas, *The Politics of Nation-Building: Making Co-Nationals, Refugees, and Minorities* (Cambridge: Cambridge University Press, 2012).

65. I define conflict here broadly, capturing violent or "lethal" conflicts as well as social/political conflict, as in minority resentments producing "contentious politics" among minority groups. Charles Tilly and Sidney Tarrow, *Contentious Politics* (Oxford: Oxford University Press, 2015). For alternative conflict definitions, see Ted Robert Gurr and Barbara Harff, *Ethnic Conflict in World Politics* (Boulder: Westview, 1994); Paul Collier and Anke Hoeffler, "Economic Causes of Civil War," *Oxford Economic Papers*, no. 50 (1998): 563–73; James D. Fearon and David D. Laitin, "Ethnicity, Insurgency, and Civil War," *American Political Science Review* 97, no. 01 (2003): 75–90; Stathis N. Kalyvas, Ian Shapiro, and Tarek Massoud, eds. *Order, Conflict, and Violence* (Cambridge: Cambridge University Press, 2008); for the case of the Kurdish Conflict, Arzu Kibris, "Funerals and Elections: The Effects of Terrorism on Voting Behavior in Turkey," *Journal of Conflict Resolution* 55, no. 2 (2010): 220–47.

66. Arend Lijphart, *Democracy in Plural Societies* (New Haven: Yale University Press, 1977); also see H. Zeynep Bulutgil, *The Roots of Ethnic Cleansing in Europe* (Cambridge: Cambridge University Press, 2016).

67. For a variation of this argument based on the causal mechanism of "double ethnic outbidding," analysis of different combinations of unity and disunity among majority and minority group elites, and comparative empirical examination of ethnic minority conflicts in Bulgaria, Montenegro, and North Macedonia, see Idlir Lika, "Nationhood Cleavages and Ethnic Conflict: A Comparative Analysis of Post-communist Bulgaria, Montenegro, and North Macedonia," PhD Dissertation, Koç University, December 2019.

68. Mahoney and Thelen, eds., *Advances in Comparative-Historical Analysis*, 27.

69. Barry Posen, "The Security Dilemma and Ethnic Conflict," in *Ethnic Conflict and International Security*, ed. Michael E. Brown (Princeton: Princeton University Press, 1993); James Fearon and David D. Laitin, "Explaining Interethnic Cooperation," *The American Political Science Review*, 90, no. 4 (1996): 715–35; James Fearon, "Commitment Problems and the Spread of Ethnic Conflict," in *The International Spread of Ethnic Conflict*, ed. David Lake and Donald Rothchild (Princeton: Princeton University Press, 1998). For ontological security dilemmas, see Paul Roe, *Ethnic Violence and Societal Security Dilemma* (New York: Routledge, 2005); Bahar Rumelili, *Conflict Resolution and Ontological Security: Peace Anxieties*, Prio New Security Studies (London: Routledge, 2015). For an application to the Kurdish Conflict, Tuncay Kardaş and Ali Balci, "Inter-Societal Security Drilemma in Turkey: Understanding the Failure of the 2009 Kurdish Opening," *Turkish Studies* 17, no. 1 (2016): 155–80.

70. Mylonas, *The Politics of Nation-Building*; Keith Darden and Harris Mylonas, "Threats to Territorial Integrity, National Mass Schooling, and Linguistic Commonality," *Comparative Political Studies* 49, no. 11 (2016): 1446–79.

71. Paul Brass, *Ethnicity and Nationalism: Theory and Comparison* (London: Sage, 1991); V. P. Gagnon, "Ethnic Nationalism and International Conflict," *International Security*, 19, no. 3 (1994–95): 130–66 and *The Myth of Ethnic War: Serbia and Croatia in the 1990s* (Ithaca: Cornell University Press, 2004); Edward D. Mansfield and Jack Snyder, *Electing to Fight: Why Emerging Democracies Go to War* (Cambridge: MIT Press, 2005).

72. Lijphart, *Democracy in Plural Societies*; Donald L. Horowitz, *Ethnic Groups in Conflict* (Berkeley: University of California Press, 1985); Michael Hechter, *Containing Nationalism* (Oxford: Oxford University Press, 2000); Steven Wilkinson, *Votes and Violence: Electoral Competition and Ethnic Riots in India* (New York: Cambridge University Press, 2004); Lars-Erik Cederman, Andreas Wimmer, and Brian Min, "Why Do Ethnic Groups Rebel? New Data and Analysis," *World Politics* 62, no. 1 (2010): 87–119.

73. Democratization can have a curvilinear relation with ethnic conflict, semi-democracies being especially vulnerable to conflict. Demet Yalçın Mousseau, "Democratizing with Ethnic Divisions: A Source of Conflict?" *Journal of Peace Research* 38, no. 5 (2001): 547–67; Mansfield and Snyder, *Electing to Fight*.

74. In addition to aforementioned discussions and conceptualizations of the roles of politics and ideas in democratization by Sheri Berman, for four seminal contributions to democratization research emphasizing political agency, Giuseppe Di Palma, *To Craft Democracies: An Essay on Democratic Transitions* (Los Angeles: University of California Press, 1990); Juan J. Linz and Alfred Stepan, *Problems of Democratic Transition and Consolidation: Southern Europe, South America, and Post-Communist Europe* (Baltimore and London: The Johns Hopkins University Press, 1996); Adam Przeworski, "Democracy as a Contingent Outcome of Conflicts," in *Constitutionalism and Democracy*, ed. Jon Elster and Rune Slagstad (Cambridge: Cambridge University Press, 1988), 59–80, and "Deliberation and Ideological Domination" in *Deliberative Democracy*, ed. John Elster (New York: Cambridge University Press, 1998), 140–60. For a recent intervention, Larry Diamond, *Ill Winds: Saving Deömocracy from Russian Rage, Chinese Ambition, and American Complacency* (New York: Penguin Press, 2019). For two contributions on Turkey, Lauren McLaren and Burak Cop, "The Failure of Democracy in Turkey: A Comparative Analysis," *Government and Opposition* 46, no. 4 (2011): 485–516; Murat Somer, "Moderation of Religious and Secular Politics, a Country's 'Center' and Democratization," *Democratization* 21, no. 2 (2014): 244–67.

75. "Resources" here can refer to material as well as nonmaterial respurces such as social capital and civil society. Fearon and Laitin, "Ethnicity, Insurgency, and Civil War"; Ashutosh Varshney, *Ethnic Conflict and Civic Life: Hindus and*

*Muslims in India* (New Haven: Yale University Press, 2002); Stathis N. Kalyvas, *The Logic of Violence in Civil War* (Cambridge: Cambridge University Press, 2006). For two microlevel and resource-based analyses of the PKK conflict, see Tezcür, "Ordinary People, Extraordinary Risks" and Belgin San-Akca, *States in Disguise: Causes of State Support for Rebel Groups* (Oxford: Oxford University Press, 2016). Competition for natural resources can be an important driver in conflict. Collier and Hoeffler, "Economic Causes of Civil War." But, as I argue in this book, this does not seem to be a main cause of the Kurdish Conflict.

76. Ted Robert Gurr, *Why Men Rebel* (Princeton: Princeton University Press, 1970); Gurr and Barbara Harff, *Ethnic Conflict in World Politics*; Lars-Erik Cederman, Kristian Skrede Gleditsch, and Halvard Buhaug, *Inequality, Grievances, and Civil War* (New York: Cambridge University Press, 2013).

77. David A. Lake and Donald Rothchild, eds., *The International Spread of Ethnic Conflict: Fear, Diffusion, and Escalation* (Princeton: Princeton University Press, 1998); Robert Hislope, "Between A Bad Peace and A Good War: Insights and Lessons from the Almost-War in Macedonia," *Ethnic and Racial Studies* 26, no. 1 (2003): 129–51.

78. Cederman, Wimmer, and Min, "Why Do Ethnic Groups Rebel?"

79. As we will see, "ethnicity" (*etnisite*) is not a frequently employed term in Turkish. Instead, other terms such as *köken* (ancestry), *kültürel grup* (cultural group), or *unsur* (component) are employed, vaguely corresponding to the meaning of ethnicity.

80. Lowell W. Barrington, "Introduction," in *After Independence: Making and Protecting the Nation in Postcolonial and Post-Communist States*, ed. Lowell W. Barrington (Ann Arbor: University of Michigan Press, 2003), 7.

81. Tariq Rahman, *Language and Politics in Pakistan* (Karachi: Oxford University Press Karachi, 1996); Paul R. Brass, *Language, Religion, and Politics in North India* (Lincoln: iUniverse, 2005).

82. Arlie Russell Hochschild, *Strangers in Their Own Land: Anger and Mourning on the American Right, a Journey to the Heart of Our Political Divide* (New York: The New Press, 2017); Jill Lepore, *This America: The Case for the Nation* (New York: Liveright, 2019); Suketu Mehta, *This Land Is Our Land: An Immigrant's Manifesto* (New York: Farrar, Straus, and Giroux, 2019).

83. Murat Somer and Jennifer McCoy, "Transformations through Polarizations and Global Threats to Democracy," *Annals of the American Academy of Political and Social Science* 681 (2019): 8–22.

84. I will not discuss in this chapter the distinctions between the legal and political definitions of internal (domestic) and external sovereignty and what I will call the "divisible and indivisible dimensions" of the concept of sovereignty (see chapter 7). For a critical argument on this subject, see among others, Neil MacCormick, *Questioning Sovereignty: Law, State, and Practical Reason* (Oxford: Oxford University Press, 1999).

85. Anthony D. Smith, *National Identity* (Reno: University of Nevada Press, 1991); Liah Greenfeld, *Nationalism: Five Roads to Modernity* (Cambridge: Harvard University Press, 1992); J. Hutchinson and A. D. Smith, eds., *Nationalism* (Oxford University Press, 1994); David Miller, *On Nationality* (Oxford: Clarendon Press, 1995); Miroslav Hrosch, *Social Preconditions of National Revival in Europe: A Comparative Analysis of the Social Composition of Patriotic Groups among the Smaller European Nations* (New York: Columbia University Press, [1985] 2000); Lowell W. Barrington, ed., *After Independence: Making and Protecting the Nation in Postcolonial and Postcommunist States* (Ann Arbor: University of Michigan Press, 2009).

86. Walker Connor, "When Is a Nation?" *Ethnic and Racial Studies* 13, no. 1 (January 1990): 92–103.

87. Crawford Young, ed., *The Rising Tide of Cultural Pluralism: The Nation-State at Bay?* (Madison: The University of Wisconsin Press, 1993). For historical/sociologist and culturalist approaches, see Afshin Marashi, "Paradigms of Iranian Nationalism: History, Theory, and Historiography," in *Rethinking Iranian Nationalism and Modernity*, ed. Kamran Scot Aghaie and Afshin Marashi (Austin: University of Texas Press, 2014), 3–24.

88. Hans Kohn, *The Idea of Nationalism: A Study in its Origins and Background* (New York: Macmillan, 1951), 4–7.

89. Hendrik Spruyt, "War, Trade, and State Formation," in *Oxford Handbook of Comparative Politics*, ed. Carles Boix and Susan Stokes (2007), 211–35. Hence, Charles Tilly discusses the historical and causal primacy of "national state": "states governing multiple contiguous regions and their cities by means of centralized, differentiated and autonomous structures . . . most states have been non-national: city-state, empires, or something else." He stresses that national state "does not necessarily mean nation-state, a state whose people share a strong linguistic, religious or symbolic identity." Charles Tilly, *Coercion, Capital, and European States* (Cambridge: Blackwell, 1990), 2–3. Also see Michael Mann, *States, War, and Capitalism: Studies in Political Sociology* (Oxford: Blackwell, 1992), in particular on the role of industrialization, social class, and militarism in the emergence of modern, territorial nation-states.

90. Andreas Wimmer, *Waves of War: Nationalism, State Formation, and Ethnic Exclusion in the Modern World* (Cambridge: Cambridge University Press, 2013).

91. Ibid.

92. Ayhan Aktar, Niyazi Kızılyürek, and Umut Özkırımlı, eds., *Nationalism in the Troubled Triangle: Cyprus, Greece and Turkey* (London: Palgrave Macmillan, 2010); Ioannis N. Grigoriadis, *Instilling Religion in Greek and Turkish Nationalism: A "Sacred Synthesis"* (New York: Palgrave MacMillan, 2013).

93. Vali, *Kurds and the State*, xiii.

94. Anatoly Khazanov, "A State without a Nation? Russia after Empire," in *The Nation-State in Question*, ed. T. V. Paul, G. John Ikenberry, and John A. Hall (Princeton: Princeton University Press, 2003), 87.

95. Anthony W. Marx, *Faith in Nation: Exclusionary Origins of Nationalism* (Oxford: Oxford University Press, 2003), 75.

96. Bozarslan, "Some Remarks on Kurdish Historiographical Discourse in Turkey."

97. *Rumeli* or *Rum ili* in Turkish (literally meaning Province (Land) of the *Rum*, i.e., Romans), refers to the historically Ottoman territories in Southeastern Europe, which Ottomans conquered from the Byzantine Empire. It was also the name of a first-level Ottoman governing unit (*beylerbeylik*) that covered most of the Balkans.

98. Roger Owen, *State, Power, and the Making of the Modern Middle East* (London and New York, Routledge, 2004). See also John Meyer, J. Boli, G. Thomas, and F. Ramirez, "World Society and the Nation-State," *American Journal of Sociology* 103, no. 1 (July 1997): 144–81; Joel S. Migdal, *Strong Societies and Weak States: State-Society Relations and State Capabilities in the Third World* (Princeton: Princeton University Press, 1988).

99. Ronald Grigor Suny, "Nationalism, Nation Making, & the Postcolonial States of Asia, Africa, & Eurasia," in *After Independence*, ed. Lowell W. Barrington, 279–95.

100. Barrington, "Introduction."

101. Ibid., 4. For examples of various and often instrumental employments of "race" and "ethnicity" in the constructions of different nations, Paul Spickard, ed., *Race and Nation: Ethnic Systems in the Modern World* (New York: Routledge, 2005).

102. Ibid., 7.

103. John Stuart Mill, "Considerations on Representative Government," in *Collected Works, J.S. Mill, XIX* (Toronto: University of Toronto Press and Routledge and Kegan Paul, [1859] 1977).

104. Walker Connor, "Nation-Building or Nation-Destroying?" *World Politics* 24, no. 3 (1972): 319–55.

105. *Lausanne Peace Conference: Proceedings and Documents*, volume 1-1, Book 1, trans. Seha L. Meray (Istanbul: Yapı Kredi Yayınları, [1923] 1993); Kemal Arı, *Büyük Mübadele* [The Great Exchange] (Istanbul: Tarih Vakfı Yurt Yayınları, 1995); Benjamin Fortna et al., *State-Nationalisms in the Ottoman Empire*; Aslı Iğsız, *Humanism in Ruins*.

106. Wimmer, *Waves of War*, 25, 108–42.

107. However, genocides and ethnic cleansing are not only carried out by nation-states and also took place before the age of nation-states. For pre-nation-state "mass political murder," Daniel Chirot and Clark McCauley, *Why Not Kill Them All? The Logic and Prevention of Mass Political Murder* (Princeton: Princeton University Press, 2010).

108. Zeynep Kezer, *Building Modern Turkey: State, Space, and Ideology in the Early Republic* (Pittsburgh: University of Pittsburgh Press, 2015); Ronald G. Suny, *"They Can Live in the Desert but Nowhere Else": A History of Armenian Genocide* (Princeton: Princeton University Press, 2015).

109. John R. Lampe, *Yugoslavia as History: Twice There Was a Country* (Cambridge: Cambridge University Press, 2000).

110. Karl W. Deutsch, *Nationalism and Social Communication* (Cambridge: The MIT Press, [1953] 1966); Eugen Weber, *Peasants into Frenchmen: The Modernization of Rural France, 1870–1914* (Stanford: Stanford University Press, 1976); Ernest Gellner, *Nations and Nationalism* (Ithaca: Cornell University Press, 1983); Roger Brubaker, *Citizenship and Nationhood in France and Germany* (Cambridge: Harvard University Press, 1992); Elie Kedourie, *Nationalism* (Malden, MA: Blackwell, 2000); Will Kymlicka, *Politics in the Vernacular: Nationalism, Multiculturalism, and Citizenship* (Oxford: Oxford University Press, 2001); Ronald Beiner, *Liberalism, Nationalism, Citizenship* (Vancouver: UCB Press, 2003). For the role of external threats, see Darden and Mylonas, "Threats to Territorial Integrity."

111. Miller, *On Nationality*. It is important to note that the processes of nation building are not only realized through purposeful state policies but that by the state but that they also emerge as a byproduct of other state policies (e.g., economic development and defense policies) and as a result of partially spontaneous social, economic, and intellectual developments. For example, nations were also spontaneously formed through the development of newspapers, which required the use of a single standard language in order to gain wide circulation with the technological possibilities of the time and the growth of print capitalism. Benedict Anderson, *Imagined Communities: Reflections on the Origin and Spread of Nationalism* (London: Verso, 1983).

112. Stepan, Linz, and Yadav, *Crafting State Nations*, xii.

113. Ibid., 5.

114. "Ideal types" à la Max Weber, are abstract group categories, which (no example of the type) "resembles fully, but all will look like in one way or another." Cas Mudde, *Populist Radical Right Parties in Europe* (Cambridge: Cambridge University Press, 2007), 13.

115. Ibid., xii.

116. Stepan, Linz, and Yadav, *Crafting State Nations*, xiv–xv.

117. Thomas Benedikter, *The World's Modern Autonomy Systems: Concepts and Experiences of Regional Territorial Autonomy* (Bolzano/Bozen: Institute of Minority Rights/EURAC Research, 2009); Marc Weller and Katherine Nobbs, eds., *Asymmetric Autonomy and the Settlement of Ethnic Conflicts* (Philadelphia: University of Pennsylvania Press, 2010).

118. See Will Kymlicka, *Multicultural Citizenship: A Liberal Theory of Minority Rights* (Oxford: Oxford University Press 1995); Matthijs Bogaards, Ludger Helms, and Arend Lijphart, "The Importance of Consociationalism for Twenty-First Century Politics and Political Science," *Swiss Political Science Review* 25, no. 4 (2019): 341–56.

119. Ashutosh Varshney, "Discovering the 'State-Nation,'" Book Review of *Crafting State-Nations: India and Other Multinational Democracies* by Alfred

Stepan, Juan J. Linz, and Yogendra Yadav (Baltimore: Johns Hopkins University Press, 2011), *Journal of Democracy* 23, no. 2 (2012): 162–66.

120. Max Weber, *Economy and Society: An Outline of Interpretive Sociology*, ed. Guenther Roth and Claus Wittich (Berkeley: University of California Press, 1978), 389.

121. Ibid.

122. Weber also noted that ethnic identities are "*künstlich*," which means "artificial" or "human-made." Michael Banton, "The Sociology of Ethnic Relations," *Ethnic and Racial Studies* 31, no. 7 (2008): 1267–85. Hence, similar to national identities, ethnic identities can be criticized as "made-up." As I highlight in this book, however, being constructed does not render social identities unreal or artificial.

123. Likening ethnic ties to family ties is a frequently used discursive strategy by nationalists to mobilize people. Horowitz, *Ethnic Groups in Conflict*, particularly chapter 2.

124. Kanchan Chandra, "What Is Ethnic Identity and Does It Matter?" *Annual Review of Political Science* 9, no. 1 (2006): 397–424.

125. Brass, *Ethnicity and Nationalism*.

126. Smith, *National Identity*.

127. In his empirical research, James Fearon also shares the view that groups that can be defined as ethnic groups must have seven characteristics. Situations where the group identity shared by members of the group and their common historical and cultural awareness is weak, are better defined as ethnic category. James Fearon, "Ethnic and Cultural Diversity by Country," *Journal of Economic Growth* 8 (2003): 201.

128. Hence, Weber also argues that "ethnic membership" (i.e., being included in an ethnic category) "does not constitute a group; it only facilitates group formation." Weber, *Economy and Society*, 389. Also see Banton, "The Sociology of Ethnic Relations."

# Chapter 2

1. For most different case analysis, George and Bennett, *Case Studies and Theory Development*.

2. Murat Somer, "Why Aren't Kurds Like the Scots and the Turks Like the Brits? Moderation and Democracy in the Kurdish Question," *Cooperation and Conflict* 43, no. 2 (2008): 220–49.

3. See Adam Przeworski, *Democracy and the Market: Political and Economic Reforms in Eastern Europe and Latin America* (Cambridge: Cambridge University Press, 1991) and Bates et al., *Analytic Narratives* for employing empirical cases this way.

4. David McCrone, *Understanding Scotland: The Sociology of a Nation* (London and New York: Routledge, 2001); Catherine Bromley, John Curtice, David McCrone, and Alison Park, *Has Devolution Delivered?* (Edinburgh: Edinburgh University Press, 2006). National Records of Scotland: https://www.nrscotland.gov.uk and UK Office for National Statistics: https://www.ons.gov.uk/ (accessed June 5, 2019).

5. Following centuries of fighting, the Scots officially joined Great Britain with the 1707 Acts of Union. Legally, the Scots and the English were thus constitutionally recognized as comprising "one sovereign people." Many Scots, however, reject the notion of "one sovereign people," while many English view that the Scots joined the union freely and voluntarily. Author's interview with Professor Bernard Crick, Edinburgh, Scotland, UK, September 2006. In addition, see: Robert Colls, *Identity of England* (Oxford: Oxford University Press, 2002). See also Michael Keating, "Brexit and the Nations," *Britain Beyond Brexit, The Political Quarterly Monograph Series* 90, no. S2 (2019): 167–76. https://doi.org/10.1111/1467-923X.12619.

6. William L. Miller, *The End of British Politics? Scots and English Political Behavior in the Seventies* (Oxford: Clarendon Press, 1981); McCrone, *Understanding Scotland*; Tom Nairn, *After Britain: New Labour and the Return of Scotland* (London: Granta Books, 2001); Michael Keating, *The Government of Scotland: Public Policy Making After Devolution* (Edinburgh: Edinburgh University Press, 2005).

7. Keating, *The Government of Scotland*.

8. David McCrone, "Be Careful What You Wish For," *Discover Society*. http://www.discoversociety.org/2014/09/30/be-careful-what-you-wish-for/ (accessed September 30, 2014)

9. Harriet Sherwood, "Is Scotland Finally Set to Bid Farewell to the Union?" *Guardian*, August 11, 2019. Also see Keating, "Brexit and the Nations."

10. Miller, *The End of British Politics? Scots and English Political Behavior in the Seventies*, 9.

11. Somer, "Why Aren't Kurds Like the Scots?"

12. Zeki Sarigil and Ekrem Karakoç, "Who Supports Secession? The Determinants of Secessionist Attitudes among Turkey's Kurds," *Nations and Nationalism* 22, no. 2 (2016): 325–46.

13. David McDowall, *The Kurds: A Nation Denied* (London: Minority Rights Group, 1992); As of the 2000s, close to one million Kurds were estimated to live in Europe. Bilgin Ayata, "Mapping Euro-Kurdistan," *Middle East Report* 38, no. 247 (Summer 2008): 18–24. Also see Vera Eccarius-Kelly, *The Militant Kurds: A Dual Strategy for Freedom* (Santa Barbara, CA: Praeger, 2011).

14. It is critical how the census takers define ethnicity and whether they define mother tongue as the language spoken at home or as the mother's native language, since the father's native language may be spoken in some households with mixed parents. For a critique of Turkish censuses, Fuat Dündar, *Türkiye*

*Nüfus Sayımlarında Azınlıklar* [Minorities in Turkey's Censuses] (İstanbul: Doz Yayınları, 1999).

15. Ibid., 29–31. See also Şener Aktürk, *Regimes of Ethnicity and Nationhood in Germany, Russia, and Turkey* (New York: Cambridge University Press, 2012).

16. Konda, *Kürt Meselesi'nde Algı ve Beklentiler* [Perceptions and Expectations in the Kurdish Question] (Istanbul: İletişim Yayınları, 2011). Also see Milliyet-Konda, *Biz Kimiz: Toplumsal Yapı Araştırması 2006* [Who Are We? Social Composition Survey] (İstanbul: Konda Araştırma ve Danışmanlık, 2007).

17. Yılmaz, "Türkiye'de Kimlikler, Kürt Sorunu ve Çözüm Süreci," 19. A further 1.8 percent reported speaking Turkish but not as well as their native Kurdish.

18. In some cases, the politically charged nature of the Kurdish Question may result in self-censorship among some survey respondents. However, the survey data discussed above suggest that at least those respondents who answered the questions about ethnicity did not feel a sense of reluctance about reporting their ethnic identities.

19. Konda, *Kürt Meselesi'nde Algı ve Beklentiler*; Peter Alford Andrews, *Ethnic Groups in the Republic of Turkey* (Wiesbaden: Reichert. 198); Servet Mutlu, "Ethnic Kurds in Turkey: A Demographic Study," *International Journal of Middle East Studies* 28, no. 4 (1996): 517–41; Ayse Gündüz-Hosgör and Jeroen Smits, "Intermarriage between Turks and Kurds in Contemporary Turkey: Interethnic Relations in an Urbanizing Environment," *European Sociological Review* 18, no. 4 (2002): 417–32. Non-systematic estimates range between 12 and 23 percent. McDowall, *The Kurds*; Bruinessen, *Ağa, Şeyh, Devlet*; Minority Rights Group International, *A Quest for Equality: Minorities in Turkey* (2007).

20. *Encyclopedia Britannica* offers the following figures for the year 2000: Turkey, 18.9 percent, Iraq, 23 percent, Syria 7.3 percent, and Iran 13 percent. http://www.britannica.com/bps/browse/atlas (accessed April 10, 2014).

21. Farideh Koohl-Kamali, *The Political Development of the Kurds in Iran: Pastoral Nationalism* (New York: Palgrave Macmillan, 2003), 24–35; Gareth Stansfield, "Kurds, Persian Nationalism, and Shi'i Rule: Surviving Dominant Nationhood in Iran," in *Conflict, Democratization, and the Kurds in the Middle East Turkey, Iran, Iraq, and Syria*, ed. David Romano and Mehmet Gürses (New York: Palgrave Macmillan, 2014), 59–84; Alireza Asgharzadeh, *Iran and the Challenge of Diversity: Islamic Fundamentalism, Aryanist Racism, and Democratic Struggles* (New York: Palgrave Macmillan, 2007), 15; Nader Entessar, "The Kurdish National Movement in Iran Since the Islamic Revolution of 1979," in *The Evolution of Kurdish Nationalism*, ed. Mohammed M. A. Ahmed and Michael M. Gunter (Costa Mesa: Mazda, 2007), 260–75; Kaveh Bayat, "Iran and the 'Kurdish Question,'" *Middle East Report* 38, no. 247 (Summer 2008); Menchinger, *The First of the Modern Ottomans: The Intellectual History of Ahmed Vasif*; Abbas Vali, *Kurds and the State in Iran: The Making of Kurdish Identity* (London: I. B. Tauris, 2011). Similar to the situation in Turkey, Iranian Kurds are geographically semi-mixed, inhabiting

disjointed and ambiguously bounded areas. Hence, to clarify the borders of a Kurdish Autonomous region both in the era of the Mahabad Republic (1945–46) and during the 1978–79 Revolution proved impossible without violating the borders of the Azerbaijan, Ilam, and Kirmanshah provinces. Nader Entessar, *Kurdish Ethnonationalism* (Boulder: Lynne Rienner, 1992), 16–31. Defining these borders in the cases of Iraq (for example, with the status of Kirkuk) and Syria is also difficult, even more so when trying to maintain a sense of geographic continuity.

22. However, Iraqi Kurds of the Sulaymaniyah region have historically been closely linked with Iran.

23. Ibid.

24. Martin van Bruinessen, *Kürtlük, Türklük, Alevilik: Etnik ve Dinsel Kimlik Mücadeleleri* [Kurdishness, Turkishness, Alevi-ness: Ethnic and Religious Identity Struggles] (İstanbul: İletişim Yayınları, 1999), 10. *Ethnologue* reports that in 2014 1,344,000 people in Turkey spoke the Zaza language (out of this, 1,160,000 spoke Southern Zaza, while 184,000 spoke either Northern Zaza or Kurmanji). Meanwhile, in 1980 it was estimated that 3.95 million people spoke Kurmanji in Turkey. Hence, as a rough estimate, one out of five Kurds (3 million) can be considered Zaza. https://www-ethnologue-com.stanford.idm.oclc.org/ (accessed June 8, 2019). These very rough estimates, however, do not take into account factors such as differential fertility rates.

25. According to these statistics, mixed Turkish-Kurdish marriages comprise 2.4 percent of the total married population in Turkey. Gündüz-Hoşgör and Smits, "Intermarriage Between Turks and Kurds," 425–26. Such figures would make any possible separation of Turks and Kurds quite difficult, but at the same time they are too low to indicate social integration between Turks and Kurds. Between 1987 and 1989 in Bosnia and Herzegovina, which would soon become the scene of bloody ethnic conflict and separatist warfare, it was estimated that 12 percent of marriages were composed of individuals from different (whether Serbian, Croat, or Bosniak) ethnic backgrounds. See Murat Somer, "Cascades of Ethnic Polarization: Lessons from Yugoslavia," *Annals of the American Academy of Political and Social Science* 573 (July 2001): 127–51.

26. *Hungarian Human Rights Foundation* (accessed March 31, 2004) http://www.htmh.hu/ reports2001/slovakia2001.htm; *CIA World Factbook*. Also see, Jiří Musil, ed., *The End of Czechoslovakia* (Budapest: Central European University Press, 1995); Sharon L. Wolchik, "The Politics of Ethnicity in Post-Communist Czechoslovakia," *East European Politics and Societies* 8, no. 1 (Winter 1994): 153–88.

27. Murat Somer, "Insincere Public Discourse, Trust, and Implications for Democratic Transition: The Yugoslav Meltdown Revisited," *Journal for Institutional Innovation, Development, and Transition* 6 (2002): 92–112; Nikolai Botev, "Where East Meets West: Ethnic Intermarriage in the Former Yugoslavia, 1962 to 1989," *American Sociological Review* 59 (1994): 461–80. Also, Somer, "Cascades of Ethnic Polarization."

28. Margaret MacMillan, *Paris 1919: Six Months that Changed the World* (New York: Random House, 2003), and *The War that Ended the Peace: How Europe Abandoned Peace for the First World War* (London: Profile Books, 2013); Reeva Spector Simon and Eleanor H. Tejirian, eds., *The Creation of Iraq, 1914–1921* (New York: Columbia University Press, 2004).

29. Jonathan C. Randal, *After Such Knowledge, What Forgiveness? My Encounters with Kurdistan* (New York: Farrar, Straus and Giroux, 1997); Çandar, *Mezopotamya Ekspresi*; Thomas E. Ricks, "Do Iraq and Syria No Longer Exist? (9): Maybe, But It Isn't Up to Us Anyways," *Foreign Policy*, November 6, 2014, https://foreignpolicy.com/2014/11/06/do-iraq-and-syria-no-longer-exist-9-maybe-but-it-isnt-up-to-us-anyways/ (accessed June 9, 2019).

30. Randal, *After Such Knowledge, What Forgiveness?*; Robert Olson, *The Kurdish Question and Turkish-Iranian Relations: from World War I to 1998* (Costa Mesa, CA: Mazda, 1998).

31. David Romano and Mehmet Gurses, eds., *Conflict, Democratization, and the Kurds in the Middle East: Turkey, Iran, Iraq, and Syria* (New York: Palgrave Macmillan, 2014), especially sections I and II.

32. Gerry Hassan, ed., *The Scottish Labor Party: History, Institutions, and Ideas* (Edinburgh: Edinburgh University Press, 2004).

33. Author's interview with Professor Crick; Colls, *Identity of England*.

34. Baki Tezcan, "The Development of the Use of 'Kurdistan' as a Geographical Description and the Incorporation of this Region into the Ottoman Empire in the 16th century," in *The Great Ottoman, Turkish Civilisation III*, ed. Kemal Çiçek (Ankara: Yeni Türkiye, 2000); "Kurdish Tourists Assaulted in Trabzon to be Deported from Turkey," *Bianet*, July 19, 2019: https://m.bianet.org/english/human-rights/210647-kurdish-tourists-assaulted-in-trabzon-to-be-deported-from-turkey (accessed August 15, 2019); "KRG 'Concerned' after Attack against Kurdish Tourists in Turkey," *Rûdaw*, July 19, 2019: https://www.rudaw.net/english/middleeast/turkey/190720191.

35. Rogers Brubaker, "Aftermaths of Empire and the Unmixing of Peoples: Historical and Comparative Perspectives," *Ethnic and Racial Studies* 18, no. 2 (1995): 198–218; Justin McCarthy, *The Ottoman Peoples and The End of Empire* (New York: Oxford University Press, 2001); Kemal H. Karpat, *Ottoman Population 1830–1914 Demographic and Social Characteristics* (Istanbul: Tarih Vakfı Yurt Yayınları, 2003); Fuat Dündar, *İttihat ve Terakki'nin Müslümanları İskân Politikası: 1913–1918* [Committee of Union and Progress's Settlement Policy for Muslims 1913–1918] (Istanbul: İletişim Yayınları, 2008); Mylonas, *The Politics of Nation-Building*; Halil İnalcık, *Türklük, Müslümanlık ve Osmanlılık Mirası* [The Heritage of Turkishness, Muslimness, and Ottomanness] (Istanbul: Kırmızı Yayınları, 2014).

36. Benjamin C. Fortna, Stefanos Katsikas, Dimitris Kamouzis, and Paraskevas Konortas, *State-Nationalisms in the Ottoman Empire, Greece, and Turkey: Orthodox and Muslims, 1830–1945* (London: Routledge, 2013); Aslı Iğsız, *Humanism*

*in Ruins: Entangled Legacies of the Greek-Turkish Population Exchange* (Stanford: Stanford University Press, 2018).

37. Among others, Baki Tezcan and Karl K. Barbir, eds., *Identity and Identity Formation in the Ottoman World* (Istanbul: Istanbul Bilgi Üniversitesi Yayınları, 2019; Norman Itzkowitz, "18th Century Ottoman Realities," in *Identity and Identity Formation in the Ottoman World,* ed. Baki Tezcan and Karl K. Barbir (Istanbul: Istanbul Bilgi Üniversitesi Yayınları, 2012), ixxx–xivi; Cemal Kafadar, "A Rome of One's Own: Reflections on Cultural Geography and Identity in the Lands of Rum," *Muqarnas* 24 (2007): 7–25; Carter Vaughn Findley, *The Turks in World History* (Oxford: Oxford University Press, 2004).

38. Mesut Yegen, "'Prospective-Turks' or 'Pseudo-Citizens': Kurds in Turkey," *The Middle East Journal* 63, no. 4 (2009): 597–615.

39. Article 3. http://confinder.richmond.edu/admin/docs/1958_Interim_Constitution__English_.PDF (accessed June 5, 2019). At the same time, and creating an unsolvable contradiction, according to Martin Van Bruinessen, Article 2 proclaimed that Iraq is a member of the Arab League. *Ağa, Şeyh, Devlet,* 50.

40. Ibid., 53.

41. Robert Lowe and Gareth Stansfield, eds., *The Kurdish Policy Imperative* (Chatham House, Royal Institute of International Affairs, 2010).

42. Meeting in Ankara in June. Cengiz Çandar, *Mezopotamya Ekspresi: Bir Tarih Yolculuğu* [Mesopotamia Express: A Journey through History] (Istanbul: İletişim Yayınları, 2012), 112.

43. Hakan Yılmaz, "Türkiye'de Kimlikler, Kürt Sorunu ve Çözüm Süreci: Algılar ve Tutumlar [Identities, the Kurdish Problem and Resolution Process in Turkey]" (Açık Toplum Vakfı ve Boğaziçi Üniversitesi, September 2014), 19. https://boun.academia.edu/HakanYilmaz/Papers. (Accessed December 15, 2014).

44. "Neşe Düzel'in Abdülmelik Fırat'la Söyleşisi," *Radkial,* 5 April 1999. Akratan Hasan Cemal, *Kürtler* (İstanbul: Doğan Kitap, 2003), 543–44. Ayrıca bkz, Ferzende Kaya, *Mesopotamya Sürgünü: Abdülmelik ırat'ın Yaşamöyküsü* (İstanbul: Alfa Yayınları, 2004).

45. One of the greatest Turkish or "Of-Turkey" writers, a Kurd, and defender of Kurdish rights.

46. Hasan Cemal, *Kürtler,* 544.

47. Elite infantry units that for centuries until their abolition in 1826 formed the backbone of the Ottoman permanent armed forces, acted as the Sultan's bodyguards, and simultaneously constituted a massive artisan social and political class, (at times rebellious) interest group, and "heterodox" Muslim religious order. Ali Yaycioglu, "Guarding Traditions and Laws—Disciplining Bodies and Souls: Tradition, Science, and Religion in the Age of Ottoman Reform," *Modern Asian Studies* 52, no. 5 (2018): 1542–1603.

48. A palace boarding school primarily for the Christian subjects of the Ottoman Empire where students were converted to Islam, trained, and recruited to Ottoman state service.

49. The Ottoman state practice of collecting young Christian boys from their families, converting them to Islam and training them for civil and military service.

50. Rauf Orbay (1881–1964) and İsmet İnönü (1884–1973) were former Ottoman officers and prominent military and political leaders of the Turkish nationalist mobilization and later of the nation-state of Turkey, and comrades of Mustafa Kemal, although Orbay later fell out with Kemal. İsmet İnönü served as prime minister, president and head of Kemal's Republican People's Party CHP until the 1970s.

51. Musa Anter, *Hatıralarım* (İstanbul: Avesta Yayınlar, 1999), 224, 263–64.

52. D. Ahsen Batur, "Ön Söz Yerine," in *Kürtleşen Türkler* (İstanbul: Selenge Yayınları, 2007), 8–9.

53. July 2007, Ankara.

54. In Turkish, "gönül bağı" i.e., literally "heart-felt bond."

55. Rogers Brubaker, *Ethnicity without Groups* (Cambridge: Harvard University Press, 2004), 116–31.

56. The terms *Turkoman* (*Türkmen*) and *Turkic* (*Türkî*) can be seen as ethnic categories but respectively denote narrower and broader categories than *Türk*. Turkoman refers to either specific Turkish-speaking tribes who settled in a very wide territory of Eurasia including Turkey—including presumably the Ottomans who originally founded the Ottoman state—or to those having a certain nomadic lifestyle and economy, and Turkic can denote any group speaking a Turkic language such as Turkish, Azeri, Tatar, Uzbek, or Kazakh. For the historically changing, adaptive-inclusive, and political/statist meanings of the Turk category, among others, see Findley, *The Turks in World History;* and Kafadar, "A Rome of One's Own."

57. Piscatori, *Islam in a World of Nation-States; Karpat, Ottoman Past and Today's Turkey;* Kurzman, ed., *Modernist Islam, 1840–1940;* Mardin, *Türk Modernleşmesi;* Findley, *Turkey, Islam, Nationalism, and Modernity.*

58. For a recent and valuable contribution and examples from the post-Ottoman world, Clayer, Giomi, and Szerek, eds., *Kemalism: Transnational Politics.*

59. Ahmet Demirel, *Birinci Meclis'te Muhalefet: İkinci Grup* [Opposition in the First Parliament of Turkey: The Second Group] (Istanbul: İletişim Yayınları, 2000); Özoğlu, *From Caliphate to Secular State.*

60. Sevan Nişanyan, *Yanlış Cumhuriyet: Atatürk ve Kemalizm Üzerine 51 Soru* [The Wrong Republic: 51 Questions about Atatürk and Kemalism] (Istanbul: Kırmızı Yayınları, 2008), 88.

## Chapter 3

1. Carter Vaughn Findley, "Continuity, Innovation, Synthesis, and the State," in *Ottoman Past and Today's Turkey*, ed. Kemal H. Karpat (Leiden: Brill, 2000), 29–46, 29.

2. Stefanos Yerasimos, "Ne Mutlu Türk'üm Diyene! [How Happy Is the One Who Says I am a Turk!]," 15–55; *Türkler: Doğu ve Batı, İslam ve Laiklik* [The Turks: East and West, Islam and Secularism] (Ankara: Doruk Yayınları, 2002), 22.

3. Niccolò Machiavelli, *The Prince*, trans. with introduction and notes by James B. Atkinson (Indianapolis: Hackett, [1976] 2008).

4. Ibid., 237.

5. Ibid., 311.

6. Ibid., 129.

7. Ibid.

8. Ibid., 131.

9. Karpat, *Ottoman Population 1830–1914*, 13; Peter Mentzel, "Conclusions: Millets, States, and National Identities," *Nationalities Papers* 28, no. 1 (2000): 199–204. This general tendency was not true for all groups, for example, Albanians.

10. Dr. Celilê CELİL, *XIX. Yüzyıl Osmanlı İmparatorluğu'nda Kürtler* [Kurds in XIX. Century Ottoman Empire] (Ankara: Öz-Ge Yayınları, 1992); İhsan Nuri Paşa, *Ağrı Dağı İsyanı* [Ararat Mountain Rebellion] (Istanbul, MED Yayınları, 1992).

11. *Türkiye Diyanet Vakfı İslam Ansiklopedisi* [Encyclopedia of Islam, the Foundation of Religious Affairs of Turkey]. https://islamansiklopedisi.org.tr/mutercim-asim-efendi.

12. Kafadar, "A Rome of One's Own," 11.

13. Ibid., 7. Among "Turks," and presumably among outsiders too, "Rumi vs. Turk" also denoted a social class distinction similar to "bourgeois vs. rustic," 11.

14. Tezcan, and Barbir, eds., *Identity and Identity Formation in the Ottoman World*.

15. Kafadar, "A Rome of One's Own," 11.

16. Itzkowitz, "18th Century Ottoman Realities," ixxx–xivi.

17. Karpat, *Ottoman Population 1830–1914 Demographic and Social Characteristics*, 24.

18. More appropriately, being an Ottoman *subject*, until the idea of "citizenship" in the modern sense emerged with Ottoman modernization in the nineteenth century.

19. David McDowall, *A Modern History of the Kurds* (New York: St Martin's Press, 1997), 1–2.

20. Tezcan, "The Development of the Use of 'Kurdistan' as a Geographical Description," 540–53.

21. Ibid., 218.

22. Karpat, *Ottoman Past and Today's Turkey*.

23. Karpat, *Ottoman Population 1830–1914*, 23.

24. Günay Göksu Özdoğan, "Turkish Nationalism Reconsidered: The 'Heaviness' of Statist Patriotism in Nation-Building," in *Nationalism in the Troubled Triangle: Cyprus, Greece, and Turkey*, ed. Ayhan Aktar, Niyazi Kızılyürek, and Umut Özkırımlı (New York: Palgrave Macmillan, 2010); Carter V. Findley,

*Turkey, Islam, Nationalism, and Modernity: A History, 1789–2007* (New Haven: Yale University Press, 2010).

25. Carter Findley notes that shifts in the sense of territorial belonging and the rise of the state as the main axis of belonging have rather been repetitive phenomena in the history of the Turkic peoples. Findley, "Continuity, Innovation, Synthesis, and the State."

26. Ibid., 11.

27. Yerasimos, "Ne Mutlu Türk'üm Diyene!," 51.

28. McDowall, *A Modern History of the Kurds*.

29. McCrone, *Understanding Scotland: The Sociology of a Nation*.

30. Michael Keating, *Nations Against the State: The New Politics of Nationalism in Quebec, Catalonia, and Scotland* (London: Palgrave Macmillan, 1996).

31. McDowall, *A Modern History of the Kurds*, 9.

32. Ibid., 217–18.

33. Hamit Bozarslan, "Kürt Milliyetçiliği: Zımni Sözleşmeden Ayaklanmaya 1919–1925 [Kurdish Nationalism: From Implicit Contract to Rebellion]," in *İmparatorluktan Cumhuriyete Türkiye'de Etnik Çatışma* [From Empire to Republic Ethnic Conflict in Turkey], ed. Erik Jan Zürcher (Istanbul: İletişim Yayınları, 2005), 89–122; Şerif Mardin, "Freedom in an Ottoman Perspective," in *State, Democracy, and the Military: Turkey in the 1980s*, ed. Metin Heper and Ahmet Evin (New York: Walter de Gruyter, 1988).

34. Tezcan, "The Development of the Use of 'Kurdistan' as a Geographical Description."

35. Vali, *Kurds and the State*, 9.

36. Bruinessen, *Ağa, Şeyh, Devlet*, 204–15.

37. Ibid., 268.

38. For a historical summary of the meanings of the terms *Alawi, Shia, and Qizilbash* see Ali Yaman, *Alevilik ve Kızılbaşlık Tarihi* [A History of Alawism and Qızılbashlik] (Istanbul: Nokta Kitap, 2007).

39. Niyazi Berkes, *The Development of Secularism in Turkey*, 1st ed. (New York: Routledge, 1998); Şerif Mardin, *Türk Modernleşmesi, Makaleler 4* [Turkish Modernization: Essays 4] (Istanbul: İletişim Yayınları, 2003).

40. Menchinger, *The First of the Modern Ottomans*, 3.

41. Baki Tezcan, *The Second Ottoman Empire: Political and Social Transformation in the Early Modern World* (Cambridge: Cambridge University Press, 2010).

42. Menchinger, *The First of the Modern Ottomans*, 8.

43. Hechter, *Containing Nationalism*.

44. Joel Migdal, *Strong Societies and Weak States*.

45. Ibid.; Timothy Mitchell, "The Limits of the State," *American Political Science Review* 85, no. 1 (1991): 77–95 and 86 (4).

46. Thomas Ertman, *Birth of the Leviathan: Building States and Regimes in Medieval and Early Modern Europe* (Cambridge: Cambridge University Press,

1997); Charles Kurzman, ed., *Modernist Islam, 1840–1940: A Sourcebook* (Oxford: Oxford University Press, 2002).

47. Spruyt, "War, Trade, and State Formation."

48. Mitchell, "The Limits of the State."

49. James Scott, *Seeing like a State* (New Haven: Yale University Press, 1997).

50. Migdal, *Strong Societies and Weak States*.

51. Margaret Levi, *Consent, Dissent, and Patriotism* (New York: Cambridge University Press, 1997).

52. Norman Naimark, *Fires of Hatred: Ethnic Cleansing in Twentieth Century Europe* (Cambridge: Harvard University Press, 2001); Michael Mann, *The Dark Side of Democracy: Explaining Ethnic Cleansing* (New York: Cambridge University Press, 2005); Philipp Ther, *The Dark Side of Nation States: Ethnic Cleansing in Modern Europe* (Oxford: Berghahn Books, 2014); H. Zeynep Bulutgil, *The Roots of Ethnic Cleansing in Europe* (Cambridge: Cambridge University Press, 2016).

53. Anderson, *Imagined Communities*.

54. Gellner, *Nations and Nationalism*; Bulutgil, *The Roots of Ethnic Cleansing*. Eric J. Hobsbawm, *Nations and Nationalism since 1780: Programme, Myth, Reality* (Cambridge: Cambridge University Press, 1992).

55. Levi, *Consent, Dissent, and Patriotism*.

56. Marc Plattner, "Sovereignty and Democracy," *Policy Review* 122 (December 2003-January 2004): 3–18; Philip Pettit, *Republicanism: A Theory of Freedom and Government* (Oxford: Oxford University Press, 2002).

57. Reinhard Bendix, *Kings or People: Power and the Mandate to Rule* (Berkeley: University of California Press, 1978); Colls, *Identity of England*; Daniel L. Unowsky, *The Pomp and Politics of Patriotism: Imperial Celebrations in Habsburg Austria, 1848–1916* (West Lafayette, IN: Purdue University Press, 2005); Ayşe Zarakol, *After Defeat: How the East Learned to Live with the West* (Cambridge: Cambridge University Press, 2011).

58. Solomon Wank, "The Habsburg Empire," in *After Empire: Multiethnic Societies and Nation-Building. The Soviet Union and the Russian, Ottoman, and Habsburg Empires*, ed. Karen Barkey and Mark von Hagen, 45–57 (Boulder: Westview, 1997), 48 and 49. For a comparative theorization: Alexander J. Motyl, *Imperial Ends: The Decay, Collapse and Revival of Empires* (New York: Columbia University Press, 2001).

59. Robert Jackson and Carl Rosberg, "Why Africa's Weak States Persist: The Empirical and the Juridical in Statehood," *World Politics* 35, no. 1 (1982): 1–24; Boli Meyer, Thomas, and Ramirez, "World Society and the Nation-State."

60. Scott, *Seeing like a State*.

61. Gellner, *Nations and Nationalism*. For the nation-building policies of "core groups," see Mylonas, *The Politics of Nation-Building*.

62. Senem Aslan, *Nation-Building in Turkey and Morocco: Governing Kurdish and Berber Dissent* (New York: Cambridge University Press, 2015).

63. James P. Piscatori, *Islam in a World of Nation-States* (Cambridge: Cambridge University Press, 1986); Kurzman, ed., *Modernist Islam*; Findley, *Turkey, Islam, Nationalism, and Modernity*; Zarakol, *After Defeat*; Touraj Atabaki, ed., *The State and the Subaltern: Modernization, Society, and the State in Turkey and Iran* (New York: I. B. Tauris, 2007); Aghaie and Marashi, eds., *Rethinking Iranian Nationalism and Modernity*.

64. Yerasimos, "Ne Mutlu Türk'üm Diyene!," 51. For Balkan nationalisms, also see Hannes Grandits, Nathalie Clayer, and Robert Pichler, eds., *Conflicting Loyalties in the Balkans: Great Powers, the Ottoman Empire, and Nation-Building* (New York: İ. B. Tauris, 2011). The foreign policies and "external patrons" of these emerging nation-states played a significant role in shaping their nation-building practices. Mylonas, *The Politics of Nation-Building*.

65. Ayhan Aktar, Niyazi Kızılyürek, and Umut Özkırımlı, "Introduction," in *Nationalism in the Troubled Triangle: Cyprus, Greece, and Turkey*, ed. Aktar, Kızılyürek, and Özkırımlı (London: Palgrave Macmillan, 2010), xiii–xxiii; Mylonas, *The Politics of Nation-Building*.

66. Karen Barkey, *Empire of Difference: The Ottomans in Comparative Perspective* (Cambridge: Cambridge University Press, 2008); Hanioğlu, "Modern Ottoman Period"; Tezcan, *The Second Ottoman Empire*; Yaycioglu, *Partners of the Empire*.

67. Yaycioglu, *Partners of the Empire*.

68. Ibid.

69. Karpat, *Ottoman Past and Today's Turkey*; Şükrü Hanioğlu, *A Brief History of the Late Ottoman Empire* (Princeton: Princeton University Press, 2010); Şevket Pamuk, *Osmanlı-Türkiye İktisadî Tarihi 1500–1914* [Ottoman-Turkish Economic History 1500–1914] (Istanbul: İletişim Yayınları, 8th ed., 2013), 140–61, 198–203; Yaycioglu, "Guarding Traditions and Laws."

70. Reşat Kasaba, *Bir Konargöçer İmparatorluk: Osmanlı'da Göçebeler, Göçmenler ve Sığınmacılar* [A Nomadic Empire: Nomads, Immigrants, and Refugees in the Ottoman Empire] (Istanbul: Kitap, 2010).

71. Hanioğlu, *A Brief History*, 22.

72. Jean-Paul Pascual quoted by Hamit Bozarslan, *Ortadoğu: Bir Şiddet Tarihi, Osmanlı İmparatorluğu'nun Sonundan El-Kaide'ye* [The Middle East: A History of Violence, from the Fall of the Ottoman Empire to Al-Qaida] (Istanbul: İletişim Yayınları, 2010), 31.

73. Kasaba, *Bir Konargöçer İmparatorluk*; Janet Klein, *Hamidiye Alayları: İmparatorluğun Sınır Boyları ve Kürt Aşiretleri* [Hamidiye Corps: The Margins of Empire and Kurdish Tribes] (Istanbul: İletişim Yayınları, 2013).

74. Previously, as Kurdish provinces were a buffer region between Iran and the Ottoman Empire, their disorganized structure, which encumbered military control by either side, represented an advantage rather than a disadvantage.

75. Klein, *Hamidiye Alayları*.

76. Bruinessen, *Ağa, Şeyh, Devlet*.

77. After 1867, the state began to use the name *Kurdistan* to refer to a geographical region. Hakan Özoğlu, *Kurdish Notables and the Ottoman State: Evolving Identities, Competing Loyalties, and Shifting Boundaries* (Albany: State University of New York Press, 2004), 37, 60–62.

78. Olson, *The Kurdish Question and Turkish-Iranian Relations*; Bozarslan, *Ortadoğu: Bir Şiddet Tarihi*.

79. Hakan Özoğlu, "Nationalism and Kurdish Notables in the Late Ottoman-Early Republican Era," *International Journal of Middle East Studies* 33, no. 3 (2001): 383–409; David McDowall, "The Kurdish Question: A Historical Review," in *The Kurds: A Contemporary Review*, ed. Phillip G. Kreyenbroek and Stefan Speri (New York: Routledge, 1992), 14.

80. Bruinessen, *Ağa, Şeyh, Devlet*, 280–84.

81. Bozarslan, *Ortadoğu: Bir Şiddet Tarihi*, 31–32.

82. Pamuk, *Ottoman-Turkish Economic History*, 204–42.

83. Clement Moore Henry and Robert Springborg, *Globalization and the Politics of Development in the Middle East* (New York: Cambridge University Press, 2010); Greenfeld, *Nationalism: Five Roads to Modernity*; Moore, *Social Origins of Dictatorship and Democracy*.

84. Nişanyan, *Yanlış Cumhuriyet*.

85. Samir Amin, *Unequal Development: An Essay on the Social Formations of Peripheral Capitalism*, trans. Brian Pierce (Sussex: The Harvester Press, 1976); Celso Furtado, *Economic Development of Latin America: Historical Background and Contemporary Problems* (Cambridge: Cambridge University Press, 1976); Richard Peet and Elaine Hartwick, *Theories of Development: Contentions, Arguments, Alternatives* (New York: The Guilford Press, 2015).

86. Doğan Avcıoğlu, *Türkiye'nin Düzeni: Dün-Bugün-Yarın, Birinci Kitap* [Turkey's Order: Yesterday-Today-Tomorrow, Book I] (Istanbul: Tekin Yayınevi, 1976).

87. Karpat, *Ottoman Population 1830–1914*, 25.

88. Ibid., 25.

89. Ibid., 25–26. Karpat cites the resistance to the Land Code of 1945 as an example of this.

90. Karpat, *Ottoman Past and Today's Turkey*.

91. Meeker, *A Nation of Empire: The Ottoman Legacy of Turkish Modernity*, xvii.

92. Yerasimos, *Türkler, Doğu ve Batı, İslam ve Laiklik*; Mardin, *Türk Modernleşmesi*; Karpat, *Ottoman Past and Today's Turkey*; Erik Jan Zürcher, *The Young Turk Legacy and Nation-Building: From the Ottoman Empire to Atatürk's Turkey* (London: I. B. Tauris, 2010).

93. Özoğlu, *Kurdish Notables and the Ottoman State*.

94. Frank Tachau, "The Search for National Identity among the Turks," *The Welt des Islams, New Series* 8, no. 3 (1963): 165–76. Füsun Üstel, "Türk Milliyetçiliğinde Anadolu Metaforu [The Metaphor of Anatolia in Turkish Nation-

alism]," *Tarih ve Toplum* [History and Society] *109* (January 1993): 51–55; also see Ayşe Hür, "Türkiye Yerine Anadolu Cumhuriyeti Dense Ne Olurdu? [What Would Have Happened If Turkey Was Called The Republic of Anatolia?]," *Radikal* newspaper, January 13, 2013.

95. Zürcher, *The Young Turk Legacy*; Mete Tunçay, *Türkiye'de Tek Parti Yönetimi'nin Kurulması: 1923–1931* [The Establishment of the Single Party System in Turkey: 1923–1931] (Istanbul: Tarih Vakfı Yurt Publications, 2005); Fuat Dündar, *İttihat ve Terakki'nin Müslümanları İskân Politikası: 1913–1918*.

96. Dündar, *İttihat ve Terakki'nin Müslümanları İskân Politikası*.

97. Taha Parla, *The Social and Political Thought of Ziya Gokalp 1876–1924* (Leiden: E. J. Brill, 1985).

98. Markus Dressler, "Rereading Ziya Gökalp: Secularism and Reform of the Islamic State in the Late Young Turk Period," *International Journal of Middle East Studies* 47, no. 03 (2015): 511–31; Nedim Nomer, "Ziya Gökalp's Idea of Cultural Hybridity," *British Journal of Middle Eastern Studies* 44, no. 3 (2017): 408–28.

99. İlker Aytürk, "The Racist Critics of Atatürk and Kemalism from the 1930s to the 1960s," *Journal of Contemporary History* 46 (2011): 308–35.

100. Document 76, December 11, 1919, in Gazi Mustafa Kemal (Atatürk), *Nutuk-Söylev: III. Cilt Belgeler-Vesikalar* [The Speech: Vol. III Documents] (Ankara: Atatürk, Kültür, Dil ve Tarih Yüksek Kurumu—Türk Tarih Kurumu, 1989), 1332.

101. Document 89, September 15, 1919 in Kemal (Atatürk), *Nutuk-Söylev: III Cilt*, 1364.

102. For Atatürk's expressions, see Ergun Özbudun, *Otoriter Rejimler, Seçimsel Demokrasiler ve Türkiye* [Authoritarian Regimes, Selective Democracies, and Turkey] (Istanbul: Bilgi Üniversitesi Yayınları, 2011), 101.

103. Tachau, "The Search for National Identity among the Turks," 165–76, 168.

104. Ibid., 166.

105. Karpat, *Ottoman Population*, 29–30.

106. It might have been the official interpreters of the Ottoman Palace who first used *millet* to mean "nation," while reporting on the 1792 war between France and Austria. Banu Turnaoğlu, *The Formation of Turkish Republicanism* (Princeton: Princeton University Press, 2017), 39.

107. As discussed in the previous chapter, Findley also observes that this was not the first time this had happened in the history of Turkic peoples. He notes that a shifting sense of belonging to a territory, and thus the state representing the main axis of belonging, have been continuous phenomena in the history of the Turkic peoples. Findley, "Continuity, Innovation, Synthesis, and the State."

108. Findley, *Turkey, Islam, Nationalism, and Modernity*, 5–6.

109. According to Tekeli and İlkin, in the aftermath of the Second Constitutional Era the movement that was dominant in both the Committee of Union and Progress and in the governance of the country was "the movement developing in Thessaloniki and its hinterland Macedonia." İlhan Tekeli and Selim İlkin,

*Cumhuriyetin Harcı: Köktenci Modernitenin Doğuşu* [The Mortar of the Republic: The Birth of Radical Modernity] (Istanbul: Bilgi Üniversitesi Yayınları, 2003), 3.

110. Wimmer, "Elementary Strategies of Ethnic Boundary Making."

111. Tezcür, *Kurdish Nationalism and Identity in Turkey.*

112. Michiel Leezenberg, "Ehmedê Xanî's Mem Û Zîn: The Consecration of a Kurdish National Epic," in *Routledge Handbook on the Kurds,* ed. Michael M. Gunter (New York: Routledge, 2019), 79–89, 79.

113. Tan, *Kürt Sorunu,* 129–30.

114. Bruinessen, *Kurds, Turks, and the Alawi Revival in Turkey,* 29–30.

115. Hamit Bozarslan, "Türkiye'de (1919–1980) Yazılı Kürt Tarihi Söylemi Üzerine Bazı Hususlar [On Some Matters Relating to the Discourse of Written Kurdish History in Turkey (1919–1980)]," in *Kürt Milliyetçiliğinin Kökenleri* [The Origins of Kurdish Nationalism], ed. Abbas Vali (Istanbul: Avesta Yayınları, 2005), 53.

116. Bozarslan, "Kürt Milliyetçiliği: Zımni Sözleşmeden Ayaklanmaya," 93; Tan, *Kürt Sorunu,* 133–34.

117. Anter, *Fırat Marmara'ya Akar; Mustafa Remzi Bucak, Bir Kürt Aydınından İsmet İnönü'ye Mektup.*

118. Özoğlu, *Kurdish Notables and the Ottoman State;* Bozarslan, "Kürt Milliyetçiliği: Zımni Sözleşmeden Ayaklanmaya"; Abbas Vali, ed., *Kürt Milliyetçiliğinin Kökenleri* [*The Origins of Kurdish Nationalism*] (Istanbul: Avesta Yayınları, 2005); Ahmed and Gunter, eds., *The Evolution of Kurdish Nationalism.*

119. Bozarslan, "Kürt Milliyetçiliği: Zımni Sözleşmeden Ayaklanmaya."

## Chapter 4

1. Mustafa Kemal (Atatürk), interview with United Press correspondent Edward Kind, 22 October 1922. *Atatürk'ün Bütün Eserleri* [The Complete Works of Atatürk], vol. 14 (Istanbul: Kaynak Yayınları, 2004), 31.

2. Minister of the Chief of General Staff İsmet İnönü, 29 May 1920. *TBMM Gizli Celse Kayıtları 1920–1934* [Records of the Proceedings of the Secret Sessions of the Grand National Assembly of Turkey 1920–1934], vol. 1 (Ankara, Türkiye İş Bankası Yayınları, [1920–21] 1985), 40.

3. Ahmed Emin Yalman, "Kürtler ve Kürdistan" [Kurds and Kurdistan], *Vakit,* August 14, 1919. Translated into modern Turkish by Ahmet Abdullah Saçmalı, "From Mudros to Lausanne: How Ahmed Emin's Perception of the 'Other' Changed," MA Dissertation, Department of History, Boğaziçi University, 2012.

4. Metin Heper asserts that these government policies should be seen as efforts to inhibit dissimilation rather than target assimilation. Heper, *The State and Kurds in Turkey.* The aim of these policies might have been to inhibit dissimilation in the eyes of some state actors, and this insight is important for reaching a

well-rounded explanation of what happened. I would add that another significant state concern might have been to prevent the dissimilation of the "Turks"—i.e., the predominantly Turkish-speaking but ethnically diverse population—or the Kurds' becoming an example that would reverse the development of national consciousness, which was a more important worry for the state builders than the Kurds, as I discuss in this book. Nevertheless, these actor-specific perceptions and intentions, however valid they were, explain only a portion of the facts on the ground. In the end, the outcome was assimilationist state policies, particularly in the public space. Regardless of how the enforcers interpreted and justified their aims in their own minds, the prohibition of the Kurdish language in most public spaces, the conversion of Kurdish place names into Turkish, and implementing bans on education in Kurdish were clear examples of actively assimilationist practices.

5. Şükrî-i Bitlisi. Tezcan, "The Development of the Use of 'Kurdistan' as a Geographical Description," 549.

6. Sudipta Kaviraj, "Disenchantment Deferred," in *Beyond the Secular West*, ed. Akeel Bilgrami (New York: Columbia University Press, 2016), 135–87.

7. Rajeev Bhargava, "An Ancient Indian Secular Age?," in *Beyond the Secular West*, ed. Akeel Bilgrami (New York: Columbia University Press, 2016), 188–214.

8. Maria Rosa Menocal, *Ornament of the World: How Muslims, Jews, and Christians Created a Culture of Tolerance in Medieval Spain* (New York: Little, Brown, 2002), 11.

9. For these concepts and the theoretical framework, see Somer, "Cascades of Ethnic Polarization"; "Turkey's Kurdish Conflict: Changing Context and Domestic and Regional Implications," *Middle East Journal* 58, no. 2 (Spring 2004): 235–53; "Failures of the Discourse of Ethnicity: Turkey, Kurds, and the Emerging Iraq," *Security Dialogue* 36, no. 1 (March 2005): 109–28.

10. Brubaker, *Citizenship and Nationhood in France and Germany*. Also see: Greenfeld, *Nationalism: Five Roads to Modernity*. For Brubaker's later views and his critique of the difference between ethnic and civic, see: Brubaker, *Ethnicity without Groups*.

11. Anter, *Fırat Marmara'ya Akar*, 187.

12. Martin van Bruinessen, "Kurdish Society, Ethnicity, Nationalism, and Refugee Problems," in *The Kurds: A Contemporary Overview*, ed. Philip G. Kreyenbroek and Stefan Speri (London: Routledge, 1992), 33–67.

13. A type of land holding granted by Ottoman sultans.

14. Here, the author could have said "the first Muslim-Turkish novel," as non-Muslim or non–Turkish Muslim novels had been produced beforehand during the Ottoman Empire. While, presumably, these could also be considered "Ottoman" novels, the author does not consider them as "ours."

15. Ancient inscriptions in an old Turkic dialect and alphabet that were erected by *Göktürks* in the eighth century and discovered in the late nineteenth century in the Orkhon Valley in today's Mongolia.

16. Taha Akyol, "Türkiyeli ve Arnavut [Of-Turkey and Albanian]," *Hürriyet* newspaper, February 13, 2013.

17. Tezcan, "The Development of the Use of 'Kurdistan' as a Geographical Description," 549.

18. Somer, "Cascades of Ethnic Polarization." For a more general definition, see Jennifer McCoy and Murat Somer, eds. *Polarizing Polities: A Global Threat to Democracy*, Special Volume of *The American Academy of Political and Social Science* 681(1) (2019).

19. Somer, "Failures of the Discourse of Ethnicity."

20. Michael Hechter and Dina Okamoto, "Political Consequences of Minority Group Formation," *Annual Review of Political Science* 4, no. 1 (2001): 189–215.

21. Jenna Krajeski, "In Taksim Square, Where Are the Kurds?" *New Yorker*, June 11, 2013. https://www.newyorker.com/news/news-desk/in-taksim-square-where-are-the-kurds (accessed on June 30, 2019). The protests nevertheless brought together individual Turks and Kurds with very different backgounds, which could form as a basis for more long-term bonds and joint collective actions. Zeynep Tufekci, *Twitter and Tear Gas: The Power and Fragility of Networked Protest* (New Haven and London: Yale University Press, 2017), xiv, 106–107.

22. Muzafer Sherif, *In Common Predicament: Social Psychology of Intergroup Conflict and Cooperation* (Boston: Houghton Mifflin, 1966); Muzafer Sherif and Carl I. Hovland, *Social Judgement: Assimilation and Contrast Effects in Communication and Attitude Change* (New Haven: Yale University Press, 1961).

23. For two fundamental social psychology arguments see, Dominic Abrams and Michael A. Hogg, eds., *Social Identity Theory: Constructive and Critical Advances* (New York: Springer Verlag, 1990); Henri Tajfel and John C. Turner, "The Social Identity Theory of Intergroup Behavior," in *Psychology of Intergroup Relations*, ed. Stephen Worchel and William G Austin (Chicago: Nelson-Hall, 1986), 775–89.

24. Güneş Murat Tezcür, "When Democratization Radicalizes: The Kurdish Nationalist Movement in Turkey," *Journal of Peace Research* 47 (November 2010): 775–89.

25. Somer, "Cascades of Ethnic Polarization."

26. For various quotes, the doublet "Turkish and Muslim" and the interchangeable use of the categories Ottoman, Muslim, and Turkish in parliamentary debates, Howard Eissenstat, "Metaphors of Race and Discourse of Nation: Racial Theory and State Nationalism in the First Decades of the Turkish Republic," in *Race and Nation: Ethnic Systems in the Modern World*, ed. Paul Spickard (New York: Routledge, 2005), 239–56.

27. *TBMM Gizli Celse Kayıtları*, vol. 1–4; Murat Somer, "Defensive and Liberal Nationalisms, the Kurdish Question and Modernization/Democratization," in *Remaking Turkey: Globalization, Alternative Modernities, and Democracy*, ed. Fuat Keyman (Oxford: Lexington Books, 2007), 103–35.

28. 14 March 1919, Communication to the Ministry of War on the *Hukuk-u Beşer* newspaper, *Atatürk'ün Bütün Eserleri*, vol. 2 (Istanbul: Kaynak Yayınları, 1999), 297.

29. Robert Olson, *Imperial Meanderings and Republican Byways: Essays on Eighteenth Century Ottoman and Twentieth Century History of Turkey* (Istanbul: The Isis Yayıncılık, 1996), 213–23; Ayşe Hür, "1922'de Kürtlere söz verildi mi? [Was a Promise Made to the Kurds in 1922?]," *Radikal*, January 23, 2013.

30. Helin Alp, "Ahmet Türk: 1922'deki 'Kürt Reform Paketi' Bizim Taleplerimizi Karşılar [Ahmet Türk: 'The Kurdish Reform Package' of 1922 Meets our Demands]," *Akşam* newspaper, January 22, 2013.

31. The Elcezire Army was founded by the national government in Ankara in June 1920, in an area where Iraqi, Syrian, and Turkish territories meet today. Its goals included fighting the French and British armies, securing Kurdish tribes' support for the National Campaign, reining in British influence and Kurdish separatism, and preventing the separation of the Mosul province. See, among others, Sadık Erdaş, "Nihad (Anılmış) Paşa'nın Elcezire Cephe Komutanlığı ve Yargılanması Meselesi [The Matter of Nihad (Anılmış) Pasha's Commandership of the Elcezire Front and Trial]," *Cumhuriyet Tarihi Araştırmaları Dergisi* 14, no. 28 (2018), 3–36.

32. Information Mustafa Kemal provided on July 22, 1922, in Grand National Assembly, on the goals and operations of the Elcezire Army headed by Nihad Pasha in 1920–21. *TBMM Gizli Celse Kayıtları*, vol. 3, 550–551; Mumcu, *Kürt-İslam Ayaklanması*, 45–46.

33. Olson, *The Emergence of Kurdish Nationalism*, 37. He states that Atatürk developed good relationships with Kurdish beys and landowners much more successfully than elite Kurdish nationalists did.

34. Bayrak, *Kürdoloji Belgeleri*, see 231–32 as well as other sections.

35. *Atatürk'ün Bütün Eserleri*, vol. 2, 390.

36. Ibid., 394.

37. In the contemporary political discourse, such "recognition" was often referred to with the term "*Kürtlerin hukuku*" (literally, the law of Kurds), which could be translated as the "lawful or just rights of Kurds."

38. Bayrak, *Kürdoloji Belgeleri*, 394.

39. "Kavim," (from *qawm* in Arabic) which can literally be translated as people, nation, race, or clan, is employed here more or less to mean what is referred to as ethnic group today.

40. Mesut Yeğen, *Müstakbel Türk'ten Sözde Vatandaşa*, 52–53.

41. Articles 1 and 3. http.//www.tbmm.gov.tr/anayasa/anayasa21.htm.

42. The official website of the Grand National Assembly of Turkey TBMM: http.//www.tbmm.gov.tr/anayasa/anayasa24.htm.

43. Even though Article 39 of the treaty fundamentally refers to non-Muslims, in the continuation there are assurances relating to linguistic rights that can be

interpreted to apply to Kurdish as well. "No restrictions shall be imposed on the free use by any Turkish national of any language in private or, commercial relations, in religion, the press, or publications of any kind or in public meetings. Notwithstanding the (undoubtfully rightful existence) of the official language, adequate facilities shall be given to Turkish nationals speaking non-Turkish languages for the oral use of their own language before the courts." (Last accessed on October 1, 2017), https://wwi.lib.byu.edu/index.php/Treaty_of_Lausanne).

44. The official website of the Grand National Assembly of Turkey TBMM: https://www.tbmm.gov.tr/anayasa/anayasa24.htm.

45. There are certainly other examples, such as Canada and Iraq, where there is more than one official language in use.

46. Hence, the article refers to the "religion of the state" as opposed to "the official religion," thereby reflecting a closer commitment to Islam than the Turkish language. However, the statement about religion was removed in 1928 and replaced with the secularism (laicism) principle in 1937.

47. The official website of the Grand National Assembly of Turkey TBMM: https://www.tbmm.gov.tr/anayasa/anayasa24.htm.

48. Vivien A. Schmidt, "Discursive Institutionalism: The Explanatory Power of Ideas and Discourse," *Annual Review of Political Science* 11 (2008): 303–26; James Mahoney, Kathleen Thelen, eds., *Explaining Institutional Change: Ambiguity, Agency, and Power* (Cambridge: Cambridge University Press, 2010); Kristin Fabbe, *Disciples of the State: Religion and State-Building in the Former Ottoman World* (Cambridge: Cambridge University Press, 2019).

49. Hasan Kayalı, *Arabs and Young Turks: Ottomanism, Arabism, and Islamism in the Ottoman Empire, 1908–1918* (Los Angeles: The University of California Press, 1997); Şerif Mardin, *The Genesis of Young Ottoman Thought: A Study in the Modernization of Turkish Political Ideas* (New York: Syracuse Univeristy Press, 2000).

50. Şeref Gözübüyük and Suna Kili, "Türk Anayasa Metinleri: 1839–1980 [Turkish Constitutional Texts: 1839–1980]," *Ankara Üniversitesi Siyasal Bilgiler Fakültesi Yayınları*, no. 496 (1982).

51. Precisely: "without distinction of whatever religion or sect they profess."

52. In this period, the word *race* was also used to refer to ethnicity not only in Turkey. For example, during the negotiations for the Lausanne Treaty, Lord Curzon used the term Turkish and Kurdish "races" in the meaning of ethnicity as he lined up the British claims related to Mosul. David Cuthell, "A Kemalist Gambit: A View of the Political Negotiations in the Determination of the Turkish-Iraqi Border," in *The Creation of Iraq: 1914–1921*, ed. Reeva Spector Simon and Eleanor H. Tejirian (New York: Columbia University Press, 2004), 85. For the politically instrumental use of the "race" category, Eissenstat, "Metaphors of Race."

53. Samim Akgönül, "Türkiye'de Din, 3B Teorisi ve AKP [Religion, 3B Theory and AKP in Turkey]," *T24*, November 27, 2013. Last accessed October 1, 2017, http.//t24.com.tr/haber/turkiyede-din-3-b-teorisi-ve-akp,244904. Also see

Eissenstat, "Metaphors of Race"; Jenny White, *Muslim Nationalism and the New Turks* (Princeton: Princeton University Press, 2013).

54. Ayhan Aktar, *Varlık Vergisi ve Türkleştirme Politikaları* [Capital Tax and Policies of Turkification] (Istanbul: İletişim Yayınları, 2000).

55. Grigoriadis, *Instilling Religion* and Fabbe, *Disciples of the State*. Also see Berna Turam, ed., *Secular State and Religious Society: Two Forces in Play in Turkey* (New York: Palgrave MacMillan 2012).

56. Bozarslan, "Kürt Milliyetçiliği: Zımni Sözleşmeden Ayaklanmaya," 102–103.

57. Ekinci, *Vatandaşlık Açısından Kürt Sorunu ve Bir Çözüm Önerisi*, 141–42. The examples Ekinci provides can be interpreted in two ways.

58. Sadi Borak, *Atatürk'ün Resmi Yayınlara Girmemiş Söylev, Demeç, Yazışma ve Söyleşileri* [Atatürk's Unofficially Published Speeches, Statements, Correspondences, and Interviews] (Istanbul: Kaynak Yayınları, 1998), 377.

59. Soner Çağaptay, "Reconfiguring the Turkish nation in the 1930s," *Nationalism and Ethnic Politics* 8, no. 2 (2002): 67–82.

60. Ibid; Eissenstat, "Metaphors of Race"; Aytürk, "The Racist Critiques"; Kezer, *Building Modern Turkey*.

61. The same trends also influenced Kurdish nationalists. For example, İhsan Nuri Pasha described the 1926–30 rebellion of Mount Ararat as a "glorious page" in the national liberation and independence war of the "aryan" Kurdish nation. Nuri Paşa, *Ağrı Dağı İsyanı*, 13.

62. Zürcher, *Savaş, Devrim ve Uluslaşma*, 48.

63. For some of the names and definitions used in this period, see Perinçek, *Kurtuluş Savaşı'nda Kürt Politikası*, 247–52.

64. Fuat Dündar, *Türkiye Nüfus Sayımlarında Azınlıklar*; Soner Cagaptay, "Race, Assimilation, and Kemalism: Turkish Nationalism and the Minorities in the 1930s," *Middle Eastern Studies* 40, no. 3 (2004): 86–101; Dündar, *İttihat ve Terakki'nin Müslümanları İskân Politikası: 1913–1918*.

65. Zürcher, *Savaş, Devrim ve Uluslaşma*, 231.

66. Ahmed Emin Yalman, "Türkçülük ve Memleketçilik [Turkism and 'Homeland'ism]," *Vakit* newspaper, October 20, 1919, in Saçmalı, "From Mudros to Lausanne," 121.

67. Saçmalı, "From Mudros to Lausanne," 129.

68. Tekeli and İlkin, *Cumhuriyetin Harcı*, 140–41.

69. Zürcher, *Savaş, Devrim ve Uluslaşma*, 238–39. Here, Zürcher uses the term *millet* in its Ottoman religious meaning.

70. Ibid., 239.

71. Ibid., 56.

72. Ibid., 276–78.

73. Tekeli and İlkin, *Cumhuriyetin Harcı*, 148–49. Also see Emel Akal, *Moskova-Ankara-Londra Üçgeninde: İştirakiyuncular, Komünistler Ve Paşa Hazretleri*

[In the Triangle of Moscow-Ankara-London: İstirakiyun-ists, Communists, and His Highness Pasha] (Istanbul: İletişim, 2013).

74. Zürcher, *Savaş, Devrim ve Uluslaşma*, 240.

75. Cited by Üstel, "Türk Milliyetçiliğinde Anadolu Metaforu," 53–54.

76. Uygun, "Federalizm ve Bölgesel Özerklik tartışmaları," 131. Also see Bülent Tanör, *Kurtuluş Kuruluş* [Liberation Foundation] (Istanbul: Cumhuriyet Kitapları, 2005).

77. *Atatürk'ün Bütün Eserleri*, vol. 14, 267.

78. Saçmalı, "From Mudros to Lausanne," 60.

79. Laitin, *Identity in Formation*; Timur Kuran, "Ethnic Norms and Their Transformation Through Reputational Cascades," *Journal of Legal Studies XXVII* (1998): 623–59; Somer, "Cascades of Ethnic Polarization"; Beissinger, *Nationalist Mobilization*; Murat Somer, "Barış Süreci ve Kürt Meselesi'nde Kimlik ve Dış Politika: Riskler ve Fırsatlar [The Peace Process and Identity and Foreign Policy in the Kurdish Question: Risks and Opportunities]," *Ortadoğu Analiz* 5, no. 57 (2013): 46–53.

80. Zürcher, *Savaş, Devrim ve Uluslaşma*, 236–40.

81. Bayrak, *Kürdoloji Belgeleri*. Also see, Zürcher, *Savaş, Devrim ve Uluslaşma*; Çandar, *Mezopotamya Ekspresi*, 471–95.

82. Mustafa Kemal (Atatürk), July 3, 1920. *TBMM Gizli Celse Kayıtları*, vol. 1, 73.

83. *Atatürk'ün Bütün Eserleri*, vol. 14, 273–74. The actual expression used in Turkish is "*öz kardeşler*" (genuine, full siblings).

84. Ibid., vol. 1, 269–70.

85. Bayrak, *Kürdoloji Belgeleri*, 263–64.

86. *Atatürk'ün Bütün Eserleri*, vol. 14, 273–74.

87. As Aleppo was invaded by the British when the Armistice of Mudros was signed, there was some ambiguity on this area. However, the general view was that the National Pact considered this area as part of the territories that were accepted as part of the homeland "without a referendum."

88. While the British asserted that they took into account a specific provision of the agreement, for the Turkish side it was clear that the British violated the terms of the armistice by taking advantage of Ali Ihsan Pasha's weaknesses. For Atatürk's citicisms of Ali İhsan Pasha, see Gazi Mustafa Kemal (Atatürk), *Nutuk-Söylev: II. Cilt 1920-1927* [The Speech: Vol. II 1920–1927] (Ankara: Atatürk Kültür, Dil ve Tarih Yüksek Kurumu Türk Tarih Kurumu Yayınları, 1984), 888–95; see also Çandar, *Mezopotamya Ekspresi*, 483–87.

89. Olson, *The Kurdish Question and Turkish-Iranian Relations*.

90. Hakan, *Türkiye Kurulurken Kürtler*.

91. McDowall, "The Kurdish Question: A Historical Review," 17. Mustafa Kemal built on his familiarity with Kurdish areas and even "personal acquaintances and ties" that he had developed with Kurdish notables when he was the

commander of the VI. Army Corps in eastern provinces in 1916–17, following his participation in the 1915 War of Galipoli and promotion to general. M. Kemal Atatürk, *Nutuk I. Cilt (1919-1920)* [The Speech, Vol. 1 (1919–1920)] (Ankara: Atatürkün Doğumunun 100.Yılını Kutlama Koordinasyon Kurulu, 1981), 56. These relations helped even his personal safety while traveling during the early years of the National Campaign. Among others, İpek Çalışlar, *Mustafa Kemal Atatürk: Mücadelesi Ve Özel Hayatı* [Mustafa Kemal Atatürk: His Struggle and Personal Life] (İstanbul: Yapı Kredi Yayınları, 2018), 204–15. Also see Akyürekli, *Türklerle Kürtler*, 107.

92. Çandar, *Mezopotamya Ekspresi*, 505, 507. İsmail Beşikçi also defends the view that "Kurdistan was divided, shredded and shared through cooperation with British and French imperialism and Arabic and Persian monarchies. Part of the nation which Mustafa referred to as "our nation" were left to the hegemony of mandatary states. This constitutes nothing other than the division, shredding and sharing of Kurdistan anew." İsmail Beşikçi, *PKK Üzerine Düşünceler: Özgürlüğün Bedeli* [Thoughts on the PKK: The Price of Freedom) (Istanbul: Melsa Yayınları, 1992], 32.

93. Cuthell, "A Kemalist Gambit."

94. Çandar, *Mezopotamya Ekspresi,* 282–83 and 516–20.

95. "İstanbul, Musul, Adana ve İzmir gibi her biri bir ukde-i hayat ehemmiyetinde en mühim vilayetlerimizin işgaliyle tahakkuka başlayan büyük tehlike." Document 97, October 2, 1919, in Kemal (Atatürk), *Nutuk-Söylev: III Cilt*, 1390.

96. *TBMM Gizli Celse Kayıtları*, vol. 4, 86–104, 112–19, 126–47, 150–91. See also: Tunçay, *Türkiye'de Tek Parti Yönetimi'nin Kurulması*, 117–19.

97. *Lausanne Peace Conference: Records of Proceedings & Documents*, vol. 1-1.

98. While the Ottomans initially granted them voluntarily for strategic purposes, over time they began to do so under pressure, which began to threaten Ottoman independence and turning it into a semi-colony. Abolishing was a major goal of Turkish nationalists during the Second Constitutional Period and War of Independence. Hanioğlu, *A Brief History*; Hasan Kayalı, "The Struggle for Independence," in *The Cambridge History of Turkey. Vol. 4: Turkey in the Modern World*, ed. Reşat Kasaba (Cambridge: Cambridge University Press, 2008), 112–46.

99. Cuthell, "A Kemalist Gambit," 90.

100. Taha Akyol, *Bilinmeyen Lozan* [Unknown Lausanne] (Istanbul: Doğan Kitap, 2014), 223–58. For Mustafa Kemal's views on the risks of prolonging the Lausanne talks until the Mosul question is resolved, see, e.g., his telegram to İsmet, *Nutuk-Söylev: II. Cilt*, 1034–35.

101. *İsmet İnönü: Hatıralar* [Memoirs], (Ankara: Bilgi Yayınevi, 1987), 100, 233.

102. Kâzım Karabekir, *Günlükler: (1906-1948) 2. Cilt* [Memoirs: (1906–1948), Volume 2], (Istanbul: Yapı Kredi Yayınları, 2009), 917–33, 981–88. Karabekir recounts that he tried to dissuade Kemal and İsmet, who had made statements

regarding their plans to launch a military operation; but it is not clear whether the announcements of the latter two reflected their real intentions or were aimed at appeasing the public opinion critical of losing Mosul.

103. Taha Akyol and Sefa Kaplan, *Açık ve Gizli Oturumlarda Lozan Tartışmaları: TBMM'de Lozan Müzakereleri Tutanakları* [Lausanne Discussions in Open and Secret Sessions: Proceedings of the Lausanne Conference at the Grand National Assembly of Turkey] (Istanbul: Doğan Books, 2013), iv–vi; Akyol, *Bilinmeyen Lozan*, 259–92.

104. Republic of Turkey, Ministry of Foreign Affairs, *50 Years of Turkey's Foreign Policy: The First Decade of the Republic and the Balkan Pact (1923–1934)* (Ankara: Directorate General of Research and Policy Planning, 1974), 82–83.

105. For Mustafa Kemal's own perspective and narrative on the events in the period, including his accusations against his critics and the possibility of a war with Britain over Mosul, see Kemal (Atatürk), *Nutuk-Söylev: II. Cilt*, 1134–41.

106. Kyle Beardsley, "Agreement without Peace? International Mediation and Time Inconsistency Problems," *American Journal of Political Science* 52, no. 4 (2008): 723–40; Milan W. Svolik, "Democracy as an Equilibrium: Rational Choice and Formal Political Theory in Democratization Research," *Democratization* 26, no. 1 (2018): 40–60.

107. Bozarslan, "Kürt Milliyetçiliği: Zımni Sözleşmeden Ayaklanmaya."

108. Tunçay, *Türkiye'de Tek Parti Yönetimi'nin Kurulması*; Özbudun, *Otoriter Rejimler, Seçimsel Demokrasiler ve Türkiye.*

109. Meeker, *A Nation of Empire*, 8.

110. Turnaoğlu, *The Formation of Turkish Republicanism*, 10.

111. For a take on nationalism, Murat Somer, "Defensive- vs. Liberal-Nationalist Perspectives on Diversity and the Kurdish Conflict: Europeanization, the Internal Debate, and *Türkiyelilik*," *New Perspectives on Turkey* 32 (2005): 73–91.

112. These perspectives may also be rooted in the "Islamic puritan" and "antinomian" currents that underlay the late Ottoman history and attempts at reordering society, military, and politics. See Yaycioglu, "Guarding Traditions and Laws."

113. Clayer, Giomi, and Szerek, eds., *Kemalism: Transnational Politics.*

114. Çalışlar, *Mustafa Kemal Atatürk*, 502.

115. Ibid., 502.

116. Clement Henry Moore, *Tunisia since Independence* (Berkeley: University of California Press, 1965); Cemil Aydin, *The Politics of Anti-Westernism in Asia: Visions of World Order in Pan-Islamic and Pan-Asian Thought* (New York: Columbia University Press, 2007); Zarakol, *After Defeat How the East Learned to Live with the West*; Daniel Ziblatt, *Conservative Parties and Birth Democracy* (Cambridge University Press: Cambridge, 2017).

117. Piscatori, *Islam in a World of Nation-States.*

118. Clayer, Giomi, and Szerek, eds., *Kemalism: Transnational Politics.*

119. Piscatori, *Islam in a World of Nation-States*.

120. Somer, "Turkish Secularism."

121. Fortna et al., eds., *State-Nationalisms*; Grandits, Clayer, and Pichler, eds., *Conflicting Loyalties in the Balkans*; Clayer, Giomi, and Szerek, eds., *Kemalism*.

122. Cihan Tuğal, *The Fall of the Turkish Model: How the Arab Uprisings Brought Down Islamic Liberalism* (New York: Verso, 2016), 35–36. See also Somer, "Turkish Secularism."

123. Fabbe, *Disciples of the State*.

124. Somer, "Turkish Secularism."

125. Fabbe, *Disciples of the State*.

126. Şükrü M. Hanioğlu, "The Historical Roots of Kemalism," in *Democracy, Islam, and Secularism in Turkey*, ed. Ahmet T. Kuru and Alfred Stepan (New York: Columbia University Press, 2012), 32–60; Tunçay, *Türkiye'de Tek Parti Yönetimi'nin Kurulması*.

127. For a counterview on the dioristic nature of positivism and materialism in Atatürk's position see, Şükrü Hanioğlu, *Atatürk: An Intellectual Biography* (Princeton: Princeton University Press, 2011).

128. Amit Bein, *Ottoman Ulema, Turkish Republic: Agents of Change and Guardians of Tradition* (Stanford: Stanford University Press, 2011), 10.

129. Dressler, "Rereading Ziya Gökalp"; Nomer, "Ziya Gökalp's Idea."

130. Findley, *Turkey, Islam, Nationalism, and Modernity*, 18.

131. Tunçay, *Türkiye'de Tek Parti Yönetimi'nin Kurulması*, 218.

132. Murat Somer, "Democratization, Clashing Narratives, and 'Twin Tolerations' between Islamic-Conservative and Pro-Secular Actors," in *Nationalisms and Politics in Turkey: Political Islam, Kemalism, and the Kurdish Issue*, ed. Marlies Casier and Joost Jongerden (London: Routledge, 2010), 28–47.

133. The term used to denote legal and trade-related concessions that the Ottoman state made to foreign, mostly Westerns states. Judicial capitulations refer to past agreements whereby the Ottoman state relinquished its judicial authorities in certain areas and vis-à-vis some of its subjects and foreign citizens to foreign governments. Hanioğlu, *A Brief History*; Kayalı, "The Struggle for Independence."

134. A pretext for judicial capitulations expressed by Western powers was that non-Muslim foreigners could not understand Islamic law Sharia, which should therefore not apply to them.

135. *Atatürk'ün Bütün Eserleri*, vol. 14, 301. The term *inkılab* can be translated as revolution, reformation, or transformation.

136. For different policies by modernizing states toward civil law and room left for law-giving authorities of religion see Yüksel Sezgin, *Human Rights under State-Enforced Religious Family Laws in Israel, Egypt, and India* (New York: Cambridge, 2013).

137. Tunçay, *Türkiye'de Tek Parti Yönetimi'nin Kurulması*, 216–17.

138. The Law on the Maintenance of Order.

139. Üstel, "Türk Milliyetçiliğinde Anadolu Metaforu," 54–55.

140. Demirel, *Birinci Meclis'te Muhalefet*.

141. Özoğlu, *From Caliphate to Secular State*, 1–2.

142. Ibid., 82.

143. Olson, *The Emergence of Kurdish Nationalism and the Sheikh Said Rebellion*; Mumcu, *Kürt-İslam Ayaklanması*; Bruinessen, *Ağa, Şeyh, Devlet*; Özoğlu, *From Caliphate to Secular State*.

144. Reşat Hallı and Kaynak Yayınları, *Genel Kurmay Belgelerinde Kürt İsyanları 1 & 2* [Kurdish Rebellions in the Documents of the General Staff I & 2] (Istanbul: Kaynak Publications, 2011). There are also other sources that cite more rebellions. See, Mehmet Ali Birand, "Kaç Kürt İsyanı Oldu? [How Many Kurdish Rebellions Happened?]," *Hürriyet*, January 3, 2008.

145. Aliza Marcus, *Blood and Belief: The PKK and the Kurdish Fight for Independence* (New York: New York University Press, 2007), 18.

146. Tezcür, "Kurdish Nationalism and Identity in Turkey."

147. Mumcu, *Kürt-İslam Ayaklanması*, 86–95.

148. Ibid.

149. Zürcher, *Savaş, Devrim ve Uluslaşma*, 58; also see, Tunçay, *Türkiye'de Tek Parti Yönetimi'nin Kurulması*, 134–86.

150. Tunçay, *Türkiye'de Tek Parti Yönetimi'nin Kurulması*, 145.

151. MPs Feridun Fikri, Kazım Karabekir (Pasha) and Halis Turgut. Mumcu, *Kürt-İslam Ayaklanması*, 89–93.

152. McDowall, *A Modern History of the Kurds*, 404.

153. Bozarslan, "Kurds and the Turkish State," 344.

154. Nicole F. Watts, "Silence and Voice: Turkish Policies and Kurdish Resistance in the Mid-20th Century," in *The Evolution of Kurdish Nationalism*, ed. Mohammad M. A. Ahmed and Michael M. Gunter (Costa Mesa: Mazda, 2007).

155. David Romano, *The Kurdish Nationalist Movement: Opportunity, Mobilization, and Identity* (Cambridge: Cambridge University Press, 2006).

156. Cemil Gündoğan, "Geleneğin Değersizleşmesi: Kürt Hareketinin 1970'lerde Gelenekselle İlişkisi Üzerine [The Devaluation of Tradition: On the Relationship Between Tradition and the Kurdish Movement in the 1970s]," in *Türkiye Siyasetinde Kürtler* [Kurds in Turkish Politics], ed. Büşra Ersanlı, Günay Göksu Özdoğan, and Nesrin Uçarlar (Istanbul: İletişim, 2012), 104. Also see, Bruinessen, *Ağa, Şeyh, Devlet*, 21–23.

157. Meeker, *A Nation of Empire: The Ottoman Legacy of Turkish Modernity*.

158. Şerif Mardin, "Turkish Islamic Exceptionalism Yesterday and Today: Continuity, Rupture, and Reconstruction in Operational Codes," *Turkish Studies* 6, no. 2 (2005): 145–65.

159. Aktürk, *Regimes of Ethnicity and Nationhood in Germany, Russia and Turkey*, 148.

160. Ibid., 147–48.

161. Igor P. Lipovsky, *The Socialist Movement in Turkey, 1960–1980* (Leiden: E. J. Brill, 1992).

162. Watts, "Silence and Voice."

163. Marcus, *Blood and Belief*, 27.

164. Arda Bilgen, "A Project of Destruction, Peace, or Techno-Science? Untangling the Relationship between the Southeastern Anatolia Project (Gap) and the Kurdish Question in Turkey," *Middle Eastern Studies* 54, no. 1 (2017): 94–113, 107.

165. For two theses on the economic aspect of the Kurdish Question, see Ahmet İçduygu, David Romano, and İbrahim Sirkeci, "The Ethnic Question in an Environment of Insecurity: The Kurds in Turkey," *Ethnic and Racial Studies* 22, no. 6 (1999): 991–1010. Servet Mutlu, *Doğu Sorununun Kökenleri: Ekonomik Açıdan* [The Origins of the Eastern Question: An Economic Perspective] (Istanbul: Ötüken Yayınları, 2002).

166. Ibid.

167. Tan, *Kürt Sorunu*, 365.

168. Ibid.

169. Tezcür, "Ordinary People, Extraordinary Risks," 262.

170. Azer Kılıç, "Interests, Passions, and Politics: Business Associations and the Sovereignty Dispute in Turkey," *Economy and Society* 46, no. 2 (2017): 275–301, 11 and 20.

171. Bilgen, "A Project of Destruction, Peace, or Techno-Science?" 100–104.

172. Tan, *Kürt Sorunu*, 364–65.

173. Ümit Cizre Sakallıoğlu, "Kurdish Nationalism from an Islamist Perspective: The Discourses of Turkish Islamist Writers," *Journal of Muslim Minority Affairs* 18, no. 1 (1998): 73–89; Hakan Yavuz, "Five Stages of the Construction of Kurdish Nationalism in Turkey," *Nationalism & Ethnic Politics* 7, no. 3 (2001): 1–24.

174. Seda Demiralp, "The Odd Tango of the Islamic Right and Kurdish Left in Turkey: A Peripheral Alliance to Redesign the Centre?" *Middle Eastern Studies* 48, no. 2: 287–302.

175. Mazlumder, *Kürd Sorunu Forumu: 28–29 Kasım 1992* [The Kurdish Conflict Forum: 28–29 November 1992] (Ankara, Ankara: Sor Yayıncılık, 1993), 12, 69–70.

176. Michael Hechter, "Internal Colonialism Revisited," in *New Nationalisms of the Developed West: Toward Explanation*, ed. E. A. Tiryakian and R. Rogowski (Boston: Allen and Unwin, 1985), 17–26; İsmail Beşikçi, *Devletlerarası Sömürge Kürdistan* [International Colony Kurdistan] (Alan Yayıncılık, 1990).

177. Barış Ünlü and Ozan Değer, eds., *İsmail Beşikçi* (Istanbul: İletişim Yayınları, 2011).

178. Rafet Ballı, *Kürt Dosyası* [The Kurdish Case] (Istanbul: Cem Yayınevi, 1991); Mehmet Ali Birand, *Apo ve PKK* [Apo and the PKK] (Istanbul: Milliyet Yayınları, 1992); İsmet İmset, *PKK: Ayrılıkçı Şiddetin 20 Yılı 1973–1992* [The PKK:

A Report on Separatist Violence in Turkey 1973–1992] (Istanbul: Turkish Daily News Publications, 1993); Marcus, *Blood and Belief.*

179. Randall, *After Such Knowledge, What Forgiveness?*; Romano, *The Kurdish Nationalist Movement.*

180. Marcus, *Blood and Belief,* 34.

181. Ibid., 37.

182. Timur Kuran, *Private Truths, Public Lies: The Social Consequences of Preference Falsification* (Cambridge: Harvard University Press, 1995).

183. Feroz Ahmad, *The Making of Modern Turkey* (New York: Routledge, 1993); Mehmet Ali Birand, Hikmet Bila, and Rıdvan Akar, *12 Eylül: Türkiye'nin Miladı* [12 September: Turkey's Point Zero] (Istanbul: Doğan Kitap, 1999).

184. Banu Eligür, *The Mobilization of Political Islam in Turkey* (New York: Cambridge University Press, 2010), 85–90.

185. Ibid., 90.

186. Cemal, *Kürtler,* 15.

187. Martin van Bruinessen, "Shifting National and Ethnic Identities: The Kurds in Turkey and Europe," in *Redefining the Nation, State, and Citizen,* ed. Günay Göksu Özdoğan and Gül Tokay (Istanbul: Eren Yayıncılık, 2000); Eva Ostergaard-Nielsen, *Transnational Politics: Turks and Kurds in Germany* (London: Routledge, 2003).

188. Eligür, *The Mobilization of Political Islam,* 90–118; Tuğal, *The Fall of the Turkish Model: How the Arab Uprisings Brought Down Islamic Liberalism,* 33–82.

189. Mumcu, *Kürt-İslam Ayaklanması.*

190. Kadri Gürsel, *Dağdakiler: Bagok'tan Gabar'a 26 Gün* [Those of the Mountains: 26 Days from Bagok to Gabar] (Istanbul: Metis Yayınları, 1996); Marcus, *Blood and Belief*; Tezcür, "When Democratization Radicalizes," and "Ordinary People, Extraordinary Risks"; Ali Kemal Özcan, *Turkey's Kurds: A Theoretical Analysis of the PKK and Abdullah Ocalan* (New York: Routledge, 2006); Joost Jongerden and Ahmet Hamdi Akkaya, "Born from the Left: The Making of the PKK"; Ahmet Hamdi Akkaya and Joost Jongerden, "The PKK in the 2000s: Continuity through Breaks?," in *Nationalisms and Politics in Turkey: Political Islam, Kemalism, and the Kurdish Issue,* ed. Marlies Casier and Joost Jongerden (New York: Routledge, 2010); Bejan Matur, *Dağın Ardına Bakmak* [Looking Beyond the Mountain] (Istanbul: Timaş Yayınları, 2011).

191. This does not mean that other Kurdish groups have not been violent. For the case of Kurdish-Islamist Hizbullah, see Mehmet Kurt, *Kurdish Hizbullah in Turkey: Islamism, Violence, and the State* (London: PlutoPress, 2017).

192. Güneş Murat Tezcür, "Violence and Nationalist Mobilization: The Onset of the Kurdish Insurgency in Turkey," *Nationalities Papers* 43, no. 2 (2015): 248–66, 248.

193. Abdullah Öcalan, *Democratic Nation* (Cologne: International Initiative Edition in cooperation with Mesopotamian Publishers, Neuss, 2017), 9.

194. Ibid., 9–10.

195. Tezcür, "Ordinary People, Extraordinary Risks," 262.

196. Oral Çalışlar, *Öcalan ve Burkay'la Kürt Sorunu* [The Kurdish Conflict with Öcalan and Burkay] (Istanbul: Pencere Yayınları, 1993); Kemal Burkay, *Anılar, Belgeler* [Memoirs, Documents], Vol. 1, 2nd ed. (Istanbul: Deng Yayınları, 2002).

197. Ceren Belge, "Civilian Victimization and the Politics of Information in the Kurdish Conflict in Turkey," *World Politics* 68, no. 2 (2016): 275–306; Juan Masullo and Francis O'Connor, "Pkk Violence against Civilians: Beyond the Individual, Understanding Collective Targeting," *Terrorism and Political Violence* (2017): 1–23. https://doi.org/10.1080/09546553.2017.1347874.

198. The same goes for the loss of state legitimacy due to state violence and other measures aimed at counterinsurgency and rendering the Kurdish population "legible." Belge, "Civilian Victimization and the Politics of Information."

199. Erica Chenoweth and Maria J. Stephan, *Why Civil Resistance Works: The Strategic Logic of Nonviolent Conflict* (New York: Columbia University Press, 2011).

200. Marcus, *Blood and Belief*, 29.

201. Ibid., 45.

202. San-Akca, *States in Disguise*, 221, 255–56.

203. Ibid., 1–2.

204. Bente Scheller, *The Wisdom of Syria's Waiting Game: Syrian Foreign Policy under the Assads* (London: Hurst, 2013), 101.

205. Paul White, *Primitive Rebels or Revolutionary Modernizers: The Kurdish Nationalist Movement in Turkey* (London: Zed Books, 2000).

206. Tezcür, "When Democratization Radicalises."

207. Tezcür, "Ordinary People, Extraordinary Risks," 261–62. For women's involvement in the PKK as well as affiliated Kurdish movement and parties, see also Zeynep Sahin-Mencutek, "Strong in the Movement, Strong in the Party: Women's Representation in the Kurdish Party of Turkey," *Political Studies* 64, no. 2 (2015): 470–87.

208. Ethnic and regional conflicts were very frequent during the Cold War but either not in the limelight or not dubbed as "ethnic." For example, see, Red Robert Gurr, Monty G. Marshall, and Deepa Khosla, *Peace and Conflict 2001: A Global Survey of Armed Conflicts, Self-Determination Movements, and Democracy* (Maryland: Center for International Development and Conflict Management, 2001).

209. Murat Güneş Tezcür, "The Ebb and Flow of Armed Conflict in Turkey: An Elusive Peace," in *Conflict, Democratization and the Kurds in the Middle East*, ed. David Romano and Mehmet Gürses (New York: Palgrave Macmillan, 2014); Correlates of War Project, http.//www.correlatesofwar.org/.

210. Grand National Assembly of Turkey Human Rights Investigation Commission, *Investigative Report on Abuses on Right to Live in the Context of Terror and Violence*, 24th Term, 3rd Legislative Year, 2013, http.//www.tbmm.gov.tr/komisyon/insanhaklari/belge/TER%C3%96R%20VE%20%C5%9E%C4%BoH

LALLER%C4%BO%20%C4%BoNCELEME%20RAPORU.pdf; last accessed November 15, 2014.

211. Banu Tuna, "4,653 Faili Meçhul Belgeseli [4,653 Unsolved Murders Documentary]," *Hürriyet* newspaper, March 20, 2005.

212. Tanel Demirel, "Lessons of Military Regimes and Democracy: The Turkish Case in Comparative Perspective," *Armed Forces and Society* 31, no. 2 (2005): 245–71; Hasan Cemal, *Türkiye'nin Asker Sorunu* [Turkey's Military Problem] (Istanbul: Doğan Kitap, 2010).

213. Tezcür, "The Ebb and Flow of Armed Conflict in Turkey: An Elusive Peace."

# Chapter 5

1. Yalman, *Kürtler ve Kürdistan*.

2. Francis Fukuyama, *The End of History and the Last Man* (New York: Free Press, 1992).

3. While I use here my own broad formulation of recognition derived from my analysis of the Kurdish Question, recognition has many different conceptualizations, which no doubt inform and motivate my discussion. Among others, Lijphart, *Democracy in Plural Societies*; Iris Marion Young, *Justice and the Politics of Difference* (Princeton: Princeton University Press, 1990); Will Kymlicka, *Multicultural Citizenship: A Liberal Theory of Minority Rights* (Oxford: Oxford University Press, 1995); John Gray, *Enlightenment's Wake: Politics and Culture at the Close of the Modern Age* (London: Routledge, 2007). Also see Elisabeth King and Cyrus Samii, *Diversity, Violence, and Recognition: How Recognizing Ethnic Identity Promotes Peace* (New York: Oxford University Press, 2020) for a cross-national empirical investigation and a definition focusing on public institutions: "Public and explicit references to ethnic groups in state institutions . . . presence (and absence) of positive statements that may be read as affirming groups' existence as part of the body politic" (4).

4. Donna Hicks, *Dignity: The Essential Role It Plays in Resolving Conflict* (New Haven: Yale University Press, 2011), 2.

5. Ibid., 3 and 5–8.

6. Joel S. Migdal, *State in Society: Studying How States and Societies Transform and Constitute One Another* (Cambridge: Cambridge University Press, 2001); Dan Slater, "Strong-State Democratization in Malaysia and Singapore," *Journal of Democracy* 23, no. 2 (2012): 19–33.

7. Somer, "Theory-Consuming or Theory-Producing."

8. Murat Somer, "Resurgence and Remaking of Identity: Civil Beliefs, Domestic and External Dynamics, and the Turkish Mainstream Discourse on Kurds," *Comparative Political Studies* 38, no. 6 (August 2005): 591–622.

9. For the sake of consistency, the count omitted articles about Kurdish organizations based outside of Turkey and active in Europe, about Iraqi refugees, or contained the use of the word *Kurdistan* as part of the name of PKK. This decision was taken because, from the perspectives of the writers, these uses do not reference an ethnic group in Turkey.

10. For methodological issues and choices in this matter, please see: Somer, "Media Values and Democratization."

11. Somer, "Resurgence and Remaking of Identity," 7.

12. Cemal, *Kürtler*, 53, 102–10.

13. Tanıl Bora, "Nationalist Discourses in Turkey," *South Atlantic Quarterly* 102, no. 2/3 (2003); Ayşe Kadıoğlu, "The Paradox of Turkish Nationalism and the Construction of Official Identity," *Middle Eastern Studies* 32, no. 2 (1997): 177–93; Mesut Yeğen, "The Turkish State Discourse and the Exclusion of Kurdish Identity," *Middle Eastern Studies* 32, no. 2 (1996): 216–29.

14. Füsun Üstel, *Makbul Vatandaş'ın Peşinde: İkinci Meşrutiyet'ten Bugüne Vatandaşlık Eğitimi* [In Pursuit of the Favorite Citizen: Citizenship Education from the Second Constitutionalist Period to Today] (Istanbul: İletişim Yayınları, 2011).

15. Özbudun, *Otoriter Rejimler, Seçimsel Demokrasiler ve Türkiye.*

16. Linz and Stepan, *Problems of Democratic Transition and Consolidation.*

17. Ballı, *Kürt Dosyası*; SHP, *Sosyaldemokrat Halkçı Parti'nin Doğu ve Güneydoğu Sorunları'na Bakışı ve Çözüm Önerileri* [Social Democratic Populist Party's Views on the Eastern and Southeastern Conflicts and Solution Proposals] (Ankara: SHP Central Executive Committee, 1990).

18. Hamit Bozarslan, "Political Crisis and the Kurdish Issue in Turkey," in *The Kurdish Nationalist Movement in the 1990s*, ed. Robert Olson (Lexington: University Press of Kentucky, 1996), 141–42.

19. For example, see Doğu Ergil, *Doğu Sorunu: Teşhisler ve Tespitler* [The Eastern Question: Opinions and Designations] (Ankara: TOBB, 1995).

20. Przeworski, "Deliberation and Ideological Domination."

21. Pippa Norris and Ronald Inglehart, *Sacred and Secular: Religion and Politics Worldwide* (Cambridge: Cambridge University Press, 2004).

22. Alpaslan Pehlivanlı, a center-right (ANAP) MP and president of the Justice Commission. Foreign Broadcast Information Services, US Government documents, FBIS-WEU-91-058, March 26, 1991, 41–42.

23. Reported private conversation with Özal on October 12, 1991. Çandar, *Mezopotamya Ekspresi*, 127.

24. Kuran, *Living with Lies.*

25. Petersen, *Resistance and Rebellion*; Somer, *Cascades of Ethnic Polarization*; Somer, "Insincere Public Discourse, Trust, and Implications for Democratic Transition: The Yugoslav Meltdown Revisited."

26. Kuran, *Living with Lies.*

27. Somer, "Cascades of Ethnic Polarization."

28. Kuran, *Living with Lies.*

29. Somer, "Resurgence and Remaking."

30. George Lakoff, *The Political Mind: A Cognitive Scientist's Guide to Your Brain and Its Politics* (London: Penguin Books, 2009).

31. Somer, "Resurgence and Remaking of Identity," 4–5.

32. Ibid.

33. Cemal, *Kürtler*, 74, 101.

34. Ibid., 245, 276.

35. Ibid., 96, 276.

36. "ABD Heyeti: Özal Bize Kürt Kökenliyim Dedi [The U.S. Delegation: Özal Told Us He Is of Kurdish Origin]," *Hürriyet*, October 10, 1989.

37. Çandar, *Mezopotamya Ekspresi*, 100.

38. Ibid., 97–98, 101, 113.

39. Muhsin Öztürk, "Kürt meselesinde Özal yalnızdı, Erdoğan ise şanslı [Özal Was Alone Whereas Erdoğan Was Lucky with the Kurdish Question]," *Aksiyon* magazine, September 28, 2009.

40. Jonathan C. Randal, *After Such Knowledge, What Forgiveness? My Encounters with Kurdistan* (Boulder: Westview, 1999), 277–83.

41. Raşit Kaya and Barış Çakmur, "Politics and the Mass Media in Turkey," *Turkish Studies* 11, no. 4 (2010): 521–37; Somer, "Media Values and Democratization." For a critical review of the intellectual and political divisions within Cumhuriyet newspaper, see Hasan Cemal, *Cumhuriyet'i Çok Sevmiştim: Cumhuriyet Gazetesindeki 'İç Savaş'ın' Perde Arkası* [I Loved the Republic: Behind the Scenes of the "Civil War" at Cumhuriyet Newspaper] (Istanbul: Doğan Books, 2005).

42. Cemal, *Kürtler*, 48–55.

43. "Demirel: Türkler çok Milliyetçi çıktı [Demirel: The Turks have turned out to be too nationalist]," interview with the Leader of Hak-Par, Abdülmelik Fırat, *Yeni Aktüel* magazine, December 5, 2005, 34–37.

44. Jack L. Snyder, *From Voting to Violence: Democratization and Nationalist Conflict* (New York: W. W. Norton, 2000); Mansfield and Snyder, *Electing to Fight: Why Emerging Democracies Go to War.*

45. Kirişçi and Winrow, *The Kurdish Question and Turkey.*

46. Cemal, *Kürtler*, 157.

47. Nicole Pope and Hugh Pope, *Turkey Unveiled: A History of Modern Turkey* (New York: The Overlook Press, 1998); Kinzer, *Crescent and Star.*

48. November 6, 1991, https://www.youtube.com/watch?v=gQaiowrL-VQ (accessed April 10, 2019).

49. Gülistan Gürbey, "The Kurdish Nationalist Movement in Turkey since the 1980s," in *The Kurdish Nationalist Movement in the 1990s: Its Impact on Turkey and the Middle East,* ed. Robert Olson (Lexington: University Press of Kentucky, 1997), 26; Kirişçi and Winrow, *The Kurdish Question and Turkey.*

50. *SHP, Sosyaldemokrat Halkçı Parti'nin Doğu ve Güneydoğu Sorunları'na Bakışı ve Çözüm Önerileri.*

51. Gürbey, "The Kurdish Nationalist Movement in Turkey since the 1980s," 27.

52. Cemal, *Kürtler*, 68–70.

53. Ibid., 69.

54. Kirişçi and Winrow, *The Kurdish Question*, 139.

55. "ABD Heyeti: Özal Bize Kürt Kökenliyim Dedi."

56. Roe, *Ethnic Violence and Societal Security Dilemma*; Rumelili, *Conflict Resolution and Ontological Security.*

57. Ayhan Kaya, *Europeanization and Tolerance in Turkey: The Myth of Toleration* (New York: Palgrave Macmillan, 2013).

58. Mehmet Ugur, *The European Union and Turkey: An Anchor/Credibility Dilemma* (Aldershot, Hants: Ashgate, 1999); Viatcheslav Morozov and Bahar Rumelili, "The External Constitution of European Identity: Russia and Turkey as Europe-Makers," *Cooperation and Conflict* 47, no. 1 (2012): 28–48.

59. The Washington Institute for Near East Policy, "German and French Leaders' Views on Turkey's EU Membership," *PolicyWatch*, 1007, June 27, 2005; https://www.washingtoninstitute.org/policy-analysis/german-and-french-leaders-views-turkeys-eu-membership.

60. Barkey, *Empire of Difference: The Ottomans in Comparative Perspective.*

61. White, *Muslim Nationalism and the New Turks*, 95–96.

62. Kaya, *Europeanization and Tolerance in Turkey.*

63. Rodrigue, "Reflections on Millets and Minorities," 36–46, 44.

64. Ali Çarkoğlu and Ersin Kalaycıoğlu, *The Rising Tide of Conservatism in Turkey* (New York: Palgrave Macmillan, 2009), 16; Hakan Yılmaz, "Two Pillars of Nationalist Euro-Skepticism in Turkey: The Tanzimat and Sèvres Syndromes," in *Turkey, Sweden, and the European Union: Experience and Expectations*, ed. Ingmar Karlsson and Annika Strom Melin (Stockholm: SIEPS, 2006), 29–40.

65. Cenk Saracoglu, " 'Exclusive Recognition': The New Dimensions of the Question of Ethnicity and Nationalism in Turkey," *Ethnic and Racial Studies* 32, no. 4 (2009): 640–58; *Şehir, Orta Sınıf ve Kürtler: İnkar'dan 'Tanıyarak Dışlama'ya* [The City, The Middle Class and the Kurds: From Denial to "Exclusive Recognition"] (Istanbul: İletişim Yayınları, 2011).

66. Saracoglu, *Şehir, Orta Sınıf ve Kürtler*, 75.

67. Saraçoğlu, "Exclusive Recognition," 640–58.

68. For an example: Gökçe Fırat, *İstila: Kürt Sorununda Gizlenen Gerçekler ve Kürt İstilası* [Invasion: The Hidden Truths in the Kurdish Problem and the Kurdish Invasion] (Istanbul: İleri, 2007); and the controversial *Türk Solu* (Turkish Left) magazine. For critiques see: "Türk Solu Dergisi Bir Kez Daha Kin Kustu [Turkish Left Magazine Once Again Spread Hatred]," *T24*, November 2, 2011. https://t24.

com.tr/haber/turk-solu-dergisi-bir-kez-daha-kin-kustu-dersimliler-hic-uzulmesin-onlar-da-dedelerinin-yanina-gi,184134 (accessed September 16, 2019).

69. Murat Ergin, "The Racialization of Kurdish Identity in Turkey," *Ethnic and Racial Studies* 37, no. 2 (2014): 322–41.

70. Necat Erder, *Türkiye'de Siyasi Partilerin Yandaş/Seçmen Profili (1994–2002)* [The Supporter/Voter Profiles of Political Parties in Turkey (1994–2002)] (Istanbul: Tüses Yayınları, Data Research, 2002). The 1996 data was taken from the 1996 report of the same research and recalculated. The data from 2003–04 was collated in the period extending from December 2003 to January 2004 by the Data Research company.

71. Rezarta Bilali, Ayşe Betül Çelik, and Ekin Ok, "Psychological Asymmetry in Minority-Majority Relations at Different Stages of Ethnic Conflict," *International Journal of Interethnic Relations* 43 (2014): 253–64.

72. Ibid., 258. Survey question no. 7. From the survey obtained from Ayşe Betül Çelik via email correspondence, December 24, 2014.

73. Meanwhile, support for Kurdish rights and freedoms also subsided.

# Chapter 6

1. Mandıracı, "Assessing the Fatalities in Turkey's Pkk Conflict." *International Crisis Group*, October 22, 2019. https://www.crisisgroup.org/europe-central-asia/western-europemediterranean/turkey/assessing-fatalities-turkeys-pkk-conflict.

2. This year featured the eruption of the Arab Uprisings and possible remaking of state borders in the Middle East, the beginning of civil war in Syria, a crucial constitutional referendum (2010) and national election (2011) in Turkey that catapulted the pro-religious elites led by the ruling AKP to hegemony, and ongoing public political and constitutional debates on the national identity. For an early formulation of the argument, see Murat Somer, "Toward A Non-Standard Story: The Kurdish Question and the Headscarf, Nationalism, and Iraq," in *Symbiotic Antagonisms in Turkey: Sources, Discourses, and Changing Nature of Turkish, Kurdish, and Islamic Nationalisms,* ed. Ayşe Kadıoğlu and Fuat Keyman (Salt Lake City: The University of Utah Press, 2011), 253–88.

3. Turkish secularism (*laiklik*) or laicism corresponds to an indigenous form of religion-state and religion-nation relationship. Murat Somer, "Turkish Secularism: Looking Forward and Beyond the West," in *Routledge Handbook on Turkish Politics,* ed. Matthew Whiting and Alpaslan Özerdem (London: Routledge, 2019), 37–54. I will discuss and argue this point in the chapters ahead.

4. For an analysis of the AKP as a "passive revolutionary" force see Cihan Tuğal, *Passive Revolution: Absorbing the Islamic Challenge to Capitalism* (Stanford: Stanford University Press, 2009) and *The Fall of the Turkish Model: How the Arab Uprisings Brought Down Islamic Liberalism.* For the revolutionary potential of the

AKP from its beginning, the shift from reformism to revolutionism, and the roles of ideology and politics in this process, see Murat Somer, "Conquering Versus Democratizing the State: Political Islamists and Fourth Wave Democratization in Turkey and Tunisia," *Democratization* 24, no. 6 (2017): 1025–43.

5. Murat Somer, "Turkey: The Slippery Slope from Reformist to Revolutionary Polarization and Democratic Breakdown," *The ANNALS of the American Academy of Political and Social Science* 681, no. 1 (2019): 42–61.

6. Berk Esen and Sebnem Gumuscu, "Rising Competitive Authoritarianism in Turkey," *Third World Quarterly* 37, no. 9 (2016): 1581–1606; Murat Somer, "Understanding Turkey's Democratic Breakdown: Old versus New and Indigenous versus Global Authoritarianism," *Southeast European and Black Sea Studies* 16, no. 4 (2016): 481–503; Berk Esen and Sebnem Gumuscu, "A Small Yes for Presidentialism: The Turkish Constitutional Referendum of April 2017," *South European Society and Politics* 22, no. 3 (2017): 303–26; Steven Levitsky and Daniel Ziblatt, *How Democracies Die* (New York: Crown, 2018).

7. Migdal, *State in Society*; Slater, "Strong-State"; Somer, "Understanding Turkey's Democratic Breakdown."

8. Somer and McCoy, "Transformations through Polarizations."

9. Necat Erder, *Türkiye'de Siyasi Partilerin Yandaş/Seçmen Profili*, 17–18.

10. Murat Somer, "Sustainable Democratization and the Roles of the US and the EU: Political Islam and Kurdish Nationalism in Turkey," *Turkish Policy Quarterly* 5, no. 3 (November 2006), 89–108.

11. Kaya, *Europeanization and Tolerance in Turkey*, 110.

12. Turkish Statistical Institute, last accessed 19 July 2014, http://www.tuik.gov.tr/UstMenu.do?metod=temelist.

13. *Turkish Statistical Institute.*

14. Tuğal, *The Fall of the Turkish Model.*

15. Korkut Boratav, "The Turkish Bourgeoisie under Neoliberalism," *Research and Policy on Turkey* 1, no. 1 (2016): 1–10; Erinç A. Yeldan and Burcu Ünüvar, "An Assessment of the Turkish Economy in the Akp Era," *Research and Policy on Turkey* 1, no. 1 (2016): 11–28.

16. Meltem Müftüler Baç, "Turkey's Political Reforms and the Impact of the European Union," *South European Society and Politics* 10, no. 1 (2005), 17–31; Kaya, *Europeanization and Tolerance in Turkey*.

17. İhsan D. Dağı, "Transformation of Islamic Political Identity in Turkey: Rethinking the West and Westernization," *Turkish Studies* 6, no. 1 (2005), 21–37; Demirel, "Lessons of Military Regimes and Democracy: The Turkish Case in Comparative Perspective"; Ümit Cizre, ed., *Secular and Islamic Politics in Turkey: The Making of the Justice and Development Party* (New York: Routledge, 2008); Somer, "Moderation of Religious and Secular Politics"; Jillian Schwedler, "Why Academics Can't Get Beyond Radicals and Moderates," *Washington Post*, February 12, 2015.

18. Somer, "Turkey: The Slippery Slope from Reformist to Revolutionary Polarization and Democratic Breakdown."

19. See interview with Duran Kalkan, a member of the Executive Council of the KCK, last accessed July 20, 2014. http://rojaciwan.com/tr/rc/99-geri-cekilme-surecini-yasayan-gerillalar-anlatiyor-dizi-iii/.

20. Cengiz Çandar, "Turkish Foreign Policy and the War on Iraq," in *The Future of Turkish Foreign Policy*, ed. Lenore G. Martin and Dimitris Keridis (London: MIT Press, 2004), 37–60.

21. Phillip Robins, "Confusion at Home, Confusion Abroad: Turkey Between Copenhagen and Iraq," *International Affairs* 79, no. 3 (2003): 547–66.

22. Among others, Stephen M. Saideman and R. William Ayres, "Determining the Causes of Irredentism," *The Journal of Politics* 62, no. 4 (November 2000): 1126–44.

23. Murat Somer, "Failures of the Discourse of Ethnicity."

24. "TSK'nın Sınır Ötesi Operasyonları [Cross-Border Operations of the Turkish Armed Forces]," *Al Jazeera*, October 19, 2011, http://wwww.aljazeera.com.tr/haber/tsknin-sinir-otesi-operasyonlari.

25. "President Barzani and Prime Minister Erdoğan open Erbil International Airport and Turkish Consulate," last accessed March 30, 2011, http://www.krg.org/a/d.aspx?s=02010100&l=12&r+223&a+39389&s=010000.

26. Tezcür, "When Democratization Radicalizes."

27. Tezcür, "The Ebb and Flow of Armed Conflict in Turkey."

28. Also see, "Erdoğan: 'Kürt Sorunu' Diyerek Yanlış Yaptım [Erdoğan: I Made a Mistake When I Referred to the 'Kurdish Problem']," *T24*, November 1, 2012, https://t24.com.tr/haber/erdogan-kurt-sorunu-diyerek-yanlis-yaptim,216461 (last accessed September 26, 2019).

29. "Kürt Sorunu Benim Sorunum [The Kurdish Problem Is My Problem]," *Yeni Şafak* newspaper, August 13, 2005, http://yenisafak.com.tr/arsiv/2005/agustos/13/p01.html (accessed June 21, 2019).

30. Mazlum-Der's survey report on the subject, Diyarbakır branch, April 6, 2006, http://www.mazlumder.org/main/yayinlar/raporlar/3/diyarbakir-olaylari-rapo-ru-06042006/1055.

31. Provinces where the DTP received more than 10 percent of the votes.

32. Ayşe Seda Yüksel, "Rescaled Localities and Redefined Class Relations: Neoliberal Experience in South-East Turkey," *Journal of Balkan and Near Eastern Studies* 13, no. 4 (2011): 444, 449.

33. For example, see interview with Altan Tan, *Yeni Şafak* newspaper, November 26, 2007.

34. For example, see Neşe Düzel's interview with former MP Haşim Haşimi, *Radikal* newspaper, August 28, 2006.

35. The success of such efforts is arguable. See Bekir Ağırdır, "HDP ve Baraj [HDP and the Threshold]," *T24*, Ocak 29, 2015.

36. Zeki Sarıgil and Ömer Fazlıoğlu, "Religion and Ethnonationalism: Turkey's Kurdish Issue," *Nations and Nationalism* 19, no. 3 (2013): 551–571. For a broad discussion, Zeki Sarigil, *Ethnic Boundaries in Turkish Politics: The Secular Kurdish Movement and Islam* (New York: New York University Press, 2018).

37. Aktürk, *Regimes of Ethnicity and Nationhood in Germany, Russia, and Turkey.*

38. Democratic Society Party, *Demokratik Toplum Partisi'nin Kürt Sorununa İlişkin Demokratik Çözüm Projesi* (The Democratic Society Party's Democratic Resolution Project about the Kurdish Conflict) (Ankara: DTP General Headquarters, September 2008). Also see Michiel Leezenberg, "The Ambiguities of Democratic Autonomy: The Kurdish Movement in Turkey and Rojava," *Southeast European and Black Sea Studies* 16, no. 4 (2016): 671–90.

39. "MİT ve PKK Arasındaki Görüşme İnternete Sızdı [The Meeting Between the MİT and the PKK Leaks Online]," *Milliyet* newspaper, September 13, 2011, http://www.milliyet.com.tr/mit-ve-pkk-arasindaki-gorusme-internete-sizdi/gundem/gun-demdetay/13.09.2011/1438049/default.htm; "AK Parti'den 'PKK ile Müzakere'ye' Yalanlama [AK Party Refutes Negotiating with the PKK]," *CNN Turk*, August 19, 2010, http://www.cnnturk.com/2010/turkiye/08/19/ak.partiden.pkk.ile.muzakereye.yalanlama/587237.0/index.html.

40. This institute went into operation in 2011. Last accessed December 24, 2013, http://tyde.artuklu.edu.tr/.

41. For example, see interview with retired Ambassador Ümit Pamir, *Milliyet* newspaper, August 7, 2009.

42. Foundation for Political, Economic and Social Research (SETA) and Pollmark, *Public Perception of the Kurdish Problem in Turkey* (Pollmark, 2009).

43. "Mehmet Zekai Özcan: MHP'yi Neden Seçtim [Mehmet Zekai Özcan: Why I Chose the MHP]," *Haberiniz.com.tr*, August 13, 2010, http://www.haberiniz.com.tr/yazilar/haber17435-Mehmet%20-Zekai-Ozcan-MHPyi_neden_sectim.html.

44. Abdullah Öcalan, *The Road Map to Democratization of Turkey and Solution to the Kurdish Question* (Cologne: International Initiative "Freedom for Abdullah Öcalan—Peace in Kurdistan," 2011), 10–11, last accessed March 29, 2014, http://kinfo.kurd-port.com/media/files/DTK%20Demokratik%20Ozerklik.pdf.

45. Amnesty International, "Turkey: KCK Arrests Deepen Freedom of Expression Concerns," Public Statement, November 10, 2011). https://www.amnesty.org/en/documents/eur44/015/2011/en (accessed June 4, 2019).

46. Leezenberg, "The Ambiguities of Democratic Autonomy," 679.

47. KCK Agreement acknowledged by Kongra Gel in May 2005 and revised in May 2007, last accessed 18 March 2014, http://www.ygk-info.com/Onderlik/sozlesme/index.html and http://rojbas3.wordpress.com/kcksozlesmesi/.

48. Öcalan, *The Road Map to Democratization*, 11. Also see, KCK (Koma Civakên Kurdistan) Agreement.

49. Leezenberg, "The Ambiguities of Democratic Autonomy," 679.

50. Kaya, *Europeanization and Tolerance in Turkey*, 113.

51. Ayşe Hür, "Devletin Demir Yumruğu: Muğlalı Paşa [The Iron Fist of the State: Muğlalı Pasha]," *Taraf* newspaper, 10 May 2009.

52. Aslan, "Incoherent State."

53. Ekrem Karakoç and Zeki Sarıgil, "Why Religious People Support Ethnic Insurgency? Kurds, Religion, and Support for the Pkk," *Politics and Religion* 13, no. 2: 245–72, 254–55, and 260. Also see Tufekci, *Twitter and Tear Gas*, 33–35.

54. Burak Bilgehan Özpek, *The Peace Process between Turkey and Kurds: Anatomy of a Failure* (New York: Routledge, 2018).

55. Mahmut Hamsici, "Barış Görüşmelerini Başlatan Pencewini: Karayılan, Gül Ve Erdoğan'a Selam Söyledi [Pencewini Who Initiated the Peace Talks: Karayılan Sent Greetings to Gül and Erdoğan]," April 18, 2016, https://www.bbc.com/turkce/haberler/2016/04/160418_pencewini_roportaj (accessed June 24, 2019); "Pkk İlk Kez Açıkladı . . . Oslo'da Neler Oldu? [Pkk Announced for the First Time . . . What Happened in Oslo?]," *Akşam* (Istanbul), 2013, https://www.aksam.com.tr/siyaset/pkk-ilk-kez-acikladiosloda-neler-oldu/haber-199057 (accessed June 24, 2019).

56. That is, although the laws did not mention the Kurdish language, to all intents and purposes, it allowed the use of Kurdish (e.g., rather than self-defense through a Turkish translator) by legalizing the conduct of these activities in "mother-tongues."

57. It is more appropriate to describe the November elections as "repeat elections" rather than as "snap elections" because only an interim government (rather than a new government) was formed based on the June elections. President Erdoğan called for new elections after the first party AKP failed to form a coalition government and without ever giving the government-forming mandate to the second party CHP. See Murat Somer, "Will Turkey's President Accept the Country's Election Results?" *Washington Post*, April 18, 2019, for a brief discussion.

58. Somer, "Turkey: The Slippery Slope from Reformist to Revolutionary Polarization and Democratic Breakdown" and "Conquering versus Democratizing."

59. Kemal H. Karpat, *Turkey's Politics: The Transition to a Multiparty System* (Princeton: Princeton University Press, 1959); Feroz Ahmad, "The Transition to Democracy in Turkey," *Third World Quarterly* 7, no. 2 (1985): 211–26 and *The Making of Modern Turkey*; Michele P. Angrist, "Party Systems and Regime Formation in the Modern Middle East: Explaining Turkish Exceptionalism," *Comparative Politics* 36, no. 2 (2004): 229–49; Meliha Altunışık, "The Turkish Model and Democratization in the Middle East," *Arab Studies Quarterly* 27, nos. 1–2 (2005): 45–63.

60. Somer, "Moderation of Religious and Secular Politics."

61. Hakan M. Yavuz, *Islamic Political Identity in Turkey* (New York: Oxford University Press, 2003); Somer, "Conquering versus Democratizing the State."

62. However, even though the transition to multiparty democracy occurred based on a remarkable agreement between the CHP and DP over ideological moderation and free and fair elections, this agreement was not strong enough to be considered as an elite "settlement" or "pact." Di Palma, *To Craft Democracies*;

Özbudun, *Contemporary Turkish Politics*, 17–18; Higley and Burton, *Elite Foundations of Liberal Democracy*. "Elite unity broke down pathologically just as the vote was given to the peasant." Frederick W. Frey, *The Turkish Political Elite*. 1st ed. (Cambridge: The MIT Press, 1965), 391.

63. Ergun Ozbudun, "Established Revolution vs. Unfinished Revolution: Contrasting Patterns of Democratization in Mexico and Turkey," in *Authoritarian Politics in Modern Society: The Dynamics of Established One Party System*, ed. Samuel P. Huntington and Clement H. Moore (London, 1970).

64. Ümit Cizre, "Ideology, Context and Interest: The Turkish Military," in *The Cambridge History of Turkey: vol. 4: Turkey in the Modern World*, ed. R. Kasaba (Cambridge: Cambridge University Press, 2008), 301–32.

65. Şerif Mardin, "Youth and Violence in Turkey," *European Journal of Sociology* 19, no. 2 (1978): 229–54.

66. Ibid; Somer, "Democratization, Clashing Narratives, and 'Twin Tolerations' between Islamic-Conservative and Pro-Secular Actors."

67. Murat Somer, "Does It Take Democrats to Democratize? Lessons from Islamic and Secular Elite Values in Turkey," *Comparative Political Studies* 44, no. 5 (2011): 511–45.

68. Özbudun, *Contemporary Turkish Politics*; Metin Heper and Sabri Sayarı, eds. *Political Leaders and Democracy in Turkey* (Lanham, MD: Lexington Books, 2002); Sabri Sayarı and Yılmaz Esmer, eds. *Politics, Parties, and Elections* (Boulder: Lynne Rienner, 2002).

69. Tuğal, *The Fall of the Turkish Model*.

70. Sultan Tepe, "Turkey's AKP: A Model 'Muslim-Democratic' Party?," *Journal of Democracy* 16, no. 3 (2005): 69–85; Ziya Öniş, "Conservative Globalism at the Crossroads: The Justice and Development Party and the Thorny Path to Democratic Consolidation in Turkey," *Mediterranean Politics* 14, no. 1 (2009): 21–40; Şebnem Gümüşçü, "Class, Status, and Party: The Changing Face of Political Islam in Turkey and Egypt," *Comparative Political Studies* 43, no. 7 (2010): 835–61; Tuğal, *The Fall of the Turkish Model*.

71. Alfred Stepan, "Religion, Democracy, and the 'Twin Tolerations,'" *Journal of Democracy* 23, no. 2 (April 2000): 37–57; Murat Somer, "Moderate Islam and Secularist Opposition in Turkey: Implications for the World, Muslims and Secular Democracy," *Third World Quarterly* 28, no. 7 (2007): 1271–89; Jillian Schwedler, "Islamists in Power? Inclusion, Moderation, and the Arab Uprisings," *Middle East Development Journal* 5, no. 1 (2014): 1–18.

72. Sinan Ciddi and Berk Esen, "Turkey's Republican People's Party: Politics of Opposition under a Dominant Party System," *Turkish Studies* 15, no. 3 (2014): 419–41.

73. Çandar, *Mezopotamya Ekspresi*, 553–59.

74. As I argued earlier, the coalition government (ANAP-DSP-MHP) before the AKP was also an example of cooperation—albeit limited—between secular and religious elites.

75. Berman, "Ideational Theorizing" and *The Primacy of Politics.*

76. Ibid.

77. Somer, "Moderation of Religious and Secular Politics"; Ciddi and Esen, "Turkey's Republican People's Party."

78. Somer and McCoy, "Transformations through Polarizations."

79. Somer, "Turkey: The Slippery Slope."

80. Senem Aydın-Düzgit and Evren Balta, *Turkey after the July 15th Coup Attempt: When Elites Polarize over Polarization* (Istanbul: Istanbul Policy Center, August 2017); S. Erdem Aytaç, Ali Çarkoğlu, and Kerem Yıldırım, "Taking Sides: Determinants of Support for a Presidential System in Turkey," *South European Society and Politics* 22, no. 1 (2017): 1–20; KONDA, *Konda Barometer* (Istanbul: 2017), available at http://konda.com.tr/en/konda-barometer; Emre Erdogan and Pınar Uyan Semerci, *Fanus'ta Diyaloglar: Türkiye'de Kutuplaşmanın Boyutları* [Dialogues in Bell Glass: The Dimensions of Polarization in Turkey] (Istanbul: Bilgi Üniversitesi Yayınları, 2018); Somer, "Turkey: The Slippery Slope."

81. Özpek, *The Peace Process*, 61.

82. Özge Mumcu, "Anayasa Uzlaşma Komisyonu: Kısa bir değerlendirme notu [Constitutional Consensus Commission: A Brief Note of Evaluation]," *T24*, January 18, 2013. https://t24.com.tr/yazarlar/ozge-mumcu/anayasa-uzlasma-komisyonu-kisa-bir-degerlendirme-notu,6121 (accessed June 30, 2019).

83. Video of Selahattin Demirtaş's meeting with members of the press, published by the HDP on December 5, 2015: https://www.youtube.com/watch?v=nVEC-1-N9gc (accessed June 30, 2019). For an evaluation of the talks from the point of view of Öcalan and HDP, see also Abdullah Öcalan, *Demokratik Kurtuluş ve Özgür Yaşamı İnşa: İmralı Notları* [Democratic Liberation and Constructing Free Life: Notes from İmralı] (Neuss, Germany: Mezopotamien Verlag, 2015). In February 2019, the German government shut down the publisher Mezopotamien Verlag citing its links with the PKK: "Almanya Mezopotamya Yayınevini Yasakladı [Germany Banned the Mesopotamia Publishing House]," *Gazete Duvar*, February 12, 2019. https://www.gazeteduvar.com.tr/dunya/2019/02/12/almanyada-mezopotamya-yayinevi-kapatildi/ (accessed March 8, 2019). Also see International Crisis Group, "Sisyphean Task? Resuming Turkey-Pkk Peace Talks," *Crisis Group Europe Briefing*, no. 77 (Istanbul/Brussels: 2015)

84. Özpek, *The Peace Process*, 64.

85. Video of Demirtaş's statement, "Selahattin Demirtaş: Seni Başkan Yaptırmayacağız [We Will Not Allow You to Become President]," published by *Al Jazeera Turk* on March 17, 2019: https://www.youtube.com/watch?v=FwKUBhyny8Y (accessed June 30, 2019).

86. "Erdoğan: 400 milletvekilini verin ve bu iş huzur içinde çözülsün [Give 400 MPs and let this [problem] be resolved with peace of mind]," *T24*, March 7, 2015: https://t24.com.tr/haber/cumhurbaskani-erdogan-gaziantepte-konusuyor,289627 (accessed June 30, 2019).

87. "Erdoğan 400 vekil istedi! [Erdoğan Asked for 400 MPs!]," *Sözcü*, February 6, 2015. https://www.sozcu.com.tr/2015/gundem/erdogan-konusuyor-100-735227/ (accessed June 30, 2019).

88. Ödül Celep, "Can the Kurdish Left Contribute to Turkey's Democratization?" *Insight Turkey* 16, no. 3 (2014): 165–80.

89. Ersin Kalaycıoğlu, "*Kulturkampf* in Turkey: The Constitutional Referendum of 12 September 2010," *Turkish Studies* 17, no. 1 (2012): 1–22.

90. Erdem Yörük and Murat Yüksel, "Class and Politics in Turkey's Gezi Protests," *New Left Review* 89 (September–October 2014): 7–8; Tufekci, *Twitter and Tear Gas.*

91. Krajeski, "In Taksim Square, Where Are the Kurds?." Also see Tufekci, *Twitter and Tear Gas* for individual Turk/Kurd experiences during the protests.

92. Sinan Ciddi, *Kemalism in Turkish Politics: The Republican People's Party, Secularism, and Nationalism* (London: Routledge, 2009); Yunus Sözen, "Politics of the People: Hegemonic Ideology and Regime Oscillation in Turkey and Argentina" (PhD Dissertation, New York University, 2010); Berk Esen, "Nation-Building, Party-Strength, and Regime Consolidation: Kemalism in Comparative Perspective," *Turkish Studies* 15, no. 4 (2014): 600–20; Yunus Emre, "Why Has Social Democracy not Developed in Turkey? Analysis of an Atypical Case," *Journal of Balkan and Near Eastern Studies* 17, no. 4 (2015): 392–407.

93. Murat Somer, *Sosyal Demokratlar ve Türkiye'de Kürt Sorunu* [Social Democrats and the Kurdish Question in Turkey] (Ankara: Bencekitap Yayınları, 2016).

94. Linz and Stepan, *Problems of Democratic Transition and Consolidation,* 61.

95. For a technical formulation of this question in terms of technical game theory, see Somer, "Why Aren't Kurds Like the Scots and The Turks Like the Brits?"

96. Barkey and Fuller, *Turkey's Kurdish Question.* Also see Kurt, *Kurdish Hizbullah in Turkey* and Gareth Jenkins, *Political Islam in Turkey: Running West, Heading East* (New York: Palgrave Macmillan, 2008).

97. Ümit Cizre, "A New Politics of Engagement: The Turkish Military, Society, and the AKP," in *Democracy, Islam, and Secularism in Turkey,* ed. Ahmet T. Kuru and Alfred Stepan (New York: Columbia University Press, 2012), 122–48.

98. Cemal, *Kürtler,* 68–70. Also see H. Akin Ünver, "Turkey's 'Deep-State' and the Ergenekon Conundrum," *The Middle East Institute Policy Brief,* no. 23 (April 2009): 1–25. Michael M. Gunter, "Turkey, Kemalism, and the 'Deep State,'" in *Conflict, Democratization, and the Kurds in the Middle East: Turkey, Iran, Iraq, and Syria,* ed. David Romano and Mehmet Gurses (New York: Palgrave Macmillan, 2014), 17–40.

99. Ersel Aydinli, "Ergenekon, New Pacts, and the Decline of the Turkish 'Inner State,'" *Turkish Studies* 12, no. 2 (2011): 227–39; Gunter, "Turkey, Kemalism, and the 'Deep State,'"; Şebnem Gümüşçü, "The Clash of Islamists: The Crisis of the Turkish State and Democracy," *POMEPS Studies* 22 (2016): 6–11; M. Hakan

Yavuz and Bayram Balcı, eds., *Turkey's July 15th Coup: What Happened and Why* (Salt Lake City: The University of Utah Press, 2018); Özpek, *The Peace Process*.

100. Cengiz Güneş, "The Rise of the Pro-Kurdish Democratic Movement in Turkey," in *Routledge Handbook on the Kurds*, ed. Michael M. Gunter (New York: Rouledge), 259–69, 262. See also Sahin-Mencutek, "Strong in the Movement, Strong in the Party."

101. Zeynep Gambetti and Joost Jongerden, eds., *The Kurdish Issue in Turkey: A Spatial Perspective* (New York: Routledge, 2015).

102. "Turkey Arrests pro-Kurdish Party Leaders amid Claims of Internet Shutdown," *Guardian*, November 4, 2016. https://www.theguardian.com/world/2016/nov/04/turkey-arrests-pro-kurdish-party-leaders-mps (accessed July 1, 2019).

103. Somer, "Why Aren't Kurds Like the Scots?"

104. *KADEP Party Program* (Ankara, 2006), 19–20.

105. Democratic Society Party, *Demokratik Toplum Partisi'nin Kürt Sorununa İlişkin Çözüm Projesi* [The DTP's Resolution Project for the Kurdist Conflict], 5. Also see "Öcalan: T.C. Vatandaşlığını Üst Kimlik Olarak Kabul Ediyoruz [Öcalan: We Accept Citizenship of the Republic of Turkey as a Supra-Identity]," *Milliyet* newspaper, December 6, 2005.

106. Among other sources, the author's interviews with members of the DTP and civil society actors in Diyarbakır, June 2006.

107. Infacto Research Workshop with the support of Istanbul Bilgi University. "Türkiye'de Milliyetçilik Araştırması [Nationalism in Turkey Research]," *Tempo* 14, no. 957 (2006): 32.

108. Milliyet-Konda, *Biz Kimiz: Toplumsal Yapı Araştırması* 2006, 35–36.

109. Somer, "Why Aren't Kurds Like the Scots?" 239; for table and corrections see http://cac.sagepub.com/content/44/2/166.full.pdf. Also see Osman Şahin, "Middle Class Formation and Democratization: Comparison of Political Islam and Kurds in Turkey," (MA Thesis in International Relations, Koç University, 2008). Also see Kılıç, "Interests, Passions, and Politics."

110. Asli S. Okyay, "Turkey's Post-2011 Approach to Its Syrian Border and Its Implications for Domestic Politics," *International Affairs* 93, no. 4 (2017): 829–46, 829. Also see Ziya Öniş, "Turkey and the Arab Revolutions: Boundaries of Regional Power Influence in a Turbulent Middle East," *Mediterranean Politics* 19, no. 2 (2014): 203–19.

111. Behlül Ozkan, "Turkey, Davutoglu, and the Idea of Pan-Islamism," *Survival* 56, no. 4 (2014): 119–40.

112. F. Stephen Larrabee, "Turkey and the Changing Dynamics of the Kurdish Issue," *Survival* 58, no. 2 (2016): 67–73.

113. "Under Kurdish Rule: Abuses in PYD-run Enclaves of Syria," Human Rights Watch Report, June 14, 2019. https://www.hrw.org/report/2014/06/19/under-kurdish-rule/abuses-pyd-run-enclaves-syria (accessed July 4, 2019).

114. Okyay, "Turkey's Post-2011 Approach to Its Syrian Border," 843.

115. Cansu Çamlıbel, "PYD lideri Salih Müslim: Ankara'nın Şam'la savaşında asker olmayız [PYD Leader Müslim: We Will not Be Soldiers in Ankara's War with Damascus]," *Hürriyet*, October 13, 2014. http://www.hurriyet.com.tr/dunya/pyd-lideri-salih-muslim-ankaranin-samla-savasinda-asker-olmayiz-27373368 (accessed July 4, 2019).

116. "Erdogan Warns Kobani Is 'About to Fall to Isis' as Militants Advance on Syria-Turkey Border Town," *Independent*, October 7, 2014. https://www.independent.co.uk/news/world/middle-east/isis-fighters-in-kobani-civilians-flee-as-militants-enter-syria-turkey-border-town-9778770.html (accessed July 4, 2019).

117. People who lost their lives included HÜDA-PAR as well as HDP supporters, Turkish ultra-nationalists, and security personnel. Ali Dağlar, "6–7 Ekim'in Acı Bilançosu: 50 Ölü [The Bitter Balance Sheet of October 6–7: 50 Deaths]," *Hürriyet*, November 6, 2014. http://www.hurriyet.com.tr/6-7-ekim-in-aci-bilancosu-50-olu-27525777 (accessed December 4, 2018). Mehmet Kurt observes that while "Hüda-Par's programme [previously] featured many elements in common with that of Hizbullah's rival HDP/BDP vis-à-vis the Kurdish issue in Turkey . . . this was reversed as a result of the Kobanê protests in 2014 . . . .The Şeyh Said Seriyyeleri (Sheikh Said Brigades), the armed wing of 'civil' Hizbullah, emerged during this period." Kurt, *Kurdish Hizbullah in Turkey*, vii. Also see Okyay, "Turkey's Post-2011 Approach to Its Syrian Border," 841–844.

118. Leezenberg, "The Ambiguities of Democratic Autonomy," 682. Also see Amy Austin Holmes, "What the Battle for Kobane Says about U.S. Overseas Military Bases," *Washington Post*, February 2, 2015.

119. Michael Keating, "What's Wrong with Asymmetrical Government," in *Remaking the Union*, ed. H. Elcock and M. Keating (London: Frank Cass, 1998), 195–218 and *The Government of Scotland: Public Policy Making After Devolution*.

120. Nebi Kesen, *Avrupa Birliği-Türkiye İlişkileri ve Kürtler* [The Relationship between the EU and Turkey, and the Kurds] (Spånga, Sweden: Apec Förlah, 2003); İbrahim Saylan, "The Europeanization Process and Kurdish Nationalism in Turkey: The Case of the Democratic Society Party," *Nationalities Papers* 40, no. 2 (March 2012): 185–202.

121. Johanna Nykänen, "Identity, Narrative, and Frames: Assessing Turkey's Kurdish Narratives," *Insight Turkey* 15, no. 2 (2013): 85–101.

122. For two opinion pieces on these subjects see Murat Somer, "Turkey's Model of 'Moderate Islamism' Can be Misleading," *The National*, October 1, 2012. http://www.thenational.ae/thenationalconversation/comment/turkeys-model-of-moderate-islamism-can-be-misleading (accessed July 4, 2019); "Demokrasiyi Müslüman Liberalizminde Arayamayız [We Can't Look for Democracy in Muslim Liberalism]," *T24*, October 28, 2013. http://t24.com.tr/yazarlar/murat-somer/demokrasiyi-musluman-liberalizmin-de-arayamayiz,7695.

123. Baskın Oran, " 'Ulus-Devlet' Fransa ["Nation-State" France]," *Radikal 2*, September 28, 2008.

124. Weber, *Peasants into Frenchmen*, 18–19, 132–35. For a recent and essential analysis of French and Turkish nation-building models see, Cengiz Aktar, "Osmanlı Kozmopolitizminden Avrupa Kozmopolitizmine Giden Yolda Ulus Parantezi [An Excursus on Nation: From Ottoman Cosmopolitanism to European Cosmopolitanism]," in *Milliyetçilik* (Nationalism), ed. Tanıl Bora (Istanbul: İletişim Yayınları, 2002), 77–80.

125. Oran, "'Ulus-Devlet' Fransa."

126. Zürcher, *İmparatorluktan Cumhuriyet'e.*

127. Ibid., 9–13.

128. Taner Akçam, "Sevr ve Lozan'ın Başka Tarihi [A Different History of the Sèvres and the Lausanne]," in *İmparatorluktan Cumhuriyete Etnik Çatışma* [Ethnic Conflict in Turkey from Empire to Republic], ed. Erik Jan Zürcher (Istanbul: İletişim Yayınları).

129. Şeker also asserts that Turkish nationalism might have evolved to become more tolerant of Christian minorities. Nesim Şeker, "Türklük ve Osmanlı Arasında: Birinci Dünya Savaşı Sonrası Türkiye'de 'Milliyet' Arayışları ya da 'Anasır Meselesi' [Between Turkishness and the Ottomans: The Quest for 'Nationality' or the 'Unity of the Elements' Post-World War I]," in *İmparatorluktan Cumhuriyete Etnik Çatışma* [Ethnic Conflict in Turkey from Empire to Republic], ed. Erik Jan Zürcher (Istanbul: İletişim Yayınları, 2005). Zürcher questions the probability of these two fictional scenarios. Zürcher, ed., *İmparatorluktan Cumhuriyete Etnik Çatışma*, 14–15.

130. Bozarslan, "Kurdish Nationalism."

131. Fikret Adanır, "Bulgaristan, Yunanistan ve Türkiye Üçgeninde Ulus İnşası ve Nüfus Değişimi [Nation-Building and Population Exchange in Bulgaria, Greece, and Turkey Triangle]," in *İmparatorluktan Cumhuriyete Etnik Çatışma* [Ethnic Conflict in Turkey from Empire to Republic], ed. Erik Jan Zürcher (Istanbul: İletişim Yayınları, 2005).

132. Cemal, *Kürtler*, 543–44.

133. White, *Muslim Nationalism and the New Turks*, 93.

134. Ibid., 95–96.

135. Kezer, *Building Modern Turkey: State, Space, and Ideology in the Early Republic.*

136. İnalcık, *Türklük, Müslümanlık ve Osmanlılık Mirası*, 21–22.

137. As one Turkish Islamist poet and intellectual expressed it in its most radical form, "One who does not perform *salaat* (Muslim daily prayers) cannot be Turkish." "İsmet Özel: Namaz Kılmayan Türk Olamaz! [İsmet Özel: One Who Does Not Perform Prayer Cannot Be Turkish!]," *T24*, February 26, 2013. http://t24.com.tr/haber/ismet-ozel-namaz-kilmayan-turk-olamaz/224563.

138. For contending views from mainstream media, see, Şahin Alpay, "Önemli Olan Ayrımcılığın Son Bulması [What Matters Is that Discrimination Ends]," *Zaman* newspaper, November 9, 2004; Can Dündar, "Atatürk'ün Sansürlenen Demeci [Atatürk's Censored Statement]," *Milliyet* newspaper, October 30,

2006; Oktay Ekşi, "Malum Rapor Üstüne [About a Certain Report]," *Hürriyet* newspaper, October 21, 2004; "Genelkurmay'dan Azınlık Tepkisi [General Staff's Minority Reaction]," *Milliyet* newspaper, November 2, 2004; Ömer Lütfi Mete, "Yine 'Türkiyelilik' Sihirbazlığına Dair [Again on the Wizardry of 'Türkiyelilik']," *Sabah* newspaper, October 29, 2004; Derya Sazak, "Cumhuriyetimiz Tek Soya İndirgenemez, Prof Kaboğlu ile Söyleşi" [Our Republic Cannot be Boiled Down to a Single Lineage, Interview with Prof Kaboğlu]," *Milliyet* newspaper, November 1, 2004; Haluk Şahin, "Türkiyeli, Türk, Alt-Kimlik, Üst-Kimlik [Türkiyeli, Turkish, Supra-Identity, Sub-Identity]," *Radikal* newspaper, October 22, 2004.

139. Hrant Dink, *Bu Köşedeki Adam* [The Man in This Corner] (Istanbul: International Hrant Dink Foundation Publications, 2009), 42; *Agos* newspaper, September 12, 2003.

140. Deniz Ülke Arıboğan, "Türk kimliği meselesi! [The Turkish identity question!]," *Akşam* newspaper, May 17, 2013.

141. The simplification belongs to me. In the original interview, it is referred to as "those who are nationalist" and "those who are Turkist."

142. Neşe Düzel, "1923 Müslümanlara 'Türk' Dedi [1923 Called Muslims 'Turkish']," interview with Hüsamettin Arslan, *Radikal* newspaper, December 19, 2005.

143. Bahar Rumelili and Ayşe Betül Çelik, "Ontological Insecurity in Asymmetric Conflicts: Reflections on Agonistic Peace in Turkey's Kurdish Issue," *Security Dialogue* 48, no. 4 (2017): 279–96, 292.

144. Berman, "Ideational Theorizing."

145. Gabriel Mitchell, "Islam as Peacemaker: The AKP's Attempt at a Kurdish Resolution," *The Washington Review of Turkish and Eurasian Affairs*, May 2012, https://www.academia.edu/1553925/Islam_as_Peacemaker_The_AKPs_Attempt_at_a_Kurdish_Resolution (accessed July 5, 2019). More nuanced studies have reached more cautious yet similar results. For example, Hakan Yavuz and Nihat Ali Özcan, "The Kurdish Question and Turkey's Justice and Development Party," *Middle East Policy* 13, no. 1 (2006): 102–19; Hüseyin Yayman, *Türkiye'nin Kürt Sorunu Algısı* [Turkey's Kurdish Conflict Recollection] (Ankara: SETA ve Pollmark, Ağustos 2009); Aktürk, *Regimes of Ethnicity*; Şener Aktürk, "İslamcılığın Kürt Açılımı [The Kurdish Opening of Islamism]," in *İslamcılık Tartışmaları* [Discussions on Islamism], ed. Seyfullah Özkurt (Istanbul: Ufuk Kitap, 2012), 297–301; White, *Muslim Nationalism and the New Turks*.

146. Durukan Kuzu, "The Politics of Turkish Nationalism: Continuity and Change," in *Routledge Handbook of Turkish Politics*, ed. Alpaslan Özerdem and Matthew Whiting (London: Routledge, 2019), 69–79, 76.

147. İlker Aytürk, "Post-Post-Kemalizm: Yeni Bir Paradigmayı Beklerken," *Birikim* 319 (2015): 34–48.

148. R. Hrair Dekmejian, "The Anatomy of Islamic Revival: Legitimacy Crisis, Ethnic Conflict, and the Search for Islamic Alternatives," *Middle East Journal* 34, no. 1 (1980): 1–12.

149. Somer and Glüpker-Kesebir, "Is Islam the Solution?,"; Mehmet Gurses and Nicolas Rost, "Religion as a Peacemaker? Peace Duration after Ethnic Civil Wars," *Politics and Religion* 10, no. 2 (2016): 339–62.

150. Christopher Houston, *Islam, Kurds, and the Turkish Nation State* (New York: Berg, 2003); Somer and Glüpker-Kesebir, "Is Islam the Solution?"; Mehmet Gürses, "Is Islam a Cure for Ethnic Conflict? Evidence from Turkey," *Politics and Religion* 8 (March 2015): 135–54.

151. Hayrettin Karaman, "Altan Tan Kardeşime [To My Brother, Altan Tan]," *Yeni Şafak* newspaper, May 24, 2012.

152. Sakallıoğlu, "Kurdish Nationalism from an Islamist Perspective: The Discourses of Turkish Islamist Writers," 77.

153. Ruşen Çakır, "Erbakan 20 yıl önce ne yapmıştı? [What did Erbakan do 20 years ago?]," *Vatan* newspaper, January 3, 2011. For a video of the speech see http://www.youtube.com/watch?v=vLVa1jLyipA. (Accessed December 25, 2013).

154. Speech by İhsan M. Arslan. Association of Human Rights and Solidarity for Oppressed People (Mazlum-Der), *Kurdish Conflict Forum 12* (Ankara: Sor Yayıncılık, 1993), 16–17.

155. *Yeni Şafak, Zaman* and *Milli Gazete,* and *Milliyet* and *Cumhuriyet* respectively.

156. Somer, "Media Values and Democratization,"; "Does It Take Democrats to Democratize?,"; Murat Somer, "Islamist Political Parties, the Turkish Case, and the Future of Muslim Polities," in *Strategies and Behavior of Islamist Political Parties: Lessons from Asia and the Middle East,* ed. Quinn Mecham and Julie Chernov Hwang (Philadelphia: University of Pennsylvania Press, 2014), 41–57; Somer and Glüpker-Kesebir, "Is Islam the Solution?"

157. Unless I state otherwise, all the differences between the sets of newspaper and between individual papers were found to be statistically significant at least within the 99 percent confidence interval, based on standard two-tail t tests. Somer, "Media Values and Democratization," 555–77. Somer and Glüpker-Kesebir, "Is Islam the Solution?"

158. Somer, "Turkey: The Slippery Slope"; "Understanding Turkey's Democratic Breakdown"; Bilge Yeşil, *Media in New Turkey: The Origins of an Authoritarian Neoliberal State* (Urbana: University of Illinois Press, 2016).

159. For definitional issues, the complexity and particularity of the religion versus secularism question and contending views in Turkey, see, among others: Somer, "Turkish Secularism: Looking Forward and Beyond the West"; Ahmet Kuru and Alfred Stepan, eds., *Democracy, Islam, and Secularism in Turkey* (New York: Columbia University Press, 2012).

160. Thus, the ideas inferred by the analysis cannot be explained either through the re-escalation of violence or the intellectual support for opposition to the government's policies in pro-government and government-critical press.

161. The pro-secular and pro-religious papers in this sample were *Hürriyet* and *Milliyet, and Zaman* and *Yeni Şafak* respectively. Analyzing issues published on the first, tenth, twentieth, and last day of each month, a total of 1,412 articles were found relevant and analyzed from a total of 384 newspaper issues.

162. Somer, "Islamist Political Parties."

163. For these findings, see, Somer, "Media Values and Democratization," "Does It Take Democrats to Democratize?" "Moderation of Religious and Secular Politics," and "Islamist Political Parties."

164. However, since there is a low number of observations, the difference between the two groups was statistically vague.

165. For the full transcript of this address, on the AKP website, visit: http.// www.akparti.org.tr/site%20haberler/1-haziran-diyarbakir-mitingi-konusmasinin-tam-metni/8230. For a video of his address, visit: http.//www.youtube.com/ watch?v=4WSrMKmMY14. (Accessed March 3, 2013). Both records were later deleted from these links.

166. Somer and Liaras, "Turkey's New Kurdish Opening: Religious and Secular Values," 152–65.

167. In principle, a lack of discussion of an issue can also reflect ideational preparedness, since well-considered and settled questions may not need discussion. In a consolidated, stable, and inclusive democracy, for example, one may not see much discussion of democracy and democratic reforms since there is widespread agreement on what democracy is and how it can be protected. However, as the previous chapters should have shown, this was clearly not the case with the Kurdish Question in Turkey. On the contrary, there was a violent conflict and a dearth of knowledge and agreement on how to resolve it.

168. "Education" (*anadilde eğitim*) refers to Kurdish being the main language of instruction in a school whereas "teaching" refers to Kurdish language courses or some subjects being taught in Kurdish.

169. However, one of the reasons behind this was that we analyzed different newspapers in 2007 and 2010.

170. Yavuz and Balcı, eds., *Turkey's July 15th Coup: What Happened and Why*; Gareth Jenkins, "Ergenekon, Sledgehammer, and the Politics of Turkish Justice: Conspiracies and Coincidences," *MERIA* 15, no. 2 (2011): 1–9 and *Political Islam in Turkey: Running West, Heading East*; Berna Turam, *Between Islam and the State: The Politics of Engagement* (Stanford: Stanford University Press, 2007); M. Hakan Yavuz and John L. Esposito, eds., *Turkish Islam and the Secular State: The Gülen Movement* (Syracuse: Syracuse University Press, 2003); Houston, *Islam, Kurds, and the Turkish Nation State.*

171. Mehmet Gürses, "Islamists, Democracy and Turkey: A Test of the Inclusion-Moderation Hypothesis," *Party Politics* 20, no. 4 (2012): 646–53.

172. Houston, *Islam, Kurds, and the Turkish Nation State.*

173. Ibid., 161.

174. Ibid., 172.

175. Sakallıoğlu, "Kurdish Nationalism from an Islamist Perspective," 80.

176. Sami Zubaida, "Introduction," in *The Kurds: A Contemporary Overview*, ed. Philip G. Kreyenbroek and Stefan Sperl (London: Routledge, 1991), 1–7.

177. Ibid., 6–7.

178. Sakallıoğlu, "Kurdish Nationalism from an Islamist Perspective"; Yavuz, "Five Stages of the Construction of Kurdish Nationalism in Turkey."

179. Gülay Türkmen, "Negotiating Symbolic Boundaries in Conflict Resolution: Religion and Ethnicity in Turkey's Kurdish Conflict," *Qualitative Sociology* 41, no. 4 (2018): 569–91, 584–85.

180. Sakallıoğlu, "Kurdish Nationalism from an Islamist Perspective," 74. Also see Cuma Çiçek, "Kurdish Identity and Political Islam under Akp Rule," *Research and Policy on Turkey* 1, no. 2 (2016): 147–63.

181. Karakoç and Sarıgil. "Why Religious People Support Ethnic Insurgency?"

182. Murat Somer, "Moderate Islam and Secularist Opposition in Turkey," in particular 1272–74.

183. Somer and Glüpker-Kesebir, "Is Islam the Solution?"; Somer, "Turkey's Model of 'Moderate Islamism,'"; "Demokrasiyi Müslüman Liberalizminde Arayamayız."

## Chapter 7

1. Constitutional court decision; Principle no: 1993/3 (closing political parties); Decision no: 1994/2; Decision date: 16/06/1994; Prosecutor: Supreme Court of Appeals Prosecutor's Office; Defendant: The Democracy Party.

2. Rodrigue, "Reflections on Millets and Minorities: Ottoman Legacies."

3. One might also mention here the absolutist rhetoric of the ruling that gave the impression that the social and political laws and conventions on which the court was ruling were as certain and immutable as well-established natural laws.

4. Durukan Kuzu, "The Politics of Identity, Recognition, and Multiculturalism: The Kurds in Turkey," *Nations and Nationalism* 22, no. 1 (2016): 123–42; Umut Ozkirimli, "Multiculturalism, Recognition, and the 'Kurdish Question' in Turkey: The Outline of a Normative Framework," *Democratization* 21, no. 6 (2013): 1055–73.

5. Anne Philips, "Democracy and Difference: Some Problems for Feminist Theory," in *The Rights of Minority Cultures*, ed. Kymlicka, 288–99.

6. Brubaker, *Ethnicity without Groups*; Kymlicka, *Multicultural Citizenship: A Liberal Theory of Minority Rights and Politics in the Vernacular*.

7. Following the court's apparent logic, it could be inferred that having minority rights makes non-Muslim citizens unequal citizens, which would be a constitutional violation.

8. Hülya Karabağlı, "Atilla Kart: Devlet Herkesin Anadilini Öğrenmesinin Yolunu Açmalı [Atilla Kart: The State Should Pave the Way for Everyone to Learn Their Native Language]," *T24*, September 16, 2013. https://t24.com.tr/haber/atilla-kart-devlet-herkesin-anadilini-ogrenmesinin-yolunu-acmali,239648 (accessed July 12, 2019).

9. For a critique and alternative account, Murat Somer, "Demokratikleşme Paketi ve Çift Dilli Eğitim [Democratization Package and Bilingual Education]," *T24*, October 6, 2013. https://t24.com.tr/haber/demokratiklesme-paketi-ve-cift-dilli-egitim,241267 (last accessed July 12, 2019).

10. *Türkiye'de yetmişiki millet var.*

11. Stepan, Linz, and Yadav, *Crafting State Nations*, 1.

12. Tan, *Kürt Sorunu*, 365.

13. Perinçek, Kemalist Devrim—4: Kurtuluş Savaşı'nda Kürt Politikası, 115.

14. Ibid., 105–106.

15. This term, or rather noun, could also be translated as "Muslim Components," "Islamic Components," or "Components of a Nation of Islam." It was a term used in late Ottoman times to refer to the ethnic/cultural peoples who made up a nation of Ottoman Muslims.

16. *Atatürk'ün Bütün Eserleri*, vol. 8, 157.

17. Republic of Turkey, Ministry of Foreign Affairs, *50 Years of Turkey's Foreign Policy*, 82.

18. *Türk Parlamento Tarihi, Milli Mücadele ve TBMM I. Dönem, 1919–1923* [History of the Turkish Parliament, the National Struggle and the Grand National Assembly of Turkey Term I, 1919–1923], vol. II (TBMM Vakfı Yayınları, 1995), 363. The provinces are Bitlis, Erzurum, Kastamonu, Mardin, Muş, Siirt, Urfa, Pozan, Diyarbakır, and Van.

19. Baskın Oran, "The Minority Concept and Rights in Turkey: The Lausanne Peace Treaty and Current Issues," in *Human Rights in Turkey*, ed. Zehra F. Kabasakal Arat (Philadelphia: University of Pennsylvania Press, 2007), 35–56.

20. Oran, "The Minority Concept and Rights."

21. Afet İnan, *Medeni bilgiler ve M. Kemal Atatürk'ün El Yazıları* [Civic Knowledge: M. Kemal Atatürk's Handwritten Writings] (Ankara: Atatürk Kültür, Dil ve Tarih Yüksek Kurumu Atatürk Araştırma Merkezi, 2000), 28.

22. Yaycioglu, *Partners of the Empire.*

23. Kristin Fabbe, *Disciples of the State?*

24. *TBMM Gizli Celse Kayıtları*, 6 March 1922–27 February 1923, vol. 3, 1153.

25. Ottoman administrative unit.

26. *Atatürk'ün Bütün Eserleri*, vol. 14, 273–74.

27. Uygun, "Federalizm ve Bölgesel Özerkilik Tartışmaları."

28. The principle formally entered the constitution in 1961.

29. Archives of the Grand National Assembly of Turkey: https://www.tbb.gov.tr/mevzuat/kanunlar/Avrupa_Yerel_Yonetimler_ozerklik_Sarti.pdf (accessed December 7, 2018); Memurlar.net, "Kamu yönetimi reformunun veto gerekçeleri

[Basis of the Veto of the Public Administrative Reform]," August 3, 2004, https://www.memurlar.net/haber/8722/ (accessed December 7, 2018).

30. Weller and Nobbs, eds., *Asymmetric Autonomy and the Settlement of Ethnic Conflicts*; Michael Keating, *Plurinational Democracy: Stateless Nations in a Post-Sovereignty Era* (Oxford: Oxford University Press, 2002).

31. Caroline A. Hartzell and Matthew Hoddie, "The Art of the Possible: Power Sharing and Post Civil War Democracy," *World Politics* 67 (2015): 37–71; Giuditta Fontana, Argyro Kartsonaki, Natascha S. Neudorfer, Dawn Walsh, Stefan Wolff, and Christalla Yakinthou, "The Dataset of Political Agreements in Internal Conflicts (Paic)," *Conflict Management and Peace Science* 38, no. 3 (2020): 338–64.

32. Stepan, Linz, and Yadav, *Crafting State Nations*, 15.

33. Keith Banning and Will Kymlicka, eds., *Multiculturalism and the Welfare* (Oxford: Oxford University Press, 2006).

34. Findley, *The Turks in World History*.

35. For example, see Mümtaz'er Türköne, "Türklük Tanımı [The Definition of Turkishness]," *Zaman*, September 18, 2007.

36. Stepan, Linz, and Yadav, *Crafting State Nations*, 13; Jan-Werner Muller, *Constitutional Patriotism* (Princeton: Princeton University Press, 2007).

37. Murat Somer, "Kürt Açılımı, Çoğul Gerçekler ve Kimlikler [The Kurdish Opening, Plural Realities and Identities]," *Radikal* newspaper, September 25, 2009; Murat Somer, "Vatandaşlık Tanımı için Atatürk Referans Alınmalı [Atatürk Should be Taken as Reference for a Definition of Citizenship]," Interview, *Akşam*, February 11, 2013. http://aksam.com.tr/roportaj/vatandaslik-tanimi-icin-ataturk-referans-alinmali/haber-168960 (last accessed July 16, 2019).

38. See note 14.

39. Roe, *Ethnic Violence*.

40. Hicks, *Dignity*.

41. Somer, "Defensive and Liberal Nationalisms."

42. Sibel Bozdoğan and Reşat Kasaba, eds., *Rethinking Modernity and National Identity in Turkey* (Seattle: University of Washington Press, 1997).

43. For example, see Vali, ed., *Kürt Milliyetçiliğinin Kökenleri*, 22–23. Özkırımlı also uses the Turkish equivalent of *imaginary community* despite stating Anderson's view that nations are not "fake," as are not other social identities. Özkırımlı, *Milliyetçilik Kuramları: Eleştirel Bir Bakış*. Also see Fisher et al., "National Identity Is Made Up."

44. Anderson, *Imagined Communities*. See also "I like nationalism's utopian elements," interview with Benedict Anderson by Lorenz Khazaleh at the Kapittel Stavanger at the International Festival of Literature and Freedom of Speech, December 15, 2005, https://www.antropologi.info/blog/anthropology/2005/interview_with_benedict_anderson_i_like (last accessed July 15, 2019).

45. Lakoff, *The Political Mind*; Jonathan Haidt, *The Righteous Mind: Why Good People Are Divided by Politics and Religion* (New York: Vintage, 2012).

46. Bozarslan, "Türkiye'de (1919–1980) Yazılı Kürt Tarihi Söylemi Üzerine Bazı Hususlar," 39.

47. For a theoretical and empirical argument on this subject, see, Somer, "Cascades of Ethnic Polarization."

48. World Values Survey (2009), 2005 Official Data File v.20090901. World Values Survey Association, Values Surveys Databank, http://www.wvsevsdb.com/wvs/WVSData.jsp (last accessed November 14, 2013).

49. The remaining percentages correlate to those who opted to express the opinion that it was "neither important nor unimportant." Konda, *Kürt Meselesi'nde Algı ve Beklentiler*, 101.

# Chapter 8

1. John Dreijmanis, ed., *Max Weber's Complete Writings on Academic and Political Vocations* (New York: Algora, 2008).

2. Berman, *The Primacy of Politics*.

3. Diamond, *Ill Winds*, 14.

4. Akyürekli, *Türklerle Kürtler*, 221. "*Kurucu*" could also be translated as "constitutive" or "foundational." A related demand has been the recognition of Kurds as a principal or constitutive component ("*asli unsur*" or "*kurucu asli unsur*"). In accordance with these discussions, a recent constitutional reform proposal suggested defining the nation as "the Turkish nation of which every citizen is a constitutive component" (*Her ferdin asli unsuru olduğu Türk milleti*). "İlk dört maddenin dili düzeltilecek" (The language of the first four articles will be fixed), *Türkiye*, September 10, 2021; https://m.turkiyegazetesi.com.tr/gundem/802665.aspx (accessed October 7, 2021).

5. Somer, "Vatandaşlık Tanımı için Atatürk Referans Alınmalı." The current article states: "Everyone bound to the Turkish state through the bond of citizenship is a Turk."

6. I am not referring to the "political and cultural nationalism" distinction discussed in nationalism studies or to the distinction between "ethnic and civic nationalism" which I discussed in chapter 2. Nor am I making any claims as to which version of nation is more "real" or "positive," nor trying to classify different nationalist movements as exclusively cultural or political. What I mean here is that for the same group, movement, and even individual, the concept of nation can be used to mean different things at different times and in different contexts.

7. "Turkic Republics on the 20th Anniversary of Their Independence," October 5–6, 2011, Kavaklıdere, Ankara. http://sam.gov.tr/conference-on-the-turkish-republics-at-the-20th-anniversary-of-their-independence/.

8. http://sam.gov.tr/tr/conference-on-the-turkish-republics-at-the-20th-anniversary-of-their-independence/. (accessed August 5, 2019).

9. Clive Church and Paolo Dardanelli, "The Dynamics of Confederalism and Federalism: Comparing Switzerland and the EU," *Regional & Federal Studies* 15, no. 2 (2005): 163–85. For the PKK demand for confederalism in Turkey, see Abdullah Öcalan, *Democratic Confederalism* (Honolulu: Transmedia Publishing, 2015). See also Ahmet Hamdi Akkaya and Joost Jongerden, "Confederalism and Autonomy in Turkey: The Kurdistan Workers' Party and the Reinvention of Democracy," in *The Kurdish Question in Turkey: New Perspectives on Violence, Representation, and Reconciliation*, ed. Cengiz Güneş and Welat Zeydanlıoğlu (London: Routledge, 2014), 186–204.

10. Rudy B. Andeweg, "Consociational Democracy," *Annual Review of Political Science* 3 (2000): 509–36.

11. Somer, "Kürt Açılımı, Çoğul Gerçekler ve Kimlikler."

12. Hence, Section 2 of the Preliminary Part of the Spanish Constitution dated 1978 states: "The Constitution is based on the indissoluble unity of the Spanish Nation, the common and indivisible homeland of all Spaniards; it recognises [*sic*] and guarantees the right to selfgovernment [*sic*] of the nationalities and regions of which it is composed and the solidarity among them all." http://www.congreso.es/portal/page/portal/Congreso/Congreso/Hist_Normas/Norm/const_espa_texto_ingles_0.pdf (accessed August 7, 2019). Also see endnote 13, ch. 7.

13. Robert Colls, *Identity of England*, 42–43.

14. Orçun Selçuk and Dilara Hekimci, "The Rise of the Democracy-Authoritarianism Cleavage and Opposition Coordination in Turkey (2014–2019)," *Democratization* 27, no. 8 (2020): 1496–1514.

15. Murat Somer, "Turkey, Kurds and Syria," *Today's Zaman*, August 8, 2012; http://mysite.ku.edu.tr/musomer/wp-content/uploads/sites/191/2021/08/Somer-Turkey-and-Kurds-TDZ-as-is-Aug2012.pdf (accessed September 10, 2021).

16. For example, see interview with Zübeyir Aydar, the PKK's EU representative, Aslı Aydıntaşbaş, "Türkiye Kürtlerle Büyür [Turkey Would Grow with the Kurds]," *Milliyet* newspaper, November 27, 2012; Hasan Cemal, "PYD Lideri: Kürt Fobisinden Kurtulsa Bütün Ortadoğu Türkiye'nin Olur! [Leader of PYD: If Turkey Overcame Its Phobia of the Kurds, the Whole of the Middle East Would be Turkey's]," interview with the leader of the PYD, *T24*, April 23, 2014, http://t24.com.tr/yazi/pyd-lideri-kurt-fobisinden-kurtulsa-butun-ortadogu-turkiyenin-olur/9089.

17. See, Introduction, Table I1.

18. "Two Years after a Disastrous Referendum, Iraq's Kurds Are Prospering," *Economist*, June 15, 2019; Joost Hiltermann and Maria Fantappie, "Twilight of the Kurds," *Foreign Policy*, January 16, 2018. A June 2013 conference organized by the PKK pronounced that Kurds have the right to self-determination but they could use this right by their own will either for "internal self-determination" (i.e., autonomy without independence) or "external self-determination" (secession). Helin Alp, "Kürt Konferansından, 'Kürt halkı kaderini kendi belirler' sonucu çıktı [The Kurdish Conference Concludes, "The Kurdish peoples will

determine their own destiny"]," *T24*, June 17, 2013. http://t24.com.tr/haber/kurt/konferansindan-kurt-halki-kaderini-kendi-belirler-sonucu-cikti/232155.

19. Also sometimes called "Muslim Bulgarians," as their language is considered a dialect of Bulgarian, Pomaks have experienced a revival of their collective identity, which has been politicized by the Bulgarian state. Ali Eminov, "Social Construction of Identities: Pomaks in Bulgaria," *JEMIE* 6, no. 2 (2007): 1–27; Mary Neuburger, "Pomak Borderlands: Muslims on the Edge of Nations," *Nationalities Papers* 28, no. 1 (2000): 181–98; Maria Todorova, "Identity (Trans)formation among Bulgarian Muslims," in *The Myth of "Ethnic Conflict": Politics, Economics, and "Cultural" Violence*, special issue in *UC Berkeley GAIA Research Series* 98, ed. Beverly Crawford and Ronnie D. Lipschutz (1998), 471–510. (Retrieved from https://escholarship.org/uc/item/7hc733q3).

20. İnalcık, *Türklük, Müslümanlık ve Osmanlılık Mirası*.

21. Harun Tunçel, "Türkiye'de İsmi Değiştirilen Köyler [Villages with Changed Names in Turkey]," *Fırat University Social Sciences Journal* 10, no. 2 (2000): 23–34.

22. Among other instances, Selahattin Demirtaş's speech in Manisa, see "Taşeron işçi yasasını Anayasa Mahkemesi'ne götüreceğim [I Will Bring the Legislation for Subcontracted Workers to the Constitutional Court]," *T24*, April 27, 2014. http://t24.com.tr/haber/taseron-isci-yasasini-anayasa-mahkemesine-goturecegim,265795.

23. Turkey's "secular" or "laic" regime has certainly been challenged and altered considerably during the last two decades. Among others, Murat Somer, "Turkish Secularism: Looking Forward and Beyond the West" and "Whither with Secularism or Just Undemocratic Laiklik? The Evolution and Future of Secularism under the AKP," in *The Uncertain Path of the 'New Turkey,'* ed. Valeria Talbot (Milan: ISPI, Instituto per gli Studi di Politica Internazionale, 2015), 23–49.

24. Mahoney and Thelen, eds., *Advances in Comparative-Historical Analysis*.

25. This, however, does not necessarily mean that structural incentives can explain the subjective motivations of individuals who participate in this conflict in one way or another, and, as I will discuss further later, the microlevel dynamics that help explain the "durability" of actors and organizations such as the PKK even after "military defeat" in the 1990s. See Güneş Murat Tezcür, "Ordinary People, Extraordinary Risks: Participation in an Ethnic Rebellion," *American Political Science Review* 110, no. 2 (2016): 247–64. Also see Jeremy M. Weinstein, *Inside Rebellion* (New York: Cambridge University Press, 2007).

26. Joel Migdal, "Studying the State," in *Comparative Politics Rationality, Culture and Structure*, ed. Mark I. Lichbach and Alan Zuckerman (Cambridge: Cambridge University Press, 1997), 208–35.

27. Bozdoğan and Kasaba, eds., *Rethinking Modernity and National Identity in Turkey*.

28. Somer, "Turkey: The Slippery Slope."

29. Hakkı Taş, "Turkey—from Tutelary to Delegative Democracy," *Third World Quarterly* 36, no. 4 (2015): 776–91; Esen and Gumuscu, "Rising Compet-

itive Authoritarianism in Turkey," "A Small Yes for Presidentialism," and "Turkey: How the Coup Failed," *Journal of Democracy* 28, no. 1 (2017): 59–73; Somer, "Understanding Turkey's Democratic Breakdown," "Turkey: The Slippery Slope from Reformist to Revolutionary Polarization and Democratic Breakdown," and "Conquering versus Democratizing"; Kerem Öktem and Karabekir Akkoyunlu, eds., *Exit from Democracy: Illiberal Governance in Turkey and Beyond* (New York: Routledge, 2017); Selçuk and Hekimci, "The Rise of the Democracy-Authoritarianism Cleavage"; Yunus Sözen, "Studying Autocratization in Turkey: Political Institutions, Populism, and Neoliberalism," *New Perspectives on Turkey* 63 (2020): 209–35; https://doi.org/10.1017/npt.2020.26; F. Michael Wuthrich and Melvyn Ingleby, "The Pushback against Populism: Running on 'Radical Love' in Turkey," *Journal of Democracy* 31, no. 2 (2020): 24–40.

30. Przeworski, "Democracy as a Contingent Outcome of Conflicts"; Nancy Bermeo, "Myths of Moderation: Confrontation and Conflict During Democratic Transitions," *Comparative Politics* 29, no. 3 (1997): 305–22 and "On Democratic Backsliding," *Journal of Democracy* 27, no. 1 (2016): 5–19.

# Bibliography

Abrams, Dominic, and Michael A. Hogg, eds. *Social Identity Theory: Constructive and Critical Advances.* New York: Springer Verlag, 1990.

Adanır, Fikret. "Bulgaristan, Yunanistan ve Türkiye Üçgeninde Ulus İnşası ve Nüfus Değişimi [Nation Building and Population Exchange in Bulgaria, Greece, and Turkey Triangle]." In *İmparatorluktan Cumhuriyete Etnik Çatışma* [Ethnic Conflict in Turkey from Empire to Republic], edited by Erik Jan Zürcher, 19–26. Istanbul: İletişim, 2005.

Afetinan, Ayşe. *Medeni Bilgiler ve M. Kemal Atatürk'ün El Yazıları* [Civic Knowledge and M. Kemal Atatürk's Handwritten Writings]. Ankara: Atatürk Kültür, Dil ve Tarih Yüksek Kurumu Atatürk Araştırma Merkezi, 2000.

Ağırdır, Bekir. "HDP ve Baraj [HDP and the Threshold]." *T24*, Ocak 29, 2015.

Ahmad, Feroz. "The Transition to Democracy in Turkey." *Third World Quarterly* 7, no. 2 (1985): 211–26.

———. *The Making of Modern Turkey.* New York: Routledge, 1993.

Ahmed, Mohammed M. A., and Michael M. Gunter, eds. *The Evolution of Kurdish Nationalism.* Costa Mesa: Mazda, 2007.

Akal, Emel. *Moskova-Ankara-Londra Üçgeninde: İştirakiyuncular, Komünistler Ve Paşa Hazretleri* [In the Triangle of Moscow-Ankara-London: İstirakiyun-ists, Communists, and His Highness Pasha]. Istanbul: İletişim, 2013.

Akçam, Taner. "Sevr ve Lozan'ın Başka Tarihi [A Different History of the Sèvres and the Lausanne]." In *İmparatorluktan Cumhuriyete Etnik Çatışma* [Ethnic Conflict in Turkey from Empire to Republic], edited by Erik Jan Zürcher, 51–87. Istanbul: İletişim, 2017.

Akgönül, Samim. "Türkiye'de Din, 3B Teorisi ve AKP [Religion, 3B Theory and AKP in Turkey]." *T24*, November 27, 2013. http://t24.com.tr/haber/turkiyede-din-3-b-teorisi-ve-akp,244904; accessed October 1, 2017.

Akkaya, Ahmet Hamdi, and Joost Jongerden, "Confederalism and Autonomy in Turkey: The Kurdistan Workers' Party and the Reinvention of Democracy." In *The Kurdish Question in Turkey: New Perspectives on Violence, Represen-*

*tation, and Reconciliation*, edited by Cengiz Güneş and Welat Zeydanlıoğlu, 186–204. London: Routledge, 2014.

Aktar, Ayhan. *Varlık Vergisi ve Türkleştirme Politikaları* [Capital Tax and Policies of Turkification]. Istanbul: İletişim, 2000.

Aktar, Ayhan, Niyazi Kızılyürek, and Umut Özkırımlı, eds. *Nationalism in the Troubled Triangle: Cyprus, Greece, and Turkey.* London: Palgrave Macmillan, 2010.

———. "Introduction." In *Nationalism in the Troubled Triangle: Cyprus, Greece, and Turkey*, edited by Aktar, Kızılyürek, and Özkırımlı, xiii–xxiii. London: Palgrave Macmillan, 2010.

Aktar, Cengiz. "Osmanlı Kozmopolitizminden Avrupa Kozmopolitizmine Giden Yolda Ulus Parantezi [An Excursus on Nation: From Ottoman Cosmopolitanism to European Cosmopolitanism]." In *Milliyetçilik* [Nationalism], edited by Tanıl Bora. Istanbul: İletişim, 2002.

Aktürk, Şener. "İslamcılığın Kürt Açılımı [The Kurdish Opening of Islamism]." In *İslamcılık Tartışmaları* [Discussions on Islamism], edited by Seyfullah Özkurt, 297–301. Istanbul: Ufuk Kitap, 2012.

———. *Regimes of Ethnicity and Nationhood in Germany, Russia, and Turkey.* New York: Cambridge University Press, 2012.

———. "Comparative Politics of Exclusion in Europe and the Americas: Religious, Sectarian, and Racial Boundary Making since the Reformation." *Comparative Politics* 52, no. 4, 2020.

Akyol, Mustafa. *Kürt Sorununu Yeniden Düşünmek* [Rethinking the Kurdish Problem]. Istanbul: Doğan Kitap, 2006.

Akyol, Taha. "Türkiyeli ve Arnavut [Of-Turkey and Albanian]." *Hürriyet*, February 13, 2013.

———. *Bilinmeyen Lozan* [Unknown Lausanne]. Istanbul: Doğan Kitap, 2014.

Akyol, Taha, and Sefa Kaplan. *Açık ve Gizli Oturumlarda Lozan Tartışmaları: TBMM'de Lozan Müzakereleri Tutanakları* [Lausanne Discussions in Open and Secret Sessions: Proceedings of the Lausanne Conference at the Grand National Assembly of Turkey]. Istanbul: Doğan Kitap, 2013.

Akyürekli, Mahmut. *Türklerle Kürtler: Bin Yıllık Geçmişin Kısa Tarihi* [Turks and Kurds: A Brief History of a Thousand Years Long Past]. Istanbul: Tarih Kulübü Yayınları, 2016.

Alp, Helin. "Ahmet Türk: 1922'deki 'Kürt Reform Paketi' Bizim Taleplerimizi Karşılar [Ahmet Türk: "The Kurdish Reform Package" of 1922 Meets Our Demands]." *Akşam*, January 22, 2013.

———. "Kürt Konferansından, 'Kürt halkı kaderini kendi belirler' sonucu çıktı [The Kurdish Conference Concludes, 'The Kurdish Peoples Will Determine Their Own Destiny']." *T24*, June 17, 2013. http://t24.com.tr/haber/kurt/konferansindan-kurt-halki-kaderini-kendi-belirler-sonucu-cikti/232155; accessed June 17, 2013.

Alpay, Şahin. "Önemli Olan Ayrımcılığın Son Bulması [What Matters is that Discrimination Ends]." *Zaman*, November 9, 2004.

Altunışık, Meliha. "The Turkish Model and Democratization in the Middle East." *Arab Studies Quarterly* 27, nos. 1–2 (2005): 45–63.

Amin, Samir. *Unequal Development: An Essay on the Social Formations of Peripheral Capitalism*. Translated by Brian Pierce. Sussex: The Harvester Press, 1 976.

Amnesty International. "Turkey: KCK Arrests Deepen Freedom of Expression Concerns." Public Statement, November 10, 2011. https://www.amnesty.org/en/documents/eur44/015/2011/en; accessed June 4, 2019.

Anderson, Benedict. *Imagined Communities: Reflections on the Origin and Spread of Nationalism*. London: Verso, 1983.

Andeweg, Rudy B. "Consociational Democracy." *Annual Review of Political Science* 3 (2000): 509–36.

Andrews, Peter Alford. *Ethnic Groups in the Republic of Turkey*. Wiesbaden: Reichert, 1989.

Angrist, Michele P. "Party Systems and Regime Formation in the Modern Middle East: Explaining Turkish Exceptionalism." *Comparative Politics* 36, no. 2 (2004): 229–49.

Anter, Musa. *Fırat Marmara'ya Akar* [The Euphrates Flows into the Marmara]. Istanbul: Avesta Yayınları, 1996.

Arı, Kemal. *Büyük Mübadele* [The Great Exchange]. Istanbul: Tarih Vakfı Yurt Yayınları, 1995.

Arıboğan, Deniz Ülke. "Türk kimliği meselesi! [The Turkish Identity Question!]." *Akşam*, May 17, 2013.

Asgharzadeh, Alireza. *Iran and the Challenge of Diversity: Islamic Fundamentalism, Aryanist Racism, and Democratic Struggles*. Palgrave: Macmillan, 2007.

Aslan, Senem. *Nation-Building in Turkey and Morocco: Governing Kurdish and Berber Dissent*. New York: Cambridge University Press, 2015.

Association of Human Rights and Solidarity for Oppressed People (Mazlum-Der). *Kurdish Conflict Forum 12*. Ankara: Sor Yayıncılık, 1993.

Atabaki, Touraj, ed. *The State and the Subaltern: Modernization, Society, and the State in Turkey and Iran*. New York: I. B. Tauris, 2007.

Atatürk, Mustafa Kemal. *Nutuk I. Cilt (1919–1920)* [The Speech, Vol. I (1919–1920)]. Ankara: Atatürk'ün Doğumunun 100.Yılını Kutlama Koordinasyon Kurulu, 1981.

———. *Nutuk-Söylev: II. Cilt 1920–1927* [The Speech: Vol. II 1920–27]. Ankara: Atatürk Kültür, Dil ve Tarih Yüksek Kurumu Türk Tarih Kurumu Yayınları, 1984.

———. *Nutuk-Söylev: III. Cilt* [The Speech: Vol. III]. Ankara: Atatürk Kültür, Dil ve Tarih Yüksek Kurumu Türk Tarih Kurumu Yayınları, 1984.

———. *Atatürk'ün Bütün Eserleri* [The Complete Works of Atatürk]. Volume 2. Istanbul: Kaynak-Yayınları, 1999.

———. *Atatürk'ün Bütün Eserleri* [The Complete Works of Atatürk]. Volume 14. Istanbul: Kaynak Yayınları, 2004.

Avcıoğlu, Doğan. *Türkiye'nin Düzeni: Dün-Bugün-Yarın, Birinci Kitap* [Turkey's Order: Yesterday-Today-Tomorrow, Book I]. Istanbul: Tekin Yayınevi, 1976.

Ayata, Bilgin. "Mapping Euro-Kurdistan." *Middle East Report* 38, no. 247 (Summer 2008): 18–24.

Aydin, Cemil. *The Politics of Anti-Westernism in Asia: Visions of World Order in Pan-Islamic and Pan Asian Thought*. New York: Columbia University Press, 2007.

———. *The Idea of the Muslim World: A Global Intellectual History*. Cambridge: Harvard University Press, 2017.

Aydın-Düzgit, Senem, and Evren Balta. *Turkey after the July 15th Coup Attempt: When Elites Polarize over Polarization*. Istanbul: Istanbul Policy Center, August 2017.

Aydinli, Ersel. "Ergenekon, New Pacts, and the Decline of the Turkish 'Inner State.'" *Turkish Studies* 12, no. 2 (2011): 227–39.

Aydıntaşbaş, Aslı. "Türkiye Kürtlerle Büyür [Turkey Grows with the Kurds]." Interview with Zübeyir Aydar, the PKK's EU representative, *Milliyet*, November 27, 2012.

Aytaç, S. Erdem, Ali Çarkoğlu, and Kerem Yıldırım. "Taking Sides: Determinants of Support for a Presidential System in Turkey." *South European Society and Politics* 22, no. 1 (2017): 1–20.

Aytürk, İlker. "The Racist Critics of Atatürk and Kemalism from the 1930s to the 1960s." *Journal of Contemporary History* 46 (2011): 308–35.

———. "Post-Post-Kemalizm: Yeni Bir Paradigmayı Beklerken." *Birikim* 319, 2015.

Baç, Meltem Müftüler. "Turkey's Political Reforms and the Impact of the European Union." *South European Society and Politics* 10, no. 1 (2005), 17–31.

Ballı, Rafet. *Kürt Dosyası* [The Kurdish Case]. Istanbul: Cem Yayınevi, 1991.

Banning, Keith, and Will Kymlicka, eds. *Multiculturalism and the Welfare*. Oxford: Oxford University Press, 2006.

Banton, Michael. "The Sociology of Ethnic Relations." *Ethnic and Racial Studies* 31, no. 7 (2008): 1267–85.

Barkey, Karen. *Empire of Difference: The Ottomans in Comparative Perspective*. Cambridge: Cambridge University Press, 2008.

Barrington, Lowell W. "Introduction." In *After Independence: Making and Protecting the Nation in Postcolonial and Post-Communist States*, edited by Lowell W. Barrington. Ann Arbor: University of Michigan Press, 2003.

———, ed. *After Independence: Making and Protecting the Nation in Postcolonial and Postcommunist States*. Ann Arbor: University of Michigan Press, 2009.

Barth, Frederick, ed. *Ethnic Groups and Boundaries: Social Organization of Cultural Difference*. Boston: Little, Brown, 1969.

Bayat, Kaveh. "Iran and the 'Kurdish Question.'" *Middle East Report* 38, no. 247 (Summer 2008): 28–35.

Bayrak, Mehmet. *Kürdoloji Belgeleri* [Kurdology Documents]. Ankara: Öz-Ge Yayınları, 2004.

Beardsley, Kyle. "Agreement without Peace? International Mediation and Time Inconsistency Problems." *American Journal of Political Science* 52, no. 4 (2008): 723–40.

Bein, Amit. *Ottoman Ulema, Turkish Republic: Agents of Change and Guardians of Tradition.* Stanford: Stanford University Press, 2011.

Beiner, Ronald. *Liberalism, Nationalism, Citizenship.* Vancouver: UCB Press, 2003.

Beissinger, Mark R. *Nationalist Mobilization and the Collapse of the Soviet State.* Cambridge: Cambridge University Press, 2002.

Belge, Ceren. "Civilian Victimization and the Politics of Information in the Kurdish Conflict in Turkey." *World Politics* 68, no. 2 (2016): 275–306.

Bendix, Reinhard. *Kings or People: Power and the Mandate to Rule.* Berkeley: University of California Press, 1978.

Benedikter, Thomas. *The World's Modern Autonomy Systems Concepts and Experiences of Regional Territorial Autonomy.* Bozen/Bolzano: EURAC Research Institute, 2009.

Bennett, Andrew, and Jeffrey T. Checkel, eds. *Process Tracing: From Metaphor to Analytic Tool.* Cambridge: Cambridge University Press, 2015.

Berkes, Niyazi. *The Development of Secularism in Turkey.* 1st ed. New York: Routledge, 1998.

Berman, Sheri. *The Primacy of Politics: Social Democracy and the Making of Europe's Twentieth Century.* Cambridge: Cambridge University Press, 2006.

———. "Ideational Theorizing in the Social Sciences since 'Policy Paradigms, Social Learning, and the State.'" *Governance* 26, no. 2 (2013): 217–37.

Bermeo, Nancy. "Myths of Moderation: Confrontation and Conflict During Democratic Transitions." *Comparative Politics* 29, no. 3 (1997): 305–22.

———. "On Democratic Backsliding." *Journal of Democracy* 27, no. 1 (2016): 5–19.

Beşikçi, İsmail. *Devletlerarası Sömürge Kürdistan* [Interstate Colony Kurdistan]. Istanbul: Yurt Kitap-Yayın, 1990.

———. *PKK Üzerine Düşünceler: Özgürlüğün Bedeli* [Thoughts on the PKK: The Price of Freedom]. Istanbul: Melsa Yayınları, 1992.

Bhargava, Rajeev. "An Ancient Indian Secular Age?" In *Beyond the Secular West,* edited by Akeel Bilgrami, 188–214. New York: Columbia University Press, 2016.

Bilal, Rezarta, Ayşe Betül Çelik, and Ekin Ok. "Psychological Asymmetry in Minority-Majority Relations at Different Stages of Ethnic Conflict." *International Journal of Interethnic Relations* 43 (2014): 253–64.

Bilgen, Arda. "A Project of Destruction, Peace, or Techno-Science? Untangling the Relationship between the Southeastern Anatolia Project (Gap) and the Kurdish Question in Turkey." *Middle Eastern Studies* 54, no. 1 (2017): 94–113.

Billig, Michael. *Banal Nationalism*. London: Sage, 1995.

Birand, Mehmet Ali. *Apo ve PKK* [Apo and the PKK]. Istanbul: Milliyet Yayınları, 1992.

———, "Kaç Kürt İsyanı Oldu? [How Many Kurdish Rebellions Took Place?]." *Hürriyet*, January 3, 2008.

Birand, Mehmet Ali, Hikmet Bila, and Rıdvan Akar. *12 Eylül: Türkiye'nin Miladı* [12 September: Turkey's Point Zero]. Istanbul: Doğan Kitap, 1999.

Bogaards, Matthijs, Ludger Helms, and Arend Lijphart, "The Importance of Consociationalism for Twenty-First Century Politics and Political Science," *Swiss Political Science Review* 25, no. 4, 2019.

Bora, Tanıl, ed. *Milliyetçilik* [Nationalism]. Istanbul: İletişim, 2002.

———. "Nationalist Discourses in Turkey." *South Atlantic Quarterly* 102, no. 2/3 (2003).

Borak, Said. *Atatürk'ün Resmi Yayınlara Girmemiş Söylev, Demeç, Yazışma ve Söyleşileri* [Atatürk's Speeches, Statements, Correspondence, and Interviews That Did Not Enter Official Publications]. Istanbul: Kaynak Yayınları, 1998.

Boratav, Korkut. "The Turkish Bourgeoisie under Neoliberalism." *Research and Policy on Turkey* 1, no. 1 (2016): 1–10.

Botev, Nikolai. "Where East Meets West: Ethnic Intermarriage in the Former Yugoslavia, 1962 to 1989." *American Sociological Review* 59 (1994): 461–80.

Bozarslan, Hamit. "Political Crisis and the Kurdish Issue in Turkey." In *The Kurdish Nationalist Movement in the 1990s*, edited by Robert Olson. Lexington: University Press of Kentucky, 1996.

———. "Some Remarks on Kurdish Historiographical Discourse in Turkey." In *Essays on the Origins of Kurdish Nationalism*, edited by Abbas Vali, 14–39. Costa Mesa: Mazda, 2003.

———. "Kürt Milliyetçiliği: Zımni Sözleşmeden Ayaklanmaya 1919–1925 [Kurdish Nationalism: From Implicit Contract to Rebellion]." In *İmparatorluktan Cumhuriyete Türkiye'de Etnik Çatışma* [From Empire to Republic Ethnic Conflict in Turkey], edited by Erik Jan Zürcher, 89–122. Istanbul: İletişim, 2005.

———. "Türkiye'de (1919–1980) Yazılı Kürt Tarihi Söylemi Üzerine Bazı Hususlar [On Some Matters Relating to the Discourse of Written Kurdish History in Turkey (1919–1980)]." In *Kürt Milliyetçiliğinin Kökenleri* [The Origins of Kurdish Nationalism], edited by Abbas Vali. Istanbul: Avesta Yayınları, 2005.

———. "Kurds and the Turkish State." In *The Cambridge History of Turkey, vol. 4: Turkey in the Modern World*, edited by Reşat Kasaba, 333–56. Cambridge: Cambridge University Press, 2008.

Bozdoğan, Sibel, and Reşat Kasaba, eds. *Rethinking Modernity and National Identity in Turkey*. Seattle: University of Washington Press, 1997.

Brass, Paul. *Ethnicity and Nationalism: Theory and Comparison*. London: Sage, 1991.

———. *Language, Religion and Politics in North India*. Lincoln: iUniverse, 2005.

Bromley, Catherine, John Curtice, David McCrone, and Alison Park. *Has Devolution Delivered?* Edinburgh: Edinburgh University Press, 2006.

Brownlee, Jasen, Tarek Masoud, and Andrew Reynolds. *The Arab Spring: Pathways of Repression and Reform*. Oxford: Oxford University Press, 2015.

Brubaker, Rogers. *Citizenship and Nationhood in France and Germany*. Cambridge: Harvard University Press, 1992.

———. "Aftermaths of Empire and the Unmixing of Peoples: Historical and Comparative Perspectives." *Ethnic and Racial Studies* 18, no. 2 (1995): 198–218.

———. *Ethnicity without Groups*. Cambridge: Harvard University Press, 2004.

Bucak, Mustafa Remzi. *Bir Kürt Aydınından İsmet İnönü'ye Mektup* [Letter from a Kurdish Luminary to İsmet İnönü]. Istanbul: Doz Basım Yayıncılık, 1991.

Bulutgil, H. Zeynep. *The Roots of Ethnic Cleansing in Europe*. Cambridge: Cambridge University Press, 2016.

Burkay, Kemal. *Anılar, Belgeler* [Memoirs, Documents]. Volume 1. 2nd ed. Istanbul: Deng Yayınları, 2002.

Caramani Daniele, ed. *Comparative Politics*. New York: Oxford University Press, 2008.

Cederman, Lars-Erik, Andreas Wimmer, and Brian Min. "Why Do Ethnic Groups Rebel? New Data and Analysis." *World Politics* 62, no. 1 (2010): 87–119.

Cederman, Lars-Erik, Kristian Skrede Gleditsch, and Halvard Buhaug. *Inequality, Grievances, and Civil War*. New York: Cambridge University Press, 2013.

Celep, Ödül. "Can the Kurdish Left Contribute to Turkey's Democratization?" *Insight Turkey* 16, no. 3 (2014): 165–80.

Celil, Celilê. *XIX. Yüzyıl Osmanlı İmparatorluğu'nda Kürtler* [Kurds in XIX. Century Ottoman Empire]. Ankara: Öz-Ge Yayınları, 1992.

Cemal, Hasan. *Kürtler* [The Kurds]. Istanbul: Doğan Kitap, 2003.

———. *Cumhuriyet'i Çok Sevmiştim: Cumhuriyet Gazetesindeki 'İç Savaş'ın' Perde Arkası* [I Loved the Republic: Behind the Scenes of the "Civil War" at Cumhuriyet Newspaper]. Istanbul: Doğan Kitap, 2005.

———. *Türkiye'nin Asker Sorunu* [Turkey's Military Problem]. Istanbul: Doğan Kitap, 2010.

———. "Başörtüsü, eşit yurttaşlık derken, ulus-devlet . . . [Talking about Headscarves and Equal Rights, but What of the Nation-State?]." *T24*, October 5, 2013. http://t24.com.tr/yazarlar/hasan-cemal/basortusu-esit-yurttaslik-derken-ulus-devlet,7570; accessed August 14, 2019.

———. "PYD Lideri: Kürt Fobisinden Kurtulsa Bütün Ortadoğu Türkiye'nin Olur! [Leader of PYD: If Turkey Overcame Its Phobia of the Kurds, the Whole of the Middle East Would Be Turkey's]." Interview with the leader of the PYD, T24, April 23, 2014. http://t24.com.tr/yazi/pyd-lideri-kurt-fobisinden-kurtulsa-butun-ortadogu-turkiyenin-olur/9089.

Center for Systemic Peace. "Death in Major Episodes of Political Violence 1946–2018." *Knoema*. https://knoema.com/xzmbnbd/death-in-major-episodes-of-political-violence-1946-2018; accessed October 15, 2019.

Chandra, Kanchan. "What Is Ethnic Identity and Does It Matter?" *Annual Review of Political Science* 9, no. 1 (2006): 397–424.

Checkel, Jeffrey T., and Peter J. Katzenstein, eds. *European Identity*. Cambridge: Cambridge University Press, 2009.

Chenoweth, Erica, and Maria J. Stephan. *Why Civil Resistance Works: The Strategic Logic of Nonviolent Conflict*. New York: Columbia University Press, 2011.

Chirot, Daniel, and Clark McCauley. *Why Not Kill Them All? The Logic and Prevention of Mass Political Murder*. Princeton: Princeton University Press, 2010.

Church, Clive, and Paolo Dardanelli. "The Dynamics of Confederalism and Federalism: Comparing Switzerland and the EU." *Regional & Federal Studies* 15, no. 2 (2005): 163–85.

Ciddi, Sinan. *Kemalism in Turkish Politics: The Republican People's Party, Secularism, and Nationalism*. London: Routledge, 2009.

Ciddi, Sinan, and Berk Esen. "Turkey's Republican People's Party: Politics of Opposition under a Dominant Party System." *Turkish Studies* 15, no. 3 (2014): 419–41.

Cizre, Ümit. "Ideology, Context, and Interest: The Turkish Military." In *The Cambridge History of Turkey: vol. 4: Turkey in the Modern World*, edited by R. Kasaba, 301–32. Cambridge: Cambridge University Press, 2008.

———. ed. *Secular and Islamic Politics in Turkey: The Making of the Justice and Development Party*. New York: Routledge, 2008.

———. "A New Politics of Engagement: The Turkish Military, Society, and the AKP." In *Democracy, Islam, and Secularism in Turkey*, edited by Ahmet T. Kuru and Alfred Stepan, 122–48. New York: Columbia University Press, 2012.

Clayer, Nathalie, Fabio Giomi, and Emmanuel Szerek, eds. *Kemalism: Transnational Politics in the Post-Ottoman World*. London: I. B. Tauris, 2019.

Collier, Paul, and Anke Hoeffler. "Economic Causes of Civil War." *Oxford Economic Papers*, no. 50 (1998): 563–73.

Colls, Robert. *Identity of England*. Oxford: Oxford University Press, 2002.

Connor, Walker. "Nation-Building or Nation-Destroying?" *World Politics* 24, no. 3 (1972): 319–55.

———. "When Is a Nation?" *Ethnic and Racial Studies* 13, no. 1 (January 1990): 92–103.

Cuthell, David. "A Kemalist Gambit: A View of the Political Negotiations in the Determination of the Turkish-Iraqi Border." In *The Creation of Iraq: 1914–1921*, edited by Reeva Spector Simon and Eleanor H. Tejirian. New York: Columbia University Press, 2004.

Çağaptay, Soner. "Reconfiguring the Turkish Nation in the 1930s." *Nationalism and Ethnic Politics* 8, no. 2 (2002): 67–82.

———. "Race, Assimilation, and Kemalism: Turkish Nationalism and the Minorities in the 1930s." *Middle Eastern Studies* 40, no. 3 (2004): 86–101.Çakır, Ruşen. "Erbakan 20 yıl önce ne yapmıştı? [What did Erbakan do 20 years ago?]." *Vatan*, January 3, 2011.

Çalışlar, İpek. *Mustafa Kemal Atatürk: Mücadelesi Ve Özel Hayatı* [Mustafa Kemal Atatürk: His Struggle and Personal Life]. Istanbul: Yapı Kredi Yayınları, 2018.

Çalışlar, Oral. *Öcalan ve Burkay'la Kürt Sorunu* [The Kurdish Conflict with Öcalan and Burkay]. Istanbul: Pencere Yayınları, 1993.

Çamlıbel, Cansu. "PYD lideri Salih Müslim: Ankara'nın Şam'la savaşında asker olmayız [PYD Leader Müslim: We Will not Be Soldiers in Ankara's War with Damascus]." *Hürriyet*, October 13, 2014. http://www.hurriyet.com.tr/dunya/pyd-lideri-salih-muslim-ankaranin-samla-savasinda-asker-olmayiz-27373368; accessed July 4, 2019.

Çandar, Cengiz. "Turkish Foreign Policy and the War on Iraq." In *The Future of Turkish Foreign Policy,* edited by Lenore G. Martin and Dimitris Keridis, 37–60. London: MIT Press, 2004.

———. *Mezopotamya Ekspresi: Bir Tarih Yolculuğu* [Mesopotamia Express: A Journey through History]. Istanbul: İletişim, 2012.

Çarkoğlu, Ali, and Ersin Kalaycıoğlu. *The Rising Tide of Conservatism in Turkey.* New York: Palgrave Macmillan, 2009.

Çiçek, Cuma. "Kurdish Identity and Political Islam under AKP Rule." *Research and Policy on Turkey* 1, no. 2 (2016): 147–63.

Dağı, İhsan D. "Transformation of Islamic Political Identity in Turkey: Rethinking the West and Westernization." *Turkish Studies* 6, no. 1 (2005), 21–37.

Dağlar, Ali. "6–7 Ekim'in Acı Bilançosu: 50 Ölü [The Bitter Balance Sheet of October 6–7: 50 Deaths]." *Hürriyet*, November 6, 2014. http://www.hurriyet.com.tr/6-7-ekim-in-aci-bilancosu-50-olu-27525777; accessed December 4, 2018.

Darden, Keith, and Harris Mylonas. "Threats to Territorial Integrity, National Mass Schooling, and Linguistic Commonality." *Comparative Political Studies* 49, no. 11 (2016): 1446–79.

Dekmejian, R. Hrair. "The Anatomy of Islamic Revival: Legitimacy Crisis, Ethnic Conflict, and the Search for Islamic Alternatives." *Middle East Journal* 34, no. 1 (1980): 1–12.

Demiralp, Seda. "The Odd Tango of the Islamic Right and Kurdish Left in Turkey: A Peripheral Alliance to Redesign the Centre?" *Middle Eastern Studies* 48, no. 2: 287–302.

Demirel, Ahmet. *Birinci Meclis'te Muhalefet: İkinci Grup* [Opposition in the First Parliament of Turkey: The Second Group]. Istanbul: İletişim, 2000.

Demirel, Tanel. "Lessons of Military Regimes and Democracy: The Turkish Case in Comparative Perspective." *Armed Forces and Society* 31, no. 2 (2005): 245–71.

Democratic Society Party. *Demokratik Toplum Partisi'nin Kürt Sorununa İlişkin Demokratik Çözüm Projesi* [The Democratic Society Party's Democratic Resolution Project regarding Kurdish Conflict]. Ankara: DTP Genel Merkezi, September 2008.

Deutsch, Karl W. *Nationalism and Social Communication.* Cambridge: The MIT Press, [1953] 1966.

Di Palma, Giuseppe. *To Craft Democracies: An Essay on Democratic Transitions.* Los Angeles: University of California Press, 1990.

Diamond, Larry. *Ill Winds: Saving Democracy from Russian Rage, Chinese Ambition, and American Complacency.* New York: Penguin Press, 2019.

Dink, Hrant. *Bu Köşedeki Adam* [The Man in This Corner]. Istanbul: Uluslararası Hrant Dink Vakfı Yayınları, 2009.

Dreijmanis, John, ed. *Max Weber's Complete Writings on Academic and Political Vocations.* New York: Algora, 2008.

Dressler, Markus. *Writing Religion: The Making of Turkish Alevi Islam.* Oxford: Oxford University Press, 2013.

———. "Rereading Ziya Gökalp: Secularism and Reform of the Islamic State in the Late Young Turk Period." *International Journal of Middle East Studies* 47, no. 3 (2015): 511–31.

DTP, *Democratic Toplum Partisi Program ve Tüzüğü [Democratic Society Program and Bylaws]*, 2005.

Dündar, Can. "Atatürk'ün Sansürlenen Demeci [Atatürk's Censored Statement]." *Milliyet*, October 30, 2006.

Dündar, Fuat. *Türkiye Nüfus Sayımlarında Azınlıklar* [Minorities in Turkey's Censuses]. İstanbul: Doz Yayınları, 1999.

———. *İttihat ve Terakki'nin Müslümanları İskân Politikası: 1913–1918* [Committee of Union and Progress's Settlement Policy for Muslims 1913–1918]. Istanbul: İletişim, 2008.

Düzel, Neşe. "1923 Müslümanlara 'Türk' Dedi [1923 Called Muslims 'Turkish']." Interview with Hüsamettin Arslan, *Radikal*, December 19, 2005.

———. Interview with former-MP Haşim Haşimi. *Radikal*, August 28, 2006.

Eccarius-Kelly, Vera. *The Militant Kurds: A Dual Strategy for Freedom* Santa Barbara, CA: Praeger, 2011.

Eissenstat, Howard. "Metaphors of Race and Discourse of Nation: Racial Theory and State Nationalism in the First Decades of the Turkish Republic." In *Race and Nation: Ethnic Systems in the Modern World*, edited by Paul Spickard, 239–56. New York: Routledge, 2005.

Ekinci, Tarık Ziya. *Vatandaşlık Açısından Kürt Sorunu ve Bir Çözüm Önerisi* [The Kurdish Question in Terms of Citizenship and a Solution Proposal]. Istanbul: Küreyel Yayınları, 1997.

Ekşi, Oktay. "Malum Rapor Üstüne [About a Certain Report]." *Hürriyet*, October 21, 2004.

Elçi, Şerafettin. "'Hür Kürtler Grubu' Parti Kuruyor ['Free Kurds Group' Forms a Political Party]." *Milliyet*, July 8, 2006. https://www.internethaber.com/hur-kurtler-parti-kuruyor-31140h.htm; accessed October 11, 2019.

Eligür, Banu. *The Mobilization of Political Islam in Turkey.* New York: Cambridge University Press, 2010.

Eminov, Ali. "Social Construction of Identities: Pomaks in Bulgaria." *JEMIE* 6, no. 2 (2007): 1–27.

Emre, Yunus. "Why Has Social Democracy not Developed in Turkey? Analysis of an Atypical Case." *Journal of Balkan and Near Eastern Studies* 17, no. 4 (2015): 392–407.

Entessar, Nader. *Kurdish Ethnonationalism*. Boulder: Lynne Rienner, 1992.

———. "The Kurdish National Movement in Iran since the Islamic Revolution of 1979." In *The Evolution of Kurdish Nationalism*, edited by Mohammed M. A. Ahmed and Michael M. Gunter, 260–75. Costa Mesa: Mazda, 2007.

Erdaş, Sadık. "Nihad (Anılmış) Paşa'nın Elcezire Cephe Komutanlığı ve Yargılanması Meselesi [The Matter of Nihad (Anılmış) Pasha's Commandership of the Elcezire Front and Trial]." *Cumhuriyet Tarihi Araştırmaları Dergisi* 14, no. 28 (2018), 3–36.

Erder, Necat. *Türkiye'de Siyasi Partilerin Yandaş/Seçmen Profili (1994–2002)* [The Supporter/Voter Profiles of Political Parties in Turkey (1994–2002)]. Istanbul: Tüses Yayınları Veri Araştırma, 2002.

Erdoğan, Emre, and Pınar Uyan Semerci. *Fanus'ta Diyaloglar: Türkiye'de Kutuplaşmanın Boyutları* [Dialogues in Bell Glass: The Dimensions of Polarization in Turkey]. Istanbul: Bilgi Üniversitesi Yayınları, 2018.

Ergil, Doğu. *Doğu Sorunu: Teşhisler ve Tespitler* [The Eastern Question: Opinions and Designations]. Ankara: TOBB, 1995.

Ergin, Murat. "The Racialization of Kurdish Identity in Turkey." *Ethnic and Racial Studies* 37, no. 2 (2014): 322–41.

Ertman, Thomas. *Birth of the Leviathan: Building States and Regimes in Medieval and Early Modern Europe*. Cambridge: Cambridge University Press, 1997.

Esen, Berk. "Nation-Building, Party-Strength, and Regime Consolidation: Kemalism in Comparative Perspective." *Turkish Studies* 15, no. 4, 2014.

Esen, Berk, and Sebnem Gumuscu. "Turkey: How the Coup Failed." *Journal of Democracy* 28, no. 1 (2017): 59–73.

———. "Rising Competitive Authoritarianism in Turkey." *Third World Quarterly*, 37, no. 9 (2016): 1581–1606.

———. "A Small Yes for Presidentialism: The Turkish Constitutional Referendum of April 2017." *South European Society and Politics* 22, no. 3 (2017): 303–26.

Fabbe, Kristin. *Disciples of the State: Religion and State-Building in the Former Ottoman World*. Cambridge: Cambridge University Press, 2019.

Fearon, James D. "Commitment Problems and the Spread of Ethnic Conflict." In *The International Spread of Ethnic Conflict*, edited by David Lake and Donald Rothchild. Princeton: Princeton University Press, 1998.

———. "Ethnic and Cultural Diversity by Country." *Journal of Economic Growth* 8 (2003): 195–222.

Fearon, James D., and David D. Laitin. "Explaining Interethnic Cooperation." *The American Political Science Review* 90, no. 4 (1996): 715–35.

———. "Ethnicity, Insurgency, and Civil War." *American Political Science Review* 97, no. 1 (2003): 75–90.

Findley, Carter Vaughn. "Continuity, Innovation, Synthesis, and the State." In *Ottoman Past and Today's Turkey*, edited by Kemal H. Karpat, 29–46. Leiden: Brill, 2000.

———. *The Turks in World History*. Oxford: Oxford University Press, 2004.

———. *Turkey, Islam, Nationalism, and Modernity: A History, 1789–2007*. New Haven: Yale University Press, 2010.

Fırat, Gökçe. *İstila: Kürt Sorununda Gizlenen Gerçekler ve Kürt İstilası* [Invasion: The Hidden Truths in the Kurdish Problem and the Kurdish Invasion]. Istanbul: İleri Yayınları, 2007.

Fisher, Max, Josh Keller, Mae Ryan, and Shane O'Neill. "National Identity Is Made Up." *New York Times*, February 28, 2018, https://www.nytimes.com/video/world/100000005660651/national-identity.html; accessed August 14, 2019.

Fontana, Giuditta, Argyro Kartsonaki, Natascha S. Neudorfer, Dawn Walsh, Stefan Wolff, and Christalla Yakinthou. "The Dataset of Political Agreements in Internal Conflicts (Paic)." *Conflict Management and Peace Science* 38, no. 3 (2020): 338–64.

Fortna, Benjamin C., Stefanos Katsikas, Dimitris Kamouzis, and Paraskevas Konortas. *State-Nationalisms in the Ottoman Empire, Greece, and Turkey: Orthodox and Muslims, 1830–1945*. London: Routledge, 2013.

Foundation for Political, Economic and Social Research (SETA) and Pollmark. *Public Perception of the Kurdish Problem in Turkey*. Pollmark, 2009.

Frey, Frederick W. *The Turkish Political Elite*. 1st ed. Cambridge: The MIT Press, 1965.

Fukuyama, Francis. *The End of History and the Last Man*. New York: Free Press, 1992.

Furtado, Celso. *Economic Development of Latin America: Historical Background and Contemporary Problems*. Cambridge: Cambridge University Press, 1976.

Gagnon, V. P. "Ethnic Nationalism and International Conflict." *International Security* 19, no. 3 (1994–95): 130–166.

———. *The Myth of Ethnic War: Serbia and Croatia in the 1990s*. Ithaca: Cornell University Press, 2004.

Gambetti, Zeynep, and Joost Jongerden, eds. *The Kurdish Issue in Turkey: A Spatial Perspective*. New York: Routledge, 2015.

Gellner, Ernest. *Nations and Nationalism*. Ithaca: Cornell University Press, 1983.

George, Alexander L., and Andrew Bennett. *Case Studies and Theory Development in the Social Sciences*. Cambridge: MIT Press, 2005.

Gözübüyük, Şeref, and Suna Kili. "Türk Anayasa Metinleri: 1839–1980 [Turkish Constitutional Texts: 1839–1980]." Ankara: Ankara Üniversitesi Siyasal Bilgiler Fakültesi Yayınları, no. 496 (1982).

Grand National Assembly of Turkey Human Rights Investigation Commission. *Investigative Report on Abuses on Right to Live in the Context of Terror and*

*Violence*. 24th Term, 3rd Legislative Year, 2013. http.//www.tbmm.gov.tr/komisyon/insanhaklari/belge/TER%C3%96R%20VE%20%C5%9E%C4%BoHLALLER%C4%BO%20%C4%BoNCELEME%20RAPORU.pdf; accessed November 15, 2014.

Grandits, Hannes, Nathalie Clayer, and Robert Pichler, eds. *Conflicting Loyalties in the Balkans: Great Powers, the Ottoman Empire, and Nation-Building*. New York: İ. B. Tauris, 2011.

Gray, John. *Enlightenment's Wake: Politics and Culture at the Close of the Modern Age*. London: Routledge, 2007.

Greenfeld, Liah. *Nationalism: Five Roads to Modernity*. Cambridge: Harvard University Press, 1992.

Grigoriadis, Ioannis N. *Instilling Religion in Greek and Turkish Nationalism: A "Sacred Synthesis."* New York: Palgrave MacMillan, 2013.

Gunter, Michael M. "Turkey, Kemalism and the 'Deep State.'" In *Conflict, Democratization, and the Kurds in the Middle East: Turkey, Iran, Iraq, and Syria*, edited by David Romano and Mehmet Gurses, 17–40. New York: Palgrave Macmillan, 2014.

Gürbey, Gülistan. "The Kurdish Nationalist Movement in Turkey since the 1980s." In *The Kurdish Nationalist Movement in the 1990s: Its Impact on Turkey and the Middle East*, edited by Robert Olson. Lexington: University Press of Kentucky, 1997.

Gurr, Ted Robert. *Why Men Rebel*. Princeton: Princeton University Press, 1970.

Gurr, Ted Robert, and Barbara Harff. *Ethnic Conflict in World Politics*. Boulder: Westview, 1994.

Gurr, Ted Robert, Monty G. Marshall, and Deepa Khosla. *Peace and Conflict 2001: A Global Survey of Armed Conflicts, Self-Determination Movements, and Democracy*. Maryland: Center for International Development and Conflict Management, 2001.

Gümüşçü, Şebnem. "Class, Status, and Party: The Changing Face of Political Islam in Turkey and Egypt." *Comparative Political Studies* 43, no. 7 (2010): 835–61.

———. "The Clash of Islamists: The Crisis of the Turkish State and Democracy." *POMEPS Studies* 22 (2016): 6–11.

Gündoğan, Cemil. "Geleneğin Değersizleşmesi: Kürt Hareketinin 1970'lerde Gelenekselle İlişkisi Üzerine [The Devaluation of Tradition: On the Relationship Between Tradition and the Kurdish Movement in the 1970s]." In *Türkiye Siyasetinde Kürtler* [Kurds in Turkish Politics], edited by Büşra Ersanlı, Günay Göksu Özdoğan, and Nesrin Uçarlar. Istanbul: İletişim, 2012.

Gündüz-Hoşgör, Ayse, and Jeroen Smits. "Intermarriage between Turks and Kurds in Contemporary Turkey: Interethnic Relations in an Urbanizing Environment." *European Sociological Review* 18, no. 4 (2002): 417–32.

Güneş, Cengiz. "The Rise of the Pro-Kurdish Democratic Movement in Turkey." In *Routledge Handbook on the Kurds*, edited by Michael M. Gunter, 259–69. New York: Routledge, 2019.

Güneş, Cengiz, and Welat Zeydanlıoğlu, eds. *The Kurdish Question in Turkey: New Perspectives on Violence, Representation, and Reconciliation*. London: Routledge, 2014.

Gürsel, Kadri. *Dağdakiler: Bagok'tan Gabar'a 26 Gün* [Those of the Mountains: 26 Days from Bagok to Gabar]. Istanbul: Metis Yayınları, 1996.

Gürses, Mehmet. "Islamists, Democracy, and Turkey: A Test of the Inclusion-Moderation Hypothesis." *Party Politics* 20, no. 4 (2012): 646–53.

———. "Is Islam a Cure for Ethnic Conflict? Evidence from Turkey." *Politics and Religion* 8, no. 1 (2015): 135–54.

———. *Anatomy of a Civil War: Sociopolitical Impacts of the Kurdish Conflict in Turkey*. Ann Arbor: University of Michigan Press, 2018, ch. 1.

Gürses, Mehmet, and Nicolas Rost. "Religion as a Peacemaker? Peace Duration after Ethnic Civil Wars." *Politics and Religion* 10, no. 2 (2016): 339–62.

Haidt, Jonathan. *The Righteous Mind: Why Good People Are Divided by Politics and Religion*. New York: Vintage, 2012.

Hakan, Sinan. *Türkiye Kurulurken Kürtler (1916–1920)* [Kurds When Turkey Was Being Founded (1916–1920)]. Istanbul: İletişim, 2013.

HAK-PAR. *Hak ve Özgürlükler Partisi Programı [The Right and Freedoms Party Program]*. Ankara, 2002.

Hallı, Reşat, and Kaynak Yayınları, *Genel Kurmay Belgelerinde Kürt İsyanları 1 & 2 [Kurdish Rebellions in the Documents of the General Staff I & 2]* Istanbul: Kaynak Yayınları, 2011.

Hanioğlu, Şükrü M. *A Brief History of the Late Ottoman Empire*. Princeton: Princeton University Press, 2010.

———. *Atatürk: An Intellectual Biography*. Princeton: Princeton University Press, 2011.

———. "The Historical Roots of Kemalism." In *Democracy, Islam and Secularism in Turkey*, edited by Ahmet T. Kuru and Alfred Stepan, 32–60. New York: Columbia University Press, 2012.

———. "Modern Ottoman Period." In *The Routledge Handbook of Modern Turkey*, edited by Metin Heper and Sabri Sayarı, 15–25. New York: Routledge, 2012.

Hartzell, Caroline A., and Matthew Hoddie, "The Art of the Possible: Power Sharing and Post Civil War Democracy." *World Politics*. 67, 2015.

Hassan, Gerry, ed. *The Scottish Labor Party: History, Institutions, and Ideas*. Edinburgh: Edinburgh University Press, 2004.

HDP. "Çözüm süreci nasıl bitti." 2015. https://www.youtube.com/watch?v=nVEC-1-N9gc; accessed June 30, 2019.

Hechter, Michael. "Internal Colonialism Revisited." In *New Nationalisms of the Developed West: Toward Explanation*, edited by E. A. Tiryakian and R. Rogowski, 17–26. Boston: Allen and Unwin, 1985.

———. *Containing Nationalism*. Oxford: Oxford University Press, 2000.

Hechter, Michael, and Dina Okamoto. "Political Consequences of Minority Group Formation." *Annual Review of Political Science* 4, no. 1 (2001): 189–215.

Helsinki Watch. "Freedom of Expression in Turkey: Abuses Continue." *News from Helsinki Watch*, June 18, 1991. https://www.hrw.org/reports/pdfs/t/turkey/turkey2916.pdf; accessed August 13, 2019.

Henry, Clement Moore, and Robert Springborg. *Globalization and the Politics of Development in the Middle East.* New York: Cambridge University Press, 2010.

Heper, Metin. *The State and Kurds in Turkey.* New York: Palgrave Macmillan, 2007.

Heper, Metin, and Sabri Sayarı eds. *Political Leaders and Democracy in Turkey* (Lanham, MD: Lexington Books, 2002).

Hicks, Donna. *Dignity: The Essential Role It Plays in Resolving Conflict.* New Haven: Yale University Press, 2011.

Higley, John, and Michael G Burton. *Elite Foundations of Liberal Democracy.* Lanham, MD: Rowman and Littlefield, 2006.

Hiltermann, Joost, and Maria Fantappie. "Twilight of the Kurds." *Foreign Policy*, January 16, 2018.

Hislope, Robert. "Between A Bad Peace and A Good War: Insights and Lessons from the Almost-War in Macedonia." *Ethnic and Racial Studies* 26, no. 1 (2003): 129–51.

Hobsbawm, Eric J. *Nations and Nationalism since 1780: Programme, Myth, Reality.* Cambridge: Cambridge University Press, 1992.

Hochschild, Arlie Russell. *Strangers in Their Own Land: Anger and Mourning on the American Right, a Journey to the Heart of Our Political Divide.* New York: The New Press, 2017.

Holmes, Amy Austin. "What the Battle for Kobane Says about U.S. Overseas Military Bases." *Washington Post*, February 2, 2015.

Horowitz, Donald L. *Ethnic Groups in Conflict.* Berkeley: University of California Press, 1985.

Houston, Christopher. *Islam, Kurds, and the Turkish Nation State.* New York: Berg, 2003.

Hrosch, Miroslav. *Social Preconditions of National Revival in Europe: A Comparative Analysis of the Social Composition of Patriotic Groups among the Smaller European Nations.* New York: Columbia University Press, [1985] 2000.

Hungarian Human Rights Foundation. http://www.htmh.hu/reports2001/slovakia2001.htm; accessed March 31, 2004.

Hutchinson, J., and A. D. Smith, eds. *Nationalism.* Oxford: Oxford University Press, 1994.

Hür, Ayşe. "Devletin Demir Yumruğu: Muğlalı Paşa [The Iron Fist of the State: Muğlalı Pasha]." *Taraf*, 10 May 2009.

———. "Türkiye Yerine Anadolu Cumhuriyeti Dense Ne Olurdu? [What Would Have Happened If Turkey Was Called The Republic of Anatolia]." *Radikal*, January 13, 2013.

———. "1922'de Kürtlere söz verildi mi? [Was a Promise Made to the Kurds in 1922?]." *Radikal,* January 23, 2013.

Icduygu, Ahmet, David Romano, and İbrahim Sirkeci. "The Ethnic Question in an Environment of Insecurity: The Kurds in Turkey." *Ethnic and Racial Studies* 22, no. 6 (1999): 991–1010.

Iğsız, Aslı. *Humanism in Ruins: Entangled Legacies of the Greek-Turkish Population Exchange.* Stanford: Stanford University Press, 2018.

International Crisis Group. "Sisyphean Task? Resuming Turkey-PKK Peace Talks." *Crisis Group Europe Briefing,* no. 77. Istanbul/Brussels: 2015.

———. "Turkey's PKK Conflict: A Visual Explainer." https://www.crisisgroup.org/content/turkeys-pkk-conflict-visual-explainer; accessed October 15, 2019.

Itzkowitz, Norman. "18th Century Ottoman Realities." In *Identity and Identity Formation in the Ottoman World,* edited by Baki Tezcan and Karl K. Barbir, ixxx–xivi. Istanbul: Istanbul Bilgi University Press, 2012.

İmset, İsmet. *PKK: Ayrılıkçı Şiddetin 20 Yılı 1973–1992* [The PKK: A Report on Separatist Violence in Turkey 1973–1992]. Istanbul: Turkish Daily News Yayınları, 1993.

İnalcık, Halil. *Türklük, Müslümanlık ve Osmanlılık Mirası* [The Heritage of Turkishness, Muslimness, and Ottomanness]. Istanbul: Kırmızı, 2014.

İriç, Banu. "Bomba Kürt Devleti Kurulacak İddiası [Explosive Allegation: Kurdish State to be Founded]." Exclusive interview with Ali Bulaç, *Internethaber,* May 4, 2013. http.//www.internethaber.com/bomba-kurt-devleti-kurulacak-iddiasi-529564h.htm; accessed August 14, 2019.

*İsmet İnönü: Hatıralar* [Memoirs]. Ankara: Bilgi Yayınevi, 1987.

Jackson, Robert, and Carl Rosberg. "Why Africa's Weak States Persist: The Empirical and the Juridical in Statehood." *World Politics* 35, no. 1 (1982): 1–24.

Jenkins, Gareth. *Political Islam in Turkey: Running West, Heading East.* New York: Palgrave Macmillan, 2008.

———. "Ergenekon, Sledgehammer, and the Politics of Turkish Justice: Conspiracies and Coincidences." *MERIA* 15, no. 2 (2011): 1–9.

Jones, Branwen Gruffydd. ed. *Decolonizing International Relations.* Lanham: Rowman and Littlefield, 2006.

Jongerden, Joost, and Ahmet Hamdi Akkaya. "Born from the Left: The Making of the PKK." In *Nationalisms and Politics in Turkey: Political Islam, Kemalism, and the Kurdish Issue,* edited by Marlies Casier and Joost Jongerden. New York: Routledge, 2010.

———. "The PKK in the 2000s: Continuity through Breaks?" In *Nationalisms and Politics in Turkey: Political Islam, Kemalism, and the Kurdish Issue,* edited by Marlies Casier and Joost Jongerden. New York: Routledge, 2010.

Kadıoğlu, Ayşe. "The Paradox of Turkish Nationalism and the Construction of Official Identity." *Middle Eastern Studies* 32, no. 2 (1997): 177–93.

Kafadar, Cemal. "A Rome of One's Own: Reflections on Cultural Geography and Identity in the Lands of Rum." *Muqarnas* 24 (2007): 7–25.

Kalaycıoğlu, Ersin. "*Kulturkampf* in Turkey: The Constitutional Referendum of 12 September 2010." *Turkish Studies* 17, no. 1 (2012): 1–22.

Kalyvas, Stathis N. *The Logic of Violence in Civil War.* Cambridge: Cambridge University Press, 2006.

Kalyvas, Stathis N., Ian Shapiro, and Tarek Massoud, eds. *Order, Conflict, and Violence.* Cambridge: Cambridge University Press, 2008.

Karabağlı, Hülya. "Atilla Kart: Devlet Herkesin Anadilini Öğrenmesinin Yolunu Açmalı [Atilla Kart: The State Should Pave the Way for Everyone to Learn Their Native Language]." *T24*, September 16, 2013. https://t24.com.tr/haber/atilla-kart-devlet-herkesin-anadilini-ogrenmesinin-yolunu-acmali,239648; accessed July 12, 2019.

Karabekir, Kâzım. *Günlükler: (1906–1948) 2. Cilt* [Memoirs: (1906–1948), Volume 2]. Istanbul: Yapı Kredi Yayınları, 2009.

Karakoç, Ekrem, and Zeki Sarıgil. "Why Religious People Support Ethnic Insurgency? Kurds, Religion and Support for the PKK." *Politics and Religion 13,* no. 2 (2020): 245–72.

Karaman, Hayrettin. "Altan Tan Kardeşime [To My Brother, Altan Tan]." *Yeni Şafak*, May 24, 2012.

Karaman, K. Kıvanç, and Şevket Pamuk. "Different Paths to the Modern State in Europe: The Interaction Between Warfare, Economic Structure, and Political Regime." *American Political Science Review* 107, no. 3 (2013): 603–26.

Kardaş, Tuncay, and Ali Balci. "Inter-Societal Security Dilemma in Turkey: Understanding the Failure of the 2009 Kurdish Opening." *Turkish Studies* 17, no. 1 (2016): 155–80.

Karpat, Kemal H. *Turkey's Politics: The Transition to a Multiparty System.* Princeton: Princeton University Press, 1959.

———. ed. *Ottoman Past and Today's Turkey.* Leiden: Brill, 2000.

———. *The Politicization of Islam Reconstructing Identity, State, Faith, and Community in the Late Ottoman State.* Oxford: Oxford University Press, 2001.

———. *Ottoman Population 1830–1914 Demographic and Social Characteristics.* Istanbul: Tarih Vakfı Yurt Yayınları, 2003.

Kasaba, Reşat. *Bir Konargöçer İmparatorluk: Osmanlı'da Göçebeler, Göçmenler ve Sığınmacılar* [A Nomadic Empire: Nomads, Immigrants, and Refugees in the Ottoman Empire]. Istanbul: Kitap Yayınevi, 2010.

Kaviraj, Sudipta. "Disenchantment Deferred." In *Beyond the Secular West*, edited by Akeel Bilgrami, 135–87. New York: Columbia University Press, 2016.

Kaya, Ayhan. *Europeanization and Tolerance in Turkey: The Myth of Toleration.* New York: Palgrave Macmillan, 2013.

Kaya, Reşit, and Barış Çakmur. "Politics and the Mass Media in Turkey." *Turkish Studies* 11, no. 4 (2010): 521–37.

Kayalı, Hasan. "The Struggle for Independence." In *The Cambridge History of Turkey. Vol. 4: Turkey in the Modern World*, edited by Reşat Kasaba, 112–46. Cambridge: Cambridge University Press, 2008.

————. *Arabs and Young Turks: Ottomanism, Arabism, and Islamism in the Ottoman Empire, 1908–1918*. Los Angeles: The University of California Press, 1997.

Keating, Michael. *Nations against the State: The New Politics of Nationalism in Quebec, Catalonia, and Scotland*. London: Palgrave Macmillan, 1996.

————. "What's Wrong with Asymmetrical Government." In *Remaking the Union*, edited by H. Elcock and M. Keating, 195–218. London: Frank Cass, 1998.

————. *The Government of Scotland: Public Policy Making After Devolution*. Edinburgh: Edinburgh University Press, 2005.

————. "Brexit and the Nations." *Britain Beyond Brexit, The Political Quarterly Monograph Series* 90, no. S2 (2019): 167–76.

Kedourie, Elie. *Nationalism*. Malden, MA: Blackwell, 2000.

Kesen, Nebi. *Avrupa Birliği-Türkiye İlişkileri ve Kürtler* [The Relationship between the EU and Turkey, and the Kurds]. Spånga, Sweden: Apec Förlah, 2003.

Kezer, Zeynep. *Building Modern Turkey: State, Space, and Ideology in the Early Republic*. Pittsburgh: University of Pittsburgh Press, 2015.

Khazaleh, Lorenz. "Interview with Benedict Anderson." December 15, 2005. https://www.antropologi.info/blog/anthropology/2005/interview_with_benedict_anderson_i_like; accessed July 15, 2019.

Khazanov, Anatoly. "A State without a Nation? Russia after Empire." In *The Nation-State in Question*, edited by T. V. Paul, G. John Ikenberry, and John A. Hall. Princeton: Princeton University Press, 2003.

Kılıç, Azer. "Interests, Passions, and Politics: Business Associations and the Sovereignty Dispute in Turkey." *Economy and Society* 46, no. 2 (2017): 275–301.

Kibris, Arzu. "Funerals and Elections: The Effects of Terrorism on Voting Behavior in Turkey." *Journal of Conflict Resolution* 55, no. 2 (2010): 220–47.

Kieser, Hans-Lukas. "Introduction." In *Turkey Beyond Nationalism: Towards Post-Nationalism Identities*, edited by Hans-Lukas Kieser, vii–xvii. London: I. B. Tauris, 2006.

King, Elisabeth, and Cyrus Samii. *Diversity, Violence, and Recognition: How Recognizing Ethnic Identity Promotes Peace*. New York: Oxford University Press, 2020.

Klein, Janet. *Hamidiye Alayları: İmparatorluğun Sınır Boyları ve Kürt Aşiretleri* [Hamidiye Corps: The Margins of Empire and Kurdish Tribes]. Istanbul: İletişim, 2013.

Kohli, Atul, Peter Evans, Peter J. Katzenstein, Adam Przeworski, Susanne Hoeber Rudolph, James C. Scott and Theda Skocpol, "The Role of Theory in Comparative Politics: A Symposium," *World Politics* 48, no. 1 (1995).

Kohn, Hans. *The Idea of Nationalism: A Study in its Origins and Background*. New York: Macmillan, 1951.

KONDA. *Kürt Meselesi'nde Algı ve Beklentiler* [Perceptions and Expectations in the Kurdish Question]. Istanbul: İletişim, 2011.

————. *Konda Barometer.* Istanbul: 2017. http://konda.com.tr/en/konda-barometer.

Koohl-Kamali, Farideh. *The Political Development of the Kurds in Iran: Pastoral Nationalism.* New York: Palgrave Macmillan, 2003.

Krajeski, Jenna. "In Taksim Square, Where Are the Kurds?" *New Yorker*, June 11, 2013. https://www.newyorker.com/news/news-desk/in-taksim-square-where-are-the-kurds; accessed June 30, 2019.

Kuran, Timur. *Private Truths, Public Lies: The Social Consequences of Preference Falsification.* Cambridge: Harvard University Press, 1995.

————. "Ethnic Norms and Their Transformation through Reputational Cascades." *Journal of Legal Studies* XXVII (1998): 623–59.

Kurban, Dilek, Ayşe Betül Çelik, and Deniz Yükseker. *Overcoming a Legacy of Mistrust: Towards Reconciliation between the State and the Displaced.* Istanbul: Turkish Economic and Social Studies Foundation TESEV, Norwegian Refugee Council and Internal Displacement Monitoring Centre, 2006.

Kurt, Mehmet. *Kurdish Hizbullah in Turkey: Islamism, Violence and the State.* London: PlutoPress, 2017.

Kuru, Ahmet, and Alfred Stepan, eds. *Democracy, Islam, and Secularism in Turkey.* New York: Columbia University Press, 2012.

Kurzman, Charles, ed. *Modernist Islam, 1840–1940: A Sourcebook.* Oxford: Oxford University Press, 2002.

Kuzu, Durukan. "The Politics of Identity, Recognition and Multiculturalism: The Kurds in Turkey." *Nations and Nationalism* 22, no. 1 (2016): 123–42.

————. "The Politics of Turkish Nationalism: Continuity and Change." In *Routledge Handbook of Turkish Politics,* edited by Alpaslan Özerdem and Matthew Whiting, 69–79. London: Routledge, 2019.

Kymlicka, Will. *Multicultural Citizenship: A Liberal Theory of Minority Rights.* Oxford: Oxford University Press, 1995.

————. *Politics in the Vernacular: Nationalism, Multiculturalism, and Citizenship.* Oxford: Oxford University Press, 2001.

Laitin, David D. *Identity in Formation: The Russian-Speaking Populations in the near Abroad.* Ithaca: Cornell University Press, 1998.

Lake, David A., and Donald Rothchild, eds. *The International Spread of Ethnic Conflict: Fear, Diffusion, and Escalation.* Princeton: Princeton University Press, 1998.

Lakoff, George. *The Political Mind: A Cognitive Scientist's Guide to Your Brain and Its Politics.* London: Penguin Books, 2009.

Lampe, John R. *Yugoslavia as History: Twice There Was a Country.* Cambridge: Cambridge University Press, 2000.

Larrabee, F. Stephen. "Turkey and the Changing Dynamics of the Kurdish Issue." *Survival* 58, no. 2 (2016): 67–73.

*Lausanne Peace Conference: Proceedings and Documents.* Volume 1-1, Book 1, translated by Seha L. Meray. Istanbul: Yapı Kredi Yayınları, [1923] 1993.

Leezenberg, Michiel. "The Ambiguities of Democratic Autonomy: The Kurdish Movement in Turkey and Rojava." *Southeast European and Black Sea Studies* 16, no. 4 (2016): 671–90.

———. "Ehmedê Xanî's Mem Û Zîn: The Consecration of a Kurdish National Epic." In *Routledge Handbook on the Kurds*, edited by Michael M. Gunter, 79–89. New York: Routledge, 2019.

Lepore, Jill. *This America: The Case for the Nation.* New York: Liveright, 2019.

Levi, Margaret. "A Model, a Method, and a Map: Rational Choice in Comparative and Historical Analysis." In *Comparative Politics Rationality, Culture, and Structure,* edited by Mark I. Lichbach and Alan Zuckerman. Cambridge: Cambridge University Press, 1997.

———. *Consent, Dissent, and Patriotism.* New York: Cambridge University Press, 1997.

Levitsky, Steven, and Daniel Ziblatt, *How Democracies Die.* New York: Crown, 2018.

Lichbach, Mark I., and Alan Zuckerman. *Comparative Politics: Rationality, Culture, and Structure.* Cambridge: Cambridge University Press, 1997.

———. *Is Rational Choice Theory All of Social Science?* Ann Arbor: The University of Michigan Press, 2003.

Lijphart, Arendt. *Democracy in Plural Societies.* New Haven: Yale University Press, 1977.

Lika, Idlir. "Nationhood Cleavages and Ethnic Conflict: A Comparative Analysis of Post-communist Bulgaria, Montenegro, and North Macedonia." PhD Dissertation, Koç University, December 2019.

Linz, Juan J., and Alfred Stepan. *Problems of Democratic Transition and Consolidation: Southern Europe, South America, and Post-Communist Europe.* Baltimore and London: The Johns Hopkins University Press, 1996.

Lipovsky, Igor P. *The Socialist Movement in Turkey, 1960–1980.* Leiden: E. J. Brill, 1992.

Lowe, Robert, and Gareth Stansfield, eds. *The Kurdish Policy Imperative.* London: Chatham House, Royal Institute of International Affairs, 2010.

MacCormick, Neil. *Questioning Sovereignty: Law, State, and Practical Reason.* Oxford: Oxford University Press, 1999.

Machiavelli, Niccolò. *The Prince.* Translated with introduction and notes by James B. Atkinson. Indianapolis: Hackett, [1976] 2008.

MacMillan, Margaret. *Paris 1919: Six Months that Changed the World.* New York: Random House Trade Paperbacks, 2003.

———. *The War that Ended the Peace: How Europe Abandoned Peace for the First World War.* London: Profile Books, 2013.

Mahoney, James, and Kathleen Thelen. *Explaining Institutional Change: Ambiguity, Agency, and Power.* Cambridge: Cambridge University Press, 2010.

————, eds. *Advances in Comparative-Historical Analysis*. Cambridge: Cambridge University Press, 2015.

Manela, Erez. *The Wilsonian Moment: Self-Determination and the International Origins of Anticolonial Nationalism*. Oxford: Oxford University Press, 2007.

Mann, Michael. *States, War, and Capitalism: Studies in Political Sociology*. Oxford: Blackwell, 1992.

————. *The Dark Side of Democracy: Explaining Ethnic Cleansing*. New York: Cambridge University Press, 2005.

Mansfield, Edward D., and Jack Snyder. *Electing to Fight: Why Emerging Democracies Go to War*. Cambridge: MIT Press, 2005.

Marashi, Afshin. "Paradigms of Iranian Nationalism: History, Theory, and Historiography." In *Rethinking Iranian Nationalism and Modernity*, edited by Kamran Scot Aghaie and Afshin Marashi, 3–24. Austin: University of Texas Press, 2014.

Marcus, Aliza. *Blood and Belief: The PKK and the Kurdish Fight for Independence*. New York: New York University Press, 2007.

Mardin, Şerif. "Youth and Violence in Turkey." *European Journal of Sociology* 19, no. 2 (1978): 229–54.

————. "Freedom in an Ottoman Perspective." In *State, Democracy, and the Military: Turkey in the 1980s*, edited by Metin Heper and Ahmet Evin. New York: Walter de Gruyter, 1988.

————. *The Genesis of Young Ottoman Thought: A Study in the Modernization of Turkish Political Ideas*. New York: Syracuse University Press, 2000.

————. *Türk Modernleşmesi, Makaleler 4* [Turkish Modernization: Essays 4]. Istanbul: İletişim, 2003.

————. "Turkish Islamic Exceptionalism Yesterday and Today: Continuity, Rupture, and Reconstruction in Operational Codes." *Turkish Studies* 6, no. 2 (2005): 145–65.

Marx, Anthony W. *Faith in Nation: Exclusionary Origins of Nationalism*. Oxford: Oxford University Press, 2003.

Masullo, Juan, and Francis O'Connor. "PKK Violence against Civilians: Beyond the Individual, Understanding Collective Targeting." *Terrorism and Political Violence* (2017): 1–23.

Matur, Bejan. *Dağın Ardına Bakmak* [Looking Beyond the Mountain]. Istanbul: Timaş Yayınları, 2011.

Mazlumder. *Kürd Sorunu Forumu: 28–29 Kasım 1992* [The Kurdish Conflict Forum: 28–29 November 1992]. Ankara: Sor Yayınları, 1993.

Mbembe, Achille Joseph. "Decolonizing the University: New Directions." *Arts and Humanities in Higher Education* 15, no. 1 (2016).

McCarthy, Justin. *The Ottoman Peoples and the End of Empire*. New York: Oxford University Press, 2001.

McCoy, Jennifer, and Murat Somer, eds. *Polarizing Polities: A Global Threat to Democracy*, Special Volume of *The American Academy of Political and Social Science* 681, no. 1 (2019).

McCrone, David. *Understanding Scotland: The Sociology of a Nation*. London and New York: Routledge, 2001.

———. "Be Careful What You Wish For." *Discover Society*, September 30, 2014. http://www.discoversociety.org/2014/09/30/be-careful-what-you-wish-for/; accessed October 30, 2014.

McDowall, David. "The Kurdish Question: A Historical Review." In *The Kurds: A Contemporary Review*, edited by Phillip G. Kreyenbroek and Stefan Speri, 14. New York: Routledge, 1992.

———. *The Kurds: A Nation Denied*. London: Minority Rights Group, 1992.

———. *A Modern History of the Kurds*. New York: St Martin's Press, 1997.

McLaren, Lauren, and Burak Cop. "The Failure of Democracy in Turkey: A Comparative Analysis." *Government and Opposition* 46, no. 4 (2011): 485–516.

Meeker, Michael E. *A Nation of Empire: The Ottoman Legacy of Turkish Modernity*. Berkeley: University of California Press, 2002.

Mehta, Suketu. *This Land Is Our Land: An Immigrant's Manifesto*. New York: Farrar, Straus and Giroux, 2019.

Menchinger, Ethan L. *The First of the Modern Ottomans: The Intellectual History of Ahmed Vasif*. Cambridge: Cambridge University Press, 2017.

Menocal, Maria Rosa. *Ornament of the World: How Muslims, Jews, and Christians Created a Culture of Tolerance in Medieval Spain*. New York: Little, Brown, 2002.

Mentzel, Peter. "Conclusions: Millets, States, and National Identities." *Nationalities Papers* 28, no. 1 (2000): 199–204.

Mete, Ömer Lütfi. "Yine 'Türkiyelilik' Sihirbazlığına Dair [Again on the Wizardry of "Türkiyelilik"]." *Sabah*, October 29, 2004.

Meyer, John, J. Boli, G. Thomas, and F. Ramirez. "World Society and the Nation-State." *American Journal of Sociology* 103, no. 1 (1997): 144–81.

Migdal, Joel S. *Strong Societies and Weak States: State-Society Relations and State Capabilities in the Third World*. Princeton: Princeton University Press, 1988.

———. "Studying the State." In *Comparative Politics Rationality, Culture, and Structure*, edited by Mark I. Lichbach and Alan Zuckerman, 208–35. Cambridge: Cambridge University Press, 1997.

———. *State in Society: Studying How States and Societies Transform and Constitute One Another*. Cambridge: Cambridge University Press, 2001.Mill, John S. "Considerations on Representative Government." In *Collected Works, J.S. Mill, XIX*. Toronto: University of Toronto Press and Routledge and Kegan Paul, [1859] 1977.

Miller, David. *On Nationality*. Oxford: Clarendon Press, 1995.

Miller, William L. *The End of British Politics? Scots and English Political Behavior in the Seventies.* Oxford: Clarendon Press, 1981.

Milliyet-Konda. *Biz Kimiz: Toplumsal Yapı Araştırması 2006* [Who Are We? Social Composition Survey]. Istanbul: Konda Araştırma ve Danışmanlık, 2007.

Minority Rights Group International. *A Quest for Equality: Minorities in Turkey.* 2007.

Mitchell, Gabriel. "Islam as Peacemaker: The AKP's Attempt at a Kurdish Resolution." *The Washington Review of Turkish and Eurasian Affairs*, May 2012, https://www.academia.edu/1553925/Islam_as_Peacemaker_The_AKPs_Attempt_at_a_Kurdish_Resolution; accessed July 5, 2019.

Mitchell, Timothy. "The Limits of the State." *American Political Science Review* 85, no. 1 (1991): 77–95.

Moore, Barrington. *Social Origins of Dictatorship and Democracy: Lord and Peasant in the Making of the Modern World.* Boston: Beacon Press, [1966] 1993.

Moore, Clement Henry. *Tunisia since Independence.* Berkeley: University of California Press, 1965.

Morozov, Viatcheslav, and Bahar Rumelili. "The External Constitution of European Identity: Russia and Turkey as Europe-Makers." *Cooperation and Conflict* 47, no. 1 (2012): 28–48.

Mousseau, Demet Yalçın. "Democratizing with Ethnic Divisions: A Source of Conflict?" *Journal of Peace Research* 38, no. 5 (2001): 547–67.

Mudde, Cas. *Populist Radical Right Parties in Europe.* Cambridge: Cambridge University Press, 2007.

Muller, Jan-Werner. *Constitutional Patriotism.* Princeton: Princeton University Press, 2007.

Mumcu, Özge. "Anayasa Uzlaşma Komisyonu: Kısa bir değerlendirme notu [Constitutional Consensus Commission: A Brief Note of Evaluation]." *T24*, January 18, 2013. https://t24.com.tr/yazarlar/ozge-mumcu/anayasa-uzlasma-komisyonu-kisa-bir-degerlendirme-notu,6121; accessed June 30, 2019.

Mumcu, Uğur. *Kürt-İslam Ayaklanması: 1919–1925* [The Kurdish-Islamist Rebellion: 1919–1925]. Ankara: Tekin Yayınevi, 1993.

Munck, Gerardo L., and Richard Snyder. *Passion, Craft, and Method in Comparative Politics.* Baltimore: The Johns Hopkins University Press, 2007.

Musil, Jiří, ed. *The End of Czechoslovakia.* Budapest: Central European University Press, 1995.

Mutlu, Servet. "Ethnic Kurds in Turkey: A Demographic Study." *International Journal of Middle East Studies* 28, no. 4 (1996): 517–41.

———. *Doğu Sorununun Kökenleri: Ekonomik Açıdan* [The Origins of the Eastern Question: An Economic Perspective]. Istanbul: Ötüken Neşriyat, 2002.

Mylonas, Harris. *The Politics of Nation-Building: Making Co-Nationals, Refugees, and Minorities.* Cambridge: Cambridge University Press, 2012.

Naimark, Norman. *Fires of Hatred: Ethnic Cleansing in the Twentieth Century Europe.* Cambridge: Harvard University Press, 2001.

Nairn, Tom. *After Britain: New Labour and the Return of Scotland.* London: Granta Books, 2001.

Neuburger, Mary. "Pomak Borderlands: Muslims on the Edge of Nations." *Nationalities Papers* 28, no. 1 (2000): 181–98.

Nişanyan, Sevan. *Yanlış Cumhuriyet: Atatürk ve Kemalizm Üzerine 51 Soru* [The Wrong Republic: 51 Questions About Atatürk and Kemalism]. Istanbul: Kırmızı, 2008.

Nomer, Nedim. "Ziya Gökalp's Idea of Cultural Hybridity." *British Journal of Middle Eastern Studies* 44, no. 3 (2017): 408–28.

Norris, Pippa, and Ronald Inglehart. *Sacred and Secular: Religion and Politics Worldwide.* Cambridge: Cambridge University Press, 2004.

Nykänen, Johanna. "Identity, Narrative, and Frames: Assessing Turkey's Kurdish Narratives." *Insight Turkey* 15, no. 2 (2013): 85–101.

Okyay, Asli S. "Turkey's Post-2011 Approach to Its Syrian Border and Its Implications for Domestic Politics." *International Affairs* 93, no. 4 (2017): 829–46.

Olson, Robert. *The Emergence of Kurdish Nationalism and the Sheikh Said Rebellion, 1880–1925.* Austin: University of Texas Press, 1989.

———. *Imperial Meanderings and Republican Byways: Essays on Eighteenth Century Ottoman and Twentieth Century History of Turkey.* Istanbul: The Isis Press, 1996.

———. *The Kurdish Question and Turkish-Iranian Relations: from World War I to 1998.* Costa Mesa, CA: Mazda, 1998.

Oran, Baskın. *Atatürk Milliyetçiliği* [Atatürk Nationalism]. Ankara: Bilgi Yayınevi, 1990.

———. "The Minority Concept and Rights in Turkey: The Lausanne Peace Treaty and Current Issues." In *Human Rights in Turkey*, edited by Zehra F. Kabasakal Arat, 35–56. Philadelphia: University of Pennsylvania Press, 2007.

———. " 'Ulus-Devlet' Fransa ['Nation-State' France]." *Radikal* 2, September 28, 2008.

Ostergaard-Nielsen, Eva. *Transnational Politics: Turks and Kurds in Germany.* London and New York: Routledge, 2004.

Owen, Roger. *State, Power, and the Making of the Modern Middle East.* London and New York, Routledge, 2004.

Ozkan, Behlül. "Turkey, Davutoglu, and the Idea of Pan-Islamism." *Survival* 56, no. 4 (2014): 119–40.

Ozkirimli, Umut. "Multiculturalism, Recognition, and the 'Kurdish Question' in Turkey: The Outline of a Normative Framework." *Democratization* 21, no. 6 (2013): 1055–73.

Öcalan, Abdullah. *The Road Map to Democratization of Turkey and Solution to the Kurdish Question.* Cologne: International Initiative "Freedom for Abdullah

Öcalan—Peace in Kurdistan," 2011. http://kinfo.kurdport.com/media/files/DTK%20Demokratik%20Ozerklik.pdf; accessed March 29, 2014.

———. *Democratic Confederalism.* Honolulu: Transmedia Publishing, 2015.

———. *Demokratik Kurtuluş ve Özgür Yaşamı İnşa: İmralı Notları* [Democratic Liberation and Constructing Free Life: Notes from İmralı]. Neuss, Germany: Mezopotamien Verlag, 2015.

———. *Democratic Nation.* Cologne: International Initiative Edition in cooperation with Mesopotamian Publishers, Neuss, 2017.

Öktem, Kerem, and Karabekir Akkoyunlu, "Exit from Democracy: Illiberal Governance in Turkey and Beyond." *Southeast European and Black Sea Studies* 16, no. 4 (2016): 469–80.

———, eds. *Exit from Democracy: Illiberal Governance in Turkey and Beyond.* New York: Routledge, 2017.

Öniş, Ziya. "Conservative Globalism at the Crossroads: The Justice and Development Party and the Thorny Path to Democratic Consolidation in Turkey." *Mediterranean Politics* 14, no. 1 (2009): 21–40.

———. "Turkey and the Arab Revolutions: Boundaries of Regional Power Influence in a Turbulent Middle East." *Mediterranean Politics* 19, no. 2 (2014): 203–19.

Özbudun, Ergun. "Established Revolution vs. Unfinished Revolution: Contrasting Patterns of Democratization in Mexico and Turkey." In *Authoritarian Politics in Modern Society: The Dynamics of Established One Party System,* edited by Samuel P. Huntington and Clement H. Moore. London: Basic Books, 1970.

———. *Contemporary Turkish Politics: Challenges to Democratic Consolidation.* Boulder: Lynne Rienner, 2000.

———. *Otoriter Rejimler, Seçimsel Demokrasiler ve Türkiye* [Authoritarian Regimes, Selective Democracies, and Turkey]. Istanbul: Bilgi Üniversitesi Yayınları, 2011. Özcan, Ali Kemal. *Turkey's Kurds: A Theoretical Analysis of the PKK and Abdullah Ocalan.* New York: Routledge, 2006.

Özdemir, Yalçın. "Kurds." *CNN Turk Programme 5N 1K,* March 22, 2007. tv.cnn-turk.com/video/2013/04/25/programlar/5n1k/5n1k/2005-03-22T1930/index.html; accessed June 17, 2014.

Özdoğan, Günay Göksu. "Turkish Nationalism Reconsidered: The 'Heaviness' of Statist Patriotism in Nation-Building." In *Nationalism in the Troubled Triangle: Cyprus, Greece and Turkey,* edited by Ayhan Aktar, Niyazi Kızılyürek, and Umut Özkırımlı. New York: Palgrave Macmillan, 2010.

Özdoğan, Günay Göksu, and Gül Tokay, eds. *Redefining the Nation, State, and Citizen.* Istanbul: Eren Yayıncılık, 2000.

Özkırımlı, Umut. *Milliyetçilik Kuramları: Eleştirel Bir Bakış* [Theories of Nationalism: A Critical Perspective]. Ankara: Doğu-Batı, 2008.

Özoğlu, Hakan. "Nationalism and Kurdish Notables in the Late Ottoman-Early Republican Era." *International Journal of Middle East Studies* 33, no. 3 (2001): 383–409.

———. *Kurdish Notables and the Ottoman State: Evolving Identities, Competing Loyalties, and Shifting Boundaries.* New York: State University of New York Press, 2004.

Özpek, Burak Bilgehan. *The Peace Process between Turkey and Kurds: Anatomy of a Failure.* New York: Routledge, 2018.

Öztürk, Muhsin. "Kürt meselesinde Özal yalnızdı, Erdoğan ise şanslı [Özal Was Alone Whereas Erdoğan Was Lucky in the Kurdish Question]." *Aksiyon*, September 28, 2009.

Pamuk, Şevket. *Osmanlı-Türkiye İktisadî Tarihi 1500–1914* [Ottoman-Turkish Economic History 1500–1914]. 8th ed. Istanbul: İletişim, 2013.

Parla, Taha. *The Social and Political Thought of Ziya Gokalp 1876–1924.* Leiden: E. J. Brill, 1985.

Paşa, İhsan Nuri. *Ağrı Dağı İsyanı* [Ararat Mountain Rebellion]. Istanbul, MED Yayınları, 1992.

Peet, Richard, and Elaine Hartwick. *Theories of Development: Contentions, Arguments, Alternatives.* New York: The Guilford Press, 2015.

Perinçek, Doğu. *Kemalist Devrim—4: Kurtuluş Savaşı'nda Kürt Politikası* [The Kemalist Revolution—4, Kurdish Policies during the Turkish War of Independence]. Istanbul: Kaynak Yayınları, 1999.

Pettit, Philip. *Republicanism: A Theory of Freedom and Government.* Oxford: Oxford University Press, 2002.

Philips, Anne. "Democracy and Differece: Some Problems for Feminist Theory." In *The Rights of Minority Cultures*, edited by Will Kymlicka, 288–299. New York: Oxford University Press, 1996.

Piscatori, James P. *Islam in a World of Nation-States.* Cambridge: Cambridge University Press, 1986.

Plattner, Marc. "Sovereignty and Democracy." *Policy Review* 122 (December 2003–January 2004): 3–18.

Pope, Nicole, and Hugh Pope. *Turkey Unveiled: A History of Modern Turkey.* New York: The Overlook Press, 1998.

Posen, Barry. "The Security Dilemma and Ethnic Conflict." In *Ethnic Conflict and International Security*, edited by Michael E. Brown. Princeton: Princeton University Press, 1993.

Przeworski, Adam. "Democracy as a Contingent Outcome of Conflicts." In *Constitutionalism and Democracy*, edited by Jon Elster and Rune Slagstad, 59–80. Cambridge: Cambridge University Press, 1988.

———. "Deliberation and Ideological Domination." In *Deliberative Democracy*, edited by John Elster, 140–60. New York: Cambridge University Press, 1998.

Rahman, Tariq. *Language and Politics in Pakistan.* Karachi: Oxford University Press Karachi, 1996.

Randal, Jonathan C. *After Such Knowledge, What Forgiveness? My Encounters with Kurdistan.* New York: Farrar, Straus and Giroux, 1997.

———. *After Such Knowledge, What Forgiveness? My Encounters with Kurdistan.* Boulder: Westview, 1999.

Restrepo, Eduardo, and Arturo Escobar. "'Other Anthropologies and Anthropology Otherwise': Steps to a World Anthropologies Framework." *Critique of Anthropology* 25, no. 2 (2016).

Ricks, Thomas E. "Do Iraq and Syria No Longer Exist? (9): Maybe, But It Isn't Up to Us Anyways." *Foreign Policy,* November 6, 2014. https://foreignpolicy.com/2014/11/06/do-iraq-and-syria-no-longer-exist-9-maybe-but-it-isnt-up-to-us-anyways/; accessed June 9, 2019.

Robins, Phillip. "Confusion at Home, Confusion Abroad: Turkey Between Copenhagen and Iraq." *International Affairs* 79, no. 3 (2003): 547–66.

Rodrigue, Aron. "Reflections on Millets and Minorities: Ottoman Legacies." In *Turkey between Nationalism and Globalization,* edited by Riva Kastoryano, 36–46. London: Routledge, 2013.

Roe, Paul. *Ethnic Violence and Societal Security Dilemma.* New York: Routledge, 2005.

Romano, David. *The Kurdish Nationalist Movement: Opportunity, Mobilization, and Identity.* Cambridge: Cambridge University Press, 2006.

Romano, David, and Mehmet Gurses, eds. *Conflict, Democratization, and the Kurds in the Middle East: Turkey, Iran, Iraq, and Syria.* New York: Palgrave Macmillan, 2014.

Rumelili, Bahar. *Conflict Resolution and Ontological Security: Peace Anxieties.* Prio New Security Studies. London: Routledge, 2015.

Rumelili, Bahar, and Ayşe Betül Çelik. "Ontological Insecurity in Asymmetric Conflicts: Reflections on Agonistic Peace in Turkey's Kurdish Issue." *Security Dialogue* 48, no. 4 (2017): 279–96.

Rustow, Dankwart Alexander. "Transitions to Democracy." *Comparative Politics* 2, no. 3 (1970): 337–63.

Şahin, Haluk. "Türkiyeli, Türk, Alt-Kimlik, Üst-Kimlik [Türkiyeli, Turkish, Supra-Identity, Sub-Identity]." *Radikal,* October 22, 2004.

Şahin, Osman. "Middle Class Formation and Democratization: Comparison of Political Islam and Kurds in Turkey." MA Thesis in International Relations, Koç University, 2008.

Sahin-Mencutek, Zeynep. "Strong in the Movement, Strong in the Party: Women's Representation in the Kurdish Party of Turkey." *Political Studies* 64, no. 2 (2015): 470–87.

Saideman, Stephen M., and R. William Ayres. "Determining the Causes of Irredentism." *The Journal of Politics* 62, no. 4 (November 2000): 1126–44.

Sakallıoğlu, Ümit Cizre. "Kurdish Nationalism from an Islamist Perspective: The Discourses of Turkish Islamist Writers." *Journal of Muslim Minority Affairs* 18, no. 1 (1998): 73–89.

San-Akca, Belgin. *States in Disguise: Causes of State Support for Rebel Groups.* Oxford: Oxford University Press, 2016.

Saracoglu, Cenk. " 'Exclusive Recognition': The New Dimensions of the Question of Ethnicity and Nationalism in Turkey." *Ethnic and Racial Studies* 32, no. 4 (2009): 640–58.

———. *Şehir, Orta Sınıf ve Kürtler: İnkar'dan 'Tanıyarak Dışlama'ya* [The City, The Middle Class, and the Kurds: From Denial to "Exclusive Recognition"]. Istanbul: İletişim, 2011.

Sarigil, Zeki. *Ethnic Boundaries in Turkish Politics: The Secular Kurdish Movement and Islam.* New York: New York University Press, 2018.

Sarigil, Zeki, and Ekrem Karakoç. "Who Supports Secession? The Determinants of Secessionist Attitudes among Turkey's Kurds." *Nations and Nationalism* 22, no. 2 (2016): 325–46.

Sarıgil, Zeki, and Ömer Fazlıoğlu. "Religion and Ethnonationalism: Turkey's Kurdish Issue." *Nations and Nationalism* 19, no. 3 (2013): 551–71.

Sayarı, Sabri, and Yılmaz Esmer, eds. *Politics, Parties, and Elections in Turkey.* Boulder: Lynne Rienner, 2002.

Saylan, İbrahim. "The Europeanization Process and Kurdish Nationalism in Turkey: The Case of the Democratic Society Party." *Nationalities Papers* 40, no. 2 (March 2012): 185–202.

Sazak, Derya. "Cumhuriyetimiz Tek Soya İndirgenemez, Prof Kaboğlu ile Söyleşi [Our Republic Cannot be Boiled Down to a Single Lineage, Interview with Prof Kaboğlu]." *Milliyet*, November 1, 2004.

Scheller, Bente. *The Wisdom of Syria's Waiting Game: Syrian Foreign Policy under the Assads.* London: Hurst, 2013.

Schmidt, Vivien A. "Discursive Institutionalism: The Explanatory Power of Ideas and Discourse Vivien A. Schmidt." *Annual Review of Political Science* 11 (2008): 303–26.

Schwedler, Jillian. "Islamists in Power? Inclusion, Moderation, and the Arab Uprisings." *Middle East Development Journal* 5, no. 1 (2014): 1–18.

———. "Why Academics Can't Get Beyond Radicals and Moderates." *Washington Post*, February 12, 2015.

Scott, James. *Seeing like a State.* New Haven: Yale University Press, 1997.

Selçuk, Orçun, and Dilara Hekimci. "The Rise of the Democracy—Authoritarianism Cleavage and Opposition Coordination in Turkey (2014–2019)." *Democratization* 27, no. 8 (2020).

Sezgin, Yüksel. *Human Rights under State-Enforced Religious Family Laws in Israel, Egypt, and India.* New York: Cambridge University Press, 2013.

Sherif, Muzafer. *In Common Predicament: Social Psychology of Intergroup Conflict and Cooperation.* Boston: Houghton Mifflin, 1966.

Sherif, Muzafer, and Carl I. Hovland. *Social Judgement: Assimilation and Contrast Effects in Communication and Attitude Change.* New Haven: Yale University Press, 1961.

Sherwood, Harriet. "Is Scotland Finally Set to Bid Farewell to the Union?" *Guardian*, August 11, 2019.

SHP. *Sosyaldemokrat Halkçı Parti'nin Doğu ve Güneydoğu Sorunları'na Bakışı ve Çözüm Önerileri* [Social Democratic Populist Party's Views on the Eastern and South Eastern Conflicts and Solution Proposals]. Ankara: SHP Merkez Yürütme Kurulu, 1990.

Simon, Reeva Spector, and Eleanor H. Tejirian, eds. *The Creation of Iraq, 1914–1921.* New York: Columbia University Press, 2004.

Skocpol, Theda. *Social Revolutions in the Modern World.* Cambridge: Cambridge University Press, 1994.

Slater, Dan. "Strong-State Democratization in Malaysia and Singapore." *Journal of Democracy* 23, no. 2 (2012): 19–33.

Smith, Anthony D. *National Identity.* Reno: University of Nevada Press, 1991.

Snyder, Jack L. *From Voting to Violence: Democratization and Nationalist Conflict.* New York: W. W. Norton.

Somer, Murat. "Cascades of Ethnic Polarization: Lessons from Yugoslavia." *Annals of the American Academy of Political and Social Science* 573 (2001): 127–51.

———. "Ethnic Kurds, Endogenous Identities, and Turkey's Democratization and Integration with Europe." *Global Review of Ethnopolitics* (now *Ethnopolitics*) 1, no. 4 (2002): 74–93.

———. "Insincere Public Discourse, Trust, and Implications for Democratic Transition: The Yugoslav Meltdown Revisited." *Journal for Institutional Innovation, Development, and Transition* 6 (2002): 92–112.

———. "Turkey's Kurdish Conflict: Changing Context and Domestic and Regional Implications." *Middle East Journal* 58, no. 2 (2004): 235–53.

———. "Defensive- vs. Liberal-Nationalist Perspectives on Diversity and the Kurdish Conflict: Europeanization, the Internal Debate, and *Türkiyelilik.*" *New Perspectives on Turkey* 32 (2005): 73–91.

———. "Failures of the Discourse of Ethnicity: Turkey, Kurds and the Emerging Iraq." *Security Dialogue* 36, no. 1 (2005): 109–28.

———. "Resurgence and Remaking of Identity: Civil Beliefs, Domestic and External Dynamics, and the Turkish Mainstream Discourse on Kurds." *Comparative Political Studies* 38, no. 6 (2005): 591–622.

———. "Sustainable Democratization and the Roles of the US and the EU: Political Islam and Kurdish Nationalism in Turkey." *Turkish Policy Quarterly* 5, no. 3 (2006), 89–108.

———. "Defensive and Liberal Nationalisms, the Kurdish Question and Modernization/Democratization." In *Remaking Turkey: Globalization, Alternative Modernities, and Democracy*, edited by Fuat Keyman, 103–35. Oxford: Lexington Books, 2007.

————. "Moderate Islam and Secularist Opposition in Turkey: Implications for the World, Muslims, and Secular Democracy." *Third World Quarterly* 28, no. 7 (2007): 1271–89.

————. "Why Aren't Kurds Like the Scots and the Turks Like the Brits? Moderation and Democracy in the Kurdish Question." *Cooperation and Conflict* 43, no. 2 (2008): 220–49.

————. "Kürt Açılımı, Çoğul Gerçekler ve Kimlikler [The Kurdish Opening, Plural Realities and Identities]." *Radikal*, September 25, 2009.

————. "Media Values and Democratization: What Unites and What Divides Religious-Conservative and Pro-Secular Elites?" *Turkish Studies* 11, no. 4 (2010): 555–77.

————. "Democratization, Clashing Narratives, and 'Twin Tolerations' between Islamic-Conservative and Pro-Secular Actors." In *Nationalisms and Politics in Turkey: Political Islam, Kemalism, and the Kurdish Issue*, edited by Marlies Casier and Joost Jongerden, 28–47. London: Routledge, 2010.

————. "Does It Take Democrats to Democratize?: Lessons from Islamic and Secular Elite Values in Turkey." *Comparative Political Studies* 44, no. 5 (2011): 511–45.

————. "Toward a Non-Standard Story: The Kurdish Question and the Headscarf, Nationalism, and Iraq." In *Symbiotic Antagonisms in Turkey: Sources, Discourses, and Changing Nature of Turkish, Kurdish, and Islamic Nationalisms*, edited by Ayşe Kadıoğlu and Fuat Keyman, 253–88. Salt Lake City: The University of Utah Press, 2011.

————. "Turkey, Kurds, and Syria." *Today's Zaman*, August 8, 2012. http://home.ku.edu.tr/~musomer/Opinion/Somer%20Turkey%20and%20Kurds%20TDZ%20as%20is%20Aug2012.pdf; accessed June 9, 2019.

————. "Turkey's Model of 'Moderate Islamism' Can be Misleading." *The National*, October 1, 2012. http://www.thenational.ae/thenationalconversation/comment/turkeys-model-of-moderate-islamism-can-be-misleading; accessed July 4, 2019.

————. "Barış Süreci ve Kürt Meselesi'nde Kimlik ve Dış Politika: Riskler ve Fırsatlar [The Peace Process and Identity and Foreign Policy in the Kurdish Question: Risks and Opportunities]." *Ortadoğu Analiz* 5, no. 57 (2013): 46–53.

————. "Demokratikleşme Paketi ve Çift Dilli Eğitim [Democratization Package and Bilingual Education]." *T24*, October 6, 2013. https://t24.com.tr/haber/demokratiklesme-paketi-ve-cift-dilli-egitim,241267; accessed July 12, 2019.

————. "Vatandaşlık Tanımı için Atatürk Referans Alınmalı [Atatürk Should be Taken as Reference for a Definition of Citizenship]." Interview, *Akşam*, February 11, 2013. http://aksam.com.tr/roportaj/vatandaslik-tanimi-icin-ataturk-referans-alinmali/haber-168960; accessed July 16, 2019.

————. "Moderation of Religious and Secular Politics, a Country's 'Center' and Democratization." *Democratization* 21, no. 2 (2014): 244–67.

———. "Islamist Political Parties, the Turkish Case, and the Future of Muslim Polities." In *Strategies and Behavior of Islamist Political Parties: Lessons from Asia and the Middle East*, edited by Quinn Mecham and Julie Chernov Hwang, 41–57. Philadelphia: University of Pennsylvania Press, 2014.

———. "Theory-Consuming or Theory-Producing?: Studying Turkey as a Theory-Developing Critical Case." *Turkish Studies* 15, no. 4 (2014): 571–88.

———. "Whither with Secularism or Just Undemocratic Laiklik? The Evolution and Future of Secularism under the AKP." In *The Uncertain Path of the 'New Turkey,'* edited by Valeria Talbot, 23–49. Milan: ISPI, Instituto per gli Studi di Politica Internazionale, 2015.

———. "Understanding Turkey's Democratic Breakdown: Old versus New and Indigenous versus Global Authoritarianism." *Southeast European and Black Sea Studies* 16, no. 4 (2016): 481–503.

———. *Sosyal Demokratlar ve Türkiye'de Kürt Sorunu* [Social Democrats and the Kurdish Question in Turkey]. Ankara: Alabanda Akademi, 2016.

———. "Conquering Versus Democratizing the State: Political Islamists and Fourth Wave Democratization in Turkey and Tunisia." *Democratization* 24, no. 6 (2017): 1025–43.

———. "Will Turkey's President Accept the Country's Election Results?" *Washington Post*, April 18, 2019.

———. "Turkish Secularism: Looking Forward and Beyond the West." In *Routledge Handbook on Turkish Politics*, edited by Matthew Whiting and Alpaslan Özerdem, 37–54. London: Routledge, 2019.

———. "Turkey: The Slippery Slope from Reformist to Revolutionary Polarization and Democratic Breakdown." *The ANNALS of the American Academy of Political and Social Science* 681, no. 1 (2019): 42–61.

Somer, Murat, and Evangelos G. Liaras. "Turkey's New Kurdish Opening: Religious versus Secular Values." *Middle East Policy* 17, no. 2 (2010): 152–65.

Somer, Murat, and Gitta Glüpker-Kesebir. "Is Islam the Solution? Comparing Turkish Islamic and Secular Thinking toward Ethnic and Religious Minorities." *Journal of Church and State* 58, no. 3 (2015): 529–55.

Somer, Murat, and Jennifer McCoy. "Transformations through Polarizations and Global Threats to Democracy." *Annals of the American Academy of Political and Social Science* 681 (2019): 8–22.

Sözen, Yunus. "Politics of the People: Hegemonic Ideology and Regime Oscillation in Turkey and Argentina." PhD Dissertation, New York University, 2010.

———. "Studying Autocratization in Turkey: Political Institutions, Populism, and Neoliberalism," *New Perspectives on Turkey* 63 (2020): 209–35.

Spickard, Paul, ed. *Race and Nation: Ethnic Systems in the Modern World*. New York: Routledge, 2005.

Spruyt, Hendrik. "War, Trade, and State Formation." In *Oxford Handbook of Comparative Politics*, edited by Carles Boix and Susan Stokes, 211–235. Oxford: Oxford University Press, 2007.

Stansfield, Gareth. "Kurds, Persian Nationalism, and Shi'i Rule: Surviving Dominant Nationhood in Iran." In *Conflict, Democratization, and the Kurds in the Middle East Turkey, Iran, Iraq, and Syria*, edited by David Romano and Mehmet Gürses, 59–84. New York: Palgrave Macmillan, 2014.

Stefanovic, Djordje, Neophytos Loizides, and Samantha Parsons. "Home Is Where the Heart Is? Forced Migration and Voluntary Return in Turkey's Kurdish Regions." *Journal of Refugee Studies* 28, no. 2 (2014): 276–96.

Stepan, Alfred. "Religion, Democracy, and the 'Twin Tolerations.'" *Journal of Democracy* 23, no. 2 (April 2000): 37–57.

Stepan, Alfred, Juan J. Linz, and Yogendra Yadav. *Crafting State Nations: India and Other Multinational Democracies*. Baltimore: The Johns Hopkins University Press, 2011.

Süleymaniye, Mahmut Hamsici. "Barış Görüşmelerini Başlatan Pencewini: Karayılan, Gül Ve Erdoğan'a Selam Söyledi [Pencewini Who Initiated the Peace Talks: Karayılan Sent Greetings to Gül and Erdoğan]." *BBC Türkçe*, April 18, 2016. https://www.bbc.com/turkce/haberler/2016/04/160418_pencewini_roportaj; accessed June 24, 2019.

Suny, Ronald Grigor. "Nationalism, Nation Making, and the Postcolonial States of Asia, Africa, and Eurasia." In *After Independence*, edited by Lowell W. Barrington, 279–95. Ann Arbor: University of Michigan Press, 2009.

———. *"They Can Live in the Desert but Nowhere Else": A History of Armenian Genocide*. Princeton: Princeton University Press, 2015.

Svolik, Milan W. "Democracy as an Equilibrium: Rational Choice and Formal Political Theory in Democratization Research." *Democratization* 26, no. 1 (2018): 40–60.

Şeker, Nesim. "Türklük ve Osmanlı Arasında: Birinci Dünya Savaşı Sonrası Türkiye'de 'Milliyet' Arayışları ya da 'Anasır Meselesi' [Between Turkishness and the Ottomans: The Quest for 'Nationality' or the 'Unity of the Elements' Post–World War I]." In *İmparatorluktan Cumhuriyete Etnik Çatışma* [Ethnic Conflict in Turkey from Empire to Republic], edited by Erik Jan Zürcher, 157–75. Istanbul: İletişim, 2005.

Tachau, Frank. "The Search for National Identity among the Turks." *The Welt des Islams, New Series* 8, no. 3 (1963): 165–76.

Tajfel, Henri, and John C. Turner. "The Social Identity Theory of Intergroup Behavior." In *Psychology of Intergroup Relations*, edited by Stephen Worchel and William G Austin, 775–89. Chicago: Nelson-Hall, 1986.

Tan, Altan. *Kürt Sorunu: Ya Tam Kardeşlik Ya Hep Birlikte Kölelik* [The Kurdish Question: Proper Brotherhood or Slavery for All]. Istanbul: Timaş Yayınları, 2009.

Tanbar, Kabir. *The Reckoning of Pluralism: Political Belonging and the Demands of History in Turkey*. Stanford: Stanford University Press, 2014.

Tanör, Bülent. *Kurtuluş Kuruluş* [Liberation Foundation]. Istanbul: Cumhuriyet Kitapları, 2005.

Taş, Hakkı. "Turkey—from Tutelary to Delegative Democracy." *Third World Quarterly* 36, no. 4 (2015): 776–91.

Taylor, Charles. *A Secular Age.* Cambridge: Belknap Press of Harvard University Press, 2007.

*TBMM Gizli Celse Kayıtları 1920–1934* [Records of the Proceedings of the Secret Sessions of the Grand National Assembly of Turkey 1920–1934]. Volume 1–4. Ankara, Türkiye İş Bankası Yayınları, [1920–34] 1985.

T. C. Dışişleri Bakanlığı, *Türkiye Dış Politikasında 50 Yıl: Cumhuriyetin İlk On Yılı ve Balkan Paktı 1923–1934* [50 Years of Turkey's Foreign Policy: The First Decade of the Republic and the Balkan Pact (1923–1934)]. Ankara: Araştırma ve Siyaset Planlama Genel Müdürlüğü, 1974.

Tekeli, İlhan, and Selim İlkin. *Cumhuriyetin Harcı: Köktenci Modernitenin Doğuşu* [The Mortar of the Republic: The Birth of Radical Modernity]. Istanbul: Bilgi Üniversitesi Yayınları, 2003.

Tepe, Sultan. "Turkey's AKP: A Model 'Muslim-Democratic' Party?" *Journal of Democracy* 16, no. 3 (2005): 69–85.

Tetlock, Philip E., and Aaron Belkin. "Counterfactual Thought Experiments in World Politics: Logical, Methodological, and Psychological Perspectives." In *Counterfactual Thought Experiments in World Politics*, edited by Philip E. Tetlock and Aaron Belkin, 3–38. Princeton: Princeton University Press, 1996.

Tezcan, Baki. "The Development of the Use of 'Kurdistan' as a Geographical Description and the Incorporation of this Region into the Ottoman Empire in the 16th century." In *The Great Ottoman, Turkish Civilisation III*, edited by Kemal Çiçek. Ankara: Yeni Türkiye, 2000.

———. *The Second Ottoman Empire: Political and Social Transformation in the Early Modern World.* Cambridge: Cambridge University Press, 2010.

Tezcan, Baki, and Karl K. Barbir, eds. *Identity and Identity Formation in the Ottoman World.* Istanbul: Istanbul Bilgi University Press, 2012.

Tezcür, Güneş Murat. "When Democratization Radicalizes: The Kurdish Nationalist Movement in Turkey." *Journal of Peace Research* 47 (2010): 775–89.

———. "The Ebb and Flow of Armed Conflict in Turkey: An Elusive Peace." In *Conflict, Democratization, and the Kurds in the Middle East*, edited by David Romano and Mehmet Gürses. New York: Palgrave Macmillan, 2014.

———. "Violence and Nationalist Mobilization: The Onset of the Kurdish Insurgency in Turkey." *Nationalities Papers* 43, no. 2 (2015): 248–66.

———. "Ordinary People, Extraordinary Risks: Participation in an Ethnic Rebellion." *American Political Science Review* 110, no. 2 (2016): 247–64.

Ther, Philipp. *The Dark Side of Nation States: Ethnic Cleansing in Modern Europe.* Oxford: Berghahn Books, 2014.

Tilly, Charles. *Coercion, Capital, and European States.* Cambridge: Blackwell, 1990.

———. "The Trouble with Stories." In *The Social Worlds of Higher Education,* edited by Bernice A. Pescosolido and Ronald Aminzade, 256–70. Thousand Oaks, CA: Pine Forge, 1999.

Tilly, Charles, and Sidney Tarrow. *Contentious Politics.* Oxford: Oxford University Press, 2015.

Todorova, Maria. "Identity (Trans)formation among Bulgarian Muslims." In *The Myth of "Ethnic Conflict": Politics, Economics, and "Cultural" Violence,* special issue in *UC Berkeley GAIA Research Series* 98, edited by Beverly Crawford and Ronnie D. Lipschutz, 471–510. 1998 (retrieved from: https://escholarship.org/uc/item/7hc733q3).

Tufekci, Zeynep. *Twitter and Tear Gas: The Power and Fragility of Networked Protest.* New Haven and London: Yale University Press, 2017.

*Turkey 2020 International Religious Freedom Report, United States Department of State.* Washington, DC: Office of International Religious Freedom, 2021.

Tuğal, Cihan. *Passive Revolution: Absorbing the Islamic Challenge to Capitalism.* Stanford: Stanford University Press, 2009.

———. *The Fall of the Turkish Model: How the Arab Uprisings Brought Down Islamic Liberalism.* New York: Verso, 2016.

Tuna, Banu. "4,653 Faili Meçhul Belgeseli [4,653 Unsolved Murders Documentary]." *Hürriyet,* March 20, 2005.

Tunçay, Mete. *Türkiye'de Tek Parti Yönetimi'nin Kurulması: 1923–1931* [The Establishment of the Single Party System in Turkey: 1923–1931]. Istanbul: Tarih Vakfı Yurt Yayınları, 2005.

Tunçel, Harun. "Türkiye'de İsmi Değiştirilen Köyler [Villages with Changed Names in Turkey]." *Fırat University Social Sciences Journal* 10, no. 2 (2000): 23–34.

Turam, Berna. *Between Islam and the State: The Politics of Engagement.* Stanford: Stanford University Press, 2007.

———, ed. *Secular State and Religious Society: Two Forces in Play in Turkey.* New York: Palgrave MacMillan 2012.

*Türk Parlamento Tarihi, Milli Mücadele ve TBMM I. Dönem, 1919–1923* [History of the Turkish Parliament, the National Struggle, and the Grand National Assembly of Turkey Term I, 1919–1923]. Volume II. TBMM Vakfı, 1995.

Türkmen, Gülay. "Negotiating Symbolic Boundaries in Conflict Resolution: Religion and Ethnicity in Turkey's Kurdish Conflict." *Qualitative Sociology* 41, no. 4 (2018): 569–91.

Türköne, Mümtaz'er. "Türklük Tanımı [The Definition of Turkishness]." *Zaman,* September 18, 2007.

Turnaoğlu, Banu. *The Formation of Turkish Republicanism.* Princeton: Princeton University Press, 2017.

Ugur, Mehmet. *The European Union and Turkey: An Anchor/Credibility Dilemma.* Aldershot, Hants: Ashgate, 1999.

Unowsky, Daniel L. *The Pomp and Politics of Patriotism: Imperial Celebrations in Habsburg Austria, 1848–1916.* West Lafayette, IN: Purdue University Press, 2005.

Uygun, Oktay. "Federalizm ve Bölgesel Özerklik Tartışmaları [Discussions of Federalism and Regional Autonomy]." In *Demokratik Anayasa: Görüşler ve Öneriler* [Democratic Constitution: Views and Proposals], edited by Ece Göztepe and Aykut Çelebi, Istanbul: Metis Yayınları, 2012.

Ünlü, Barış, and Ozan Değer, eds. *İsmail Beşikçi.* Istanbul: İletişim, 2011.

Ünver, H. Akin. "Turkey's 'Deep-State' and the Ergenekon Conundrum." *The Middle East Institute Policy Brief,* no. 23 (2009): 1–25.

Üstel, Füsun. "Türk Milliyetçiliğinde Anadolu Metaforu [The Metaphor of Anatolia in Turkish Nationalism]." *Tarih ve Toplum* [History and Society] 109 (1993): 51–55.

———. *Makbul Vatandaş'ın Peşinde: İkinci Meşrutiyet'ten Bugüne Vatandaşlık Eğitimi* [In Pursuit of the Favorite Citizen: Citizenship Education from the Second Constitutionalist Period to Today]. Istanbul: İletişim, 2011.

Vali, Abbas. *Kurds and the State in Iran: The Making of Kurdish Identity.* London: I. B. Tauris, 2011.

———, ed. *Essays on the Origins of Kurdish Nationalism.* Costa Mesa: Mazda, 2003.

———, ed. *Kürt Milliyetçiliğinin Kökenleri* [The Origins of Kurdish Nationalism]. Istanbul: Avesta Yayınları, 2005.

van Bruinessen, Martin. "Kurdish Society, Ethnicity, Nationalism, and Refugee Problems." In *The Kurds: A Contemporary Overview,* edited by Philip G. Kreyenbroek and Stefan Speri, 33–67. London: Routledge, 1992.

———. *Kürtlük, Türklük, Alevilik: Etnik ve Dinsel Kimlik Mücadeleleri* [Kurdishness, Turkishness, Alevi-ness: Ethnic and Religious Identity Struggles]. İstanbul: İletişim, 1999.

———. "Shifting National and Ethnic Identities: The Kurds in Turkey and Europe." In *Redefining the Nation, State, and Citizen,* edited by Günay Göksu Özdoğan and Gül Tokay, 91–108. Istanbul: Eren Yayıncılık, 2000.

———. *Ağa, Şeyh, Devlet* [Agha, Sheikh, State]. İstanbul: İletişim, [1992] 2003.

Varol, Ozan O. "The Democratic Coup d'Etat," *Harvard International Law Journal* 53, no. 2 (2012): 291–356.

Varshney, Ashutosh. *Ethnic Conflict and Civic Life: Hindus and Muslims in India.* New Haven: Yale University Press, 2002.

———. "Discovering the "State-Nation." Book Review of *Crafting State-Nations: India and Other Multinational Democracies* by Alfred Stepan, Juan J. Linz, and Yogendra Yadav. Baltimore: Johns Hopkins University Press, 2011, *Journal of Democracy* 23, no. 2 (2012).

Washington Institute for Near East Policy. "German and French Leaders' Views on Turkey's EU Membership." *PolicyWatch*, 1007, June 27 2005, https://www.washingtoninstitute.org/policy-analysis/german-and-french-leaders-views-turkeys-eu-membership.

Watts, Nicole F. "Silence and Voice: Turkish Policies and Kurdish Resistance in the Mid-20th Century." In *The Evolution of Kurdish Nationalism*, edited by Mohammad M. A. Ahmed and Michael M. Gunter, 52–77. Costa Mesa: Mazda, 2007.

Weber, Eugen. *Peasants into Frenchmen: The Modernization of Rural France, 1870–1914*. Stanford: Stanford University Press, 1976.

Weber, Max. *The Methodology of the Social Sciences*. New York: Free Press, [1905] 1949.

———. *Economy and Society: An Outline of Interpretive Sociology*. Edited by Guenther Roth and Claus Wittich. Berkeley: University of California Press, 1978.

Weinstein, Jeremy M. *Inside Rebellion*. New York: Cambridge University Press, 2007.

Weller, Marc, and Katherine Nobbs, eds. *Asymmetric Autonomy and the Settlement of Ethnic Conflicts*. Philadelphia: University of Pennsylvania Press, 2010.

White, Jenny. *Muslim Nationalism and the New Turks*. Princeton: Princeton University Press, 2013.

White, Paul. *Primitive Rebels or Revolutionary Modernizers: The Kurdish Nationalist Movement in Turkey*. London: Zed Books, 2000.

Wilkinson, Steven. *Votes and Violence: Electoral Competition and Ethnic Riots in India*. New York: Cambridge University Press, 2004.

Wimmer, Andreas. "Elementary Strategies of Ethnic Boundary Making." *Ethnic and Racial Studies* 31, no. 6 (2008): 631–65.

———. *Waves of War: Nationalism, State Formation, and Ethnic Exclusion in the Modern World*. Cambridge: Cambridge University Press, 2013.

Wolchik, Sharon L. "The Politics of Ethnicity in Post-Communist Czechoslovakia." *East European Politics and Societies* 8, no. 1 (Winter 1994): 153–88.

Wuthrich, F. Michael and Melvyn Ingleby. "The Pushback against Populism: Running on 'Radical Love' in Turkey," *Journal of Democracy* 31, no. 2 (2020): 24–40.

Yalman, Ahmed Emin. "Türkçülük ve Memleketçilik [Turkism and 'Homeland'ism]." *Vakit*, October 20, 1919. Quoted in Ahmet Abdullah Saçmalı, "From Mudros to Lausanne: How Ahmed Emin's Perception of the 'Other' Changed." MA Dissertation, Department of History, Boğaziçi University, 2012.

———. *Kürtler ve Kürdistan* [Kurds and Kurdistan]. *Vakit*, August 14, 1919. Translated into modern Turkish by Ahmet Abdullah Saçmalı, "From Mudros to Lausanne: How Ahmed Emin's Perception of the 'Other' Changed." MA Dissertation, Department of History, Boğaziçi University, 2012.

Yaman, Ali. *Alevilik ve Kızılbaşlık Tarihi* [A History of Alawism and Qızılbashlik]. Istanbul: Nokta Kitap, 2007.

Yavuz, M. Hakan. "Five Stages of the Construction of Kurdish Nationalism in Turkey." *Nationalism & Ethnic Politics* 7, no. 3 (2001): 1–24.

———. *Islamic Political Identity in Turkey.* New York: Oxford University Press, 2003.

Yavuz, M. Hakan, and Nihat Ali Özcan. "The Kurdish Question and Turkey's Justice and Development Party." *Middle East Policy* 13, no. 1 (2006): 102–19.

Yavuz, M. Hakan, and Bayram Balcı, eds. *Turkey's July 15th Coup: What Happened and Why.* Salt Lake City: The University of Utah Press, 2018.

Yavuz, M. Hakan, and John L. Esposito, eds. *Turkish Islam and the Secular State: The Gülen Movement.* Syracuse: Syracuse University Press, 2003.

Yaycioglu, Ali. *Partners of the Empire: The Crisis of the Ottoman Order in the Age of Revolutions.* Stanford: Stanford University Press, 2016.

———. "Guarding Traditions and Laws—Disciplining Bodies and Souls: Tradition, Science, and Religion in the Age of Ottoman Reform." *Modern Asian Studies* 52, no. 5 (2018): 1542–1603.

Yayman, Hüseyin. *Türkiye'nin Kürt Sorunu Algısı* [Turkey's Kurdish Conflict Recollection]. Ankara: SETA ve Pollmark, Ağustos 2009.

Yeğen, Mesut. "The Turkish State Discourse and the Exclusion of Kurdish Identity." *Middle Eastern Studies* 32, no. 2 (1996): 216–29.

———. *Müstakbel Türk'ten Sözde Vatandaş'a: Cumhuriyet ve Kürtler* [From Prospective Turks to So-Called Citizens]. Istanbul: İletişim, 2006.

———. " 'Prospective-Turks' or 'Pseudo-Citizens': Kurds in Turkey." *The Middle East Journal* 63, no. 4 (2009): 597–615.

Yeldan, Erinç A., and Burcu Ünüvar. "An Assessment of the Turkish Economy in the AKP Era." *Research and Policy on Turkey* 1, no. 1 (2016): 11–28.

Yerasimos, Stefanos. *Türkler: Doğu ve Batı, İslam ve Laiklik* [The Turks: East and West, Islam and Secularism]. Ankara: Doruk Yayımcılık, 2002.

Yeşil, Bilge. *Media in New Turkey: The Origins of an Authoritarian Neoliberal State.* Urbana: University of Illinois Press, 2016.

Yıldız, Ahmet. *"Ne Mutlu Türküm Diyebilene": Türk Ulusal Kimliğinin Etno-Seküler Sınırları 1919–1938* ["How Happy Is the One Who Can Say I am a Turk": The Ethno-Secular Limits of Turkish National Identity 1919–1938]. Istanbul: İletişim, 2001.

Yılmaz, Hakan. "Two Pillars of Nationalist Euro-Skepticism in Turkey: The Tanzimat and Sèvres Syndromes." In *Turkey, Sweden, and the European Union: Experience and Expectations*, edited by Ingmar Karlsson and Annika Strom Melin, 29–40. Stockholm: SIEPS, 2006.

———. "Türkiye'de Kimlikler, Kürt Sorunu ve Çözüm Süreci: Algılar ve Tutumlar [Identities, the Kurdish problem, and Resolution Process in Turkey]." Açık Toplum Vakfı ve Boğaziçi Üniversitesi, September 2014. https://boun.academia.edu/HakanYilmaz/Papers; accessed December 15, 2014.

Young, Crawford, ed. *The Rising Tide of Cultural Pluralism: The Nation-State at Bay?* Madison: The University of Wisconsin Press, 1993.

Young, Iris Marion. *Justice and the Politics of Difference.* Princeton: Princeton University Press, 1990.

Yörük, Erdem, and Murat Yüksel. "Class and Politics in Turkey's Gezi Protests." *New Left Review* 89 (2014): 7–8.

Yüksel, Ayşe Seda. "Rescaled Localities and Redefined Class Relations: Neoliberal Experience in South-East Turkey." *Journal of Balkan and Near Eastern Studies* 13, no. 4 (2011): 444–49.

Zarakol, Ayşe. *After Defeat: How the East Learned to Live with the West.* Cambridge: Cambridge University Press, 2011.

Ziblatt, Daniel. *Conservative Parties and Birth Democracy.* Cambridge: Cambridge University Press, 2017.

Zubaida, Sami. "Introduction." In *The Kurds: A Contemporary Overview*, edited by Philip G. Kreyenbroek and Stefan Sperl, 1–7. London: Routledge, 1991.

Zürcher, Erik Jan. *Savaş, Devrim ve Uluslaşma, Türkiye Tarihi'nde Geçiş Dönemi: 1908–1928* [War, Revolution, and Nation-Formation, The Transition Period in the History of Turkey: 1908–1928]. İstanbul: Bilgi Üniversitesi Yayınları, 2005.

———, ed. *İmparatorluktan Cumhuriyete Etnik Çatışma* [Ethnic Conflict in Turkey from Empire to Republic]. Istanbul: İletişim, 2005.

———. *The Young Turk Legacy and Nation-Building: From the Ottoman Empire to Atatürk's Turkey.* London: I. B. Tauris, 2010.

# Index

9 781438 486727